THE PREHISTORY OF FOOD

The production and consumption of food can tell us much about how different cultures constructed and perceived their environment. The distinction between what is regarded as edible and inedible and the ecological systems in which people live are not just a passive backdrop to life but important indications of prevailing social and cultural systems. *The Prehistory of Food* discusses the changing uses of food in prehistory and sets subsistence firmly within its social context.

This collection presents studies from across the globe examining the interrelationships of food, biology and ecology. The contributors investigate the different roles food plays in culture: as an object of consumption and, subsequently, an important factor of socioeconomic change, as an agent of innovation affecting agriculture and methods of preparation and cooking, as a vital part of the landscape and as an important influence on the history of humans and plants. *The Prehistory of Food* contains case studies ranging from the rainforest groups of South America, to peoples of the desert fringes of Asia, to farmers in the Highlands of New Guinea. The book charts the movements of plants over the last 5,000 years, and with an impressive wealth of archaeological, genetic, botanical and linguistic evidence it tells the complex and fascinating story of the relationship between humans and their food.

The Prehistory of Food is of interest to all students and academics in the fields of archaeology, anthropology and archaeobotany.

Chris Gosden is Lecturer in Archaeology and curator at the Pitt Rivers Museum, University of Oxford. **Jon Hather** is Lecturer in Archaeology at the Institute of Archaeology, University College London.

ONE WORLD ARCHAEOLOGY
Series Editor: P. J. Ucko

THE PREHISTORY OF FOOD
Appetites for change

Edited by

Chris Gosden and Jon Hather

London and New York

First published 1999
by Routledge
11 New Fetter Lane, London EC4P 4EE

Simultaneously published in the USA and Canada
by Routledge
29 West 35th Street, New York, NY 10001

Routledge is an imprint of the Taylor & Francis Group

Typeset in Bembo by RefineCatch Limited, Bungay, Suffolk
Printed and bound in Great Britain by
TJ International Ltd, Padstow, Cornwall

British Library Cataloguing in Publication Data
A catalogue record for this book is available from the British Library

Library of Congress Cataloging in Publication Data
Gosden, Chris, 1955–
    The prehistory of food : appetites for change / Chris Gosden and
Jon Hather.
        p.   cm. – (One world archaeology)
    Includes bibliographical references and index.
    (hardbound : alk. paper)
    1. Prehistoric peoples – Food.   2. Food habits – History.
I. Hather, Jon G., 1963– . II. Title. III. Series.
GN799.F6G67   1999
306.4 – dc21   98–20445
                CIP

ISBN 0–415–11765–8

Contents

Figures

Tables

Contributors

Tim Bayliss-Smith, Department of Geography, University of Cambridge, Downing Place, Cambridge CB2 3EN, UK.

Soren Blau, Division of Society and Environment, Research School of Pacific and Asian Studies, Australian National University, Canberra, ACT 0200, Australia.

Ann Butler, Institute of Archaeology, UCL, 31–34 Gordon Square, London WC1H 0PY, UK.

Catherine D'Andrea, Department of Archaeology, Simon Fraser University, Burnaby, British Columbia, Canada V5A 1S6.

Edmond De Langhe, Laboratory of Tropical Crop Improvement, KU Leuven, Kardinal Mercierlaan, 92, B-3001 Heverlee, Belgium.

Pierre de Maret, Department of Archaeology, CP150, University of Brussels, av. Fr. D. Roosevelt, 50, B-1050 Brussels, Belgium.

Richard Fullagar, Division of Anthropology, Australian Museum, 6–8 College Street, Sydney, NSW 2000, Australia.

Jack Golson, Division of Society and Environment, Research School of Pacific and Asian Studies, Australian National University, Canberra, ACT 0200, Australia.

Chris Gosden, Pitt Rivers Museum, University of Oxford, 64 Banbury Road, Oxford OX2 6PN, UK.

Randi Haaland, Historical Museum, University, 5007 Bergen, Norway.

Alejandro F. Haber, Escuela de Arqueologia, Universidad Nacional de Catamarca, Salas Martinez 464, 4700 Catamarca, Argentina.

Christine A. Hastorf, Department of Anthropology, University of California, Berkeley, California 94720, USA.

Jon Hather, Institute of Archaeology, UCL, 31–34 Gordon Square, London WC1H 0PY, UK.

Lesley Head, School of Geosciences, University of Wollongong, Wollongong, New South Wales 2522, Australia.

Robert Kuhlken, Department of Geography and Land Studies, Central Washington University, Lind Hall 119, 400 E. 8th Avenue, WA 98926–7420, USA.

Helen M. Leach, Department of Anthropology, University of Otago, PO Box 56, Dunedin, New Zealand.

Kevin MacDonald, Institute of Archaeology, UCL, 31–34 Gordon Square, London WC1H 0PY, UK.

K.L. Mehra, 38 Munirka Enclave, New Delhi 110067, India.

Sarah Milledge Nelson, Department of Anthropology, University of Denver, 2130 Race Street, Denver, Colorado 80208, USA.

Carol Palmer, Department of Archaeology and Prehistory, University of Sheffield, Northgate House, West Street, Sheffield S1 4ET.

Deborah M. Pearsall, American Archaeology Division, University of Missouri, Swallow Hall 103, Columbia, Missouri 65211, USA.

Gustavo G. Politis, Aqueologia, Facultad de Ciencias Naturales y Museo, Universidad Nacional de La Plata, Paseo del Bosque, La Plata 1900, Argentina.

Elizabeth J. Reitz, Museum of Natural History, University of Georgia, Athens, GA 30602–1882, USA.

Christophe Sand, Département Archéologie, Service des Musées et du Patrimonie de Nouvelle-Calédonie BP: 2393, Nouméa, New Caledonia.

Andrew Sherratt, Department of Antiquities, Ashmolean Museum, University of Oxford, Beaumont Street, Oxford OX1 2NP, UK.

Michael Therin, Department of Archaeology and Anthropology, The Faculties, Australian National University, Canberra, ACT 0200, Australia.

Ken Thomas, Institute of Archaeology, UCL, 31–34 Gordon Square, London WC1H 0PY, UK.

Robin Torrence, Division of Anthropology, Australian Museum, 6–8 College Street, Sydney, NSW 2000, Australia.

Willem van Zeist, Biologisch-Archaeologisch Instituut, Rijksuniversiteit Groningen, Postsraat 6, 9712 ER Groningen, Holland.

Yuri E. Vostretsov, Institute of History, Archaeology and Ethnology of the Peoples of the Far East, Russian Academy of Sciences, Far Eastern Branch, 89 Pushkinskaya St., Vladivostok 690 600, Russia.

George Willcox, CNRS, Institut de Préhistoire Orientale, Jales 07460, Berrias, France.

Preface

This book is based around a session at the Third World Archaeological Congress, held in New Delhi in December 1994, but it also differs from the structure of that session in a number of significant respects. First, not all of the papers given at the session have been published here. In particular, there was a group of papers by Indian contributors, which, for a variety of reasons, have not come to publication. On the other hand, the editors (aided, as ever, by Peter Ucko) have recruited new papers to attempt to ensure a good geographical coverage and consideration of a wide range of topics. In the end, consideration of different regions has been reasonably wide, although we had hoped for more papers on Africa and certainly more by African scholars. The fact that Europe has recieved little attention is unintentional, but not of concern given the general rate of publication on European topics.

The editors would jointly like to thank Mekund Kajale for the very active role he played in encouraging Indian papers given at the conference and to the actual organization of the conference session itself. Deborah Pearsall was active in recruiting American contributions for the conference, but was precluded by pressures of work from engaging in the editing of this volume. We thank David Harris for the active role he played within the original conference session. Peter Ucko has recruited some of the papers for this volume and has provided encouragement and applied pressure when needed, to both authors and editors. Chris Gosden would like to thank the Research School of Pacific and Asian Studies at the Australian National University in Canberra where he carried out much of his editing whilst a Visiting Fellow during 1997.

Introduction

CHRIS GOSDEN

FOOD: WHERE BIOLOGY MEETS CULTURE

The study of food is one of the growth areas within academia at present. Food is good for thought, as well as eating, because it spans all areas of human life. It is obvious that food is necessary for physical survival, but it has become equally apparent that food is vital in constructing culture. Anthropologists have analysed the political and sensual uses of food in constructing cultural categories, but archaeologists have also come to realize that cultures are constructed over long periods of time and in the process of this construction the interaction between people and plants has been vital. Discussions of plants take us into the realm of biology where the genetic and biochemical properties of plants come to the fore, plus also the long-term interaction of people and plants. It is this interaction of people and plants that marries and blurs our dichotomous notions of nature versus culture. Although it is true that people have shaped plants over many millennia, it is equally so that plants have altered human patterns of life; we are therefore dealing with a mutual dependence of people and plants in intertwined histories.

The central thread of this book is the meeting of the cultural and biological in terms of both the material being studied and the disciplinary emphasis of those doing the studying. In order to understand the long-term history of food we need detailed knowledge of the ecological requirements of plants, their genetic changes over time, and we need methods suitable for the recovery of plant material from archaeological sites. Of equal necessity is a knowledge of how people construct the world around them through the categories of their culture, how they approach landscapes, divide edible from inedible things and attempt to change the world to their benefit. There has been all too little communication between those with a sound ecological and genetic knowledge and those interested in how cultures work and change. This is partly because food has been studied as lying within the ecological and the economic realms, whereas culture has been about artefacts and their meanings. But if food is culture as well as nutrition, then these divisions start to break down. This book aims to help break down such divisions and, although it is not possible or desirable to come up with a seamless synthesis of differing points of view, it may be possible to explore common ground and create new forms of dialogue.

Archaeological discussions of food and subsistence have tended to be rather limited, concentrating mainly on food as the basis for the economy, rather than as an element of culture. In this, archaeology still takes its lead from the nineteenth-century view that subsistence was one of the main motors for history, which created such abiding dichotomies as that between hunter-gatherers (or savages in L.H. Morgan's ([1877] 1985) scheme) and farmers (barbarians for Morgan). These ideas were given more theoretical bite and empirical richness in Childe's idea of the neolithic revolution as a great leap forward which underwrote those other revolutions, the Urban and the Industrial. Human history has been seen to march on its stomach and this view has some truth to it, but the major concentration on the production of calories and surplus has led to a concentration on domestication and its role in the invention of agriculture. Recent work by Harris (1989, 1990) has shown that farming and hunting and gathering are not polar opposites, but that there is a whole spectrum of practices ranging from the cultivation of wild plants to intensive agriculture based on domesticated forms. Here the degree of alteration of the landscape as a whole, the effort put into tillage and the genetic alteration of particular species interact in a complex and changing manner which cannot be encapsulated in the simple division between farming and gathering. Once a greater complexity of techniques and processes is acknowledged, this opens the way for a broader consideration of choice and why people take certain options not others. Choice leads us back to culture and the cultural logics underlying approaches to the landscape and food.

This book tackles the broad issue of setting subsistence in its social context but also attempts to make use of new evidence coming out of genetics and new syntheses of archaeological evidence of plant exploitation. In this introduction I want to look at the range of topics to which the study of food can lead us and these include introductions (or resistance to introduced crops), conceptions of landscapes, the social imperatives for landscape use and the linked history of plants and peoples to show the various ways they are being embraced by the rich mixture of chapters in the present volume.

FOOD AND CULTURE

Much effort has been expended by anthropologists in demonstrating that food is a cultural category which provides the raw material for systems of thought, as well as reflecting social divisions (Douglas 1972; Goody 1982; Lévi-Strauss 1969). Less work has been done along these lines by archaeologists, although Hodder's *Domestication of Europe* is an honourable exception here. Hodder (1990) has attempted to rethink the notion of domestication and sees neolithic societies as attempting to domesticate themselves as a means of coping with the tensions brought about by a new, settled form of life. Social domestication involves the creation of a plethora of new symbolic forms, developed to cope with the threat that nature, in the form of wildness and death, poses to culture. Hodder's work is deliberately provocative, using the overall structuralist tradition of thought to demonstrate that there was more to early neolithic life than the breeding of plant and animal species which gave higher yields in nutritional terms.

A number of the chapters in the present volume take a somewhat similar tack, but in a manner which links the argument about cultural categories and their changes more directly to food. Sherratt argues against the notion of subsistence and feels that means of growing plants throughout Eurasia changed due to a complex series of motives of taste and economics, such that innovation often occurred in plants that might be considered to be luxuries and not the staples. This follows arguments he has made elsewhere (Goodman *et al.* 1995) about the importance of situating food and drugs within patterns of consumption as a whole. One of the benefits of emphasizing consumption is to tie food into material culture, so that the pots to prepare or eat food are indicative of where and how consumption took place, plus the sets of cultural categories lying behind different forms of food and drink.

Hastorf explores similar themes in the Andes, making the point that plants adding taste and zest to food, like chillies, were the first to be domesticated and reflect profound social changes rather than an improvement in the economic basis of society. Also in South America, Haber tackles the notion of domestication and the ambiguous position of llamas in this respect, pointing out that animal herding cannot be divorced from the use of space both domestically and within the landscape as a whole. Once again subsistence is being brought home as an element of culture and culture change.

Appadurai (1981, 1988) has shown how the sensory nature of food, which is able to evoke memory and create present associations, is a powerful element within contemporary Hindu politics and culture. Anthropologists are less able to deal with long-term change in these aspects of life than archaeologists, and a number of studies in this volume look at both domestication of local resources and the adoption of new crops from elsewhere. Mehra, discussing the Indian subcontinent and providing some potential prehistory for Appadurai's argument, argues that although introductions of wheat, millet or rice have been vital in shaping southern Asian agronomy, the importance of locally domesticated crops should not be underestimated and it is the interaction of the local and the novel that holds the real key to agriculture in the subcontinent. There may be some deep structure to the distinctions that Appadurai sees people making in the present, deriving from the prehistoric use of plants.

More contemporary examples of change and resistance are provided by Blau and Leach. Leach looks at the specific introduction of the *Solanum* potato in New Zealand and how far its use fitted into existing Maori practices of food processing, particularly of the sweet potato (itself a prehistoric introduction into New Zealand). She also makes fascinating contrasts between the history of the potato in the Pacific and its original reception in Europe (see also Salaman 1985), where it passed from ornamental to staple with considerable speed. Similar complex histories are found with other plants, such as sugar (Mintz 1985). Blau makes a broader link between changes in the post-war period in the United Arab Emirates due to the sale of oil, which has brought in new foods and lifestyles, and periods of change in prehistory in the same area judged from skeletal analysis viewed against a background of the botanical evidence. Once again diet is viewed as an element of lifestyle, as people change their habits to maintain their place within a changing cultural field.

The question of the acceptance of novel and foreign resources is not a trivial one, as much of the world's food grown over the past 5,000 years has been introduced from other areas. Introductions are so important and widespread that they can provide a basis for global comparisons. A number of chapters explore the impact of crops from a more strictly economic point of view. The domestication and spread of rice has long been controversial (Glover and Higham 1996) within Asian prehistory, Nelson explores the impact of rice as a new crop in Korea and its links to new forms of monumentality and society. Working on a broad range of plant species, Andrea looks at the complexity of ecological and economic factors influencing the introduction of new domesticates into one area of Japan, the north-east. A reverse case, which combines archaeological and historical evidence, is provided by Reitz for Florida from the Spanish period onwards. Here rejection was the main response to new animal species, which could not be fitted within existing cultural categories and patterns of practice.

FOOD AND THE LANDSCAPE

A major area of present interest within both archaeology and anthropology is in the landscape as both a producer and product of social forces (Bender 1993; Hirsch and O' Hanlon 1995). All aspects of the social process have some spatial expression, and space is not an abstract geometry but is lived and worked on. Landscapes are human creations, but equally people are shaped by the landscapes they have made, these being the material settings into which the young are socialized and which become part of their social being. Landscapes have implications for the manner in which practical skills are developed and deployed, plus differences in the use of the landscape deriving from gender or social standing. Bayliss–Smith and Golson look at the most famous prehistoric agricultural site in Papua New Guinea: Kuk swamp, which has a sequence spanning some 9,000 years. Their careful analysis of the ditches that drained the swamp in one phase in terms of the social forces that created them is one of the most detailed pieces of work linking features of the landscape to the organization of labour, gender and political aspirations. On a broader and necessarily more superficial level, Gosden and Head explore the old question of the distinction between Australia and Papua New Guinea, making the point that if subsistence is taken as the main point of distinction, it is only possible to emphasize differences between Australia as a continent of hunter-gatherers and Papua New Guinea, a country of farmers. However, if different elements of attachment to the landscape are emphasized then more of the shared history of the two areas comes into focus. Also in the Pacific, Sand emphasizes the human creation of the landscapes of New Caledonia throughout the period of human occupation over the last 3,000 years, particularly the construction of widespread terraced systems only abandoned after the coming of Europeans. Kuhlken takes a different tack and looks at the manner in which social forces, especially the political competition that impelled groups in Fiji towards warfare, were a major impetus for intensification of agriculture. Farming and fighting, which could be glossed as ploughshares and swords in the western idiom, might seem to us to be contrasting elements of life, but in many areas of the world have been joined through the demands of the political process.

In a very different cultural context, Palmer looks at the links between history and land in Jordan and links the history of the social relations of the group to patterns of land ownership and how both of these have changed in the recent past as the result of local people becoming enmeshed in changing external political structures. The parcelling up of land in both a social and a legal sense is part of a knot of social forces stretching way beyond the group, but is also worked through on a daily basis through labour on the land.

Thomas's chapter explores the impact that landscapes on the frontier of different geographical zones have had on human history. In his case, it is the borderlands between Pakistan and Afghanistan which are of interest, with their mix of mountains and plains which create a complex of long-distance routes to be travelled by pastoralists and basins between the mountains where settled agriculturalists dwelt. Since the Neolithic, the balance between pastoralism and settled agriculture has been crucial to local ways of life, but also to long-distance connections with Central and Southern Asia. Vostretsov is most concerned with the impact that changing sea-levels throughout the Holocene have had on the coastal economies of mainland areas north of the Japan Sea. Coastal change has not only affected people living near the sea, but also the balance between coastal and inland economies and the complexity of their development through the Holocene. Similarly, for West Africa MacDonald argues that individual aspects of the economy cannot be considered in isolation. It is especially the case that settled forms of life and pastoralism have been mutually influencing, although it is an unfortunate fact of archaeological life that the mobile lives of pastoralists have left only ephemeral evidence behind them. At a micro-scale, van Zeist's detailed consideration of the Balikh Valley, Syria from the point of view of plant crops, emphasizes the shifting balance between the cultivation of the valley bottom and the higher plateau regions. He lays out the complex of forces influencing choices in this regard, which range between the level of population and the social demands for a particular quality of crop, reminding us that choices about growing food link the demographic and the social.

PLANTS AND PEOPLE

Plants could be said to have a social life and a history as they participate in people's creation of space and time. As mentioned earlier, a simple scheme of domestication and then intensive cultivation may not be adequate to look at such histories. We also need to look both at the cosmological schemes within which plants are used and at what might be called their context in the world system. Many plants are moved around through sets of social connections and trading connections, and their eventual domestication or diversification into new species may happen well outside their original ranges. We are not looking at delimited hearths of domestication, where new types of animals and plants were bred into being, but rather at complex overlapping histories of plants and people which may not alter the plants genetically at all.

Balée (1994) has looked at how history is created and maintained through people's knowledge of trees within the Amazonian rainforest. Politis explores the ideology lying behind rainforest exploitation by the Nukak and shows how plants and animals are used to create cultural categories and histories. The rainforest, which appears to western eyes as an untouched wilderness, is used according to a set of cosmological schemes and is also a historical product altered continuously by its human inhabitants. Particular plant species have complex linked histories with people, as De Lange and de Maret show for the banana. The banana is now dependent on people for its propagation, but many groups rely on different sorts of bananas for a major part of their livelihood. This linked history spans many millennia and can be elucidated through a combination of genetic, archaeological and linguistic research. Sorghum in the Nile is the focus of Haaland's attention, and she explores the problem of the sequence of cultivation and domestication and uses sorghum as a possible example of a plant domesticated outside its area of origin. Together the chapters by De Lange and de Maret and Haaland show the complexity of the movement of plants in areas around the Indian Ocean and that plants have moved both east and west to alter people's lives fundamentally.

The slow adoption of a plant also seems to be the case in Ecuador, where people took up the use of maize over a period of centuries rather than suddenly. An important element of Pearsall's story concerns our ability as archaeologists to recover evidence, such as phytoliths, in a consistent manner which can provide a rounded picture of long-term change. Therin, Fullagar and Torrence report a potential breakthrough in the recognition of starch in archaeological sites. In the Pacific, as many other areas of the world, starch from root and tree crops plays a large role in people's diet, past and present. Evidence for starchy foods is extremely difficult to recover, especially in the humid tropics. New techniques of recovery and analysis may make it possible to discover starch both on the edges of stone tools and in the sediments which compose archaeological sites. Therin *et al.* are cautious in their conclusions, stressing much future work on techniques is necessary, but they foresee the possibility of tracking changes in the uses of food over the last few millennia which will open up new areas of understanding of the role of food in prehistory.

A final emphasis on the complexities of influences on the growing of food, and consequently the sets of evidence we need to combine in order to understand food in prehistory, is provided by the chapters by Butler and Wilcox. Butler provides a uniquely broad survey of the range of seed cropping systems which exist in temperate areas of the Old World, plus the botanical and ecological limits on these systems which can allow an understanding of the biological parameters within which prehistoric peoples worked and thus the constraints on social choice. Wilcox tackles that hardy perennial, the origins of agriculture in the Near East, using an impressive range of sources ranging from a botanical understanding of wild species, to experimental work and the results of analyses of early neolithic plant assemblages, again showing the range of change that happened in different areas and time periods.

CONCLUSIONS

In anthropology food has become a major topic because all human life is there: the landscape and its histories, patterns of consumption as an element in the creation of cultural categories, problems of aesthetics and taste (to use this latter term in two senses), links to the body and embodied experience and food as a reflection of symbolism and structures of thought. Archaeology can tackle all these topics related to food, albeit in a manner consonant with the nature of our evidence, which emphasizes the long-term histories of food and people. Where anthropology can look at food as a cultural category, archaeology can probe the long-term differentiations and changes in the cultural uses of food. An anthropological analysis of landscape has limits as far as time depth is concerned, but through archaeology there is the possibility of a linked history of sediments, society and plants. A more novel area which needs much further exploration is the conjoined history of people and particular plant species, where there has been a mutual process of

8 C. GOSDEN

domestication, so that people's patterns of life are partly structured around the requirements of plants in the same manner as the physical needs of the plants have been reconfigured by people.

Archaeology differs from anthropology not just through the possibility of understanding long-term change, but also in the indirect nature of our evidence. Much work needs to be done to develop new recovery techniques, especially for ephemeral plant remains, and to understand the requirements of climate and soil of different species. An archaeological interest in food will always hover on the borderland of the technical and the social in a manner which will be both productive and uncomfortable. Some, including a number of contributors to this volume, will feel that I have here emphasized the social and cultural side of food rather than the environmental and the economic, and all our views echo deep divisions within archaeology between the humanistic and the scientific. My aim here has not been to assert the primacy of the humanistic, but to indicate that an interest in the prehistory of food can help provide dialogue across the divide, even though the division itself still remains. The chapters in this book show that thoughts about food in prehistory are changing and that with a proper combination of the theoretical and the technical a rounded disciplinary approach is possible, which will do justice to the richness of the subject-matter.

REFERENCES

Appadurai, A. 1981. Gastro-politics in Hindu south Asia. *American Ethnologist* 8, 494–511.
Appadurai, A. 1988. How to make a national cuisine: cookbooks in contemporary India. *Comparative Studies in Society and History* 30, 3–24.
Balée, W.L. 1994. *Footprints of the Forest. Ka'apor ethnobotany: the historical ecology of plant utilization by an Amazonian people.* New York: Columbia University Press.
Bender, B. (ed.) 1993. *Landscape: politics and perspectives.* Oxford: Berg.
Douglas, M. 1972. Deciphering a meal. *Daedalus* 101, 61–82.
Glover, I.C. and C.F.W. Higham. 1996. New evidence for rice cultivation in South, Southeast and East Asia. In *The Origins and Spread of Agriculture and Pastoralism in Eurasia*, D.R. Harris (ed.), 413–41. London: UCL Press.
Goodman, J., E. Lovejoy and A. Sherratt (eds) 1995. *Consuming Habits: drugs in history and anthropology.* London: Routledge.
Goody, J. 1982. *Cooking, Cuisine and Class.* Cambridge: Cambridge University Press.
Harris, D.R. 1989. An evolutionary continuum of people–plant interaction. In *Foraging and Farming: the evolution of plant exploitation*, D.R. Harris and G.C. Hillman (eds), 11–26. London: Unwin Hyman.
Harris, D.R. 1990. *Settling Down and Breaking Ground: the evolution of plant exploitation.* Twaalfde Kroon-Voordracht. Amsterdam: Stichting Nederlands Museum voor Anthropologie en Praehistorie.
Hirsch, E. and M. O'Hanlon (eds) 1995. *The Anthropology of Landscape: perspectives on space and place.* Oxford: Oxford University Press.
Hodder, I. 1990. *The Domestication of Europe.* Oxford: Basil Blackwell.
Lévi-Strauss, C. 1969. *The Raw and the Cooked.* London: Jonathan Cape.

Mintz, S.W. 1985. *Sweetness and Power: the place of sugar in modern history.* Harmondsworth: Penguin.

Morgan, L.H. [1877] 1985. *Ancient Society.* Tucson: University of Arizona Press.

Salaman, R.N. 1985. *The History and Social Influence of the Potato.* Cambridge: Cambridge University Press.

Part I

FOOD AND CULTURE

1 Cash-crops before cash: organic consumables and trade

Andrew Sherratt

Archaeology, like the rest of western thought, suffers from over-compartmentalization. Too often its procedures take the form of analysis – breaking down, dividing – rather than combining and synthesizing. Such separating procedures are useful where they foster specialist skills, but dangerous if their subject-matter is left in isolation. The purpose of this contribution is to assert that the word often used to describe an important part of our subject-matter – 'subsistence' – is not an autonomous domain, but is best considered as one aspect of a larger set of relationships. 'Subsistence' is a misleading category within which to work; the textbook division between 'subsistence and settlement' and 'trade and exchange' should be abolished as a hindrance to understanding.

THE MYTH OF 'SUBSISTENCE'

Although masquerading as a neutral, descriptive term, 'subsistence' is in fact heavily freighted with intellectual baggage. It has two principal uses in modern English: to describe the economies of far-away regions, and to specify an element of allowable *per diem* expenses after second-class travel by rail. Its use in the latter context clearly has a moral content: it is a bureaucratic warning against the temptation to potlatch. 'Mere subsistence' implies just enough to keep body and soul together: enough to stay alive without transmitting messages about social superiority. The very employment of the term implies the constant danger of the behaviour which it forbids. Such motives also underlie its more general usage: the whole concept is actively constructed in opposition to an accurate depiction of everyday reality. It is, in short, a rhetorical rather than a scientific term: a utopian representation of a world without ostentation and cupidity. Like many other unstated assumptions of contemporary discourse (because social theorists are usually also social reformers), it has its roots in Puritanism, and in a moral stance in relation to conspicuous consumption rather than as an accurate description of the real world.

Whence, therefore, its widespread employment in archaeology as a general term to describe food-getting, which in everyday experience is so rarely divorced from considerations of social image and ideological negotiation? The answer lies in the recent intellectual history (and disciplinary politics) of development studies and economic anthropology. Careful to avoid the established territory of classical economics, with its focus on the market, these newer discplines defined their subject-matter as those societies which were so far untouched by the blandishments of 'the market' and market forces. Such a conception was inevitably the reconstruction of a postulated past reality rather than the description of a present one, since the societies in question had almost without exception been subjected to the classic sequence of contacts: merchants, soldiers, missionaries, colonial administrators, anthropologists; and following the Heisenberg principle which governs anthropological investigation (the fact that by the time you can observe a community, it is no longer what it was before contact), had to reconstruct conjecturally what might have been its pristine condition. Mentally removing the Levis and substituting bark loincloths, therefore, they described a community existing completely without external contacts and living entirely by autosubsistence – ignoring the fact that the imported commodities replaced precisely those indigenous meaning-laden manufactured products which were most likely to have been traded and negotiated between communities. They thus replicated the romantic myth of western anthropology, of a set of isolated communities comprehensible as independent social microcosms – created by purging what they could actually observe from the supposed 'pollution' of outside influence, in an ironic parody of their own description of the thought-processes of the natives.

In so far as there exist communities which might be described as possessing 'subsistence' economies, it is not those as yet untouched by the world system, but rather those most closely enmeshed in it but impoverished by it. Throughout the Third World there exist peasantries which dutifully pay their taxes to local elites, but whose countries are systematically exploited by the unequal balance of exchange between raw material producers and metropolitan manufacturers who cream off the added value ('the man from Del Monte says "Yes"', as the television advertisement succinctly encapsulated it). Doubly burdened by their international and national position in contemporary social structures, the peasantries of such countries unsurprisingly have little disposable income with which to acquire much beyond the bare necessities if life – if that. They might thus, with justification, be described as representing a 'subsistence economy'. To treat such societies as in any way paradigmatic of the natural condition of humankind, however, is to extrapolate a late and atypical situation as a model for the greater part of human existence. This is methodologically unsound. The attempt to isolate a sphere of prehistoric existence as 'subsistence behaviour' is bound to fail. We should, in fact, be more alert to the tradable potential of many organic products.

SHEEP AND OLIVE TREES: 'SUBSISTENCE' OR 'EXCHANGE'?

At a trivial level, the point is an obvious one. There are no sharp dividing-lines along a continuum of prehistoric objects constituted as follows: a rock like marble, traded for making ornaments; a mollusc like *Spondylus*, traded for its shell; a mollusc like *Ostrea*, gathered for its meat; and a sea-bird, shot or caught for food. Even in the last case, there may be feathers which can be used – and even traded, if they are attractive; most animals yield non-food products such as bones, sinews, hides, and so on, many of which are widely in demand. (Think how many antler picks a neolithic flint-miner would get through.) Nor are plants usually restricted simply to providing food. Here, too, exploited species are often characterized by multiple uses, like hemp as fibre (stem) and narcotic (flower, leaves); or palms, which support a huge range of products and uses. Corn-stalks can be used for thatching, or even for making corn-dollies – and straw baskets have actually been found in the PPN B desert cave of Nahal Hemmar, Israel, dating back 10,000 years almost to the beginnings of Old World cereal cultivation (Kislev and Bar-Yosef 1988: 176). This is not, therefore, a trivial consideration. Besides the food element, there is almost always some other product – which is usually called 'secondary', even though in many cases (like *Spondylus* shell, which lives in deeper water than *Ostrea* and is usually found washed up) the non-food element is of primary interest, and the meat is a secondary consideration, if not irrelevant. There is often a long-term shift from primary to secondary products: palaeolithic hunters ate elephant-meat but left the tusks; now ivory-poachers leave the meat to rot.

The term 'secondary products' is principally employed to describe those products that can be extracted continuously without killing the organism – like milk and wool, as opposed to meat. This does not generally include bones, horn, hide, etc., though these might usefully be called secondary terminal products – a useful reminder that the more precise term for milk and wool would be secondary *live* products. In this sense, the analogy with the vegetable kingdom would be something like rubber, which can be tapped throughout the life of the tree: the term applies particularly to perennials, including many kinds of fruit trees. Olive-oil, in this sense, is a 'secondary product' of the olive tree. What these secondary live products often have in common, whether they are derived from animals or plants, is that the materials which they continuously yield can often be converted to more valuable forms by some further kind of work. This is what unites sheep and rubber trees: they yield commodities. While the types of economy that specialize in tree-crops, and those that specialize in animal products, might be considered as somehow antithetical – since the former demands sedentism while the latter is often associated with mobility – this does not mean that they are unrelated. Indeed, in the history of Old World farming, they were closely associated. Both appeared some time after the initial development of farming, but before the onset of urbanism, in the Chalcolithic (sixth to fourth millennia cal. BC); and they involved species or breeds which had not been represented amongst the earliest domesticates. The Ghassulian culture of the southern Levant was a pioneer in both tree-crops and animal-herding for milk (much as the earliest inhabitants of Jericho simultaneously attempted to grow cereals and chase gazelle); although these soon became the activities of specialized social groupings, they were initially common responses within a single society and historical context (Levy 1992). (Moreover the Ghassulians were also spectacularly expert copper metallurgists, symptomatic of their extensive search for raw materials and ability to trade in them.) Their common incentive was the specialized secondary live products: wool and milk on the one hand, olive and grape on the other. These products have some further properties in common: they are commodities which can be traded, and especially so if they have been processed to some degree. Indeed, all of them share the property that they can be processed to many degrees, and with the appropriate skill and knowledge can gain in value at each transformation, until one has such valuable products as the robe of Athena (the *palladion*), or a *premier grand cru*. In this respect these products perhaps resemble metals or semi-precious stones as much as they do cereal-porridge or a lump of meat; organic commodities have as much potential for trade as inorganic ones.

CASH-CROPS BEFORE CASH

There is thus a measure of parallelism in the human uses not only of animals and plants but also of inanimate materials: wool, olive-oil and copper are coeval. All require technological knowledge, skill and investment both in productive facilities and in distributive networks. Whilst the specialist study of their remains requires differing backgrounds in zoology, botany and metallurgy, their archaeological significance lies in their common social and cultural contexts and uses. This common field is the domain of value and exchange: quite the opposite of what is commonly implied by the word 'subsistence', which has the sense of basic nourishment – but nothing more. Best, then, to drop the phrase 'subsistence systems' altogether, since one of the deleterious side-effects of this phrase is to create an artificial expectation that inorganic products can be traded but organic products are largely consumed locally. This is reinforced by their differential survivorship in the archaeological record. It is taken as a truism that attractive stones or sea-shells are typical objects of stone age trade, often transmitted over long distances, without pausing to consider that furs may have been equally mobile, or even narcotics (a highly desirable item of Australian aboriginal exchange systems is, of course, *pitcheri*). Feathers, in particular, are known ethnographically (especially, because of their colourfulness, from tropical regions) as traded commodities of high value. But there may also have been traded subsistence products, or at least diet-enhancers (like salt, often traded over long distances among groups with a largely vegetable diet) even in the Palaeolithic. In a recent article, Schmitt (1994) has suggested that seals, abundant on islands in the nutrient-rich waters of the Yoldia Sea narrows in the Late Glacial, were extensively culled for the procurement of blubber and the production of train-oil (nothing to do with oiling railway-trains, but cognate with German *Tränen*, tears or droplets, obtained by boiling the blubber), that was widely desired amongst the hunting populations of the North European Plain, because of the problems caused by a diet consisting predominantly of lean meat. (Where such maritime products are not available, Boreal hunters may expend much energy in rendering reindeer bones to produce 'bone-grease', which has similar nutritional/dietetic properties.) Marek Zvelebil has reconstructed the circulation of similar commodities for the Mesolithic in the Baltic region (1996: figs 18.7, 18.8); and among the illustrations of the equipment of the north-east Siberian Samoyed in Friedrich Ratzel's *Anthropo-Geographie* of 1882 is a container made from a swan's foot for carrying this substance. (It takes imagination to restore this item to the archaeology of Mesolithic Denmark!)

Traffic in substances such as these, even after the beginning of farming, would make sense of the cultural prominence of islands like Orkney, which (in the Neolithic and Bronze Age, when they have an especially rich artefactual and monumental record) were not stepping-stones on routes of long-distance communication to larger areas but constituted a terminus or *ultima Thule* at the end of the known world. It is their richness in high-vitamin sea-products, concentrating a huge radius of marine productivity through their bird and sea-mammal faunas, which provided compact and desirable products that could be traded to the mainland and potentially far beyond. Accustomed now to industrial substitutes, we have lost our appreciation for commodities (like goose-grease) still valued only a generation or so ago. As Grahame Clark records (1952: 77), some of the inhabitants of Orkney paid their rent in seal-oil in the last century. Such commodities take their place alongside the many other kinds of organic materials and products known ethnographically as important items of trade, including plants cultivated specifically for this purpose. There is archaeo-logical evidence for the movement of honey over rather a long distance, and of pig fat probably over a somewhat shorter one (Dickson 1978; Needham and Evans 1987).

Recognition of the importance of organic products in trade allows us to 'unfreeze' a useful concept, hitherto confined to the historical period, and to generalize it for further use: the idea of cash-crops. The defining characteristic of a cash-crop is that it is grown specifically for exchange, rather than for local consumption. In this sense, most modern cereal-growing is undertaken on this basis, though the term is usually used of commodities other than the basic calorific staples. Tree-crops are almost always in this class, since plantations require long-term investment and economies of scale. The appearance of vine and olive through the Mediterranean was thus embedded in a process of economic and infrastructural development, as discussed below (pp. 19–21). Products such as olive-oil are highly exchangeable commodities, and were exported long before the formal appearance of 'cash' (coinage) in the sixth century BC – though the term usefully reminds us that the economic liquidity of such transaction networks depends critically on a medium of exchange, and usually a metallic one (typically silver, though copper/bronze performed an analogous function in earlier contexts). Metallic media of exchange are not, however, a *sine qua non*; for on occasion tree-crops themselves have served as currency (standards and media of exchange), much as Marlboro cigarettes – narcotic leaf-crop products – did in parts of the former USSR. The use of theobromine-rich cacao as precisely such an exchange medium in Classic Mesoamerica gave Rene Millon the opportunity to use the only genuinely humorous dissertation title I know: 'When Money Grew on Trees' (1955). This is perhaps the most literal kind of cash-crop: the crop itself is the cash. Many of the crops brought into cultivation in the 'second phase' of farming (parallel to the emergence of secondary animal products, uses and domesticates) were cash-crops in the less literal sense of producing commodities for exchange, and thus forming part of a spatial process of regional specialization.

The examples cited above, however, show that certain species had been exploited primarily for the exchange-value of their products even by palaeolithic groups: 'cash-crops' not merely before cash, but even before farming and domestication. In this respect, the contrast between stone age Sweden, exporting seal-oil, and the bronze age Levant, exporting olive-oil and wine in specialized containers (jars and jugs) by sea to Egypt and Cyprus, is one of degree rather than of kind. In principle, there is no difference: stone age economies were not *ipso facto* simply subsistence economies. What opens up as a field of research and a fruitful area of model-building is the story of trade in organic commodities (both alive and dead, raw and processed), as part of the story of trade and exchange as much as of subsistence and settlement. Indeed, to the extent that 'subsistence' is a dangerously misleading concept, its abolition opens the possibility of telling the story primarily as a chapter in cultural and social history, instead of part of some autonomous realm of economics or simple nutrition. Cash-crops are about value, and thus about evaluation, desire and culturally constructed modes of consumption.

Such a process of valuation necessarily creates opportunities for middleman profit. All crops possess some kind of rarity value when they are initially in short supply; and if they have some generally desirable characteristics (taste, ease of digestion, appearance) may be 'cash-crops' all around the perimeter of the area within which they are grown, and beyond which they are desirable novelties. It is this point which was grasped ten years ago by Runnels and van Andel in 'Trade and the origins of agriculture' (1988), following an older insight by Kent Flannery; if agriculture is essentially the movement of plants and animals out of their natural habitats to new niches under human agency, then their transmission between people is a negotiated transaction, and can be considered under the general rubric of 'trade'. 'In a sense we are saying that "cash-crop" farming was a phenomenon as old as, and perhaps older than, subsistence farming' (Runnels and van Andel 1988: 97). I would go further: what is called 'subsistence farming' is the exception – a late phenomenon of global specialization which has little to do with prehistory.

ROLE AND POSITION: WORLD-SYSTEM ZONATION

The initially paradoxical concept of seals as a 'cash-crop' in a pre-cash, pre-agricultural economy is repeated more recently in a whole range of commodities, such as ivory, leopard skins and ibex horns, which are acquired by hunting but are nevertheless traded over long distances across the zones of the world system. Interestingly, such commodities have been the subject of an arcane controversy amongst world-systems enthusiasts over the status of Canada and Siberia within the European world-system of the eighteenth century. This argument (i.e. that of a 'fur periphery') can only be reconciled with Wallerstein's concept of the periphery if such hunted commodities as slaves and furs are to be equated with 'cash-crops, agricultural or analogue forms of primary sector production' (Wallerstein 1989: 138). If Wallerstein accepts timber and dye-wood, which are collected in natural forests, why not furs and slaves? Instead these are only accepted at the first stage of transition when an external arena becomes incorporated (Nitz 1993: 17–18). It is not necessary to follow the scholastic finesse of this argument to recognize that the outer edges of the world system are characterized by the exploitation of natural resources by the cropping of wild populations, rather than the more capital-intensive process of rearing and culling. It is instructive that this description could apply to the economy of Egypt in the fourteenth century BC as easily as it could be accepted for the world two centuries ago. (It is also amusing that the phrase 'leopard-skin accessories' is applied today in parody of the contemporary motor trade – when the 'leopard skin' is an ersatz printed textile – in a way precisely parallel to that in which an Egyptian chariot-maker, using the real thing, might have described the vehicles of Tuthmosis or Tutankhamun!)

The cropping of wild resources on the outer edge of the system (like King Solomon's Red Sea expedition to Tarshish in I Kings 10.22, bringing back 'gold, silver, ivory, apes, and peacocks') makes sense in an arrangement where the value is added nearer to the centre, on the Del Monte principle alluded to above; as the system grows and differentiates, it develops a zonation in which native populations are used as intermediaries in the outermost zone in exploiting primary terminal products, through a zone in which unfree labour is used in exploiting secondary live products, to an inner zone in which skilled (though often dependent) labour is used to add value to the products of the other two in a variety of manufacturing processes. The first of these produces largely raw materials, the second of them half-finished commodities, and the innermost one the fully manufactured product. The characteristic of the core, therefore, is its lengthened chains of processing, which often require highly specific processes and ingredients in small quantities at appropriate points in the manufacturing process – like valonia acorns (the cups of *Quercus aegilops macrolepsis*, used in tanning fine leather), or *Murex* shellfish and saffron for the purple and orange dyes used in the production of luxury cloth. The central zone is thus characterized particularly by its knowledge (both technological and spatial), and by its reticulating web of contacts. Such areas produce not just olive-oil but perfumed olive-oil, enhanced by added extracts and fragrances. The multitude of often small, specialist product-flows are what necessitate a generally acceptable medium of exchange, to balance the transactions.

The focal areas where such systems emerge – the 'nuclear' areas of early civilizations – are typically geographically unusual areas of complex ecology, where complementary exchanges between contrasting ecological zones can easily occur. These are often parts of the same regions which were nuclear for the origins of farming, which can be seen as an exchange of the crops themselves, moving them from natural habitats to a wider distribution; the second stage of exploiting such ecological complementarity included in addition the systematic exchange of specialist products (like oil and wine) rather than just the organisms themselves. The development of economic core regions sets the context of production in an ever-enlarging hinterland, where characteristic patterns of zonation develop. Unlike the highly developed macro-von Thünen rings of the advanced world system, however, the earlier phases of such a zonally differentiated structure were characterized by rather loose articulation between the nuclear core (with its peripheral sustaining area) and its outer supply zone – often reached by periodic expeditions like those of Solomon and earlier rulers like Hatshepsut and Tuthmosis III (see p. 30). The formation of early states was often accompanied, therefore, by the development of semi-independent opportunist mobile populations, either on land or sea, who simultaneously exploited specialist ecological niches, and occupied an articulating role in the economy (which later on was taken over by specialist merchants). These were typically pastoralists and sea peoples (Artzy 1994). It was the increasing flow of organic commodities which made possible such regional specialization, and bulkier products were increasingly commoditized as the system grew in scale and transport capacity (especially by sea) increased. Increasing capitalization makes possible ranching and the plantation of tree-crops. At the same time the need for highly specific ingredients means that routes for rare materials can open up over long distances, and may be supplied from very different socio-economic settings – like the camphor gathered by south-east Asian rainforest tribes for the Chinese. As the system expands, so the 'zones' are experienced successively by any particular location as a series of 'phases' of development (which may give the impression of an endogenous evolutionary sequence); but as the system increases in scale there are also qualitative transformations, so experiences are not merely replicated but can be seen as new types of phenomena, particularly in the degree of area-specialization and the facilities required for their integration. The nature of animal and plant exploitation, including the balance between staples and non-staples, and between primary and secondary products (whether live or terminal), is increasingly determined by position in such a system.

SPATIAL OPPORTUNITY AND LOCATIONAL ADVANTAGE

This growing complexity of exchanges, usually channelled through nodal points on transport networks, offers opportunities for the system to be manipulated for individual or sectional advantage. Zonal centrality thus corresponds to network complexity. The spread of new cultigens (first the products, then the crops themselves, in a series of episodes of import-substitution) leads to novel forms of consumption practice, values, and patterns of social emulation. Access to exotic goods and consumables is a well-known way of constructing power. In these negotiated transactions, particular social actors or groups stand to gain a competitive advantage, particularly where they can control the flow of goods and more particularly the processes of adding value by creating more complex products with special social meanings through their association with rituals and festivities. (Perfumed oil for anointing would be a classical example; or special foods imbued with mythical significance.) It is by these mechanisms that social differentiation and incipient economic stratification begins to occur. Nascent elites, however, have a common interest in restricting exotic materials so that supplies remain within their control; and for this reason patterns of local specialization may appear, which preserve the 'exotic' character of the goods and delay or prevent the process of 'import substitution'. This may be a fast-moving game, for it reflects patterns of competition both within and between communities. These possibilities of diverting and monopolizing flows are naturally greater in proportion to the volume (and value) of the flows. The possibility of riverine or maritime transport (whose costs are about one-tenth of those over land) greatly enhances the conditions for developing such a pattern. In particular, they open up possibilities for the exploitation of middlemen positions – areas whose locational advantage lies not in terms of immediate natural resources such as soils or minerals, but in terms of their structural position within a differentiating system. These factors are particularly powerful in primitive transport conditions with a high friction of distance, where route choices may be highly constrained; and it is at choke points, convergence nodes and trans-shipment (break-of-bulk) points along these routes that spectacular accumulations of wealth may occur.

Although these points are often made in connection with the growth of urban economies, they are equally true of much smaller-scale trading systems like those of coastal Melanesia. Here, advantageously placed islands – often without outstanding natural resources of their own – may come to specialize in middleman trading, and come to cultivate 'cash-crops' for which they have a steady market, such as tree-crop products. The classic example are the Siassi of the Vitiaz Strait, between the Huon peninsula of New Guinea and the island of New Britain (Harding 1967; Brookfield and Hart 1971: 328–32). The inhabitants of the Siassi islands exploit their nodal position in the network to specialize in middleman trading, at a considerable profit. A series of transactions with different partners might yield the following sequence: 12 coconuts → 3 pots → 1 pig → 10 sago packets → 100 pots → 10 pigs (Harding 1967: 139). The Siassi exploit their superior knowledge (and exchange-partners' ignorance) by outrageous advertising claims: pots, for instance, are described – to the inhabitants of non-pottery-producing areas – as the shells of deep-water molluscs, obtained by dangerously deep dives! (Herodotus' description of the gold-guarding ants of Bactria suggests a similar hype.) The Siassi also grow coconuts, in which they possess a near monopoly; and it is notable that they deliberately break the exported coconuts to prevent their being grown elsewhere.

Another property exemplified by trading networks of this kind is the principle of intervening opportunity. In the Melanesian example mentioned above, some locations specialize in the manufacture of pots, using the flow of other products to subsidize added-value production from relatively cheap raw materials, which 'piggyback' on the movements of other goods. Specialization is thus made possible by an advantageous position on routes of inter-regional contact. A similar situation explains the growth of wool production in the English Cotswolds in the Late Iron Age, since the area of the Jurassic limestone ridge west of Oxford is the crossing-point from the Severn catchment to the Thames catchment, and saw an increase in traffic past the developing *oppida* of Minchinhampton, Bagendon, Salmonsbury, and Oxfordshire Grim's Ditch, where surplus wool was profitable (Sherratt 1996b). The area has been famous for its wool-production ever since (and two hundred years ago made the blankets which the Hudson Bay Company exchanged for furs, in a classic core export of manufactures for peripheral high-value raw materials). This area has no inherent environmental advantages as grazing country by comparison with many other areas (for instance other parts of the Jurassic scarp). It is the combination of suitable environmental conditions with an assured outlet for its products that has produced the emphasis on wool-production – like much of Mediterranean transhumant pastoralism. The element of production for exchange tends to be ignored in prehistory, because of the pervasive belief in purely 'subsistence' production, locally consumed; but an advantageous location in relation to flows of trade would have been an important factor in determining the crops grown and livestock kept.

How, therefore, are more complex systems generated? It is relatively easy to see how a large-scale world system works, and why it should expand; but how do such structures begin? In particular, how do nuclear patterns build up sufficient internal differentiation *before* the onset of urbanization? It is here that regional diversity exercises a critical influence on the genesis of complex social systems – and the stress on human motivations must be complemented by a consciousness of the possibilities provided by the environment.

THE DEVELOPMENT OF SECONDARY FARMING IN SOUTH-WEST ASIA

The differentiation of farming systems in the nuclear region of the western Old World (Sherratt 1996a) offers a well-studied example, which may provide a paradigm for other areas which have given rise to similar structures (Figure 1.1). The initial (PPN) phase of farming, in the ninth and eighth millennia cal. BC, was a limited form of simple groundwater-dependent cultivation to which the keeping of domestic livestock (principally sheep and goat) was slowly added. After a phase of restructuring in the Levant around 7000 cal. BC, a rapid extension out of the Near East, both to Europe across the Iranian Plateau, took place in the early seventh millennium, associated with the domestication both of cattle and free-threshing species of wheat; while by the later seventh and sixth millennia there is evidence from Greater Mesopotamia for small-scale irrigation and indications that cattle traction may have been used for ploughing. For these three or four millennia, the initial crop complex – essentially providing carbohydrate-rich cereals and protein-rich legumes – remained dominant; variety was perhaps supplied by locally gathered oil-bearing plants (since many later specialized crop-plants – the 'variety crops' – must have replaced small indigenous sources of these types of food). From the sixth millennium onwards it was variety crops rather than the staple crops which were added to the suite of cultigens and domesticates; and many of them were perennials such as tree-crops, propagated vegetatively to fix desirable strains (Zohary and Hopf 1993).

It is this process which needs to be seen in terms of the phenomena discussed in earlier sections, and particularly in terms of dietary diversification. The development of storable and transportable commodities was thus an important element of the growth of exchange: and especially products with high value and low bulk, which could nevertheless be produced in quantity at certain locations – oil-rich or sugar-rich species; aromatics or plants with a distinctive taste; fibre-plants and dyes. Many of these products could be combined, to create further consumable commodities. Such a description calls to mind the complex maritime trade of the Bronze Age; at the beginning of this process, in the Chalcolithic, distances were smaller and formulae simpler – but the principle was the same. The incentive to expand milk production, by keeping larger numbers of mature female sheep, was no doubt due in part to the fact that nutritious and relatively long-lasting cheeses could be produced, which would form useful items of exchange with neighbouring communities in environments slightly less advantageous for

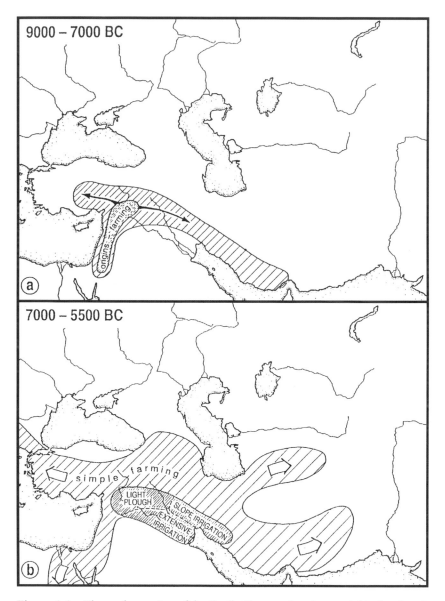

Figure 1.1 The nuclear region of the Fertile Crescent (south-west Asia), showing the spread of simple farming (horticulture) in the Neolithic (9000–7000 cal. BC) and the subsequent emergence of secondary farming (agriculture and arboriculture) in the Chalcolithic (7000–3500 cal. BC), culminating in the domestication of specialized transport-animals in the period or urbanization (3500–2500 cal. BC). Note that simple farming continued to spread during the time in which more advanced forms were emerging in the nuclear area (Sherratt 1997).

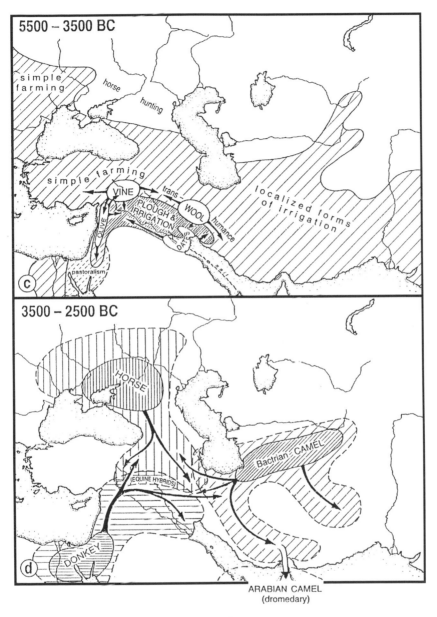

Figure 1.1 continued

raising animals. Wool provided a similar though longer-lasting product that could be traded over greater distances, and which could itself be made up into a variety of locally specified artefacts: it thus had the cross-cultural advantage of prime value, like metals (Renfrew 1986). Moreover the wool-bearing breeds of sheep would be an item of trade in themselves: to some extent 'hoarded' as 'trade secrets' – like the Siassi with their coconuts, since exchanging viable organisms would be the equivalent of giving away capital – but potentially available to seal a particularly valuable trading partnership. These considerations form the fine detail of the process of crop dispersal.

So also did the kinds of food produced. New ingredients and supplies must have had their effects on cuisine. Fruit crops, in particular, brought their own fungi, such as the yeasts; and new forms of what might be called micro-domesticates developed: genera such as *Saccharomyces*, probably transfered from fruits to sprouting (malted) cereals, to make beer and leavened bread; just as the bacterium *Lactobacillus* was tamed to make cheese and yoghurt (Englund 1995; Stol 1993; Teuber 1995). Transfers of techniques between crop complexes thus enhanced the range of products. These products made their parent cultigens more desirable, but they surely also had meanings for particular social groups (like tea for middle-class Europe), and provided cultural content to social differentiation. Alcoholic beverages were particularly important in this respect, helping to create the hard-drinking, landowning elite against which a tea-drinking bourgeoisie would make its cultural protest some 5,000 years later (Smith 1995).

The variety of crops (olive and date) evidenced at Nahal Mishmar on the edge of the Dead Sea by 4000 BC (Bar-Adon 1980) indicates that a lively series of exchanges around the edges of the Fertile Crescent had already taken place. It is possible to postulate separate areas of origin for the various elements of this secondary farming complex. Each of them appears to have been situated just beyond the inner arc of the Crescent where agrarian expansion in Greater Mesopotamia was most marked in the seventh and sixth millennia (Figure 1.2). They thus appear as 'variety crops' around the zone most suitable for producing carbohydrate staples. In the north, a variety of forms of evidence situate the domestication of the vine (and perhaps pomegranate) in eastern Anatolia, in the Mediterranean hill-country perhaps along the upper courses of the Euphrates and Tigris. On the evidence of tartaric acid in residues, McGovern *et al.* (1996) has identified grape-wine – not only from mid-fourth-millennium Godin Tepe in Kermanshah but even from sixth-millennium Hajji Firuz Tepe near Lake Rezaiyeh. Other tree-crops such as olive, fig and almond seem to have their origins further to the south-west, in the Mediterranean hill-country of the Levant. On the other hand, the date-palm was abundant in palm-groves at the head of the Persian Gulf, and is likely first to have been extensively utilized there; date-stones were recovered from the Ubaid (fifth millennium) levels at Eridu, in southern Iraq. Sheep are native to Iran, and the earliest evidence for a wool-bearing variety comes from Kermanshah, which would conform to this model of areas linked to the network of contacts that constitutes the Fertile Crescent. These elements were exchanged and diffused, in appropriate niches, around the area of Greater Mesopotamia during the fifth millennium. The close cultural and economic articulation of all these areas is indicated by the spread of the late Ubaid culture around northern Mesopotamia as well as its southern part, and

10000 BC cal.	**FERTILE CRESCENT**
	NATUFIAN
	(Younger Dryas)
9000	*(Holocene)*
	EARLY CULTIVATION
	OF PRIMITIVE CEREALS
8000	
	AND FIRST INTEGRATION
	OF DOMESTIC ANIMALS
	– CRISIS TRANSITION –
7000	
	SPATIAL EXPANSION AND
	SPREAD OF INNOVATIONS
	(cattle and free-threshing wheat)
	DEVELOPMENT OF
6000	PLOUGH CULTIVATION
	AND IRRIGATION
	(first farmers in the delta plain)
	DIVERSIFICATION
	OF PRODUCTS
5000	(tree-crops and secondary
	live and animal products)
	DENSE NETWORK OF
	EXCHANGES OF NEW PRODUCTS
	AROUND FERTILE CRESCENT
4000	
	RIVERINE BYPASS TRADE
	(centrality of plain/delta)
	GENESIS OF CENTRE/
	PERIPHERY INTERACTION
3000	(colonies)
	RIVAL SECONDARY STATES
	AND MILITARIZATION
2000	FIRST EMPIRES

Figure 1.2 Chronological diagram of the succession of agrarian regimes (and their political consequences) in the nuclear area of the western Old World in the earlier Holocene, *c.* 9000–2500 cal. BC (Sherratt 1997).

the chain of influences through the Levantine Chalcolithic cultures down to Egypt. This created a sphere of common interests and modes of consumption (not least of alcoholic drinks), within which a degree of regional specialization and inter-regional trade began to optimize productivity on a Ricardian (comparative advantage) model. Linking northern and southern parts of this sphere, the Euphrates in particular became a great highway which brought middleman opportunities to the Sumerians – the super-Siassi of Mesopotamia. Like the medieval Low Countries at the mouth of the Rhine, the logical response was the development of a woollen textile industry, adding value to the product; and it was on this basis, around the temple-centres with their flocks, herds and dependent labour, that the economic basis of Mesopotamian civilization was created.

It was the growing emphasis on storable and tradable secondary live products which characterized the agro-pastoral systems of this increasingly nuclear area. Even if some aspects of this development represented an 'adaptation' to an increasing range of environments, from coastal swamps to desert margins, it was to an equal if not greater extent 'auto-adaptive', in that the whole range of innovations were complementary and mutually adjusted through exchange. It is in this sense that the diversifying range of cultigens can be considered as cash-crops, and analysed from an economic as well as an ecological point of view. In this analysis, the products of cultivation differ in no fundamental respect from other forms of material culture. The development of techniques of processing and refinement, mixing and manufacture into commodities is precisely parallel to contemporary developments in metallurgy, from smelting to alloying and complex casting. These are not separate processes, but rather aspects of the same long-term trend towards the elaboration of material culture and more complex patterns of its social circulation.

THE SPREAD OF CROPS: 'DISPERSAL' OR 'TRADE'?

A growing complexity of diet and cuisine, in parallel to the evolution of more complex social and technological structures, is a continuing feature of cultural development. Archaeological textbooks sometimes give the impression that 'farming' had its 'origins' and then 'spread', after which nothing much happened except 'intensification'. In fact the farming systems of the world were in continuous flux, constantly absorbing new cultigens from their neighbours, and at the same time accommodating them socially and culturally in the complex ways hinted at above. Individual regions and their civilizations were not isolated, but interacted on an increasing scale – of which the 'globalization' of the world economy, so much discussed today, is but the final episode. These interactions have led to the dispersal of certain crops on a continental and intercontinental scale. Such exchanges between regional crop complexes form important episodes in world history. The most spectacular was, of course, the post-Columbian exchange of New and Old World crops which took place from AD 1500 onwards, and involved a whole spectrum of important and useful plants, from tobacco to the potato – to cite only two New World members of a single family, the Solanaceae. This has been chronicled, *inter alia*, by Alfred Crosby (1972), who has also considered the expansion of European crops, weeds, and especially livestock – with which the New World was relatively underendowed – in his 1986 book. This latter work has been criticized, however, for its failure to situate the biological process within a framework of economic and cultural imperialism, including the global specialization in production which came to characterize the modern world-system (Wallerstein 1974). Simple models of diffusion, or the ecological concept of colonization, are an inadequate tool to deal with the complexities of the historical process; and a more sophisticated approach is discussed below.

Some idea of the range of edible species which has dispersed in this way is provided by the *Oxford Book of Food Plants* (Harrison *et al.* 1969), which gives a compendium of species currently used for eating – whether by elites or mass consumers – across the world. Only about a fifth of these species could be considered calorific staples: the rest might collectively be termed 'variety crops'. (The statistic is rather artifical, in counting only the numbers of species, but it is worth defining more precisely: taking 'staples' to include grains, legumes and major root-crops, and 'non-staples' as fruits, herbs and leaf-vegetables, Harrison *et al.* (1969) lists *c.* seventy species or important varieties of the former, and *c.* 350 of the latter. A mere handful of calorie-rich species account for the great bulk of the world's production; the rationale of the rest is precisely in their diversity and variety – and these non-staple crops well deserve the name of 'variety crops'.) To this should be added not only the species which have now fallen from use (e.g., through replacement by more attractive – or commodified – equivalents), but also the great range of plants exploited for their non-food products, and together these provide the materials for a continuing process of exchange which has been going on without cessation since the inception of farming.

The 'Columbian exchange' was only the latest and best known of the inter-continental encounters, such as those between the western and eastern Old World (along the Silk Route), or between India and Africa (across the Indian Ocean). These clearly defined exchanges between biogeographic zones, however, are themselves only the most obvious of the subtle network of exchanges between regional centres of farming, and between secondary foci of domestication, which have accompanied the encounters of civilizations. Partly because of the association of the early Old World cereals with a demographic 'wave of advance', the spread of crops is curiously one of the few remaining fields in which migrationism is consistently invoked by prehistorians (e.g., Renfrew 1987), perhaps in the effort to avoid the reductionism of 'diffusion'; but both deserve a more sophisticated alternative. The spread of new crops, and of newly domesticated forms of livestock, is a *social* process: that is to say, part of the sphere of competition, emulation, negotiation, performance and communication like the rest of material culture usage. Simply because its products are consumable in the literal sense should not exclude them from the field of the anthropology of consumption!

One book which offers a model for the historical analysis of such a cultural transformation in which crops and livestock have played a prominent (but not exclusive) part is Andrew Watson's *Agricultural Innovation in the Islamic World: the diffusion of crops and farming techniques 700–1100* (1983). In longer perspective, the process described by Watson is a further phase of that *orientalización* of the western Mediterranean that had begun with the Phoenicians (who introduced the donkey and the olive – two features which had made their appearance in the Early Bronze Age of the eastern Mediterranean), and continued to some extent under the Romans. It was these elements, reinforcing earlier arrivals such as wool-bearing breeds of sheep, which *created* the Mediterranean environment and vegetation as we know it today (Huntley and Birks 1983). Rice and sugar-cane were Islamic introductions in Spain, as well as citrus fruits and cotton, marking the arrival of South Asian species in western Europe; and with them came new techniques of irrigation, including the water-wheel. (Watson also discusses sorghum, banana, coconut, watermelon, spinach, artichoke, colocasia, eggplant and mango.) This was the most important movement of crops before the Columbian exchange; and, indeed, the spread of sugar-cane to Spain made possible its export and establishment across the Atlantic as a major high-value commodity-producing crop in the colonial world of the early modern period.

This 'diffusion', however was not simply a continuous and inexorable spread, but rather an episodic process which usually happened rapidly, when many of the right conditions coincided, or not at all. Among the relevant factors were trade and prosperity, the regular use of certain routes, political and cultural compatibility, the fostering of demand, and the leading role of certain rulers in initiating transfers. That such factors were not novel ones is indicated by Egyptian 18th Dynasty records of Hatshepsut's expedition to Punt, or Tuthmosis III's conquests in the Levant, both of which resulted in the importation of foreign species, to be grown under royal patronage in Egypt (Manniche 1989). Islamic rulers were equally proud of their propagation of new species – some of which simply proclaimed the prestige of the exotic, though others were important as medicinal or spice plants, and some ultimately became widely grown food- or fibre-crops. Changed habits in diet and dress were sometimes necessary before they became widespread; though some introductions were simply locally grown substitutes for materials imported as luxuries (like sugar). Some of the imported species fitted the climate of the southern shore of the Mediterranean better than the existing suite of plants derived from a winter-rainfall complex: rice, cotton, sugar-cane, colocasia, eggplant, watermelon and sorghum were irrigated summer crops, and like Indian *kharif* crops (as opposed to winter-grown *rabi* crops, such as the wheats) formed complementary seasonal products. The agricultural 'revolution' was bound up with demographic changes and the settlement of new areas, often pushing far into the desert (where contacts could be maintained by camel), as well as with the process of urbanization. (This situation might be seen as a scaled-up version of the kind of agriculture typical of lowland western Asia since the fourth millennium, combining tree-crops, notably date-palms, with pastoralism, using camels instead of donkeys.) New products from introduced crops were often traded over long distances, now usually through the intermediacy of a merchant class. These factors show how farming innovation was embedded in a pattern of social, cultural and economic change. Watson refuses to separate agrarian history from general history: 'what one glimpses ... is an agricultural sector developing within an economy which was also developing, each acting on the other to determine the overall pattern of growth' (1983: 134). (Similar remarks would apply to the 'Ipomoean Revolution' in highland New Guinea, where the incentive to introduce the sweet potato was partly to sustain pig-feasting.)

Mediterranean sophistication – supported by a maritime trade that articulated with overland desert routes linking to the monsoon routes of the Indian Ocean – was slower to penetrate into temperate Europe beyond the Alps. It was only in the fourteenth century that the courts of Christian Europe began to develop a sophisticated, spice-based cuisine (Sherratt 1995: 14, and references therein), and during the sixteenth century there was a rapid development of tableware and serving equipment appropriate to the density of messages encapsulated in the now highly elaborate meals of the aristocracy and their bourgeois imitators. As the competitive display of this rising class came to challenge the aristocracy's monopoly of conspicuous consumption, so the older-established elite replied by emphasizing access to game and the subtlety of flavouring achieved by an expert *chef-de-cuisine*. Such manoeuvrings correspond well to the strategies and counter-strategies of social emulation described for instance by Miller (1982) as characteristic of the human uses of material culture; and food and food-crops are no exception to such generalizations. Just as the equipment of elite consumption practices (precious metal vessels) was imitated in less expensive media (Greek painted pottery or 'vases') by a broadening class of consumers in fifth-century BC Athens (Vickers and Gill 1994), so in our own times we have seen dogfish come to be described as 'rock-salmon', and served to the masses as if it were fresh from a Scottish salmon stream; or fizzy fermented pear-juice sold as 'Babycham', with the implication that it has some relationship to champagne. Here, then, lies an important dynamic of agrarian change: the desire of rising social groups for symbols of distinction, and consumption rituals (like the eighteenth-century middle-class tea ceremony) appropriate to their new-found class and station. Such is the fine detail of the process which on the map is represented by the successive isochrons of 'dispersal'.

CONCLUSION

This chapter has argued against the dualism that pervades archaeological analysis: the desire to set up oppositions between 'subsistence' and 'trade', and between 'ancient' (or 'prehistoric') and 'modern'. These lead to false dichotomies. The past was different from the present in many ways, not least in scale; but not so fundamentally that human motivations do not provide a thread of continuity.

I have therefore attempted to shift the subject-matter of 'subsistence' from the realm of the calculable determinism of economics into the interpretative domain of culture. This does not, however, demand a retreat into relativism and the assertion of cultural uniqueness. Food behaviours (and other forms of consumption) are not so environmentally or economically determined as to be fully predictable, but not so arbitrary as to preclude useful comparison. Values are socially constructed, but they are constructed for similar purposes in different cultures. There is no abstract, measurable quality called 'value'; but the desire to possess (and thus to mobilize goods for exchange) follows certain characteristic human propensities. 'Added value' is always the impression of meaning as well as simply the manufacture of a commodity: it carries an imprinted message (however much that message can be reinterpreted by its ultimate recipients). Even such dissimilar commodities as woollen textiles and wine have comparable properties in this respect. Wool made possible the manufacture of more plentiful and more elaborate textiles (Barber 1991; Winiger 1995). Texiles are intimately connected with the presentation of the body in everyday life, and thus with the creation and transmission of social meanings (Gittinger 1985; Weiner and Schneider 1989); hence also with concepts of civility and systems of social control. Roche (1994: 506) has talked of the 'production and commercialisation of appearances'. It is no coincidence that foreign missionaries tell the natives they are naked, and foreign merchants then sell them clothes: the ideological and the practical are two aspects of the same concept of 'civilization' and the *mission civilatrice*. It is not surprising, therefore, that an expansion of sheep-rearing has accompanied the spread of urban civilization in the Old World. Alcohol, too, is intimately connected with the sense of civilized identity which characterizes the region of central Eurasia extending from the Mediterranean to the Far East. This is not a simple addiction (though this element is undoubtedly present), but is testimony to the power of wine in particular to convey a subtle spectrum of meanings (both sacred and secular) concerning physical and spiritual well-being and social worthiness (Sherratt 1995). Similar observations could be made for olive-oil in relation to anointment, purification, body odour and social acceptability. Both wool-sheep and tree-crops have sustained social relations in this way since the Chalcolithic. Although they manifest them in a particularly powerful way, these properties are not confined to the consumables of civilizations; they are an aspect of all forms of consumption, whether in everyday cuisine or more particularly in rarer forms of ceremony and feasting.

Recognition of this fact does not imply neglect of the limits set by calories and bioenergetics, still less a denigration of the work of archaeologists who work with questions of sustenance and agrarian intensification. But there is a continuing tendency in the archaeological literature to cede responsibility to 'subsistence change' (even if no longer so explicitly to demographic pressure) as the principal motor of change in human societies. The perspective offered here would deny that population growth (or even agrarian improvement) is an independent variable; instead it would assert that societies grow and thrive as they successfully interact with their neighbours, and not least in the mutual provision of consumable commodities.

REFERENCES

Artzy, M. 1994. Incense, camels and collared rim jars: descrt trade routes and maritime outlets in the second millennium. *Oxford Journal of Archaeology* 13, 121–47.

Barber, E.J.W. 1991. *Prehistoric Textiles: the development of cloth in the Neolithic and Bronze Ages.* New Jersey: Princeton University Press.

Bar-Adon, P. 1980. *The Cave of the Treasure: the finds from the caves in Nahal Mishmar.* Jerusalem: Israel Excavation Society.

Brookfield, H.C. and D. Hart, 1971. *Melanesia: a geographical interpretation of an island world.* London: Methuen.

Clark, J.G.D. 1952. *Prehistoric Europe: the economic basis.* London: Methuen.

Crosby, A. 1972. *The Columbian Exchange: biological and cultural consequences of 1492.* Westport, Conn.: Greenwood Press.

Crosby, A.W. 1986. *Ecological Imperialism: the biological expansion of Europe, 900–1900.* Cambridge: Cambridge University Press.

Dickson, J.H. 1978. Bronze Age mead. *Antiquity* 52, 108–13.

Englund, R.K. 1995. Late Uruk period cattle and dairy products: evidence from proto-cuneiform sources. *Bulletin on Sumerian Agriculture* 8, 35–50.

Gittinger, M. 1985. *Splendid Symbols: textiles and tradition in Indonesia.* Oxford: Oxford University Press.

Harding, T.G. 1967. *Voyagers of the Vitiaz Strait.* Seattle: University of Washington Press.

Harrison, S.G., G.B. Masefield, and M. Wallis (with B.E. Nicholson, illustrator) 1969. *The Oxford Book of Food Plants.* Oxford: Oxford University Press.

Huntley, B. and H.J.B. Birks, 1983. *An Atlas of Past and Present Pollen Maps for Europe 0–13,000 years ago.* Cambridge: Cambridge University Press.

Kislev, M.E. and O. Bar-Yosef. 1988. The legumes: earliest domesticated plants in the Near East? *Current Anthropology* 29, 175–8.

Levy, T. 1992. Transhumance, subsistence, and social evolution in the northern Negev desert. In *Pastoralism in the Levant: archaeological materials in anthropological perspective,* O. Bar-Yosef and A. Khazanov (eds), pp. 65–82. Madison, Wis.: Prehistory Press.

McGovern, P.E., D.L. Ginsker, L.J. Exner and M.M. Voigt. 1996. Neolithic resinated wine. *Nature* 381, 480–1.

Manniche, L. 1989. *An Ancient Egyptian Herbal.* London: British Museum Press.

Miller, D. 1982. Artefacts as products of human categorisation. In *Symbolic and*

Structural Archaeology, I. Hodder (ed.), 17–25. Cambridge: Cambridge University Press.

Needham, S. and J. Evans. 1987. Honey and dripping: neolithic food residues from Runnymede Bridge, *Oxford Journal of Archaeology* 6, 21–8.

Nitz, H.-J. 1993. Introduction. In *The Early-Modern World-System in Geographical Perspective*, H.-J. Nitz (ed.), 1–25. Stuttgart: Franz Steiner Verlag.

Renfrew, A.C. 1986. Varna and the emergence of wealth in prehistoric Europe. In *The Social Life of Things: commodities in cultural perspective*, A. Appadurai (ed.), 141–68. Cambridge: Cambridge University Press.

Renfrew, A.C. 1987. *Archaeology and Language: the puzzle of Indo-European origins*, London: Cape.

Roche, D. 1994. *The Culture of Clothing: dress and fashion in the ancien regime*. Cambridge: Cambridge University Press.

Runnels, C. and Tj.H. van Andel. 1988. Trade and the origins of agriculture in the eastern Mediterranean. *Journal of Mediterranean Archaeology* 1, 83–109.

Schmitt, L. 1994. The Hensbacka: a subsistence strategy of continental hunter-gatherers, or an adaptation at the Pleistocene–Holocene boundary? *Oxford Journal of Archaeology* 13, 245–64.

Sherratt, A.G. 1995. Alcohol and its alternatives: symbol and substance in early Old World cultures. In *Consuming Habits: drugs in history and anthropology*, J. Goodman, P. Lovejoy and A. Sherratt (eds.) 11–46 London: Routledge.

Sherratt, A.G. 1996a. Plate tectonics and imaginary prehistories; structure and contingency in agricultural origins. In *Origins and Spread of Agriculture*, D. R. Harris (ed.), 130–40. London: UCL Press.

Sherratt, A.G. 1996b. Why Wessex? The Avon route and river transport in later prehistoric Britain. *Oxford Journal of Archaeology* 15, 211–34.

Sherratt, A.G. 1997. *Economy and Society in Prehistoric Europe: changing perspectives*. Edinburgh: Edinburgh University Press.

Smith, W.D. 1995. From coffeehouse to parlour: the consumption of coffee, tea and sugar in north-western Europe in the 17th and 18th centuries. In *Consuming Habits: drugs in history and anthropology*, J. Goodman, P. Lovejoy and A. Sherratt (eds), 148–64. London: Routledge.

Stol, M. 1993. Milk, butter and cheese. *Bulletin on Sumerian Agriculture* 7, 99–113.

Teuber, M. 1995. How can modern food technology help to identify dairy products mentioned in Sumerian texts? *Bulletin on Sumerian Agriculture* 8, 23–31.

Vickers, M. and D. Gill. 1994. *Artful Crafts: ancient Greek silverware and pottery*. Oxford: Clarendon Press.

Wallerstein, I. 1974. *The Modern World-System: capitalist agriculture and the origins of the world-economy in the 16th century*. New York: Academic Press.

Wallerstein, I. 1989. *The Modern World-System: the second great expansion of the capitalist world-economy, 1730–1840*, New York: Academic Press.

Watson, A. 1983. *Agricultural Innovation in the early Islamic World: the diffusion of crops and farming techniques, 700–1100*. Cambridge: Cambridge University Press.

Weiner, A. and J. Schneider (eds). 1989. *Cloth and Human Experience*. Washington, DC: Smithsonian Institution Press.

Winiger, J. 1995. Die Bekleidung des Eismannes und die Anfänge der Weberei nördlich der Alpen. In *Der Mann im Eis: neue Funde und Ergebnisse* (The Man in the Ice, 2), K. Spindler, E. Rastbichler-Zissernig, H. Wilfing, D. zur Nedden and H. Nothdurfter (eds), 199–87. Vienna: Springer-Verlag.

Zohary, D. and M. Hopf. 1993. *Domestication of Plants in the Old World: the origin and spread of cultivated plants in West Asia, Europe and the Nile Valley*. Oxford: Clarendon Press.

Zvelebil, M. 1996. The agricultural frontier and the transition to farming in the circum-Baltic region. In *The Origins and Spread of Agriculture and Pastoralism in Eurasia*, D.R. Harris (ed.), 323–45. London: UCL Press.

2 Cultural implications of crop introductions in Andean prehistory

CHRISTINE A. HASTORF

INTRODUCTION

Plants participate in political processes at many levels: civic, ceremonial, ritual, as well as daily practice, creating and recreating the world that people perceive and live in through the meals that are prepared and eaten, the tools that are produced and used, the kin groups that exist across the landscape. Through plant patterns in the archaeological record, archaeologists can identify cultural activities. In this chapter, I shall look at the onset of agriculture and the entrance of crop use seen archaeologically along the west coast of Peru with a focus on the tempo of uptake of foreign crops. With that evidence, I shall explore what plant use might illustrate about the social dynamics in these early sedentary groups. I will use the example of Peruvian coastal plant data, spanning the time of the first plants up to the evidence for the political developments of the Early Horizon. The dates and traditional phase names span the Preceramic and the Initial Phases:

- Preceramic Phase III (8000–6000 BC);
- Preceramic Phase IV (6000–4200 BC);
- Preceramic Phase V (4200–2500 BC);
- Preceramic Phase VI (2500–2100 BC) – Cotton Preceramic;
- Initial Period (2100–1400 BC).[1]

The greater Andean region of South America is considered one of the centres of pre-modern civilization. This area includes modern Ecuador, Peru, Bolivia, northern Chile and north-west Argentina. It lies along the main spine of the South American continental mountain range. It is notable for its diverse environmental zones that can be very close together. The area this study focuses on is the Peruvian coast, along hundreds of kilometres of very dry coastline. Many scholars describe this long time-span there, like the Neolithic in Europe, as a unified, homogeneous cultural and economic trajectory. But, looking at this time-span from another angle, I think we can see diversity in this sequence that illustrates the growth and maintenance of cultural identities as well as the values of the plants that were farmed.

My question is not why did intensive agriculture take so long to develop on the coast of Peru, which it did, but what can the introductions of the crops and their distributions during this long time period illustrate about the political and cultural processes that were occurring? Here I shall view the creation of cultural difference through food and its preparation and to investigate what meanings might have accompanied such a process. By moving on from the well-discussed models of population pressure and climatic constraints of the coast, I think we can see a dynamic of cultural difference along the coast in the preceramic phases between 8000–1400 BC that only minimally relates to environmental differences (Lanning 1967). Many ideas have been put forward for why agriculture began and why it spread. While most models hold a grain of truth, none satisfy the archaeological community with an explanation. I think we can gain further understanding about this transition by looking at the differences in these changes more closely.

Marek Zvelebil, in his edited volume on the transition to farming in Eurasia, presents a series of models for agrarian onset with an eye towards geographical and temporal differences. In the concluding chapter he makes a case that this innovation occurs for different reasons in different settings. He lists a series of traditional causes for taking up agriculture in different geographical settings. These include filling gaps in the local resources (Lewthwaite 1986), contact with farmers (Zvelebil 1986), a decline in resources through climate change, environmental stress or population pressure and thus the need for increased calorific output (Cohen 1978, 1981), social competition (Bender 1978, 1985; Hayden 1990), and colonization (Ammerman and Cavalli-Sforza 1984). This last model for the uptake of agriculture outside of a plant (or animal) domestication core suggests that when a set of crops were adopted, they were accompanied by new technologies, paraphernalia, and people. Zvelebil (1986) notes that when crops arrived as a package, people were probably moving into the region, bringing along their own cultural traits and subsistence strategies. While this should be the most easily visible model in the archaeological record, it does not have supporting evidence along the coast of Peru.

The other above-mentioned models are well known and have been suggested for the Peruvian onset of agriculture, therefore I will not elaborate on these models here. I claim that these models do not provide us with the closest explanations for the onset and spread of agriculture. I would like to re-focus our view of this transition by taking a slightly different look at the agricultural evidence to see if we cannot get closer to the changes during the preceramic years, setting the stage for the later, rich, and elaborate Andean political (pre) histories.

SOME MODELS

The traditional economic models of agricultural origins do not fit most individual examples, their scales are not correct. This challenges us to seek out new perspectives about domestication, directing us to look at the smaller events in food use. Perhaps these events are more tied to inter-community relations, settlement configuration, marriage patterns and exchange (Goody 1982), harvesting shifts (Hillman and Davies 1990; Bohrer 1991), as well as the definition of the people's ethnicities through daily practice.

What were the first domesticates and what might have been their value to the people tending them? A traditional model for Peruvian agriculture is that people were hungry so they focused on producing high carbohydrate foods to ease resource pressure and feed their growing population (Cohen 1978; Wilson 1981). Food shortage could have been brought about by many causes, including climate change, change in the resource base, or just more people in the area. I find these models particularly dubious for the Peruvian coast. The Peruvian coast is one of the richest marine food resource areas in the world (Moseley 1975; Quilter and Stocker 1983). Models for the onset of agriculture also include the impact of the periodic torrential storms (El Niño) and the need for storage along the Peruvian coast (Osborne 1977). This storm model is curious because periodic storms, which occur in many places of the world, have not been used as a model for agricultural origins in other regions.

Of the two main classes of foragers who adopt agriculture world-wide, one is mobile with small groups following clustered, patchy resources, the other is more sedentary with larger communities and steady, local resources. Zvelebil (1986) suggests that farming was more likely to be taken up by mobile foragers first, while more sedentary and complex foragers would accept it more slowly and for different reasons. Sedentary coastal foragers with good marine and littoral resources, like Peru, at some point in time would have had access to and knowledge about the use of various crops but clearly chose *not* to add their production and tending to their daily activities, nor to change their cuisine and symbolic economy for some time – if ever in some cases.

The *regular* use of domestic crops in the early days of farming, especially among the more sedentary foragers, seems to be more about cultural symbols and kinship relationships than hunger. Farrington and Urry's model for domestication (1985) suggests that the first domesticated plants were herbaceous plants of a tasty, oily or spicy flavour, consumed to diversify meals rather than to bulk them up; exotic (even medicinal) foods added to special family or group meals rather than to ward off starvation. While the authors do not speculate beyond the desirability of this food type, their refreshing model prompts one to ask how and why *specific* plants may have entered into a group's daily practice? Can we suggest that the tasty plants that were taken up also had some special meaning or identity due to their links with places, events, or peoples? I would think that the new foods had to have a (positive) meaning in order to be added into the cuisine.

The Farrington and Urry model is a variation of the idea proposed by Braidwood for grain domestication in the Near East (1953). He suggests that early grain cultivation was due to an interest in beer production; people took the extra time for plant tending to provide a bit of 'spice' in their daily routine with the consumption of fermented beverages and all that might have entailed culturally and socially (Braidwood 1953). The role of fermented beverages and hallucinogens in early agriculture comes and goes in the archaeological literature, but I think they probably played a larger part in initiating new activities than archaeologists give them credit for.

A more politically driven model for the use of domesticates is seen in Barbara Bender's (1978) and Brian Hayden's (1990) ideas that people adopted and cultivated crops because of an increased interest in political activities and exchange. They assume that agricultural produce would provide exchangeable goods, thus making groups regularly operate in a larger network. Gaining items for exchange can be linked to an increased desire for public display, alliance building and group construction of identity through feasts and food gifts. These political acts would probably be initiated by important families, leaders, or religious persons, keen to introduce plants and encourage the cultivation of crops once they were present. Such acts, however, seem to occur after the cultural changes that are initiated with agriculture in changing daily practice. This political stage, involved in the growth of hierarchy and surplus, is a different level of interest and access than the differences being formed in early agriculture.

We see more appropriate small-scale beginnings without overt political pressures (but probably covert social pressures) in the model proposed by Watson and Kennedy (1991). They suggest that women gatherers first initiated the cultivation of plants in North America, through their tending of wild taxa that were of interest to them in their daily rounds of food and medicine gathering. Women thus were the plant nurturers that instigated the morphological and genetic changes that we associate with domestication, not as an economic behaviour, but as nurturers of, and experimenters with, people and plants. This point cannot be overemphasized. Women foragers are constantly collecting and experimenting with plants for nibbling, spicing foods, and medicines. The female Barasana of Colombia, a foraging, swidden farming group, are the collectors of plants. They bring back cuttings, exchange with friends and kin, in a constantly nurturing mode of plant and family raising (Hugh-Jones, pers. comm.). Women also are involved in tending specific taxa that they inherit along their family lines; special family crops that have symbolic meanings linked to the origin myths of their ancestors. These would be carried with women when they moved, planted in each new home, and fed to their families. Their neighbours would recognize that specific variety as that family's plant, with all of its connotations.

Helping us develop a different model of agricultural onset in Peru are the activities from modern Amazonian forager-farmers. Current evidence suggests that small-scale familial inter-regional relationships have wide-ranging catchments, due to exogamous marriage patterns. Through these networks of periodic visits or while on hunting and gathering journeys away from home-base villages, plants are brought back from near and far, not for gain but for curiosity, pleasure and value (Hugh-Jones and Posey, pers. comm.). These plants are planted along local paths and in encircling kitchen gardens and include exotics, medicinal, magical, industrial, mind-altering, and spicy food plants. In this way, plants enter into a people's cuisine because of experimentation, interest, and curiosity. Further, in the Amazon, some plant varieties are community markers. Communities have specific taxa or varieties that are associated with their community identity (Hugh-Jones, pers. comm.). These plants are passed on through the generations to grow and eat, especially at feasts in the process of defining ethnicity. As ethnic markers their neighbours emphasize different plants in their own feasts and myths. Thus these plants move with the people as part of their rituals, renewing their social ties past and present as well as marking their territory.

Such a scenario for plant entry is likely for the Peruvian coast, as most plants were brought in from elsewhere, and thus had to be cared for as special things within the landscape from the start. In fact, the earliest coastal evidence suggests that the plants were grown in a world that was not domesticated nor sedentary. We don't know much about the pre-agricultural sites, but probably there was movement from the coast seasonally inland with fishing and foraging in the *lomas* cloud forests on the coast and gathering and hunting inland, even up into the intermontane region and over into the jungle. We have evidence for cave use and tool processing sites, but coastal sites hint at sedentism only by around 4000 BC.

ABOUT DOMESTICATION

How does domestication first become possible and then active in a group? Hodder (1991) has addressed this question for the European Neolithic by suggesting that people first had to create the concept of domestication before actions could be taken. I suggest that the physical and social development and maintenance of the kin-line and family was an active ingredient in initiating the concept of both farming and territoriality. Things and places would begin to be associated with activities that surround families. A jurisdiction over a plant, tree, or place on a stream (a loose ownership) was probably developed through using the thing or place in special ritual time. This concept could have been expanded upon and other *things* could then become 'domesticated' or incorporated into a family's array of collective memories and associated things. This could include clay for pottery, springs for water, plants and where they grow, resources for building shelters and making tools, as well as whole landscapes for living in. The objects have to take on new meanings and identities. Human influence (impact, power, or a sense that humans have made a difference) is linked to meaningful interactions with a thing ('a loose form of domestication'), and this interaction creates a sense of identity.

How did people change their view of the landscape such that they began to see it as a place and a territory rather than just something they move through? Thomas (1993) has suggested that, as seasonal rounds became more regular and as locations were repeatedly visited by the same people, a series of encounters with these specific locales would become incorporated into the people's collective memories and cosmologies. Each place became invested with past memories and meanings. These special places in turn influenced the activities that occurred there, creating group identity and social relations within the group (Thomas 1993: 82). Such locations and associated remembrances would have existed where specifically charged interactions transpired. At times these would have been events that included the use of the local vegetation and animals. These marked places could have become special, expressly because they were where certain plants or animals inhabited and/or where these life-forms interacted with humans. These places or plants could have gained meaningful identity through such recurring activities. People identify with and therefore signify ('domesticate') places, as well as flora and fauna, probably well before morphologically defined domestication is evident in the archaeological record.

Social identity therefore is associated with food preferences. As individuals and families begin to identify with a place or with specific activities, they also begin to identify with the food they eat together there (Appadurai 1981; Douglas 1984). A version of this is seen in the totems of many societies, where kin groups identify with certain taxa. So too, food presentations have meanings, associated with people, events, and spatial or temporal places where they are consumed. Foods and activities can be social markers used in group affiliation, often without other material signs that archaeologists look for are visible and well before hierarchy is codified. Food can separate one sub-group from another not only in fasting and taboos (males and females, young and old), but also in foods that are feasted. This is done through identifying preferences such as one group eating maize at their feast, while their neighbours down the road feast on manioc. Further, cultural and political differences can be negotiated and accentuated through food preparation and presentation (Hastorf and Johannessen 1993; Welch and Scarry 1995).

Plants that were adopted by groups early on surely had special meanings or identities due to their links with places, events and histories. It is up to us now to search for and propose what these associations and meanings might have been in the groups we study. One goal therefore is to chart the acceptance of domestic plants and the social and political changes that must have accompanied these processes.

We see in various examples around the world that, after local plant cultivation began and the concepts of domestication and territory were initiated, groups incorporated foreign plants, but these often provided only a small portion of the diet for a long time. Why did people take up some crops and not others into their diet either as new foods or as substitutes of something previously foraged? Was it that these plants had different meanings for the farmers, that some plants were brought in with a mythology while others were connected to their neighbours' mythology? What can we learn from a sequence of plant additions into diets and cuisines about cultural developments?

THE PERUVIAN CASE

Returning to the earlier models, the Peruvian coastal environmental situation fits the sedentary forager model of rich marine resources best. Yet, it is one of driest places in the world, with habitable areas restricted to the coast and along the rivers. What we find is that hundreds and sometimes thousands of years passed before certain coastal valley residents adopted some of the crops that their neighbours were growing and consuming. We will see in the data that, while there are several different patterns of crop adoption, in general crops entered the region in a patchy manner. I do not think there is strong evidence for stress on resources during these times. The evidence reflects different selective cultural strategies and meanings at each site.

The data we have for coastal Peru are of irregular quality but of superb preservation. With more than twenty sites that have botanical remains on or near the coast, the data are in no way complete or systematic. Over the years, many different collection strategies have been implemented, making it impossible to quantitatively compare the samples. Because of this, I present the plant taxa qualitatively, as either present or absent.[2]

The first evidence for crop plants on the coast comes in the Preceramic III phase, 8000–6000 BC. However, substantial agriculture, with a regular array of fifteen to twenty crops growing up and down the coast, occurs only by the end of the Initial phase, 2100–1400 BC, some 4–5,000 years later. By this time we have irrigation systems associated with civic architecture.

The plant material
Figures 2.1–2.5[3] present a selective set of twelve crop taxa in five archaeological phases spanning the earliest crop evidence through large ceremonial centres and semi-urban ways of life. Most of these crops occur regularly at coastal sites after the Initial Period, after 1400 BC. By then we have evidence for a qualitatively different form of hierarchy and stratification in the record of both difference within and between communities. Not all plant taxa found on the sites are included in this presentation. I have chosen only a range of crops to focus on the trends. The point of this subset is to

look at general trends of taxa introduction through time. The plants are plotted on the maps by presence only, so that the viewer can see the general pattern through time without too many plants to comprehend at one time. My hope is that patterns and trends of plant entry will be clearer if we track fewer plants. I selected a representative array of plants from three major plant categories to give a balanced perspective of the most important plant entries. These plants include three locally 'domesticated' plants, begonia (*Begonia geraniifolia*), cotton (*Gossypium barbedense*), and bottle gourd (*Lagenaria siceraria* (Mol.) Standl.) and nine introduced, foreign plants.

These nine plants encompass several plant life-forms that are important when thinking about people actually planting and tending the crops; in other words, the types of human–plant interactions necessary for the successful growing of the plant. These plant categories include root crops: manioc (or yucca *Manihot esculenta* Crantz), achira (*Canna edulis*), potatoes (*Solanum* spp. L.), and begonia; annuals: chile peppers (*Capsicum* spp., *chinensis* and *baccatum*), common bean (*Phaseolus vulgaris),* lima bean (*Phaseolus lunatus*), bottle gourd, cotton, and maize (*Zea mays* L.), and perennial trees, avocado (*Persea americana*) and guava (*Psidium guajava*). Most of these plants come from the eastern slopes of the central Andes or from the tropics in the northern part of the continent (Pickersgill 1969; Bergh 1976; Pickersgill and Heiser 1977; Pearsall 1992). In those places planting can occur all year long. It is becoming more accepted that the first South American domesticates were root crops, probably initially cultivated in the moister regions of southern Mesoamerica and northern South America (Sauer 1952; Harris 1969; Roosevelt 1980; Stone 1984).

Along the west coast, differences in plant use cannot be attributed to different climatic or storm patterns, although there are slight differences in the moisture regimes and micro-environments. There is variation in water availability between the valleys. The southern valleys are drier with more seasonal water flowing down the rivers from the Andes; the northern valleys are larger and have perennial water. The northern valleys have sandy beaches from which to launch boats and to net fish, while south of the Santa Valley the shoreline is rocky, which is good for rock-pool animals. The sea and especially the rocky littoral had abundant foods and there was regular *lomas* (cloud forest) plant exploitation. Given that the bulk of the plants in the archaeological record up and down the coast are non-local, the pattern of plant uptake suggests social and symbolic processes at work as much as if not more than economic and environmental.

Annual plants

Six annual crops are plotted on the maps, including the most prominent plants through prehistory. The earliest, chile pepper, is the *Capsicum baccatum*, domesticated in southern Peru or eastern Bolivia. The second South American pepper, *C. chinense*, arrived on the coast also from the eastern slopes (Pickersgill 1969). Both peppers are hardy plants that need warmth and water. The lima bean arrived earlier in Peru than the common bean. While both beans are from the eastern slopes of the Andes, they were taken up differentially along the coast while becoming important crops (Gepts *et al.* 1986; Kaplan 1980). Gourds, like cotton, are first found on the north coast and in the highlands but are thought to have been harvested wild on the west coast of South America from locally growing varieties that existed naturally along the lower river banks on the South American coastline. Andean cotton is a hybrid of several cotton species from the New World and Africa, considered to have been naturally dispersed (Stephens and Moseley 1974). Both gourds and cotton seem to have been harvested for a long time before visible morphological change occurred. These two plants grow well along the sunny coastline.

Maize is an interesting crop and actually seems to arrive quite late into the Andean region, given its locus of origin in the Rio Balsas region of western Mexico and early evidence in lowland Central and South America (Benz 1994; Bush *et al.* 1989; Pearsall 1994). It is an annual that must be tended by humans to survive, though it is quite flexible genetically and can adapt to many different environments. Its route into the western Andes was either down the western coast and/or over the mountains to the coast from the eastern slopes.

Vegetatively reproduced plants

Of the four tuberous plants, manioc is the earliest in the region. Several locations of origin have been suggested for manioc: north-eastern Brazil (the driest locale), southern Mexico–Guatemala, the Orinoco River Basin, or Venezuela, all places with a dry and a wet season (Harris 1969; Rogers 1963: 52; Rogers and Appan 1972: 1). The South American locations are considered the most likely loci of origin. This perennial shrub can produce bitter or sweet root-tubers. It is thought that the sweet variety spread first into the Andes, requiring little processing to make it edible (Hawkes 1989: 486). Since it can be harvested year-round this is a very useful crop, except that a protein source must accompany it to make a balanced diet. It is propagated by replanting cuttings, and thus is not as easy to domesticate as other tubers. The archaeological evidence supports its domestication because of its spread to new locations from its homeland.

Achira is thought to have been domesticated in mid-elevation valleys, perhaps even in the western-slope Andean valleys of South America or in the eastern mid-elevation valleys (Ugent *et al.* 1984; Hawkes 1989: 492). It propagates by its tubers, and thus is very easy to cultivate. Like manioc, there is no clear evidence for domestication other than its geographical spread. Its regular presence suggests that it was easily and quickly adapted to the coast.

The potato's most likely wild progenitors come from the greater Titicaca Basin and its nearby valleys and could have spread across the Andes and down into the western valleys reasonably quickly (Hawkes 1989: 495). It is a stem tuber in that the storage organs grow off stems under the ground. It propagates by planting the previous year's tubers, which generate more underground storage tubers. It is easy to plant and can become feral easily. Begonia is a west coast *lomas* plant that was intensively used and perhaps cultivated at the Chilca sites, but seemed never to spread much beyond there (Quilter 1989).

Perennial trees

I have included two trees, one a protein-rich food and the second a fruit tree. The avocado tree species found in Peru comes from northern South America (Bergh 1976). Its high protein and fat content would make it a very desirable food – especially so because this South American variety can yield all year round and produces for many years. It is a tree propagated by seed, and thus cropping such a plant would take dedication to plant and maintain with regular visits and/or local residence to harvest it. It would be some years before the first yield, and its presence suggests people had a long-term interest in a locale and planned for such a crop to produce years in the future. Guava is also a tree species, growing in warm, moist settings, requiring years to produce mature fruit. Its locus of domestication is unclear at this point. Guava first occurs archaeologically in mid-elevations in the Andes and could have been brought in from nearby, over the mountains (Harlan 1975).

THE SEQUENCE OF CROP INTRODUCTIONS

At the beginning of this sequence pre-8000 BC coastal people were living on a combination of *lomas* seasonal cloud forest plants and animals as well as a wide range of marine life. The northern coast stabilized to what we see today only by 4000 BC, the reason we have no early coastal sites in the north. What coastal evidence we do have from the south coast, like La Paloma in the Chilca Valley, indicates that people lived near and between the *lomas* and the coast (Quilter 1989). The inland Santa Valley Guiterrero Cave foodstuffs could have arrived from the eastern rivers originally but were probably grown locally (Lynch 1980). We are not yet able to reconstruct what type of communication networks existed between the western valleys and the eastern slopes. It is not surprising that foraging people moved easily across this space and that at least some members of the coastal groups travelled regularly up the western valleys into and over the mountains to the eastern areas.

In the first phase, the Preceramic III during the seventh millennium, the earliest crops in the north are beans and chile peppers, with potato and manioc to the south in the Chilca Valley and the Tres Ventanas Cave (Figure 2.1). Most of this plant evidence is of questionable identification. The best documented material comes from the Guiterrero Cave (Lynch 1980), although there has been a reassessment of the early beans using AMS dating which places the bean later in time (Kaplan 1994). While I am not convinced

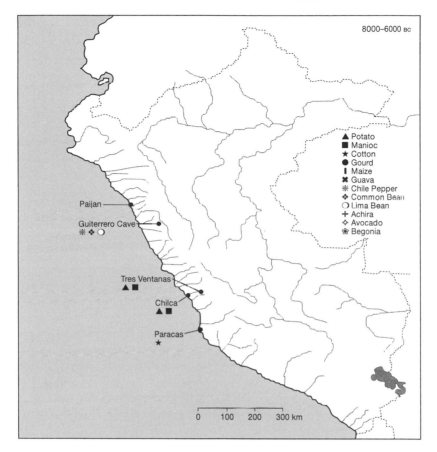

Figure 2.1 Twelve domestic plant taxa distributions of the Preceramic III: 8000–6000 BC from the central Andean region, based primarily on Lanning (1967) and Pearsall (1978, 1992).

of the security of the date and stratigraphy of the tubers at Tres Ventanas Cave in the Chilca Valley, some scholars support the early dates, a millennium earlier than Guiterrero Cave (Engel 1973; Martins-Farias 1976). All crops are introduced from afar except perhaps the potato at Tres Ventanas Cave.

While tubers do not become common over the next 5,000 years, beans continue to be the most common crops in the excavations, from 6000 to 4200 BC (Figure 2.2), with beans, gourd and guava entering the south coast at La Paloma (Quilter 1989). Because of the high frequencies of begonia at La Paloma, Quilter suggests that it was intensively harvested and perhaps cultivated at that site. This, however, is the only site where such evidence exists at this time.

When very little else was grown, beans were cultivated. Could they have been introduced as a taste treat, fitting the Farrington and Urry model? More importantly, half of the edible crops from these first two phases (chiles, beans

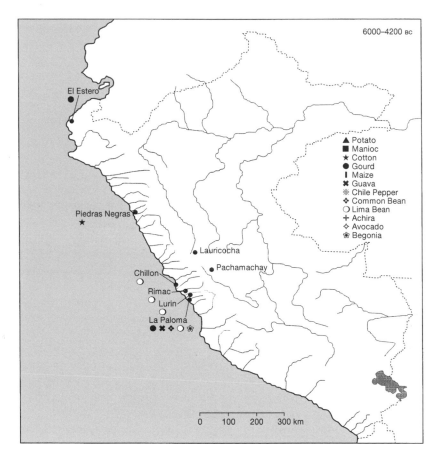

Figure 2.2 Twelve domestic plant taxa distributions of the Preceramic IV: 6000–4200 BC from the central Andean region, based primarily on Lanning (1967) and Pearsall (1978, 1992).

and guava) are savoury treats. Chile peppers are still the quintessential spice in the New World; toasted beans are a common snack food today. Perhaps early starchy foods occurred in the western valley caves, but then there is a hiatus in site occupation evidence until about 2500 BC, leaving us without much solid evidence for plant use there. The annual crops are moderately hardy and could be left to grow on their own along the river banks in the same areas where riparian plants, gourds, and cotton could grow, suggesting that people could have still been making seasonal rounds well through 4000 BC. This is when the climatic patterns of today probably began (periodic El Niños).

In the Preceramic V phase (4200–2500 BC), we see the continued occurrence of beans, with both bean taxa present on the south and the central coast (Figure 2.3). It is towards the end of this phase that achira and avocado enter the region. Several new crops occur at La Galgada, a ritual site in the mid-elevations of the Santa Valley (Smith, in Grieder *et al.* 1988:

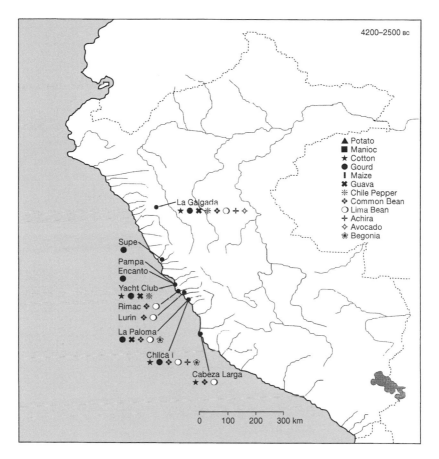

Figure 2.3 Twelve domestic plant taxa distributions of the Preceramic V: 4200–2500 BC from the central Andean region, based primarily on Lanning (1967) and Pearsall (1978, 1992).

125–51). This site is a ceremonial centre *en route* between the coast and the eastern slopes. Therefore, it is not surprising that it has the first evidence for achira and avocado from the east. The other achira evidence is from the Chilca Valley. Beans are most frequent at the coastal sites. The other common crops now are the industrial cotton and gourd. Cotton occurs irregularly with gaps of three or four valleys between. Cotton and gourd at the highland site of La Galgada diminish the thesis that these two crops were initially farmed because of their benefit to fishing (Moseley 1975).

Intriguing is the evidence that C. Earle Smith found at La Galgada that the ritual structures' central hearths contain chile peppers (Grieder *et al.* 1988). He posits that they were burned in rituals to create a potent smoke that caused irritation and therefore memorable events within these early, small, enclosed structures. Stephen Hugh-Jones relates a similar idea from groups in the modern Colombian Amazon, where, in the past, their ancestors used to throw peppers into fires to drive away demons and purify the people. La Galgada inhabitants seem to have also participated in such rituals. Chile peppers seem to be a particularly charged plant across the Americas.[4]

Looking at the distribution of the guava tree, previously it had been found only at La Paloma, and now it is also present three valleys to the north at the Yacht Club site near the Chillon Valley and at La Galgada further north and inland. It is not found to the south of the Chilca Valley. Guava's distribution gives us a sense that some groups chose to plant guava while others did not, if the data we have at present are reliable. Thousands of years after agriculture began along the coast, tasty, nutritious crops have the greatest presence. They are the only crops of the twelve that are found at every site. This phase of plant remains gives us the best explanatory view of the earliest introduced plants. The reasons for their uptake seems to be symbolic, social, and flavourful.

In the Cotton Preceramic VI (2500–2100 BC), domestic plants are more common at all sites and we see new, intriguing patterns (Figure 2.4). There are now two main complexes of crops that co-occur at the sites. First, beans and peppers co-occur (with squash as well) throughout the coast, building on earlier trends. The second cluster of crops that co-occur, especially on the central coast, are gourd, cotton, achira, and guava. These plants were present in the previous phase; industrial, one starchy food, and one fruit. Maize, avocado, potato, and manioc are present during these 400 years, but sporadically.

At this time, maize is present only every three valleys or so along the coast: in the valleys of Viru, Supe, Chancay, and Chilca, as well as in the Ayacucho Caves. Maize has a large seed and is easy to identify if present in plant collections. Avocado only occurs in the north, not south of the greater Moche region. The potato is a difficult plant to identify. It has been found at Huaynuná in the Casma Valley (Ugent *et al.* 1982) and perhaps in the Ayacucho Caves (MacNeish *et al.* 1980). Manioc is found only at Guiterrero Cave in the central region, but it too is difficult to identify.

By this time, after four or five thousand years of agriculture, we can begin to assess what some of these patterns might mean socially. Manioc is especially intriguing. From the research that has been carried out on manioc and its probable early domestication in northern South America, we learn that it can produce more calories than other staple crops in low fertility soils, hence its great modern importance throughout the lowlands of Meso-america and South America (Rogers 1963; Rogers and Appan 1972). Given that it might have been present in the region by 6000 BC at Tres Ventanas Cave (Engel 1973), it is curious that it did not become as ubiquitous as achira did over the next 4,000 years. If manioc was first in the region, it did not become the most common, whereas achira, also a lowland staple and equally difficult to identify, arrives in the Preceramic V and becomes ubiquitous within 500 years of its entry. Their very different patterns of distribution through space and time suggest that these two lowland, high carbohydrate root crops had different entrance routes and values associated with them.

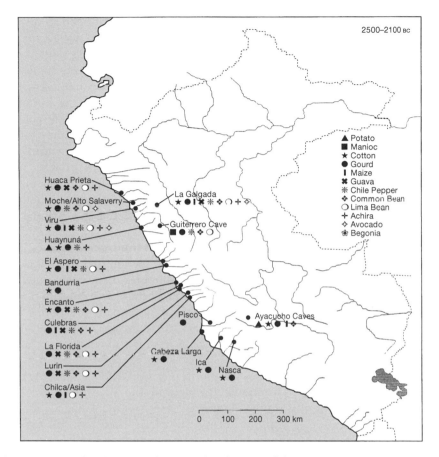

Figure 2.4 Twelve domestic plant taxa distributions of the Preceramic VI: 2500–2100 BC from the central Andean region, based primarily on Lanning (1967) and Pearsall (1978, 1992).

Manioc does not seem to have had the same connotations as achira. A closer look at the specific sites where manioc or achira occur should give us further clues to their meanings, and hence if these were in fact ethnicity markers as well as dietary supplements during this time period.

It is also during Preceramic Phase VI that the first evidence for ritual space exists, with small walled enclosures and a sunken court at La Galgada (Grieder *et al.* 1988). By the end of this phase, the forerunner of the U-shaped mound and plaza at Huaynuná is also built (Pozorski and Pozorski 1993: 47). The ceramics have similar designs up and down the coast, though they still make up a simple assemblage. We assume that most inhabitants who practised farming were using simple river flood-water farming. Achira and guava became regular in this phase, with continuing sporadic finds of maize, avocado, potato and manioc. Avocado is common in the northern valleys, but not to the south. Maize is found in some central and south-central valleys

only, with manioc solely at Guiterrero Cave. The potato has been so difficult
to identify we only have secure evidence for it in the Casma Valley, making
its distribution and that of manioc difficult to assess at this time (Ugent *et al.*
1982). These four crops have continued to have a selective use, suggesting
they might have arrived as ethnicity identity markers.

The plant distributions in these last two phases (V and VI) begin to suggest
that the northern valley inhabitants, down to the Santa Valley, differentiated
themselves through the food they grew and ate. Did the Santa Valley form a
cultural boundary between these coastal settlements? Even within that
northern coastal sector there are further differences in plant use. Some
northern river valley folk ate avocado along with beans and chilees but no
maize (in the Moche River). To the south of the Viru Valley, sites have maize
but no avocado. As these domesticates were being differentially planted and
consumed by the inhabitants, overt ritual activity and associated architectural
features increased in evidence. Locations where we find dense domesticates
do seem to be where there is special architecture; La Galgada, Huaynuná, El
Aspero, and Huaca Prieta, thus supporting the idea that more intensive
political–religious interests included more, yet particular, foodstuffs as key
elements in their cultural constructions as well as in the daily practice of food
consumption. As these plants seem to be part of the initial complex of a new
intensity in political identity it would be informative to view from which
contexts these plant taxa originate.

By the end of the next phase, the Initial Period (2100–1400 BC), these
twelve crops occur more commonly throughout the sites that have been
sampled, but by no means are they ubiquitous (Figure 2.5). While all sampled
sites have evidence for agriculture during this phase, there are still regional
and individual crop-use differences. The chile peppers and the beans occur
everywhere, suggesting their continued highly charged value. Achira is still
common, with manioc and potato hardly present on the coast. Avocado
continues only in the north. Guava has a patchy pattern, present in two
neighbouring valleys, then none for six valleys, then grown in two adjacent
valleys, then none for three more valleys.

Maize continues to have a curious history during this period also.
Throughout the Initial Period it is found in one valley but not the next; at
Gramalote in the Moche Valley but not in the Chicama Valley just next door.
Then there is a break, with no maize for six valleys to the south, until it
occurs again at Culebras and El Aspero on the central coast. Like the avocado
and the guava, there does seem to be something culturally noteworthy about
the scattered distribution of maize. We know that maize is a highly charged
crop throughout the New World by AD 1000 and that it probably was well
before that. In these times we might be seeing the use of maize, and probably
also avocado and guava, in defining different, neighbouring cultural identities
along the coast through farming practices, cuisines and feasts.

Around 2100 BC civic architecture began to be constructed up and down
the coast, although at a small, visually and audibly accessible scale up through

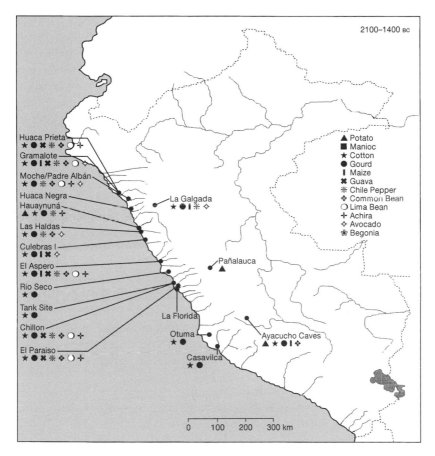

Figure 2.5 Twelve domestic plant taxa distributions of the Initial Period: 2100–1400 BC from the central Andean region, based primarily on Lanning (1967) and Pearsall (1978, 1992).

the Initial Period (1400 BC) (Jerry Moore pers. comm.). These structures began with segmented U-shaped compounds, that were then elaborated on through time (Williams 1985). Around 1400 BC, with the start of the Early Horizon Period, the architecture changed in scale and scope, becoming larger with a more hierarchical orientation, seen in the spatial separation of the masses from the select ritual participants. Whereas the rituals were at a small scale earlier (with everyone hearing, seeing and probably consuming at the events), after the Initial Period most people could only see from afar as the rituals changed in scale and probable strategy. By the end of the Initial Period, hierarchy became codified in several places along the coast, like El Aspero, Huaynuná, El Paraiso and La Florida. It is in the Early Horizon where the crop taxa are more regular and irrigation is more commonplace. Now there are larger scale polities, where agricultural surplus goes hand-in-hand with political development.[5]

DISCUSSION

One conclusion we can draw from this sequence is that the individual crops had very different life histories along the Peruvian coast. Some crops entered at 6000 BC and were planted and consumed in many places, like beans, chile peppers, cotton and gourds. Other crops entered early as well but remained irregularly present up and down the coast for many millennia, like guava, manioc and potatoes. Still other crops entered later in a second wave of crop introductions in the Preceramic V (4200–2500 BC), but then were taken up quickly, like achira. And still other crops were within this second wave of entry but were not taken up quickly, occurring more selectively for some years, like maize and avocado.

Both annuals and tree crops were planted in the first and second entries, and thus one cannot suggest differential access to technology as the reason for differential acceptance of crops. Rather there was a varying sense of territoriality and farming, interest in these specific crop-plants, as well as perhaps connections with other peoples. The different crop histories make it clear that even when crops arrived in a region they were not all adopted automatically by neighbours. Whatever maize, manioc, guava, or avocado represented, they were each charged with a usefulness and a meaning that led some to propagate them while others did not. These plants should be studied more closely for their specific contextual and use patterns in these early phases.

Scholars like Cohen (1978) have suggested that the Preceramic VI saw a population increase that required agriculture to augment the food supply and ward off starvation. Alternatively, I support Quilter and Stocker (1983) who suggest that the marine food base could sustain the populations that existed at that time and even into the Initial Period. Quilter (1989: 9) rightly suggests that during the severe El Niño storms, the coastal inhabitants' menu would have altered but not disappeared.

Within this sequence, we can see that there are hints at cuisine development and the formations of group identities, even with such patchy data and only a subset of the actual plants addressed in this chapter. Early on, there are tasty beans and peppers, with a guava fruit treat. Later on we see the culturally selective use of other tasty foods, with avocado or maize occurring at different sites.

The role of food in cultural identity and politics

Social identity is closely bound to food preferences, and changes in food consumption entail an alteration in self-identification (Appadurai 1981; Goody 1982; Douglas 1984; Rao 1986). People identify themselves with the food they eat and give meaning to each item served or consumed. Further, groups separate themselves from others through different items, dishes and cuisines. Therefore, when we see that the different settlements along the coastal valleys adopted different combinations of crops, I propose that we are seeing the development of different social identities at each community through different cultural constructions. The northern valleys (e.g., the Moche and Chicama valleys) have different crops than the Santa–Casma valleys and this crop combination varies from the Ancon–Chillon area. These three areas also each have early but distinct ritual evidence. We are probably seeing ethnic differences emerging through time, each with different food traditions, highlighted by the avocado eaters and the maize eaters.

Let's return briefly to the onset of agriculture and our Peruvian example. These pre-8000 BC coastal residents were fairly sedentary, with rich coastal resources. The early coastal plant data and crop introductions reflect, in part, the Farrington and Urry model of non-local, tasty food first beginning the agricultural process, with local, industrial crops entering later. The western valley caves have local, highland plants, suggesting local plant use well before foreign incorporation. Almost none of these coastal crops present up to 4000 BC are the staples of hungry people. Nor do we see crops entering as packages. We do not see the evidence of one ethnicity nor polity expanding over a wide territory. Rather, we see an irregular and diverse scattering of plants with little spatial or temporal patterning. Regional variations exist, but even neighbouring valleys have different crops. These patterns imply that local villagers decided for themselves what they would take up and when; probably plants were brought in by visitors or marriage. Pozorski and Pozorski (1993: 49) note this same localized difference in their study of ceremonial architecture and ceramic use along the north coast. They find distinct polities choosing to build different styles of monuments as well as a different acceptance rate of ceramics at different sites.

It seems likely that the motives for the acceptance of plants changed over this time-span. In the earlier phases food production was influenced by the development of social identity and place, and the concept of domestication was active at many levels. The early material indicates that agricultural and food exchanges were based on curiosity and far-away trade, with an interest in community difference and changing relations with the local landscape. Plants were adopted along different pathways, not all from east to west nor north to south. In the later periods, political motives of aggrandizement and political power are more evident in the data. In the Initial Period, with increasing civic–ceremonial construction, we see more of the Bender–Hayden dynamics: crop production and use with a political edge of hierarchy and internal difference. This generation of surplus food and labour begins 4000 years after the onset of agriculture.

Summary

A likely scenario for the Preceramic periods was increasing socio-symbolic activities at certain locations, such as La Galgada, Huaynuná, the Yacht Club, El Aspero and Huaca Prieta. As ritual centres came into existence, people clearly were using and reusing certain locales symbolically as well as economically. The earliest evidence of substantial building too is ritual, not domestic. Each population's identity was emerging. This process included building structures and developing special community acts, including eating a cuisine using local and foreign foods – foods marked by the lineages that were participating. These identities were based on links with other peoples, places, and meanings across the Andean region. In some ways these links (linking arguments) were arbitrary signs that the inhabitants constructed to give their lives meaning. At the same time, each region's population seemed to be differentiating themselves from their neighbours. Most likely, the inhabitants received or brought in plants from other locales as gifts or curiosity items in the early years, and began to make them special, to nurture and to raise them, to cultivate them. It is not surprising therefore to find discontinuous distributions of some species across these ecologically similar valleys.

We must now look carefully at each of these sites to see what other material forms of cultural identity can be associated with the domestic plant uptake suggested by the patterns traced here, as well as more specifically discovering the contexts of plant use at these sites (as already seen in the different architectural trajectories at north coast sites that the Pozorskis note). Clearly, plant use in special activities and in daily consumption would culturally construct meanings for each plant. We need to learn what the meanings of these plants were to the people at the individual sites, such as Huaynuná or La Galgada. We have hints, like the chile pepper at La Galgada, where people burned them in their sunken hearths, either for the smoke or as a food to be consumed in the enclosures. In this way we will get closer to the meanings of the people that participated in these cultural and political changes along the Peruvian coast before hierarchy became institutionalized.

Crop plants appear to have been brought in individually over the first 6,000 years of cultivation, with regional combinations distinct by the time groups became consolidated into larger polities. Changes in ritual activities are tied to political developments. By the end of the Initial period, such changes were not only evident in new public structures but also in the form of associated ceremonies, including feasting that accompanies public events. Political explanations for the increase in certain foodstuffs can be suggested by this phase, where the production of surplus food became important for social aggrandizement (Nassenay 1987; Hayden 1990; Hastorf and Johannessen 1994). In the earlier days, the goals of plant production may not have been for more food, but for more food of a certain kind.

More subtle is the use of certain types of dishes and cuisines, not just to gain political power but simply to unite a community through shared participation in meals and ceremonies. Some plants were highly charged, like the chile pepper that could have meaning continuities over 4,000 years. This is what is suggested for the Preceramic phases along the coast. These meals of avocado, or guava or maize, became part of the memory of things and places, of ancestors and lineages, and thus helped create the social world as well as domesticate the landscape. This trajectory eventually expanded and increased the desire to plant and tend crops. In the early phases, domestication is wrapped up in identity, in influence, and in the memory of the symbolic activities that occurred across the landscape.

ACKNOWLEDGMENTS

My trip to the New Delhi World Archaeological Congress where this paper was presented was supported by the Stahl Foundation and the Academic Senate's Committee for Research at the University of California, Berkeley. I have gained much insight about this subject from working with Sissel Johannessen. I also benefited from talking with Jerry Moore about early Andean architecture and ritual and Stephen Hugh-Jones about Amazonian beliefs. Chris Gosden helped this chapter with his thoughtful editing.

NOTES

1 The phases are an updating of Lanning (1967: 25) and Rowe and Menzel (1967: ii).
2 For brevity's sake, I have worked here only with the presence or absence of these plants and tried to look at general trends rather than giving too much credit to any one find. I have not included data from two sites that are still controversial in terms of dates relating to their botanical remains and mixing of levels. These two sites are Los Gavilanes (Bonavia 1982) and the early levels of the Ayacucho Caves (MacNeish 1977).
3 The data in these figures are primarily extracted from Pearsall (1978, 1992), as well as many of the references that she refers to in those two articles – especially Heiser (1965), Lanning (1967), Engel (1973), Kaplan (1980), Lynch (1980), Pozorski (1983), Pozorski and Pozorski (1987), and Smith in Grieder et al. (1988). The maps were drawn on a computer by Matt Bandy and William Whitehead, in part based on plant distribution maps by Jan Greenough who kindly shared her maps with me. The choice of the taxa, sites, and dates are mine, but based primarily on the Rowe–Menzel scheme.
4 This use is also reminiscent of using chile peppers in the initiations of young boys in the American Southwest by pouring peppers onto lacerated tongues, or in the Amazon Basin where male initiates pour pepper juice on their faces and up their nostrils to become stronger and purify the body (Hugh-Jones, pers. comm.). Peppers also have many sexual connotations: 'hot and spicy' even today is used in many different settings.
5 While harder to see without detailed excavations, the lineage-identity use of plants during this larger-scale political phase would also have continued. Further evidence would have to be gained only in very specific archaeological contexts.

REFERENCES

Ammerman, A.J. and L.L. Cavalli-Sforza. 1984. *The Neolithic Transition and the Genetics of Population in Europe*. Princeton: Princeton University Press.
Appadurai, A. 1981. Gastro-politics in Hindu South Asia. *American Ethnologist* 8, 494–511.

Bender, B. 1978. Gatherer-hunter to farmer: a social perspective. *World Archaeology* 10, 204–22.

Bender, B. 1985. Prehistoric development in the American midcontinent and in Brittany, northwest France. In *Prehistoric Hunter-gatherers: the emergence of complexity*, T.D. Price and J.A. Brown (eds), 21–57. Orlando: Academic Press.

Benz, B. 1994. Reconstructing the racial phylogeny of Mexican maize: where do we stand. In *Corn and Culture in the Prehistoric New World*, S. Johannessen and C.A. Hastorf (eds), 157–79. Boulder: Westview Press.

Bergh, B.O. 1976. Avocado *Persea americana* (Lauraceae). In *Evolution of Crop Plants*, N.W. Simmonds (ed.), 148–51. London: Longman.

Bohrer, V.L. 1991. The relation of grain and its method of harvest to plants in prehistory. *Reviews in Anthropology* 16, 149–56.

Bonavia, D. 1982. *Preceramic Peruano: Los Gavilanes, mar, desierto y oasis en la historia del hombre*. Lima: Cooperación Financiera de desarollo S.A. and the German Institute of Archaeology.

Braidwood, R.J. 1953. Query to symposium; did man once live by beer alone? *American Anthropologist* 55, 515–16.

Bush, M.B., D.R. Piperno and P.A. Colinvaux. 1989. A 6000 year history of Amazonian cultivation. *Nature* 340, 303–5.

Cohen, M.N. 1978. Archaeological plant remains from the central coast of Peru. *Nawpa Pacha* 16, 23–50.

Cohen, M.N. 1981. Pacific coast foragers: affluent or overcrowded. In *Affluent Foragers*, S. Koyama and D.H. Thomas (eds), 275–95. Osaka: Senri Ethnological Studies 9, National Museum of Ethnology.

Douglas, M. 1984. *Food in the Social Order: studies of food and festivities in three American communities.* New York: Russell Sage Foundation.

Engel, F. 1973. New facts about pre-Colombian life in the Andean *lomas. Current Anthropology* 8, 287–97.

Engel, F. 1981. *Prehistoric Andean Ecology, Man, Settlement, and the Environment in the Andes. The deep south.* New York: Humanities Press.

Farrington, I.S. and J. Urry. 1985. Food and early history of cultivation. *Journal of Ethnobiology* 5, 143–57.

Gepts, P.T., C. Osborn, K. Rashka and F.A. Bliss. 1986. Phaseolin-protein variability in wild forms and landraces of the common bean (*Phaseolus vulgaris*): evidence for multiple centers of domestication. *Economic Botany* 40, 451–68.

Goody, J. 1982. *Cooking, Cuisine and Class.* Cambridge: Cambridge University Press.

Grieder, T., A.B. Mendoza, C.E. Smith and R.M. Malina. 1988. *La Galgada, Peru: a preceramic culture in transition.* Austin: University of Texas Press.

Harlan, J. 1975. *Crops and Man.* Madison, Wis.: American Society of Agronomy.

Harris, D.R. 1969. Agricultural systems, ecosystems and the origins of agriculture. In *The Domestication and Exploitation of Plants and Animals*, P.J. Ucko and G.W. Dimbleby (eds), 3–16. London: Duckworth.

Hastorf, C.A. and S. Johannessen. 1993. Pre-Hispanic political change and the role of maize in the central Andes of Peru, *American Anthropologist* 95, 115–38.

Hastorf, C.A. and S. Johannessen. 1994. Becoming corn-eaters in prehistoric America. In *Corn and Culture in the Prehistoric New World,* S. Johannessen and C.A. Hastorf (eds), 427–43. Boulder, Colo.: Westview Press.

Hawkes, J.G. 1989. The domestication of roots and tubers in the American tropics. In *Foraging and Farming: the evolution of plant exploitation,* D.R. Harris and G.C. Hillman (eds), 481–503. London: Unwin Hyman.

Hayden, B. 1990. Nimrods, piscators, pluckers, and planters: the emergence of food production. *Journal of Anthropological Archaeology* 9, 31–69.

Heiser, C.B. 1965. Cultivated plants and cultural diffusions in nuclear America. *American Anthropologist* 67, 930–49.

Hillman, G.C. and M.S. Davies. 1990. Domestication rates in wild wheats and barley under primitive cultivation and their archaeological implications. *Journal of World Prehistory* 4, 157–222.

Hodder, I. 1991. *The Domestication of Europe,* Oxford: Basil Blackwell.

Kaplan, L. 1980. Variation in the cultivated beans. In *Guiterrero Cave,* T. Lynch (ed.), 145–8. New York: Academic Press.

Kaplan, L. 1994. Accelerator mass spectrometry dates and the antiquity of *Phaseolus* cultivation. *Annual Report of the Bean Improvement Cooperative* 37, 131–2.

Lanning, E. 1967. *Peru Before the Incas,* Englewood Cliffs, N.J.: Prentice-Hall.

Lewthwaite, J. 1986. The transition of food production: a Mediterranean perspective. In *Hunters in Transition,* M. Zvelebil (ed.), 53–66. Cambridge: Cambridge University Press.

Lynch, T.F. 1980. *Guiterrero Cave.* New York: Academic Press.

Lynch, T.F., R. Gillespie, J.A.J. Gowlett and R.E.M. Hedges. 1985. Chronology of Guiterrero Cave, Peru. *Science* 229, 864–7.

MacNeish, R.S., R.K. Vierra, A. Nelken-Terner and C.J. Phagen, 1980. *Prehistory of the Ayacucho Basin, Peru. Volume 3: Nonceramic Artifacts.* Ann Arbor: University of Michigan Press.

Martins-Farias, R. 1976. New archaeological techniques for the study of ancient root crops in Peru. Unpublished Ph.D. thesis, University of Birmingham.

Moseley, M.E. 1975. *The Maritime Foundations of Andean Civilization.* Menlo Park, Calif.: Cummings Press.

Nassenay, M.S. 1987. On the causes and consequences of subsistence intensification in the Mississippi alluvial valley. In *Emergent Horticultural Economies of the Eastern Woodlands,* W.F. Keegan (ed.), 129–51. Carbondale: Southern Illinois University, Occasional Paper no. 7, Center for Archaeological Investigations.

Osborne, A.J. 1977. Strandloopers, mermaids, and other fairy tales: ecological determinants of marine resources utilization – the Peruvian case. In *For Theory Building in Archaeology,* L. Binford (ed.), 157–205. New York: Academic Press.

Pearsall, D. 1978. Paleoethnobotany in western South America: progress and problems. In *The Nature and Status of Ethnobotany,* R.I. Ford, M.F. Brown, M. Hodge and W.L. Merrill (eds), 389–416. Ann Arbor: University of Michigan, Anthropological Papers, no. 67, Museum of Anthropology.

Pearsall, D. 1992. The origins of plant cultivation in South America. In *Origins of Agriculture: an international perspective,* C.W. Cowan and P.J. Watson (eds), 173–205. Washington, D.C.: Smithsonian Institution Press.

Pearsall, D. 1994. Issues in the analysis and interpretation of archaeological maize in South America. In *Corn and Culture in the Prehistoric New World,* S. Johannessen and C.A. Hastorf (eds), 245–72. Boulder, Colo.: Westview Press.

Pickersgill, B. 1969. The archaeological record of chili peppers (*Capsicum* spp.) and the sequence of plant domestication in Peru. *American Antiquity* 34, 54–61.

Pickersgill, B. and C.B. Heiser Jr. 1977. Origins and distribution of plants domesticated in the New World tropics. In *Origins of Agriculture,* C.A. Reed (ed.), 803–35. The Hague: Mouton Publs.

Pozorski, S. 1983. Changing subsistence priorities and early settlement patterns on the north coast of Peru. *Journal of Ethnobiology* 3, 15–38.

Pozorski, S. and T. Pozorski. 1987. *Early Settlement and Subsistence in the Casma Valley, Peru.* Iowa City: University of Iowa Press.

Pozorski, T. and S. Pozorski. 1993. Early complex society and ceremonialism on the Peruvian coast. In *El mundo ceremonial,* L. Millones and Y. Onuki (eds). Osaka: Senri Ethnological Studies 37, 45–68.

Quilter, J. 1989. *Life and Death at Paloma.* Iowa City: University of Iowa Press.

Quilter, J. and T. Stocker. 1983. Subsistence economies and the origins of Andean complex societies. *American Anthropologist* 85, 545–62.

Rao, M.S.A. 1986. Conservatism and change in food habits among the migrants in India: a study of gastrodynamics. In *Food, Society and Culture*, R.S. Khare and M.S.A. Rao (eds), 121–40. Durham, N.C.: Carolina Academic Press.

Rogers, D.J. 1963. Studies of *Manihot esculenta* Crantz and related species. *Bulletin of the Torrey Botanical Club* 90, 43–54.

Rogers, D.J. and S.G. Appan. 1972. Cassava (*Manihot esculenta* Crantz), the plant, world production and its importance in world food supply. In *A Literature Review and Research Recommendations on Cassava* (Manihot esculenta Crantz), C.H. Hendershoot (ed.), AID Contract No. csd/2492. Athens: University of Georgia.

Rowe, J.H. and D. Menzel. 1967. Introduction. In *Peruvian Archaeology, Selected Readings*, J.H. Rowe and D. Menzel (eds), v–x. Palo Alto, Calif.: Peek Publications.

Sauer, C. 1952. *Agricultural Origins and Dispersals*. New York: The American Geographical Society.

Stephens, S.G. and M.E. Moseley. 1974. Early domesticated cottons from archaeological sites in central coastal Peru. *American Antiquity* 39, 109–22.

Thomas, J. 1993. The hermeneutics of megalithic space. In *Interpretative Archaeologies*, C. Tilley (ed.), 73–97. Oxford: Berg.

Ugent, D., S. Pozorski and T. Pozorski. 1982. Archaeological potato tuber remains from the Casma valley of Peru. *Economic Botany* 36, 401–15.

Ugent, D., S. Pozorski and T. Pozorski. 1984. New evidence for ancient cultivation of *Canna edulis* in Peru. *Economic Botany* 38, 417–32.

Watson, P.J. and M. Kennedy. 1991. The development of horticulture in the Eastern Woodlands of North America: a woman's role. In *Engendering Archaeology*, J. Geo and M. Conley (eds), 205–75. Oxford: Basil Blackwell.

Welch, P. and C.M. Scarry, 1995. Status-related variation in foodways in the Moundville chiefdom. *American Antiquity* 60: 397–419.

Williams, C. 1985. A scheme for the early monumental architecture of the central coast of Peru. In *Early Ceremonial Architecture in the Andes*, C. Donnan (ed.), 227–40. Washington, D.C.: Dumbarton Oaks.

Wilson, D. 1981. Of maize and men: a critique of the maritime hypothesis of state origins on the coast of Peru. *American Anthropologist* 38, 93–120.

Zvelebil, M. 1986. Mesolithic prelude and Neolithic revolution. In *Hunters in Transition*, M. Zvelebil (ed.), 5–15. Cambridge: Cambridge University Press.

3   Uywaña, *the house and its indoor landscape: oblique approaches to, and beyond, domestication*

ALEJANDRO F. HABER

Domestication is one of the major issues in archaeology in different parts of the world. Sometimes seen as progress and evolution, sometimes as a backward step, domestication is one of the topics in the western conceptualization of the nature–culture relationship. Domestication of nature as a goal of human social action implies the belief in a utilitarian rationality that leads towards intensified subsistence. Essentialist and reified views of social being underlie this notion of the rationality of subsistence. But also the concepts of domestication and subsistence are historically constructed and imply views of nature and the uses to which they can be put.

We are used to thinking of deserts as the most difficult environment to which humans are compelled to adapt themselves for their subsistence. Natural constraints are so strong in deserts that human life can only be seen as being at the mercy of the environment. The Puna de Atacama, a high altitude desert, seems a paradigmatic instance of a harsh environment (Figure 3.1). The Puna de Atacama was seen by its first explorers as an extreme environment. The people of the Puna were accordingly seen as marginal people. Geography and archaeology are in a sense intermingled in the visions of the Puna de Atacama. But both are dependent on the construction of the Puna de Atacama as the extreme case of marginality. Marginality in this case seems justified on environmental and historical grounds, but it can be seen as part of the cultural construction of western urban people. In some way it can be said that it is a construction of a landscape, but it is really the construction of a set of views on landscape (see Bender 1993; Cosgrove 1993; Olwig 1993). Archaeology has a social origin, just as archaeology searches for the origins of societies. We need to be aware of the links between the construction of the archaeology of the Puna de Atacama from the standpoint of a landscape viewer and the construction of us as Argentines and/or as part of modern civilization (Friedman 1992).

In the first part of this chapter I aim to show the links between cultural and political meanings of the self and otherness in archaeological discourse on the Puna de Atacama; in other words, how the Puna de Atacama was

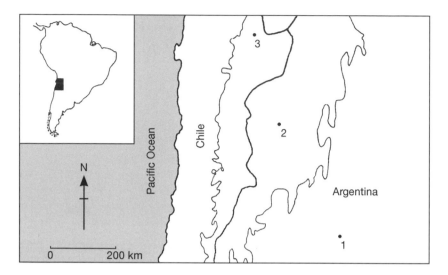

Figure 3.1 Map of the South-Central Andes, including the Puna de Atacama. Contour lines of 3,000 metres above sea level. (1) San Fernando del Valle de Catamarca city; (2) Tebenquiche Chico archaeological site; (3) town of San Pedro de Atacama.

constructed as a marginal landscape and how its people were described through the framework of subsistence. In the remainder of this chapter, based on my own ethnoarchaeological and archaeological research, I will draw on some countercultural ways of interpreting the archaeology of the Puna de Atacama, emphasizing what I think have been the cultural and political meanings of the definition of the self and the other within the Puna de Atacama. Starting with a comparison of the notion of domestication with the Aymara concept of *uywaña*, I explore an oblique route between the dichotomies of nature and culture and self and other, in the form of a house and its contained landscape.

PUNA DE ATACAMA: AN EXPLORATION OF THE MARGINS

Introducing the reader to the geography and culture of the Puna de Atacama cannot be accomplished without the risk of reproducing the essentialist and reified notions that I am trying to deconstruct (Keesing 1990; Vayda 1990). Thus, I prefer to present the landscape as it was historically constructed; explorers and voyagers will aid the reader in this 'exploration' of the Puna de Atacama.

The whole area of the Puna de Atacama was not an important region in colonial Hispanic times, and only the extraction of minerals justified some settlement, confined to specific locales and of short duration. After Independence and the civil wars of the Río de la Plata region, spanning almost all of the first half of the nineteenth century, the Puna de Atacama was included in the territorial domain of Bolivia, whose state structures were rarely a presence in the region. After the 'War of the Pacific Ocean' between the Peru–Bolivia Confederation and Chile, and the consequent expansion of Chile to the north, the Puna de Atacama was incorporated into its territory (Delgado and Göbel 1995). The Argentine Republic, whose elites were building up and consolidating the national state since the last third of the nineteenth century, claimed the territory of the Puna de Atacama based on historical considerations (colonial administrative jurisdictions) and geographical features (watershed divisions). The Argentinian adviser was Francisco Moreno, at the same time one of the pioneers of Argentine archaeology.

At the turn of the century the Puna de Atacama was declared, by an international arbiter, part of Argentine territory. The Los Andes National Territory was created under military control. The other military territories created in those times were in the Pampa, Patagonia and Chaco regions, where Indian peoples had been recently subjugated after several military campaigns. Even if the annexation of the Puna de Atacama was done through diplomatic means and not through force of arms, the administration of its land and people was seen by the Argentine state as a military issue. The first governor of the Territory, General Daniel Cerri, visited the Puna de Atacama twice, and produced an interesting report full of descriptions of the desert, its poor people and their laziness, the scarcity of resources and the difficulty of communications. In short he described the troubles faced by the Argentine state to take control and advantage of the Territory and its people. His whole description was imbued with a sense of an extremely marginal land, and the high costs of its incorporation into the modern nation that his generation was willing to build (Cerri 1906). Although the administrative unworkability of this territory was realized since the first attempts to establish state control of the area, it was not until the mid-twentieth century that the national state divided the Territory of Los Andes in three, and gave the contiguous provinces of Jujuy, Salta and Catamarca a part each, thus transferring to these provincial states the costs of setting up state control over the Territory and its people.

The Puna de Atacama is the southernmost part of the great Andean high plains, which extend over the north-west of Argentina, the north-east of Chile, the west of Bolivia and the south-east of Peru. Given that in the high plains there is a gradient of decreasing humidity and vegetation from north to south and from east to west, the Puna de Atacama is the driest and most desert-like area. Ranging between 3,500 and roughly 6,500 m above sea level, salt plains, extensive barren lands, volcanoes and volcanic rock outcrops are the main features of the landscape. A naturally treeless area, the Puna de Atacama has three main types of vegetation: tiny oasis-like marshes with short grass and reeds alongside the few springs, open shrubs (less than 10 per cent of vegetation cover) and open fields of tall and resistant gramineae over 4,000 m above sea level (with less than 20 per cent of vegetation cover). Snowfall is almost confined to over 4,000 m above sea level, and rain fall is less than 100 mm per year, with dry periods of several years without a single drop of rain. Temperatures are below freezing at night almost all the year round and over 40°C at noon. Primary production is very low, the growing season is short, strong winds and electric storms are common. Population is very low and concentrated in the few oases where agriculture, pastoralism, and working for the state are the main occupations, beside a small number of foreign capital investments in mineral extraction and survey.

These desert-like features are well reflected in the stories of the voyagers of the last decades of nineteenth century and the first ones of the twentieth century (Bertrand 1885; San Román 1896; Maldones 1899; Cerri 1906; Boman 1908; Bowman 1924; Brackebusch 1990). They described the desert as imposing in its extent and hostility, and, in accordance with this image, its people were described as simple, superstitious, with little invention, and poor or starving. Their stories emphasize the risks and dangers of travelling across the Puna, the difficulties in managing both mules and guide-men. The trails in the desert were the major images of these narrations, only interrupted by passing through hamlets located in oases. The landscape was conceived from a foreigner's perspective, from the risky experiences of travelling across the Puna, but with the certainty that they were only visitors. The possibilities of the incorporation of the Territory into the national market were explored in terms of utility, but there was not much optimism. In fact, the national state did not risk very much. The construction of the railway line between Salta (in Argentina) and Antofagasta (in the Chilean Pacific coast) was supported by the state. It was a huge enterprise justified by the need to set up a means of communication with the Pacific coast. The railway line was constructed across the Puna de Atacama; so, it can be said, the state's investment in the Puna de Atacama was in creating a way to cross this area quickly. The Puna de Atacama was an obstacle, and the train was the way of crossing it.

The Puna de Atacama was *de jure* inside the nation but was *de facto* on the fringes, and was only just incorporated within it. The Puna de Atacama was perceived as a true frontier, both in geographical and cultural terms. The archaeology of the Puna de Atacama was to be constructed on these foundations. The political dimension of the cultural construction of the Puna de Atacama through archaeology is of some importance, provided that we are able to see the territorial and political expansion of the state and the construction of the national and provincial bodies as one and the same process.

THE HISTORY OF ARCHAEOLOGY OF THE PUNA DE ATACAMA: PRE-HISPANIC SETTLEMENT AS A MARGINAL LANDSCAPE

The first archaeological expedition to the Puna de Atacama was that of Francisco Moreno in 1893 (Ten Kate 1893). His trip was conceived as an archaeological exploration of the north-west of the country, but, as the contemporary witness Samuel Lafone Quevedo wrote in his personal diary, the scientific justification of the voyage masked geopolitical concerns (Márquez Miranda 1958–9). Moreno turned to the Puna de Atacama as the rest of the group went on gathering archaeological material in the valleys of Calchaqui. He himself was gathering topographical information to be used by the government in the disputes over boundaries with Chile. But the work of Moreno was actually a study of the border, as he conceived the Andes as the border of the national geography and national self, something under construction at that time. The Puna de Atacama was beyond the border and nationhood became delimited in relationship to the geography of the border. Argentine archaeology was beyond the border of the history of the nation as well, as Indian materials were not part of the civilizing process that gave birth to the Argentine nation but instead were part of the natural landscape encountered by the first Europeans; the Argentine elites continued to encounter them as a matter of scientific enquiry (Haber 1992–4). Archaeology was one of the practices through which the national state could manage to build up its self-image of being able to control, know and possess the entirety of nature on which it was being built. The Puna de Atacama was the extreme case of otherness, at the fringes of the self, a true delimitation of the nationhood and its modern self-understanding. Naturalism has deep roots in Argentine archaeology, because individuals are socialized in reference to the collective self, defined through a set of dichotomized constructs involving history–culture–Europe–modernity on one side and archaeology–nature–Indian–savagery on the other.

The so-called father of Argentine archaeology, Juan Bautista Ambrosetti, produced another early report on the archaeology of the Puna de Atacama (Ambrosetti 1904, 1905), in line with his predecessor but emphasizing the links of the archaeological vestiges with those of the neighbouring Calchaqui area (Ambrosetti 1902, 1903). His nationalism was so deeply rooted that he even managed to dismiss the Inca occupation of the north-west of Argentina. The Inca civilization was known at that time as Peruvian, and, as with other South American states, Argentina was constructed with the emphasis on its difference to neighbouring countries. Ambrosetti passionately argued against Eric Boman, a Swedish archaeologist who lived in Argentina and worked for Swedish and French expeditions. Boman argued for a dependence of the Calchaqui civilization on the Peruvian civilization, and he refused to acknowledge a long temporal depth of the human occupation of the north-west (Lejeal and Boman 1907). Beside these issues, which embroiled him in a long dispute with Ambrosetti and his successors on the control of archaeological state institutions, Boman contributed to the description of the Puna de Atacama as a wild landscape, and of its people as hostile and unconfident (Boman 1908).

It was not until mid-century that other archaeologists became interested in this territory (apart from a couple of expeditions in the 1920s aimed at the gathering of artefacts and proving their authenticity for collectionism). It was the late Pedro Krapovickas, then an advanced student, who produced the first archaeological report of the site of Tebenquiche, in the heart of the Puna de Atacama (Krapovickas 1955). The report consisted of a rough sketch of structures and a description of the pots and sherds he discovered in two stone-chambered burials and a third chamber which was already opened. His discovery of a golden pectoral ornament in one of the burials, beside his description of the irrigation canals and agricultural terraces and fields, provided an image of richness and complexity that was at odds with that of marginality. He could not manage to date his findings but suggested an *atacameño* affiliation – that is, a close relationship with San Pedro de Atacama (Figure 3.1), a lower oasis located towards the north-west of the Puna de Atacama, with milder conditions and a very rich archaeology.

Nevertheless, characterizations of the archaeology of the Puna de Atacama remained inventories of artefacts, stressing homogeneity, scarcity of decoration and 'symbolism' on artefacts, and highlighting the long duration of the same stylistic poverty during different periods (Bennett *et al.* 1948; Krapovickas 1959). The difficulties of reproducing the culture-chronological charts that were being made for neighbouring areas during the 1950s and 1960s led to the definition of an all embracing so-called 'Puna Complex'. Thus the culture of the Puna de Atacama went on being ignored as a historical phenomenon.

The Puna de Atacama was included in the regional synthesis of the south-central Andes and north-western Argentina emphasizing its dependence on neighbouring regions. Long-distance trade organized through caravans of llamas was the main topic in Puna de Atacama research when culture-historical and functionalist accounts were in fashion. The Puna de Atacama was seen as an intermediate step in the influence of San Pedro de Atacama on La Aguada or vice versa, or changing dependencies on San Pedro de Atacama and La Aguada were underlined (González 1977). Evidences of long-distance trade were put forward, linking the region with almost all the neighbouring valleys (Núñez and Dillehay 1979; Tarragó 1984; Dillehay and Núñez 1988; Olivera 1991).

In the 1980s and 1990s the subsistence basis of llama herding was brought in as a major theme, and the domestication and pastoralism of llamas as a local process became one of the preferred issues of research (Haber 1988, 1991, 1992, 1993; Olivera 1988, 1991; Aschero *et al.* 1991; García 1991; Yacobaccio and Madero 1991; Olivera and Nasti 1993; Olivera and Podestá 1993; Aschero 1994; Yacobaccio 1994; Yacobaccio *et al.* 1994). Broadly speaking, these interpretations of the Puna de Atacama are in the same line as that inaugurated in the late nineteenth century, reformulating the language of marginality, in that they construct past societies in terms of subsistence activities, and subsistence change is the major area of concern. The overall image of the Puna de Atacama that underlies archaeological accounts of it is that of a marginal landscape. That is why a critical understanding of the archaeology of the region should begin by deconstructing this image, given that it is constitutive of archaeological discourse.

Rethinking the marginal landscape

Landscapes are perceived, and that is true both for prehistoric actors and for archaeologists. But landscapes are perceived, in both cases, as original views undifferentiated from the land. The idea of landscape is not only one of a view of the countryside but one of viewing it at a distance, objectifying it, as one is physically confronted by a depicted landscape. So, in a word, it could be said that the whole idea of landscape is a matter of understanding the place as seen from the outside (Tilley 1994). This is a good metaphor for archaeology, and particularly for the archaeology of the Puna de Atacama. We archaeologists tend to view past societies as if they were at a distance from ourselves; we see deposits from the top of the ground, and we see the land from the perspective of a map-viewer: the land is there to be seen, landscapes are distant and apprehensible through the eyes. Our places of everyday life are apprehended in many, unaccountable directions, and more on the basis of routine and ritual actions linked to the emotional aspects of everyday practice than from an exclusively visual perspective. Lived places cannot be objectified as if they were a picture, for through living in places the actor is performing on the stage and not sitting in front of it. Objects and atmospheres are densely charged with so many internal meanings that they cannot be objectified through the act of acquiring a distant metrical perspective on them (Thomas 1993; Barrett 1994).

It is not my aim to discuss here the current theoretical literature on landscape archaeology (see Bender 1993; Criado 1991; Gosden and Head 1994; Tilley 1994), but only to suggest that through transcending the perspective of landscape we can pretend a deeper understanding of the archaeology of the Puna de Atacama, as well as a critical understanding of our own pre-construction of the area which bridges the dichotomies of subjectivity/objectivity, material/symbolic, nature/culture, self/other. Land-scapes are constructed as part of the same process through which actors are constructed; and to wonder if landscapes or actors come first is as sterile as to imagine that isolated individuals or natural lands are more than abstract artificial constructions of the mind. A landscape perspective is useful in bridging opposite ideas, but it pre-theoretically retains the idea of space as an objective dimension, apprehended through perception.

Marginality, the second component of the image of the Puna de Atacama, has been referred to previously in relation to the construction of nationhood.

There is a relational definition of the other that integrates the self-understanding of the Argentine people, where the repression of meaning assumes a relevant role. Each individual or group is positioned on an axis of discrimination from Buenos Aires, the capital of the country, to the Puna (or any other Indian marginland). So, for example, people from Catamarca city perceive themselves as much nearer to Buenos Aires than to the Andes, whose people are derogatively called 'Kolla'. In the towns situated around the Puna, people considered Kolla by those from the capital do not perceive themselves as Kolla but ascribe all the people from the Puna to this category. People from the Puna do not consider themselves to be Kolla, but the Kolla are people from more distant hamlets situated in the more isolated areas of the desert, whose people in turn do not see themselves as Kolla. But this is not a matter of names. It is a matter of discrimination, differential access to political and administrative power and to cultural resources necessary to be able to manage oneself in the broader society.

In archaeological discourse marginality gained renewed importance when, during the 1980s and 1990s, issues of domestication and herding were raised as part of an increasing concern with the subsistence basis and adaptation to the environment (Haber 1988, 1991, 1992, 1993; Olivera 1988, 1991; Aschero et al. 1991; Yacobaccio and Madero 1991; Olivera and Nasti 1993; Olivera and Podestá 1993; Yacobaccio 1994; Yacobaccio et al. 1994). Apparently the Puna de Atacama, and its extreme marginal environmental conditions, is the best test arena for adaptationist theses. Llama domestication was seen as an adaptation to the environment due to subsistence risk reduction.

CLASSIFICATIONS OF NATURE AND CULTURE

The domestication of camelids cannot be recognized as a cultural issue because it was culturally constructed as a matter of nature. As part of the cultural construction of nationality, Argentine identity is as much a matter of invention of the other in terms of proximity/distance of the pre-European world. So, this world must be constructed in terms of nature and accordingly subjected to methodological control and stripped of cultural meaning.

There are four South American camelid species, two of them domesticated (llamas and alpacas) and two of them wild (vicuñas and guanacos). The four give cross-fertile offspring and in the Andes they share the same geographical distributions (Franklin 1982; Wheeler 1984; Kent 1987). Particularly in the Puna de Atacama vicuñas and guanacos (both wild) and llamas (domesticated) share not only the same general area, but in certain cases the same grazing areas. As we do not know the exact relationship between speciation and domestication, and palaeontological and zooarchaeological explanations of them depend one on the other, there is no way to assert objectively whether we are viewing the bone specimen of a domesticated or wild animal. A previous decision, an interpretation, has to be made at the same point that we start the interpretation. And usually this decision rests on what is presumably inter-subjectively acceptable. Moreover, it reproduces and reinforces the cultural meanings of the past and the other, as well as its political implications.

Even ethnographically the question of llama pastoralism is so ambiguous that there are authors who doubt if the relationship between humans and llamas can be termed pastoralism (Rabey 1989), given that the nature of the herder behaviour with llamas does not accord with biologically oriented definitions of domestication (Bökönyi 1989). If the herds are alone (they are not herded) almost all the year round, and they reproduce without human control, it cannot be said that pastoralism exists. Rejecting this interpretation, and as in many sheep-herding societies (Corse herders for instance), the llama herder puts to the service of pastoralism the species' natural sociology (Tomka 1992). Regarding camelids this means gregarious behaviour, polygyny, marked territoriality, daily movements between open feeding areas and protected sleeping areas, and group leadership by only one male. Llamas herd themselves (or the dominant male herds them), and they protect themselves from dangers (such as the vicinity of predators or windy snowstorms). Moreover, to control the breeding practices directly is unnecessary; the selection of the dominant male through castration, or killing of non-wanted males, means the selection of 50 per cent of the genotype of the offspring, and 75 per cent of the second generation. Llamas are objects of property, marked with distinctive cuts in their ears. Llamas are also objects of inheritance and exchange. Nevertheless, nobody would pretend to appropriate, inherit or exchange vicuñas, yet vicuñas can live beside llama herds, eat the same grass and drink the same water (and sometimes mixed familiar groups are formed). Given that llamas are *uywa* (domesticated, owned) and vicuñas are *salqa* (wild, not owned, the herd of the mountain), the different behavioural attitudes are contained in the symbolic world developed by a culture made through the interaction with these animals (Grebe Vicuña 1984).

But here we have another problem, and it is related to the implications of our own language. Speaking of culture and nature is part of our modern self-understanding, and also part of our language of domestication (Hodder 1990). The western concept of domestication maintains both the Indo-European root and the close historical and semantic links with a broad set of words: from 'domination' to 'house', from 'dome' to 'sir' ('*don*' in Spanish), that cannot be seen as neutral nor outside of history. A basic idea in the western concept of domestication is the control or dominance of nature by humans. This idea has been implied in archaeological approaches to llama domestication, trying to identify the time when llamas have been subjected to control by Andean people through a behavioural change towards animals. Thus it is supposed that this process would have left archaeologically visible prints in camelid and/or cultural remains.

CONFRONTING MINDSCAPES OF NATURE AND SELF: FROM DOMESTICATION TO *UYWAÑA*

Let me introduce at this point some details of Andean linguistic meanings concerning what we call domestication. But I am not attempting to use ethnographic analogy for interpretation, as I am convinced that Andean culture is a result of historical process and cannot be transported to the past as a model of interpretation. I prefer to think using other meaningful terms because they help me to rethink otherness. And I prefer an Andean language because it is supposedly much nearer than my own (Spanish) to the frames of meaning which gave sense to the reality I am trying to interpret.

I do not mean that an Andean ethnography or ethnoarchaeology can provide an approach to the Andean hermeneutic from which the human–llama relationship was originally constructed, because present Andean cosmology (if such a thing exists) is the result of the human–llama relationship (besides being the product of many other historical factors). To approach the 'Andean thought' with the aim of constructing an analogue for archaeological interpretations would not be acceptable if we agree that cultural life has a historical context. The opposite approach would be to fall into the alternative of essentialism and naturalism, two ways through which political and cultural discrimination are legitimized.

Perhaps the Andean word that best accounts for the human–llama relationship is Aymara *uywaña*, but it is far from connoting only dominance or control (Martínez 1989). *Uywaña* is the nurtured, the loved, whether children or animals. The human–llama relationship is defined by this idea of nurturing and protection. But the concept of *uywaña* itself implies more than the human–animal relationship, for it accounts as well for the relationship between the mountain as a sacred place and the house of the herder family (see the entry '*vyvatha*' in Ludovico Bertonio's Aymara vocabulary, the earliest dictionary of that language written in colonial times). The whole set of concepts linguistically related through the root *uywa-* gives an idea of the structure of meaning operating in the perception of the human, the natural, and supernatural beings: the raised animal (llamas and alpacas), the herder (who raises animals), the children, to nurture for oneself, the loved thing, to protect, the sacred place, the sacred or protecting mountain, are some of the linked concepts. Thus, it is protection, love and obedience that defines the relationship between humans and domesticated animals, but also between the family and the sacred mountain, and between parents and children (as well as between the living and the dead, and between the living and *antiguos* – pre-Hispanic people). It is a feeling of love and fear at once, situating humans at the centre of the reciprocal metaphors of the natural and the supernatural, so the herder (as nurtured being) is analogous to llama, but again (as nurturing being) he is analogous to the mountain. Thus, pastoralism or domestication cannot be separated from the dense fabric of meaning in which human–animal relationships make sense, and from which they are reproduced. In this sense the house is the constructed arena of performances in which the relationships of protection and nurturing reproduce those of being protected and nurtured.

With these ideas in mind, and with the self-critical understanding of the links between archaeological discourse on domestication and the cultural construction of the self and the other, I would like in the rest of this chapter to turn to what I interpret as the cultural and political meanings of the definition of the self and the other from the Puna de Atacama in pre-Hispanic times. Previous discussion of landscape, marginality, domestication and *uywaña* will be merged in the discussion of the excavation of a house and its broader context at the Tebenquiche Chico site.

A LITTLE HOUSE IN THE PUNA

The site is located inside an old exploded volcanic crater transformed by glacial activity. The moraine deposits are split by a permanent watercourse that eroded to form a creek. Both terraces thus formed are the locus of archaeological remains of buildings, as well as the slopes of the creek and the western slope of the valley. The altitude of the site is from 3,500 m above sea level along the creek in an almost continuous distribution up to 4,000 m above sea level. Archaeological remains are found on the upper slopes too. A long temporal span of occupation can be suggested for the site, on the basis of typological comparisons of pottery with neighbouring areas and through radiocarbon chronology. Radiocarbon dates span from the third to the eighteenth centuries AD, but ceramic comparisons indicate an occupation from the last centuries BC. More than eight centuries of almost continuous 14C dates are found in the deposits inside a house excavated at Tebenquiche Chico (Table 3.1). This house was composed of two main rooms which were contiguous and connected by an entrance that was originally sealed with mud and buried under the fallen stones of a wall (Figure 3.2).

Table 3.1 Uncalibrated 14C dates for the house excavated in Tebenquiche Chico

LP-736	270 ± 50 BP
LP-780	880 ± 60 BP
Beta-44660	900 ± 70 BP
LP-739	1050 ± 45 BP
LP-741	1130 ± 70 BP
LP-763	1240 ± 50 BP
LP-795	1350 ± 80 BP
LP-774	1360 ± 60 BP
LP-745	1430 ± 60 BP
LP-764	1460 ± 60 BP
LP-724	1610 ± 70 BP

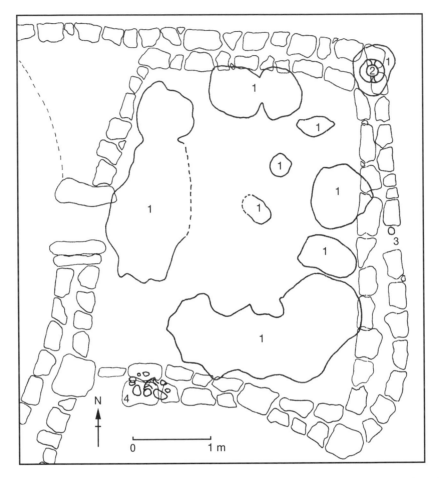

Figure 3.2 Plan of the easterly room of the house at Tebenquiche Chico. Note double walls and entrances. (1) pits; (2) vessel deposited inside a pit within the walls of the house, at the north-east corner; (3) little bottle deposited below the first line of stones of the outer wall; (4) infant interment below the wall and beside the main entrance.

The rooms are double walled. They are formed by two parallel walls made of non-worked stone separated by an inner space *c.* 0.5 m wide, filled with mud, smaller stones, and other inclusions, mainly archaeological material broken and unbroken (pottery, lithics, bone, metal). Stone walls are used for other structures as well as for houses. Courtyards, terraces, fields, canals and tombs are built with stone walls, but it is usually only houses that have double walls (occasionally some other structures do). The double walls in this house were filled with archaeological material, and all the walls (even the wall between both rooms) shared this characteristic. This starts to highlight the importance of walls, and of house walls in particular. The walls of the house can be seen as a container, but it seems as if their function as a container had twofold implications: as a house wall it contained the inner space of the house, and as a wall it contained the fill of mud and objects.

There are three special deposits linked with the building of the house. One was placed beneath the outer east wall and consisted of a little earthenware bottle with a face modelled on the everted neck, placed upside down just below the first line of stones. The little bottle was found without evident contents. A second special building deposit was placed inside a pit that was dug in the interior space between the inner and the outer eastern walls, near the north-east corner of the house. It consisted of a medium-sized vessel, nearly 0.4 m in diameter, placed with the mouth up. It contained nothing in particular, beside a filling of sand and stones which had probably fallen in during the collapse of the wall. A second vessel of the same type was found broken in many pieces and dispersed between the fill of the eastern wall and the collapse of this wall inside the room. These two types of deposits mark the room, and especially its eastern wall. Two (or three) vessels were placed there during the construction of the building. A little modelled bottle and two utilitarian vessels were included before the initial sedimentation of the living space near the eastern wall. The third special deposit was placed beneath a huge stone that served as pillar for the entrance to the house. Marked by several small stones (that at the same time helped to support the weight of the pillar) a prematurely born infant (in his/her eighth lunar month; Bernardi 1996) was placed, in a foetal position (as is normal in this region for all ages of interments), with the head to the south and looking to the east (so leaning on his/her right side). No grave goods were recovered. Beneath the infant's body, a 15 cm pit was dug up and filled. All the sediment was fine sieved, but nothing was found.

So, it seems as if the walls were specially charged with symbolic meaning, as meaningful objects and beings were placed beneath and inside the wall as it was built; but the floor was reconstructed, before and during the habitation of the house. The space was levelled, and two steps were left there where the eastern wall was going to be built. Slightly before, during or after the construction, several pits were dug in the interior of the room, all along the walls. The only space left without pits was that of the entrance to the room and the communication with the western room. The pits were cut into hard soil and filled with ashes, earth, charcoal, broken bones (several of them burnt and some painted with red ochre), pottery sherds, discarded lithics, beads and pigment. Some of the pits, and the fills, were stratigraphically below the walls, and some of them above it. There is also some evidence for several re-excavations of some of the pits.

Again, the whole construction and preparation of the living place, now marked through the removal and deposition of material in the pits, emphasizes the walls, as the pits are parallel with the inner wall. Where there is no wall, as in the entrance, there are no pits, and every area of wall was marked by pits. So the wall, as a functional marker and as separation of the inside and outside space, is paralleled by the pits and their fills. As the walls hold the roof, it can be said that the pits hold the floor. The inner space is very clearly demarcated from the outer space. The communication between outer and inner space is not interrupted by walls or pits, but is marked with a shallow stone placed across the entrance, two big stones serving as pillars at each side of the entrance, and, beneath the eastern one, the remains of the dead baby. The living place was transformed, not only through enclosing it but also through the removal of the natural floor and the construction of an artificial one, a mix of mud, ashes and refuse. It is unlikely that the room was used with all the pits left open. The steep neat walls of the pits clearly show that they were filled in quickly. Even some of the fills were underneath the walls. So, it can be said to be highly probable that in some cases the pits were dug and filled in before the building of the house. But several other pits were repeatedly dug up and filled with the same type of deposit. An interpretation of the pits as part of the preparation of the house floor seems plausible, and in line with this the house floor was prepared parallel to the walls. Also, the continued reuse of the pits allow for a continued reshaping of the house floor, as the house was being inhabited. At the centre of the house a hearth was placed, and beside it a little pit surrounded by standing slabs which could be a post-hole for the central wooden column supporting the roof.

The complex stratigraphy resulting from the repeated digging and filling of pits (sometimes several refillings of the same pit) produces some ambiguity in the phasing of stratigraphy. Based on radiocarbon determinations, stratigraphy and artefactual dating (in the case of artefacts of European origin, assumed to be from the sixteenth century onwards, for example) a long period of occupation from *c.* AD 350 to *ca.* AD 1750 can be seen. The initial construction of the house can be dated to the Early/Middle Ceramic Periods, in the early part of the occupational history. This house was occupied, perhaps intermittently, over a very long time, and it was reoccupied after a period of abandonment. Important changes occurred in the south Andean region as a whole (one of them being the arrival of Europeans), but this house was repeatedly selected for habitation by local people.

Much more astonishing is the long duration of patterns of deposition of some particular artefacts. For instance, whole vessels, or whole (or almost whole) bases of vessels, were found beside the eastern wall, and never elsewhere. On the other hand, projectile points (of many different types) were found in the south-western corner, near the entrance, and in the area of communication with the room to the west, but in no other part of the room. Three additional projectile points were found beneath the mud seal of the doorway to the western room. It seems as if projectile points and ceramic pots were two opposite categories, constructed as such through their differential usage and placement. But more striking is the fact that the symbolic relationships between these categories were so attached to the meanings of the house as to endure more than ten centuries – as long as the house was still standing.

While I am not implying that those living in the house at the end of its occupation had direct knowledge of the ritual deposits performed during the construction of the house, other evidence is available for the continuity of practice within the house. The opposed placing of vessels and projectile points, and the continued action of digging and filling pits with the same sets of artefacts, is evidence for the long duration of cultural categories constructed and reconstructed in the daily practices inside the house. The vessels are preferentially located near the wall whereas the projectile points are located in the areas which are walked on. So, if there is such a differential relation between pots and projectile points it can be traced in relationship to the enacted meanings attached to the wall (as container and content) and the experience related to the fluidity of transit. Projectile points can be related to the outer world, and certainly they are not functionally related to the interior of the house. The exact opposite cannot be said in reference to pots, but it seems reasonable as pots, like walls, can be containers and contained.

There are not, then, true spatial oppositions, but relationships between spaces and objects in terms of container/contained and the broader landscape. The wall and the pottery are related to the pits, and they imply the alteration of natural floors. Just as the wall derives from the action of construction (choosing and carrying suitable stones, placing them in suitable manner) and the pits to the action of digging the soil (activities linked with spades and the turning of the soil), both of them are related to everyday agricultural activities. Construction of agricultural fields and irrigation systems also involve the construction of walls, digging the soil, working with stones, earth and water – not to dominate them, but to make them do the best for people.

Inside the wall is included an infant body. Offering the first child to appease the forces of the earth can be seen as a way of asking for the best for the people. The dead baby (dead when not yet a social person, as the difference with all the other burials in the region would suggest) was interred in the house, beneath the wall, beneath the pillar of the wall, on top of a pit, by the entrance, and not inside an underground cyst chamber, as the common burial pattern shows. Perhaps his or her liminality as not being a person yet and being already born made him/her not suitable for being separated from the house. The placing of the body beneath the wall and by the entrance reinforces this idea of liminality and inclusion. The other dead were placed inside underground cyst chambers built with slabs, single or in groups, accompanied by pots, bows, arrows, beads, and other objects. The chambers are sometimes arranged in groups and sometimes isolated on the neighbouring hills. But these chambers are constructed as if they were houses for the dead, combining both the idea of the wall and that of the pit, but at the same time secluding the entrances and fluidity that are marked as a component of the houses of the living.

Thus, it can be said that there is a group of material settings obliquely linking space and time through the definition of the wall as a monumentalized house. The present construction of the wall contains the filling of rubbish of the past, and the same can be said for pits. But what is inside the house and contained by it is again marked in its relationship with the outside world, in an apparent opposition between the wall and the entrance, the pots and the projectile points, the fixity of agriculture and the fluidity of going into and out of the house, the closeness of familial relationships and experience of walking the trails across the desert. So, in this way, the experienced landscape of the outer world is included inside the inner world of the house, turning upside down, mirroring and inverting the reciprocal relationships between society and nature. On the reverse side of a textile, figures change their colours, but their relationships can be determined nevertheless. The house is a constructed monument meaningfully related to domestic and agricultural–pastoral activities, where the reproduction of society is enacted, but it seems to be containing the objects connected with the outside world in areas of fluidity, relating both concepts. Now let us put this house in the context of the whole valley.

BROADER CONTEXTS

Six or seven domestic compounds of stone walls can be observed, each of them involving a house of two to four rooms, attached courtyards, agricultural fields of two types (yards over the gentle slope of the moraine and terraces over the steep slopes of the creek) and irrigation canals (Figure 3.3). In some of the domestic compounds there is a standing stone near the house. Several groups of tombs can be identified, all of them underground cyst chambers made of slabs, being some of the groups of tombs relating to the domestic compounds and others isolated from them.

One of the most astonishing features of the site is that all along the time-span of successive or continuous occupations the same domestic level of settlement arrangement is conserved. Even if there are substantial differences between each domestic compound in relation to the disposition of the architectural elements, they are always built up in a domestic arrangement, and the different elements are significantly present. This is very different to what happens in neighbouring regions of the south-central Andes – for instance, the aggregation of households in small villages, or the centralization of ritual monuments, or the formation of hill-forts during the Late Period. Tebenquiche seems to contradict the general tendency, showing long-term conservatism in the domestic arrangement of space and society. Burial patterns also remain over a long period of time. The typical underground cyst chamber is used from the Early till the Hispanic-Indian Periods, again in contrast to what happens in neighbouring regions, where burial patterns change from urn interments of infants, to burials in the ground and back to urns, or there are other regional traditions of cave burials or adult interment in large urns. Again Tebenquiche shows a very long stability of the same patterns.

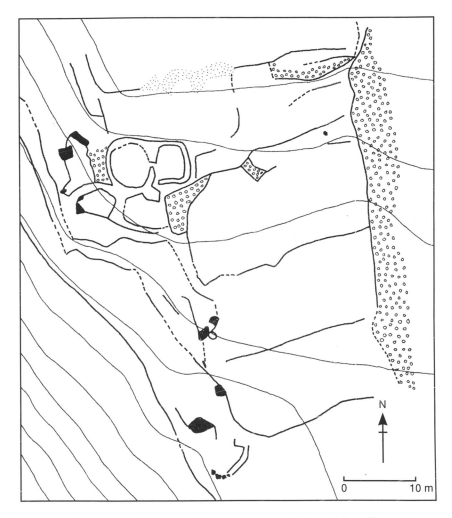

Figure 3.3 The excavated household compound at Tebenquiche Chico. Note the agricultural fields at the centre right; standing stone (black dot at the upper right) within the fields; two-roomed house, at the upper left (including the excavated room shown in Figure 3.2); irrigation canals entering the fields from the upper left.

Thus, domestic activity as the organiser of society appears as an important feature in the history of Tebenquiche, and both houses and burials are related in this way. It seems that the long-term duration of patterns of definition of the place of the living and the dead was a major goal in itself, for the reproduction of society seems closely linked to reproducing relationships with the ancestors and the past. Thus, a constellation of concepts can be suggested, linking the house, agriculture, herding, canal construction and maintenance, everyday activities, storing, preparing and serving food, caring for children, and the ancestors, the past, the place of everyday life as a point fixed in time-space. Everyday ritualization of agriculture and domestic activities is linked to the longer-term ritualization of the life cycle, either through individual deaths or in the construction of a new house. The house and all its related aspects can be seen as the arena of performances in which the relationships of protection and nurturing reproduce those of being protected and nurtured.

However, the world of life defined through the domestic house, including the everyday life spoken of in a language of domesticity, involves an oppositional as well as an inclusive relationship with the experience of the outside world. An important aspect of the artefactual remains excavated at the site, both from the domestic compound and in earlier excavations of underground chamber, is the very persistent occurrence of exotic elements: sea shells from the Pacific Ocean; seeds from the lower valleys; and pots from neighbouring regions. It is worth recalling here that 'neighbouring regions' usually means a journey of several hundreds of kilometres through desert and mountains. The nearest lowland valley lies around ten days away for a llama caravan. The importance of the llama caravan trade network has been raised by the interpretations of the Puna on its regional dimension since the 1970s (for instance, Núñez and Dillehay 1979; Tarragó 1984; Dillehay and Núñez 1988; Olivera 1991). These interpretations stressed the economic and the social implications of the caravan, but not the experiential context in which the llama caravan could have been undertaken. The llama caravan was not a special occasion, but a repetitive experience both for the caravanners and for those who stayed at home; an occasion of risks for the lives of caravanners and pack animals, as well as for the transported goods. Even economically speaking the caravan was a risky enterprise (Browman 1987), a fact not to be overlooked in the interpretation of the daily experience of caravan trade.

The insistence on defining and preserving the experience of the domestic place as fixed in time and space is perhaps related to the uneasy production and reproduction of a social unit that involves the uncertainties of impermanence and absence of some members. For those who stay at home maintaining the agricultural fields, irrigating them and caring for the children (and I do not necessarily mean by females), and for those who spend several weeks walking along the trails of the desert, facing the risks of the high mountain passes and the white storms to meet distant peoples, the close links with the place and the household can be related to the expectation of renewed encounter. The social domestic unit was constructed through symbolic and ritual over-elaboration because it could not be constructed as a social whole through everyday practice. For symbolic and economic reasons, and through emotional life as well, the domestic sphere was an important and inescapable link for the caravanners. The reproduction of caravans (animals and caravanners) cannot be accounted for without reference to the domestic sphere. And the fixed place for caravanners would be a place to die, if not a place to live.

Finally, from a broader perspective, the south-central Andes Tebenquiche site and the Puna de Atacama show some other interesting points I would like to highlight. As a contrast to neighbouring regions, the Puna de Atacama has been very difficult to understand through cultural historical sequences, and it has been very difficult to define any particular 'archaeological culture' in the area. The great persistence of ceramic, settlement and burial patterns over successive periods can be seen as an explanation for this sort of invisibility of idiosyncratic successive styles, as opposed to what are relatively clearly defined 'cultures' or 'polities' in the surrounding valleys. But if we introduce a conceptual split into what are described as cultures and what can be seen as material objectifications of the collective self, the Puna de Atacama region, and the area of Tebenquiche in particular, seems to have been in contact with several and different neighbouring ethnicities but not to have been dependent on any of them, nor to have constructed an objectified collective self through the creation of cultural boundaries. Unlike in other regions, there is no such a thing as a distinctive iconography or any material element involved in the reification of society as a totality. If this was the case, a different sense for marginality could be put forward, involving a negotiation of self-inclusion within several other polities in regard to the acquisition and maintainance of social and economic relationships, extending kinship, and at the same time defending self-exclusion as a matter of the independence of caravan enterpreneurs, mediating between different valleys separated by the Puna. It could have been the case that the house reinforced a sense of belonging at a local level, and a sense of marginality in relationship to other more developed and populated areas. Although not implying a sort of cynical self-understanding put into practice for taking advantage of commercial and social links with the outside world, belonging and marginality could have been negotiated as social resources in the broader context. The outside world was already introduced into the house in its contents, involving the experience of the outside world and the caravans within the language of domesticity elaborated and reproduced as part of the day-to-day experience of living in the house. A very developed notion of attachment to the place and the time would have existed as a local domestic experience, and a large-scale fluidity of identities and boundary construction was part of the experience of walking the desert trails, but the broader scale was included in the construction of meanings of domesticity. In some sense, the definition of the self was not necessarily implying a closed boundary, given that the ideas of the self were different but at the same time contained those of contact with the others. The other was introduced inside the house, in the practice of a rationality that involved the self and its dependence towards the other as one and the same symbolic complex.

SUMMARY AND CONCLUSIONS

We have seen how the landscape of the Puna de Atacama was constructed as an imaginary other, first by explorers and then by archaeologists, creating an image of marginality that reduced human action to the logic of subsistence. We need to view one of the major issues of recent archaeological research in the area, the domestication of camelids, in this context. Aymara linguistics and meanings are useful for building alternative views to those culturally rooted in modern western rationality. The constellation of meanings represented by *uywaña* implies a non-oppositional but mutually referential representation of nature, culture and supernature, linked to practice rather than discourse, to bodily experience more than to symbolic structures. I have tried to show through the description and interpretation of the archaeological remains of a house, how the kind of relationships illuminated both theoretically and methodologically by *uywaña* can be represented in the house as a way of understanding the self and the other.

Current discussion of domestication in the Andes is expressed in terms of the logic of subsistence. Meanwhile, Old World theoreticians have recently advanced positions giving preference to symbolic forms of domestication over economic ones (Hodder 1990; Thomas 1991). But an understanding of domestication cannot be reduced to economic forces or symbolic structures. Domestication is an ongoing representation of reality, and I hope that the relevance of the linguistic, ethnographical and archaeological data suggesting alternative representations helps support this criticism. Our own subjectivities as Argentine individuals were formed in part through the suppression of meaning in pre-Hispanic history and the construction of others as a means of domination. The historical content of the different constructions and cultural meanings of otherness is relevant both for archaeology and for society. Speaking of the domestication of nature we speak of domestication of society, both past and present, and archaeology has a part in such multiple domestications.

Linking the spatial and temporal dispositions of the house with the experience of landscape produces an oblique way of linking particular constructions of the natural body (domesticating nature) and the social body (domesticating society). *Uywaña* provides us with a particularly apt image, stressing the mutual implications of the same type of relations and emphasizing practices instead of objectified concepts. But *uywaña* does not provide us with an interpretive analogy, nor does it point out specific relations between elements or symbols. *Uywaña* involves a particularly acute way of understanding the performances of domestication: one that highlights the experience of reflexivity of the social action and the representation of society and history. Domestication as a set of actions involving animals and plants implies that the agent is herself or himself domesticated at the same time. Building the walls of the house involves the inclusion inside the house of the experience of the outer world. The construction of the social self involves the experience of transcending it. Also, the construction and the understanding of the landscape, its history and its people, necessitates defining the interpreter as well. *Uywaña* provides both an image for interpreting the domestication of domesticates and for interpreting the domestication of domesticators, and, at the same time, for the domestication of the images of domestication.

ACKNOWLEDGEMENTS

The fieldwork relevant to this chapter was done in 1988, 1989, 1993 and 1995, with Research Grants from the Secretary of Science and Technology of the University of Catamarca and a Research Fellowship from the Secretary of Science and Technology of the University of Buenos Aires (in 1988 and 1989). Pato Bernardi (Argentine Team of Forensic Anthropology) kindly analysed the human skeletal remains. Marcos Quesada drew the map and figures. A very large number of people contributed their efforts to the research, including the inhabitants of the Puna de Atacama, undergraduate students of Archaeology of the Universities of Catamarca and La Plata, local and provincial state officials, and authorities of the University of Catamarca. Elina Silvera de Buenoden supported the archaeological research as far as she was able. My writing also benefited from the comments on previous versions of this chapter by Silvina Ahumada de Haber, Carlos Baied, Robin Boast, Mirta Bonnin de Laguens, Felipe Criado, Daniel Delfino, Chris Gosden, Ian Hodder, Andrés Laguens, Pepe Pérez Gollán, Cynthia Pizarro de Cruz, Penny Spinkins, Joan Gero, Myream Tarragó and several participants of the Ethnoarchaeology session in WAC3 in New Delhi, chaired by Betty Meehan, and the 1996 Lent Term Research Seminars of the Department of Archaeology of the University of Cambridge; not one of them is responsible for the errors. This chapter is dedicated to my parents, Sabina and Tito, for their constant love.

REFERENCES

Ambrosetti, J.B. 1902. La civilisation Calchaqui. Région préandine des provinces de Rioja, Catamarca, Tucuman, Salta y Jujuy (République Argentine). *Congrès International des Américanistes. XIIe session tenue a Paris en 1900*, 293–7. Paris: Ernest Leroux éditeur.
Ambrosetti, J.B. 1903. I Calchaqui. *Bollettino della Societá Geografica Italiana* I, 3–18.
Ambrosetti, J.B. 1904. *Viaje a la Puna de Atacama de Salta á Caurchari*. Buenos Aires: Imprenta y litografía 'La Buenos Aires'.
Ambrosetti, J.B. 1905. Apuntes sobre la arqueología de la Puna de Atacama. *Revista del Museo de La Plata* XII, 3–30. La Plata: Museo de La Plata.
Aschero, C.A. 1994. Reflexiones desde el arcaico tardío (6000–3000 ap). *Rumitacana. Revista de antropología* 1, 13–17. San Fernando del Valle de Catamarca: Dirección de Antropología de Catamarca.

Aschero, C.A., D. Elkin and E. Pintar. 1991. Aprovechamiento de recursos faunísticos y producción lítica en el precerámico tardío. Un caso de estudio: Quebrada Seca 3 (Puna meridional argentina). *Actas del XI Congreso Nacional de Arqueología Chilena, Volumen II*, 101–14. Santiago: Museo Nacional de Historia Natural and Sociedad Chilena de Arqueología.

Barrett, J.C. 1994. *Fragments from Antiquity. An archaeology of social life in Britain, 2900–1200 BC*. Oxford: Blackwell.

Bender, B. 1993. Stonehenge – contested landcapes (Medieval to present-day). In *Landscape. Politics and perspectives*, B. Bender (ed.), 245–79. Providence: Berg.

Bennett, W.C., E.F. Bleiler and F.H. Sommer. 1948. Northwest Argentine archaeology. *Yale University Publications in Anthropology* 38. New Haven: Yale University Press.

Bernardi, P. 1996. Unpublished report on file.

Bertrand, A. 1885. *Memoria sobre la cordillera del desierto de Atacama y rejiones limítrofes.* Santiago de Chile: Imprenta Nacional.

Bökönyi, S. 1989. Definitions of animal domestication. In *The Walking Larder. Patterns of domestication, pastoralism, and predation*, J. Clutton-Brock (ed.), 22–7. London: Unwin Hyman.

Boman, E. 1908. *Antiquités de la région Andine de la République Argentine et du désert d'Atacama.* T. I et II. Paris: Imprimerie National.

Bowman, I. 1924. *Desert trails of Atacama.* New York: American Geographical Society.

Brackebusch, L. 1990. Viajes en las cordilleras de la República Argentina. In *Por los caminos del norte*, 65–96. San Salvador de Jujuy: Universidad Nacional de Jujuy.

Browman, D.L. 1987. Agro-pastoral risk management in the Central Andes. *Research in Economic Anthropology* 8, 171–200.

Cerri, D. 1906. *El territorio de Los Andes (República Argentina). Reseña geográfica descriptiva por su primer Gobernador, el General Daniel Cerri.* 2nd edition. Buenos Aires: Talleres Gráficos de la Penitenciaría Nacional.

Cosgrove, D. 1993. Landscapes and myths, gods and humans. In *Landscape. Politics and perspectives*, B. Bender (ed.), 281–305. Providence: Berg Publishers.

Criado, B.F. 1991. Construcción social del espacio y reconstrucción arqueológica del paisaje. *Boletín de antropología americana* 24, 5–29. México: Instituto Panamericano de Geografía e Historia.

Delgado, F. and B. Göbel. 1995. Departamento de Susques: la historia olvidada de la Puna de Atacama. In *Jujuy en la historia. Avances de investigación II*, M. Lagos (ed.), 117–42. San Salvador de Jujuy: Unidad de Investigación en Historia Regional, Facultad de Humanidades y Ciencias Sociales, Universidad Nacional de Jujuy.

Dillehay, T. and L. Núñez. 1988. Camelids, caravans, and complex societies in the South-central Andes. In *Recent Studies in Pre-Columbian Archaeology*, N.J. Saunders and O. de Montmollin (eds), 603–34. Oxford: BAR.

Franklin, W.L. 1982. Biology, ecology, and relationship to man of the South American camelids. In *Mammalian Biology in South America*, M.A. Mares and H.H. Genoways (eds), 457–90. Pittsburgh: University of Pittsburgh Press.

Friedman, J. 1992. The past in the future: history and the politics of identity. *American Anthropologist* 94, 837–57. Washington, D.C.: American Anthropological Association.

García, L.C. 1991. Etnoarqueología de pastores andinos: un aporte hacia la visualización e interpretación de sitios arqueológicos. *Shincal* 3 (1). San Fernando del Valle de Catamarca: Escuela de Arqueología, Universidad Nacional de Catamarca.

González, A.R. 1977. *Arte precolombino de la Argentina. Introducción a su historia cultural.* Buenos Aires: Filmediciones Valero.

Gosden, C. and L. Head. 1994. Landscape – a usefully ambiguous concept. *Archaeology in Oceania* 29, 113–16.

Grebe Vicuña, M.E. 1984. Etnozoología andina: concepciones e interacciones del hombre andino con la fauna altiplánica. *Estudios Atacameños* 7, 455–72. San Pedro de Atacama.

Haber, A.F. 1988. El recurso del método. *Precirculados de las ponencias científicas presentada a los simposios del IX Congreso Nacional de Arqueología Argentina*, 40–51. Buenos Aires: Instituto de Ciencias Antropológicas, Facultad de Filosofía y Letras, Universidad de Buenos Aires.

Haber, A.F. 1991. La estructuración del recurso forrajero y el pastoreo de camélidos. *Actas del XI Congreso Nacional de Arqueología Chilena. Volumen II*, 139–50. Santiago: Museo Nacional de Historia Natural and Sociedad Chilena de Arqueología.

Haber, A.F. 1992. Pastores y pasturas. Recursos forrajeros en Antofagasta de la Sierra (Catamarca) en relación a la ocupación formativa. *Shincal* 2, 15–23. San Fernando del Valle de Catamarca: Escuela de Arqueología, Universidad Nacional de Catamarca.

Haber, A.F. 1993. Camelidae resource potentiality in formative Puna. *Arqueología contemporánea* 4, 99–105.

Haber, A.F. 1992–4. Supuestos teórico-metodológicos de la etapa formativa de la arqueología de Catamarca (1875–1900). *Publicaciones del CIFFYH – Arqueología* 47. Córdoba: Centro de Investigaciones de la Facultad de Filosofía y Humanidades, Universidad Nacional de Córdoba.

Hodder, I. 1990. *The Domestication of Europe. Structure and contingency in Neolithic societies*. Oxford: Basil Blackwell.

Keesing, R. 1990. Theories of culture revisited. *Canberra Anthropology* 13, 46–60.

Kent, J.D. 1987. The most ancient South: a review of the domestication of Andean camelids. In *Studies in the Neolithic and Urban Revolutions. The V. Gordon Childe Colloquium, Mexico, 1986*, L. Manzanilla (ed.), 169–84. Oxford: BAR.

Krapovickas, P. 1955. El yacimiento de Tebenquiche (Puna de Atacama). *Publicaciones del Instituto de Arqueología* III. Buenos Aires: Instituto de Arqueología, Facultad de Filosofía y Letras, Universidad de Buenos Aires.

Krapovickas, P. 1959. Arqueología de la Puna argentina. *Anales de arqueología y etnología* XIV–XV, 53-113. Mendoza: Universidad Nacional de Cuyo.

Lejcal, L. and E. Boman. 1907. La question *Calchaquie. Congrès International des Américanistes. XVe session tenue a Québec en 1906, Tome II*, 179–86. Québec: Dussault and Proulx, Imprimeurs.

Maldones, E. [E.M.] 1899. *Catamarca y la Puna de Atacama (recopilación ó extracto)*. Buenos Aires: Imprenta, litografía y encuadernación de J. Peuser.

Márquez Miranda, F. 1958-9. Noticias antropológicas extraídas del 'Diario íntimo', inédito, de D. Samuel A. Lafone-Quevedo. *Runa. Archivo para las ciencias del hombre* IX (1–2), 19–30. Buenos Aires: Departamento de Ciencias Antropológicas, Facultad de Filosofía y Letras, Universidad de Buenos Aires.

Martínez, G. 1989. *Espacio y Pensamiento. I. Andes meridionales*. La Paz: Hisbol.

Núñez, L. and T. Dillehay. 1979. *Movilidad giratoria, armonía social y desarrollo en los Andes meridionales: patrones de tráfico e interacción económica (ensayo)*. Antofagasta: Universidad del Norte.

Olivera, D.E. 1988. La opción productiva: apuntes para el análisis de sistemas adaptativos de tipo Formativo del Noroeste Argentino. *Precirculados de las ponencias científicas presentada a los simposios del IX Congreso Nacional de Arqueología Argentina*, 83–101. Buenos Aires: Instituto de Ciencias Antropológicas, Facultad de Filosofía y Letras, Universidad de Buenos Aires.

Olivera, D.E. 1991. El formativo en Antofagasta de la Sierra (Puna meridional argentina). Análisis de sus posibles relaciones con contextos arqueológicos agro-alfareros tempranos del noroeste argentino y norte de Chile. *Actas del XI Congreso Nacional de Arqueología Chilena, Volumen II*, 61–78. Santiago: Museo Nacional de Historia Natural and Sociedad Chilena de Arqueología.

Olivera, D.E. and A. Nasti. 1993. Los pastores de los Andes y su registro arqueológico: prolemas y perspectivas metodológicas. *Arqueología. Revista de la Sección Prehistoria* 3, 251–8. Buenos Aires: Instituto de Ciencias Antropológicas, Universidad de Buenos Aires.

Olivera, D.E. and M.M. Podestá. 1993. Los recursos del arte: arte rupestre y sistemas de asentamiento-subsistencia formativos en la Puna meridional argentina. *Arqueología. Revista de la Sección Prehistoria* 3, 93–141. Buenos Aires: Instituto de Ciencias Antropológicas, Universidad de Buenos Aires.

Olwig, K. 1993. Sexual cosmology: nation and landscape at the conceptual interstices of nature and culture; or what does landscape really mean? In *Landscape. Politics and perspectives*, B. Bender (ed.), 307–43. Providence: Berg.

Rabey, M.A. 1989. Are llama herders in the south central Andes true pastoralists? *The Walking Larder. Patterns of domestication, pastoralism, and predation*, J. Clutton-Brock (ed.), 269–76. London: Unwin Hyman.

San Román, F.J. 1896. *Desierto i cordilleras de Atacama*. Santiago de Chile: Imprenta Nacional.

Tarragó, M.N. 1984. La historia de los pueblos circumpuneños en relación con el altiplano y los Andes meridionales. *Estudios atacameños* 7, 116–32. San Pedro de Atacama: Instituto de Investigaciones Arqueológicas R.P. Gustavo Le Paige S.J., Universidad del Norte.

Ten Kate, H.F.C. 1893. Rapport sommaire sur une excursion archéologique dans les provinces de Catamarca, de Tucuman et de Salta. *Revista del Museo de La Plata* V, 331–48. La Plata: Talleres del Museo de La Plata.

Thomas, J. 1991. *Rethinking the Neolithic*. Cambridge: Cambridge University Press.

Thomas, J. 1993. The politics of vision and the politics of landscape. In *Landscape. Politics and perspectives*, B. Bender (ed.), 19–48. Providence: Berg.

Tilley, C. 1994. *A Phenomenology of Landscape. Places, paths and monuments*. Oxford: Berg.

Tomka, S.A. 1992. Vicuñas and llamas: parallels in behavioral ecology and implications for the domestication of Andean camelids. *Human Ecology* 20, 407–33.

Vayda, A.P. 1990. Actions, variations, and change: the emerging anti-essentialist view in anthropology. *Canberra Anthropology* 13, 29–45. Canberra.

Wheeler, J.C. 1984. On the origin and early development of camelid pastoralism in the Andes. *Animals and Archaeology: 3. Early herders and their flocks*, J. Clutton-Brock and C. Grigson (eds), 395–410. Oxford: BAR.

Yacobaccio, H.D. 1994. Hilos conductores y nudos gordianos. Problemas y perspectivas en la arqueología de cazadores-recolectores puneños. *Rumitacana. Revista de antropología* 1, 19–21. San Fernando del Valle de Catamarca: Dirección de Antropología de Catamarca.

Yacobaccio, H.D., D. Elkin and D.E. Olivera. 1994. ¿El fin de las sociedades cazadoras? El proceso de domesticación animal en los Andes centro-sur. *Arqueología contemporánea* 5.

Yacobaccio, H.D. and C. Madero. 1991. ¿Qué hacían los pastores con los huesos? *Comechingonia. Revista de antropología e historia* 7, 15–28. Córdoba.

4 Of water and oil: exploitation of natural resources and social change in eastern Arabia

Soren Blau

INTRODUCTION

Focusing on a particular part of Arabia, the United Arab Emirates (UAE), this chapter examines examples of human interaction with, and adaptation to, the environment. Whether it be food, mythology, landscape, costume, or resources, certain aspects of any unfamiliar area tend to integrate into popular culture. In the case of Arabia, it is spices, tales of Aladdin and jinn, vast deserts, a fanaticism linked with religion, and (more recently) oil which constitute current stereotypical associations. The Arabian Gulf (also known as the Persian Gulf depending on which side of the water you live) is situated in a sedimentary basin which holds roughly two-thirds of the world's proven reserves of oil (Long 1978: 1). It has been stated, for example, that without this oil 'the Gulf would elicit little interest for any but the people who inhabit its shores' (Long 1978: 1; see also Auchterlonie 1986: 54). While such generalizations are beginning to be dislodged as the tourist industry makes access to such countries increasingly easy, disciplines such as archaeology and anthropology are also contributing information about the long-term history of the region.

In refutation of simplistic statements such as that quoted above, the climatic extremes and geographical location of the UAE provide an interesting background for the study of human interaction with the environment, especially in terms of humans accessing and manipulating natural resources, and the subsequent social changes which may result from such actions. Further, such studies are particularly interesting because it is possible to juxtapose examples of human adaptation both in the past and in the present. Although restricted in detail, archaeological evidence provides insights into the effects which long-term developments in techniques of exploiting fresh water had on settlement patterns and health. In contrast, anthropological studies provide details concerning the effects of the more recent exploitation of oil on areas such as occupation, housing, demographics and health.

THE UNITED ARAB EMIRATES: BACKGROUND

Of the many countries bordering the Gulf, the UAE (Dawlat al-Imaaraat al-Arabiyya al-Muutahidah in Arabic) has only relatively recently begun to be of interest to western scholars. Extending across the Tropic of Cancer, the UAE is situated between the latitudes of 22°50' and 26° north and longitudes 51° and 56°25' east (Peck 1986: 4). The UAE spreads from the base of the Qatar Peninsula in the west, to the borders of the Sultanate of Oman in the north (the Musandam Peninsula) and the south-east, and the Hasa or Eastern Province of Saudi Arabia in the south-west (Zahlan 1978: 1) (Figure 4.1). Located on the southern shores of the Arabian Gulf, the UAE forms part of the geographical subdivision of south-eastern Arabia and is also considered part of the greater geographical unit of South-west Asia (formerly the 'Middle East') (Heard-Bey 1982: 6).

Because of its geographical position at the cross-roads of three continents, situated between the Arabian Gulf and the Red Sea, parts of the great land mass of Arabia have been visited, explored and inhabited for millennia (Wilson 1928: 1). Although there are early historical references which suggest the waters of the Gulf were known and traversed in Antiquity (see for example, Trench 1986: 74), early European land exploration focused predominantly on southern and inland Arabia, with eastern Arabia (the area of modern day UAE) being comparatively by-passed (Blau in prep.[a]; see also Brent 1977; Freeth and Winstone 1978; Trench 1986). Further, the lack of antiquarian interest in the UAE compared to north-western Arabia and other South-west Asian countries such as Iran and Iraq (where tangible evidence for the biblical record was sought), contributed to the traditional western scholarly opinion that the UAE was peripheral.

Being part of 'Arabia', there has been a tendency to generalize about the type of landscape found in the UAE, which has often been considered to consist only of desert (which in turn has fostered racist notions about the 'simplistic' lifestyles of the people – see for example, Lorimer in Bidwell 1971: xvi). While the desert certainly constitutes a large area of the country, different environmental areas do exist and contribute to the nature of human interaction within the landscape. Four main environmental zones have been identified, and include coastal, desert, mountainous and alluvial plain regions (Heard-Bey 1982: 8–11). These different environments host a variety of exploitable terrestrial and marine resources: the most significant of these in terms of impact on the people are fresh water and oil.

HUMANS AND RESOURCES IN PREHISTORY

Although the UAE has a relatively short history of archaeological research (Potts 1997: 78–81), archaeological investigations over the last thirty-nine

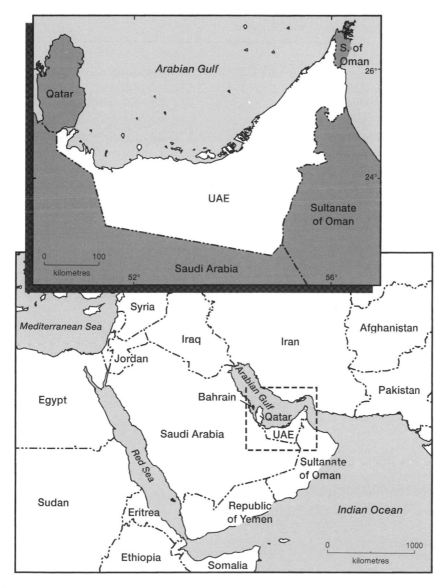

Figure 4.1   Location of the United Arab Emirates

years have 'revealed a rich archaeological record which . . . suggests the UAE was, and is, anything but peripheral' (Blau 1995: 125). The majority of archaeological investigations have concentrated on establishing chronologies for the region (Table 4.1) and examining the UAE in its wider geographical context, especially in terms of the development of ancient trade (see for example, Potts 1990). To date, there is no knowledge of the hominoid and early hominid occupation of eastern Arabia between the early Miocene and

Table 4.1 Chronology of pre-Islamic archaeology in
the United Arab Emirates

Period	Date
Arabian Bifacial Tradition	*c.* 5000–3100 BC
Hafit	*c.* 3100–2500 BC
Umm an-Nar	*c.* 2500–2000 BC
Wadi Suq	*c.* 2000–1200 BC
Iron Age	*c.* 1300–300 BC
Late Pre-Islamic (A–B)	*c.* 300–0 BC
Late Pre-Islamic (C)	*c.* 0–200 AD
End of Pre-Islamic	*c.* 240–635 AD

early Holocene (Potts 1990: 12), the majority of archaeological evidence
dating from the last four to five thousand years.

Environmental evidence has been used to suggest that while the Gulf
experienced wet phases during the Pleistocene and early Holocene,
conditions deteriorated to the current hyper-arid conditions about five to six
thousand years ago (Stanger 1994: 97; cf. Gebel *et al.* 1989: 24). This is
significant in terms of attempting to understand human ecology in the past
because it can be assumed that the people who created the archaeological
evidence experienced the same climatic conditions as today. These climatic
conditions include exceptionally hot and humid summers (May to
September) with temperatures reaching up to 45°C, while the winter months
(December to February) tend to be cooler with temperatures averaging 10–
30°C (Potts 1990: 22; Stanger 1994: 89; Morbin 1995: 138). The UAE can
thus be described as lying in a subtropical arid zone.

The discovery of stone tools and debitage throughout the UAE indicates
that humans were interacting with, and manipulating, their environment from
around 6,500 years ago (Potts 1993a: 169; Rice 1994: 330). However,
evidence for formal organization and control of natural resources does not
appear until the third millennium BC. The crucial natural resource in
question, fresh water, has been, and largely remains, of great importance. The
two main sources of water in the UAE are rainfall (the mean annual
precipitation being only around 100 mm – Satchell 1978: 201; Mitchell
1980b: 547) and underground aquifers which run at shallow depths, either
providing oases where the water rises naturally to the surface, or are exploited
where wells can be dug (Peck 1986: 11).

Archaeologically, wells which topped an underground lens of fresh water
have been found in the UAE as early as the mid-third millennium BC (in the
so-called Umm an-Nar period – *c.* 2500–2000 BC – Table 4.1), both at coastal
sites such as Tell Abraq (Potts 1993b: 118), as well as inland sites such as Hili 8
(Cleuziou 1989) (see Figure 4.2). Given the scarcity of rainfall, farming
which relies on rainfall alone (200 mm is generally considered necessary –
Potts 1990: 82) was probably impossible (Potts 1993a: 165). Different types of
archaeological evidence suggest that water drawn from wells provided an

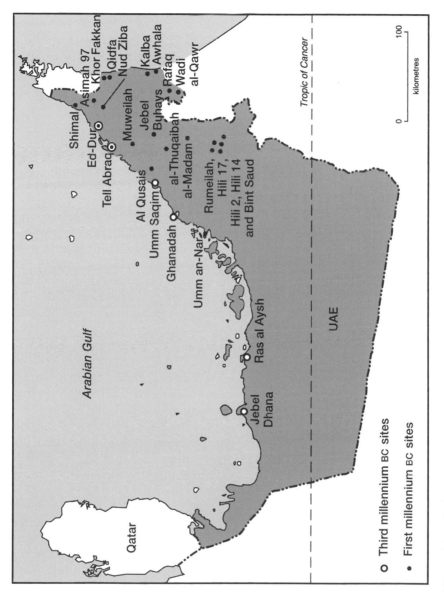

Figure 4.2 Third and first millennium BC sites in the United Arab Emirates

adequate source for irrigation of some kinds of crops. Although relatively little work has been carried out on palaeobotanical remains from Arabia (Potts 1994: 236) (which is probably a combination of the results of poor preservation as well as the false notion that arid environments could not sustain agricultural populations), palaeobotanical evidence of barley and wheat has been recovered from Umm an-Nar sites such as Tell Abraq and Hili 8 mentioned above (Potts 1990: 80; Willcox and Tengberg 1995: 130, 134).

Given the numerous date seeds found at some of the Umm an-Nar sites in the UAE, the cultivation of date palms (*Phoenix dactylifera*) was almost certainly carried out in the vicinity of settlements associated with wells. It is possible, therefore, that date plantations were nurtured purely by means of the water from wells, which in turn provided shade, a 'micro-climate', to cultivate other crops (Blau 1996: 166). This system was used by the traditional agriculturalists of the UAE prior to the discovery of oil (Heard-Bey 1982, quoted in Cleuziou 1989: 79), and remains in use in some areas of Oman and the UAE today.

Other evidence supporting the idea that water was available for crop production includes the hundreds of fragments of grinding stones as well as fired clay ovens which have been recovered from various sites (Potts 1991: 30–2). Such evidence suggests that grain processing was being carried out. Although the function of the clay ovens has not been proved, it is possible that bread production was being carried out given that they resemble the modern *tanours* or ovens used primarily to cook bread in Western Asia today (Potts 1990: 36).

Further, an analysis of some of the human foot bones from Tell Abraq revealed a number of interesting changes. Transformations of articular surfaces and/or the formation of osteophytes were observed on many of the first metatarsals, and those with alterations were significantly shorter than those without (Blau 1996). Similar alterations found in other studies have been explained as so called 'occupational changes'; that is, skeletal changes due to the frequent adoption of a posture such as kneeling. Based on ethnographic studies such changes have been interpreted as perhaps developing in 'the preparation of the grain for eating' (Molleson 1994: 71; see also Ubelaker 1979). Consumption of bread in which the grain has been hand ground and, therefore, not always completely refined, has been shown to affect the dentition severely (Molleson 1994). Studies of human dental remains from a number of archaeological sites in the UAE dating to the third millennium BC show high levels of attrition (Kunter 1983: 339; Blau in prep.[b]). The mastication of dry bread is likely to have been one factor contributing to this degradation.

It is not until about two thousand years later that evidence of new forms of water exploitation occur in the UAE. In the so-called Middle Iron Age, dating to *c.* 1100–600 BC (Magee 1996b: 249), there is evidence for innovative forms of environmental manipulation with the introduction of an irrigation system known as the *falaj*. Believed to be Iranian in origin (Potts 1990:

391–2), the *falaj* systems (of which there are three different types – Costa 1994: 276) involve channelling water either from surface flow or mountain aquifers, and transporting it via subterranean and surface channels (English 1968; Costa 1983). Such a system requires openings cut along the under-ground stream to regulate and ventilate the water supply, to remove silt and allow for general maintenance.

The implications of such innovations for social change are many. While archaeological evidence for settlements and burials have been documented as early as the fifth millennium BC in the UAE, it is not until the first millennium BC that settlement numbers, particularly inland and in the piedmont areas, increase in a way 'unrivalled in the peninsula's history up to that point' (Potts 1990: 354). While location of habitation sites does not change (that is, sites dating from the third to the first millennium BC have been identified both inland and on the coast), the number of settlements increases (Figure 4.2). The introduction of the *falaj* systems inevitably resulted in more efficient and easy access to water leading to agricultural intensification. This in turn probably accounted for the 'increase and diversification of settlement distribution' (Magee n.d.).

Archaeological evidence also reveals changes in building styles and techniques. In the Umm an-Nar period, the principal architectural style was based on a solid compartmented circular building made of white limestone and finished with mud-brick, usually about 25 metres in diameter (see for example, Potts 1990: 100–2; Potts 1993b: 118; Orchard 1994: 63), (although an example of a 40 m diameter tower has also been recovered – Potts 1993b: 118). It is believed that defence was a major motivation in construction (Potts 1990: 102). In contrast, settlements dated to the Iron Age tend to consist of buildings constructed of mud-brick, which are entirely rectangular in shape and lack fortifications (Potts 1990: 366; Naayeem 1994: 75–81) (although the results of a recent excavation on the east coast of the UAE have shown an exception to this design – Potts *et al.* 1996).

Although settlement numbers increased during the Iron Age, it is only possible to speculate about whether population numbers also increased (see for example, Magee 1996a: 338–9) and, if so, what this meant for society. It is possible, for example, that if population numbers were increasing, then so too was a susceptibility to so-called 'crowd diseases' such as tuberculosis or leprosy (Manchester 1983: 44; Lancaster 1990; Dodson 1992). Further, perhaps the closer proximity of water to the community would have provided a suitable environment for the development of diseases such as malaria (an affliction which 'has been endemic in the region for a considerable time' – Dar *et al.* 1993; see also Gelpi 1983: 229).

An informative means of investigating human health in the past is through the studies of archaeological skeletal remains. Although diseases such as malaria cannot be detected through studies of bone itself[1], other pathologies may indicate certain changes in liefstyles, including diet and occupation. Preliminary reports on skeletal remains from nearby Oman (Kunter 1981,

1983) for example, suggest that dental remains dating to the third and second millennium BC show extreme attrition of the molars, while evidence of the formation of dental calculus (plaque), caries and ante-mortem tooth loss are rare. Dental remains of skeletons dated to the first millennium BC (that is, contemporary to the introduction of the *falaj*), however, show little molar attrition, but quite extreme frontal attrition and extreme ante-mortem tooth loss, perhaps explained by an increase in the incidence of caries (Kunter 1983: 339–40).

While date plantations probably existed in the third millennium BC, it is not until the first millennium BC, with an innovation in technology, that such plantations were truly exploited for both economic and nutritional purposes. The percentage of dates and date-related foods such as vinegar and liquor (Vanhove 1994) which were consumed may have increased, thus explaining the significant change in frequencies of dental caries. Further, the changes observed in dental attrition between the third and first millennium BC may also be a reflection of changes in subsistence. The high frontal wear observed on the dentition of skeletons dating to the Iron Age may suggest that teeth were used as tools (for example, in the processing of palm fronds for wickerwork), and again may be indicative of a change in economy. Current analysis of skeletal remains from different sites throughout the UAE will provide further information about the ways in which health altered in this area at the time of the introduction of the *falaj* (Blau in prep.[b]).

Whether indirectly in the case of water, or directly in the case of a raw material such as copper (which was mined in the mountains in the UAE bordering Oman) (Potts 1990: 89–90, 114–25; Nayeem 1994: 224–31), exploitation of natural resources in the past undoubtedly enhanced the development of trade networks. Archaeological evidence from the UAE including stone weights and storage jars from Harappa (ancient India), pottery from Bahrain and Mesopotamia, soft stone vessels from Iran, as well as an unique ivory comb from Bactria (northern Afghanistan) (Potts 1993b: 123–4) illustrates that as early as 4,000 years ago 'a major phenomenon of contact extending from the steppes of Central Asia to the shores of Arabian Sea took place' (Potts 1993c: 595). 'Contact' may not only have provided a means by which new pathogens were introduced into previously unexposed groups potentially having far-reaching repercussions for health (as documented in the European colonization of countries such as Australia and the United States – see for example, Curson 1985; Webb 1995: 284–9), but may also have affected the gene pool.

Given that the 'morphological expression of discrete and metric dental traits can be considered at a fundamental level of gene expression' (Biggerstaff 1979: 215), the morphology of dentition from archaeological sites throughout the UAE is currently being studied in order to contribute finer details to questions concerning the so-called racial affinity of indigenous people in the UAE in Antiquity (Blau in prep.[b]). Preliminary analyses are also currently being undertaken on archaeological skeletal material from the UAE to investigate the possibility of survival of ancient DNA and proteins. Such molecular studies may provide information about an individual's predisposition to disease, as well as evidence concerning racial affinity.

Based on assumptions drawn from studies of contemporary people, the genetic evidence for population origins in the UAE suggests an admixture of people from the African continent and Mediterranean countries (Kamel 1979; Kamel et al. 1980: 482–3; White et al. 1986: 250) as well as Baluchistan (now Iran, Afghanistan and Pakistan) (Quaife et al. 1994: 60) occurred at some time in the past. This certainly supports the archaeological evidence outlined above. While it can be assumed that people came with the goods, it is only possible to surmise at present the extent to which the gene pool began to be mixed and over what time period this merging took place (Blau in prep.[a]). It is likely, however, that the diversity seen in the current UAE population is only the most recent manifestation of similar episodes in the past (see p. 92).

While the exploitation of water was evidently a fundamental part of subsistence in the UAE (and the Oman peninsula in general) in antiquity, the implementation of the *falaj* system in the first millennium BC had obvious repercussions for local communities. As a result of the introduction of this technology examples of changes between the third and first millennia BC have been documented in settlement numbers and in architectural styles, as well as in human health. One can only assume that social dynamics in general must have been affected. Although manipulating water resources continues to be vital to the UAE today (illustrated by the 'massive investment in coastal desalination plants' – Al Abed et al. 1996: 164), social changes are more evident as a result of relatively recent exploitation of a different natural resource.

HUMANS AND RESOURCES IN THE PRESENT

Attempting to understand the ways in which humans in the past in the UAE managed natural resources, such as water, provides insights into the ways in which such manipulations may be related to social norms. More recently, the change in relationship between humans in the UAE and their environment has implemented social change which can be recognized much more easily. Again, these social changes have come about due to processes of managing natural resources – namely oil.

Although the presence of petroleum in the Gulf was first mentioned by Pliny the Elder (in his *Natural History*, AD 77) who used the term 'naphtha' to describe the way in which areas around the borders of Persia (modern-day Iran) burned brightly during the night (Wilson 1928: 45), unlike water, oil has been exploited for less than half a century (Bulloch 1984: 184). In 1958 the first oil well was drilled in the territorial waters of Abu Dhabi and an oil boom followed in the 1970s (Hamad 1986: 167). The immense wealth resulting from exporting this resource has transformed what were considered fairly unknown backwaters into modern cities, banking centres and world financial powers (Bulloch 1984: 2). Once again, the manipulation of a natural resource has altered social dynamics in the UAE in nearly every aspect of life, including occupation, housing, demographics and health (not to mention providing funds for research into the study and preservation of cultural heritage – Costa 1983: 273; 1994: 269).

Both pearling and fishing have traditionally provided significant sources of income for the people of the UAE (Vine and Casey 1992: 81–2, 86–91). However, since the discovery, and subsequent export of oil many of the traditional techniques used in pearl diving have been lost. While fish remain an important commodity the frequent oil spills in the Gulf severely affect the industry (Peck 1986: 14).

The other prominent area of social change is in health. An increasing prevalence, for example, of obesity has been observed among younger people in the UAE (Amine and Samy 1996). This has been attributed to the fact that energy intake has increased without a concomitant increase in levels of physical activity. For example, changing lifestyles where aspects of modern life such as fast-foods have replaced conventional foods, and have been integrated with traditional behaviour such as long afternoon napping to cope with the heat. The affluent urban lifestyle of the majority of Arabs in the UAE has also led to coronary heart disease emerging as the leading cause of mortality (el-Mugamer et al. 1995).

Other health problems also relate to the presence of many different nationalities in the UAE. Once oil production became a prominent industry there was a recognized need for diverse job skills. A shortage of indigenous labour saw an increasing number of foreign immigrants entering the country, mainly from Iran, India, Pakistan and other Arab countries, as well as the Philippines and South Korea (Abdelfattah 1992: 11). This has not only resulted in the Arabs now being a minority (one-quarter of the population) in their own country (Homouda et al. 1982: 49; Anon. 1995: 3110), but has also affected health trends. For example, although a concerted malaria eradication programme in the UAE has reduced local transmission to a very small level, the large immigrant workforce from countries such as the Sudan and Pakistan has meant that malaria has been imported into the UAE (Dar et al. 1993).

The presence of many different nationalities in the UAE also has social and cultural implications. For example, in many Emirati homes nannies from foreign countries are employed to look after the children, the result being that the children are often brought up speaking English and bits of the nanny's language, with little acquaintance of their native Arabic (Peck 1986: 71).

Because the rate of change has been so fast in the UAE, accompanying aspects of development, such as modern health practices, are resisted. It is interesting to note, for example, that traditional practices in the UAE such as the use of the so-called 'chewing sticks' (a fibrous root of the Miswak tree which contains natural antiseptic – Mauger 1988: 56) to fight oral bacteria are still widely used (and, interestingly, actively encouraged by the World Health Organization as an effective tool for oral hygiene – Al-lafi and Ababneh 1995).

CONCLUSION

Although more is known about contemporary use of resources than prehistoric uses, it is obvious that in both cases many aspects of lifestyles were, and continue to be, affected. Although environment is only one of *many* variables which affect human action and socialization, in harsh climatic conditions such as those experienced in the UAE, accessing and exploiting fresh water was a major undertaking in the past, influencing many aspects of life. The importance of water has only recently been superseded by the exploitation of oil. Rapid social change has followed this shift, especially in areas of life such as settlement and health.

Whereas water in the form of oases, wells and the *falaj* systems once formed the focus of social organization, the oases are now 'low order centres on the peripheries of the settled regions' (Wilkinson 1978: 3). The government is now trying to settle the relatively few remaining nomadic and semi-nomadic peoples (Peck 1986: 63). Thus, traditional tribal life and practices such as techniques of date cultivation or the use of the sun, stars and colour and depth of the water as navigational aids (Heard-Bey 1982: 184) are slowly disappearing. Where once stood the traditional *barastis* huts, mud-brick structures with roofs of palm fronds, now stand luxury hotels, apartments, broad boulevards, Burger Kings, and Seven-Elevens (Bulloch 1984: 18). Traditional architectural features such as wind towers (tall structures employed to catch any breath of air and direct it into the house) have also been lost, primarily to modern air conditioning.

The discovery of oil has also contributed to shifts in attitudes towards the land, in turn relating to local conflict within the UAE. Formerly, the land itself, with its relative shortage of fresh water, had little intrinsic value. Rather than having a strong bond with the land, people's affiliation lay predomin-antly with particular family or group leaders (Lienhardt 1957: 56; 1975: 64; Balfour-Paul 1982: 46; Blau 1993: 46). The formal division of the UAE is largely the heritage of British presence, and to some extent is still permeated by tribal, clan and family relations (Wilkinson 1991: 29). However, the presence of oil has given land monetary importance. Because oil has not been discovered in all of the Emirates questions of drilling rights have resulted in increasing disputes regarding boundaries of the individual Emirates (Burrell and McLachlan 1980; Clark 1980: 497; Mitchell 1980a: 560; Litwak 1981: 41–72; Petrie-Ritchie 1981: 57; Peck 1986: 4; Butt 1995: 101).

Thirty years ago the UAE was among the poorest countries in the world

(Peck 1986: 65), and yet today per capita income in the UAE is among the highest (Gause 1994: 9). Given that the government has been able to establish a welfare system whereby all citizens can enjoy social benefits such as free health care and education, then it must be acknowledged that there are certainly positive aspects of social change accompanying the discovery of oil. It is inevitable that the manipulation of natural resources (both in the past and the present) has allowed society in the UAE to break out of and change its environmental constraints (Stevens 1974: 144). In the UAE today, this has resulted in a country which presents a bewildering blend of traditional and modern elements in its cultural and social life. While oil has put the UAE on the international map, it is also possible that there were similar occurrences in the past, where exploitation of resources may have similarly expanded foreign contact.

While the great capacity of traditional society to absorb massive change has been noted (Peck 1986: 67), this fast pace of change has more recently triggered a backlash by some of the older Emirati locals who are afraid that many of the traditional practices and knowledge will soon be lost forever. Consequently, there has been an increase in support for museums and the public display of symbolic icons which, it is hoped, will preserve aspects of the country's heritage. Continued research into the ways in which people in the past interacted with their environment is thus supported. Although traditionally considered peripheral by most western scholars, the UAE is an area where examples of human interaction and adaptation and the consequent social changes can be traced and documented both in antiquity and the present.

ACKNOWLEDGEMENTS

I would like to thank the Australasian Society for Human Biology for providing me with the opportunity to present a version of this chapter at its tenth annual conference. I am also extremely grateful to Paul Rainbird, Chris Gosden, Alan Thorne and Peter Magee for their comments on this chapter. Responsibility for the content is mine.

NOTE

1 If continuity can be assumed between archaeological skeletal remains recovered in the UAE and contemporary Emirati's then it is possible that malaria may have affected people in the past. Sickle cell anaemia exists among nationals today (Walters 1954: 389–91; White 1983; White et al. 1986) and is believed to be an adaptational response to malaria (El-Hazmi 1982: 48–9; Gelpi 1983; Carola et al. 1992: 573).

REFERENCES

Abdelfattah, S.H. 1992. Higher education in the United Arab Emirates: University of United Arab Emirates and its development. Unpublished Ph.D. thesis, The University of Texas.

Al Abed, I., P.J. Vine and P. Vine (eds) 1996. *The United Arab Emirates Yearbook 1996.* London: Trident Press.

Al-lafi, T. and H. Ababneh. 1995. The effect of the extract of the Miswak (chewing sticks) used in Jordan and the Middle East on oral bacteria. *International Dental Journal* 45, 218–22.

Amine, E.K. and H. Samy. 1996. Obesity among female university students in the United Arab Emirates. *Journal of the Royal Society of Health* 116, 91–6.

Anon. 1995. *The Europa World Year Book.* Vol. 2. London: Europa Publication.

Auchterlonie, P. 1986. Some western views of the Arab Gulf. In *Arabia and the Gulf: from traditional society to modern states*, I.R. Netton (ed.), 43–56. London: Croom Helm.

Balfour-Paul, H.G. 1982. How and why: the making of the Emirates. *South* 15, 46–7.

Bidwell, R. (ed.) 1971. *The Affairs of Arabia 1905–1906.* Vol. 1. London: Frank Cass and Co.

Biggerstaff, R.H. 1979. The biology of dental genetics. *Yearbook of American Journal of Physical Anthropology* 22, 215–27.

Blau, S. 1993. Observing the present – reflecting the past: attitudes towards archaeology in the United Arab Emirates. Unpublished BA Hons thesis, The University of Sydney.

Blau, S. 1995. Observing the present – reflecting the past: attitudes towards archaeology in the United Arab Emirates. *Arabian Archaeology and Epigraphy* 6, 116–28.

Blau, S. 1996. Attempting to identify activities in the past: preliminary investigations of the third millennium BC population at Tell Abraq. *Arabian Archaeology and Epigraphy* 7, 143–76.

Blau, S. (in prep.[a]). Studies of Human Skeletal Remains in the United Arab Emirates: where are we now?

Blau, S. (in prep.[b]). Health in Antiquity in the United Arab Emirates: a reassessment.

Brent, P. 1977. *Far Arabia: explorers of the myth.* London: Weidenfeld and Nicolson.

Bulloch, J. 1984. *The Persian Gulf Unveiled.* New York: Congdon and Weed.

Burrell, R.M. and McLachlan, K. 1980. The political geography of the Persian Gulf. In *The Persian Gulf States: a general survey*, J. Cottrell (ed.), 121–39. Baltimore: Johns Hopkins University Press.

Butt, G. 1995. *The Lion in the Sand: the British in the Middle East.* London: Bloomsbury.

Carola, R., J.P. Harley and C.R. Noback. 1992. *Human Anatomy and Physiology.* 2nd edition. New York: McGraw-Hill.

Clark, B.D. 1980. Tribes of the Persian Gulf. In *The Persian Gulf States: a general survey*, J. Cottrell (ed.), 485–509. Baltimore: Johns Hopkins University Press.

Cleuziou, S. 1989. Excavations at Hili 8: a preliminary report on the 4th to 7th campaigns. *Archaeology in the United Arab Emirates* 5, 61–87.

Costa, P.M. 1983. Notes on traditional hydraulics and agriculture in Oman. *World Archaeology* 14, 273–95.

Costa, P.M. 1994. *Studies in Arabian Architecture.* Hampshire: Variorum.

Curson, P.H. 1985. *Times of Crisis: epidemics in Sydney 1788–1900.* Sydney: Sydney University Press.

Dar, F.K., R. Bayoumi, T. Al Karmia, A. Shalabi, F. Beidas and M.M. Hussein. 1993.

Status of imported malaria in a control zone of the United Arab Emirates bordering an area of unstable malaria. *Transactions of the Royal Society of Tropical Medicine and Hygiene* 87, 617–19.

Dodson, A. 1992. People and disease. In *The Cambridge Encyclopedia of Human Evolution*. S. Jones, R. Martin and D. Pilbeam (eds), 411–20. Cambridge: Cambridge University Press.

El-Hazmi, M.A.F. 1982. Haemoglobin disorders: a pattern for thalassaemia and haemoglobinopathies in Arabia. *Acta Haematologica* 68, 43–51.

el-Mugamer, I.T., A.S. Ali-Zayat, M.M. Hossain and R.N. Pugh. 1995. Diabetes, obesity and hypertension in urban and rural people of bedouin origin in the United Arab Emirates. *Journal of Tropical Medicine and Hygiene* 98, 407–15.

English, P.W. 1968. The origin and spread of Qanats in the Old World. *Proceedings of the American Philosophical Society* 112, 170–81.

Freeth, Z. and H.V.F. Winstone. 1978. *Explorers of Arabia: from the Renaissance to the end of the Victorian era*. London: Allen and Unwin.

Gause, G.F. 1994. *Oil Monarchies*. New York: Council of Foreign Relations Press.

Gebel, H.G, C. Hannes, A. Liebau and W. Raehle. 1989. The late quaternary environment of 'Ain al-Faidha/Al-'Ain, Abu Dhabi Emirate. *Archaeology in the United Arab Emirates* 5, 9–49.

Gelpi, P. 1983. Agriculture, malaria and human evolution: a study of genetic polymorphism in the Saudi oasis population. *Saudi Medical Journal* 4, 229–33.

Hamad, A. 1986. *United Arab Emirates: 1971–1986 fifteen years of progress*. Abu Dhabi: Ministry of Information and Culture.

Heard-Bey, F. 1982. *From Trucial States to United Arab Emirates: a society in transition*, London: Longman.

Homouda, A., D. Peiris, H.G. Balfour-Paul and R.S. Zahlan. 1982. The UAE experiment: A decade of federation. *South* 15, 43–80.

Kamel, K. 1979. Heterogeneity of sickle cell anaemia in Arabs: review of cases with various amounts of foetal haemoglobin. *Journal of Medical Genetics* 16, 428–30.

Kamel, K., R. Chandy, H. Mousa and D. Yunis. 1980. Blood groups and types, hemoglobin variants, and G-6-PD deficiency among Abu Dhabians in the United Arab Emirates. *American Journal of Physical Anthropology* 52, 481–4.

Kunter, M. 1981. Bronze und eisenzeitliche skelettefunde aus Oman. bemerkungen zur bevölkerungsgeschichte Ostarabiens. *Homo* 32, 197–210.

Kunter, M. 1983. Chronologische und regionale unterschiede bei pathologischen zahnbefunden auf der Arabischen Halbinsel. *Archäologisches Korrespondenzblatt* 13, 339–43.

Lancaster, H.O. 1990. *Expectations of Life: a study in the demography, statistics and history of world mortality*. New York: Springer-Verlag.

Lienhardt, P. 1957. Village politics in Trucial Oman. *Man*, 56.

Lienhardt, P. 1975. The authority of shaykhs in the Gulf: an essay in nineteenth-century history. *Arabian Studies* 2, 61–75.

Litwak, R. 1981. *Security in the Persian Gulf: sources of inter-state conflict*. Vol. 2. London: Gower, for the International Institute for Strategic Studies.

Long, D.E. 1978. *The Persian Gulf: an introduction to its people, politics and economics*. Colorado: Westview Press.

Magee, P. 1996a. Cultural change, variability and settlement in southern Arabia. Unpublished Ph. D. thesis, University of Sydney.

Magee, P. 1996b. The chronology of the southeast Arabian Iron Age. *Arabian Archaeology and Epigraphy* 7, 240–52.

Magee, P. n.d. Agricultural intensification and social complexity in the southeast Arabian Iron Age. Unpublished manuscript in possession of author.

Manchester, K. 1983. *The Archaeology of Disease*. Bradford: University of Bradford.

Mauger, T. 1988. *The Bedouins of Arabia*. Souffles: France.

Mitchell, K. 1980a. Natural regions – appendix C. In *The Persian Gulf States: a general survey*, J. Cottrell (ed.), 548–64. Baltimore: Johns Hopkins University Press.

Mitchell, K. 1980b. Climate and oceanography – appendix B. In *The Persian Gulf States: a general survey*, J. Cottrell (ed.), 543–8. Baltimore: Johns Hopkins University Press.

Molleson, T. 1994. The eloquent bones of Abu Hureyra. *Scientific American* 275, 70–5.

Morbin, A. 1995. United Arab Emirates. In *Middle East Review*, 133–41. 20th edition. London: Kegan Paul.

Nayeem, M.A. 1994. *The United Arab Emirates: prehistory and protohistory of the Arabian Peninsula*. Hyderabad: A.C. Guards.

Orchard, J. 1994. Third millennium oasis towns and environmental constraints on settlement in the Al-Hajar region. Part 1: the Al-Hajar oasis towns. *Iraq* 61, 63–100.

Peck, M.C. 1986. *The United Arab Emirates: a venture in unity*, London: Croom Helm.

Petrie-Ritchie, M. 1981. Dubai and Sharjah settle border dispute. *Middle East Economic Digest* 25, 57.

Potts, D.T. 1990. *The Arabian Gulf in Antiquity: from prehistory to the fall of the Archaemenid Empire*, Vol. I. Oxford: Clarendon Press.

Potts, D.T. 1991. *Further Excavations at Tell Abraq: the 1990 season*. Copenhagen: Munksgaard.

Potts, D.T. 1993a. The late prehistoric, protohistoric, and early historic periods in eastern Arabia (ca. 5000–1200 B.C.). *Journal of World Prehistory* 7, 163–212.

Potts, D.T. 1993b. Four seasons of excavation at Tell Abraq (1989–1993). *Proceedings of the Seminar for Arabian Studies* 23, 117–26.

Potts, D.T. 1993c. A new Bactrian find from southeastern Arabia. *Antiquity* 67, 591–6.

Potts, D.T. 1994. Contributions to the agrarian history of eastern Arabia II. The cultivars. *Arabian Archaeology and Epigraphy* 5, 236–75.

Potts, D.T. 1997. History of the field: archaeology in the Arabian Peninsula. In *The Oxford Encyclopedia of Archaeology in the Near East*, E.M. Meyers (ed.), 77–81 (Vol. 3). Oxford: Oxford University Press.

Potts, D.T., L. Weeks, P. Magee, E. Thompson and P. Smart. 1996. Husn Awhala: a late prehistoric settlement in southern Fujairah. *Arabian Archaeology and Epigraphy* 7, 214–39.

Quaife, R., L. Al-Gazali, S. Abbes, P. Fitzgerald, A. Fitches, D. Valler and J.M. Old. 1994. The spectrum of β thalassaemia mutations in the UAE national population. *Journal of Medical Genetics* 31, 59–61.

Rice, M. 1994. *The Archaeology of the Arabian Gulf*. London: Routledge.

Satchell, J.E. 1978. Ecology and environment in the United Arab Emirates, *Journal of Arid Environments* 1, 201–26.

Stanger, G. 1994. Part II: Environmental factors affecting early settlement south of the Jabal al-Akhdar, Oman. *Iraq* 61: 89–100.

Stevens, J.H. 1974. Man and environment in eastern Saudi Arabia. *Arabian Studies* 1, 135–45.

Trench, R. 1986. *Arabian Travellers*, London: Macmillan.

Ubelaker, D.H. 1979. Skeletal evidence for kneeling in prehistoric Ecuador. *American Journal of Physical Anthropology* 51, 679–86.

Vanhove, M. 1994. The making of palm vinegar at al-Hiswah (near Aden) and some other crafts related to palm trees. *New Arabian Studies* 2, 175–85.

Vine, P. and P. Casey. 1992. *United Arab Emirates: heritage and modern development*. London: Immel Publishing.

Walters, J.H. 1954. Uncommon endemic diseases of the Persian Gulf area. *Transactions of the Royal Society of Tropical Medicine and Hygiene* 48, 385–94.

Webb, S. 1995. *Palaeopathology of Aboriginal Australians: health and disease across a hunter-gatherer continent*. Cambridge: Cambridge University Press.

White, J.M. 1983. The approximate gene frequency of sickle haemoglobin in the Arabian Peninsula. *British Journal of Haematology* 55, 563–4.

White, J.M., M. Byrne, R. Richards, T. Buchanan, E. Katsoulis and K. Weerasingh. 1986. Red cell genetic abnormalities in peninsular Arabs: sickle haemoglobin, G6PD Deficiency, and α and β thalassaemia. *Journal of Medical Genetics* 23, 245–51.

Wilkinson, J.C. 1978. *Problems of Oasis Development*. Research Paper 20. Oxford: Oxford Publishing.

Wilkinson, J.C. 1991. *Arabia's Frontiers: the story of Britain's boundary-drawing in the desert*. London: IB Tauvist and Co.

Willcox, G. and M. Tengberg. 1995. Preliminary report on the archaeobotanical investigations at Tell Abraq with special attention to chaff impression in mud brick. *Arabian Archaeology and Epigraphy* 6, 129–38.

Wilson, A. 1928. *The Persian Gulf: an historical sketch from the earliest times to the beginning of the twentieth century*, London: Allen and Unwin Ltd.

Zahlan, R.S. 1978. *Origins of The United Arab Emirates: a political and social history of the Trucial States*, London: Macmillan Press.

5 Plant exploitation among the Nukak hunter-gatherers of Amazonia: between ecology and ideology

GUSTAVO G. POLITIS

INTRODUCTION

Human exploitation of plants has traditionally been seen as a global evolutionary process, with the beginnings of cultivation and crop domestication being incorporated into different regions at varying times in the past. This perspective has reduced the classification of groups to a dichotomy between two main categories: 'hunter-gatherers' and 'agriculturalists'. Orthodox concepts of plant domestication have recently changed in the context of people–plant interaction (Hecht and Posey 1989: 185–6; Harris 1989: 18). The distinction between domesticated and undomesticated is no longer clear. Between these two categories exists a wide spectrum of plants which, without having been domesticated in the classic use of the term, are manipulated by human intervention (Posey 1984a, 1984b; Rindos 1984; Harris 1989). Clement (in Dufour and Wilson 1994: 115) proposed the terms 'semi-domesticated', 'cultivated' and 'managed' as three main intermediate stages. Other authors include concepts such as 'tolerated', 'protected' (see Dufour and Wilson 1994), 'tamed' (Groube 1989) or 'plant husbandry' (Higgs and Jarman 1972; Shipek 1989). Harris (1989) uses the concepts of manipulation and transformation to examine two aspects of human intervention between the extremes of wild and domesticated. The confusion and overlap in the use of these terms reflects the difficulties of distinguishing the different degrees of mutual interaction between human societies and their environment.

The Nukak are a hunter-gatherer group from the Amazonian rainforest which collects, manipulates and cultivates plants to varying degrees. Their multiple exploitation strategies allow them to manage the rainforest and increase its productivity. Improvement of productivity is not only related to the adoption of new crops or to the development of better agricultural techniques, but is also directly linked to the manipulation of non-domesticated plants. This practice still provides a high percentage of the Nukak subsistence base (see Politis and Martínez 1992; Politis and Rodríguez

1994; Cabrera *et al.* 1994, Politis 1996b). The way they use most plant resources may be clearly placed between two poles: purely wild species and completely domesticated cultivars.

The interaction between people and plants has been seen as a complex continuum in which both populations affect each other to different degrees (Rindos 1984; Harris 1989). Domestication is considered by some authors to be a co-evolutionary process of taxon divergence in which all domesticated plants have undergone genetic modification through direct or indirect human intervention in their habitat (Rindos 1984). For others, domestication is perceived as a 'human social and cultural process relating to the structured knowledge by which individuals and groups agree upon certain interpretations of the natural realm of plants and animals and carry out their routine daily actions on the basis of this interpretation' (Chase 1989: 47). In this chapter I explore this idea, on the basis that the use of plants, animals and minerals by native Amazonian people is determined not only by the ecology of the resources but also by their cosmology and their ideological framework. Amazonian cosmology has been called 'ecosophy' (Arhem 1990), and it can be summarized in a basic concept: unlike the western perception of nature, humans are not in any superior position in the natural order. Animals, plants and inanimate objects are integrated in several hierarchical levels; their use and exploitation is mediated by a complex mythical system in which spirits/ancestors played a significant role being the 'owners' of places and the 'managers' of situations (among many others Reichel-Dolmatoff 1971, 1996; Reichel 1989; van der Hammen 1992). Dreams, traditions and daily events are taken into account when decisions are to be taken about game-hunting or plant exploitation, and people constantly need to negotiate with the spirits/ancestors/owners of the non-human beings.

Cosmologies such as this, where people are not in any upper hierarchy – rather they are not significantly different from non-human beings – are not restricted to the native people of the Amazonia. For example, the Chewong of the Malay rainforest do not place people apart from other beings, and the ontological distinctions between humans and other classes of being are extremely difficult to establish since humans and non-humans can change their appearance at will (Howell 1996; Descola and Pálsson 1996: 7). The people of Marovo Lagoon, in the Solomon Islands, do not identify living and non-living components of the environment as constituting a different realm of nature distinct from human society (Hviding 1996). For the Cree and other northern hunters of North America, personhood is open equally to humans and non-humans (including non-animals) and is therefore assigned to humans, animals, spirits and certain geographical agents (Ingold 1996: 131).

In the Amazonian rainforest several studies address the multidimensional character of local environment manipulation and management by indigenous people (see Posey 1984a, 1984b, 1987; Balée 1989; Descola 1994). The ecological relationship between foragers and plants has been a subject of recent debate in relation to the origins of domestication, and has been explained by the concept of incidental domestication (Rindos 1984). Hynes and Chase (1982) developed the concept of *domiculture*, which was later refined by Chase (1989) who considered the social and ideological aspects related to the use of natural resources and suggested that the process of plant (and other) resource exploitation needed to be viewed from the perspective of localized social groups intersecting spatially and temporally with particular environments:

> This intersection results in a series of hearth-based areas of exploitation (*domuses*), each carrying with it a package of resource location, restrictions upon open-ended exploitation (religious prohibitions, strategic planning for delayed harvesting, etc.) and localized technologies to fit particular domuses. We suggested the term *domiculture* for these localized packages of interaction between people and resources.
>
> (Chase 1989: 43)

In this chapter I summarize and analyse how the Nukak exploit, manipulate and generate rainforest plant resources and I apply the concept of *domiculture* to understand this process. I also discuss social and ideological factors, advocating that they are crucial in order to highlight different aspects of the continuum of ecological change involved in the people–plant interaction. My aim is not to examine or offer hypothetical explanations concerning the origins of agriculture/horticulture, using the Nukak as potential living representatives of a past evolutionary stage in the development of plant domestication. I do not consider them to be 'proto-cultivators' or 'incipient farmers' who are involved in an irreversible process of plant domestication towards an agricultural/horticultural stage. Instead I want to describe and examine the processes involved in the use of plants and warn about their effects on contemporary and past societies.

This chapter is the result of a wider ethnoarchaeology project among the Nukak that started in 1990 and which is part of the research programmes of the Instituto Amazónico de Investigaciones Científicas SINCHI (Colombia) since 1995. A large amount of original data has been obtained, part of which has been recently published (Ardila and Politis 1992; Politis 1992; Politis and Martínez 1992; Politis and Rodríguez 1994; Politis 1995; Politis 1996a, 1996b), while another part is still in press (Politis in press; Politis *et al.* 1997) or remain as manuscripts (Cárdenas and Politis n.d.; Politis and Saunders n.d.) The data summarized in this chapter was collected between 1990 and 1996 during seven field seasons led by the author, and with the participation of Julián Rodríguez (Universidad Nacional, Colombia), Dairon Cárdenas (Instituto SINCHI, Colombia) and Gustavo Martínez (CONICET – Universidad Nacional del Centro de la Pcia. de Buenos Aires, Argentina). The total period of fieldwork was 185 days.

THE PRESENT SITUATION

The Nukak are an indigenous group that lives in the area between the Guaviare and Inirida rivers, in the Colombian sector of the Amazonian rainforest (Figure 5.1). This group began regular contact with Colombian colonists only very recently – since 1988, when a band of forty-three Nukak people appeared in the small village of Calamar (Guaviare District), without any western products in their possession and with no knowledge of Spanish whatsoever (Wirpsa and Mondragón 1988; Reina 1990; Zambrano 1993). A few other Nukak bands had had previous contact with New Tribes missionaries who had settled in the east of the territory a few years earlier. Since 1988 this ethnic group has undergone an increasing process of acculturation, especially in the western part of their territory where colonization is following a land route. Several cultural aspects, however, still remain quite traditional, especially among the eastern bands, whose settlement/mobility patterns and subsistence strategies show little impact caused by recent contact with colonists (peasants) or with missionaries. The fact that the Nukak have begun regular contact with westerners only recently does not mean that until the 1980s they had been completely isolated. They

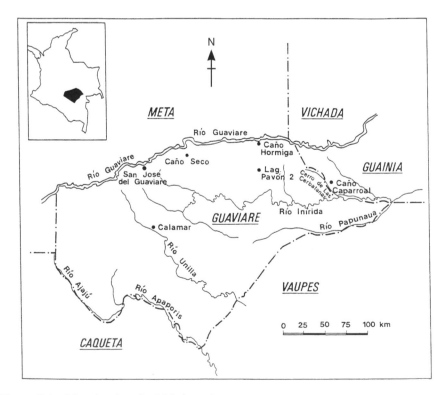

Figure 5.1   Map showing the Nukak territory.

were not 'pristine' or 'intact' (see summaries of the 'revisionist' debate in Stiles 1992 and Lee 1992). Undoubtedly they were probably involved in complex exchange networks which included other, basically horticulturist, neighbours (i.e., Tukanos, Kurripacos, Puinaves, etc.). Through them, the Nukak would have received information about the colonists and eventually they would have had occasional contact with them. The sociopolitical and historical contexts in which the Nukak are embedded have been summarized by several authors (see Ardila and Politis 1992; Caycedo Turriago 1993; Cabrera *et al.* 1994; Politis 1996b). Thus, the term 'traditional', in this context, does not imply in any case that the Nukak remained without changes throughout their history (see discussion in Politis 1996b: 22–3). The Nukak did have their own history, which was embedded in an Amazonian indigenous people tempo. At present, the dynamic of transformation is being changed due to recent contact. Nowadays several bands, especially the western ones, have already adopted some of the colonist practices. Although the Nukak continue to maintain their ethnic identity, they are under constant danger. The Division of Indigenous Affairs of the Government Ministry and other governmental institutions are making significant attempts to protect the Nukak and their territory, although results are still largely disappointing.

The Nukak belong to a heterogeneous group called Makú which includes several terra firma hunter gatherers of the north-western part of the Amazonian Basin (Koch-Grunberg 1906; Metraux 1948; Correa 1987). Linguistically, the Nukak belong to the Makú-Puinave family and their closest affiliation is with the two nearest Makú groups: Bará and Jupdu (see Mondragón n.d; Reina 1990; Cabrera *et al.* 1994). Most of the Makú people, such as the Bará and Jupdu, have changed their way of life in the last decades and nowadays are basically settled in villages and, although they still hunt and gather, their subsistence depends to a great extent on yucca and industrialized products (Silverwood-Cope 1972; Reid 1979; Milton 1984).

In contrast to other Makú groups, the Nukak still maintain a nomadic foraging way of life. Reichel-Dolmatoff (1967) made a brief reference to Makú groups living in the Guaviare–Inirida inter-fluvial area, but he did not mention them as Nukak. With respect to the colonists who began to settle in great numbers along the Guaviare following the 'coca bonanza' at the end of the 1970s (Molano 1987; Acosta 1993), the Nukak were wary and evaded contact, moving deeper into the forest as tree clearing and colonists advanced (Politis 1996b: 358–62). A number of local stories tell of Nukak killings and the abduction of women and children (Mondragón n.d.)

New Tribe missionaries established a mission, called Laguna Pavón, in the late 1970s on the southern banks of the Guaviare river and later in 1986 moved further into Nukak territory. This new mission was called Laguna Pavón 2 and from it the missionaries began a more regular contact with the Nukak, who frequently arrived at the mission seeking medical treatment and to trade their goods for metal pots, machetes and matches. Nevertheless this situation did not settle the Nukak since they usually only stayed for a few days until treatment was completed. Laguna Pavón 2 was completely abandoned in mid-1996 when the missionaries left Nukak territory. At the end of the 1980s the missionaries estimated a total Nukak population of from 700–1,000 individuals, of which they have had direct contact with 350 (unpublished reports from New Tribes). Current Nukak population has been estimated at from 400–450 persons. Only Reina (1992: 63) has a larger population estimate of about 2,000 individuals. The sources for this figure remain unknown.

The land which the Nukak presently occupy is a rainforest characterized by a tropical climate and a short dry season. Annual precipitation fluctuates between 2,500 and 3,000 mm (Domínguez 1985). The rainy period is moderated by a dry season which, due to its relatively high average temperature (25–27 degrees Celsius), has notorious effects on the forest structure. During most of the year precipitation is abundant, producing a rainy season (or winter) between April and the middle of November, with an apogee between June and August (with an average monthly precipitation of approximately 400 mm). The dry season (or summer) peaks in January and February when rainfall is at its lowest (with an average monthly precipitation falling between 50 and 100 mm).

Current knowledge about Nukak territory indicates that they occupy the land between the Guaviare and Inirida rivers, comprising an area of about 10,000 sq. km. The western limit is defined by an always-advancing line of peasant colonization towards the east, while 'Cerro de las Cerbatanas' (Blowpipe Hill) and the Caño Caparroal mark the eastern limits (Figure 5.1). Some researchers have proposed that in the recent past Nukak territory was much more extensive, with its southern limits reaching as far as Río Papunaua and Caño Aceite and its western limits extending as far as the headwaters of the Inilla, Utilla, and Ajajú rivers (Torres 1994; Mondragón n.d.). All research up to now, however, has concentrated on the area between the Guaviare and Inirida rivers (i.e., Ardila 1992; Mondragón n.d.; Torres 1994; Cabrera et al. 1994) and it seems that there are no Nukak bands south or west of this area (Cárdenas and Politis n.d.).

The Nukak recognize five territorial dimensions (Politis 1996b: 147–53). The first is the area habitually exploited by a band or co-resident group and comprises an area of between 200 and 500 sq. km. This dimension would be equivalent to what Chase (1989: 45) called a *domain*. A second, and larger territory, is that exploited by the greater affiliation (i.e., the regional group), within which band members can move with little or no restriction, to visit other camps and exploit local resources. The surface of this territory varies from 1,000 to 2,000 sq. km. The third is composed of distant regions which are sometimes occupied by bands with which they have had no or only sporadic previous contact. In this territory there are some places, such as 'Cerro de las Cerbatanas', which are visited by parties of men at least once a year in order to get the proper canes to make blowpipes. This territory may be considered as a sort of annual range (in the sense of Binford 1982). A fourth dimension is represented by distant places (or sites outside the Nukak world) whose existence is known to the Nukak, but which none or very few of them have ever visited. The existence of this territory is passed on by oral tradition, rather than personal experience, and is basically the territory of 'the others'. The fifth and final dimension is the mythical domain, whose perception is in the core of Nukak cosmology. This domain is composed of three stratified levels: the 'intermediate', or the surface of the earth, where the Nukak are living; the 'underworld' where the Nukak came from and where powerful spirits still live; and the 'overworld', where the main spirit of the ancestors prevails and where the Nukak-sun and the Nukak-moon live (unpublished New Tribe report 1989; Politis 1996b: 65–70). The 'intermediate' level has two sub-levels: the surface, the actual place where they and the rest of the people exist during life, and the subsurface where the second spirits (yore'hat) live. In this second level we find the 'house of the danta' (tapir), where spirits/ancestors inhabit. These spirits/ancestors take the appearance of sacred animals (tapir, jaguar, deer, etc.) in order to go to the surface during the night. Other 'houses', such as the one which includes aquatic beings, are also found here.

Strong solidarity, patterns of sharing and a lack of hierarchy characterize Nukak social–political organization, which can be labelled as that of a band (in the sense of Lee 1992: 31). During our fieldwork, bands or co-resident groups usually comprised between 10 to 27 individuals and formed a few nuclear families (generally no more than five). On only one occasion, a band of forty-one people was recorded in the north-eastern part of the territory. Other authors have given ranges of 12–35 (Mondragón n.d.) and 6–30 people (Torres 1994). Band composition is not fixed due to regrouping, movement of individuals from one co-resident group to another, and intermarriage. However, some families frequently live together for several years. In certain circumstances, two or three bands (or band segments) may place their camps closer together in order to facilitate inter-band ritual activities (a reunion called bak-waad). Inter-band movements of individuals depend on kinship rules which regulate interchange or the relocation of band members (Franky et al. 1995). Individual psychological factors such as dissatisfaction or distrust among members also cause relocation. The bands are joined into larger groups called munu; within these larger groups inter-band movements, marriages, social visits and rituals take place.

One of the main characteristics of Nukak bands is high residential mobility (in the sense of Hitchcock 1982: 258). This is a factor directly linked with camp construction and the occupation of the landscape (Figure 5.2). Camps are integrated by dwellings or domestic units; every dwelling is occupied by a couple with their children and sometimes some affiliated members. On a few occasions a widow with her children occupies a single structure.

Data obtained in our fieldwork reveals different seasonal patterns of residential mobility (Politis 1996a). In winter the mean distance between camps was 3.85 km (n = 12) and the mean camp occupation was 5 days

Figure 5.2 Interior of a rainy season residential camp.

(n = 13). During the summer, distances between residential camps reveal a pattern with a mean distance of 8.94 km (n = 13) and a mean occupation of 3 days (n = 15) in each camp. The pattern is, therefore, that in the rainy season the Nukak stay longer in each residential camp and move shorter distances between camps, while in the dry season they occupy the camp for a shorter time but move longer distances. Combining the data from both seasons it could be estimated that bands which still maintain a traditional way of life make from 70–80 residential moves per year. This figure coincides with the one provided by Franky et al. (1995) and is among the highest mobility rates when compared with other foragers of the world (see for example table 4.1 in Kelly 1995: 112–15), but the average distances between camps is lower. On the other hand, daily logistical mobility, beyond the exploitation of the residential camp surroundings (roughly considered less than a radius of 1 km), maintained a similar pattern in both seasons: x = 8.52 km (round-trip) in winter (n = 14; min = 3.50 km; max = 19.19 km) and x = 8.30 km (round-trip) in summer (n = 13; min = 3.00 km; max = 14.56 km). The annual average is then 8.41 km (n = 27).

Traditional Nukak subsistence is based on hunting, and gathering of plant and animal products such as honey, turtle eggs and 'mojojoy' (insect larvae of the genus *Rhynchophorus*, commonly referred to as palm grubs). Fishing and small-scale horticulture is also practised. The Nukak are increasingly obtaining both unprocessed vegetables (papaya, yucca, corn, etc.) and processed foods (rice, sugar and pasta) from the colonists. Food from the colonists is only important when the Nukak camps are located close to their settlements. During the period of fieldwork the bands were moving into the deep forest. As a result the supplies from the colonists decreased immediately and were insignificant (always less than 5 per cent by weight) in their diet.

Among the animals, primates are the preferred game. During our fieldwork the Nukak hunted monkeys two out of three days. Monkeys are hunted exclusively by young and adult males, using blowguns and darts with curare-poisoned tips. Hunting parties move along established paths in search of prey, and consist of between one to four persons, each one with his own blowgun and numerous darts (from 20–40). The most commonly hunted monkeys are howler (*Alouatta* sp.), capuchins (*Cebus apella*), woolly (*Lagothrix lagotricha*), titi (*Callicebus torquatus*) and tamarins (*Saguinus negricollis*). Once killed, the carcasses are carried back to the camp where they enter the female domain; women are responsible for butchering, preparation, and cooking. Portions of butchered monkey are later distributed among the members of the band, but the hunter's family keep the head, which is forbidden to be eaten by the hunter.

Other hunted animals are peccaries, in particular the white-lipped peccary (*Tayassu pecari*). The presence of herds of peccary, usually comprising several tens of individuals, is occasional and unpredictable, and when one is encountered the band hunters participate in a communal hunt in order to exploit the resource intensively. The weapon used on such occasion is a wooden spear with fire-hardened conical points at both ends. During these hunting episodes it is common to obtain around three or four animals, which are later cooked and smoked over a large fire in the residential camp surroundings. The peccary is taboo to women,[1] and the idea of eating the peccary meat causes them great distaste. On the other hand, men eat this animal's meat in great quantities for up to three days after the hunt. Eating peccary is also taboo for children of both sexes.

Land turtles (*Testudo* sp.) are frequently consumed by the Nukak, and every four or five days at least one is captured. Birds are also regularly hunted, but more intensely during the summer season. During our fieldwork other animals were occasionally killed, including agouti (*Dasyprocta* sp.), caiman (*Caiman sclerops*) and armadillo (*Dasypus novemcinctus*). Other researchers (Cabrera *et al.* 1994; Mondragón n.d.) also mention the hunting of other species such as collared peccary (*Tayassu tajacu*), American opossum (*Didelphis marsupialis*), paca (*Agouti paca*) and coatimundis (*Nasua nasua*).

For the Nukak, most of the larger animals are subject to formal taboo. Tapir (*Tapirus terrestris*), deer (*Mazama* sp.) and jaguar (*Panthera onca*) are proscribed, at least in part because they are considered sacred, and appear in an anthropomorphized form in the mythical framework which supports Nukak spiritual life. They are considered 'like people', and in fact the Nukak say that spirits of the 'house of danta' wear the body of these animals to reach the surface during the night. Other, smaller animals, such as the lapa, are also subject to either total, gender, age, or situation-dependent restrictions. Although we do not have sufficient information to construct a detailed table of gradations in food taboos, a broad but nevertheless insightful outline can be attempted (see Politis and Saunders n.d.).

Nukak taboos surrounding smaller animals appear to be highly selective. In general, Nukak women cannot eat all that men eat, particularly when pregnant, and children can eat even less than women. For example, when a woman is pregnant her husband can only bring her certain kinds of food, such as toucan (*Ramphastidae* sp.), and certain unspecified types of tortoises. Pregnant women, as well as their husbands, are banned from eating foods which at other times they can consume. Parents of a recently born baby are forbidden to eat certain kinds of animal food, such as howler monkey, and various kinds of birds and fishes, for up to a month. During certain times, the father does not hunt monkeys and family diet is based on vegetables, both wild and domesticated, woolly monkey and honey (Politis and Saunders n.d.). Some species of fish, duck and birds appear to have a status as 'anti-food', inasmuch as they may cause wasting. When adults or children are sick, they are also forbidden to eat certain kinds of animal food which at other times are permissible.

Periodically palm grubs are collected by all members of the band. During the rainy season, 'mojojoy' were collected almost every day, while in summer this activity decreases. It was not possible to weigh the amount of palm grubs that were consumed since they were eaten immediately. Nevertheless, it is possible to estimate that the Nukak consume between 0.05 and 0.10 kg per person/day during the winter months. There is no quantitative information for the transitional months.

As well as wild and manipulated plant species, game and palm grubs, the Nukak also have two other important seasonal resources. During the dry season fishing, using water poison ('barbasco') and collecting honey and hive contents, such as royal jelly, propolis and larvae, make a significant contribution to their diet. During fieldwork in 1994 fishing produced on average 0.4 kg per person per day, while the collection of honey (including hive products) averaged 0.7 kg per person per day. Honey was occasionally collected during the winter and did not provide a significant amount of food. Cabrera *et al.* (1994: 191) found that large amounts of honey were collected between May/June and October/November.

THE USE OF VEGETABLE RESOURCES

The other pillar of Nukak economy consists in gathering wild and 'manipulated' plant species (Politis and Martínez 1992; Politis and Rodríguez 1994; Cabrera *et al.* 1994; Politis 1996b; Mondragón n.d.). Women, men and children leave the camp to collect fruits, seeds, and roots daily. They carry the plant products in bunches, or they separate the fruits from the stalk and transport them in expedient bags (*burup*), baskets, and occasionally in metal and pottery bowls. During these walking trips and during the procurement parties, people usually eat fruits and nuts close to the trees.

Previous ethnobotanical studies indicate that the Nukak exploit a variety of vegetal resources. Cabrera *et al.* (1994) counted the use of fifty-seven species, of which forty-one were edible. They recorded twenty-two cultivated species and thirty-five non-cultivated ones. In a confusing thesis,[2] Gutierrez Herrera (1996) mentioned the use of fifty-three species, including forty-three non-cultivated and ten cultivated species found in the 'chagras' (small multistrata cultivated plots). Among the non-cultivated species, thirty-three were used as food while eight cultivated species were eaten. Finally, Cárdenas and Politis (n.d.) identified 113 used species, which encompass the plants recorded in the two previous studies. Among this list of species, ninety are non-cultivated and twenty-three are cultivated (the great majority were incorporated in the last decade). Seventy-six of these species are used as food. All these figures have to be considered as a minimum, since more ethnobotanical research has to be done in order fully to identify the whole range of used plants. However, comparing the data obtained by the authors mentioned above, and from other authors who mention plant utilization (i.e., Reina 1990; Ardila 1992; Mondragón n.d.), it seems that the main plant food resources have already been recorded. The most represented family is Arecaceae (Palmae) with fifteen species. Its palm products are used as food, and also for making artefacts, building lean-to dwellings and as a bed for the 'mojojoy'. The Moraceae family, whose fruits are used exclusively as food, is ranked second with ten species. In third place is the Burseraceae, with five species used mostly as food (Cárdenas and Politis n.d.).

During the annual cycle, 'seje' (*Oenocarpus bataua*) and 'platanillo' (*Phenakospermum guianensis*) fruits are regularly exploited in great quantities.[3] The Nukak also collect fruits of 'moriche' (*Mauritua flexuosa*), 'piassava' (*Attalea* sp.),'mamita' or *coróp'anat* (*Iryanthera ulei*), patatá (*Helicostylis cf. tormentosa*), 'palma real' (*Maximiliana maripa*), popere (*Oenocarpus mapora*), 'patabá' or *yuabutu* (*Oenocarpus bacaba*), guaná (*Dacryodes peruviana*), kupé (*Dacryodes chimantensis*), 'juansoco' (*Couma macrocarpa*), and many others. The majority of these fruits are collected in great quantities (see tables 1 and 2 in Politis and Rodríguez 1994 and tables 4.1 to 4.12 in Politis 1996b). In the case of 'seje', *popere*, 'patabá', 'piassava' and *guaná* the fruits are mashed to extract oils and other nutritional substances and are ingested in a milk-like form or 'chicha', which increases the nutritional value of the fruit (Politis and Martínez 1992; Politis 1996b). It has also been observed that some tubers such as *chidna* and *hum* provide important quantities of carbohydrates. This food element is also significant in 'platanillo' seeds, which are ground into a flour which is boiled wrapped in green leaves.

Other components of subsistence are products which the Nukak cultivate in 'chagras' dispersed throughout the forest. There are three main types of fields. The first seems to be the most traditional and is very small, usually consisting of a few chontaduro palms or 'pipire' (*Bactris gasipaes*) and sometimes achiote (*Bixa orellana*) or plantain (*Musa paradisiaca*). These orchards are spots which have been utilized for generations, and their importance is both economic and symbolic. In, or around, these orchards certain dead people are buried, significant events are said to occur (i.e., 'we discarded the stone axes in the "pipireras" when we got the metal axes'), and they are frequently used as 'meeting places' for *bak-waad* reunions (Politis 1996b; Mondragón n.d.). Generally, chontaduro orchards are found far away from colonized areas, having been established by 'the elders', and can be traced back to at least three generations. This species (chontaduro) appears in Nukak origin myths; when the first Nukak emerged to the 'intermediate world' from the 'underworld', they brought chontaduro in bags with them. It is interesting to note that the mythical antiquity of chontaduro coincides with botanical studies, which indicate chontaduro was domesticated in the north-west Amazon, where larger and more evolved varieties of the plant exist (Clement 1989). Chontaduro is also an important palm for most of the Amazonian groups. Cabrera *et al.* (1994) suggest that the Nukak traditionally cultivated other species such as bitter yucca in the past, but that this practice later disappeared. Information gathered by the missionaries during the 1980s also supports this hypothesis.

Larger gardens with a greater variety of species are generally found a few kilometres from the colonized borders, but still in the rainforest, or close to Laguna Pavón 2 (Figure 5.3). A number of domesticated species are cultivated, including sweet yucca, sugar-cane, plantains, pepper, tavena potato, ñame, pineapple and papaya, which have been introduced through contact with colonists or missionaries.

Nukak bands usually control a few 'chagras' of both types within their

Figure 5.3 Portion of the forest recently cleared to open a 'chagra'.

circle of mobility, and sometimes they camp nearby to exploit some of the cultivated plants or to carry out agricultural tasks such as slashing and burning or sowing. In the area close to the Laguna Pavón 2, there are several chontaduro orchards as well as larger 'chagras', each of them controlled by a different group. It is highly probable that the presence of the Mission attracted Nukak bands and influenced the location of the 'chagras'. On the other hand, the area was already a frontier between the territory of several bands belonging to two *munu* (*Wayari* and *Muhabeh*) and nowadays has an unusual concentration of cultivated fields.

The third field type is very recent and is obviously an adoption of colonist practices. This type is characterized by a large slash-and-burn area and usually consists of more than one hectare. Slash-and-burn fields are generally located very close to the colonist settlements and sometimes adjoining them. This type of horticulture is now practised by the bands which have become semi-sedentary and who, in addition to spending most of the time near the colonists, are occasionally employed by them to harvest coca. We observed a couple of these fields near the colonist settlements on the western limits of the Nukak territory.

In spite of the use of domesticated species, it seems clear that the Nukak economy still revolves around the exploitation of non-domesticated plants and animals (Politis and Martínez 1992; Politis and Rodríguez 1994; Cabrera *et al.* 1994; Mondragón n.d.). In fact, the collection of products such as 'seje', 'platanillo', *coróp'anat,* 'moriche', *guaná* and others greatly exceeds the quantity and variety of resources obtained from cultivation. During the rainy season, the 'seje–platanillo' duplex plays an important role. It serves not only as food, but also as a source of other products important to Nukak life: leaves for the lean-to roofs and expedient basket construction, fibres for dart manufacture, and bed for 'mojojoy' breeding.

DISCUSSION

The way that the Nukak people exploit the plant resources of the tropical rainforest could be included in what Harris (1989) has called 'wild plant-food production'. It has been widely accepted for some time now (Rindos 1984, 1989) that after long periods of time human feeding behaviour alters local flora. In this manner, certain plant species are placed at a competitive advantage (Rindos 1989: 29) or in some way 'protected'. The Nukak are a good example of this. They make residential movements and occupy a new exploitation area (or *foraging radius*, after Binford 1982: 7–8) before an observable decline occurs in the available resources obtained from the surrounding area (see tables 1 and 2 in Politis and Rodríguez 1994: 180–1, and tables 4.1 to 4.13 in Politis 1996b). Their well-balanced and varied diet indicates that no clear limitation in food resources exists which would prevent a longer residential camp existence or a higher population density. I argue that high mobility is related to a strategy aimed at concentrating and managing forest resources as well as it being the result of social and ideological factors.

Residential movements are made far before any depletion in the resources can be observed (at least in quantitative terms). In this sense, mobility can be seen as a result of placing the residential camps close to certain resources when they are abundant. This means being in a place during a certain time of the year where the availability of some food resources is at its highest, using them appropriately and then moving on to another area before making a great negative impact on the production of these resources. During the dry season, economic decisions would be associated with channel and stream access, where one can obtain fish in abundance, and in areas with beehive concentrations. In January and February, during the harvest, chontaduro orchards and 'chagras' are also a focus of attraction. In winter, access to patches of certain palms, plus hunting strategies, play a major role in organizing mobility. This complex process is a part of what the concept of *domiculture* means.

Nukak mobility is partially a consequence of a sophisticated strategy for the management and use of forest resources. This implies that while a modification in the phenotype or genotype of a particular species does not occur, its natural distribution is affected and becomes concentrated in certain forest sectors. Within this spectrum one finds palms such as 'seje', 'platanillo', and the *popere* and *guaná* trees which are in unusual concentrations throughout the rainforest. The high density of some of these species in the Nukak territory was also noted by other authors (Cabrera *et al.* 1994; Gutierrez Herrera 1996) and by the New Tribes missionaries (Andres Jiménez, pers. comm.). The manipulation of these and perhaps other species seems to be associated with activities relating to Nukak mobility. One such activity is the cutting of trees and plants during residential camp movements, or during hunting or gathering outings. This is forest management through selective clearing, subtle and insignificant in the short run but probably significant in the long run. Another activity that favours concentration of certain species is residential movement. When the Nukak abandon their camps the ground is left covered with large amounts of seeds of fruits consumed during occupation (Figure 5.4). This high concentration of seeds places some species in an advantageous situation in a tropical rainforest environment, which is typically highly competitive for sunlight and nutrients. These favoured species are precisely those which the Nukak intensively consume: 'seje', 'platanillo', *guana, popere,* and possibly a few others; it also modifies in different degrees the natural distribution of every plant consumed by the Nukak. The frequent movement of residential camps, then, produces various derived food sources in the form of 'wild orchards', which the Nukak frequent in their cycles of mobility. In other words, the Nukak leave a resource patch behind when they abandon and relocate a camp. They are creating *domuses* to which they can return in times of high productivity.

Figure 5.4   Consumption of wild fruits inside the residential camp.

Residential camp construction encourages the generation of these wild orchards. The surface area of these camps oscillates between 32 and 178 m^2, depending on the number of domestic units (see Table 5.1). There are no significant variations between seasons. In the process of camp construction the herb layer, shrubs, small and sometimes medium-sized trees are cut and removed. The majority of the medium trees, and all the large trees are left, so that the camp area remains covered by the forest canopy (Figure 5.5), to

Figure 5.5   Schematic profile of the forest layers with the location of a residential camp.

Table 5.1 Residential camp surface areas.

Construction date	Number of units	Number of individuals	Length of stay	Surface area (m^2)
Rainy season				
25-6-91	2	10	14	32.5
10-7-91	2	10	4	43.5
14-7-91	2	10	1 (night)	42.6
15-7-91	2	12	1 (night)	37.6
16-7-91	2	12	1 (night)	47.2
17-7-91	2	12	2	—
19-7-91	2	12	2	33.7
21-7-91	2	12	more than 2	36.3
17-7-91	4	26	10	85
27-7-91	4	22 + 16*	more than 2	170
28-8-92	5	24	14	114
10-9-92	5	24	3	105
13-9-92	4	18	more than 6	104
Dry season				
21-1-94	5	27	3	129.9
24-1-94	5	27	2	108.6
26-1-94	5	27	3	111.5
29-1-94	5	27	3	103.8
1-2-94	5	27	more than 3	114
19-1-95	4	14	2?	60
21-1-95	3	14	3	78
24-1-95	4	14	2	—
26-1-95	4	14	8	68
4-2-95	4	16	1	—
5-2-95	4	16	1	45
6-2-95	8	46	2	130
8-2-95	7	46	2	112
10-2-95	6	41	2	99
16-2-95	6	41	6	—
12-1-96	3	11	7	38.8
17-1-96	5	23	2	66.4
19-1-96	5	26	—	80.6
19-1-96	2	9	2	49.6
20-1-96	6	41	3	178.9
24-1-96	6	38	1 (night)	122.3
25-1-96	3	21	1 (night)	—
26-1-96	5	34	2	141
28-1-96	3	18	more than 6	74.9

Note: *Camp where a *bak-waad* took place. Two bands get together for one night.

create a filtered shade typical in tropical rainforests. As a result, when camps are abandoned there is no cleared gap in the camp area and the plot is not invaded by vines and shrubs which grow quickly and aggressively in areas exposed to direct sunlight (Kricher 1989: 81) and would otherwise successfully compete with 'seje', 'platanillo', and the seeds of other plants frequently consumed by the Nukak in the camps. Thus, the abandoned camps do not become a 'jungle' with a tangled vegetation. Due to the fact that abandoned camps are not reoccupied, edible wild species are not destroyed by subsequent human activity. During the summer the dry roof leaves which still remain are sometimes burned, as well as the garbage piles (Figure 5.6), creating a fine layer of ash which increases the fertility of the compacted soil.

This pattern of behaviour creates patches of edible plants throughout different parts of the territory. The Nukak construct a residential camp, which, after being abandoned, becomes transformed into a type of wild orchard, which augments the resource potential of the area. This sophisticated settlement and mobility system is also connected to the rainforest layers, as the Nukak displace the lowest stratum of the rainforest ecosystem, and leave the forest canopy intact. This is a sort of horizontal displacement in order to create patches without disturbing the natural stratification of the tropical rainforest (Figure 5.5). In the long term one can conclude that residential camps are not established where there is a high concentration of resources since the concentration is promoted by the establishment and subsequent abandonment of residential camps. This pattern alters the density and

Figure 5.6 Nukak woman burning a pile of garbage in the border of a dry season residential camp.

distribution of edible plants through means other than domestication (see also Brosius 1991: 131–2). Nevertheless, not every concentration of trees has to be automatically interpreted as caused by human agency, as Gutierrez Herrera (1996) did, since there are several palms – such as 'moriche' and 'platanillo' – which naturally form large dense stands which make them an attractive resource (Dufour and Wilson 1994: 119; Cárdenas and Politis n.d.). In terms of archaeological visibility, the reflection in the record of this so-called *tethered nomadism* would also produce patches of resources which in turn would increase the attraction to certain geographical locations.

Other indigenous groups also have their own ways of concentrating edible plants without being involved in classical horticultural practices. The Alyawara from Australia discard watermelon seeds after eating, returning about a year later to gather watermelons in the old camps (Lewis Binford, pers. comm. 1997). Laden observed that the Efe's forest-use pattern concentrates edible plants along the paths and around ancient camps (Bailey and Headland 1991: 266). Among Amazonian native people it has been observed that 'managed plants would also include plants that grow in cultivated areas or around living sites from seeds discarded after snack' (Dufour and Wilson 1994: 116). Hutterer (1983: 175) also recognized the constant influence of human population with minimal or no horticultural practices and concluded that 'certain aspects in the patchy distribution of plants in tropical forest may be an effect of long-range and continuous human presence'.

Although until very recently domesticated plants were consumed only in small quantities, they are not critical or 'keystone' resources (in the sense of Stearman 1991). Nukak keystone resources are the patches of wild edible plants which are created during the foraging circuit. These patches supply not only food but also raw materials. I am not denying the importance of cultivated gardens, especially in recent times, but they are important only in terms of food yield and not for raw materials (with the exception of achiote for painting). In addition they do not provide any exclusive nutritional elements, either in terms of quantity or quality.

Women usually depend on men for collecting plant products, especially palms, since the trees have to be cut or someone has to climb to bring down the bunches. Both tasks are generally carried out by men or, in the second case, by boys. The kinds of fruits that can be gathered by women by themselves are, therefore, those which grow in a lower position (such as 'platanillo', *coróp'anat* or the tubers). This does not imply that women do not participate significantly in gathering fruits as in most hunter-gatherer societies, but in this case it is different as a result of the fact that most fruits are in the canopy. Usually men have to cut down the trees, leaving women and children gathering the fruits. The typical example of the last situation is the harvest of *guaná*. Women and children are more active in harvesting in the 'chagras', when the camps are located close (less than 1 km), since most of the cultivated products are easily gathered without any help or tool.

There are important derivations for archaeological interpretation in Nukak behaviour. Most of the fruits with juicy pulps, like the Moraceae (i.e. *patatá*, *yeéd* [*Perebea xanthochyma*], *yé* [*Maquira guianensis*], etc.) are eaten in the forest, close to the tree, without processing, and not transported to the residential camps. This means that their seeds usually remain around the fallen tree or are randomly dispersed by human faeces.[4] In this case archaeological visibility will be almost non-existent (other than possibly in coprolites), even with good preservation. Most palm fruits and tree nuts, on the other hand, need some kind of processing and, therefore, have to be taken to the residential camps in order to be prepared for consumption (taking the shell off, boiling, smashing, etc.) (Figure 5.7). In this second case, their seeds have many more chances of being discarded in the camp and being incorporated into the process of increasing the wild orchards (Figure 5.8); these species will have much higher archaeological visibility. This situation makes us think about human diet reconstructions based on vegetable remains of any kind in the archaeological deposits, in as much as certain fruits and nuts would be clearly over-represented. In this context we would expect an under-representation of fleshy fruits (see discussion in Cárdenas and Politis n.d.) and hold the illusion of low diversity of plant use during the formation of the archaeological deposit (see also King 1994: 189).

The pattern of Nukak land use, where places are given names, gardens created and forests managed, albeit at a low level of intensity, provides a framework of landscape use into which the newly introduced crops can be readily fitted. This emphasizes the point that the categories of forager and

Figure 5.7   Nukak woman in the residential camp extracting the seeds from 'platanillo' fruit with a small stick.

Figure 5.8   Residential camp floor with a high concentration of 'seje' seeds and 'platanillo' shells (ruler is 20 cm long).

farmer are not determined by what is eaten, grown or hunted but rather by the mode and means of production. The Nukak will remain foragers as long as a system of tenure which recognizes surface area, fields, or territory as a unit of social and economic production and reproduction does not exist (Politis and Gamble 1996).

   The location and production of resources are not the only causes which influence mobility and use of the rainforest. It seems quite clear that the Nukak do not move residential camps in order to minimize distance between 'home' and food resources like the !Kung (Howell 1986: 168), nor to avoid the over-exploitation of local resources, as has been postulated as an interpretation of most hunter-gatherers' mobility (i.e., Hayden 1981; Bettinger 1991; Stein Mandryk 1993). Mobility among the Nukak is not only a way of intersecting and creating *domuses* but is also the result of a myriad of factors framed by cosmology. The forest is not perceived as an easily depleted environment as some anthropological studies suggest (i.e., Sponsel 1986; Bailey and Headland 1991) but is considered a rich, bountiful milieu and a dimension of the cosmos, partly given, partly created by ancestors/spirits, with whom the Nukak need to negotiate the use of mineral, floral and faunal components in a similar way to that employed by most Amazonian native people. In this sense, food procurement strategies, including plant exploitation, mobility, social practices and rituals are strongly articulated in a complex web shaped by ideology. Prohibitions and permissions in the kinship system, as well as a variety of social rules, play a key role within society in order to operationalize the ideational order. The

Nukak example supports the culturalist view of the landscape, which states that it is a 'particular cognitive or symbolic ordering of space' (Ingold 1993: 152). One cannot understand any of these cultural aspects in isolation, and by no means are abundance, distribution and the structure of natural resources the dominant factors which shape Nukak behaviour.

Within this cosmological framework, the Nukak move across their territory, place residential camps, develop procurement strategies and use the resources. Their motivation varies greatly; satisfying nutritional needs is one, but there are many others actively influencing the whole set of daily life decisions. During the dry season, the accumulation of garbage is crucial in order to decide to leave the residential camp and move away ('it smells bad' is one of the answers). When *bak-waad* is scheduled, bands move quickly throughout the forest in order to get close to the neighbouring band to perform the meeting ritual (see for example the movements of two bands in the map displayed in fig. 3.6 in Politis 1996b: 149). The death of a person may be the reason to abandon or to stay longer in a camp, depending on the situation and status of the deceased. The location of an ancient burial in a spot is a strong reason for not camping nearby: its *nemep*[5] may be around and disturb people during the night.

Plants are part of this universe of spirits/ancestors/owners. The production of edible fruits is related to how much people/spirits of the 'overworld' eat; if they eat a lot, the trees of the 'intermediate world' will produce in abundance. In the case of the *coróp'anat*, the abundance of fruits is a direct derivation of the sexual activity in the 'overworld'. Some plots in the forest where the herb layer is not developed are considered to be *nemep wopyi*,[6] places used and managed by the *nemep*. These spots are dangerous at night and should be avoided. Camping nearby is not advisable. Several plants have mythical connotations and their use is ritualized. For example, curare has been created by Nanabet, the wife of Maúrótjumjat (the ancestral hero) who urinated over the forest in ancient times, impregnating some large creeping plants and trees, leaving behind the substance from which the Nukak get the poison.

As we said, the *domuses* are built integrating prohibitions and permissions in an ideological context. The conceptualization of environment exploitation is framed in the Nukak cosmology, resulting in a 'map' of the territory where places are favoured or forbidden and where the spirits/ancestors/owners integrate the perception and determine the access to them. One interesting derivative of the Nukak ideology in the landscape is the attitude towards the 'salados' (salty ponds where mammals go to drink). While for many Amazonian groups these are preferred spots for hunting big animals, for the Nukak the 'salados' are the 'gates' to the 'house of danta', which connect the surface with the subsurface level. They believe that tapirs, jaguars, deer and other animals, whose tracks can be frequently seen in the 'salados', use these ponds to come up to surface at night. Thus, the 'salados' are conceived as sacred places rarely visited and strongly avoided during the night. The spiritual meaning of the 'salados' is also present in other Amazonian groups, despite their use as a strategic hunting spot. Among the Yukuna, the 'salados' are not only places to hunt animals but also have mythical connotations. Each 'salado' has its 'owner' with whom the shamans have to negotiate the hunting of certain species (van der Hammen 1992).

Other spots of intense significance are the chontaduro orchards. These places are related to the ancestors since the palms connect past with contemporary generations. The elders planted them or used these plots for cultivation; the descendants are now consuming the fruits of chontaduro. In addition, achiote is cultivated in these orchards and is essential for all kinds of rituals. Red painting, obtained from the achiote fruits, is used on a regular basis for body decoration and to give colour to several objects (hammocks, spears, etc.). Red painting is present in Nukak daily life, and the colours and the designs have a variety of meanings. The connections reflected in the orchards are between the past and the present, and between the food (chontaduro) and the ritual (achiote). One of the main representations of the symbolic aspects of the chontaduro orchards is the performance of *bak-waad*, in or near these spots and the inhumation of the deceased.

In summary, we need to understand the complexity of the exploitation of the plant resources and the use of space, and also to recognize that decisions relating to exploitation and mobility are not taken purely on economic or energetic grounds. Ethnographic accounts show how significant the spirits/ ancestors/owners who inhabit or control animate and inanimate components of the universe are for non-western people. This pattern of rationality or ideational order shaped the behaviour of past societies (see discussion in Hernando Gonzalo 1995) and if we want to understand which factors significantly motivate or affect a people's decisions, we cannot deny their importance and influence.

CONCLUSION

In this chapter I argue that the Nukak cannot be considered as being ecologically passive in a supposedly pristine rainforest. They modify the floral structure of the landscape, not only by the clearing of 'chagras' but, more importantly, by behavioural patterns which are not included under the category of horticulture/agriculture. In this sense, rainforest floral structure could be modified by long-term hunter-gatherer occupations. The impact of these populations would be through 'accidental' or 'unconscious' actions (in the sense of Chase 1989) or, otherwise, would be the effect of a carefully planned strategy to improve the food production of the forest. In any case, it seems clear that mobility among the Nukak cannot be seen exclusively as a consequence of avoiding the over-exploitation of an easily depleted environment. On the contrary, the Nukak are environmental managers, promoting some species over others, and increasing the productivity of the forest.

The Nukak landscape is impregnated with ideological connotations; their perception of it is embedded in the Amazonian native peoples' cosmology and the categories that they use to describe their function in the environment are analogic codes or metaphors rather than binary oppositions such as nature–culture, human–non-human, wild–domesticated (Descola and Pálsson 1996). Plant exploitation patterns and mobility are a consequence of both ecological and ideological factors, which have to be examined with the same intensity when we approach the study of present and past societies. Subsuming the symbolic and ideological aspects to economic/energetic factors is assuming that non-western people have our logic and motivations, our pattern of rationality. The Nukak are showing that this is not the case.

ACKNOWLEDGEMENTS

Fieldwork between 1991 and 1994 was funded by two grants given by the Wenner-Gren Foundation for Anthropological Research. Since 1995, financial and logistical support has been given by the Instituto Amazónico de Investigaciones Científicas SINCHI (Colombia), where this project is now settled. I am grateful to both for making my research possible.

Dairon Cárdenas, Gustavo Martínez and Julián Rodríguez (who led the 1995 fieldwork) were excellent companions during field seasons. Many points made in this chapter were refined and clarified in the course of discussion with them. Karina Obregón (Universidad Nacional de La Plata) helped me with the drawing. All statements made herein are, however, my own responsibility.

NOTES

1 It is not clear whether this taboo includes all women or is stronger in the Wayari-munu groups where the peccary hunting events have been recorded during our fieldwork.
2 This thesis is confusing because there are several discrepancies between the taxonomic determination of the plant used by the Nukak and the one done by Cárdenas and Politis (n.d.). Unfortunately the botanical collection done by Gutierrez Herrera could not be located in order to check and contrast the samples.
3 All the taxonomic determinations have been made by botanist Dairon Cárdenas.
4 It is not clear yet if the seeds still maintain germinative potential after passing through the human digestive system.
5 The *nemep* is the third spirit of a person and is associated with the person's shadow during life. This spirit remains on the surface, in the 'intermediate' world, hiding inside certain trees and usually bothers people at night. It is basically a malicious spirit.
6 The term *wopyi* is generic and seems to be used by the Nukak to refer to any place transformed by human or spirit agency. In this sense the Nukak call a residential camp a *wopyi*, as well as a chagra or a place used or modified by a *nemep*.

REFERENCES

Acosta, L. 1993. *Guaviare, puente a la Amazonia*. Bogotá: Corporación Colombiana para la Amazonia-Araracuara.

Ardila, G. 1992. Los Nukak-Makú del Guaviare: mi primer encuentro con la gente de las palmas (etnografía para la arqueología del poblamiento de América), *América Negra* 3, 171–89.

Ardila, G. and G. Politis. 1992. La situación actual de los Nukak de la Amazonía Colombiana: Problemas y Perspectivas. *Revista de la Universidad Nacional de Colombia* 26, 2–6.

Arhem, K. 1990. Ecosofía Makuna. In *La Selva Humanizada*, F. Correa (ed.), 105–22. Bogotá: ICAN.

Bailey, R. and T. Headland. 1991. The tropical rain forest: is it a productive environment for human foragers? *Human Ecology* 19, 261–85.

Balée, W. 1989. The culture of Amazonian forest. *Advances in Economic Botany* 7, 1–21.

Bettinger, R. 1991. *Hunter-gatherers: archaeological and evolutionary theory*. New York: Plenum.

Binford, L. 1982. The archaeology of place. *Journal of Anthropological Archaeology* 1, 5–31.

Brosius, J.P. 1991. Foraging in tropical rain forest: the case of the Penan of Sarawak, East Malaysia (Borneo). *Human Ecology* 19, 123–50.

Cabrera, G., C. Franky and D. Mahecha. 1994. Aportes a la Etnografía de los Nukak y su lengua– Aspectos sobre Fonología Segmental. Unpublished graduate degree thesis, Universidad Nacional de Colombia.

Cárdenas, D. and G. Politis. n.d. Territorio, movilidad, etnobotánica manejo del bosque de los Nukak orientales (Amazonía Colombiana). On file in Instituto Amazónico de Investigaciones Científicas SINCHI, Santafé de Bogotá, Colombia.

Caycedo Turriago, J. 1993. Los Nukak: transformaciones socioculturales y articulación étnica en una situación regional. In *Encrucijadas de Colombia Amerindia*, F. Correa (ed.), 141–57. Bogotá: ICAN.

Chase, A.K. 1989. Domestication and domiculture in northern Australia: a social perspective. In *Foraging and Farming. The evolution of plant exploitation*, D.R. Harris and G. Hillman (eds), 42–54. London: Unwin Hyman.

Clement, C.R. 1989. *Origin, Domestication and Genetic Conservation of Amazonian Fruit Tree Species*. Manaus: INPA, 19.

Correa, F. 1987. Makú. In *Introducción a la Colombia Amerindia*, F. Correa (ed.), 123–34. Bogotá: ICAN.

Descola, Ph. 1994. *In the Society of Nature. A native ecology in Amazonia*. Cambridge: Cambridge University Press.

Descola, Ph. and G. Pálsson (eds) 1996. *Nature and Society. Anthropological perspectives*. London: Routledge.

Domínguez, c.A. 1985. *Amazonia Colombiana*. Bogotá: Banco Popular.

Dufour, D. and W. Wilson. 1994. Characteristics of 'wild' plant foods used by indigenous populations in Amazonia. In *Eating on the Wild Side*, N. Etkin (ed.), 114–42. Tucson: The University of Arizona Press.

Franky, C., G. Cabrera and D. Mahecha. 1995. *Demografía y movilidad socio-espacial de los Nukak*. Santafé de Bogotá: Fundación GAIA.

Groube, L. 1989. The taming of the rain forests: a model for Late Pleistocene forest exploitation in New Guinea. In *Foraging and Farming. The evolution of plant exploitation*, D.R. Harris and G. Hillman (eds), 292–304. London: Unwin Hyman.

Gutierrez Herrera, R. 1996. Manejo de los recursos naturales (flora y fauna) por los Nukak. Unpublished graduate degree thesis, Universidad Nacional de Colombia.

Harris, D.R. 1989. An Evolutionary continuum of people–plant interaction. In

Foraging and Farming. The evolution of plant exploitation, D.R. Harris and G. Hillman (eds) 11–24. London: Unwin Hyman.

Hayden, B. (1981). Subsistence and ecological adaptation of modern hunter/gatherers. In *Omnivorous Primates. Gathering and hunting in human evolution*, R.S.O. Harding and G. Teleki (eds), 344–421. New York: Columbia University Press.

Hecht, S.B. and D.A. Posey. 1989. Preliminary results on soil management techniques of the Kayapó indians. *Advances in Economic Botany* 7, 174–88.

Hernando Gonzalo, A. 1995. La etnoarqueología hoy: una vía eficaz de aproximación al pasado. *Trabajos de Prehistoria* 52, 15–30.

Higgs, E.S. and M.R. Jarman. 1972. The origin of animal and plant husbandry. In *Papers in Economic Prehistory*, E.S. Higgs (ed.), 3–13. Cambridge: Cambridge University Press.

Hitchcock, R. 1982. Pattern of sedentism among the Basarwa of Botswana. In *Politics and History in Band Societies*, E. Leacock and R. Lee (eds), 223–67. Cambridge: Cambridge University Press.

Howell, N. 1986. Feedbacks and buffers in relation to scarcity and abundance studies of hunter-gatherer populations. In *The State of Population Theory: forward from Malthus*, D. Coleman and R. Schofield (eds), 156–87. Oxford: Basil Blackwell.

Howell, S. 1996. Nature in culture or culture in nature? Chewong ideas of humans and other species. In *Nature and Society. Anthropological Perspective*. Ph. Descola and G. Pálsson (eds), 127–44. London: Routledge.

Hutterer, K. 1983. The natural and cultural history of Southeast Asian agriculture. Ecological and evolutionary considerations. *Anthropos* 78, 169–212.

Hviding, E. 1996. Nature, culture, magic, science: on meta-languages for comparison in cultural ecology. In *Nature and Society. Anthropological perspective*. Ph. Descola and G. Pálsson (eds), 165–84. London: Routledge.

Hynes, R.A. and A.K. Chase. 1982. Plants, sites and domiculture: aboriginal influence among plant communities in Cape York Peninsula. *Archaeology in Oceania* 17, 38–50.

Ingold, T. 1993. The temporality of the landscape. *World Archaeology* 25, 152–64.

Ingold, T. 1996. Hunting and gathering as ways of perceiving the environment. In *Redefining Nature. Ecology, culture and domestication*, R. Ellen and K. Fukui (eds), 117–55. Oxford: Berg.

Kelly, R.L. 1995. *The Foraging Spectrum*. Washington, D.C.: Smithsonian Institution Press.

King, F. 1994. Interpreting wild plant food in the archaeological record. In *Eating on the Wild Side*, N.L. Etkin (ed.), 185–209. Tucson: The University of Arizona Press.

Koch-Grunberg, T. 1906. Die Makú. *Anthropos* 1, 877–906.

Kricher, J. 1989. *The Neotropical Companion*. Princeton, N.J.: Princeton University Press.

Lee, R. 1992. Art, science or politics? The crisis in hunter-gatherer studies. *American Anthropologist* 94, 31–54.

Metraux, A. 1948. The hunting and gathering people of the Rio Negro Basin. In *Handbook of South American Indians*, Vol. 3, J. Steward (ed.), 861–7. Washington, DC: Bureau of American Ethnology, Bulletin 143.

Milton, K. 1984. Protein and carbohydrate resources of the Makú indians of northwestern Amazonia. *American Anthropologist*, 86, 7–25.

Molano, A. 1987. *Selva Adentro. Una historia oral de la colonización del Guaviare*. Bogotá: El Ancora Editores.

Mondragón, H. (n.d.). Estudio para el establecimiento de un programa de defensa de la comunidad indígena Nukak. Informe final presentado al programa de Rehabilitación Nacional (PNR) de la Presidencia de la República de Colombia.

Politis, G. 1992. La arquitectura del nomadismo en la Amazonía Colombiana. *Proa* 412, 11–20.

Politis, G. 1995. *Mundo de los Nukak. Amazonia Colombiana*. Bogotá: Fondo de Promoción de la Cultura.
Politis, G. 1996a. Moving to produce: Nukak mobility and settlement patterns in Amazonia. *World Archaeology* 27, 492–510.
Politis, G. 1996b. *Nukak*. Bogotá: Instituto Amazónico de Investigaciones Científicas SINCHI.
Politis, G. In press. La formación de sitios de cazadores- recolectores en las Tierras Bajas sudamericanas: un caso de estudio etnoarqueológico. In *Arqueología de Tierras Bajas*, R. Bracco (ed.). Montevideo, Uruguay.
Politis, G. and C. Gamble. 1996. Los Nukak y los límites ambientales de los foragers. In *Nukak*, G. Politis (ed.), 270–88. Santafé de Bogotá: Instituto Amazónico de Investigaciones Científicas SINCHI.
Politis, G. and G. Martínez. 1992. La subsistencia invernal de un Grupo de los Nukak Nor-Occidental del Guaviare. Paper presented at 6th Congreso Nacional de Antropología de Colombia. Symposium 'Pasado y Presente de los Cazadores-recolectores en América del Sur'. Bogotá, July.
Politis, G. and J. Rodríguez. 1994. Algunos aspectos de la subsistencia de los Nukak de la Amazonía Colombiana. *Colombia Amazónica* 7, 169–207.
Politis, G. and N. Saunders. n.d. Archaeological correlates of ideological activity: food taboos and spirit-animals in an Amazonian hunter-gatherer society. (Submitted for publication.)
Politis, G., G. Martínez and J. Rodríguez. 1997. Caza y recolección como estrategia de explotación de recursos en ambientes de Forestas Tropicales: los Nukak de la Amazonía Colombiana. *Revista Española de Antropología Americana*, 167–97.
Posey, D. 1984a. A preliminary report on diversified management of tropical forest by Kayapó Indians. *Advances in Economic Botany* 1, 112–27.
Posey, D. 1984b. Keepers of the Campo. *Garden* 8, 8–12.
Posey, D. 1987. *Alternatives to Destruction: Science of the Mebengorke [Kayapó]*. Belem: Museu Paranaense Emilio Goeldi.
Reichel, E. 1989. La danta y el delfín. Manejo ambiental e intercambio entre dueños de malocas y shamanes. El caso Yukuna-Mataapí (Amazonas). *Revista de Antropología* 5 (1–2), 69–133. Bogotá: Universidad de los Andes.
Reichel-Dolmatoff, G. 1967. A brief report on urgent ethnological research in the Vaupes area, Colombia, South America. *Bulletin of International Committee on Urgent Anthropological Research* 9, 53–62.
Reichel-Dolmatoff, G. 1971. *Amazonian Cosmos: the sexual and religious symbolism of the Tukano Indians*. Chicago: The University of Chicago Press.
Reichel-Dolmatoff, G. 1996. *The Forest Within. A world-view of the Tukano Amazonian Indians*. Devon: Themos Books.
Reid, H. 1979. Some aspects of movement, growth, and change among the Hupdu Makú indians of Brazil. Unpublished Ph.D. thesis, Cambridge University.
Reina, L. 1990. Actividades relacionadas con los Nukak. *Mopa-Mopa* 5, 17–25.
Reina, L. 1992. Los Nukak: cacería, recolección y nomadismo en la Amazonía. In *Diversidad es riqueza*, 62–4. Bogotá: ICAN.
Rindos, D. 1984. *The Origins of Agriculture: an evolutionary perspective*. Orlando: Academic Press.
Rindos, D. 1989. Darwinism and its role in the explanation of domestication. In *Foraging and Farming. The evolution of plant exploitation*, D.R. Harris and G. Hillman (eds), 29–39. London: Unwin Hyman.
Shipek, F.C. 1989. An example of intense plant husbandry: the Kumeyaay of southern California. In *Foraging and Farming. The evolution of plant exploitation*, D.R. Harris and G. Hillman (eds), 159–70. London: Unwin Hyman.
Silverwood-Cope, P. 1972. A contribution to the ethnography of the Colombian Makú. Unpublished Ph.D. thesis, Cambridge University.

Sponsel, L.E. 1986. Amazon ecology and adaptation. *Annual Review of Anthropology* 15, 67–97.

Stearman, A. 1991. Making a living in the tropical forest: Yuqui foragers in the Bolivian Amazon. *Human Ecology* 19, 245–58.

Stein Mandryk, C.A. 1993. Hunter-gatherer social costs and nonviability of submarginal environments. *Journal of Anthropological Research* 49, 39–72.

Stiles, D. 1992. The hunter-gatherer 'revisionist' debate. *Anthropology Today* 8, 13–17.

Torres, W. 1994. Nukak: aspectos etnográficos. *Revista Colombiana de Antropología* 31, 197–234.

Van der Hammen, C. 1992. *El manejo del mundo. Naturaleza y sociedad entre los Yukuna de la amazonia colombiana.* Bogotá: Tropenbos.

Wirpsa, L. and H. Mondragón. 1988. Resettlement of Nukak Indians, Colombia. *Cultural Survival Quarterly* 12, 36–40.

Zambrano, C. 1993. Los Nukak en Calamar: encuentro posible de culturas distantes. In *Diversidad es riqueza*, 65–7. Bogotá: ICAN.

Part II

INTRODUCTIONS

Food processing technology: its role in inhibiting or promoting change in staple foods

HELEN M. LEACH

The introduction of new foods which subsequently became staples, to cultural groups previously unfamiliar with that type of food, has given rise to a special class of anecdote which seems designed to explain why they were slow to adopt what is now highly valued. Two examples are given below – one from Britain concerning the introduction in the late sixteenth century of the root crop *Solanum tuberosum*, the potato, to the Irish who had no long-standing familiarity with a starchy root crop, and one from New Zealand which describes the introduction in the early nineteenth century of the first wheat crop to the Maori whose staples had been previously confined to root crops. In each story there is a key figure (the agent of introduction) who uses his inside knowledge to show both how ignorant the local people are and how valuable the new crop will be.

From Henry Phillips's *History of Cultivated Vegetables* (1822) we have this story about the potato:

> Sir Walter Raleigh is said to have given some potatoes to his gardener in Ireland as a fine fruit from America, and ordered them to be planted in his kitchen-garden. In August the plants flowered, and in September produced the fruit; but the berries were so different to what the gardener expected, that in an ill humour he carried the potatoe-apples to his master. 'Is this (said he) the fine fruit from America you praised so highly?' Sir Walter either was, or pretended to be ignorant of the matter; and desired the gardener, since that was the case, to dig up the weed and throw it away. The gardener, however, soon returned with a good parcel of potatoes.
>
> (Phillips 1822, II: 81)

Five years earlier, in 1817, the missionary Samuel Marsden wrote about the experiences of the Maori chief Ruatara who had visited the Church Missionary Society training establishment in New South Wales and returned to New Zealand with wheat for cultivation:

When he was landed from the *Ann*, he took with him the wheat
he had received at Parramatta for seed, and immediately informed
his friends and the neighbouring chiefs of its value, and that the
Europeans made biscuit of it, such as they had seen and eaten on
board of ships. He gave a portion of wheat to six chiefs and also
some to his own common men, and directed them all how to sow
it, reserving some for himself and his uncle Shungi [Hongi]. All
the persons to whom Duaterra [Ruatara] had given the seed-
wheat put it into the ground and it grew well; but before it was
well ripe many of them grew impatient for the produce, and as
they expected to find the grain at the roots of the stems, similar to
their potatoes, they examined the roots, and finding there was no
wheat under the ground, they pulled it all up and burnt it,
excepting Shungi . . .

(Nicholas 1817, II: 389)

In time Ruatara's and Hongi's crops ripened and were reaped and threshed.
Ruatara's claim that biscuit could be made from the grain was still not
believed, so he borrowed a pepper or coffee mill from a whaling ship's
master, but it was too small. Marsden then sent him a steel mill and a sieve:

He soon set to work and ground some wheat before his
countrymen, who danced and shouted for joy when they saw the
meal. He told me that he made a cake, and baked it in a frying
pan, and gave it to the people to eat, which fully satisfied them of
the truth he had told them before, that wheat would make bread.

(Nicholas 1817, II: 392–3)

The truth of these stories is not at issue here, though the Raleigh 'legend'
incorporates some elements now known to be incorrect, such as the
procurement of the potato from Virginia (Salaman 1985: 51; Hawkes 1990:
39). These apocryphal stories are important because they emphasize that
knowledge of cultivation methods, of what constitutes the edible part, of the
processing techniques, as well as the equipment for processing the crop, are
essential for a successful introduction of a new staple. The desire for the
product is not sufficient on its own.

For the Maori chief Ruatara, and for most of his contemporaries, wheat
flour was a desirable commodity. Their experience of it as ship's biscuit
seems not to have deterred them, despite the modern belief that this dried
bread was frequently mouldy or weevil-infested. Besides the ship's biscuit
which Ruatara had eaten for long periods on European vessels, he would
have encountered leavened bread at Parramatta when he lived there with
Marsden.

It was not so much the cultivation techniques that held back the adoption
of wheat as a crop, as the lack of processing equipment. Thus the Marsden
story emphasized the importance of having an appropriate type of mill, as

well as sieves. The frying pan of the story was not so vital to the success of the venture, as flat cakes of processed berries or bulrush pollen were already part of Maori culinary repertoire. Wrapped in leaves or in a woven container, these were either cooked in the ashes or in the underground oven (Leach 1986).

The initial euphoria at producing wheat flour seems to have dissipated when the energy costs of hand-milling and sifting were realized by the Maori. One of the missionaries whom Marsden employed to teach agricultural techniques in the Bay of Islands, Richard Davis, wrote in 1826:

> I have not yet been able to succeed in getting any of the native chiefs to cultivate land for wheat, Taiwanga excepted. Some of those chiefs who promised to sow wheat for themselves . . . were supplied with seed by Mr Kemp; which they sowed, but never reaped. In endeavouring to inforce the cultivation of wheat on these people, they argue in this way – 'We cannot cultivate wheat, nor do we wish to cultivate it; because it is attended with so much labour and has to go through so many processes before it can be eaten as bread. If we clear a piece of land and plant it with sweet Potatoes, we get a good crop of food which we like, and which we can eat immediately out of the ground.' [Presumably they meant after cooking the potatoes.]
>
> (Davis, MS letter of 10/11/1826)

Equipment was still a problem twelve years later when in 1838 William Wade noted that the inhabitants of Kaikohe Pa were still waiting to get grindstones for their wheat (Wade 1842: 27).

In contrast, the Solanum potato never seems to have suffered any setbacks to its acceptance by the Maori. In 1806 Savage found Bay of Islands' Maori growing two crops a year and commented:

> Though the natives are exceedingly fond of this root they eat them but sparingly, on account of their great value in procuring iron by barter . . .
>
> (Savage 1939: 63)

Twenty years later Richard Davis compared the roles played by the sweet potato and Solanum potato in the Bay of Islands economy:

> At present, the wants of the New Zealanders are but few. He can bring a few potatoes to us, for which he gets tools. He then selects a piece of good land in a wood, falls the timber, burns it off, plants the land with potatoes, takes his produce to the shipping, and sells it for muskets and powder, which things make him a great man. As those potatoes are, what is termed by them, a winter crop, as soon as he returns from the ship with his muskets and powder he

> begins to prepare his land for a second crop, which is generally
> sweet potatoes . . . I believe the Bay of Islanders would not care
> much for planting common potatoes, were it not for selling them
> for articles they want.
>
> (Davis, MS letter 14/11/1826)

Davis, in the same letter, was of the opinion that these Maori preferred to eat
sweet potatoes, Indian corn, taro, turnips and fernroot 'which is a thing they
eat from choice and not from necessity'.

It is hard to assess the extent to which the Maori valued Solanum potatoes
as food, given the importance of the crop in trade throughout the country.
That fernroot remained in use into the 1840s in areas where potatoes were
grown in large acreages suggests that the potato was not the preferred staple
for some 40–70 years after its introduction, despite the ease with which it
could be gathered and prepared (Leach 1969: 56). Alternatively, the fernroot
may have remained important for times when the potato was out of season,
though this in itself might indicate that the desire for maximum quantity for
trade overruled the need for storage for personal consumption. Potatoes were
grown in similar fashion to the sweet potato and cooked in the earth oven
well into the 1840s (e.g., Angas 1847, II: 131). The alternative method,
boiling, depended on the spread of iron cooking pots. Marshall (1836: 70)
described the use by two Maori women of an 'English swing pot of cast iron'
for boiling potatoes inland from the Bay of Islands in 1834. Pot boiling took
over progressively as a day-to-day preparation technique for potatoes, but for
ceremonial and festive occasions potatoes are still a major ingredient of the
hangi cooked in the *umu* (earth oven).

Falling between the rapid acceptance of the potato and the disillusionment
with early wheat introductions, we find the experimentation with 'Indian'
corn or maize. In view of the reliance of the pre-European Maori on root
crops, it might be expected that quite a long period of trial and error would
be required to learn the correct cultivation techniques. Maori were used to
planting the bottle gourd from seeds, so the planting of similarly large seeds of
Zea mays would not have been unfamiliar. But there is evidence that plant
spacings were initially too close for good results. At the time of the early
wheat-growing attempts in the Bay of Islands, Nicholas described some small,
apparently experimental plots of maize on Moturoa Island:

> We saw some plantations, in one of which there were about an
> hundred stalks of Indian corn, but of a very unpromising
> appearance. We told the chief that he did not understand the
> cultivation of this grain; that the stalks, instead of being only
> twelve and eighteen inches asunder, as he had them, should be
> separated from each other by a distance of four feet, and the
> intermediate space not planted with potatoes as was the case.
>
> (Nicholas 1817, II: 82–3)

Nicholas went on to comment on the processing of corn which one might at first expect to have no precedent in Maori culinary technology:

> As these people understand nothing of grinding, nor have any means to perform that process, they roast the ears of the corn in the fire, in the same manner as the original natives do at New South Wales.
>
> (Nicholas 1817, II: 83)

In this respect corn possessed a considerable advantage over wheat. Its much larger heads were encased in husks which would have been readily appreciated as natural leaf wrappers by people accustomed to the use of leaf wrappers in day-to-day cooking in the hearth or *umu* (Leach 1982). However, this form of processing may not have rendered more mature corn on the cob particularly palatable. Instead a technique of fermentation was adapted from traditional wild food processing, formerly applied to cooked karaka kernels and hinau drupes (Leach 1986: 133–4).

In 1827 Augustus Earle visited the inland Bay of Islands area:

> Indian corn was likewise very abundant, but as the natives did not possess any means or knowledge of grinding it, they were not aware of its true value. Their only method of cooking it was one very disgusting to Europeans. They soaked the ear in water until it was quite soft and sour, the smell from which was exceedingly offensive; they then placed it in their earth ovens to bake ...
>
> (Earle 1909: 111)

Further south in the Waikato district, Angas observed in 1844 that

> Railed enclosures of some twenty feet square are erected in the water, near these river-side settlements, expressly for the purpose of preparing the favourite stinking corn. The cobs of maize are placed, when in a green state, in flax baskets, and put under the water for some weeks, until quite putrid: they are then taken out as occasion may require, and made up into the disgusting cakes before mentioned. At other times, the putrid mass is put into a *kohue*, or large pan, and, when mixed with water and boiled over the fire, is converted into a species of gruel that sends forth an effluvia over the whole settlement.
>
> (Angas 1847, II: 28–9)

The result was the still esteemed *kanga pirau*. Such anaerobic fermentation was not practicable for the much smaller mature wheat heads. From its introduction in 1793 (Thomson 1859: 158), maize cropping appears to have undergone an experimental phase of 20–30 years, after which the plant rapidly became established as an important Maori crop throughout the warmer parts of New Zealand.

In summary, traditional Maori culinary technology offered various processing techniques that could be adapted to maize because of its seed-head size, but were not appropriate for wheat. Solanum potatoes required no modification of traditional technology, though they seem not to have been particularly valued for many decades after their early introduction despite their importance in trade. Thus we have a food preference ranking, ranging from the highly desired wheat flour (the European staple), through corn, to the common potato, inversely correlated to the relative ease of cultivation and processing.

COMPARATIVE CASES

Turning to the northern hemisphere for comparison, we can examine the case of the arrival of the potato in cereal-growing cultures. What should not be forgotten is that the sweet potato (*Ipomoea batatas*) actually preceded the Solanum potato into Europe by some decades, reaching Spain and Portugal possibly in the first half of the sixteenth century. Climatically the sweet potato was not a viable crop in Britain, nor any other part of northern Europe. Although parts of France were certainly suitable, the sweet potato never became important in the French kitchen (Wheaton 1983: 85). Instead it was established in Spain and Italy and was shipped to northern centres such as London as roots or as candied sweetmeats with a widespread reputation as an aphrodisiac (Gerard 1597: 780–1). Elizabethan references to the potato leave little doubt that it is the sweet potato that is meant, judging by its textual association with other aphrodisiacs and the quoted prices for the roots (Salaman 1985: 424–8). Although there was considerable confusion between the two potatoes in the kitchens of the wealthy, with the Solanum potato having lust-procuring powers attributed to it as a result of the shared names, there was no possibility of the sweet potato's cultivation methods facilitating the adoption of the Solanum potato anywhere in the British Isles. The latter entered the British garden without precedents. At that time there were no root vegetable crops that were propagated from tubers. Existing root vegetables, namely parsnips, carrots, turnips and skirrets, were grown as annuals or biennials from seed, not vegetatively propagated (Salaman 1985: 231, 434, 436). The practice of vegetable gardening was largely confined to the vicinity of large towns, and the country estates of the wealthy. However, the professional gardeners involved in these enterprises might be expected to have applied general principles of vegetative propagation to the potato through their familiarity with ornamental plants such as the iris.

The extent to which ignorance of propagation techniques delayed acceptance of the potato is probably less than the influence of day-length on the early European cultivars. Hawkes (1967: 289–93) has argued convincingly that it was the short–day–length–adapted Andean potato that reached Europe in the sixteenth century. Requiring a maximum 12-hour day-length in order to initiate tuber formation, it was not till the end of September that the crop began to develop. An early autumn frost would prove disastrous. Until selection for longer day-length tolerance occurred, Hawkes (1990: 39) believes the potato was confined to milder regions such as southern Spain and western Ireland. Thus we should not argue for culinary or technological barriers to widespread acceptance until the potato was acclimatized to European summer day-lengths.

In those milder areas, however, cultural factors can be invoked right from the time of introduction, believed to be about 1590 in Ireland (Hawkes 1990: 38), or a little earlier (Salaman 1985: 221). Salaman (1985: 220) argued that war in Ireland between 1586 and 1601 created such conditions of turmoil and disruption of normal peasant life that 'innate prejudices' against the new food were rapidly broken down. How rapidly it was transferred from the well-stocked kitchen gardens of English and Scottish settlers is still debated (Cullen 1992: 45). Before the adoption of the potato, the Irish peasantry had subsisted on oats and barley (and lesser amounts of wheat), with dairy products as a source of fat and protein. Cereals were normally eaten as porridges prepared in iron pots, and as flat breads such as oatcakes cooked on a stand or on an iron griddle (Danaher 1962: 46–8; Cullen 1992: 51; O'Danachair 1981). Traditional hearth cooking offered two methods for cooking the newly arrived potato: boiling in the cauldron, as was practised with cereals, roots and greens, or baking in the embers, sometimes using a cabbage leaf as a wrapper (Danaher 1962: 50). No additional equipment was required and the potato was probably originally treated as a sustaining but nevertheless supplementary vegetable. There was no indication that the potato would become a staple, let alone a mono-staple, until famine, civil war, drastic changes in land tenure, and, not insignificantly, a desire for a cash income, deprived Irish peasants of the cereals and cattle that had been their mainstay (Cullen 1992: 48). This process began in the mid-eighteenth century and by the nineteenth the stage was set for the Great Famine of 1845–8, triggered by the arrival of potato blight. There is no evidence that the potato was ever seen as a substitute for bread or preferred to bread.

In Scotland, the potato was also introduced via the kitchen garden, with the earliest references to it falling in the late seventeenth century (Salaman 1985: 344–5). In the Lowlands it slowly spread from the gardens of the wealthy to field cultivation by labourers. As a kitchen garden vegetable for those with French or English tastes, the potato was recommended to be treated as a parsnip. However, the majority of Scots appear to have eaten only one vegetable at this time, the hardy kale, which was simmered in broth. Potatoes were added to this dish and thus required no additional equipment for their processing. By the mid-eighteenth century, the potato's cultivation as a field crop was encouraged by the rising prices of meat and cereal for which it became an unwelcome substitute in the diets of the lower classes (Salaman 1985: 395–6).

The situation in the Scottish Highlands was similar to that in parts of Ireland. Oats and occasionally barley were the only feasible cereals and were prepared as oatcakes, porridge or gruel, and barley broth. Peas and beans were sometimes stored as dried pulses and boiled as required. The only green vegetable cultivated by the small farmers, the kale or colewort, was also boiled (Salaman 1985: 335, 348). The potato was adopted in the Western Isles in the first half of the eighteenth century, some decades earlier than in the Highlands or Northern Isles. As in Ireland it entered via the kitchen gardens of the lairds and bigger tenant farmers, who were familiar with carrots, parsnips, skirret and artichokes as early as 1693 (Fenton 1978: 421). When the crofters adopted potatoes, they boiled them in the standard three-legged pots used for gruel and broth, or for supper roasted them in their skins in the peat fire embers (Fenton 1978: 420). The potato thus required no investment in new culinary technology, and indeed needed even less than oats and barley for which querns and rubbers, dehusking or knocking stones, sieves and sometimes drying kilns had been necessary equipment for several thousand years.

An obvious conclusion is that the potato, with its minimal technological investment needs, both in cultivation and cooking, spread widely among the rural poor because it offered opportunities to decrease their investment in capital equipment, or to escape dependency on those such as millers and bakers who owned the processing equipment. It appealed to employers and reformers since wages did not need to be increased to meet the steeply rising costs of wheat and bread in Britain at the end of the eighteenth century. A contemporary writer praised the potato (and denigrated the poor) in the following terms:

> The lower classes, to whom this vegetable is now the greatest blessing that the soil produces – forming flour without a mill, and bread without an oven – and at all seasons of the year an agreeable and wholesome dish, unaided by expensive or injurious condiments – were the last to become acquainted with this valuable root. So difficult is it to overcome prejudices in ignorant minds.
>
> (Phillips 1822: 86–7)

However, the enclosure campaigns of eighteenth-century England deprived the poorest of the fuel necessary to boil potatoes. For them indigestible raw potatoes were the only option when their bought loaves of bread had been consumed.

CONCLUSIONS

This brief comparison of the introductions to selected island groups of certain foods that later became staples has shown that three factors operated relatively independently: cultural taste preferences, technological costs, and economic potential. The case has been made that in each of the areas considered, the potato changed its status from just another vegetable (like carrot or parsnip) to starch staple, not because of taste preference but because it was technologically undemanding and economically important. For some groups in Britain and Ireland, potatoes allowed the selling of formerly consumed cereals to obtain a small cash income. For other communities it substituted for cereal crops when the people were evicted from land where cereals were viable or were forced to squat on marginal strips like roadsides and coastlines where cereals could not be grown. In New Zealand, potatoes achieved importance as an item of trade and exchange, rather than as a preferred starch staple. They enabled the Maori to purchase many desirable goods, including wheat flour which they rated much more highly as a source of starch. It was the technological costs of wheat production that discouraged Maori farmers from growing it themselves.

From such case studies, there are several lessons for prehistorians concerning the acceptability of introduced crops and the speed at which crops move between cultures. First, such crops are unlikely to be transferred as staples; initially they are added to existing cereal or vegetable inventories as minor components, and often treated like existing crops both agronomically and gastronomically. At this stage they are unimportant and archaeologically almost invisible, since the processing technology is frequently adapted from that for existing crops. Transformation to staple status is far more likely to be linked to a major environmental and/or social disruption, and may remain regional as in the cases of rice in Spain, and maize and rice in Italy, or affect entire nations. As staple status is attained, the archaeological record is much more likely to show the concomitant changes in land use, in agricultural and culinary technology including storage devices, and in the diets of consumers.

REFERENCES

Angas, G.F. 1847. *Savage Life and Scenes in Australia and New Zealand.* 2 volumes. London: Smith, Elder, and Co.

Cullen, L.M. 1992. Comparative aspects of Irish diet, 1550–1850. In *European Food History: a research review*, H.J. Teuteberg (ed.), 45–55. Leicester: Leicester University Press.

Danaher, K. 1962. *In Ireland Long Ago*. Cork: The Mercier Press.

Davis, R. MSS Letters and Journals 1824–1863. Hocken Library, Dunedin, New Zealand.

Earle, A. 1909. *A Narrative of a Nine Months' Residence in New Zealand in 1827*. Christchurch: Whitcombe and Tombs Ltd.

Fenton, A. 1978. *The Northern Isles: Orkney and Shetland*. Edinburgh: John Donald Publishers Ltd.

Gerard, J. 1597. *The Herball or Generall Historie of Plants*. London. [reprint 1974 by Walter J. Johnson, Norwood, N.J. and Theatrum Orbis Terrarum Ltd, Amsterdam]

Hawkes, J.G. 1967. The history of the potato. *Journal of the Royal Horticultural Society* 92, 207–24, 249–62, 288–302.

Hawkes, J.G. 1990. *The Potato: evolution, biodiversity and genetic resources*. Washington: Smithsonian Institution Press.

Leach, H.M. 1969. *Subsistence Patterns in Prehistoric New Zealand*. Studies in Prehistoric Anthropology 2. Dunedin: Department of Anthropology, University of Otago.

Leach, H.M. 1982. Cooking without pots: aspects of prehistoric and traditional Polynesian cooking. *New Zealand Journal of Archaeology* 4, 149–56.

Leach, H.M. 1986. A review of culinary and nutritional adaptations involving wild plant foods following Polynesian settlement of New Zealand. In *Archaeology at ANZAAS, Canberra*, G.K. Ward (ed.), 131–40. Canberra: Canberra Archaeological Society.

Marshall, W.B. 1836. *A Personal Narrative of Two Visits to New Zealand in His Majesty's Ship Alligator A.D. 1834*. London: James Nisbet and Co.

Nicholas, J.L. 1817. *Narrative of a Voyage to New Zealand*. 2 volumes. London: James Black and Son.

O'Danachair, K. 1981. Bread in Ireland. In *Food in Perspective*, A. Fenton and T.M. Owen (eds), 57–67. Edinburgh: John Donald Publishers Ltd.

Phillips, H. 1822. *History of Cultivated Vegetables*. 2 volumes. London: Henry Colburn and Co.

Salaman, R.N. 1985. *The History and Social Influence of the Potato* (revised impression). Cambridge: Cambridge University Press.

Savage, J. 1939. *Some Account of New Zealand*. Wellington: L.T. Watkins Ltd.

Thomson, A.S. 1859. *The Story of New Zealand*. London: John Murray.

Wade, W.R. 1842. *A Journey in the Northern Island of New Zealand*. Hobart Town: George Rolwegan.

Wheaton, B.K. 1983. *Savouring the Past : the French kitchen and table from 1300 to 1789*. London: Chatto and Windus.

7 Subsistence changes in India and Pakistan: the Neolithic and Chalcolithic from the point of view of plant use today

K.L. MEHRA

INTRODUCTION

Most summaries of the prehistoric evidence for subsistence from India and Pakistan emphasize the introduction of crops from South-west Asia (wheat, barley, peas, lentils and flax) or from Asia and Africa (rice and the millets) (Meadow 1996; Glover and Higham 1996). This initial emphasis on introduction has been in many ways warranted, as new crops have transformed subsistence systems in the subcontinent over the last 5,000 years. However, much less effort has been expended on attempting to understand the interaction of introduced crops and indigenous ones. In looking at local food plants there are two main sources of evidence: the distribution of such plants in the present and their use in agricultural or hunter-gatherer systems in the present and recent past. This chapter concentrates on the former set of evidence, making only brief comments on how such plants are presently used and how far these uses provide some window on the longer-term past. It should be stressed at the outset that what follows does not represent a full survey of the evidence, as this is too massive a task for such a large region for which the evidence is patchy at best. Rather, I indicate the potential of studies of present-day food plants and provide some sketch as to how these might be combined with the evidence from prehistory.

Inferences about possible means of subsistence in pre-Neolithic times can be drawn from the present-day uses of biodiversity, especially by peoples living in tribal belts of India where agricultural practices are only part of people's subsistence practices, and people continue to depend on forest products. Reviews of plant and animal species identified from different archaeological sites have mostly provided information on the presence of certain plant and animal species at specific sites, rather than broader sequences of change (Vishnu-Mittre 1977; Randhawa 1980; Kajale 1991; Saraswat 1992).

RECENT CROP USE

Surveys of the use of wild plants have revealed that of over 20,000 plant species found in India, only 778 species, belonging to 96 families, possess edible plant parts (Singh and Arora 1978; Vishnu-Mittre 1981; Jain 1981). Of these, 648 species provide edible plant parts which are easily separable from the whole and thus are especially useful. These include tuberous starchy roots and rhizomes (95 species), leaves and shoots (250 species), flower and flower buds (46 species), fruits (383 species), seeds including nuts and kernels (110 species), and other plant parts (14 species); while 130 species provide more than one edible plant part. Despite such a great number of potential domesticates, only about 80 plant species (only 33 prior to the Iron Age) have been found in the archaeological contexts, partly because of the preservation conditions in India, coupled with the different recovery techniques used on various excavations and Indian archaeobotanical studies in general (Kajale 1991).

Based on the list of wild, edible plant species presently used in different regions of India (Singh and Arora 1978), Mehra and Arora (1985) provided a list of plant species (*Vigna capensis, Moghania vistata, Erisoema Chinense*) which were perhaps used as tubers and rhizomes which could be eaten raw, followed by those (*Amorphophallus, Dioscorea, Colocasia, Alocasia*)), containing calcium oxalate crystals and other chemicals which had to be subjected to boiling and cooking to make them edible. Taro and yams supported the initial tuber-based cultures of the humid tropical and subtropical regions, and their domestication could only have occurred after fire was discovered and boiling which would have needed suitable containers. More sophisticated processing would be required for those plant species (*Codonopsis ovata, Dioscorea hispida, Cyperus bulbosus, Curcuma angustifolia, Tacca leontopetaloides*) which yielded edible starch, especially tubers which could be dried and made into flour. Dried tubers would have increased storage for lean periods. No archaeo-botanical records of such species are available from India. Similarly, the earliest edible leaves and tender shoots came from species which could be eaten raw, and more sophisticated use as salad and condiments probably followed at a later date (for a list see Mehra and Arora 1985). The use of raw fruits for pulps may have preceded the practice of pickling and preserving. Similarly, the use of edible grains and seeds which could be eaten raw might have preceded those needing boiling. Thus, the development of culinary techniques and preferences played a significant role in which plants were used and for what purposes.

CROP DOMESTICATION

A wide range of cereals, millets and legumes was gathered and used for subsistence long before some of them were domesticated (Vishnu-Mittre

1985). The heritage of 'unconventional' staple millets/cereals still cultivated by groups in various parts of India may be very meaningful in this context. Such plants are as follows: *Coix lachryma jobi, Dactyloctenium aegyptium, Digitaria cruciata, D. cruciata* var. *esculenta and D. sanguinalis* sub sp. *aegyptiaca* var. *frumentacea, Echinochloa colona* (sawa millet), *E. crus galli, E. frumentacea, Panicum miliaceum, P. sumatrense (*syn. *P. milliare), Paspalum scorbiculatum* (kodo millet), *Pennisetum orientale, Setaria glauca, S. italica and Urochloa panicoides. Digitaria cruciata* was domesticated in India (Harlan 1975). Kodo millet, *Paspalum scorbiculatum*, was domesticated across its range of present-day cultivation in India (de Wet *et al.* 1983). Wild, weed and cultivated, non-shattering kinds of *P. scorbiculatum* hybridize with each other, and weedy types are harvested along with the crop. Sawa millet, *Echinochloa colona*, is a tropical species domesticated in India, and differs from *E. crus galli*, a temperate species, in having smaller spikelets with membranous rather than chartaceous glumes. Sawa millet matures in less than two months and is often planted on poor soils. *Echinochloa colona* is often planted mixed with *Setaria italica* (Italian millet) or *Eleusine corocana* (finger millet). Since the growing periods of these three millets differ, present-day farmers usually harvest them in sequence to have a regular supply of staple food. This practice was also perhaps followed in the past. *Panicum sumatrense* (syn. *P milliare)* is a native of India. Wild, weed and cultivated, non-shattering kinds occur in India. *Setaria viridis* is the ancestor of Italian millet, *Setaria italica*, grown in tropical and temperate regions of the world. Italian millet perhaps originated in eastern Asia, probably China, but it diffused into India prior to the diffusion of South-west Asian cereals. In *Coix lacryma jobi*, another Indian domesticate, cultivated and wild types form a euploid series (Koul 1974). Many of these minor millets were identified from several archaeological sites of India. Green gram (*Vigna radiata*) and black gram (*Vigna mungo*) are related morphologically and cytologically to their ancestral wild types, *V. radiata* var. *sublobata* and *V. mungo* var. *sylvestris*. Both species were domesticated in India (Jain and Mehra 1980).

Phyto-geographic distribution patterns of cultivated and closely related wild plants suggest that there are specific regions that have high diversities of economic plants and their closely related wild species (Mehra and Arora 1985). For cereals, there is a concentration of rice, *Coix* and *Digitaria* in the north-eastern region and of *Paspalum* sp. and *Panicum milliare* in the southern and east peninsular regions. The entire peninsular region has both green and black grams, although the wild progenitor form of *Vigna radiata* (*Vigna sublobata*) is concentrated more in the Western Ghats, particularly in the Maharashtra region. *Dolichos uniflorus*, related to the horse gram (*D. biflorus*), is localized in the eastern and southern peninsular regions, while *Lablab niger*, related to *L. purpureus*, occurs on the eastern coast of India (Arora and Nayar 1984).

THE ARCHAEOLOGICAL EVIDENCE

There is the possibility that agriculture started in the Belan and Ganga Valley, Uttar Pradesh with the domestication and cultivation of rice in the mid-sixth millennium BC (Savithri 1976; Sharma 1980, 1985), although these early dates have been strongly disputed (Meadow 1996). However, we can be sure that rice culture had spread to different regions of India by the mid-second millennium BC.

Leaving rice aside, the indigenous peoples of India domesticated the minor millets, grain legumes, oilseeds and other crops (see Smartt and Simmonds 1995 for a complete list). They developed several culinary preparations, and experimented with many different ways of utilizing the plant biodiversity.

Several species of winter cereals, legumes and other crops were domesticated in South-west Asia (Smartt and Simmonds 1995), and several of these are found at Mehrgarh, Pakistan (seventh millennium BC) (Meadow 1984; Costantini and Costantini-Biasini 1985). Similarly, sorghum, finger millet and pearl millet were domesticated in Africa (Harlan 1975; Mehra 1991; Smartt and Simmonds 1995), and these crops diffused into India around 2000 BC (Mehra 1991). South-west Asian crops are adapted to winter cultivation, while those from Africa are suited for cultivation in the summer rainy season (July to September) in north India. African crops can also be grown from September–November in certain parts of India. These African crops are dual purpose (grains for humans and fodder for animals). In north India, indigenous chalcolithic farmers practised agriculture in only one season (July–September), and they had no crop to cultivate in winter. The introduced winter season crops provided an opportunity to practise crop rotation, resulting in high surplus food production to feed people who were not food producers. Legume cultivation, in both seasons, sustained soil fertility to a large extent. Crop cultivation in winter is comparatively easier than that of rice during the summer rainy season. Domesticated non-shattering minor millets, rice and grain legumes of Indian origins were identified, along with South-west Asian crops from the same occupational levels of several sites of north and central India. Therefore, it is likely that agriculture had a strong indigenous component, a fact which has been ignored as a result of continuously focusing on 'introductions'.

Not only were indigenous crops important in the early stages of agriculture but they were also important in the diversified agricultural systems from 2000 BC onwards. The identification of seventeen different crops cultivated at seven pre-Harappan and Harappan sites, has revealed that farmers cultivated only South-west Asian crops at Kalibagangan, but at other sites exotic crops were sown after harvesting the indigenous crops sown in the summer season (July–September). At all sites there is evidence of diversity in the combination of local and exotic crops that were grown and in this people were responding to local environmental conditions and food preferences. The exotic crops did not all diffuse together, but may have moved in sequence so that naked barley arrived after hulled barley, bread wheat after dwarf and club wheats, several legume species after one another, and finger millet after sorghum.

Changes in subsistence patterns were brought about by (i) gradually replacing emmer, dwarf and club wheats by high yielding bread wheat; (ii) incorporating several species of grain legumes, oats, and fenugreek for cultivation in winter; (iii) cultivating additional species of Indian legumes and other economic plants especially rice; (iv) replacing Italian millet with jowar and finger millet; (v) using more species of wild economic shrubs and trees, many of which were indigenous. Increasing economic prosperity was ensured when farmers began to raise twenty-three crops and five fruits/vegetables suited to different agro-climatic situations under dryland and wetland farming systems during summer, rainy and winter seasons. Extensive land use, crop rotation, crop diversification, animal husbandry, herding, hunting and fishing practices, enhanced surplus food and animal production.

A limited number of plant species were identified from plant remains recovered from several sites. This may be either due to the cultivation of only a few species at several sites, or efforts and techniques of collection and examination of samples may not have been adequate. The processing and identification of meticulously recovered samples from Hulas, Narhan and Senuwar have provided evidence of cultivation of several crops at these sites. The same is true of plant materials collected at Surkotada (Savithri 1976) and Rojdi (Weber 1991).

Crop diversification (seventeen crops at Hulas, thirty at Narhan and fourteen at Senuwas) was an obvious subsistence strategy of the Chalcolithic period. Crops suited to drylands and wetlands were available for cultivation in both seasons, leading to better land use. There were also choices between cereals (barley being more drought-resistant than wheat), oilseeds (sesame, rape and mustard, safflower serving different culinary purposes), millets and legumes. All legume species (exotic and indigenous) can be grown under rainfed conditions, but they differ in drought resistance. They are especially useful for different purposes; that is, as dried grains (lentil, green gram, black gram), dried and immature seeds (field-pea, pigeon-pea, chick-pea), dried grain and immature seeds/pods (hyacinth-bean, cow-pea, horse-gram, *moth* bean). Early cultivars of all legume species were of indeterminate type, with pods maturing at periodic intervals. Thus, farmers could harvest green pods/immature seeds for daily use and finally harvest different crops based on their specific maturity periods. All legume species provided green/dry fodder (although to varying extents) for use as animal food, and some of them like cow-pea, hyacinth-bean and horse-gram were amenable for regrowth after cutting (for fodder) to provide grain harvest. Such subsistence strategies ensured food security in both seasons, and farmers could then decide their cropping patterns based on their culinary preferences and land use. This traditional system is still practised today in India by subsistence farmers.

A major subsistence change almost equal to the use of South-west Asian crops for winter cultivation and crop rotation was that brought about through the use of African crops. The subsistence economies of Rajasthan, Madhya Pradesh and Maharashtra were based on minor millets and agro-pastoral systems, using species of *Panicum, Setaria, Echinochloa* and *Paspalum*. Farmers probably cultivated two or more minor millet species of different maturity periods, since mixtures of species were recovered from several archaeological sites. Farmers harvested different millets at periodic intervals from the same field. Multi-crop mixtures acted as food security for humans (seeds as staple food) and animals (vegetative parts used as fodder) because the vagaries of weather promote a differential response by different species, so that one or more species could be harvested for subsistence. This subsistence pattern is likely to have been practised by the Chalcolithic farmers of India and it is still practised by 'tribal' peoples in several parts of India. This situation began to change with the diffusion of pearl millet, sorghum and finger millet due to their specific plant characteristics and adaptability to different agro-climatic situations. Pearl millet can be grown in low rainfall (250–800 mm) areas, on poor sandy/very light/light/heavy, even red, soils; can tolerate drought; and can be stored well. Its range of adaptation is high under different day-lengths, temperatures and moisture stress. Sorghum yields are very high compared to other millets; it can be grown in medium to heavy soils, in 400–1,000 mm rainfall, and can tolerate temperature fluctuations. Finger millet has good grain storage capacity, even for ten years; can be grown in areas with rainfall ranging from 50 to 100 cm and in irrigated soils, in red loams, black and sandy soils. Thus, each millet has a special ecological niche and can also yield some grains in adverse soil and climatic conditions. All of these African crops also provided fodder for animals and they rapidly started replacing minor millet cultivation (Mehra 1991).

African sorghum and millet culture thus played an important role in the agricultural history of India following the opening up of opportunities for rainfed agriculture and mixed (crop cultivation and animal husbandry) farming systems (Mehra 1991). This led to a change in settlement patterns. Instead of urban centres with neighbouring food-producing villages, several small villages began to emerge over large stretches of land. The new system progressed rapidly because the centrally controlled production and distribution system, so characteristic of the Indus Valley civilization, could not operate (Mehra 1991). Similarly, the incorporation of pearl millet in the dryland agriculture of Gujarat seems responsible for the sudden increase in the number of settlements during Rangpur phases B and C.

In conclusion, it can be seen that the introduction of winter cereals and legumes led to a system of crop rotation, African crops replaced or supplemented minor millet cultivation, and appropriate land-use systems gradually developed with increasing crop diversification. All these strategies continued to produce surplus food and other products. Domesticated animals provided animal products, hunting of wild animals and fishing supplemented animal products, and increased exploitation of forest biodiversity served several useful purposes.

CONCLUSIONS

There is no doubt of the importance of introduced crops in increasing yields and in extending the range of crops that can be grown in different seasons. However, indigenous plants also played an important role and this has been consistently underestimated. The minor millets and the grams may have been important in the origins of domestication and were sets of species with which people were more familiar than the introduced species. Also, in many periods from the Chalcolithic to the present, people have cultivated a large range of crops, suitable to varying soil and climatic conditions and producing food at different seasons of the year. Although there has been an overall trend towards intensification in food production this has rarely led to the sorts of monocultures found in many other parts of the world. In looking at both origins and the long-term histories of agricultural systems in India the indigenous plants have had an important and underestimated role to play.

REFERENCES

Arora, R.K. and R. Nayar. 1984. *Wild Relatives of Crop Plants in India*. New Delhi: National Bureau of Plant Genetic Resources.

Costantini, L. and L. Costantini–Biasini. 1985. Agriculture in Baluchistan between the seventh and the 3rd millennium B.C. *Newsletter of Baluchistan Studies* 2, 16–30.

de Wet, J.M.J., K.E. Prasada Rao, M.H. Mangesha and D.E. Brink. 1983. Diversity in Kodo millet. *Economic Botany* 37, 159–63.

Glover, I.C. and C.F.W. Higham. 1996. New evidence for early rice cultivation in south, southeast and east Asia. In *The Origins and Spread of Agriculture and Pastoralism in Eurasia*, D.R. Harris (ed.), 413–41. London: UCL Press.

Harlan, J.R. 1975. *Crops and Man*. Madison, Wis.: American Society of Agronomy.

Jain, H.K. and K.L. Mehra. 1980. Evolution, adaptation, relationships and uses of the species of *Vigna* cultivated in India. In *Advances in Legume Science*, vol. I, R.J. Summerfield and R. Bunting (eds), 459–68. Kew: Royal Botanic Gardens.

Jain, S.K. 1981. *Glimpses of Indian Ethno-botany*. New Delhi: Oxford and IBH Publ. Co.

Kajale, M.D. 1991. Current status of Indian palaeoethnobotany: introduced and indigenous food plants with a discussion of the historical and evolutionary development of Indian agriculture and agricultural systems in general. In *Recent Developments in Palaeo-ethnobotany*, J. Renfrew (ed.), 155–89. Edinburgh: Edinburgh University Press.

Koul, A.K. 1974. Job's tears. In *Evolutionary Studies in World Crops; diversity and change in the Indian subcontinent*, Sir Joseph Hutchinson (ed.), 63–6. Cambridge: Cambridge University Press.

Meadow, R.H. 1984. Notes on faunal remains from Mehrgarh, with a focus on cattle (*Bos*). In *South Asian Archaeology*, B. Allchin (ed.), 34–40, Cambridge: Cambridge University Press.

Meadow, R.H. 1996. The origins and spread of agriculture and pastoralism in northwestern South Asia. In *The Origins and Spread of Agriculture and Pastoralism in Eurasia*, D.R. Harris (ed.), 390–412. London: UCL Press.

Mehra, K.L. 1991. Pre-historic Ethiopia and India: contacts through sorghum and millet genetic resources. In *Plant Genetic Resources of Ethiopia*, J.M.M. Engels, J.G. Hawkes and M. Worde (eds), 160–8. Cambridge: Cambridge University Press.

Mehra, K.L. and R.K. Arora. 1985. Some considerations on the domestication of plants in India. In *Recent Advances in Indo-Pacific Prehistory*, V.N. Misra and P. Bellwood (eds), 275–80. New Delhi: Oxford and IBH Publ. Co.

Randhawa, M.S. 1980. *A History of Agriculture in India*. New Delhi: Indian Council of Agricultural Research.

Saraswat, K.S. 1992. Archaeobotanical remains in ancient cultural and socio-economical dynamics of the Indian subcontinent. *Palaeobotanist* 40, 514–45.

Savithri, R. 1976. Studies in archaeobotany together with its bearing upon socio-economy and environment of Indian Proto-Historic cultures. Unpublished Ph.D. thesis, University of Lucknow.

Sharma, G.R. 1980. *History to Prehistory: archaeology of Ganga Valley & Vindhyas*. Allahabad: Allahabad University Publications.

Sharma, G.R. 1985. From hunting and food gathering to domestication of plants and animals in the Belan and Ganga Valleys. In *Recent Advances in Indo-Pacific Prehistory*, V. N. Misra and P. Bellwood (eds), 369–71. New Delhi: Oxford and IBH Publ. Co.

Singh, H.B. and R.K. Arora. 1978. *Wild Edible Plants of India*. New Delhi: Indian Council of Agricultural Research.

Smartt, J. and N.W. Simmonds. 1995. *Evolution of Crop Plants*. Harlow: Longman.

Vishnu-Mittre. 1977. Changing economy in ancient India. In *The Origin of Agriculture*, C.A. Reed (ed.), 569–88. The Hague: Mouton and Co.

Vishnu-Mittre. 1981. Wild plants in Indian folk life – a historical perspective. In *Glimpses of Indian Ethnobotany*, S.K. Jain (ed.), 37–58. New Delhi: Oxford and IBH Publ. Co.

Vishnu-Mittre. 1985. The uses of wild plants and the processes of domestication in the Indian sub-continent. In *Recent Advances in Indo-Pacific Prehistory*, V.N. Misra and P. Bellwood (eds), 281–91. New Delhi: Oxford and IBH Publ. Co.

Weber, S.A. 1991. *Plants and Harappan Subsistence : an example of stability and change from Rojdi*. New Delhi: Oxford and IBH Publ. Co.

8   Megalithic monuments and the introduction of rice into Korea

SARAH MILLEDGE NELSON

The relationship between increasingly complex societies and their subsistence base has long been known to be neither simple nor direct, but the various strands of complexity have been elusive and difficult to separate. One of the important findings of a symposium on transitions to agriculture was that the adoption of agriculture 'entails major, long-term changes in the structure and organization of the societies that adopt this new way of life' (Gebauer and Price 1992: 1). The adoption of rice in Korea is an example of agricultural origins in a 'secondary setting' (Cowan and Watson 1992: 209), which allows an examination of the effect of introducing a new and more productive crop into a society which already practised cultivation (with millets and perhaps other cultigens) (Nelson 1982a). While once it was thought that a new group of people had swept into the Korean peninsula with rice, dolmens, bronze and horses (e.g., Kim W.-Y. 1983: 20), the increasing time-span of the introduction of rice into Korea and the level of detail which can be teased out of recent excavations present a decidedly different view. What emerges is a picture of the slow formation of an elite class, based on the greater productiveness of rice. Visible traces of the burgeoning elite include megaliths and their contents, especially burnished red jars and polished stone knives, later to be joined by bronze artefacts and jade beads. The introduction of rice into Korea is thus not a wave of advance nor does it represent independent invention; it is, rather, a slow absorption of a new crop with important local consequences.

This interpretation is different from that usually proffered in Korea, and that difference requires a few words of explanation. Megalithic monuments and domesticated rice appeared in the Korean peninsula at roughly the same time, from an archaeological perspective, in the first half of the second millennium BC. This apparent contemporaneity has led to a number of assertions about movements of peoples and ideas, with surprisingly little discussion of societal changes. That is, the assumption has been that rice arrived as part of a complex package. In earlier papers I have suggested that the megalithic monuments are indicators of social hierarchies in Korea

(Nelson 1991), and that they could have functioned as territorial markers (Nelson 1993: 159), either of which are compatible with a migration theory or a theory of development in place. Here I will argue that the migration of rice farmers is unlikely, and I suggest that dolmens represent a local response to changes initiated by the adoption of rice agriculture in Korea – not immediately, but following the first rice cultivation by several hundred years. This discussion is complicated by wide differences in interpretations of the evidence, and even what kinds of data can be accepted as evidence, among archaeologists in North and South Korea and elsewhere, as will be discussed in more detail.

Cultivated rice as a foreign resource is at least one fact that is beyond question; the plant is not native to Korea, and must have arrived in the peninsula fully domesticated (Im 1988; Ho 1991; Shim 1982; Zheng 1992). Emphasis among archaeologists in Korea is on the movement of the plant, rather than the effects of domesticated rice on the existing culture. For example, most of the discussions about the introduction of rice to the Korean peninsula concern the era of its arrival (e.g., Kim B.-M. 1981a), the route (or routes) of transmission (e.g., Choe 1982; Shim 1991), or the accompanying stone tools which might delineate its route and arrival (e.g., Chon 1982, 1992).

The origin of dolmens, on the other hand, is more controversial. Megaliths are sometimes considered to be an indigenous invention (Kim W.-Y. 1986: 36), but many scholars consider them to be another import (see papers in Kim B.-M. 1981a). Often the same kinds of questions (when, where and how) are applied to these megaliths as are asked of the import of rice, either representing a diffused idea or as an indication of migration of peoples (Kim B.-M. 1981b). In my opinion, these topics have been wrung dry, without bringing about any consensus. A change in perspective is in order.

The new perspective suggested here must rest fundamentally on the relative and absolute chronology of rice and dolmens as well as an understanding of conditions in the peninsula when rice was introduced. Therefore I begin with the archaeological evidence for pre-rice cultivation and the social structure of the Chulmun period in Korea. Then I examine various indicators of rice cultivation: the sites where charred rice grains, rice phytoliths, rice impressions or rice pollen have been found; accompanying pottery and stone tools and the light they may shed on the organization of rice production; and the types, numbers, and arrangements of dwellings in these and related sites. Next I present the known data on the dolmens: their age, distribution, contents, and so forth. In particular it is necessary to distinguish early dolmens from their later counterparts, in order not to confuse the argument about changes in social structure with traits much later in time, such as bronze daggers and horse gear. With these data in mind, I pursue the questions of hierarchies, symbolism, and both social and ideological changes that appear to be the result of the introduction of rice cultivation. But first, a short excursion into the problem of nomenclature.

THE BRONZE AGE PROBLEM

In many publications on Korean archaeology, Mumun (Plainware) (see Figure 8.2) is equated with the Bronze Age. What I have referred to as the Megalithic period (Nelson 1992b, 1993) is often called in the Republic of Korea (ROK: South Korea) the Bronze Age (e.g., Choi 1984), and in the Democratic People's Republic of Korea (DPRK: North Korea) is always referred to as Bronze Age (e.g., Anon. n.d.: headings on 140ff.; Kim and So 1972). From the archaeological evidence to be detailed below it is evident that some Mumun pottery is at least a millennium earlier than the appearance of bronze in ROK, and assertions about the contemporary status of Mumun and bronze in DPRK have not been followed by any discussion of the issues or attempts to persuade the sceptical reader of the presence of bronze in the third millennium BC. In ROK the dates of both bronze and Mumun are assumed to be later than the third millennium, thus preserving the contemporaneity of Mumun and bronze but contradicting the dates from DPRK. Of course there are individuals in the south, and possibly also in the north, who diverge from these views, but they do not represent the consensus opinion.

In this chapter I attempt to distinguish the effects of the earliest rice production, although on a rather coarse chronological scale, from the later impetus given to social organization by the addition of bronze, warfare (to judge from the ubiquity of weapons), and probably horses. The chronology of bronze is thus a complicating factor which needs to be taken into account at the outset. While bronze is associated with some Mumun pottery, it is not at all clear, or even likely, that bronze and Mumun are completely contemporaneous. The first bronze artefacts probably cannot be earlier than about 1000 BC, based on dates of related artefacts in Liaoning Province, China; many bronzes, of course, are much later. Mumun pottery, however, has associated C14 dates beginning around 2000 BC, especially on the south coast of Korea. Thus, my discussion of rice and dolmens must emphasize the earliest sites.

One problem is, of course, that the sites are not dated with sufficient precision, which has allowed sweeping generalities concerning the Megalithic period which fail to distinguish between pre-bronze and bronze-containing sites. This assumption was not the result of faulty logic, but inadequate data; until recently rice, megaliths, Mumun and bronze were thought to be all imported together into the Korean peninsula. A mass migration of Tungusic people has often been posited, even naming these immigrants as Ye-Maek, a name used in the *Weishu*, a Chinese history of the third century AD (e.g., Kim W.-Y. 1975b: 106). Although few of the megaliths can be dated, the associated artefacts do help to distinguish broad chronological stages. The rice, fortunately, is more amenable to standard dating procedures.

BEFORE RICE

Millets and other crops were grown all over the Korean peninsula before the introduction of rice. Charred millet grains were found at several sites associated with Chulmun pottery, often inside inverted Chulmun jars. These grains probably indicate Incidental Domestication (Rindos 1984: 154–8), beginning in the sixth millennium BC. Chulmun spread to sites on the east and south coasts by the middle of the fourth millennium BC (Nelson 1990, 1992a, 1992b, 1994) achieving a level of Specialized Domestication as defined by Rindos (1984: 158–64).

Millets may have been locally domesticated in Korea, but more likely they were an import, for millets appear in northern China as early as 7000 BC. At the same time as millets were undergoing domestication in northern China, rice was domesticated in the south (Yan 1991, 1992; Wa 1992). Both crops were thus not far from the Korean peninsula across the Yellow Sea, but the northern route of diffusion began to operate about three millennia before that of the south. One possible explanation is proximity; an overland route is possible into the north-western part of the peninsula, while on the south coast boats were necessary to reach China. Since the earliest coastal sites in Korea imply boats, a more likely explanation for the time gap is that rice could not be planted in Korea until it became adapted to colder and shorter growing seasons. All the early rice in Korea is the *japonica* variety, which has shorter, rounder grains that are cold-adapted. Transverse reaping knives, with two holes, often associated with rice cultivation, are found at the site of Shaungtouzi as early as 2000 BC (Xu 1989), suggesting that at least by this date *japonica* was grown near northern Korea.

Little of the material culture of China arrived with rice, although both reaping knives and the stepped adze are exceptions which did diffuse to Korea. In the north, the semi-lunar stone knife has been thought to be associated with the spread of rice, and its occurrences in various forms are used to mark diffusion routes (e.g., Watson 1971). The stepped adze is similarly used by those who favour a southern route for the diffusion of rice into China. Although stone tools associated with rice production did diffuse to Korea, pottery did not. It is particularly important to note that tripod vessels are virtually ubiquitous in China by 2000 BC, having spread even to the far north-east (Tan *et al.* 1995), but do not appear in Korea before 100 BC, and even at that time they are rare. These observations will be discussed below, after considering the evidence for rice and dolmens.

EARLY SITES WITH IDENTIFIED RICE

Although there are several iron age sites containing rice grains which date to the first century BC, earlier sites with rice are few, and have been discovered only in recent years. The most northerly of these sites is Namkyongni, nea

Pyongyang, North Korea, in an agricultural basin where rice can still be grown. The other sites are in the Han river basin and further south, including locations near the south–east coast (Figure 8.1).

The most recent study of rice remains has successfully recovered and identified phytoliths of rice in potsherds from two sites in south–eastern Korea (Kwak 1995). As a result of this research these two sites, Nongsori and Kumgokdong, have become the oldest sites with definitive evidence for rice cultivation on the Korean peninsula. The environment for survival of organic remains is poor in most of Korea, making the recovery of actual grains or pollen unlikely except in unusual circumstances. The discovery that phytoliths could be identified in low–fired pottery (Fujihara 1976) opened the way for a better understanding of Korea's earliest agriculture. The technique of identifying phytoliths in pottery is particularly useful since it leaves no doubt of the association of the rice phytoliths with the pottery, and therefore with the particular phases of the sites to which the pottery belongs. In each case the phytoliths were embedded in Mumun ware, a largely undecorated class of pottery having deep bowls and jars as its two major shapes, which has long been identified with both late neolithic and bronze age sites (Figure 8.2). The two sites with rice phytoliths have similar pottery but are otherwise somewhat different from each other.

Kumgokdong is a site within the present boundaries of the city of Pusan. Although it is a small site, and in the excavated area lacks evidence of architecture except for a possible stone pavement feature, it is particularly useful because of the association of its radiocarbon date of 3580±75 BP (Kim and Chung 1980: 56), which calibrates to 2120–1865 BC cal. (Nelson 1992b: 114), with Mumun pottery. With the rice phytoliths in the potsherds and the associated C14 date, it is quite certain that rice, as a crop, came to Korea at least as early as the beginning of the second millennium BC.

Two sherds were selected for phytolith analysis, one from a bowl with a doubled rim (a common feature of Mumun, called Ichungko (Figure 8.2:1)), the other from a jar with a few incisions near the rim. Most of the Mumun vessels have pointed rather than flat bases, the flat bases being more characteristic of sites farther north. Stone tools found at the site were fashioned by chipping, except for a single ground projectile point with a diamond–shaped cross–section (Kim and Chung 1980).

The Nongsori site is a shellmound 5 km from Kimhae, near the mouth of the Naktong river. Most of the artefacts were found in layers of mixed earth and shell, beneath a pure shell layer. The pottery is similar to that of Kumgokdong, especially Mumun with pointed bases (Figure 8.2). Associated stone tools were all chipped rather than ground. No architectural features were discovered (Kim Y.-K. 1965). The sherd used for phytolith analysis came from an undecorated wide-mouthed bowl with a pointed base.

Phytoliths of other crops in addition to rice were identified. The inclusion of sorghum (*susu*), broomcorn millet (*kichang*), reed (*kalde*), and *Miscanthus sacchariflorus* (*okse*) demonstrates that several crops were grown (for descriptions

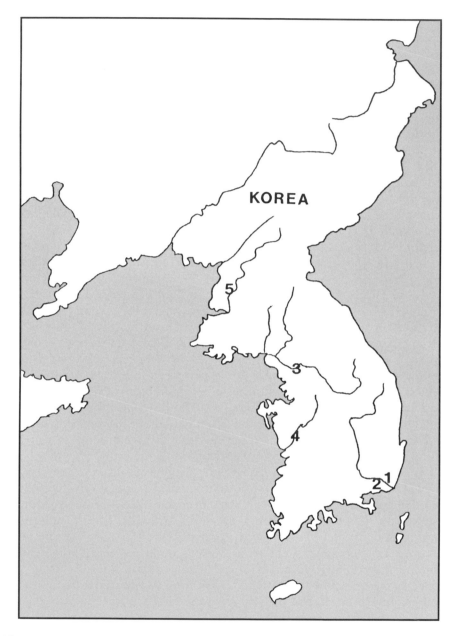

Figure 8.1 Locations of sites with early rice: (1) Kumgokdong, (2) Nongsori, (3) Hunamni, (4) Songgungni, (5) Namkyongni.

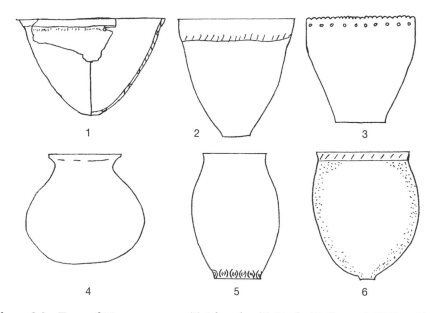

Figure 8.2   Types of Mumun pottery: (1) Ichungko, (2) Karak, (3) Gongyul, (4) Burnished jars, (5) Songgungni, (6) Kakhyung.

of the plants, see Lee 1966). Thus, even in sites where the stone tools do not indicate rice cultivation (or that of any other plant), rice phytoliths are found. An important lesson to be learned from this site is that the stone tool inventory cannot be relied upon to distinguish agricultural sites from those dependent only upon fishing and foraging. Furthermore, these are both small sites without known dwellings. They were simple villages at 2000 BC or so, growing rice on a small scale, not unlike small villages that dotted the Korean countryside through the 1970s, and still present in smaller numbers today. It seems likely that if phytolith testing were to be applied widely to Mumun pottery, the extent of rice-growing would be found to coincide with the presence of Mumun pottery.

While phytolith analysis is a new technique in Korea, recovery of carbonized plant material has been possible in a few unusual sites in Korea, in which all or part of the site burned and was not reoccupied. Grains of rice and other cereals were found at Songgungni in Cholla Puk Do, Hunamni on the South Han river, and Namkyonghi near Pyongyang (see Figure 8.1 for site locations). The Mumun pottery in these sites is flat-bottomed, but otherwise has traits in common with those of the southern coast in terms of the paste and firing of the bowl and jar shapes, and doubled rims with minimal decoration.

Hunamni was the first site in South Korea to yield carbonized grains ssociated with Mumun pottery. In addition to rice, barley (*boli*), fox-tail illet (*cho*) and sorghum (*susu*) were identified (SNU 1978: 37). Two radiocarbon dates from House 12, the location of the grain discoveries, place the rice around 1400 BC, the earliest dates from the site. House 8 was dated to the tenth–ninth centuries BC. These two earlier houses were placed higher on the hill slope than House 7 and House 14, both at the foot of the hill and having iron age dates. In spite of the varying dates for the houses at the site, they are all similar in size and shape – rectangular, about 6–7 m long and 3–4 m wide. The pottery is generally Mumun, with two varieties – a flat based doubled-rim deep bowl called Karak ware (Figure 8.2:2), and a group with punctates under the rim and a scalloped lip, named Gongyul (Figure 8.2:3). Both are found widely in west-central Korea. Burnished red pottery is found for the first time at this site in houses instead of dolmens (Figure 8.2:4).

The stone tool inventory is considerably more extensive and varied than the stone assemblages of Kumgokdong and Nongsori. Polished stone daggers and arrowheads having diamond-shaped cross-section are notable because they are also found in dolmens. Tubular clay beads are interesting, too, as they echo the tubular jade beads often associated with dolmens. Spindle whorls and loom weights attest to weaving, again suggesting more complex activities at this site than are demonstrated in the southern sites with phytoliths. Axes, hoes, reaping knives and grinding stones presumably all had agricultural functions. Scrapers and whetstones suggest further industrial activities (Kim et al. 1973; SNU 1974, 1976, 1978).

While Hunamni represents a small village, Songgungni is notable for having produced more than a dozen houses from the Mumun area of the site with much of it unexcavated (the other area is from the Paekche period, AD 300–668). Most of the semi-subterranean houses had burned, probably in one grand fire that caused the abandonment of the site. The houses were about 4 m square, with a hearth in the floor space of each dwelling. Charred wooden posts had fallen onto the floors, making it possible to approximate the superstructure of the buildings.

Red burnished jars, which are frequently found in dolmens, were located here in the dwellings, in addition to the more common Mumun jars and bowls. A Mumun ware with thumb prints along the base is called Songgungni type, and has been thought to be later than Karak and Gongyul. Tubular jade beads and polished stone daggers, other hallmarks of dolmens, were found at the site as well. These artefacts tie the dolmens to the site and thus relate the dolmen to rice cultivation.

Whetstones, small projectile points with diamond-shaped cross-sections, harvesting knives, sickles, spindle whorls, grooved adzes, axes, plane and chisels were also among the tools discovered at Songgungni (Figure 8.2:5). A wooden spade and the wooden handle of a dagger are reminders of the richness of perishable artefacts that has been lost (Chi et al. 1986; An et al. 1987). Calibrated C14 dates place the site in the ninth–fifth centuries BC (Nelson 1992b: 114).

The Namkyong site in Pyongyang, North Korea contained remains of broomcorn millet, soybeans (appearing for the first time in Korea), and foxta millet in addition to rice. Several houses were unearthed, each with a hearth in the centre (Kim and Suk 1984). The Mumun pottery is a type called Paengi, or Kakhyung (top-shaped), because of its very small flat bases making it seem unstable, like a spinning toy (Figure 8.2:6). The vessels are constructed by adding a small round foot to an otherwise rounded or pointed base. Thus the pots are very similar to those of the south coast, including in some cases the double rim. Stone tools include axes, grinding stones and net sinkers. The site is attributed to 2500–2000 BC (Anon. n.d.).

Rice impressions in Mumun pottery have been known for some time, but their significance went unrecognized until recently. It seems likely that additional rice impressions might be found in existing collections if a systematic search were undertaken. For example, some imprints of rice hulls were reported from the Puan area (illustrated in Kim W.-Y. 1975a: plate 8). The imprints found at Konamni, on an island off the south-west coast of Korea, attracted particular attention because this was the first 'bronze age' shell mound ever discovered. Other food remains included carbonized millet from House 3, and a charred peach seed in Midden 2. Faunal remains, well preserved by the shell midden environment, consist largely of deer and boar. Fish bones are abundant, especially sea bream.

The two oval shell mounds, mostly containing oysters, covered the houses, thus the houses antedate the shell. The houses are smaller than average for Mumun sites, about 3 × 4 m. Each has a central hearth. The artefact inventory is even more varied than that of Songgungni, with fishhooks, arrowheads and needles made of bone, shell ornaments, and a curved jade *gokok* in addition to stone arrowheads, axes, knives, grinding stones and hammer stones. The pottery includes both Mumun and red burnished ware. Mumun styles were both the doubled-rim variety and the Songgungni type, found together throughout the layers. Thus it seems that the difference between these two types is regional, not chronological as had been previously thought (HUM 1990a, 1990b).

Rice pollen is another obvious indication of the presence of rice, but it is not commonly found in archaeological sites in Korea. Pollen has been collected from dated peat bogs, however, allowing inferences to be made about the presence of rice cultivation. A bog at Kimpo, near the mouth of the Han river (Im 1992), has abundant rice pollen, and has been dated to about 2000 BC (Choe 1991). Yasuda and Kim (1980) earlier found rice pollen in Naju dated to 1500 BC, but this was largely discounted due to lack of supporting evidence (e.g., Kim W.-Y. 1981: 28). The supporting evidence is now at hand, and it seems likely that the beginning of rice cultivation in Korea occurred prior to 1500 BC, and probably as early as 2000 BC.

Since there is no reason to suppose that archaeologists would chance to uncover the very first occurrence of rice in the peninsula, it seems possible to conclude from these data that rice made its appearance in Korea at least as early as 2000 BC. Rice is consistently associated with Mumun pottery in one or more of its several variants, thus it is also reasonable to infer that the presence of Mumun pottery coincides with rice cultivation. This likelihood is supported by the distribution of Mumun variants in the regions of the west and south of the peninsula where rice is widely grown at present. It is interesting and pertinent that these are also the regions where megalithic monuments are most prevalent. There are no dolmens at all in Hamgyong Province, in the far north-east, where rice does not grow.

MEGALITHIC STRUCTURES

Megalithic monuments in Korea are divided into two basic types, menhirs and dolmens, whose names were taken from similar structures in western Europe. (Using this terminology is simply conventional; it does not imply any connection between the megaliths of Asia and those of Europe.) The single standing stones called menhirs are far less common than the structures with capstones known as dolmens. The menhirs that remain standing suggest that they may have had functions similar to village guardian posts (changsung) which into the twentieth century were carved from wood in male/female pairs.

Dolmens are of two major types, although some scholars have made further subdivisions and the terminology can become quite complex (Whang 1981; Mikami 1961; Chi 1982). One of the major types is the high table dolmen, also called Northern dolmen, in which the capstone is raised above the ground on three or four stone slabs arranged like a box. The capstone is the 'lid' of the box, although it always projects a considerable distance beyond the upright slabs. So-called Southern dolmens are built with the capstone on or near the ground, either propped on small stones or simply covering a burial in a stone cist, or less frequently a jar coffin (Figure 8.3). Geographical distributions of the two types actually overlap considerably, but in general the taller type is found more in the north and the lower in the south.

Few Northern dolmens contain any remaining artefacts. One dolmen from the Liaodong peninsula was excavated and found to contain a burial (Mikami 1961), but if these structures commonly were burial monuments, most of the evidence has vanished, looted long ago. On the other hand, Southern dolmens, being more difficult to distinguish from stray boulders as well as more difficult to break into, frequently have an intact burial when they are excavated. Contents of Northern dolmens, when found, include red burnished jars and polished stone daggers; the Southern-type may additionally contain Liaoning style bronze daggers (characterized by bracket-shaped edges) and tubular jade beads in addition to red jars and polished daggers.

Without biological material for radiocarbon dating, and with few artefacts for relative dating, estimates of the age of dolmens have varied widely. Absolute dates associated with dolmens are quite inconsistent. Yangsuri, north-east of Seoul in the Paldang Dam area, produced a date of 2665–2140 cal. BC, which is acceptable as related to rice cultivation only on the mor

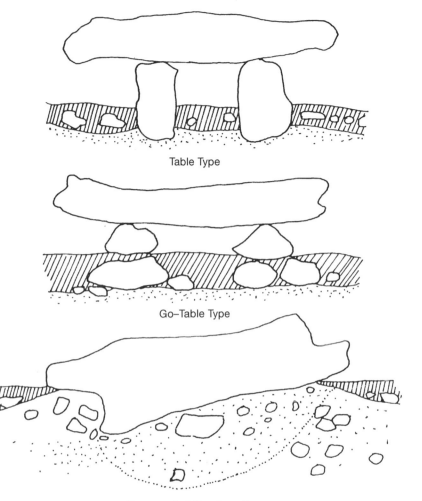

Table Type

Go–Table Type

Unsupported Capstone Type

Figure 8.3   Dolmen types in Korea.
Source: Kim B.-M. 1981.

recent end of the range. Other dates are later; Hwangsongni No. 13 near Chejon, with an even greater standard deviation, has a date of 835–0 cal. BC. This is a bone sample, and possibly not reliable. Sangjapori No. 4, also excavated as a result of the Paldang Dam survey, has a late date of 390–160 cal. BC (Lee 1977; Nelson 1992b). These dates are not useful for establishing the origin of dolmen-building, although they may reveal something about the length of time over which they were erected. It appears that dolmens continued in use as burial markers as late as the Iron Age, especially in the south.

Relative chronologies of dolmens all depend on typological arguments based on either the shapes of the dolmens themselves or varieties of Mumun, with additional assumptions about the direction of diffusion. Rhee (1984) derives the dolmens from the south, and asserts that the Southern style is earlier, while the consensus (e.g., Kim W.-Y. 1981; Choi 1984) looks to the north, and gives precedence to the Northern style. Similarly, there is no agreement about the chronology of Mumun. For example, Whang (1981) believes that the chronological order of Mumun varieties is Kakhyung, modified Kakhyung; Gongyul (which appears in the Han river basin and its tributaries); Karak (the flat-based doubled rim of central-west Korea); and red burnished pottery. One difficulty with this scheme is that it omits the south coast pottery, which is earliest by C14 dates. It seems more reasonable to posit that these are regional variants of Mumun, not chronological ones.

Estimates of the numbers of dolmens in Korea tend to rise with each new area surveyed. Given the density of dolmens of the Southern type, it is not unreasonable to estimate that 100,000 of them may still exist in the Korean peninsula (Nelson 1993: 147). Although this is a large number, it would account for only a small percentage of the population (assuming they are all burials), given the 1,000–2,000 years during which they were constructed, at best 100 dolmens per year for the entire Korean peninsula.

Dolmens tend to be found in groups, from the tens to the hundreds. They are often lined up along streams, sometimes clustered into groups of ten to twelve within the longer lines (Kim and Yun 1967). Usually their relationship to a nearby archaeological site is clear. Rhee (1984: 321) states that in his survey of the Ungok valley, the presence of dolmens always alerted him to the likelihood of a village site nearby. He noted further that habitation sites could be found 500–1,500 m from dolmens, usually on a ridge facing south, near a wide valley and overlooking the dolmens.

Sizes of dolmens vary greatly. The capstones are always large, weighing several tons, but some are enormous – for example the capstone at Maesonni weighs 160 tons (Rhee 1984: 328). Dolmens may also be mixed according to type, with one Northern dolmen on a hill above a row of Southern dolmens, as at Maedongni, where there are three Southern dolmens and one Northern type (Chi 1977). Some examples of recently excavated dolmens include Sasuri (Lee, Ha and Choi 1988), Chongnyongni and Changchonni (MUM 1984). The dolmens in these sites included both types of Southern dolmens, all of them burial markers. Burial goods included pottery vessels, polished stone knives, stone projectile points, grinding stones, and semi-lunar reaping knives. At Chongnyongni, six dolmens were excavated, along with two dolmens at Changchonni. No bones remained, but the burial chambers indicated extended burials. Dolmen No. 1 at Changchonni contained a bronze dagger and pommel. A nearby village was excavated, where Mumun pottery, grinding stones, semi-lunar knives, and small diamond-shaped projectile points were found. In central Korea, a group of dolmens was discovered at Hwangsongni (Lee, Ha and Choi 1988), in which excavations revealed extended burials in stone cists with burnished red pottery, tubular beads, and gokuk (curved beads).

Dolmens are densest in the Korean peninsula, but their distribution extends into Kyushu, the southwesternmost of Japan's large islands, and into the Liaodong and Shandong peninsulas of China. In China only Northern dolmens are found, often with dressed stones instead of the rough stones characteristic of Korean megaliths, while in Kyushu both Northern and Southern types are found. Although there have been proposals to derive them from elsewhere, from south India to Europe, their distribution and density suggest that they are likely to be a local Korean creation, or at least to have been a response to local needs.

Some archaeologists suggest that Korea's dolmens were designed after the model of stone cists, arguing that a dolmen is nothing more than an enormous, above-ground stone cist. Stone cists have a continuous distribution from the Karasuk culture of Siberia through a number of variants in China's Dongbei. However, the direct inspiration for Korean stone cist burials appears to be the Xituanshan culture centred in Jilin province, China which includes both villages and cemeteries. Although most of the burials are simple, with few grave goods, Xituanshan also features tubular beads and occasional small bronze artefacts (Liu 1995). Stone cist burials are thus associated with bronze age sites in north-eastern China, including some high status tombs containing Liaoning daggers, bronze mirrors decorated with lined triangles and zigzags, and horse trappings. Thus while it is likely that the idea of stone cist burials did enter into the Korean peninsula from the north, given their associated artefacts (including bronzes), they are considerably later than the earliest dolmens. On the other hand, some stone cists, as at Bidangni (Yi 1971) and Tangsan (Kang 1980) both near Puyo, and Sajikdong in Tangnai yielded polished stone daggers and no bronze. They may be earlier, but dates are lacking.

The tangled chronology of Korean dolmens is thus not easy to unravel. The earliest southern sites with rice have dolmens nearby, but their contents suggest that they are much later. North Koreans ascribe dolmens above stone cists, surrounded by a layer of pebbles, to the second millennium BC (Anon. n.d.: 239–43). Other dolmens are called 'Bronze Age (1st millennium BC)'. Some of these, for example the Hwangsongni dolmens, contained polished stone projectile points and daggers in red jars in stone cists, but no bronze. Other excavated dolmens also lacked bronze. Thus it seems possible to consider dolmens without bronze as likely to antedate the Bronze Age. Common associated artefacts in both north and south are red jars and polished daggers.

Given the diffusion of rice into Korea without other evidence of population movement (the semi-lunar knife and stone adze are tools that may be directly related to grain harvesting and paddy clearing, and so can be treated as functional rather than stylistic additions), it can be argued that the building of large dolmens is local response to rice agriculture. The implications of this argument will be drawn out below.

IMMIGRANTS OR ADOPTERS OF A NEW CROP

This returns us to the question of the effects of rice cultivation on the social organization and symbolic life of the inhabitants of the Korean peninsula in the second millennium BC. Various occurrences of rice, in a wide range of places, demonstrate that rice was grown in Korea during this time period, in roughly the same regions where rice is now grown. The first dolmens are somewhat later. They do not coincide spatially with the earliest evidence of rice, which is in the south, but rather arise when rice is more widespread, and in the centre of the peninsula, suggesting that dolmens are a response to the increasing incidence of rice agriculture rather than simply an import.

As a short aside, it is useful to consider again the intrusion scenario which hypothesizes a new people with rice who overran the peninsula (Kim W.-Y. 1986: 35). Kim gives us an explicit model. He assumes a small population (2,000–3,000 in the entire peninsula) of millet growers (the 'Chulmun' people), assimilated by immigrants (the 'Mumun' people). The argument runs that a number of new elements appeared at once: Mumun ware, burnished red jars, ground stone, polished stone daggers, rice, and dolmens. In addition, the location, size, and density of sites changed. Instead of being found predominantly along the coasts and interior riverbanks, villages were built on hill slopes, and tended to be larger and more densely packed in the landscape. (This omits the complicating feature of bronze, but since I believe the latest phytolith work makes it quite clear that rice preceded bronze by roughly one millennium, it seems that it can be safely set aside.)

Explanations other than migrations of peoples can account for these factors. Rice cultivation itself is likely to have been responsible for the change in village location. Millets and other crops were easily planted on the treeless edges of the rivers – treeless due to the annual flooding (Bartz 1972), which allowed only annual plants to flourish. These were herbs and forbs, easily uprooted to allow for crops, without extensive felling of trees. Furthermore, this was rainfall agriculture, for which the spring and summer rains provided ample moisture. Rice, on the other hand, requires relatively still ponded water in which to grow. This environment cannot be provided by the larger rivers, which become raging torrents in the rainy season. As a result, in Korea rice agriculture tends to tap smaller mountain streams, spreading them out into terraced plots that course from paddy to paddy down the hillside. Hillside houses were thus closer to the farmland, and simply handier for the cultivation of rice. The size and density of villages could be explained by the productivity of rice; more people could be fed and the population could grow.

The Mumun pottery, polished stone tools, and so forth could have been adopted along with rice, and some of them undoubtedly were. It is evident that the rice-growers received their initial rice seeds from outside the peninsula; therefore they were open to outside influences. The many coastal sites, some with evidence of deep-sea fishing as early as 6000 BC at the latest

(Nelson n.d.), show that contact with other fishing folk from the continent as well as nearby islands was not only possible but likely. The only question then becomes, why did it take them so long to adopt rice? The unsuitability of southern rice for the Korean climate is the likely answer.

But did people migrate to Korea with rice, or did the established millet farmers add rice to their crops? This argument could become a stalemate between two equally plausible interpretations, were it not for one crucial and telling circumstance: the lack of tripod vessels in Korea, when they are all but ubiquitous in China. I have noted the significance of this in a general way (Nelson 1982b: 130; 1993: 158), but here I would like to extend the argument and make it more specific. If the new elements in the peninsula were the result of immigrants from any part of China, why did they not bring tripods with them? Some tripod vessels were culinary, made to boil or steam food above a small fire. These jars had fat legs in which water could be placed. Others may have been ceremonial, as some tripods became elaborate and finely executed. In either case, it seems that immigrants would not abandon their customary cuisine (especially as it was rice-based, and the rice *was* brought to Korea), nor would they abandon their rituals and beliefs. This tips the balance in favour of an acceptance of a new, productive food source, into ongoing agricultural practices, and away from any theory of mass migration. It suggests that established cooking habits in Korea required the rejection (or lack of adoption) of the vessels in which rice had been cooked on the continent. The inhabitants of Korea did shift from Chulmun to Mumun pottery, but changed the vessel shapes only gradually, as a response to internal needs. The same general argument applies to the use of tripods as ritual paraphernalia. Migrants would have brought with them their customary ritual and ceremonial objects, or at least would have reconstructed them as closely as possible in their new surroundings. The lack of ritual tripods suggests that the occupants of Korea already had rituals sufficient to their needs. The ceremonies left no recognized traces, although it is not unreasonable to assume an animism that was based on mountains, rocks, rivers and trees (Nelson 1995). It is reasonable to posit that these rituals led to the construction of dolmens.

HIERARCHIES AND DOLMENS

Dolmens are often taken to be evidence of a hierarchical social structure (e.g., Rhee and Choi 1992). The argument rests on the assumption that they are burial markers, but too few of them were erected to account for the majority of the population. Dolmens also contain non–utilitarian objects, which may belong to only a subset of the population. In particular the polished red jars and polished stone knives are labour-intensive artefacts which may have been made for a special class of people by a group of artisans trained in these special skills.

If the migration argument for dolmens is rejected, and we recall that although dolmens are found also in south-western Japan and north-eastern China they are most numerous in the Korean peninsula and therefore likely to be indigenous, then it is possible to consider dolmens as a response to rice agriculture. The fact that the productivity of rice makes possible a division of labour between primary producers and others, such as full-time artisans or managers, does not demonstrate that rice is the cause of that division. Nevertheless, such division of labour seems to be reflected in the labour intensity required to manufacture the red jars and polished daggers, as well as the special skills needed. Furthermore, neither object appears to have any practical use. The daggers are made of patterned limestone, and are usually too fragile for any functional application. Most of the red jars are an appropriate size for individual servings and their jar shape suggests liquid; perhaps they held an alcoholic potable associated with rituals. *Makkoli* (rice wine) is used in shamanic ceremonies (*kut*) even at present in Korea. Although they have been found in dwellings (see pp. 150–6), those dwellings might simply be the locus of their manufacture; or they could have had a ritual function within the household or only in some households, in addition to the ritual function which resulted in deposition within the burial.

The unequal size of villages suggests central places and subordinate places. The larger villages may have been sites of intermittent markets, where dried fish and seafood from the coasts, perishable crafts such as basketry, cloth, and wooden items, and perhaps even pottery were exchanged. The larger sites, such as Soktalli (Nelson 1993: 143), are associated with many more dolmens than smaller sites, reflecting the larger population but perhaps also the greater importance of the larger villages or towns.

I suggest that the dolmens, which unlike those of Europe do not contain multiple burials, are unlikely to be territorial markers as I have briefly suggested previously (Nelson 1993: 159). They fail in an analogy with western European dolmens in several ways. Not only are they for the most part individual burials, but they are found in groups, not scattered on the landscape like those of Rouay (Renfrew 1973). Thus they are less comparable to tribal indicators, and more compatible with an emerging elite, who could use the dolmens to trumpet their power and their ability to mobilize labour with megalithic structures.

This elite seems to have developed gradually, since sites with the earliest rice lack dolmens. Thus, with the new evidence of early rice in Korea, the invention and growth of dolmens can be seen as a response to the new crop. With the addition of bronze, the elite rapidly consolidated their position, but the slow growth of power and hierarchy is the tale told by early rice and dolmens.

REFERENCES

An S.-M., Cho H.-J. and Yoon K.-J. 1987. *Songgungni Site III*. Report of the Research of Antiquities, Volume 19. Seoul: National Museum of Korea. (In Korean.)

Anon. n.d. *The Illustrated Book of Ruins and Relics of Korea Primitive Ages*. Pyongyang: The Archaeology Research Institute.

Bartz, P.M. 1972. *South Korea: A Descriptive Geography*. Oxford: Oxford University Press.

Chi K.-G. 1977. Excavation of Dolmens at Naedongni, Taedok. *Paekche Yongu*, 8, 107–28.

Chi K.-G. 1982. A study of dolmen distribution in north-eastern Asia. *Hanguk Kogo Hakbo* 12, 245–61. (In Korean.)

Chi K.-G., An S.-M. and Song U.-J. 1986. *Songgungni Site II*. Report of the Research of Antiquities, Volume 28. National Museum of Korea. (In Korean.)

Choe C.-P. 1982. The diffusion route and chronology of Korean plant domestication. *Journal of Asian Studies* 41, 519–29.

Choe C.-P. 1991. A critical review of research on the origin of Koreans and their culture. *Hanguk Sangkosa Hakbo* 8, 7–43.

Choi M.-L. 1984. Bronze Age in Korea. *Korea Journal* 24, 23–33.

Chon Y.-N. 1982. Chronology of Korean stone daggers and arrowheads. *Mahan-Paekche Munhwa* 4–5. (In Korean.)

Chon Y.-N. 1992. Introduction of rice agriculture into Korea and Japan: from the perspective of polished stone implements. In *Pacific Northeast Asia in Prehistory: hunter-fisher-gatherers, farmers, and socio-political elites*, C.M. Aikens and S.N. Rhee (eds), 161–9. Pullman: Washington State University Press.

Cowan, C.W. and P.J. Watson. 1992. Some concluding remarks. In *The Origins of Agriculture: an international perspective*, C.W. Cowan and P.J. Watson (eds), 207–12. Washington, D.C.: Smithsonian Institution Press.

Fujihara K. 1976. The transition from Jomon to Yayoi as seen through plant opals. *History Journal* 1, 63–70. (In Japanese.)

Gebauer, A.B. and T.D. Price. 1992. Foragers to farmers: an introduction. In *Transitions to Agriculture in Prehistory*, A.B. Gebauer and T.D. Price (eds), 1–10. Madison, Wis.: Prehistory Press.

Ho M.H. 1991. Origin and introduction of domesticated rice in Korea. *Hanguk Kogo Hakbo* 27, 63–104. (In Korean.)

HUM (Hanyang University Museum), 1990a. *The Excavation Report of Konamri Shellmound (I) At Anmyondo Island*. The University Museum Research Series No. 10. Hanyang University Museum.

HUM. 1990b. *The Excavation Report of Konamri Shellmiddens (II) At Anmyondo Island*. The University Museum Research Series No. 11. Hanyang University Museum.

Im H.-J. 1988. Prehistoric agriculture in Korea. *Papers of the 5th International Congress of Korean Studies*. 384–93. Songan: Academy of Korean Studies. (In Korean.)

Im H.-J. 1992. Prehistoric rice agriculture in Korea. In *Pacific Northeast Asia in Prehistory: hunter-fisher-gatherers, farmers, and socio-political elites*, C.M. Aikens and S.N. Rhee (eds), 157–60. Pullman: Washington State University Press.

Kang I.-G. 1980. Stone cist at Tangsan in Puyo. *Yoksa Hakbo* 88, 1–18.

Kim B.-M. 1981a. Megalithic remains in Chinese continent. In *Monographs, No. 2 Megalithic Cultures in Asia*, Kim Byung-mo (ed.), 164–90. Seoul: Hanyung University Press.

Kim B.-M. 1981b. Excavations uncover new evidence. *Korean Culture* 2, 40–1.

Kim C.-W. and Yun M.-B. 1967. *Studies of Dolmens in Korea*. National Museum of Korea, Vol. 6. (In Korean.)

Kim J.-H. and Chung J.-W. 1980. *Kumgokdong Rock Shelter and Shell Mound*. Pusan University Museum. (In Korean.)

Kim W.-Y. 1975a. *Archaelogy in Korea 1973*. Seoul National University Museum, Vol. 1. (In Korean, with English summary.)

Kim W.-Y. 1975b The neolithic culture of Korea. In *The Traditional Culture and Society of Korea: Prehistory*, R.J. Pearson (ed.), 61–111. Honolulu: The Center for Korean Studies, The University of Hawaii Press.

Kim W.-Y. 1981. Korean archaeology today. *Korea Journal* 21, 22–43.

Kim W.-Y. 1983. *Recent Archaeological Discoveries in the Republic of Korea*. Tokyo: The Centre for East Asian Studies, UNESCO.

Kim W.-Y. 1986. *Art and Archaeology of Ancient Korea*. Seoul: The Taekwang Publishing Company.

Kim W.-Y., Im H.-J., Choi M.-L., Yeo J.-C. and Kwak S.-H. 1973. *The Hunamri Site – a prehistoric village site on the Han River* – Progress Report 1972, 1973. Volume 4. Archaeological and Anthropological Papers of Seoul National University. Seoul: The University Museum, Seoul National University.

Kim Y.-G. and So G.-T. 1972. Sopohang prehistoric remains report. *Kogo Minsok* 4, 31–145. (In Korean.)

Kim Y.-G. and Suk K.-J. 1984. *Namgyong Site Research*. Pyongyang: Kwahak Paek Kwa Sachon Chulgwansa.

Kim Y.-K. 1965. *Excavation and Investigation of the Shell Mound Located at Nongsori*. Pusan National University Museum. (In Korean.)

Kwak J.-C. 1995. Rice plant-opal detected in pottery of neolithic period. *Hanguk Koko Hakbo* 32, 149–62. (In Korean.)

Lee Y.-J. 1977. A new interpretation of the prehistoric chronology of Korea: the application of MASCA theory. *Hanguk Sa Yongu* 15, 3–43. (In Korean.)

Lee Y.-J., Ha M.-S. and Choi S.-K. 1988. Sasuri Taejon Dolmens. *Juam Dam Report II*. Chonnam University. (In Korean.)

Lee Y.-J., Lee Y.-M., Dong M.-S. and Woo J.-Y. 1988. *Dolmens at Usanni, Gokchon*. Chonnam University. (In Korean.)

Lee Y.-N. 1966. *Manual of Korean Grasses*. Seoul: Ewha Women's University.

Liu J.-W. 1995. Bronze culture in Jilin Province. In *The Archaeology of Northeast China Beyond the Great Wall*. S.M. Nelson (ed.), 206–24. London: Routledge.

Mikami T. 1961. *The Dolmens and Stone Cists in Manchuria and Korea*. Tokyo: Yoshikawa Kobunkan. (In Japanese with English summary.)

MUM (Mokpo University Museum). 1984. *Dolmens in Chongnyongni and Changchonni in Yongamgun*. Mokpo University Museum Monographs. (In Korean.)

Nelson, S.M. 1982a. The effects of rice agriculture in prehistoric Korea. *Journal of Asian Studies* 41, 531–43.

Nelson, S.M. 1982b. Recent progress in Korean archaeology. In *Advances in World Archaeology Volume 1 1982*, F. Wendorf and A.E. Close (eds), 99–149. New York: Academic Press.

Nelson, S.M. 1990. The Neolithic of northeastern China and Korea. *Antiquity* 64, 234–48.

Nelson, S.M. 1991. Mumumtogi and megalithic monuments: a reconsideration of the dating. *Papers of the British Association of Korean Studies* 3, 183–94.

Nelson, S.M. 1992a. The question of agricultural impact on sociopolitical development in prehistoric Korea. In *Pacific Northeast Asia in Prehistory: hunter-fisher-gatherers, farmers, and socio-political elites*, C.M. Aikens and S. Rhee (eds), 179–81. Pullman: Washington State University Press.

Nelson, S.M. 1992b. Korean archaeological sequences from the first ceramics to the introduction of iron. In *Chronologies in Old World Archaeology*, R.W. Ehrlich (ed.), 430–8. Chicago: University of Chicago Press.

Nelson, S.M. 1993. *The Archaeology of Korea*. Cambridge: Cambridge University Press.

Nelson, S.M. 1994. Millet and pigs in Korea and Manchuria. In *Theme Papers: Change in Agrarian Systems World Archaeological Congress 3*. Paper No. 10, unpaginated. New Delhi: WAC.

Nelson, S.M. 1995. Roots of animism in Korea, from the earliest inhabitants to the Silla kingdom. In *Korea's Cultural Roots*, T. Koh and D. Lee (eds), North Park College Symposium Papers.

Nelson, S.M. n.d. Korean foraging and fishing sites in the Holocene. Paper presented at the From the Jomon to Star Carr conference, Universities of Cambridge and Durham, Sept. 4–8, 1995.

Renfrew, C. 1973. *Before Civilization: the radiocarbon revolution and prehistoric Europe*. New York: Alfred A. Knopf.

Rhee S.N. 1984. Emerging complex society in prehistoric southwest Korea. Unpublished Ph.D. thesis, University of Oregon.

Rhee S.N. and Choi M.-L. 1992. Emergence of complex society in prehistoric Korea. *Journal of World Prehistory* 6, 51–95.

Rindos, D. 1984. *The Origins of Agriculture: An Evolutionary Perspective*. Orlando, Fla.: Academic Press.

SNU (Seoul National University). 1974. *The Hunamri Site – a prehistoric village site on the Han river*. Progress Report 1974, Volume 5. Archaeological and Anthropological Papers of Seoul National University. Seoul: The University Museum, Seoul National University.

SNU. 1976. *The Hunamri Site 3 – a prehistoric village site on the Han river*. Progress Report 1975 (fourth year), Vol. 7. Archaeological and Anthropological Papers of Seoul National University. Seoul: The University Museum, Seoul National University.

SNU. 1978. *The Hunamri Site 4 – a prehistoric village site on the Han river*. Progress Report 1976, 1977, Vol. 8. Archaeological and Anthropological Papers of Seoul National University. Seoul: The University Museum, Seoul National University.

Shim B.-K. 1982. A study on the origin of rice cultivation in Korea. *Busan Sahak* (Pusan Historical Review) 6, 11–64. Tong-A University.

Shim B.-K. 1991. Prehistoric rice cultivation in Korea. *Hanguk Kogo Hakbo* 27, 5–61. (In Korean.)

Tan Y., Sun X., Zhao H. and Gan Z. 1995. The Bronze Age of the Song-Nen plain. In *The Archaeology of Northeast China: beyond the Great Wall*, S.M. Nelson (ed.), 225–49. London: Routledge.

Wa Y. 1992. Neolithic tradition in northeast China. In *Pacific Northeast Asia in Prehistory: hunter-fisher-gatherers, farmers, and socio-political elites*, C.M. Aikens and S. Rhee (eds), 139–56. Pullman: Washington University Press.

Watson, W. 1971. *Cultural Frontiers in Ancient East Asia*. Edinburgh: University Press.

Whang Y.-H. 1981. The general aspect of megalithic culture of Korea. In *Monographs No. 2: Megalithic Cultures in Asia*, Kim B.-M. (ed.), 41–64. Seoul: Hanyang University Press.

Xu Y. 1989. A highlight of bronze culture during the Shang and Zhou dynasties. *Liaohai Wenwu Xuegan* 2, 63–70.

Yan W. 1991. China's earliest rice agriculture remains. *Indo-Pacific Prehistory 1990 Volume 1, Papers from the 14th IPPA Congress, Yogakarta*, P. Bellwood (ed.), 118–26.

Yan W. 1992. Origins of agriculture and animal husbandry in China. In *Pacific Northeast Asia in Prehistory: hunter-fisher-gatherers, farmers, and socio-political elites*, C.M. Aikens and S. Rhee (eds), 113–23. Pullman: Washington University Press.

Yasuda Y. and Kim J.-M. 1980. *History of Ecological Changes in Korea*. Tokyo.

Yi K.-S. 1971. A prehistoric burial from Bidangni, Puyo. *Kogohuk* 4, 75–80.

Zheng Y. 1992. History of rice farming in the Korean peninsula. *Agricultural Archaeology* 1, 64–9.

9 The dispersal of domesticated plants into north-eastern Japan

CATHERINE D'ANDREA

INTRODUCTION

The origin and dispersal of domesticated plants has long been a focus of archaeological research, and has become an important aspect of palaeoethno-botanical studies. Large compendia of articles dealing with this research problem have been available since the late 1960s (Ucko and Dimbleby 1969; Struever 1971; Reed 1977; Harris and Hillman 1989; Cowan and Watson 1992; Gebauer and Price 1992). Studies of *in situ* agricultural origins have developed considerably over the past twenty years, progressing from deterministic, causal models (e.g. Cohen 1977; Wright 1977) to discussions on evolutionary factors in human–plant interaction (Rindos 1984), and domestication rates in plants (Hillman and Davies 1990; Blumler and Byrne 1991). Modelling the subsequent spread of agriculture has progressed beyond ideas of simple dispersal (e.g. Ammerman and Cavalli-Sforza 1973, 1984). Recent work in agricultural dispersals has emphasized the complexity of forager–farmer interactions tempered by cultural, technological, and ecological factors (e.g. Zvelebil 1986; Gregg 1988).

In Japan, there has been considerable theorizing about the origins of agriculture. The focus of research has been on dispersals, specifically of wet-rice agriculture, although there is some discussion of the possibility of *in situ* plant domestication. Wet-rice agriculture is thought to have originated in a broad region including South Asia, southern China, and South-east Asia, and spread into south-western Japan, eventually reaching the north-east (Chang 1976; Kanaseki and Sahara 1978; Akazawa 1981, 1986a, 1986b). Comparisons have been drawn with agricultural dispersals into north-western Europe (Rowley-Conwy 1984), and north-eastern North America, where tropical cultigens (maize, beans, and squash) were adopted by groups inhabiting temperate regions (Aikens 1981; Crawford 1983). Explanations for the spread of agriculture have been largely in the form of models emphasizing environmental (Kanaseki and Sahara 1978; Akazawa 1986a) and socio-economic factors (Aikens 1981; Hayden 1990). In addition to these ideas, some researchers have proposed the existence of temperate swidden horticulture based on millets, barley, buckwheat, and other crops that pre-dates wet-rice cultivation (e.g. Fujimori 1963, 1970; Nakao 1966; Ueyama 1969; Sasaki 1971). Kotani (1981) refers to these models collectively as the 'Jomon Farming Hypothesis' which holds that wet-rice agriculture was introduced to populations that had prior knowledge of farming techniques. More recently, the shift to agriculture in Japan has been described as a series of four transitions, beginning with indigenous gardening during the Jomon, the introduction of wet-rice paddy farming during the Yayoi, followed by two transitions associated with the northeastward dispersal of cultigens (Crawford 1992b). Data are accumulating that demonstrate the presence of Jomon domesticates (e.g. Crawford 1983, 1992a; Tsukada et al. 1986; Kudo and D'Andrea 1991; D'Andrea 1995a, 1995b; D'Andrea et al. 1995; Okada 1995). More extensive research is required, however, to determine the nature of any associated husbandry practices.

This chapter provides a brief review of the evidence for Jomon cultigens, emphasizing the Tohoku region of north-eastern Japan (Figure 9.1). It has been argued that some form of horticulture was practised by Jomon groups, based on archaeobotanical (Crawford 1983, 1997; D'Andrea et al. 1995), palynological (Tsukada et al. 1986) and ecological/historical data on agricultural practices in adjacent regions (D'Andrea 1995b; D'Andrea et al. 1995). While the available archaeobotanical database is not extensive, it does indicate a steady dispersal of domesticated plants to Japan from the mainland beginning early in the Jomon period. It is possible that once introduced, these crops, which eventually included rice, may not have disrupted Jomon cultural or subsistence systems, at least on the same scale as is evident during the later infiltration of wet-rice paddy and other Yayoi cultural elements. The Jomon lifestyle of sedentary village occupation, in fact, may have facilitated the spread of these early cultigens propagated in small gardens or swidden fields. Moreover, sedentism and familiarity with horticulture on the part of Jomon cultures also may explain what is now viewed as a relatively rapid dispersal northwards of later Yayoi wet-rice paddy technology.

EVIDENCE FOR JOMON DOMESTICATES

Jomon culture is commonly portrayed as comprising several temporally and regionally diverse groups of affluent foragers, occupying more or less sedentary villages, and producing large quantities of cord-marked pottery (Figure 9.2). Subsistence is thought to have been similarly heterogeneous, dominated by fishing, terrestrial and marine mammal hunting and plant gathering (Ikawa-Smith 1980; Aikens and Higuchi 1982). The question of Jomon horticulture has been debated for many years, and although most archaeologists now agree that some form of cultivation was practised, it is considered to have been of minor economic significance (Akazawa 1982;

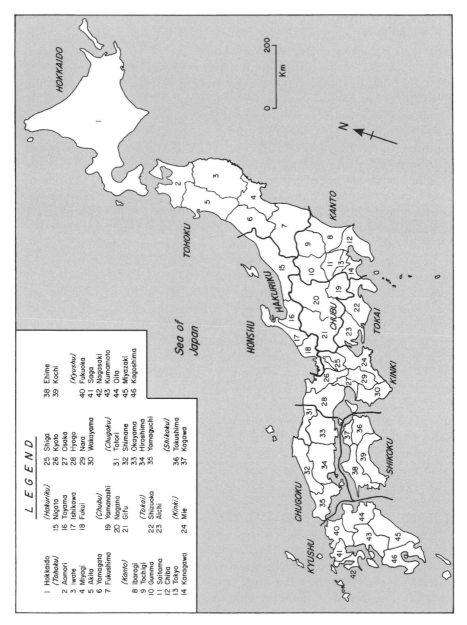

Figure 9.1 Japan: prefectures and districts.

LEGEND

1 Hokkaido
(Tohoku)
2 Aomori
3 Iwate
4 Miyagi
5 Akita
6 Yamagata
7 Fukushima

(Kanto)
8 Ibaragi
9 Tochigi
10 Gumma
11 Saitama
12 Chiba
13 Tokyo
14 Kanagawa

(Hokuriku)
15 Niigata
16 Toyama
17 Ishikawa
18 Fukui

(Chubu)
19 Yamanashi
20 Nagano
21 Gifu

(Tokai)
22 Shizuoka
23 Aichi

(Kinki)
24 Mie

25 Shiga
26 Kyoto
27 Osaka
28 Hyogo
29 Nara
30 Wakayama

(Chugoku)
31 Tottori
32 Shimane
33 Okayama
34 Hiroshima
35 Yamaguchi

(Shikoku)
36 Tokushima
37 Kagawa

38 Ehime
39 Kochi

(Kyushu)
40 Fukuoka
41 Saga
42 Nagasaki
43 Kumamoto
44 Oita
45 Miyazaki
46 Kagoshima

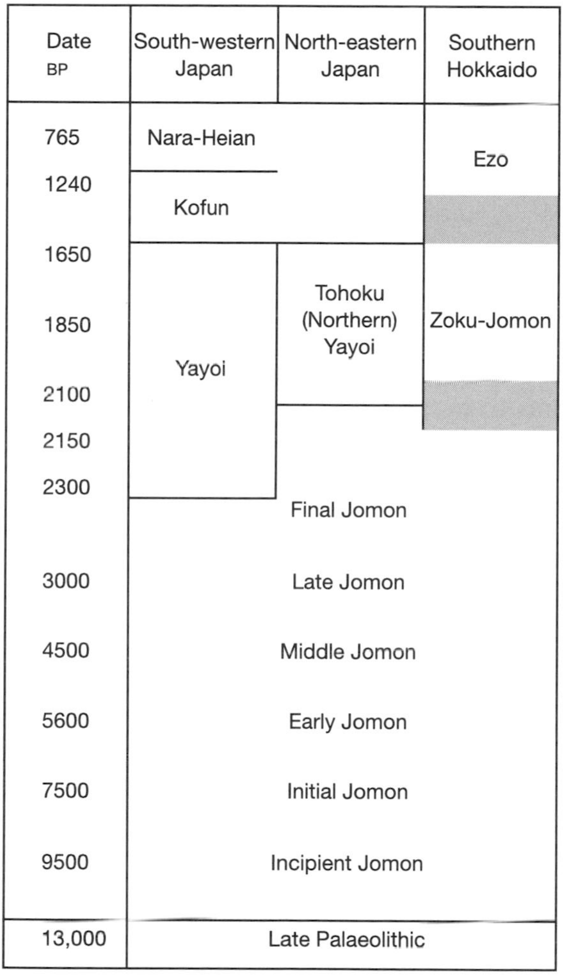

Date BP	South-western Japan	North-eastern Japan	Southern Hokkaido
765	Nara-Heian		Ezo
1240	Kofun		
1650	Yayoi	Tohoku (Northern) Yayoi	Zoku-Jomon
1850			
2100			
2150			
2300		Final Jomon	
3000		Late Jomon	
4500		Middle Jomon	
5600		Early Jomon	
7500		Initial Jomon	
9500		Incipient Jomon	
13,000		Late Palaeolithic	

Figure 9.2 Generalized cultural chronology for Japan (after Ikawa Smith 1980; Aikens and Higuchi 1982; Suzuki 1986; Barnes 1988).

Kasahara 1984; Higuchi 1986; Crawford 1992b; Barnes 1993a: 91). As will be demonstrated, evidence does indeed point to the existence of cultivation at certain times during the Jomon, but it is argued that at present these data are insufficient to suggest the nature and economic importance of plant husbandry activities.

Although the main focus of this chapter is on the Tohoku region (Figure 9.1), it is instructive to summarize briefly the evidence for Jomon domesticates throughout Japan, and ideas concerning the possibility of associated plant husbandry practices. This review is by no means exhaustive, but it will serve to indicate the extent to which existing archaeobotanical evidence bears on the question of Jomon cultivation. Most cultigens appearing during the Jomon originated on the East Asian mainland, or at least have their primary centres of diversity in that region (Zeven and de Wet 1982). Given other general indications of continental influences on Jomon culture (e.g. Groot 1951; Chard 1974; Sample 1978), the presence of these domesticates throughout much of the Japanese archipelago may constitute additional evidence of contact with the mainland.

The earliest domesticated plants date to the Initial Jomon (Figure 9.2), and consist of one seed each of bottle gourd (*Lagenaria siceraria*) and *shiso* (*Perilla frutescens* var. *crispa*) at the waterlogged Torihama Shell Mound, Fukui. However, it is during the following Early Jomon that evidence for several domesticates is present throughout much of Japan. In addition, this period is characterized by the development of increased sedentism and substantial village settlements (Ikawa–Smith 1980; Nishida 1983). A growing number of plant remains recovered from Early Jomon sites suggests that forms of subsistence in addition to hunting, fishing and plant collecting were practised at that time. Deposits at Torihama have produced remains of bottle gourd, adzuki (*Vigna angularis* var. *angularis*), *shiso*, egoma (*P. frutescens* var. *japonica*), paper mulberry (*Broussonetia papyrifera*), great burdock (*Arctium lappa*), and hemp (*Cannabis sativa*) (Okamoto 1979, 1983). The identifications of adzuki and bottle gourd, however, have been questioned (Akazawa 1982; Crawford 1992a). Minamiki *et al.* (1986, in Crawford 1992a) report the finding of peach stones (*Prunus persica*) at the Ikiriki site, Nagasaki, dating from 5660 ± 90 BP to 5950 ± 30 BP. At the Otsubo site, Chiba, seeds and rind fragments of bottle gourd are known from Early Jomon levels (Kokawa 1978).

The Hamanasuno site in Minamikayabe, south-western Hokkaido, has produced one buckwheat achene (Crawford *et al.* 1976). The presence of this Early Jomon domesticate is further indicated by the recovery of buckwheat pollen dating to 6600 ± 75 BP at Ubuka Bog, Yamaguchi (Tsukada *et al.* 1986). This cultigen is not native to Japan, and Tsukada (1986: 44) contends that it was imported from the Yunnan Plateau of China which he suggests is a centre of buckwheat domestication. Other sources note that buckwheat originated in temperate Asia, and its probable wild ancestor, *Fagopyrum cymosum*, is native to northern India and China (Campbell 1976). In addition, Tsukada *et al.* (1986) suggest that swidden horticulture is evidenced by the nature of charcoal fragments recovered in the Ubuka Bog pollen cores. Although these fragments could equally suggest clearance for other purposes (Barnes 1986), the existence of swidden is not unreasonable given the occurrence of cultigens during this and subsequent periods. Recently, Okada (1995) has announced the recovery of several domesticates from Early–Middle Jomon (5500–4000 BP) levels at the Sannai Maruyama site in Aomori City, Aomori. Preliminary reports indicate the presence of a planned village with ceremonial platforms supporting as many as 500 people. Crop plants recovered include barnyard millet (*Echinochloa utilis*), great burdock, gourd, *egoma*, and beans. Okada (1995) suggests the site was occupied by sedentary, horticultural populations.

The existence of agriculture in the Middle Jomon has generated considerable discussion, but, unfortunately, little in the way of archaeobotanical material is available to support the models that have been proposed. Several hypotheses are based on archaeological evidence from the Chubu district of central Honshu which indicates a marked phase of cultural fluorescence during the Middle Jomon. Populations inhabiting large villages in this region are postulated to have developed agricultural systems based on nuts (e.g. Esaka 1959; Sakazume 1959, 1961; Ueyama 1969; Ueyama *et al.* 1976; Fujimori 1970; Nishida 1983), yam, taro and other crops (e.g. Esaka 1959; Nakao 1966, 1967; Kamikawana 1968; Sasaki 1971; Turner 1979). Several of these models have been discussed elsewhere (D'Andrea 1992).

Unequivocal evidence for domesticated plants in the Middle Jomon is known from central and north-eastern Japan. The charred Idojiri 'cakes' recovered from sites in Nagano, Gifu, and Fukushima initially were thought to have been made from starchy plant sources, including millet, barnyard millet, taro, rice, oats, and nuts (Kidder 1968: 25; Ikawa-Smith 1980). Matsutani (1983) identifies *shiso* as a major component of the cakes. In addition, Crawford (1983) suggests the possibility of Early and Middle Jomon gardening based on evidence from the Hamanasuno and Usujiri B sites in south-western Hokkaido. At these localities, the grain size of barnyard grass (*Echinochloa crus-gali*) is shown to increase steadily over a 4,000 year period. It is suggested that this species was cultivated by Middle Jomon occupants of Hamanasuno. Barnyard grass is the wild ancestor of Japanese barnyard millet (Yabuno 1966: 320–1), and is the only species postulated to have been a prehistoric indigenous Japanese domesticate (Crawford 1983, 1992b). Additional evidence for Middle Jomon cultigens comes from Usujiri B, where foxtail (*Setaria italica* ssp. *italica*) and Japanese barnyard millet have been identified (Crawford 1992b). The importance of anthropogenic environments to these populations is outlined by Crawford who suggests that disturbed habitats may be the result of activities associated with forest clearance (Crawford 1992b, 1997).

It is during the Late and Final Jomon periods that rice (*Oryza sativa* var. *japonica*) and barley (*Hordeum vulgare*) are added to the list of cultigens present throughout Japan. At the Kuwagaishimo site in Fukui, remains of charred rice, barley, and adzuki were recovered from Late Jomon deposits (Tsunoda and Watanabe 1976). Rice has been reported from Late to Final Jomon sites in Kyushu, such as Nabatake (Kasahara 1982, 1984), Uenoharu (Kotani 1972), and several other localities (for reviews see Hudson 1990; Crawford 1992b). The Uenoharu remains consist of rice grains and phytoliths and one barley caryopsis. Rice phytoliths are known from other Late Jomon sites in north-western Kyushu, and the earliest known rice pollen dates to 3200 BP at Itatsuke (Tsukada 1986). In the north-east, the evidence for Late Jomon cultigens comes from the Kyunenbashi site, Iwate, where Yamada (1980) reports the presence of buckwheat pollen. In addition, rice, barnyard and foxtail millet have been recovered from the Kazahari site in south-eastern

Aomori. Two rice grains were dated by AMS (Accelerator Mass Spec-trometry) to 2540 ± 240 BP and 2810 ± 270 BP (Kudo and D'Andrea 1991; D'Andrea et al. 1995). The presence of rice in northern Tohoku during this period has fostered a reconsideration of models dealing with processes of rice dispersals into north-eastern Japan. In particular, the Kazahari data indicate that the arrival of rice as a domesticate and Yayoi wet-rice paddy technology represent two separate events (D'Andrea 1992, 1995b; D'Andrea et al. 1995).

Wet-rice cultivation was established in Tohoku by Final Jomon times, contemporary with the Early Yayoi of south-western Japan (Figure 9.2). At Kamegaoka and other sites in Aomori, rice remains are associated with Final Jomon Obora A ceramics (Sato 1984). It has been suggested that a precocious variety of rice was introduced directly to Tohoku from Kyushu via the Japan Sea (Hoshikawa 1984). At the Sunazawa site, Aomori, extensive rice paddy fields contemporary with the Early Yayoi have been recovered. In addition, Ongagawa type pottery and other Yayoi artefacts, such as glass beads, are known from Sunazawa and other Sunazawa phase sites in Aomori (Murakoshi 1988). Although Tohoku Final Jomon rice was often interpreted as a trade item obtained from south-western Yayoi populations (Ikawa-Smith 1988), the discovery of the Sunazawa rice paddies (Suzuki 1986; Murakoshi 1988) demonstrates that rice was being cultivated in Aomori during the Early Yayoi.

In addition to rice, other Final Jomon cultigens include barley from Uenoharu and bottle gourd from Itatsuke and Shimpukuji in Kyushu. Buckwheat pollen has been recovered from the Kasori site and other localities along Tokyo Bay, dating to ca. 2800 BP, and by 1500 BP, the quantities increase markedly (Tsukada 1986). At Kamegaoka, palynological data also indicate the presence of Final Jomon buckwheat (Yamanoi and Sato 1984). Several cultigens have been identified at Nabatake: one foxtail millet grain (2680 ± 80 BP), twenty-two shiso seeds (3330–2500 BP), and two rice grains (2620 ± 60 BP – 3230 ± 100 BP) (Kasahara 1982, 1984). In addition, mung beans (Vigna radiatus var. radiatus) have been reported in Final Jomon levels at Nabatake (Watanabe and Kokawa 1982).

A north–south dichotomy in Tohoku ceramic chronology is evident at the end of the Final Jomon, and this continued into the subsequent Tohoku Yayoi. The southern Tohoku sequence seems to have been more heavily influenced by south-western Yayoi cultures, while northern groups main-tained local Jomon ceramic styles (Itoh 1966; Crawford and Takamiya 1990). It was initially believed that Yayoi populations did not penetrate northern Tohoku, and cultures represented there were referred to as Zoku-Jomon (or continuing Jomon) (Katoh and Suto 1986). However, in 1984, Itoh suggested the presence of a Yayoi period in Tohoku based on his observation that pottery from the Inakadate site, Aomori, was more similar to south-western Yayoi ceramics than to local Obora forms. Most archaeologists did not believe in the existence of late prehistoric wet-rice farming in Tohoku until rice paddy fields at Tareyanagi were dated to the first century AD, contemporary with the Middle Yayoi of south-western Japan (Itoh 1984; Kuraku 1984; Katoh and Suto 1986). Rice paddies also are known in southern Tohoku such as those recovered at the Tomizawa site in Miyagi (Crawford and Takamiya 1990). There is evidence that crops in addition to rice were grown by Final Jomon–Tohoku Yayoi populations. Phytoliths of a *Panicum* species, possibly broomcorn millet, have been identified at the Babano II site in Iwate (Itoh 1984). Also, pithouse contexts at Kazahari have produced substantial quantities of rice, in addition to hemp (*Cannabis sativa*), broomcorn and foxtail millet (D'Andrea 1992, 1995b).

Although outside the time frame of the Jomon, the Ezo period farming system of south-western Hokkaido is worthy of mention in the context of north-eastern Japanese agricultural development (Figure 9.2). Many of the traditional views of agricultural dispersals to the north-east were thrown into question with the discovery of a ninth century AD millet-based dryland agricultural complex in south-western Hokkaido at the Sakushu-Kotoni River site (Crawford 1986). The Sakushu-Kotoni archaeobotanical evidence points to the presence of intensive dry field agriculture in this region, practised by Ezo populations who are considered the immediate ancestors of the ethnohistorically known Ainu (Crawford and Yoshizaki 1987; Crawford and Takamiya 1990). At present, the origin and development of this millet-based farming system have not been established; however, routes of introduction directly to Hokkaido from the north Asian mainland (e.g. Katoh 1986; Kuzmin *et al.* 1994) and from Tohoku (Hayashi 1969; Crawford and Yoshizaki 1987) have been proposed. Recent discussions of this problem have emphasized the likelihood of several introductions of domesticated plants to Hokkaido from both Asian and Tohoku area sources (cf. Yamada and Tsubakisaka 1995).

NEW DIRECTIONS IN THE STUDY OF JOMON SUBSISTENCE

As evidence mounts in support of Jomon cultivation, several workers have developed models to explain the origin and development of these plant husbandry activities. Previous explanations, such as those given by Ueyama *et al.* (1976) and others, suggest that the development of horticulture was a conscious response by Jomon populations to the resource-poor broad-leaved forest regions of south-western Japan. More innovative models emphasizing socioeconomic factors have been proposed (e.g. Aikens 1981; Hayden 1990), but their applicability is hampered because of difficulties in establishing correlations between social complexity and the appearance of the earliest domesticates. As is pointed out by Crawford (1992b), the earliest cultigens in Japan predate evidence for social complexity. Others have emphasized the role of ecology and anthropogenesis in the development of Jomon plant husbandry. They view Jomon populations as active agents in the generation of disturbed environments upon which they became increasingly dependent

(Crawford 1983, 1992b, 1997; Nishida 1983). In this regard, the study of archaeobotanical weed seed assemblages from several sites in north-eastern Japan has indicated that compared to earlier periods anthropogenic environments from the Early to Late Jomon were more widespread. Furthermore, these weed assemblages comprise species that differ from later periods when wet-rice paddy cultivation was practised. These anthropogenic communities are thought to be the result of ecological disruption associated with sedentary village life and related activities, which may have included gardening (Crawford 1997).

Perhaps the key to explaining the development of Jomon plant husbandry lies in first obtaining a clearer understanding of the nature of these practices, and then viewing their evolution within the context of Far Eastern agricultural history. A first step towards this goal would involve undertaking more archaeobotanical sampling in the north-east, in addition to re-examining other categories of archaeological evidence, such as settlement and seasonality/scheduling patterns. The relationship between increased sedentism and the appearance of several domesticates during the Early Jomon should be further investigated. This kind of work may serve to demonstrate how plant husbandry could be successfully integrated into established Jomon foraging subsistence patterns. The question of whether Kazahari Late Jomon and other contemporary northern groups were cultivating crops or acquiring them through exchange remains open (D'Andrea 1992, 1995b). Although irrigation works were present in contemporary China (Ho 1977; Chang 1983) this technology is not evident in north-eastern Japan until the Sunazawa phase, contemporary with the Early Yayoi (Murakoshi 1988). Based on ecological and historical data, it has been argued that some form of cultivation was possible, such as non-irrigated swamp cultivation or swidden (D'Andrea 1995b; D'Andrea et al. 1995). Several methods of rice growing have been described in the ethnographic literature, many of which do not require irrigation (e.g. Lambert 1985). In addition, Fujiwara (1993) has reported sizable yields of rice produced on experimental non-irrigated swidden plots in the mountains of Kyushu. His research on phytoliths indicates that swidden cultivation of rice in Miyazaki was practised until 1945 (Fujiwara et al. 1985). This approach, in addition to palynology, holds much promise for the identification of ancient swidden fields.

The East Asian evidence points to the existence of two distinct prehistoric agricultural complexes, dryland millet farming in the north (6500–5000 cal. BC) that predates wet-rice agriculture in the south (5000 cal. BC) (Chang 1986, 1989; Crawford 1992a). Based on recent AMS dates from Primorye, in the Russian Far East, it has been proposed that following its origin in northern China, millet agriculture diffused to Korea, Primorye and Japan sometime during the fourth and third millennia BC (Kuzmin et al. 1994; Kuzmin pers. comm.). Although the earliest unequivocal evidence for a millet-based agricultural complex in Japan dates to the ninth century AD Ezo period (Crawford and Yoshizaki 1987), the origin of this system may be related to a temperate north-east Asian farming adaptation based on the cultivation of small seeded cereals, such as millets, and other dry field crops (D'Andrea 1992, 1995b). The Early to Middle Jomon suite of domesticates, including buckwheat, barnyard millet and other crops, seems to mirror this continental pattern, but more evidence is needed to establish links between northern Asian mainland and Japanese farming traditions.

The spread of cultigens into Japan prior to the Yayoi perhaps should be viewed as a fluid process, with species arriving at various times beginning by the Early Jomon, and incorporated into small-scale gardens or horticultural fields. These dispersals also included rice by Late Jomon times. The new resources may not have caused major socioeconomic disruption of Jomon foraging patterns, but may have inspired the cultivation of local herbaceous plants, such as barnyard grass (Crawford 1992b). Whether the route was overland from Kyushu or directly from the mainland via sea traffic (e.g., Im 1995), however, remains to be established. Assuming the dispersals were overland, their progression does not seem to have been significantly slowed by cultural or ecological factors.

The Jomon case may have some general similarity to that observed in the prehistoric American Southwest. Minnis (1992) has argued that the introduction of Mesoamerican domesticates to Late Archaic populations of the south-western United States did not result in major changes in economy or sociocultural frameworks. Instead he suggests that plant cultivation was integrated into the pre-existing seasonal scheduling of subsistence activities, and eventually it led to substantial increases in resource productivity. When first adopted, maize was probably grown in small garden plots, and it was not until at least a thousand years following the Late Archaic introduction of domesticates that irrigated field agriculture grew to dominate subsistence systems. Several introduced crops, such as maize, gourds, squashes, and beans, do not require constant attention, and as such Minnis argues that the 'casual cultivation' of these plants can produce adequate yields. In support of this position, he cites eighteenth- and nineteenth-century accounts of Apache populations who planted maize fields in the late spring, and leaving them for the most part untended, returned to harvest in the autumn (Minnis 1992).

Several of the earliest Jomon domesticates, particularly millets, do not require intensive tending to produce respectable yields. Foxtail, broomcorn and Japanese barnyard millet can tolerate extreme ranges in environmental conditions, and the latter two may have the lowest water requirements of any cultivated cereal. These species are well adapted to both semi-arid and high altitude conditions with low precipitation and poor soils. Foxtail millet is not as tolerant to drought, but it can survive a wide range of soil conditions (Purseglove 1972; Simmonds 1976; Chang 1983). Purseglove (1972: 199) also points out that broomcorn millet was often cultivated by 'nomads' because of its ability to mature very quickly, sometimes within six weeks. Other millets also mature in a short period of time, and in general these species require less tending than many cereals (Chang 1983). Although there is not universal agreement on the view of agricultural origins in the American Southwest presented by Minnis (cf. Wills 1990), and the culture and ecology of the south-western United States is not directly comparable to that obtaining in prehistoric Japan, the American example may be of heuristic value in the development of new models of Jomon subsistence.

The introduction of wet-rice paddy farming dominates the literature dealing with the Final Jomon and the Jomon–Yayoi transition, and the significance of other cultigens, such as barley and millets, is often ignored (for exceptions see Hudson 1990; Crawford 1992a). Yayoi culture represents an incursion of populations from the Asian mainland, who introduced wet-paddy farming as well as several other technological innovations (e.g. Hanihara 1990, 1991; Brace *et al.* 1989). The spread of wet-rice farming was thought to have taken place in two stages (e.g., Kanaseki and Sahara 1978; Akazawa 1981, 1982; Aikens and Higuchi 1982). The first dispersal was apparently rapid, going from northern Kyushu to western Tokai in the space of a few hundred years. It was believed that rice farming cultures did not penetrate northern Tohoku until a second phase of expansion, contemporary with the Middle Yayoi of south-western Japan (Minato 1977; Kanaseki and Sahara 1978). It was further proposed that rice cultivation in the south-west diffused along coastal areas, but that in the north-east it moved inland because marine-oriented coastal foragers, with their stable fishing and hunting way of life, resisted the shift to farming (Kanaseki and Sahara 1978; Akazawa 1981, 1982). Rice agriculture supposedly did not arrive in Hokkaido until the nineteenth century when the Japanese state encouraged the Ainu to undertake farming (Watanabe 1972).

The two-stage model explaining the spread of Yayoi cultural elements (e.g. Kanaseki and Sahara 1978; Akazawa 1981, 1982) has been reconsidered in light of recent evidence. New perspectives on the Jomon–Yayoi transition emphasize that the transformation in Kyushu took somewhat longer than was previously thought. Furthermore, it is now believed that the subsequent spread of rice agriculture to the north-east occurred more quickly than was proposed in the two-stage model (Murakoshi 1988; Crawford 1992b; Barnes 1993b; D'Andrea 1995b). In the south-west, at least 1,000 years separates the initial appearance of rice and the initiation of intensive farming practices (Hudson 1990). Although rice is present in Kyushu by Late Jomon times, paddy fields appear during the following Final Jomon, at sites such as Itatsuke. These early paddies are located in low-lying areas, and consist of mud ridges and ditches designed for drainage control (Higuchi 1986). Fully developed irrigation was not in evidence until the Middle Yayoi, when it may have been introduced from northern China, together with Chinese mirrors and iron weapons (Kanaseki 1986). The period between the first introduction of rice farming and the beginning of the Early Yayoi (300 cal. BC) has been referred to as the Initial Yayoi (Hudson 1990).

Several workers have proposed viable alternatives to the two-stage model, which has been characterized by Hudson (1990) as a 'wave of advance' model. He suggests that concepts of forager–farmer interaction (cf. Crawford and Takamiya 1990) have more relevance in understanding the Jomon–Yayoi transition (Hudson 1990). Following on this theme, Barnes (1993b) finds Dennell's (1985) 'imitation' model useful in explaining the introduction of rice farming to south-western Japan. This process involved imitation and adoption of new technologies by Kyushu Jomon populations from a variety of sources, where the relationship between recipients and donors was rather distant. Evidence in support of this view includes the intensification of food production on the part of local groups, a long-distance exchange of technology where agriculture is one of the earliest transmissions, and the lack of a clear demarcation between Final Jomon and Initial Yayoi cultures (Barnes 1993b: 184). Barnes has further suggested that the spread of Yayoi cultural elements, including wet-rice farming, out of northern Kyushu was a complex process involving both migrations and diffusion (1993b: 184–5). This is attested to by the high degree of variability in archaeological assemblages of south-western Japan, especially in the Osaka Bay area, where there is evidence for the coexistence of Jomon and Yayoi cultures.

The apparent cultural dichotomy between south-western/central Japan and northern Tohoku suggests that the spread of Yayoi culture and technology to the north-east was more a function of acculturation than colonization, as was the case in south-western Japan. This is evidenced by the persistence of Jomon cultural elements well into the Tohoku Yayoi period (Crawford and Takamiya 1990). Although the processes by which rice-paddy farming was adopted by north-eastern Jomon groups remain to be understood, evidence indicates that the technology arrived relatively quickly (e.g. Murakoshi 1988). This suggests that the dispersal of wet-paddy techniques was facilitated by Jomon sedentary lifestyles, which may have included the swidden cultivation of rice, millets and other crops. As such, these conditions could have produced a cultural milieu that was receptive to the adoption of new agricultural technologies.

CONCLUSION

The Jomon period presents several intriguing problems concerning the origins of East Asian plant husbandry. Over the past several years, archaeobotanical research in north-eastern Japan has demonstrated the presence of buckwheat, millets, rice and several other domesticates in Jomon contexts. It has been shown that buckwheat and millets occur by the Early Jomon, while rice, barley, and other millets appear by the Late Jomon. Subsistence interpretations based on archaeobotanical studies in all areas have been plagued by small sample sizes from too few sites. Although it is now generally accepted that plant cultivation was a component of Jomon subsistence prior to the arrival of Yayoi wet-paddy technology, the nature of these plant husbandry practices remains to be elucidated. It is precisely this kind of basic issue that needs to be addressed before examining questions relating to the economic importance of these activities. It does appear, however, that dispersals of rice and other cultigens during the Jomon were not substantially delayed by cultural or ecological factors, and once introduced, the cultivation of these plants may not have instigated substantial cultural change. Moreover, various aspects of Jomon lifeways, such as sedentism and horticulture, could have acted to facilitate the later introduction of Yayoi wet-rice paddy farming.

ACKNOWLEDGEMENTS

I would like to thank the participants of a graduate seminar on the Origins of Agriculture held at the Department of Archaeology, Simon Fraser University in 1994, during which some of the issues discussed in this chapter were raised: Bob Muir, Mike Clark, Dave Schaepe and John Wolf. Many thanks to both Gary Crawford and Larry Pavlish of the University of Toronto who provided useful criticisms of various drafts of this chapter.

REFERENCES

Aikens, C.M. 1981. The last 10,000 years in Japan and eastern North America: parallels in environment, economic adaptation, growth of societal complexity, and the adoption of agriculture. In *Affluent Foragers*, S. Koyama and D.H. Thomas (eds), 261–73. Osaka: National Museum of Ethnology, Senri Ethnological Studies No. 9.

Aikens, C.M. and T. Higuchi. 1982. *Prehistory of Japan*. New York: Academic Press.

Akazawa, T. 1981. Maritime adaptation of prehistoric hunter-gatherers and their transition to agriculture in Japan. In *Affluent Foragers*, S. Koyama and D.H. Thomas (eds), 213–60. Osaka: National Museum of Ethnology, Senri Ethnological Studies No. 9.

Akazawa, T. 1982. Cultural change in prehistoric Japan: receptivity to rice agriculture in the Japanese archipelago. In *Advances in World Archaeology* Volume 1, F. Wendorf and A.E. Close (eds), 151–211. New York: Academic Press.

Akazawa, T. 1986a. Hunter-gatherer adaptations and the transition to food production in Japan. In *Hunters in Transition*, M. Zvelebil (ed.), 151–66. Cambridge: Cambridge University Press.

Akazawa, T. 1986b. Regional variation in seasonal procurement systems of Jomon hunter-gatherers. In *Prehistoric Hunter-Gatherers in Japan: new research methods*, T. Akazawa and C.M. Aikens (eds), 73–89. The University Museum, University of Tokyo, Bulletin No. 27.

Ammerman, A.J. and L.L. Cavalli-Sforza. 1973. A population model for the diffusion of early farming in Europe. In *The Explanation of Culture Change*, A.C. Renfrew (ed.), 343–59. London: Duckworth.

Ammerman, A.J. and L.L. Cavalli-Sforza. 1984. *The Neolithic Transition and the Genetics of Population in Europe*. Princeton: Princeton University Press.

Barnes, G.L. 1986. Japanese agricultural beginnings. *Nature* 322, 595–6.

Barnes, G.L. 1993a. *China, Korea and Japan*. London: Thames and Hudson.

Barnes, G.L. 1993b. Miwa occupation in wider perspective. In *The Miwa Project*, G.L. Barnes and M. Okita (eds), 181–92. Oxford: BAR.

Blumler, M.A. and R. Byrne. 1991. The ecological genetics of domestication and the origins of agriculture. *Current Anthropology* 32, 23–61.

Brace, C.L., M.L. Brace and W.R. Leonard. 1989. Reflections on the face of Japan: a multivariate craniofacial and odontometric perspective. *American Journal of Physical Anthropology* 78, 93–113.

Campbell, C.G. 1976. Buckwheat. In *Evolution of Crop Plants*, N.W. Simmonds (ed.), 235–7. London: Longman.

Chang, K.C. 1986. *The Archaeology of Ancient China*. New Haven: Yale University Press.

Chang, T.-T. 1976. The origin, evolution, cultivation, dissemination, and diversification of Asian and African rices. *Euphytica* 25, 425–41.

Chang, T.-T. 1983. The origins and early cultures of the cereal grains and food legumes. In *The Origins of Chinese Civilization*, D.N. Keightley (ed.), 65–94. Berkeley: University of California Press.

Chang, T.-T. 1989. Domestication and the spread of cultivated rices. In *Foraging and Farming*, D.R. Harris and G.C. Hillman (eds), 408–17. London: Unwin Hyman.

Chard, C.S. 1974. *Northeast Asia in Prehistory*. Madison: University of Wisconsin Press.

Cohen, M.N. 1977. *The Food Crisis in Prehistory*. New Haven: Yale University Press.

Cowan, C.W. and P.J. Watson (eds). 1992. The *Origins of Agriculture: an international perspective*. Washington, D.C.: Smithsonian Institution Press.

Crawford, G.W. 1983. *Paleoethnobotany of the Kameda Peninsula Jomon*. Ann Arbor: Museum of Anthropology, University of Michigan, Anthropological Papers No. 73.

Crawford, G.W. 1986. The Sakushu-Kotoni River site: the Ezo-Haji component plant remains. In *Sakushu-Kotoni Gawa Iseki* [*The Sakushu-Kotoni River Site*], Hokkaido Daigaku (ed.), 146–58. Sapporo: Hokkaido Daigaku Bungakubu.

Crawford, G.W. 1992a. Prehistoric plant domestication in east Asia: the Japanese perspective. In *Agricultural Origins in World Perspective*, P.J. Watson and C.W. Cowan, (eds), 7–38. Washington, D.C.: Smithsonian Institution Publications in Anthropology.

Crawford, G.W. 1992b. The transitions to agriculture in Japan. In *The Transitions to Agriculture*, A.B. Gebauer and T.D. Price (eds), 117–32. Madison: Prehistory Press.

Crawford, G.W. 1997. Anthropogenesis in Prehistoric Northeastern Japan. In *People, Plants, and Landscapes: studies in palaeoethnobotany*, K.J. Gremillion (ed.), 86–103. Tuscaloosa: University of Alabama Press.

Crawford, G.W. and H. Takamiya. 1990. The origins and implications of late prehistoric plant husbandry in northern Japan. *Antiquity* 64, 889–911.

Crawford, G.W. and M. Yoshizaki. 1987. Ainu ancestors and early Asian agriculture. *Journal of Archaeological Science* 14, 201–13.

Crawford, G.W., W.M. Hurley and M. Yoshizaki. 1976. Implications of plant remains from the Early Jomon Hamanasuno site. *Asian Perspectives* 19, 145–53.

D'Andrea, A.C. 1992. Palaeoethnobotany of Later Jomon and Yayoi cultures of northeastern Japan: northeastern Aomori and southwestern Hokkaido. Ann Arbor, Mich.: University Microfilms International.

D'Andrea, A.C. 1995a. Archaeobotanical evidence for Zoku-Jomon subsistence at the Mochiyazawa site, Hokkaido, Japan. *Journal of Archaeological Science* 22, 583–95.

D'Andrea, A.C. 1995b. Later Jomon subsistence in northeastern Japan: new evidence from palaeoethnobotanical studies. *Asian Perspectives* 34, 195–227.

D'Andrea, A.C., G.W. Crawford, M. Yoshizaki and T. Kudo. 1995. Late Jomon cultigens in northeastern Japan. *Antiquity* 69, 146–52.

Dennell, R.W. 1985. The hunter-gatherer/agricultural frontier in prehistoric temperate Europe. In *The Archaeology of Frontiers and Boundaries*, S.W. Green and S.M. Perlman (eds), 113–39. London: Academic Press.

Esaka, T. 1959. *Jomon bunka no jidai ni okeru shokubutsu saibai kigen no mondai ni kansuru ichikosatsu* [On the problems of the origin of plant cultivation in the Jomon period culture]. *Kokogaku Zasshi* 44, 10–16.

Fujimori, E. 1963. Theory of Jomon agriculture and its development. *Kokogaku Kenkyu* 10, 21–33.

Fujimori, E. 1970. *Jomon Agriculture.* Tokyo: Gakuseisha.

Fujiwara, H. 1993. Research into the history of rice cultivation using plant opal analysis. In *Current Research in Phytolith Analysis: applications in archaeology and palaeoecology*, D.M. Pearsall and D.R. Piperino. (eds), 147–59. Philadelphia: MASCA, University Museum of Archaeology and Anthropology, University of Pennsylvania.

Fujiwara, H., A. Sasaki and S. Sugiyama. 1985. Fundamental studies of plant opal analysis (6). *Archaeology and Natural Science* 18, 111.

Gebauer, A.B. and T.D. Price (eds). 1992. *Transitions to Agriculture in Prehistory.* Madison, Wis.: Prehistory Press.

Gregg, S.A. 1988. *Foragers and Farmers.* Chicago: Chicago University Press.

Groot, G.J. 1951. *The Prehistory of Japan.* New York: Columbia University Press.

Hanihara, K. 1990. *Emishi*, Ezo and Ainu: an anthropological perspective. *Japan Review* 1, 35–48.

Hanihara, K. 1991. Dual structure model for the population history of the Japanese. *Japan Review* 2, 1–33.

Harris, D.R. and G.C. Hillman (eds). 1989. *Foraging and Farming.* London: Unwin Hyman.

Hayashi, Y. 1969. Ainu no noko bunka [Ainu Agriculture]. Tokyo: Keiyusha.

Hayden, B. 1990. Nimrods, piscators, pluckers, and planters: the emergence of food production. *Journal of Anthropological Archaeology* 9, 31–69.

Higuchi, T. 1986. Relationships between Japan and Asia in ancient times. In *Windows on the Japanese Past*, R.J. Pearson (ed.), 121–6. Ann Arbor: Center for Japanese Studies, University of Michigan.

Hillman, G.C. and M.S. Davies. 1990. Measured domestication rates in wild wheats and barley under primitive cultivation and their archaeological implications. *Journal of World Prehistory* 4, 157–222.

Ho, P.-T. 1977. The indigenous origins of Chinese agriculture. In *Origins of Agriculture*, C.A. Reed (ed.), 411–84. Paris: Mouton.

Hoshikawa, K. 1984. *Wagakuni no kodai inasaku ni tsuite no sakumotsu gaku teki na kansatsu to ni, san no jikken* [A few experiments and observations on our ancient rice agriculture.] In *Kobunkazai no Shizen Kagakuteki Kenkyu* [*National Scientific Research of Antiquities*], Kobunkazai Henshu-Iinkai (ed.), 611–16. Tokyo: Dotosha.

Hudson, M. 1990. From Toro to Yoshinogari: changing perspectives on Yayoi archaeology. In *Hoabinhian, Jomon, Yayoi, Early Korean States*, G.L. Barnes (ed.), 63–112. Oxford: Oxbow Books.

Ikawa-Smith, F. 1980. Current issues in Japanese archaeology. *American Scientist* 68, 134–45.

Ikawa-Smith, F. 1988. The Kamegaoka social networks. Paper presented to the Symposium on Approaches to Japanese Archaeology at the Fifty-Third Annual Meeting of the Society for American Archaeology, Phoenix, Arizona, April 1988.

Im, H.-J. 1995. *Korea Newsreview* 10 September–8 October.

Itoh, G. 1966. *Tohoku.* In *Yayoi Jidai* [*The Yayoi Period*], S. Wajima (ed.), 203–20. Tokyo: Kawaide Shobo.

Itoh, N. 1984. *Aomori-ken ni okeru inasaku noko-bunka no keisei* [The development of rice agriculture in Aomori prefecture]. In *Hoppo Nihon Bunka no Kenkyu* [*Study of Northern Cultures of Japan*], T. Katoh (ed.), 1–26. Sendai: Tohokugakuin Daigaku Tohoku Bunka Kenkyusha.

Kamikawana, A. 1968. Sites in Middle Yamanashi-ken and Middle Jomon agriculture. *Asian Perspectives* 11, 53–68.

Kanaseki, H. 1986. The evidence for social change between the Early and Middle Yayoi. In *Windows on the Japanese Past*, R.J Pearson (ed.), 317–34. Ann Arbor: Center for Japanese Studies, University of Michigan.

Kanaseki, H. and M. Sahara. 1978. The Yayoi Period. *Asian Perspectives* 19, 15–26.

Kasahara, Y. 1982. *Nabatake iseki no maizo shushi no bunseki dotei kenkyu* [Analysis and identification of ancient seeds from the Nabatake site]. In *Nabatake*, Tosu-shi Kyoiku Iinkai (ed.), 354–79. Tosu-shi: Tosu-shi Kyoiku Iinkai.

Kasahara, Y. 1984. *Maizo Shushi Bunseki ni Yoru Kodai Noko no Kensho (2) – Nabatake iseki no sakumotsu to zasso no shurui o yobi to rai keiro* [Examination of ancient agriculture from the perspective of archaeological seed analysis (2) – species and routes of introduction of crops and weeds at the Nabatake site]. In *Kobunkazai no Shizen-Kagakuteki Kenkyu*, Kobunkazai-Henshu Iinkai (ed.), 617–29. Tokyo: Dotosha.

Katoh, M. and T. Suto. 1986. *Tohoku*. In *Iwanami Koza Nihon Kokogaku*, Y. Kondo (ed.), 155–97. Tokyo: Iwanami Shoten.

Katoh, S. 1986. *Siberia no Senshi noko to Nihon eno eikyo* [Prehistoric agriculture in Siberia and its influence on Japan]. In *Hatasku-bunka no tanjo* [The origin of dry field farming]. K. Sasaki and T. Matsuyama (eds), 215–35. Tokyo: Nihon Hoso Kyokai.

Kidder, J.E. 1968. Agriculture and ritual in the Middle Jomon. *Asian Perspectives* 11, 19–41.

Kokawa, S. 1978. Study of ancient life and environment based on plant remains. *Annual Report of Scientific Research on Antiquities for 1977*, 149–58.

Kotani, Y. 1972. Economic bases during the Later Jomon periods in Kyushu, Japan: a reconsideration. Ann Arbor, Mich: University Microfilms International.

Kotani, Y. 1981. Evidence of plant cultivation in Jomon Japan: some implications. In *Affluent Foragers*, S. Koyama and D.H. Thomas (eds), 201–12. Osaka: National Museum of Ethnology, Senri Ethnological Studies No. 9.

Kudo, T. and A.C. D'Andrea. 1991. An Accelerator Radiocarbon Date on Rice from the Kazahari Site. *Project Seeds News* 3, 5.

Kuraku, Y. 1984. *Tohoku chiho ni okeru kodai inasaku o saguru* [The search for ancient rice agriculture in the Tohoku region]. In *Kobunkazai no Shizen Kagakuteki Kenkyu* [*Natural Scientific Research of Antiquities*], Kobunkazai Henshu Iinkai (ed.), 603–10. Tokyo: Dotosha.

Kuzmin, Y.V., L.A. Orlova, L.D. Sulerzhitsky and A.J.T. Jull. 1994. Radiocarbon dating of stone and bronze age sites in Primorye (Russian Far East). *Radiocarbon* 36, 359–66.

Lambert, D.H. 1985. *Swamp Rice Farming*. Boulder, Colo.: Westview Press.

Matsutani, A. 1983. *Egoma-Shiso*. In *Jomon Bunka no Kenkyu* [*Research on the Jomon culture*], S. Katoh, T. Kobayashi and T. Fujimoto (eds), 50–62. Tokyo: Yuzankaku.

Minamiki, M., S. Nohjo, S. Kokawa, S. Kosugi and M. Suzuki. 1986. *Shokubutsu itai to kokankyo* [Plant remains and ancient environment]. In *Ikiriki Iseki* [*The Ikiriki Site*], Tarami-cho Kyoiku Iinkai (ed.), 44–53. Tarami-cho: Tarami-cho Kyoiku Iinkai.

Minato, M. 1977. *Japan and its Nature*. Tokyo: Heibonsha Ltd.

Minnis, P.E. 1992. Earliest plant cultivation in the desert borderlands of North America. In *Agricultural Origins in World Perspective*, P.J. Watson and C.W. Cowan (eds), 121–42. Washington D.C.: Smithsonian Institution Publications in Anthropology.

Murakoshi, K. 1988. *Sunazawa iseki* [The Sunazawa site]. In *Yayoi Bunka no Kenkyu* [*Research on the Yayoi culture*], H. Kanaseki and M. Sahara (eds), 211–13. Tokyo: Yuzankaku.

Nakao, S. 1966. *Saibai Shokubutsu to Noko no Kigen* [*Cultigens and the origin of agriculture*]. Tokyo: Iwanami Shinsho.

Nakao, S. 1967. Origins of agriculture. In *Natural History Ecological Studies: contributions in honour of Dr. Kinji Imanishi on the occasion of his sixtieth birthday*, M. Morishita and T. Kira (eds), 329–494. Tokyo: Chukoronsha.

Nishida, M. 1983. The emergence of food production in neolithic Japan. *Journal of Anthropological Archaeology* 2, 305–22.

Okada, Y. 1995. *Ento doki bunka no kyodai shuraku* [A large village of the Ento pottery culture]. *Kikan Kokogaku* 50, 25–30.

Okamoto, I. 1979. *Torihama Kaizuka* [*The Torihama shell mound*]. Fukui: Fukui Kyoiku Iinkai.

Okamoto, I. 1983. *Torihama Kaizuka* [*The Torihama shell mound*]. Fukui: Fukui Kyoiku Iinkai.

Purseglove, J.W. 1972. *Tropical Crops: Monocotyledons*. London: Longman.

Reed, C.A. (ed.). 1977. *Origins of Agriculture*. Paris: Mouton.

Rindos, D. 1984. *The Origins of Agriculture: an evolutionary perspective*. New York: Academic Press.

Rowley-Conwy, P. 1984. Postglacial foraging and early farming economies in Japan and Korea: a west European perspective. *World Archaeology* 16, 28–42.

Sakazume, N. 1959. A tentative theory on primitive agriculture in Japan. *Journal of the Archaeological Society of Nippon* 42, 1–12.

Sakazume, N. 1961. *Nihon Jomon Sekki Jidai Shokuryo Sosetsu* [*Complete description of food in neolithic Jomon Japan*]. Kyoto: Doyokai.

Sample, L.L. 1978. Prehistoric cultural relations between western Japan and southeastern Korea. *Asian Perspectives* 19, 172–5.

Sasaki, K. 1971. *Pre-Rice Cultivation*. Tokyo: N.H.K. Books (No. 147).

Sato, T. 1984. *Kamegaoka iseki Sawane chiku B-ku shutsudo no ine eika narabe ni tanka mairyu* [Rice caryopses and carbonized rice from the Kamegaoka site, Sawane Locality B]. In *Kamegaoka Iseki* [*The Kamegaoka site*], Aomori Kenritsu Kyodokan (ed.), 218–24. Aomori: Aomori Kenritsu Kyodokan, Archaeology Report 16.

Simmonds, N.W. 1976. Hemp. In *Evolution of Crop Plants*, N.W. Simmonds (ed.), 203–4. London: Longman.

Struever, S. 1971. *Prehistoric Agriculture*. New York: Natural History Press.

Suzuki, K. 1986. *Nihon no Kodai Iseki 29: Aomori* [*Ancient sites in Japan 29: Aomori*]. Tokyo: Hoikusha.

Tsukada, M. 1986. Vegetation in prehistoric Japan. In *Windows on the Japanese Past*, R.J. Pearson (ed.), 11–56. Ann Arbor: Center for Japanese Studies, University of Michigan.

Tsukada, M., Y. Tsukada and S. Sugita. 1986. Oldest primitive agriculture and vegetational environments in Japan. *Nature* 322, 632–4.

Tsunoda, B. and M. Watanabe. 1976. *Kuwagaishimo Iseki* [*The Kuwagaishimo site*]. Kyoto: Heian Hakubutsukan.

Turner, C.G., III. 1979. Dental anthropological indications of agriculture among the Jomon people of central Japan. *American Journal of Physical Anthropology* 51, 619–36.

Ucko, P.J. and G.W. Dimbleby (eds). 1969. *Domestication and Exploitation of Plants and Animals*. London: Duckworth.

Ueyama, S. (ed.). 1969. *Laurel Forest Culture*. Volume 1. Tokyo: Chukoronsha.

Ueyama, S., K. Sasaki and S. Nakao. 1976. *Laurel Forest Culture*. Volume 2. Tokyo: Chukoronsha.

Watanabe, H. 1972. *The Ainu Ecosystem*. Tokyo: University of Tokyo Press.

Watanabe, M. and S. Kokawa. 1982. *Nabatake Jomon Banki (Yamanotera-so) kara shutsudono tanka gobo, adzuki, egonoki to mitanka meron shushi no dotei* [Identification of carbonized *gobo*, adzuki, *egonoki*, and uncarbonized melon seeds from the Final Jomon (Yamanotera) level at Nabatake]. In *Nabatake*, Tosu-shi Kyoiku Iinkai (ed.), 447–54. Tosu-shi: Tosu-shi Kyoiku Iinkai.

Wills, W.H. 1990. Cultivating ideas: the changing intellectual history of the introduction of agriculture in the American Southwest. In *Perspectives on Southwestern Prehistory*, P. Minnis and C. Redman (eds), 319–22. Boulder, Colo.: Westview Press.

Wright, H.E. 1977. Environmental change and the origins of agriculture in the Old and New Worlds. In *Origins of Agriculture*, C.A. Reed (ed.), 281–320. Paris: Mouton.

Yabuno, T. 1966. Biosystematic study of the genus *Echinochloa*. *Japanese Journal of Botany* 19, 277–323.

Yamada, G. 1980. *Iwate-ken Kitakami-shi Kyunenbashi iseki no kafun bunseki ni tsuite* [Analysis of pollen from the Kyunenbashi site, Kitakami City, Iwate Prefecture]. In *Kyunenbashi Iseki [The Kyunenbashi site]*, Kitakami Board of Education (ed.), 63–75. Kitakami: Kitakami Bunkazai Chosa Hokoku.

Yamada, G. and Y. Tsubakisaka. 1995. Propagation of cultivated plants from the continent. In *Final Reports on Research Project of the Historical and Cultural Exchange of the North*, 107–34. Sapporo: Historical Museum of Hokkaido.

Yamanoi, T. and M. Sato. 1984. *Kamegaoka iseki no kafun bunseki* [Palynological research at the Kamegaoka site]. In *Kamegaoka Iseki [The Kamegaoka site]*, K. Suzuki (ed.), 189–99. Aomori City: Aomori Kenritsu Kyodoken.

Zeven, A.C. and J.M.J. de Wet. 1982. *Dictionary of Cultivated Plants and Their Regions of Diversity*. Wageningen: Centre for Agricultural Publishing and Documentation.

Zvelebil, M. (ed.). 1986. *Hunters in Transition*. Cambridge: Cambridge University Press.

10   Native Americans and animal husbandry in the North American colony of Spanish Florida

ELIZABETH J. REITZ

It is sometimes assumed that Native American subsistence strategies in North America rapidly incorporated European domestic animals and changed to accommodate European foodways. However, archaeozoological evidence for vertebrate use by Native Americans at North American proto-historic and historic sites indicates that domestic animals did not supplant traditional animals and were not adopted at all by some communities on the Atlantic coastal plain (Figure 10.1). There is also little evidence that changes occurred in other aspects of animal use. Those changes that did occur indicate these were shaped by previous indigenous experiences rather than by European models.

This survey is in some respects premature. Ideally groups of clearly prehistoric, proto-historic, and historic data should be compared. These terms encompass a continuum of increasingly frequent interaction from intermittent contact with explorers marked by the presence of a few trade items; occasional trading relationships through Native American intermediaries such as the Apalachee and Occaneechis, marked by more substantial trade goods; and finally direct contact with colonists marked by construction of forts, trading posts, and missions (Holm 1994: 15; Kelley 1994: 24; Jeter and Williams 1989: 171–2). In many locations this continuum ended with the demise of native peoples rather than their assimilation into colonial society. Hypothetically, however, animal use may have varied depending upon the intensity of interaction with colonists. Future work should attempt to estimate the degree of interaction between native communities and colonists.

Other important variables are also not considered below. Perhaps the most important of these is the extent to which the cultural traditions of both Native Americans and colonists influenced the degree and direction of subsistence change and continuity. While European colonies in North America are commonly referred to in terms of the nation in whose name the lands were claimed (i.e. Spain, The Netherlands, England, France), in reality colonists were of many nationalities. In the case of Spanish Florida, it is particularly important to recognize that some of the colonists were from

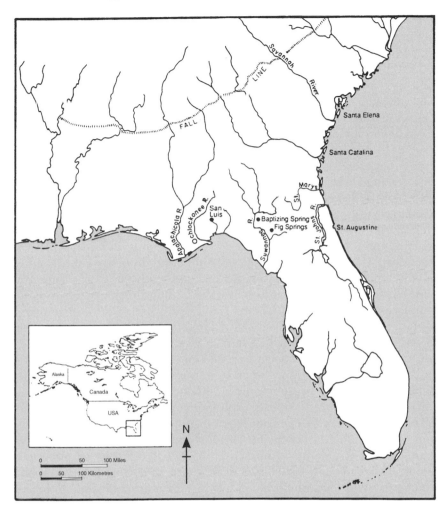

Figure 10.1 Map of Atlantic coastal plain, south-eastern United States

Africa. Much more research into this time period and the ethnicity of the colonists must be completed before such temporal and cultural variables can be controlled.

Most models of culture contact assume that Native Americans were rapidly assimilated into European traditions. However, in a recent test of this assumption, Kristen Gremillion (1993) found that Native Americans of the south-eastern interior of North America adopted few Euro-African food crops before the late eighteenth century. Only peach (*Prunus persica*) was widely accepted, although watermelon (*Citrullus vulgaris*) and cowpea (*Vigna unguiculata* ssp. *unguiculata*) were also adopted. These crops have cultivation requirements similar to traditional plants, have relatively high yields, and are less risky than other Euro-African crops. They could, therefore, be more easily incorporated into traditional cultivation patterns. They did not require new husbandry techniques and served as supplements to traditional foods. Gremillion concluded that traditional subsistence activities satisfied the needs of Native Americans. None of the Euro-African plants offered clear advantages such that they replaced traditional crops. Only those items which did not interfere with long-standing practices were adopted.

Even fewer domestic animals may have been accepted. When colonization began in the 1540s the only domestic animal Native Americans on the North American Atlantic coast had was the dog (*Canis familiaris*), an animal which required little or no care. When considering animal husbandry we must recognize that elsewhere in the world most other domestic animals exist in the context of plant cultivation, and that animal husbandry often conflicts with plant husbandry. A mixed economy with both domestic plants and animals requires careful management of the scheduling and energy demands of these two very distinct resources. Incorporating domestic animals into an economy which previously had experience only with domestic plants would require changes in schedules, land-use patterns, cultivation practices, use of wild resources, and the division of labour. Traditional patterns of both animal *and* plant use would have to be altered for domestic animals to be incorporated into south-eastern economies. Even without the addition of domestic animals, we might expect changes in wild animal use to be found only where such changes offered a distinct advantage in terms of time, effort and yield.

When colonization began in the 1540s, traditional European domestic animals were introduced. Archaeozoological evidence indicates that few of these were adopted by Native Americans during the two centuries of Spanish colonial rule. Biological reasons for this include climatic constraints, parasites and predators. These domestic animals probably had difficulty adapting to the subtropical climate and may have been quite rare. Social forces such as unfamiliarity with the techniques of animal husbandry and social dislocation associated with depopulation probably also restricted the adoption of introduced domestic animals by Native Americans.

In the following section, archaeozoological evidence for animal use by Native Americans at Spanish missions during the two centuries of Spanish colonial rule will be presented. A summary of the vertebrate faunal data from each of the regions of Spanish Florida will demonstrate that domestic livestock were not widely adopted by Native Americans living here except, perhaps, in Apalachee Province. The reasons for this will be elaborated. First, however, a brief history of the colony is given.

SPANISH FLORIDA

The data presented here are from a portion of the North American Atlantic coast known as Spanish Florida (Figure 10.1). Spanish Florida was a Spanish province founded in 1565 by Pedro Menéndez de Avilés, thus beginning the First Spanish Period. Originally Spain claimed all of North America south of Newfoundland and west of the Atlantic Ocean indefinitely (Gannon 1967: 1); however, the actual occupation was a strip along the Atlantic coast from Santa Elena southward to St. Augustine, and west across the north-central portion of peninsular Florida to the Apalachicola river. The real boundaries of Spanish Florida varied considerably throughout the First Spanish Period.

Spanish Florida remained under Spanish governance for two hundred years. Menéndez founded two towns, Santa Elena and St. Augustine, and established a series of fortifications. Many of the original fortifications, as well as Santa Elena, were abandoned by the end of the sixteenth century. This was in response to a variety of forces, including native resistance to Spanish intrusions, attacks by competing European nationals, disease, and natural disasters. During the seventeenth century new fortifications, missions, and cattle ranches were established. Spanish Floridians re-established their claims northward along the Atlantic coast and westward throughout the north-central portion of peninsular Florida to the Apalachicola river and perhaps beyond. The eighteenth century was also a time of turmoil for Spanish Florida. Raids by English colonists and their Native American allies destroyed outlying missions, fortifications, and cattle ranches by 1704, forcing Spaniards and missionized Native Americans to retreat to St. Augustine. The First Spanish Period ended in 1763 when Spain ceded Spanish Florida to England, and most Spaniards and missionized Native Americans evacuated the town (Dunkel 1955). Spain regained most of the Florida peninsula in 1783 (the Second Spanish Period), but ceded it to the United States of America in 1821.

Efforts to convert the native residents of Spanish Florida to Roman Catholicism were initiated early and continued throughout the First Spanish Period. The first missionaries were Jesuits, but they abandoned their efforts in 1572 and were replaced by Franciscans. Although both Jesuits and Franciscans founded missions in the sixteenth century, it was during the seventeenth century that the Spanish mission system reached its greatest extent. After 1606, a series of missions were established westward from St. Augustine to the Apalachicola river, and the abandoned chain of missions north of St. Augustine along the Georgia coast was re-established. Native Americans and a few Spaniards lived at the missions. Not only were these missions a source of fish, game, and native produce for St. Augustine, but missionized Native Americans may have raised several varieties of Old World plants (Hann 1988: 239), though recent archaeobotanical research does not support archival evidence for this (Gremillion 1993). Spaniards in St. Augustine traded with nearby Native Americans, and may also have relied heavily upon livestock, game, fish, and produce from more distant missions. St. Augustinians had to compete with French, Dutch, English, and Cuban traders as well as Franciscans for access to the Native American trade (Boyd et al. 1951: 46; Bushnell 1981: 92–5, 99).

Spanish Florida was subdivided into several administrative units roughly defined by the cultural identity of Native Americans living in each. Precise boundaries for these provinces are not agreed upon. The Guale primarily occupied the sea islands and estuaries which border the Atlantic coast and the adjacent mainland north of the St. Marys River. Timucua Province included the islands and estuaries of the Atlantic coast as well as the mainland from the southern border of Guale and the north-central third of peninsular Florida (Hann 1990: 423; Milanich 1978). Timucua extended from the Atlantic coast westward to beyond the Suwannee river. The southern boundaries are poorly defined, but extended southward some distance from St. Augustine. Timucua was a region of pine–oak hammocks and sand hills punctuated by numerous freshwater lakes and rivers. The Western Timucua occupied the area west of the St. John's river, while the Eastern Timucua lived between the St. John's and the Atlantic Ocean (Milanich 1978). Apalachee Province is associated with the panhandle of peninsular Florida. The eastern boundary was shared with the Western Timucua and the western boundary was defined by the Ochlockonee river (Hann 1988: 1). The southern edge was formed by the Gulf of Mexico, but the northern boundary is not well defined. The Apalachee mission headquarters, San Luis de Talimali, was located towards the north-west edge of Apalachee. Apalachee was characterized by rolling hills and numerous lakes and streams.

ARCHAEOZOOLOGICAL DATA

Animal use at missions in Guale Province is represented by faunal samples from Fallen Tree, a Native American pueblo or village located immediately adjacent to Mission Santa Catalina de Guale on St. Catherines Island, Georgia. The mission was founded in the late sixteenth century and abandoned in the early 1680s (Thomas 1987: 56–7). Fallen Tree materials were recovered by David Hurst Thomas and Allen May (Dukes 1993). Domestic animals are extremely rare in this collection. Based on estimates of the minimum number of individuals (MNI), a pig (*Sus scrofa*) and a chicken (*Gallus gallus*) were the only introduced domestic animals present (Dukes 1993; Table 10.1). The bulk of the subsistence effort appears to have emphasized locally available wild resources, which constituted 83 per cent of the individuals. Estuarine fishes and deer (*Odocoileus virginianus*) were the primary resources used, although small mammals, turkeys (*Meleagris gallopavo*), and turtles were also common.

Excavations at the Fountain of Youth Park site under the direction of Kathleen A. Deagan provide the only archaeozoological information from an Eastern Timucua mission (Merritt 1983). The site is located about a kilometre north of the capital of Spanish Florida, St. Augustine, and was associated with the Nombre de Dios mission. The village attracted many Native Americans throughout the First Spanish Period. Faunal remains were

Table 10.1 Native American faunal summaries from Spanish Florida

	Fallen Tree		Fountain of Youth		Baptizing Spring		San Martin		Apalachee Village	
	MNI	%	MNI	%	MNI	%	MNI	%	MNI	%
Domestic mammals	1	1.7			3	8.6	1	2.0	3	75.0
Domestic birds	1	1.7					6	12.2		
Deer	10	16.7	7	1.6	12	34.3	3	6.1		
Other wild mammals	11	18.3	12	2.7	2	5.7	1	2.0	1	25.0
Wild birds	8	13.3	4	0.9	1	2.9				
Turtles/alligators	7	11.7	13	2.9	15	42.9	10	20.4		
Sharks/rays/fishes	14	23.3	398	88.2	1	2.9	26	53.1		
Commensal taxa	8	13.3	17	3.8	1	2.9	2	4.1		
Total	60		451		35		49		4	

Note: Fallen Tree data from Dukes (1993); Fountain of Youth data from Reitz (1991); Baptizing Spring data from Loucks (1993); San Martin data from Newsom and Quitmyer (1992) and Quitmyer (1991); Apalachee Village data from Reitz (1993).

recovered from both late sixteenth/early seventeenth-century and late seventeenth/early eighteenth-century mission components (Reitz 1985, 1991). Timucuans were joined by other Native American groups who wanted to be near the mission and the protection of the Spanish town during the First Spanish Period. The early mission animal remains probably represent Timucuan and Guale subsistence primarily. Later mission remains may have been deposited by a variety of Native American groups from throughout Spanish Florida, as the outlying missionized Native Americans were withdrawn to St. Augustine during the late seventeenth/early eighteenth centuries and settled in nearby mission villages.

The faunal collection from the Fountain of Youth site indicates that, in spite of the proximity to St. Augustine, the prehispanic focus on marine resources remained intact throughout the First Spanish Period (Reitz 1991; Table 10.1). Only 4 per cent of the vertebrate individuals identified in the Fountain of Youth assemblage were terrestrial mammals. No introduced domestic animals were identified. Deer contributed less than 2 per cent of the vertebrate individuals, while marine vertebrates contributed 90 per cent. This pattern is consistent in both the late sixteenth/early seventeenth-century and late seventeenth/early eighteenth-century components and is very similar to that available for the prehispanic components at this site (Reitz 1985, 1991). The emphasis on marine resources even in the late seventeenth/early eighteenth-century component is surprising given that by the eighteenth century Native Americans from many non-coastal locations throughout Spanish Florida had moved to the missions around St. Augustine. Animal use at Fountain of Youth appears to contrast dramatically with that suggested for Native Americans in Guale. None the less, the basic pattern is the same: limited use of domestic livestock and primary use of locally available wild resources.

Native American archaeofaunal data are available from excavations at two seventeenth-century, north-central Florida mission sites. One of these is known as Baptizing Spring and was excavated by L. Jill Loucks. The identity of the mission is unknown, although it was probably occupied during the first half of the seventeenth century (Hann 1990: 470; Loucks 1993). Thirty-five vertebrate individuals were identified from the Native American village associated with Baptizing Spring (Loucks 1993; Table 10.1). Introduced domestic animals, two pigs and a cow (*Bos taurus*), contributed 9 per cent of the individuals, while indigenous wild fauna comprised the rest of the individuals. The most common of these were deer and the terrestrial, burrowing gopher tortoise (*Gopherus polyphemus*).

The second Western Timucua mission faunal collection was recovered from the Fig Springs site under the supervision of Brent Weisman (Newsom and Quitmyer 1992; Quitmyer 1991). This was probably Mission San Martín de Ayaocuto, which was established about 1607 and abandoned around 1656 following a Timucuan uprising (Hann 1990: 461, 473). Faunal samples were taken from a Native American structure near the convento and church as well as from the village. An estimated forty-nine vertebrate individuals were identified from San Martín. A single pig was identified, the remainder of the individuals were indigenous wild fauna (Table 10.1). Deer contributed 12 per cent of the individuals in the collection and turtles 20 per cent. The terrestrial gopher tortoise alone contributed 10 per cent of the individuals. However, freshwater fish contributed most of the individuals. Access to marine resources from the site was demonstrated by an earlier faunal study which identified two species of whelk and three species of marine clams (Deagan 1972). Use of fine-meshed screen to collect artefacts during excavation, as was the case for San Martín, usually enhances the recovery of fish remains. Hence, the San Martín data probably provide the most accurate picture currently available for the life of Native Americans at one of the western missions in Spanish Florida.

Summarizing the Western Timucua materials, introduced domestic animals were probably rarely used by Native Americans at Western Timucua missions. Chickens may have been uncommonly consumed or else were absent in the diet. On the other hand, locally available wild resources were heavily used. Native Americans appear to have made extensive use of two wild native species: deer and gopher tortoises. The contrasts between Baptizing Spring and San Martín (Fig Springs) in terms of the role of fish in the diet may be a reflection of the fine-screen recovery techniques used at San Martín.

Faunal remains from Native American contexts in Apalachee Province during the First Spanish Period are very rare. Some data are available from the Apalachee village associated with San Luis de Talimali, the capital of the Spanish mission chain in Apalachee from 1656 to 1704. This was the largest mission village in Apalachee Province and was occupied by Spanish soldiers, civilians, friars, and Native Americans. Historical records tell us that the Apalachee played a major role in supplying livestock, tallow, lard, hides, and other agricultural products to St. Augustine as well as the Caribbean (Boniface 1971: 200–1; Boyd et al. 1951; Hann 1988: 136). Presumably Apalachee would not be exporting products such as hams, lard, tallow and chickens if colonists living at the missions were unable to satisfy their own preference for these products. Hence, it seems likely that faunal remains from one of the Apalachee missions, especially those from the capital of the western mission chain, might be dominated by domestic animals. The limited data available from the Apalachee village suggest this may have been the case (Reitz 1993; Table 10.1). Morphometric data also indicate that Apalachee cattle were somewhat larger than cattle from St. Augustine (Reitz and Ruff 1994).

DISCUSSION

Although these vertebrate data are biased by lack of control over stratigraphy, depositional environment, recovery techniques, sample size, and cultural context, they offer strong evidence that few Native Americans adopted Euro-African domestic animals. They indicate that animal use at missions in

Guale, Eastern Timucua, Western Timucua, and Apalachee provinces was regionally distinctive and that introduced domestic animals played a minor role in the diet in all of them except Apalachee. It appears unlikely that cattle, pigs, or chickens replaced wild animals in the diet of missionized Native Americans to any great extent in spite of frequent references to introduced livestock in colonial accounts. Most of these accounts actually were associated with Apalachee, which supports the impression obtained in this study that introduced domestic animals were uncommon everywhere else. If the Fountain of Youth data are reliable, the intensity of cultural interaction does not appear to be an important variable.

In many respects, these data indicate that the animal-based portion of the Native American diet at missions was similar to that practised prior to missionization. The percentages of wild taxa in Native American faunal assemblages range from 83 per cent (Fallen Tree) to 96 per cent (Fountain of Youth), 89 per cent (Baptizing Spring), 94 per cent (San Martín), and 25 per cent (Apalachee Village) of the estimated individuals. By contrast, domestic animals are absent from one of these mission assemblages and rare in all of the others except that from the Apalachee village.

There are two variables that probably influenced the degree to which introduced livestock were adopted by Native Americans: environmental variables and tribal affiliation. Environmental variables influenced the ability of livestock to adapt and flourish in this new setting. Biological stresses encountered by introduced domestic animals included high humidity, local competition for food, parasites and predators. Florida's climate is permanently humid, with warm winters – an environment which can be difficult for cattle and hogs and almost impossible for sheep (*Ovis aries*). Florida soils are leached, low in fertility, acidic, and poorly drained, so graze is less nutritious. Wolves (*Canis lupus*) and bears (*Ursus americanus*) would also have posed a significant problem to introduced herds, especially sheep. The presence of native deer in Spanish Florida indicates that indigenous ruminant diseases were present and these might have quickly infected introduced animals with no natural immunity to these new diseases. Today, mineral deficiencies, screw-worm, and fever tick continue to be major problems for Florida cattle (Rouse 1973: 371).

Cattle may have had a difficult time adapting in most of Spanish Florida, especially under the free-range conditions that characterized the colony (Arnade 1961). The coastal missions in Guale and Eastern Timucua were on low-lying, poorly drained soils overlooking Atlantic coast estuaries. Western Timucua soils were also poor. Apalachee, however, was recognized early as a rich province with an agreeable climate and good soils. From the faunal data it appears that cattle flourished only in this province. This is not to say that Spanish cattle did poorly everywhere in Spanish Florida. By the late seventeenth century British colonists newly arrived in North America stole cattle from Spanish Florida because they were bigger and more hardy than the newly introduced British cattle (Hann 1986: 200).

Cultural factors such as unfamiliarity with the techniques of animal husbandry, conflicts with traditional plant husbandry practices, depopulation, and social unrest also deterred Native Americans from adopting domestic animals. While farmers might find it relatively easy to incorporate new domestic plants into their traditional complex of crops (although see Gremillion 1993); domestic animals required a new set of skills for which no pre-colonial activities would have prepared native Floridians. They also would require substantial alterations in plant cultivation techniques as well as in labour systems, seasonal schedules, and residential patterns. Adoption of animals by people unfamiliar with tending livestock could be a lengthy and difficult process. The Apalachee may have been able to do so because the land was fertile and cattle could do well without skilful husbandry. In addition, the Apalachee were known as highly productive farmers, while there is some uncertainty of the degree to which Guale and Timucua were farmers prior to the First Spanish Period. The social institutions necessary for successful animal husbandry may have been more readily developed by the Apalachee than by the other native peoples. The Apalachee also had more time. Guale and Timucua tribes rapidly succumbed to European diseases. By about 1680, most Guales and Timucuans had died and the survivors incorporated into other tribal units by Spanish administrators. The Apalachee survived as a recognizable group for several more decades.

These data also indicate that the animal-based portion of the Native American diet was similar to that prior to colonization. The percentages of wild taxa in Native American vertebrate assemblages from sites occupied during the colonial period range from 100 to 83 per cent of the estimated individuals (Table 10.1). The variety and relative proportions of wild animals used prior to colonization does not seem to have been altered in most cases. The few changes that did occur indicate that these were shaped by previous experiences rather than by European husbandry models.

Continuity rather than change is suggested by these data. It appears that native peoples in the south-east were highly selective of colonial products. They did not abandon their traditions in favour of novelties but adopted those that could be accommodated comfortably into previous strategies. Domestic animals were not easily incorporated into traditional strategies and were by and large ignored. This also underscores the degree to which pre-Columbian foodways met the biological and cultural needs of both Native Americans and colonists in the south-eastern United States.

Foodways are highly conservative. It is likely that wherever evidence for substantial subsistence change is found, it will be in the context of major alterations in cultural and environmental elements which were even more disruptive than what we know took place in the south-east. The absence of Euro-African plants and animals in these assemblages may also indicate that adopting novel domestic food sources would be a slow and cautious process. These two observations may offer insights into the progress of domestication elsewhere, especially in Europe where many domestic species were introduced rather than locally domesticated. The adoption of domestic plants and animals is not to be taken for granted; it occurs only where they offer a clear subsistence advantage.

CONCLUSION

This survey of vertebrates from sixteenth- and seventeenth-century Native American sites finds no single pattern of resource use and little evidence of subsistence change. Subsistence strategies are conservative and not expected to change rapidly under normal circumstances. Even intense interaction with Spanish colonists did not result in fundamental changes. This indicates that European patterns of animal use were not an improvement upon native ones in many colonial environments and may not have been viable in others. It also indicates the strength of pre-Columbian subsistence patterns as well as the degree of cultural change that must accompany changes in subsistence patterns.

ACKNOWLEDGEMENTS

I would like to thank Kathleen A. Deagan (Florida Museum of Natural History), David Hurst Thomas (American Museum of Natural History), and Bonnie G. McEwan (Florida Bureau of Archaeological Research) for the opportunity to examine materials from the Fountain of Youth Park site, St. Catherine's Island, and the San Luis Archaeological and Historic Site. Funding was provided in part by the Florida Bureau of Historic Preservation (No. 85030610); the University of Florida Division of Sponsored Research; the Edward John Noble and St. Catherine's Island Foundation; the State of Florida Conservation and Recreation Lands (CARL) Trust Fund; and the National Endowment for the Humanities (No. RO–22177–91).

REFERENCES

Arnade, C.W. 1961. Cattle raising in Spanish Florida. *Agricultural History* 35, 3–11.
Boniface, B.G. (1971) A historical geography of Spanish Florida, circa 1700. Unpublished Masters thesis, Department of Geography, University of Georgia.
Boyd, M.F., H. Smith and J. Griffin. 1951. *Here They Once Stood*. Gainesville, Fl.: University Press of Florida.
Bushnell, A. 1981. *The King's Coffer*. Gainsville, Fl.: University Presses of Florida.
Deagan, K.A. 1972. Fig Springs: the mid-seventeenth century in north-central Florida. *Historical Archaeology* 6, 23–46.
Dukes, J.A. 1993. Change in vertebrate use between the Irene Phase and the seventeenth century on St. Catherine's Island, Georgia. Unpublished Masters thesis, Department of Anthropology, University of Georgia.
Dunkel, J.R. 1955. St. Augustine, Florida: a study of historical geography: Unpublished Ph.D. thesis, Worcester, Massachusetts, Clark University.

Gannon, M.V. 1967. *The Cross in the Sand: the early Catholic Church in Florida 1513–1870*, Gainesville, Fl.: University of Florida Press.

Gremillion, K.J. 1993. Adoption of Old World crops and processes of cultural change in the historic southeast. *Southeastern Archaeology* 12, 15–20.

Hann, J.H. 1986. Translation of Alonso de Leturiondo's memorial to the King of Spain. *Florida Archaeology* 2, Tallahassee, Fl.: Florida Bureau of Archaeological Research.

Hann, J.H. 1988. *Apalachee: the land between the rivers*. Gainesville, Fl.: University Presses of Florida.

Hann, J.H. 1990. Summary guide to Spanish Florida missions and *visitas* with churches in the sixteenth and seventeenth centuries. *The Americas* 46, 417–513.

Holm, M.A. 1994. Continuity and change: the zooarchaeology of aboriginal sites in the North Carolina piedmont. Unpublished Ph.D. thesis, Department of Anthropology, University of North Carolina.

Jeter, M.D. and G.I. Williams Jr. 1989. Late prehistoric cultures, A.D. 1000–1500. In *Archeology and Bioarcheology of the Lower Mississippi Valley and Trans-Mississippi South in Arkansas and Louisiana*, M.D. Jeter, J.C. Rose, G.I. Williams, Jr. and A.M. Harmon (eds) 170–220. Fayetteville, Ark.: Arkansas Archeological Survey Research Series 37.

Kelley, D.B. (ed.). 1994. *The McLelland and Joe Clark sites: prohistoric-historic Caddoan farmsteads in southern Bossier Parish, Louisiana*. Prepared by Coastal Environments, Inc. for US Army Corps of Engineers, Baton Rouge, Louisiana, Vicksburg District.

Loucks, L.J. 1993. Spanish–Indian interaction on the Florida missions: the archaeology of Baptizing Spring. In *The Spanish Missions of La Florida*, B.G. McEwan (ed.), 193–216. Gainsville, Fl.: University Press of Florida.

Merritt, J.D. 1983. Beyond the town walls: the Indian element in colonial St. Augustine. In *Spanish St. Augustine: the archaeology of a colonial Creole community*, K.A. Deagan (ed.), 125–47. New York: Academic Press.

Milanich, J.T. 1978. The Western Timucua: patterns of acculturation and change. In *Tacachale: essays on the Indians of Florida and Southeastern Georgia during the historic period*, J. Milanich and S. Proctor (eds), 59–88. Gainesville, Fl.: University Presses of Florida.

Newsom, L. and I.R. Quitmyer. 1992. Archaeobotanical and faunal remains from Fig Springs Mission (8Co1). In *Excavations on the Franciscan Frontier: archaeology at the Fig Springs Mission*, B. Weisman (ed.), 206–33. Gainesville, Fl.: University Press of Florida.

Quitmyer, I.R. 1991. Faunal remains from Fig Springs Mission (8Co1). Manuscript on file, Florida Museum of Natural History, University of Florida, Gainesville.

Reitz, E.J. 1985. A comparison of Spanish and aboriginal subsistence on the Atlantic coastal plain. *Southeastern Archaeology* 4, 41–50.

Reitz, E.J. 1991. Animal use and culture change in Spanish Florida. In *Animal Use and Culture Change*, P.J. Crabtree and K. Ryan (eds), 62–77. Philadelphia, Pa.: Museum of Archaeology and Anthropology, University of Pennsylvania, MASCA 8.

Reitz, E.J. 1993. Vertebrate remains from the Apalachee Village at San Luis de Talimali. Manuscript on file. Museum of Natural History, University of Georgia, Athens.

Reitz, E.J. and B. Ruff. 1994. Morphometric data for cattle from North America and the Caribbean prior to the 1850s. *Journal of Archaeological Science* 21, 699–713.

Rouse, J.E. 1973. *World Cattle: cattle of North America*, Volume III. Norman, Okla.: University of Oklahoma Press.

Thomas, D.H. 1987. *The Archaeology of Mission Santa Catalina de Guale: 1. Search and discovery*, New York: Anthropological Papers of the American Museum of Natural History 63 (2).

Part III

FOOD AND THE LANDSCAPE

11 The meaning of ditches: deconstructing the social landscapes of New Guinea, Kuk, Phase 4

TIM BAYLISS-SMITH and JACK GOLSON

This chapter is an attempt to go beyond what is strictly known about the agricultural history of New Guinea. What is known derives mainly from the highlands of Papua New Guinea. It also derives disproportionately from highly indirect forms of evidence, such as pollen diagrams and estimated rates of soil erosion, and from the archaeological record of ditches — especially those at the Kuk site near Mount Hagen and at Tari. These sources can be used to generate a history of the *longue dureé* (Golson and Gardner 1990; Bayliss-Smith 1996; Golson 1997), but in these accounts there is a striking lack of detail about the lives of the people who shaped this prehistory.

However, within this broad historical geography of environmental impacts and responses, small patches of drainage activity at Kuk can be reconstructed in extraordinary detail (Bayliss-Smith and Golson 1992a, 1992b). The excavations of Golson at Kuk swamp have uncovered evidence of thousands of ditches and field drains, which in many cases can be shown to be contemporary features because of the distinctive types of volcanic ash (tephra) present in their infill (Golson 1976, 1977). For Phase 4 in the Kuk sequence, between about 2000 and 1200 BP, these buried agricultural landscapes take the form of systems of small fields defined by the shallow ditches that enclose them. The field drains are linked to major disposal channels which themselves connect to the natural river drainage of the upper Wahgi valley (Figure 11.1). In this chapter an attempt is made to interpret these ditches as a *social landscape* of wetland drainage.

DRAINED WETLANDS AS SOCIAL LANDSCAPES

Natural landscapes of the upper Wahgi

The upper Wahgi valley which provides the setting for this wetland drainage activity has a lower montane humid tropical climate. The average temperature is about 19°C. and there is about 2,700 mm of rainfall each year, with rather little seasonal or year-to-year variation. The annual water

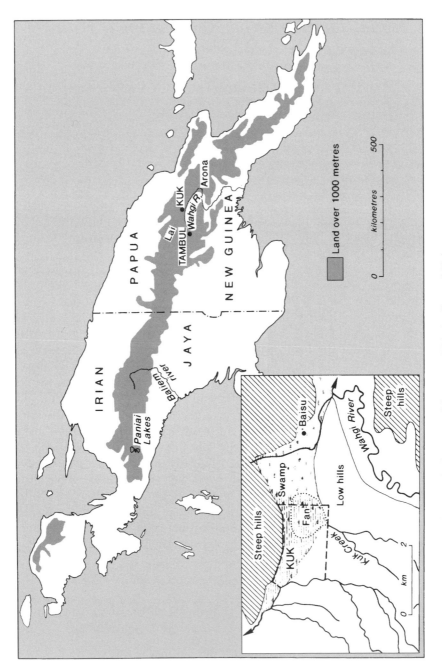

Figure 11.1 New Guinea, showing the location of the upper Wahgi valley and Kuk swamp.

surplus (precipitation minus evapotranspiration) is estimated at about 1,700 mm (McAlpine *et al.* 1983; Hughes *et al.* 1991). All this surplus has to flow as runoff across a wide valley floor whose topography is interrupted by Pleistocene volcanic ash deposits eroded into low conical hills known as lahar mounds.

Kuk swamp is at an altitude of 1,580 m. According to Pain *et al.* (1987) it was formed, perhaps 200,000–400,000 years ago, by a disruption to the local drainage pattern caused by a mass movement of volcanic ash deposit. This landslide blocked off the outlet of Kuk creek and created a lake basin which, by the late Pleistocene around 30,000 years ago, had become infilled to form a swamp. Since 9000 BP this swamp has been the object of repeated attempts to improve its drainage by the digging of ditches (Golson 1976, 1977; Golson and Hughes 1980). In this chapter we suggest ways in which we should consider the landscapes of drainage that were created by these interventions. We focus on the phase of drainage so far published in the most detail, Phase 4 (Bayliss-Smith and Golson 1992a, 1992b).

Social landscapes of the upper Wahgi

Landscapes of wetland reclamation are, by definition, social landscapes, the result of actions planned, organized and carried out by local communities with the intention of transforming a swamp into something more productive and therefore, inevitably, something more meaningful. It can be argued that all landscapes modified in this way are social products. Indeed, some writers reject altogether the use of the term 'natural' in relation to 'landscape', preferring instead to consider the concept of landscape as intrinsically 'cultural' or 'social'. From this standpoint the landscape is defined as an artefact modified from nature, or portrayed in art or literature, or residing in the mind of an observer (Cosgrove and Daniels 1988; Ingold 1993; Tilley 1994).

However, in the context of Melanesia, Gosden (1989, 1994) has argued that it is not helpful to place an excessive emphasis on the symbolic meanings encoded within the landscape. While the landscapes formed by agricultural activities are clearly social products, Gosden suggests that they are not primarily symbolic constructs or landscapes of the mind:

> Rather they are spaces carved out by patterns of action, which then help to channel future action. The symbolic aspect of the landscape is derived from the actions carried out in it: a conscious gloss on unthought practice.
>
> (Gosden 1994: 81)

In this way Melanesians carve out social space from ecological space. Their social actions (for example, agricultural activities) have a dialectical relationship with the ecosystem's responses (for example, changes in soils following drainage). Furthermore, Gosden argues, the formation of a social landscape by people interacting with their environment is not primarily the outcome of a series of conscious acts, but should be seen instead as reflecting mainly 'unthought practice'. On the other hand the way in which symbolic value is given to artefacts within the landscape is much more the result of a conscious construction of meaning.

Gosden's distinction between what is conscious and what is unthought practice may help us to disentangle some confusions that can emerge in the interpretation of archaeological evidence. In the New Guinea highlands ditches are going to form an important source of evidence about the history of agriculture and the societies dependent upon it, so it important for us to sort out in our minds what a ditch does and does not represent. Was the digging of ditches a matter of habit, and therefore of actions that were carried out as 'unthought practice'? Or was each ditch designed consciously, and made so that it became the spatial representation of an idea that existed in the mind of the person who dug it, or in the mind of whomever it was that instructed and controlled that digger?

THE SOCIAL LANDSCAPE AS ARTEFACT

Conscious and unconscious acts

'Unthought practice' is Gosden's model of what most material culture actually represents. It is similar to Giddens's (1979) earlier notion of practical rather than discursive consciousness, but as Hodder (1992) points out, as far back as Aristotle distinctions were being drawn between the theoretical thinking of people who ask 'why?' questions and the practical thinking of artisans who want to get things done. Gosden argues that the landscape and its artefacts have been formed by a complex interplay of conscious and unconscious acts. The conscious acts result from decisions that become necessary in situations where a problem arises, and where that problem cannot be overcome by actions that are more directed by habit than by thought. He provides the example of the complex processes needed to establish a garden in the Arawe Islands off New Britain, Papua New Guinea (Gosden 1994: 18–19).

Laying out a garden on Arawe requires a set of skills, both conscious and unconscious. To overcome the main practical problems requires the clan as a whole to co-operate together, to choose a site and to clear the rainforest, and there is also decision-making by heads of families about their own resources and needs, present and future. These include food requirements and exchange obligations, labour resources, the planting material available, and the likelihood that the spiritual standing of the clan will be sufficient to ensure the fertility of certain crops. All these are essential preparations. However, 'once the work starts much unconscious knowledge is brought into play in the use of axes, fire and digging sticks' (Gosden 1994: 19). It is a matter of habit also for the leader of a group to work out what combination of men, women and children is possible or desirable for carrying out a set of tasks.

Establishing a new garden is therefore a complex operation, but it becomes manageable because so much of the work does not have to be thought out. The actions needed for managing both landscape and people become second nature to the participants, who know what sort of project to take on given the human, physical and spiritual resources that they have at their disposal.

The resulting garden is a social landscape which we can see as a space created by actions of various kinds. Normal everyday skills are sufficient for most tasks, and this will result in the reproduction of a cultural landscape that is regarded as distinctively 'traditional' because of the repetition of known and trusted styles and motifs in the layout of fields, fences and ditches. Only where problems arise that require particular solutions is it necessary for the men or women in control to decide consciously that a certain task must be carried out in a certain way. In such a case the artefact created will be distinctive, the particular outcome of deliberate decision-making, within a landscape that may have been mainly shaped by other kinds of actions.

Social and spiritual problems

Gosden has suggested that in Melanesia the predominance of reciprocal gift exchange, or 'social debt', as an overriding motive for production creates a distinctive type of social landscape. He calls the resulting pattern of settlements and sites for specialized production a 'landscape dominated by debt' (Gosden 1986, 1989). On the other hand where there was a centralization of chiefly power, as in the high islands of Polynesia, this will have generated a different type of social landscape, one that contains concentrations of landesque capital (e.g., irrigated taro fields) and places of elite residence and consumption (*marae* and fortified sites). Here the dominant social principle was chiefly privilege. Patrick Kirch reconstructs some remarkable examples of such landscapes in his recent work on Futuna and Alofi (Kirch 1994).

The spiritual meaning that resides in the landscape may in some cases become the dominant principle. Archaeologists have tried to reconstruct the 'sacred landscapes' of the past, in societies whose world-view seems dominated by the sites where religious activity was focused and by the spiritual meaning that resided in the landscape itself (e.g., Pryor 1991: 71; Bender 1992; Carmichael et al. 1994; Sognnes 1994). A recent example is Tilley's (1994) reinterpretation of Mesolithic and Neolithic sites in Wessex and south-west Wales. Basing his argument on selected evidence from present-day hunter-gatherers (especially Aborigines) and small-scale agriculturalists, Tilley concludes the concept of 'economic base' is irrelevant to an understanding of how people in such societies perceived their resources or related to their landscapes. Instead, he believes, 'landscape is intimately related to myth and obeys the same kind of logic as that which structures myth, viz. metaphor, allegory, synedoche, etc.' (Tilley 1994: 67).

This is an extreme view that focuses so exclusively on the symbolic world that fundamental problems of subsistence and survival are completely overlooked. We must reintroduce ecological and social dimensions if we are to achieve a more balanced view. Based on his study of the Huli of the New Guinea Southern Highlands, Ballard (1994: 145) comes to a similar conclusion: 'The promise of a social landscape approach lies in the scope it offers for working with a series of overlapping constructs, different landscapes of meaning that address a variety of perspectives.' The comparative study of how cultural meanings vary in time and in space shows us that, within the constraints of what is ecologically feasible, there are many alternative and successful ways in which space can be socially organized and symbolically ordered. This can be demonstrated at scales that range from domestic space within houses to the 'sacred geography' of monuments or mountains visible over a vast area.

The landscape as text?

The rich cultural variations in the ordering of space have led some scholars to treat space as a kind of 'text' (Shanks and Tilley 1987; Duncan 1990; Storli 1993; Tilley 1994). If material culture has symbolic meaning and plays an important role in social agency then, the argument runs, surely its organization in space has meanings that can be deconstructed? Henrietta Moore (1986) provides a revealing demonstration of how the use of space among the Marakwet of Kenya can be interpreted as a 'spatial text'. The text is made meaningful by the social actions of men and women, in the same way that a book becomes meaningful through the act of reading it.

The analogy with text can be taken even further. Just as speaking or writing is a continual process of augmentation, with new meanings being established all the time by the coining of new words and new metaphors, so perhaps the social landscape is being 'spoken' and 'read' in new ways by the social actors who move through it and rework it to meet their own needs and aspirations. In literary interpretation the *context* of the text is important, because we need to understand the relation of the text to the social and historical conditions within which it was produced (Moore 1986: 85). The context of landscape needs to be deconstructed in the same way. The land-scape contains within it many traces of past actions as well as the resources that provide an opportunity for renewed social action, but its meaning to those who 'read it' is not fixed. Actors can either take steps physically to reshape the landscape, or they can reinterpret it to endow it with new symbolic meaning.

The historical geographer Kirk was one of the first to explore this idea of an interplay between *text* and *context* in landscape, using the analogy of a theatre (Kirk 1952: 155). The scenery in the theatre is the landscape, while the unfolding story of human actions past and present is the play. Kirk pointed out that, like the landscape and its occupants, 'stage and actors are in a dynamic relationship both in space and time'. An example of this dialectical relationship is provided by the islands of eastern Fiji, where

> Present-day human actions are merely the latest episode in a long-running 'evolutionary play' that is happening within the ecological theatre. This play is one in which every scene necessarily takes place amid a scenery newly created, but in part inherited from past scenes, some of them quite remote from the actions taking place at any given moment.
>
> (Bayliss-Smith *et al.* 1988: 12).

Different island ecosystems in Fiji have proved to be rather different settings for the 'plays' that have emerged, resulting in some very contrasted social landscapes. Ecologically resilient, fertile islands like Koro have not been degraded by millennia of shifting cultivation, and so have not seen the emergence of the unproductive and hence problematic ecological settings that might encourage agricultural intensification. By contrast, vulnerable islands like Lakeba have seen deforestation and soil erosion, which has infilled valleys with sediment and produced alluvial swamps. In this new setting of degraded hill slopes and potentially productive wetlands, powerful leaders have emerged who compete for control of the surplus gained from intensive cultivation of wetland taro (Bayliss-Smith *et al.* 1988: 41–2; Kirch 1994: 309). In the islands of southern Vanuatu a similar story can be told, of contrasted social landscapes that sustain different degrees of social stratification (Spriggs 1986).

Summary

To summarize: the 'play' is the social text that we wish to interpret. The ecological 'theatre' is the social landscape, and to unravel its meaning we need to consider both its historical origins and the way in which it has been modified by social actors to meet their present needs. In staging the play (in other words, in meeting the social goals of everyday life), actors encounter problems. We can classify these problems as being either economic, or social, or spiritual in character. At the same time, most of the 'stagecraft' that enables the play to go on does not have to be thought out by the actors in a conscious way.

Therefore the artefacts that are added to the social landscape, which once they are constructed then become part of the 'scenery' within which people's lives unfold, may or may not be 'texts' heavy in economic, social or symbolic meaning. It will depend upon whether these artefacts were the carefully designed solutions to important perceived problems, or whether they were instead artefacts of normal ('traditional') design that were produced in a more unthinking way, by force of habit more than by conscious action.

DECONSTRUCTING KUK AS A SOCIAL LANDSCAPE

If we transpose these ideas from the social landscapes of the Arawe Islands, Wessex or Fiji to the New Guinea highlands, then we can ask new questions about how the social landscapes of prehistoric drainage should be interpreted. Kuk swamp in the upper Wahgi valley was the object of repeated attempts at drainage for crop cultivation, starting perhaps 9,000 years ago (Golson 1977, 1997). These drainage ditches constitute important evidence for the prehistoric societies of the highlands. Can these apparently mundane artefacts reveal more than has been supposed about the purpose and meaning of swamp drainage?

The social meaning of drainage

What meanings are revealed by an analysis of the design of ditches? Are the ditches that have been uncovered at Kuk the result of everyday production, or is there a consciously economic, social or spiritual meaning in their hidden 'style' of construction? Although the question has not been asked in an explicit way, most of those who have written about Kuk have tried to infer some social meaning from the buried landscapes of drainage that have been uncovered there.

Phase 3 of drainage at Kuk provides an example. The onset of gardening activity in Phase 3 has been seen as signalling the emergence of a new form of agriculture based upon taro, *Colocasia esculenta* (Bayliss-Smith 1996: 517) – although the presence of taro in the Highlands at a much earlier period is also a possibility (Golson 1997). Taro was originally a swidden crop, but in certain areas where the accessible forests became degraded to grassland, as in the upper Wahgi valley by about 4000 BP, taro cultivation was able to move into the wetlands using a more labour intensive technology and a swamp fallow rather than a forest fallow (Bayliss-Smith and Golson 1992a).

Gorecki interprets the new Phase 3 ditch systems that we begin to see at Kuk around 4000 BP as follows:

> It appears that the whole gardening activity was now planned, and the organisation and management were now communal rather than individual as during . . . [previous phases]. The overall pattern had a geometric aspect, with major channels regularly spaced and receiving tributaries at right angles.
>
> (Gorecki 1986: 163)

By about 2000 BP this change in the way that wetlands were used had evolved into the 'grid' pattern of Phase 4, the period with which this chapter is concerned. Golson (1977) remarked in relation to these later ditch features:

> The field ditches, typically gutter-like features deeper than wide (30–50cm as against 20–40 cm) and much more closely spaced

than the field drains of Phase 3, are disposed in grids . . . They seem to represent a far more systematic and perhaps specialised use of the swamp . . .

(Golson 1977: 623)

Golson has recently suggested that Phase 4 is the first of the systems at Kuk which show 'standardized patterns based on long, straight ditches parallel and at right angles to each other that enclosed square to rectangular plots' (Golson 1997: 45). These plots are interpreted as planting areas for a single crop, probably taro.

The archaeologist is here uncovering social meanings from the style that has been glimpsed in a buried landscape. On the basis of ethnographic analogues, Golson implies that the wetland landscape of Phase 4 is the conscious outcome of a set of decisions, through which Kuk swamp is organized in a particular way. Wetland land use becomes 'systematic', 'specialized' and 'standardized'.

Gorecki (1986) goes further, in interpreting the ditches of Phase 4 as revealing a change towards a more 'communal' social organization. Following Golson (1977: 623–4; 1981: 57–8), he interprets the ditch pattern as representing a switch from polyculture in wetlands to crop segregation, with dryland gardens (not preserved archaeologically) side by side with wetland monoculture, probably for taro. In this way the people he calls 'sedentarised swamplanders' were in an excellent position to develop trade networks based on their productive surplus (Gorecki 1986). It is possible that the adoption of yam cultivation about 2500 BP is what permitted the intensification of production at this time (Bayliss-Smith 1996: 517). Agriculture would now have involved soil tillage in both dryland sites (based on yams) and in the wetland taro gardens.

Archaeologists looking at evidence from outside the valley swamps have, since the 1970s, sought to find some echo of the social processes that are implied by the intensification of land use in the wetland sites. John Burton (1984: 228), for example, interpreted the lithic evidence from Kamapuk rockshelter as showing the onset, between 2,500 and 1,500 years ago, of large-scale stone-axe quarrying at Tuman, designed to serve regional exchange systems and not just local demand for stone. At contact (early 1930s) Tuman was the prime source of high-grade stone in the Central Highlands, and the Kamapuk evidence suggests a chronology for the onset of large-scale production at Tuman which matches quite well the dates for Phase 4 (c.2000–1200 BP). Feil's (1987) reinterpretation of the prehistory of the Eastern Highlands, an area devoid of wetland sites, is also consistent with this model. Thus, at a rather generalized level of interpretation, there has been no significant dissent from the idea that the system represented at Kuk by Phase 4 had 'revolutionary' potential for social relations, in that it had the capacity to produce and sustain both subsistence and surplus within a Central Highlands valley that was otherwise degraded by deforestation (Golson and Gardner 1990; Bayliss–Smith and Golson 1992a, 1992b).

Deconstructing ditches

At a more detailed level of interpretation we shall be arguing that progress is being hindered by an inadequate understanding of what ditch digging actually signifies. To what extent should the fields, drains and disposal channels of Phase 4 be seen as a social landscape invested in symbolic meaning because it has been consciously designed to solve key problems? Should we rather see it as a landscape formed by unthought practice to serve mundane and purely functional purposes? We can reduce the social landscape model of Gosden (1994) to a series of hypotheses testable with the archaeological evidence from Kuk, if we are prepared to regard conscious and unconscious actions in the environment as binary alternatives, rather than being the opposite ends of a continuum of variation in behaviour, which is perhaps nearer to Gosden's original intention.

The conscious actions of a person will normally generate artefacts that, potentially at least, are interpretable to others because they are the outcome of deliberate design. However, we should not expect that unconscious acts will produce artefacts that appear random or even idiosyncratic. On the contrary, when a preconceived model of how the artefact *ought* to be produced is followed, then the action can proceed smoothly without pause for thought or the need for conscious choice about style. Such a procedure would result in drainage ditches that conformed to 'traditional' design, but such ditches would have been dug without reference to the precise local circumstances. Following Gosden (1994), we can assume that only when these circumstances constitute a perceived *problem* does conscious design have to enter into the process.

Perhaps arbitrarily we can subdivide such problems as being primarily either (a) ecological, or (b) social, or (c) spiritual in character. If only one set of problems predominates, then the solutions that are adopted in each case will conform to the perceived need, respectively, either

(a) to optimize the function of the artefact so as to achieve economic efficiency; or
(b) to shape or locate the artefact so that it reflects social meanings to onlookers; or
(c) to produce an artefact in a way that will convey symbolic meaning to others who share the same magico–religious ideas.

To classify motives in such a way does not necessarily help us to remove ambiguity, since the same features in a social landscape can simultaneously serve different functions. In a Melanesian swidden a garden fence might be constructed in order to keep out destructive pigs (solving an economic problem), and to serve as a boundary between clan territories (solving a social problem), and also to provide a site for ritual sacrifice (solving a religious problem). At the same time, the height and method of construction of this fence might conform very closely to all other fences constructed by the same ethnic group. It might indeed have been built by someone subordinate to a leader, and therefore by a man or woman who was only partially aware of the anticipated economic, social and religious problems that the fence was designed to overcome. The actual construction of the fence might therefore result from the habits and practices of unconscious action, even though it conveys to others quite different meanings.

An example from fenland

An archaeological example of the ambiguity of artefacts in the social landscape comes from English fenland (Pryor 1991). At Fen Gate near Peterborough there are well-preserved traces of thousands of wooden posts that were initially interpreted as marking the line of a track or causeway that ran across the shallow waters of the flooded fen. The line of posts was constructed in the early Bronze Age to link the farming settlement at Fen Gate to a platform in the middle of Flag Fen. The posts had been split from logs, mostly oak, with their ends sharpened in the usual way, so that as individual artefacts they appear to differ not at all from the usual products of bronze age woodmanship, each post shaped by unconscious acts and habitual skills.

However, once the decision had been implemented to place them in a straight line for 900 m across the waters of Flag Fen, then we have a bold reworking of the landscape which requires a different type of interpretation. According to Pryor (1991), who has been excavating this site since 1971, the posts may mark the position of the causeway that provided access to a platform in Flag Fen, and so they might have served a purely utilitarian function. At the same time they mark a boundary between the dry land of the fen margin to the south and the open waters to the north, and they seem therefore to symbolize an important division in social space. The posts also provided a site for the ritual deposition in water of deliberately broken metalwork, such as bronze axes, daggers, bracelets and pins. These objects are recovered today mostly within 30 m of the line of posts and along its southern side, and they must represent the outcome of some form of religious ritual. For a society to focus its religious ceremonial along a boundary might suggest an increase in political tensions, or even the increasing economic problems that were posed in the later Bronze Age by rising water levels (Pryor 1991: 121).

Any landscape can, of course, be demarcated conceptually, and its various natural features can convey symbolic meanings, without the land itself being altered in any way, for example by ditches, fences or lines of posts. The Flag Fen example suggests that the layout of large-scale 'artefacts' in the landscape is the outcome of design, the result of a conscious act of problem-solving and therefore a rich source of economic, social or religious meaning. On the other hand any large-scale feature is made up of many individual components, each of which (e.g., each post) may be just an everyday object produced by a series of unconscious acts, by using habitual skills and according to usual, customary styles. We might therefore expect that in a drained field, for example, each individual ditch will convey less meaning than the network of which it is a part. The layout, the location and the very existence of the whole system of ditches represents a significant investment of labour, skill and social organization, and is likely to result from conscious and co-ordinated actions to tackle certain perceived problems.

Phase 4 at Kuk: alternative hypotheses

The Phase 4 ditches at Kuk will now be considered in the light of these alternative ideas about the meaning of landscape artefacts. Two areas at Kuk have so far been analysed in detail: block A9 of the archaeological site, in a relatively elevated and less waterlogged part of Kuk swamp, and blocks A10/A11 which is a more low-lying area and therefore probably a more difficult area to drain. Various interpretations for the Phase 4 ditches dug in these contrasted sites can be proposed, and these are models which perhaps can be tested.

Model A. Unconscious practice in an unproblematic context. According to this model those who dug ditches at Kuk in Phase 4 times did not consider the context of their actions to be problematic in any way, so the task was not part of some carefully conceived design. Ditches were therefore dug in all areas of Kuk swamp in the same way, and according to preconceived mental models of the 'correct' depth, shape and spacing. On the other hand we might expect some random variations in ditches, perhaps linked to the age, sex or personal idiosyncrasy of the digger.

Model B. Conscious acts to maximize economic efficiency. This is the conventional 'functionalist' model, which says that ditches would be dug differently in different areas when a change in their size or spacing was thought to be necessary to solve particular ecological problems. On a more elevated site with fewer problems of waterlogging (e.g., in block A9), then either the depth of the ditches or the density of the network would be less, in comparison to more swampy sites (e.g., blocks A10/A11).

Model C. Conscious acts to promote a social project. The project could be connected to the need to extend territorial boundaries, or to produce more food because of a forthcoming marriage or festival, or to serve as a visible reminder of the power or the skills of a leader or a group. The resulting landscape can tell us much about its role in social agency, because many of its features will reflect social relationships and the prestige that can derive from production surplus or public display. In the case of the Phase 4 ditches at Kuk, if they were dug more for symbolic than for functional purposes then it might mean the workforce following some preconceived plan or layout for the ditches. A strict ordering of social space that cannot be interpreted in functional terms implies the imposition of strong social control over a previously uncontrolled domain, the undrained swamp.

Model D. Conscious acts to create a sacred landscape. The fourth possibility, that networks of ditches served as a means to mediate relations with the supernatural world, is a logical possibility but actually seems implausible because it receives no support from New Guinea ethnography. Sacred space in the highlands finds its focus today in the open ceremonial grounds that are located on flat, dry ground or on ridges (Strathern 1971). Alternatively it is represented more diffusely in the sacred geography of the forests and the mountains (Ballard 1994). If, in the prehistoric cultures in Phase 4 times, ditch digging was designed to create spiritually meaningful space in the Kuk swamps, then we might anticipate a lack of evidence for ecological or social function or individual idiosyncrasy. However, the recognition of spiritual meaning in the landscape is always likely to be speculative unless some ethnographic support is forthcoming, as Tilley's (1994) doomed effort to interpret the spiritual meaning of mesolithic sites in Britain so amply demonstrates.

In practice, distinguishing between the artefacts generated by these various models might be impossible. The 'severe' organization of space implied by the pursuit of social projects (Model C) might not be distinguishable from the more casual, habitual landscape of everyday subsistence practice (Model A). However, ditch design as a pursuit of hydraulic efficiency (Model B) ought to be detectable in the archaeological record, although of course the ditch digger's attempt to enhance efficiency need not exclude other, non-economic motives.

The difficulty we have in isolating the symbolic meaning of an artefact or landscape from its more functional significance may in part be intrinsic to the way meaning itself is constructed. Hodder (1992) has discussed why the symbolic meaning of material culture is so difficult to define. He points out that where an artefact can be given alternative meanings by the society responsible for its production, then these alternatives may tend to reinforce each other in ways that serve the interests of dominant groups. For example, if something is designed to be an object that symbolizes prestige, then it is far better if the time, energy, skill and aesthetic sense devoted to it can also be justified in terms of what is necessary for functional efficiency. Hodder gives the hypothetical example of a projectile point that is made in an elaborate way ostensibly so that it does the best possible job in killing prey, but whose production in fact serves to legitimate male prestige:

> The careful flaking of the projectile point does not seem arbitrary and it does not refer in a direct way to prestige. Nevertheless the pragmatic knowledge has the effect of locating prestige in the domain of hunting and giving a secondary role to other activities.
>
> (Hodder 1992: 206)

As a general conclusion, we can say that if the material basis for prestige is concentrated on what is seen to be a necessary technology to achieve economic efficiency, then the ideologies that are sustained by the artefacts will have what Hodder (1992: 209) calls 'a non-arbitrary, natural logic'. The ideology becomes less transparent and less open to critique – it becomes necessary.

It seems likely that ditches may also be liable to the same conflation of different meanings. Their symbolic meaning may be the more hidden because the 'real' meaning of ditches seems so self-evident: they drain the swamp. As Hodder suggests, this self-evident quality is what masks or hides the references that are being made: 'the ideological messages are hidden behind the supposed non-communicative nature of material culture' (Hodder 1992: 207). We therefore need to consider a fifth possibility for Phase 4 ditches at Kuk: *Model E. Conscious acts designed to hide the ideological meaning of a social landscape that was produced behind a façade of functional justification.*

We now turn to the empirical evidence that might enable Models A–E to be tested.

BLOCKS A10 AND A11 AT KUK

Methods

The area chosen for the testing of these hypotheses is in the south-eastern part of Kuk swamp, which was one of the principal areas investigated by Golson and his team from 1972–7 (Figure 11.2). Phase 4 in the Kuk sequence is dated from about 2000 to 1200 BP, and at this time the major disposal channels in use in this south-eastern area were Ketiba's and Neringa's Barets, both named after members of Golson's team of workmen ('baret' being the Pidgin word for ditch). After Ketiba's joins Neringa's the combined channel runs NNW across the study site towards its outfall at the River Guga (Figure 11.2).

Apart from some small lahar mounds along the south-western margins, the surface topography of Kuk swamp is very gentle. The process which has dominated the geomorphology of the swamp in between periods of drainage activity has been the deposition of an alluvial fan by the stream known as Kuk Creek (Hughes *et al.* 1991). According to the contour map produced by the Department of Agriculture, Territory of Papua, at the time when Kuk first became a government station in 1969, the surface slope of the fan in the lower parts of blocks A10 and A11 is only about 1:350 (Figure 11.3). The area was completely waterlogged in 1969, and its drainage would have been a major challenge for the hydraulic engineers of prehistory.

Block A9 is where we have already investigated the Phase 4 ditches in some detail (Bayliss-Smith and Golson 1992a, 1992b). The middle of this block had a surface elevation in 1969 that was at least 6 feet (1.8 m) above the level of the northern parts of A10/A11. It is therefore reasonable to predict that cultivators in A10/A11 would have experienced severe problems of seasonal waterlogging. Gorecki (1985: 325) has emphasized the difficulty

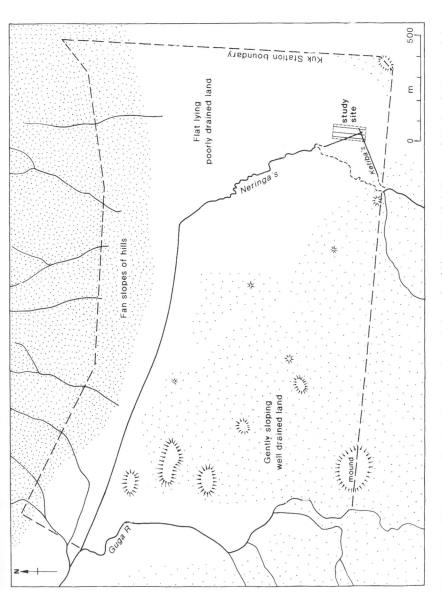

Figure 11.2 Kuk swamp, showing the major disposal channels of Phase 4, Ketiba's Baret and Neringa's Baret, and the location of the study sites in blocks A10/A11. (The channel shown as a dotted line to the west of the study site is Nema's Baret, which in our earlier paper was shown as a Phase 4 channel (Bayliss-Smith and Golson 1992a: Figure 2). The evidence for its Phase 4 status now looks more doubtful but is still under review.)

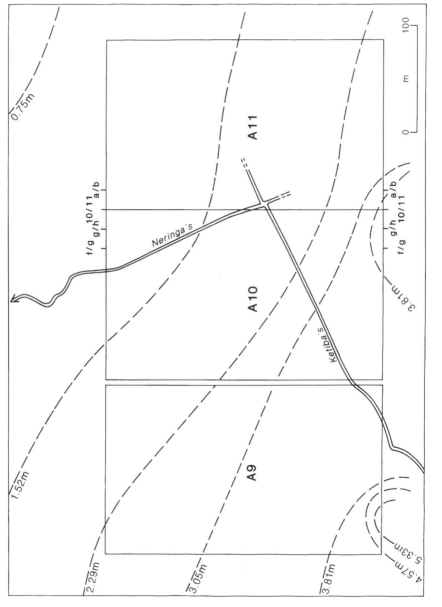

Figure 11.3 Blocks A9, A10 and A11 at Kuk, showing topography and approximate positions of the major disposal channels (excluding Nema's Baret – see Figure 11.2).

of defining what is wet and what is dry at Kuk, because 'most of the drylands become wetlands during the wet season, whereas swamplands become wetlands, and even drylands on their margins, during dry spells'. Undoubtedly the lower parts of A10/A11 would actually have been under water up until 1969. Mick Leahy recalled that in 1933 'in the swamp we had to put kunai under the small dogs and [carry] two of them across part of it – it was so deep' (Gorecki 1979b: 26). This part of Kuk would never have been other than wetland, even under favourable conditions of drought or drainage.

We have described elsewhere the techniques used for analysing the archaeological record made by Golson and others from 1972–4 (Bayliss-Smith and Golson 1992a). Our information comes from the exposure of the cross-sections of prehistoric ditches, usually visible in both walls of the modern drains that were dug from 1969 onwards. The modern drains run north–south and are about 1 m wide and 22 m apart. We can reconstruct the prehistoric landscape from a knowledge of the orientation of the Phase 4 ditches. Assuming that the ditches run more or less in straight lines, the grid pattern of Phase 4 drainage can therefore be reconstructed. From the basal elevations of these ditches, the direction of water flow can also be established.

What emerges from the analysis is a large sample of ditch cross-sections, and also maps of the reconstructed grid network of the small ditches which we call 'field drains'. The grid defines a pattern of rectangular plots, which we are calling 'fields' and which we assume were the gardens used for the cultivation of taro and perhaps other crops like sugar cane and green vegetables. Exactly the same methods for drawing cross-sections and maps were used for A10/A11 in this study as were used for A9 in our earlier paper.

We are able to reconstruct the social landscape in this way because all of the Phase 4 ditches that are used in the analysis contain Olgaboli tephra as part of their infill. The evidence therefore enables us to trace the microtopography of fields and ditches that existed at the time of this volcanic event, which is well known from tephra sequences across the highlands and is dated to around 1200 BP (Golson 1976: 212; Blong 1982: 10). The fall of Olgaboli signalled the end of Phase 4 at Kuk, and was followed by a long period of swamp abandonment (Golson 1977). With one or two dubious exceptions there are in fact no ditches in A10/A11 identifiable by their size and shape as Phase 4 ditches but lacking Olgaboli tephra. Such ditches would be interpreted as dating from early in the phase rather than the period immediately prior to the fall of Olgaboli tephra. Their absence from blocks A10/A11, in contrast to A9, itself suggests that the more difficult part of the swamp had been avoided until the very end of Phase 4. In fact the absence of earlier ditches in A10/A11 makes the task of interpretation easier, so that quite a large area of drained fields can be reconstructed (Figure 11.4).

The depth of field drains

In A10/A11 there are 105 field drains for which both depth and elevation measurements are available. Some examples of these cross–sections are shown

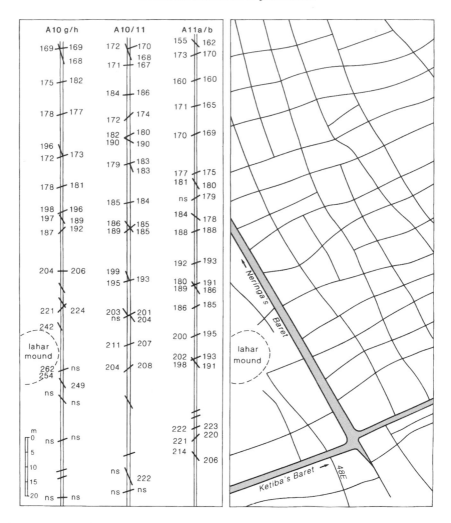

Figure 11.4   (Left) Evidence for the orientation and elevation above local datum of Olgaboli ditches in drains A10 g/h, A10/11 and A10 a/b; and (right) a reconstruction of the social landscape of drained fields and major disposal channels. *Note:* Drain cross-sections marked 'ns' are those where the elevation of the base of the ditch above local datum is not stated in the field record. Other elevations are given in centimetres.

in Figure 11.5. These ditch cross-sections resemble closely those that we described for block A9 (Bayliss-Smith and Golson 1992a: fig. 3), but in A10/A11 there are fewer of the very wide ditches that we believe were formed by repeated cycles of re-cutting. We have suggested that it was when an area was being reclaimed from swamp fallow that ditches were re-dug in order to re-establish the drainage network and, in the process, the ditches were sometimes accidentally widened. An example of this effect was revealed by open-site excavation in block A9, and is illustrated in Golson (1976: 215, fig.

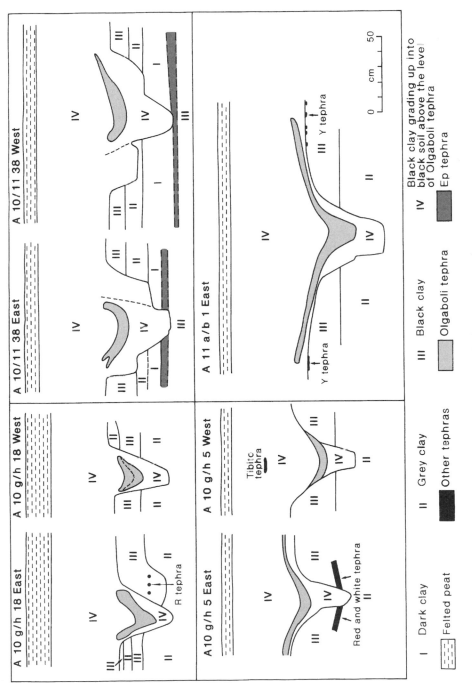

Figure 11.5 Examples of the cross-sections of Phase 4 ditches in blocks A10/A11, Kuk.

8). The fact that the ditches in A10/A11 show little evidence of widening or deepening again supports the idea that this low-lying area was not brought into production until the end of Phase 4.

As in A9, ditch depth was measured from the base which in most cases was clearly outlined by the soft black clay infill against the grey clay substrate into which the ditches were incised. The top of the bank of each ditch could only be defined by the level of the top of the black clay which overlies the grey clay. There must have been a soil horizon overlying this black clay, as can be detected in some cases from the gap that exists between the top of the black clay and the overlying Olgaboli tephra. (For an example, see ditch A10g/h 5 East in Figure 11.5, where 2–16 cm of black peaty clay, interpreted as the Phase 4 soil, is found beneath the tephra and on top of the black clay banks of the ditch). However, only in some cases can the thickness of this palaeosol be defined precisely, so for present purposes depth is measured as the distance from each ditch's base to the top of the black clay.

There are 105 ditches in A10/A11 for which this measure of depth is available, which by coincidence is exactly the same number of depth measures as were available in A9. As can be seen from Figure 11.6, there is no significant difference between the two areas in the depth of the field drains. Mean depth in A9 was found to be 41.1 cm (Bayliss-Smith and Golson 1992a: 7), whereas in A10/A11 it is 40.4 cm. The modal depth class in A9 was 40–44 cm, little different from the 35–39 cm modal class in A10/A11. Statistical analysis of the two areas would suggest that we are looking here at two subsets of the same population of ditches.

At first sight this is a surprising finding, given our expectation that the greater hydraulic problems of A10/A11 would have demanded, as a conscious response, that the ditches there be dug deeper than in A9 at the margins of the swamp. To investigate this further for A10/11, the relationship between ditch depth and field elevation was examined. The height above local datum of the black clay surface into which the Phase 4 ditches were dug was compared with the depth of their incision (Figure 11.7). Whereas the elevation of the palaeo-surface varies within A10/A11 by more than a metre (from 197 to 302 cm above local datum), and whereas the depth of ditches ranges from 20 to 64 cm, the two variables are not in any way correlated. The lowest parts of A10/A11 are not necessarily where the deepest ditches are to be found, and nor are the more elevated parts necessarily where we find the shallower ones. Instead, most ditches have a rather standard depth (around 40 cm), and the small variations that exist are not correlated with the elevation of the local land surface.

The spacing of field drains

Another way in which people can adapt the design of wetland drainage at a site, as a conscious response to the ecological (hydraulic) problems they encounter, is by making an adjustment to the spacing of the drains. In a low-lying area with a higher water table the soil has to be drained through slow

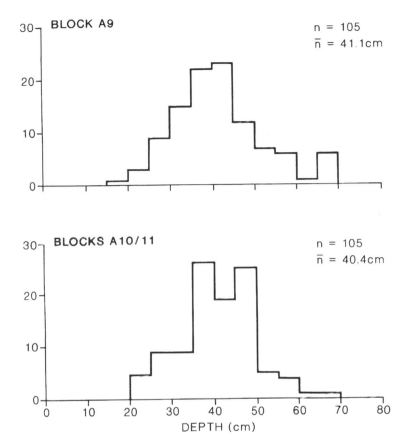

Figure 11.6 Depths of the Phase 4 Olgaboli ditches at Kuk: block A9 compared to blocks A10/A11.

lateral seepage into the field drains, and if these drains are dug at the same depth but closer together then the fields will be drained more quickly.

In the earlier study in A9 it was found that in the four sub-areas where fields could be reconstructed, their average dimensions were 12.2 × 8.6 m (Bayliss-Smith and Golson 1992a: 12). These dimensions are for the longer and shorter sides, respectively, and represent the average of the four separate areas in A9. A re-measuring of the thirty 'complete' fields (pooled data for the aggregate sample) gives very similar dimensions of 13.6 × 8.7 m.

These field sizes at Kuk can be compared with measurements made on present-day ditches in the upper Kaugel valley, which were being dug in 1980 for taro cultivation. The ditches in the Kaugel define almost square fields with sides that vary between 5 and 8 m in length (Bayliss-Smith 1985: 297; Bayliss-Smith and Golson 1992b: 22). In our earlier paper we provided an ecological explanation for the difference between the fields of Phase 4 in the upper Wahgi valley (altitude 1,580 m) and those in the upper Kaugel

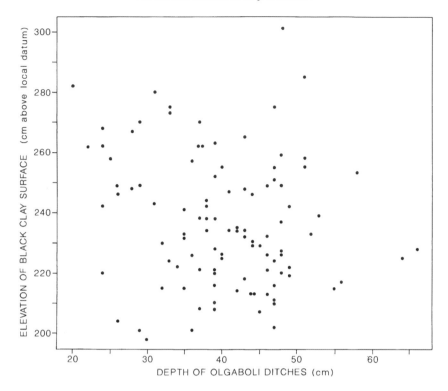

Figure 11.7   Relationship between elevation of the black clay palaeo-surface and the depth of the Phase 4 Olgaboli ditches dug into that surface, blocks A10/A11, Kuk.

valley (altitude 2,200 m) today: 'in the cooler and damper climate of the upper Kaugel valley it is not unreasonable to expect a higher drainage density' (Bayliss-Smith and Golson 1992a: 12). Can the same line of argument be applied to contrasted areas within Kuk swamp?

A sample of sixty 'complete' fields is available in A10/A11 (see Figure 11.4). The longer sides of the fields average 13.32 m in length, and the shorter ones 8.83 m. Once again there is absolutely no significant difference between block A9 (13.6 × 8.7 m) and blocks A10/A11. The absence of any difference in either ditch depth or field size, despite the contrasted elevation of the two areas, forces us to rethink our assumptions about the ditch-digging behaviour of New Guinea highlanders of the Phase 4 period. Clearly waterlogging of the fields was not regarded as a distinctive problem for late Phase 4 cultivators in blocks A10/A11, despite the area's low-lying and hence potentially problematic character. The ditches dug there differed neither in depth, nor spacing, nor orientation from those on the margins of the swamp.

This finding suggests that the field drainage system in blocks A10/A11 was not specially designed to solve a new and different problem, but instead was a set of standard artefacts produced in the normal way as part of unconscious practice. We conclude that in searching for the meanings of these field patterns the 'economic efficiency model' (Model B) should not be given the most emphasis. Model A (unconscious practice in an unproblematic context) receives more support, while Models C and E remain possibilities.

The major disposal channels

We can conclude that at the end of Phase 4 the same type of agricultural system was being extended into the low-lying parts of Kuk swamp as was already well established on the swamp's margins. To understand what made this process possible we need to widen our view of the social landscape, and consider in more detail the major disposal channels. Without some means to evacuate out of the swamp the water that was draining from the fields, the field drains would have had no function other than as territorial boundaries. At Kuk, digging and maintaining channels to enable the water to flow unimpeded towards the Guga river outfall was the most fundamental challenge facing anyone who intended to cultivate the swamp.

Unfortunately the data that we have available to address this question within blocks A10/A11 are not altogether satisfactory. The field drains recorded in those blocks in large numbers all articulate with Ketiba's Baret or with the northward-flowing channel that Ketiba's joins, called Neringa's Baret (see Figure 11.2). This latter channel is exposed in oblique section in the modern drain called A10/11, but its complex stratigraphy and disturbance by later phases of drainage made the Phase 4 channel difficult to detect. The position of its north bank could be established, but not its width. However, Ketiba's Baret is somewhat better preserved. Where its western extension crosses the modern drain A10/11 there are two clear cross-sections through its south bank (Figure 11.8), and there is enough evidence to locate the northern bank and so establish its width.

Ketiba's Baret at this point is about 2.4 m wide. Further east the extension of the same channel crosses the modern drain A11 a/b, and here it has an estimated width of 2.0 m. However, the total depth of Ketiba's Baret cannot be established from the archaeological data available. At the time of record in 1973 it proved impossible to see the base of the Phase 4 channel, which was below the level of standing water in the modern drain. The 1973 water level was at an elevation of 195 cm above local datum. The sections reproduced in Figure 11.8 show Olgaboli tephra mantling the side of the palaeo-channel. The bank of this channel, as defined by the Olgaboli tephra, dips at an angle of 26 degrees down towards the 1973 water level. The base of the channel must be somewhere just below this elevation. If the original channel was roughly symmetrical in cross-section, then considering its width it would seem unlikely that Olgaboli tephra can extend for more than a few centimetres below the 1973 water level; but lack of data prevents us from being more definite on this point.

Nevertheless, even the minimum level of the base of Ketiba's (195 cm above local datum) is quite a substantial depth. As Figure 11.7 has shown, all of the 105 field drains in blocks A10/A11 have basal elevations that are above this 195 cm level, so that even at this minimum level Ketiba's Baret would have been effective in draining the surrounding fields. We can prove this by reference to the nearest field drain (A10/11 48 East), which joins Ketiba's about 3 metres upstream from the sections of this channel that are shown in Figure 11.8. At a point 9 metres upstream from this junction the field drain, which at this point has a depth of 43 cm and is altogether a typical Phase 4 ditch, has a basal elevation of 222 cm above local datum. The difference in elevation between this drain and Ketiba's Baret suggests that in this area the cultivated fields were at least 27 cm 'high and dry' above a water table controlled by the water level in the disposal channel.

Ketiba's Baret in block A10 is far away from the ultimate outfall of the water, which is the River Guga to the north-west (see Figure 11.2). From the point where Neringa's Baret joins Ketiba's to the River Guga is a distance of about 2.4 km, with a fall in level of only 5.5 m. The average water slope of 1:440 represents a rather modest hydraulic gradient, and would have necessitated careful grading of the channel for its hydraulic efficiency to be maintained.

DISCUSSION: THE ORGANIZATION OF PHASE 4 DRAINAGE

Labour input

The labour costs of the original construction of major disposal channels like Neringa's and Ketiba's can be very roughly estimated. We assume first an average width of 2.5 m and a depth of 1.0 m, so that to excavate each kilometre length would have involved the digging of 2,500 cubic metres of saturated peat and clay. The experimental data from a range of sites suggest a mean productivity for men using wooden spades and digging sticks in Phase 4 of 0.5 cubic metres per hour (Bayliss-Smith and Golson 1992a: 21). This rate of digging could be kept up for perhaps five hours per day (Gorecki 1985: 341).

On the basis of these assumptions we can estimate that each kilometre of major disposal channel would have required about 1,000 man-days of digging, which represents about two months' work for a gang of sixteen men. To dig Neringa's Baret, from its origin near to the junction with Ketiba's to its outfall in the Guga, would have required the same group of sixteen men to work continuously for two and a half months. It would clearly have been a substantial undertaking, in terms of both the investment of effort and the necessary social organization.

Social organization

Any discussion of the organizational needs of Phase 4 drainage must be heavily dependent on ethnographic analogy. We can find close parallels to Kuk in the Tari basin of the Southern Highlands, in the Baliem valley of

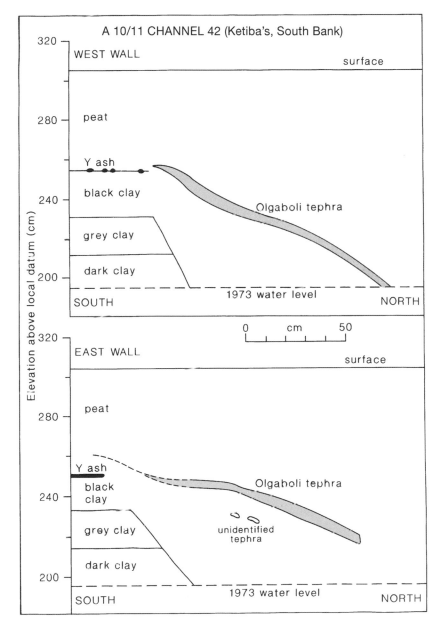

Figure 11.8 Two sections through the south bank of Ketiba's Baret at its intersection with drain A10/A11, Kuk

Irian Jaya, and in the upper Wahgi itself. Although Kuk swamp and all the adjacent wetlands were abandoned at the time of contact, since 1969 the Kawelka tribe have been returning to the area. Pawel Gorecki's (1985) detailed studies of the colonization process show, when establishing new gardens in swampland, the Kawelka always follow an important rule. Drainage begins with the establishment of a disposal channel, which starts at a point where water can run off the garden site into an outlet. They then work upslope towards the chosen site for the garden itself. In anticipation of future needs a major ditch is often dug longer than is necessary for the initial area of drained garden that it serves, and such ditches are often established along the boundaries of clan or sub-clan territories (Gorecki 1985: 325).

Co-ordination by a large group is needed for the initial construction, but subsequent maintenance of the disposal channel is the responsibility of the particular people cultivating the adjacent gardens. On the margins of the wetland, on the other hand, drainage can be a more individual project. A short disposal drain can feed straight into the swamp, which itself provides the outfall. Warfare, the clogging of ditches, and normal fallowing practices are all reasons for a formerly drained area to be abandoned (Gorecki 1979a; 1985: 329).

Most of these general findings are confirmed by Heider's observations of the drainage practices of the Dugum Dani in the Baliem valley, Irian Jaya (Heider 1970; Gardner and Heider 1968: 46–8). Across most of their territory the Dugum Dani's drainage activities focused on the maintenance of existing ditches, since the swamps were already fully reclaimed. The ditches were rarely less than 2 m wide, and the main channels could be up to 5 m in width.

> Because of the muddy bottoms of the ditches in use, the depth is hard to measure exactly, but often the head of a man standing in a ditch does not reach above the adjacent garden bed . . . Some men stand in the ditches, up to their waist in water and mud, cutting into the mud with the broad-bladed digging sticks and heaving it on to the banks with their hands; other men or women on the banks then spread this mud out evenly with their feet.
>
> (Heider 1970: 40, 42)

Among the Dani the cleaning of ditches was communal work, carried out by a 'co-operative work party' (Heider 1970: 39–40). The system as it operated in the 1960s was focused on sweet potato cultivation, which allowed about half of the swamp to be in production and half in fallow. Just as warfare could lead to swamp abandonment at Kuk, so in the Baliem valley the breakdown of political alliances could have the same effect. Across one valley floor there was a 2 km strip of 'no-man's-land' along a disputed frontier: 'in time of peace the people of the two alliances push out to farm and live in the no-man's-land' (Heider 1970: 42, 78). Episodes of swamp drainage can therefore reflect the vicissitudes of local politics rather than being a response to regional economic or ecological problems.

These ethnographic analogues were used by Golson (1976: 218–19; Powell et al. 1975) to suggest what might have been the proximate cause of the abandonment of Kuk at the end of Phase 6, 250 years ago:

Part of the answer no doubt lies in the complexity of the regime, whereby the draining of large areas was dependent on a limited number of outlets into a remote outfall. Such a system was highly vulnerable to upsets of all kinds, both natural and political.

(Powell *et al.* 1975: 49)

During Phase 6 the dramatic changes that were underway in the agricultural economy following the arrival of the sweet potato may have provided a sufficient 'upset'. If so, then a political explanation for swamp abandonment at that time is unnecessary (Golson and Gardner 1990). However, in relation to Phase 4 it is an explanation that we would like to revive.

Implications for Kuk Phase 4

The evidence of New Guinea ethnography suggests that digging a major disposal channel such as the Ketiba/Neringa ditch was a large-scale, co-operative project, and a necessary pre-condition for the establishment of individual drained gardens such as those in blocks A10/A11. It is unfortunate that the precise character of Ketiba's and Neringa's Barets cannot be better described, but the data available indicate that their total length, their straightness, their depth and their width represent the outcome of a major, planned investment of time, skill and effort by a relatively large co-operating group. In the terms proposed by Gosden (1994), the meaning of the resulting artefact relates to its production by conscious design in order to solve a particular set of problems.

It was the construction of the major disposal channels that made possible more individual efforts to establish gardens, such as those shown in our reconstruction (see Figure 11.4). These drained gardens are artefacts which convey a rather different meaning. In the spacing of the field drains and in their actual digging, unconscious practice could take over from deliberate design. We have shown that everywhere the dimensions of fields and ditches deviate not at all from a norm which must represent customary Phase 4 practice. The small variations that we see in these small ditches and fields could be individual, idiosyncratic or even accidental. The size and shape of fields must have had their principal meaning in the division of space between households or between different crops, as well as conforming to the basic requirements of hydraulic efficiency.

These conclusions follow from a rigorous testing of alternative hypotheses about the meaning of these artefacts, using a large sample of archaeological evidence. However, the evidence itself does not enable us to deduce how far the Phase 4 social landscape as a whole should be seen as a 'social' rather than an 'economic' project (i.e. Model C rather than Model B). Perhaps we should be considering also Models D and E. Is this a landscape of drainage in which the artefacts convey an ostensible message about their self-evident functional purpose, but where they are actually designed to mask a deeper symbolic, or even sacred, meaning? As an artefact the Phase 4 system of channels and ditches seems to be functionally effective, but to what ultimate purpose?

Our reading of Melanesian ethnography discourages us from proposing simple, single-cause explanations for a phenomenon like agricultural intensification. Intensification always generates a landscape which is simultaneously a technical, a social and an ideological construct. There is no reason why the New Guinea past should be less complex than the present. The conscious design of a major disposal channel must have been a 'social' as well as an 'economic' project, within a society where coercive big-man leadership and a gendered division of labour were latent if not dominant features. There is no way of knowing if, in the second millennium before present, coercion rather than co-operation was the main basis for group activity, or whether 'pressure' rather than opportunity was the main motive for drainage. Is Phase 4 a gendered landscape, reflecting male projects to display prestige or solidarity (the digging of major disposal channels) alongside female projects of household production (the drained fields)? The hypothesis is plausible, but cannot be supported except by a fragile web of ethnoarchaeological speculation.

Stone axe quarrying: an analogue?

We would, however, draw attention to the total abandonment of swamp drainage immediately after the fall of Olgaboli tephra. The abandonment was so complete that the Phase 4 ditches became completely infilled with peat and alluvium and so disappeared as topographic features, and for this reason have survived as archaeological evidence. The fall of Olgaboli tephra must have been at least as dramatic as the fall of Tibito tephra around AD 1700, an event still remembered in highlands legend as 'the time of darkness' (Blong 1982). Although innovations in the dryland sphere of agriculture can be invoked, and although these may have provided an incentive for swamp abandonment (Golson 1977, 1997; Golson and Gardner 1990), we suggest that the fall of Olgaboli tephra at precisely the end-point of Phase 4 cannot be a coincidence. We take it to be further evidence for the fragility of the social and political arrangements which made possible the digging of the major disposal channels.

There is a parallel between the digging of major disposal drains in New Guinea and other kinds of large-scale social projects, such as pig festivals, warfare or stone axe quarrying. The Tuman quarries 15 km south-east of Kuk have been utilized in recent times by the Tungei tribe, and up until 1933 expeditions were mounted by the Tungei at intervals, in order to re-open the quarries and so provide a new supply of axe blanks for use in local exchange. Burton (1984: 72) points out that a period of political stability was necessary before an expedition to the quarry could be mounted. Stability was perhaps less critical for quarrying than for holding a pig festival, but none the less it was important. During the 1920s for example there was such a long period of fighting that some of the quarries became overgrown (Burton 1984: 72).

Another pre-condition for quarrying was an effective social organization, probably on a consensus basis but under big-man leadership:

> The process of arranging for a mass of men to coordinate their labour for months on end is likely to have been more important than the technical [knowledge necessary for quarrying] . . . The organisation of the labour force at the Tuman quarries was highly idiosyncratic, but it is obvious that the overall system was an extremely effective means of extracting axe stone . . . The Tuman example shows – if demonstration were needed – that non-ranked, non-hierarchical societies can organise themselves for large-scale productive ventures when a range of conditions are met.
>
> (Burton 1984: 81, 88)

In the Tuman case, and for other large-scale projects in the upper Wahgi valley, these pre-conditions include:

(a) peace or at least a truce in normal inter-tribal warfare;
(b) a continuing belief in the ideology that underlies male solidarity and the division of labour between men and women; and
(c) a sufficient number of skilled men who can remember how success was achieved during a previous expedition.

Although it can be effective, Burton (1984: 88) argues that this form of labour organization is also highly volatile. The group project can easily be undermined if one of the conditions that make it possible is no longer met. In the Tuman case stone axe quarrying came to an abrupt end in 1933. It ceased after the expedition that was actually in progress on 27 March when Jim Taylor (government patrol officer) and Mick Leahy (gold prospector) flew past on their reconnaissance flight which first revealed the existence of the Central Highlands to the outside world. After four or five years the supply of stone that the Tungei had quarried in 1933 had been used up, and this might have been the stimulus for planning a new cycle of quarrying, but circumstances had changed. Shifts in the pattern of local alliances and the coming of steel tools had removed both the means and the incentive for any leader to mobilize a labour force, and quarrying was abandoned forever.

Swamp drainage: social problem or ecological problem?
Rather than seeing stone axe quarrying at Tuman in economic terms, as a local response to the regional demand for these valuable exchange items, Burton (1984) emphasizes instead the fragile social and political base upon which quarrying as a group activity depended. It is tempting to transpose this model into the Wahgi valley wetlands, and suggest that episodes of swamp drainage might also have required a precise balance of social and political relations. It is possible, therefore, that we should interpret the social landscapes of drainage at Kuk more as an expression of co-operation and male solidarity

under big-man leadership than as symptoms of economic response to ecological problems.

A sociopolitical explanation for drainage makes it easier to explain the sudden abandonment of Kuk swamp after the volcanic eruption known as Olgaboli. Unlike the coming of the white man in 1933, the fall of Olgaboli tephra about 1200 BP was a temporary disturbance to the economy and society of the Wahgi valley, but clearly it was a sufficiently disastrous event to have transformed the pre-conditions for large-scale drainage activity. The volcanic ash which fell from the sky and was washed into the field drains was never afterwards disturbed by a new cycle of ditch maintenance. The swamp was abandoned and drainage of Kuk swamp was not resumed until the onset of Phase 5, some 800 years later (Golson 1977).

CONCLUSION

A drained swamp is a wetland ecosystem transformed into a social landscape. It is something shaped by decisions and actions so as to fulfil human needs. At the time of its original formation such a landscape would have conveyed many meanings to those who created it, and to others. In the case of Kuk swamp in Phase 4 only the ditch network has survived as archaeological evidence, but in a rather complete form. We therefore believe it is worth trying to analyse it as a distinctive artefact, the meaningful product of decisions and actions.

This chapter is an attempt to deconstruct the meanings which underlie the actions that created the Phase 4 landscape. Gosden (1994: 35) has argued that 'much action is unthought, but problems which arise in the structure of habit are brought to consciousness'. Such problems require particular solutions, and may result in artefacts that are consciously designed to convey symbolic meanings to others. Perhaps some of these meanings can be conveyed to us today. Can Phase 4 ditches be deconstructed in this way?

We have presented evidence to show that the Phase 4 field drains have a standard size and spacing which is insensitive to variations in local topography. This standardization suggests that these ditches were dug not as a response to local problems of hydraulic efficiency, but instead as habitual practice in order to reproduce an agricultural landscape which conformed to the cultural norms of Phase 4 society. Social space of a familiar kind was thereby created, in the repeated patterns of small rectangular fields extending across the swamp.

The conscious actions which made possible this replication of a standard pattern of small fields were instead focused on the design of the major disposal channels. Once they were dug, these long, deep, straight ditches lowered the water table so effectively that even in low-lying areas 'unthought practice' (i.e. standard field drainage) was adequate for the task of draining individual fields.

We interpret the disposal channels as representing the successful culmination of a social project that would have required political alliances between groups as well as intra-group co-operation and leadership. The sudden abandonment of the system following the fall of Olgaboli tephra is testimony to the fragile nature of the Phase 4 project, possibly in terms of its ideological underpinnings as well as its sociopolitical base.

However, while arguing that the proximate causes of drainage episodes at Kuk should be explained in this way, we are not proposing that we should ignore the *longue dureé* or structural prehistory of the highlands, which provides the context for shorter-term cyclical actions such as those we can document at Kuk. We need to understand the long-term technological, demographic and environmental changes which affect the material basis for highlands subsistence. As Golson (1977) originally argued, this shifting context for action may be critical in deciding whether group decisions are directed towards the intensification of wetland agriculture, or whether equivalent but different social projects take place elsewhere, perhaps in some corner of the social landscape that is much less archaeologically visible.

REFERENCES

Ballard, C. 1994. The centre cannot hold. Trade networks and sacred geography in the Papua New Guinea Highlands. *Archaeology in Oceania* 29, 130–48.

Bayliss-Smith, T.P. 1985. Pre-Ipomoean agriculture in the New Guinea Highlands above 2000 metres: some experimental data on taro cultivation. In *Prehistoric Intensive Agriculture in the Tropics* (part i) I.S. Farrington (ed.), 285–320. Oxford: BAR.

Bayliss-Smith, T.P. 1996. People–plant interactions in the New Guinea highlands: agricultural heartland or horticultural backwater? In *The Origins and Spread of Agriculture and Pastoralism in Eurasia*, D.R. Harris (ed.), 499–523. London: UCL Press.

Bayliss-Smith, T.P. and J. Golson. 1992a. A Colocasian revolution in the New Guinea Highlands? Insights from Phase 4 at Kuk. *Archaeology in Oceania* 17, 1–21.

Bayliss-Smith, T.P. and J. Golson. 1992b. Wetland agriculture in New Guinea highlands prehistory. In *The Wetland Revolution in Prehistory*, B. Coles (ed.), 15–27. Exeter: The Prehistoric Society and Wetland Archaeology Research Project.

Bayliss-Smith, T.P., R.D. Bedford, H.C. Brookfield and M. Latham. 1988. *Islands, Islanders and the World. The Colonial and Post-Colonial Experience of Eastern Fiji.* Cambridge: Cambridge University Press.

Bender, B. 1992. Theorising landscapes, and the prehistoric landscapes of Stonehenge. *Man* 27, 735–55.

Blong, R.J. 1982. *The Time of Darkness. Local legends and volcanic reality in Papua New Guinea.* Canberra: Australian National University Press.

Burton, J. 1984. *Axe makers of the Wahgi. Pre-colonial industrialists of the Papua New Guinea Highlands.* Unpublished Ph.D. thesis, Australian National University, published by Prehistory Department, R.S.Pac.S., ANU.

Carmichael, D.L., J. Hubert, B. Reeves and A. Schanche (eds.) 1994. *Sacred Sites, Sacred Places.* London: Routledge.

Cosgrove, D. and S. Daniels. 1988. *The Iconography of Landscape. Essays on the symbolic representation, design and use of past environments.* Cambridge: Cambridge University Press.

Duncan, J. 1990. *The City as Text. The Politics of Landscape Representation in the Kandyan Kingdom.* Cambridge: Cambridge University Press.

Feil, D.K. 1987. *The Evolution of Highland Papua New Guinea Societies.* Cambridge: Cambridge University Press.

Gardner, R. and K.G. Heider. 1968. *Gardens of War. Life and death in the New Guinea Stone Age.* New York: Random House.

Giddens, A. 1979. *Central Problems in Social Theory.* London: Macmillan.

Golson, J. 1976. Archaeology and agricultural history in the New Guinea highlands. In *Problems in Economic and Social Archaeology,* G. de G. Sieveking, I.H. Longworth and K.E. Wilson (eds), 201–20. London: Duckworth.

Golson, J. 1977. No room at the top: agricultural intensification in the New Guinea Highlands. In *Sunda and Sahul: Prehistoric studies in Southeast Asia, Melanesia and Australia,* J. Allen, J. Golson and R. Jones (eds), 601–38. London: Academic Press.

Golson, J. 1997. From horticulture to agriculture in the New Guinea highlands: a case study of people and their environment. In *Historical Ecology in the Pacific Islands: prehistoric environmental and landscape change,* P.V. Kirch and T.L. Hunt (eds), 39–50. New Haven and London: Yale University Press.

Golson, J. and D.S. Gardner. 1990. Agriculture and sociopolitical organisation in New Guinea Highlands prehistory. *Annual Review of Anthropology* 19, 395–417.

Golson, J. and P.J. Hughes. 1980. The appearance of plant and animal domestication in New Guinea. *Journal de la Société des Océanistes* 36, 294–303.

Gorecki, P.P. 1979a. Population growth and abandonment of swamplands: a New Guinea Highlands example. *Journal de la Société des Océanistes* 35, 97–107.

Gorecki, P.P. 1979b. The Kuk obelisk, Western Highlands Province. *Oral History* 7, 19–28.

Gorecki, P.P. 1985. The conquest of a new 'wet and dry' territory: its mechanism and its archaeological consequences. In *Prehistoric Intensive Agriculture in the Tropics* (part i), I.S. Farrington (ed.), 321–45. Oxford: BAR.

Gorecki, P.P. 1986. Human occupation and agricultural development in the Papua New Guinea Highlands. *Mountain Research and Development* 6, 159–66.

Gosden, C. 1986. The interpretation of Mailu prehistory: the tyranny of distance. *Archaeology in Oceania* 21, 180–6.

Gosden, C. 1989. Prehistoric social landscapes of the Arawe islands, West New Britain province, Papua New Guinea. *Archaeology in Oceania* 24, 45–58.

Gosden, C. 1994. *Social Being and Time.* Oxford: Basil Blackwell.

Heider, K.G. 1970. *The Dugum Dani. A Papuan culture in the Highlands of West New Guinea.* Viking Fund Publications in Anthropology 49. New York: Wenner-Gren Foundation.

Hodder, I. 1992. Material practice, symbolism and ideology. *Proceedings of Theoretical Archaeology Conference, Bergen.* Bergen: Historical Museum. (Reprinted in I. Hodder, *Theory and Practice in Archaeology.* London: Routledge, 1992, 201–12.)

Hughes, P.J., M.E. Sullivan and D. Yok. 1991. Human-induced erosion in a Highlands catchment in Papua New Guinea: the prehistoric and contemporary records. *Zeitschift für Geomorphologie* suppl. Bd. 83, 227–39.

Ingold, T. 1993. The temporality of landscape. *World Archaeology* 25, 152–74.

Kirch, P.V. 1994. *The Wet and the Dry. Irrigation and agricultural intensification in Polynesia.,* Chicago and London: University of Chicago Press.

Kirk, W. 1952. Historical geography and the concept of the behavioural environment. In *Silver Jubilee Souvenir and N. Subrahmanyam Memorial Volume,* Indian Geographical Society, 152–60. (Reprinted in F.W. Foal and D.N. Livingstone (eds). 1989. *The Behavioural Environment. Essays on reflection, application and re-evaluation.* London and New York: Routledge, 18–32.)

McAlpine, J.R. and G. Keig, with R. Falls. 1983. *The Climate of Papua New Guinea.* Canberra: Australian National University Press.

Moore, H.L. 1986. *Space, Text and Gender. An anthropological study of the Marakwet of Kenya.* Cambridge: Cambridge University Press.

Pain, C.F., C.J. Pigram, R.J. Blong and G.O. Arnold. 1987. Cainozoic geology and geomorphology of the Wahgi valley, central highlands of Papua New Guinea. *BMR Journal of Australian Geology and Geophysics* 10, 267–75.

Powell, J.M., A. Kalunga, R. Moge, C. Pono, F. Zimike and J. Golson. 1975. *Agricultural Traditions of the Mount Hagen Area.* Occasional Paper 12, Port Moresby: Department of Geography, University of Papua New Guinea.

Pryor, F. 1991. *Flag Fen, Prehistoric Fenland Centre.* London: Batsford/English Heritage.

Sognnes, K. 1994. Ritual landscapes. Towards a reinterpretation of stone age rock art in Trondelag, Norway. *Norwegian Archaeological Review* 27, 29–50.

Shanks, M. and C. Tilley. 1987. *Social Theory and Archaeology.* Cambridge: Polity Press.

Spriggs, M. 1986. Landscape, land use and political transformation in southern Melanesia. In *Island Societies: archaeological approaches to evolution and transformation,* P.V. Kirch (ed.), 6–19. Cambridge: Cambridge University Press.

Storli, I. 1993. Sami Viking Age pastoralism, or the 'Fur Trade Paradigm' revisited. *Norwegian Archaeological Review* 26, 1–20.

Strathern, A. 1971. *The Rope of Moka. Big-men and ceremonial exchange in Mount Hagen, New Guinea.* Cambridge: Cambridge University Press.

Tilley, C. 1994. *A Phenomenology of Landscape: places, paths and monuments.* Oxford: Berg.

12 Different histories: a common inheritance for Papua New Guinea and Australia?

CHRIS GOSDEN AND LESLEY HEAD

Bernard Shaw once described the British and the Americans as two people divided by a common language. We feel much the same is true of academic views of Australia and Papua New Guinea, which have become divided through the use of a particular form of discourse, emphasizing subsistence and the differences in all other aspects of life which are seen to flow from the production of food. Central to the division of Australia from its northern neighbour is the notion that it is a continent of hunter–gatherers next to an island of farmers. This has long called for explanation. The need for explanation has been increased by the common history of the two landmasses, which were joined when people first entered the larger continent some 50,000 years ago and were only separated by rising sea levels around 8,000 years ago, by which time agricultural systems had already been established in the Highlands of New Guinea. The comparison of the two areas has not been open-ended, but has centred round one question: why did Aboriginal groups not adopt agriculture when they must have known about it through contacts with agriculturalists? (White 1971; Harris 1995; Yen 1995).

We shall look at the structure of thought that lies behind the comparison of a 'neolithic' Papua New Guinea and a 'palaeolithic' Australia and suggest that such a structure misleads in the following ways. First, when people consider either Australia or Papua New Guinea separately they stress diversity in forms of subsistence and culture. When they are compared each becomes a monolith, representing a category rather than a living entity. Second, the basis for this monolithic categorization is the assumption that subsistence is the major influence on all other areas of life, such that all hunter-gatherers must be more similar to each other in social structure, attachment to the land and ritual life than they will be to any farming group. Third, the key to a comparison of the prehistory of Australia and Papua New Guinea is teleological, in that Papua New Guineans from the earliest evidence are seen to be on the way to farming, whereas Australian prehistory reveals a series of hunter-gatherer ways of life which make them look less dynamic than their northern farming neighbours.

Positive comparisons between Australia and Papua New Guinea, on the other hand, can allow us to probe whether the two areas shared a joint history which had effects not just in the period when the two were joined as a single continent but also throughout the Holocene, after the great divide. The deepest divide we see is that imposed by European thought which, since the last century, has created a chasm between hunter-gatherers and farmers which is still divisive today. We shall first briefly state our own argument, and then review the history of thought on hunter-gatherers and farmers in this part of the world as well as looking at how people are starting to rethink a similar boundary between hunter-gatherers in Europe and then how we intend to rework this distinction in the Australia and Papua New Guinean case around the possibilities of a long-term history.

CULTURE, FOOD AND HISTORY

A major part of our argument is that the production of food is not the motor for history. To provide broader and deeper histories we need a more rounded view of culture. Our view is that cultures represent a complex field of relations in which all areas of life are interlinked and mutually influencing and that none of these can be seen to be more influential than any other. Culture has to do with people's mutual involvement in a material and physical world. A practice-based approach looks at the engagement in the world of the whole person, not just, or primarily, their mental faculties. Skills necessary for coping with the world are embodied and represent a series of dispositions to action that lead people to engage deeply with some areas of the world and not others (Ingold 1994: 332). Material things are not passive technical instruments guided by thought but a vital part of people's engagement with the world. Patterns of action unfold over time and space through the deployment of human skills, but these skills only exist fully when they are worked out on the recalcitrant material world. The things being worked on and with thus represent a series of triggers to action, mnemonic devices which help activate the next step in sequences of production or consumption. These sequences are rarely carried out by isolated individuals, but rather in particular social settings, where the triggers to and breaks in action are complex and derive from multiple connections between people and people, and people and things (Gosden 1994).

In this view culture is a set of resources, both human and physical, which are interwoven to create patterns of action in time and space. Skilled human action is given pattern and direction through the material world, so that the form of the landscape (itself shaped under human influence), the houses, the containers, clothing, cooking equipment and ritual gear all help shape acts of production and consumption, in the same way as they are products of human acts.

Within such a notion of culture, food is bound to loom large. Food is a constant need, something that people consume every day and around which there is often considerable cultural elaboration. Appadurai (1981) has pointed out that food is a powerful element in the battle for various cultural resources and coined the term 'gastro-politics' when looking at the Hindu case, where he shows that the sensory nature of food acts as a powerful evocation of memory, bringing situations far distant from the present into reach, making it a potent element in battles for power within the family and beyond. This one example will have to stand for many, in showing that food is not just a bundle of nutritional requirements but an integral part of the cultural field. There is, then, no such thing as subsistence. Subsistence is often seen as a basic cause in human life unlike any other, as it is felt that so much time and effort goes into the growing and eating of food that this effort must structure all other areas of social relations and cultural forms. The importance of subsistence is especially taken for granted when the change from hunter-gathering to farming is looked at, which is seen to involve the move to a greater intensity of effort in food production, sedentism and more intense forms of social co-operation and conflict. Irrespective of whether the stance is predominantly economic and ecological (Binford 1968) or symbolic and social (Hodder 1990), the importance of this transition is still assumed.

The stance taken here is that culture is a seamless whole of resources in which the production and consumption of food has a vital role. We cannot see subsistence as a thing apart, or as a major source of cause more important than other areas of life and which will have predictable effects. Instead we need to integrate the growing and eating of food within a notion which stresses that material things are in constant interaction with human skills and contain triggers to action, that help ensure that acts are performed in due sequence and within their proper spaces. At the analytical level the stance we are developing here encourages an holistic, rather than reductionist, analysis seeing linkages between different areas of life, without privileging any one element of life as more causative than any other.

The relational field of culture does not just exist in the present, but changes in a manner that is not random but is rather integral to that cultural field itself.

MYTH, HISTORY, LANDSCAPE AND GIFT

The notion of a cultural field is misleading as an image in one respect: it contains no suggestion of depth and of the structured nature of change. One of the possibilities that the dichotomy between Australia and Papua New Guinea has caused us to ignore is that of a long-term shared history. If people have been in both areas for at least 40,000 years and Australia and New Guinea were only sundered 8,000 years ago, then five-sixths of the period of the settlement of the continent occurred while the two areas were joined. This raises the possibility of long-term historical continuities which still have some influence today, ancient inheritances being reworked to suit local exigencies. We will present possible empirical evidence for such long-term continuities below, but first we need to consider how to develop a model of history which has both long- and short-term dimensions to it which can allow us comparison and contrast throughout Australia and New Guinea.

One of the commonest explanations given for why Aboriginal people did not adopt agriculture is that their ritual attachment to land made it impossible to change the land through cultivation. The Dreamtime is a potent notion here, both for Europeans and Aboriginal groups, as a collection of accounts of the activities of ancestors in forming the landscape and providing a set of guidelines for right action within any one landscape. Yen gives a recent version of this view where he says that Aboriginal groups humanized the landscape through ritual and that Dreamtime notions were inherently conservative, leading to a rejection of new ideas. Aboriginal ritual is to do with the landscape as a whole, whereas Melanesian ritual concerns productivity which is needed to fund exchange relationships (Yen 1995: 845). However, Rumsey (1994) has attempted to look at the way Aboriginal groups' relations to the land were both historical and mythical and he starts with a distinction between myth and history which is useful in the present context. Rumsey takes up a distinction made by Turner (1988) in which myths view the structure of human society as a product of superhuman forces, natural powers or pre-social forces, which are beyond the reach and influence of human agency. History, by contrast, is an awareness that social relations are not predetermined by mythical structures, but are shaped by individual or collective action. History shows an openness to, and awareness of, contingency and of the power of human agency. History also operates in a time continuous with the present, even if change is acknowledged, whereas mythical structures refer back to a previous state of the world, where human beings either did not exist or had no power and where processes of cause and effect manifest themselves differently. It might seem at first as if these distinctions echo Lévi-Strauss's categories of hot and cold societies, whereby in the latter elaborate systems of social and natural classification, ultimately grounded in myth, absorb contingent events so as to render them unimportant and not socially efficacious. Similarly, Sahlins made the distinction between prescriptive forms of history in which societies assimilate contingent historical circumstances through a denial of their contingent character, unlike performative societies who make events the spur for change. In both these distinctions Aboriginal societies are seen as an archetypal expression of cold or prescriptive forms of history (Rumsey 1994: 118).

Rumsey's main point is that myth and history are not mutually exclusive, so that only one or the other can be found in a particular social group, but that they are linked means of dealing with the past, which can easily coexist. He goes on to look at the centrality of landscape to both myth and history in Aboriginal Australia and shows that landscape is the main locus of social memory with both myth and history inscribed in the landscape. Stories, songs, dance and paintings are all means of retrieving memories and meanings from the country, working together as social memory and showing the paradoxical combination of extreme and long-term continuity and considerable negotiability (Rumsey 1994: 127–8).

If we now combine the distinction between myth and history with the different emphases that can be put on mobile material culture and the landscape, we come up with a matrix for possible different emphases in social action. These range from groups where much social effort is concentrated on myth and myth is inscribed in the landscape to people who emphasize myth, but have access to mythical powers or times primarily through material culture (such as saints' relics etc.), to those who emphasize history and ascribe historical forces to the landscape and see a close connection between human agency and the landscape, to those who connect history and human agency with material things and the exchange of gifts in order to construct and alter human relations is the best known possibility here. Land, material things, history and myth are not truly separate entities and therefore are not formally distinguishable in analytical terms. Before looking in more detail at this matrix of possibilities we must look briefly at why these have not been explored before; this necessitates a short historical account of the subject.

HISTORY OF THOUGHT ON HUNTER-GATHERERS AND FARMERS

A historical perspective on the problem of comparisons of Australia and Papua New Guinea shows how the construction of categories and definitions within a context of eighteenth- and nineteenth-century colonialism continues to structure thought-patterns and debates today. Coming closer to the present, we can query why various challenges to the categories did not result in them being jettisoned. Was it because they remain the best representation of reality we have, or because a particularly powerful categorization was entrenched and maintained?

The colonization of the entire Australian continent by a single nation has been seen to exacerbate perceptions of external difference and internal unity in several different contexts. Australia has been treated as a single archaeological region precisely because of this colonial history. The corollary of such a perception is that differences between Australia and the island of New Guinea were emphasized. Historian Attwood (1989) examined the construction of Aboriginality as a category arising very much out of the needs and perceptions of the colonizers. It is important to also note Mulvaney's caution that the northern hemisphere commentators were drawing on and reworking the same relatively small body of ethnographic literature, resulting in 'circular and misleading argument more often than has been recognised' (Mulvaney 1990: 34). The creation of Australia as a single nation-state, the use of a limited set of ethnographic examples to represent the continent, and the concerns of northern hemisphere commentators led to a limited view of Australian Aboriginal social and economic forms. These limitations are in many ways still with us today.

A brief overview of the role of early ethnography in establishing conceptualizations of Australians compared with New Guineans is relevant here. It shows that several processes, operating simultaneously, contributed to a very entrenched division between hunters (later hunter-gatherers) and farmers. First, hunting was central to the definition of savages. Second, the imperative of classification had both spatial and temporal dimensions. Degrees of primitiveness were correlated with the three islands under discussion: New Guinea, Australia and Tasmania. Tasmania was most distant in both space and time. Third, the geological heritage of many of those active in the debates contributed to a layered, teleological view of evolutionary change.

Although emphasis varied between authors, central criteria to discussions of levels of civilization were the relationship to nature, in particular the extent of control over nature (e.g. Prichard 1855; Ratzel 1896), the role of subsistence (e.g. Morgan [1877]1907) and the complexity of the material culture (e.g. Tylor 1891). Williams (1986) shows the close relationships between these discussions and the development of English property law. Hunting savages, representing the lowest stage, were considered to live 'in a state of nature in which concepts of property had not yet come into being' (Williams 1986: 129).

With the acceptance of deep time in geology and the Darwinian revolution in biology, it was a short step for the classification across space to become one across time:

> It being shown that the details of Culture are capable of being classified in a great number of ethnographic groups of arts, beliefs, customs, and the rest, the consideration comes next how far the facts arranged in these groups are produced by evolution from one another.
>
> (Tylor 1891: 4)

Nowhere is this more explicit than in the chapter structure of Sollas's 1915 volume *Ancient Hunters and Their Modern Representatives*; various 'modern representatives' are interspersed with archaeological stages. The Tasmanians (chapter IV) come after chapter III (Eoliths) and before chapter V (The Most Ancient Hunters). The Australian Aborigines (chapter VII) come between the Lower Palaeolithic and the Aurignacian Age. The particular position of the Tasmanians in schema such as these has been discussed in greater detail by Murray (1992) and Jones (1992). Looking at the other side of the divide, in 1891 the missionary/ethnographer Codrington wrote:

> The Melanesians are a horticultural people; the skill and care with which gardens are kept and planted could not from the first fail to

strike their visitors, and marked them off by a distinction that
cannot be mistaken from the natives of Australia.

(Codrington 1891: 303)

Around the turn of the century, the influence of the environment on
people was debated in terms of both civilized and savage. It is bound up in
what Livingstone (1992) calls the 'moral economy of climate', and is part of a
bigger discussion on whether it was possible for the white races to prosper in
the tropics. This question was of course central to the colonial enterprise on
a global scale. The discussion was also tied in to European attempts to come
to terms with the very different physical environment of Australia; it was self-
evident to many of these writers that Australia was hardly a surprising place
to find the archetypal primitive. 'Australia, the most insular of all the quarters
of the globe, has received a larger share than all the others of that culture-
stunting gift – vacant coasts' (Ratzel 1896: 333; see also Prichard 1855: 263;
Peschel 1876: 324).

> The social development visibly deteriorates both from north to
> south and from east to west; that is to say, in proportion to the
> distance from Cape York, the chief point of which has served to
> connect Australia with the Old World, the customary mode of life
> of the natives becomes more and more degraded.
>
> (Peschel 1876: 330)

The recognition of a continuum between hunter-gatherers and farmers
continued into the ethnographically influenced archaeology of the 1960s and
1970s. For example, White (1971: 182), in quoting Captain John Moresby's
widely quoted comparison between the Aborigines of Cape York and their
Papuan neighbours, recognized in his first sentence that Moresby got it
wrong about hunter-gatherers when he described them as wandering about,
'living precariously' on whatever wild fruits and animals they could catch.
Jones (1975) highlighted a number of ways in which Australian evidence did
not fit the categories; planting of yams and fruits, use of fire to curate the
landscape, the possible cause of megafaunal extinctions. Harris (1977) very
explicitly argued for a continuum, in subsistence terms. Yet once again the
discussion did not go to the point of jettisoning the categories. In fact, where
the dichotomy was challenged, it was usually in subsistence terms.

In fact it was not the stress on subsistence *per se* that led nineteenth-
century thinkers in particular directions of thought prejudicial to Aboriginal
people, but was rather the link seen between subsistence, property in land,
material culture and the political process. Without notions of property there
would be no attempts at improvement of land and the production of surplus
food which could then support a dynamic social and political process.
Hunter-gatherers were, by this definition, people without history. In many
ways we are still burdened by the weight of nineteenth-century expectations,
and this is demonstrated by recent attempts to give Aboriginal people a

dynamic history by making them look more like farmers. There is an inescapable gender dimension to the nineteenth-century observations, all made by male explorers and ethnographers, and who perceived as peripheral any subsistence activity other than hunting to the savage life. Indeed we have found no reference to Australians being referred to as 'hunter-gatherers' before the 1968 'Man the Hunter' conference.

There are a number of ways that Australian evidence, already in the nineteenth century, could be taken to be subversive of the various categories that scholars had constructed as relevant. For example, clear expressions of Aboriginal land ownership were noted by Lubbock (1870: 312); Prichard (1855: 269) and Ratzel (1896: 348). Sollas commented (1915: 229) on the importance of the rule of law. Most relevant for this discussion are the numerous references to Aboriginal people being engaged in agricultural practices. For example, Haddon put forward the curious proposition that they cultivated plants but not the soil:

> The Australians can rarely depend on regular supplies of food . . . Cultivation of the soil is unknown, except that on the west coast the natives invariably re-insert the head of the wild yams they have dug up so as to be sure of a future crop. The cultivation of purslane [*Portulaca oleracea*] seems to be a well-established fact.
>
> (Haddon 1924: 22)

Grey's descriptions of warran (*Dioscorea*) plantations in the south-west of Western Australia were also widely quoted (e.g., Ratzel 1896: 363).

However, it was the rule not the exceptions which dominated views of the continent and this is true into this century and even includes the major challenge to the old framework: the so-called intensification debate.

'INTENSIFICATION': A CHALLENGE TO AHISTORICAL MODELS OF HUNTER-GATHERERS?

The most influential theoretical discussions on the Australian Holocene in the last couple of decades have centred around the notion of 'intensification'. In a nutshell, this debate, which was mainly sparked by the work of Lourandos (1980, 1997), was concerned with whether Aboriginal groups were developing more intensive forms of subsistence, trade and political hierarchy in the late Holocene which made them more similar to New Guinean Big Man systems than had been recognized and these trends would have continued had it not been for white colonialism from the late eighteenth century. Lourandos and Ross (1994) argued that the contribution of this debate was twofold. First, and most well known, it challenged environmentally deterministic views about hunter-gatherer societies. Second, it questioned the dichotomy between hunter-gatherers and agricultural societies. 'This new debate demonstrated the similarities between these societies, with respect to social organisation, economy, demography and change, in both the long- and short-term' (Lourandos and Ross 1994: 54–5). For example, Lourandos (1980: 248) presented a table of population densities for Australian hunter-gatherer and New Guinea shifting agricultural societies 'showing an unbroken continuum of energy harnessing technologies' and population densities.

We do not want to discuss the specifics of the intensification debate here – it has been canvassed extensively elsewhere – but are more interested in the way it affected views of the dichotomy. In both the original expression of the intensification theory, and in the way it was taken up by others, the similarities identified between hunter-gatherers and agriculturalists were expressed in such a way as to make the former seem more like the latter, or at least be on a trajectory heading in that direction. For example, 'intensification of social and economic relations would appear to have been increasingly taking place during the Holocene period on the Australian mainland, the process being nipped in the bud by the coming of the Europeans' (Lourandos 1983: 92). The Australian material was often tied into broader debates about 'complex' as opposed to 'simple' hunter-gatherers. Whether inadvertently or otherwise, the dominance of the intensification view in recent Australian archaeology has reinforced perceptions of a teleological relationship between hunter-gathering and farming, where the former are only complex and progressive where they are about to become farmers.

Criticisms came from several directions; two are of note here. First, Horton discussed 'the feeling that hunter/gatherers are somehow second class citizens in comparison to farmers and that we must therefore see them as being more like farmers' (Horton 1982: 248). While he was actually criticizing Jones's fire-stick farming model, and the reaction against hunter-gatherers being seen as 'in harmony with the environment', the sentiment was reflected in a number of other works written during the intensification debate. Frankel discussed the way Aboriginal environmental management (for example, fish traps and fire use) was 'seen by some as still reflecting an attitude that farmers are "better" than foragers, and that it would be good to establish that Aborigines were, to some degree, farmers, thereby raising them a step on the ladder of social evolution' (Frankel 1984: 14). On the other hand their embodiment as environmental damagers also had a political dimension. A second line of criticism came from those who argued that, whatever the scale of change on mainland Australia during the Holocene, it was still very different from Melanesia (Beaton 1983).

There have been few attempts to rethink the categories. In his review of Zvelebil (1986), Davidson (1989) challenged the idea of agricultural lifeways being an evolutionary outcome of fishing-gathering-hunting. He suggested instead that fishing-gathering-hunting and agriculture were two different choices made by different groups, and that each were separate outcomes of the more generalized subsistence strategies at the end of the Pleistocene. The differences between the two, and the reason for agriculture's widespread dominance, lie in the way that land and resources are appropriated. Following Ingold (1980, 1986) these were characterized as collective appropriation for fishing-gathering-hunting and individual appropriation for agriculturalists. Instead of the Mesolithic being a meaningful transition between the latter and the former, Davidson argued that 'it is an artefact of the methods of study of archaeologists – not a fundamental division in the progress of human evolution' (Davidson 1989: 75).

Our view is that the Papua New Guinea–Australia case shows that there is no progressive movement from hunter-gathering to farming and nor is farming a dominant form of subsistence within the area as a whole, despite the long antiquity of farming within Papua New Guinea. Further light can be shed on this point if we look at an instance where farming did appear to spread.

BOUNDARIES BETWEEN HUNTER-GATHERERS AND FARMERS: THE CASE OF NORTHERN EUROPE

There are a number of areas of the world in which hunter-gatherers lived in close proximity to farmers, often for long periods of time before adopting a farming way of life. We will take just one case as comparison, as one of the best-researched prehistoric instances of interactions between hunter-gatherers and farmers, which encompasses the region from Holland to northern Poland on the one hand and central Europe on the other. Around 4000 BC farmers, known archaeologically as Linearbandkeramik users, moved from Hungary to southern Holland, spreading across much of central Europe in the process. In an arc to the north, from northern Holland to the shores of the eastern Baltic, they encountered hunter-gatherer groups, the best known of which are the Danish and Swedish Ertebølle and Ellerbek groups. These people lived on fish, shellfish, seals, wild pig, nuts, roots and a range of other plant foods and probably had higher population densities than the early groups of mobile farmers (Zvelebil 1996: 331). Over a long period, between 4000 and 1000 BC, there was increasing contact between farmers and hunter-gatherers which has traditionally been seen as hunter-gatherers taking up first the material culture of farmers, such as pottery, axes and adzes, bone combs and rings, and later the resources of farmers, like cows and cereals (Zvelebil 1996: figures 18.5, 18.6). Thomas (1996) has recently provided a corrective to the overly simple view that the movements of materials and ideas was one-way, from farmers to hunter-gatherers, and feels that hunter-gatherer groups only took what they wanted from their southern neighbours. More importantly, he feels that hunter-gatherer groups would have been socially open, willing to experiment, and sources of social novelty and their new ideas may have caused change in farming groups, so rather than talking of the 'Neolithicization' of hunter-gatherer groups we should think of the 'Mesolithicization' of southern farming groups. Furthermore, neither the Neolithic nor hunting and gathering represented a cultural package of which people had to accept all or nothing, but formed a set of strategies and series of practices which could be deployed in new ways in new settings.

Brief consideration of the Papua New Guinean and Australian case shows that even a more open-ended view of the question, such as that of Thomas, is not broad enough to throw light on the similarities and differences between the two parts of Sahul. If the same history had been in place there should have been a movement of agricultural techniques out of the Highlands after 9000 BP, first into surrounding areas of Papua New Guinea and then later further south to Australia. As it is, the situation is more complex and hence more interesting. There was some spread of agricultural crops from Papua New Guinea to Australia, but these were not accompanied by full-blown agriculture. Equally some sets of plants may have a joint history of human manipulation in both places. Finally, the frontier is not an absolute divide: there are people who live a virtually hunter-gatherer lifestyle in Papua New Guinea and some intensive forms of subsistence are and were practised in Australia.

There have been long arguments about the nature and date of domestication of the crops used in Papua New Guinean agriculture since its beginnings in the early Holocene, and we shall start with this argument as it leads us into the joint history of Australia and New Guinea and their shared biological heritage. In Papua New Guinea in the present the principal crops are those of the taro–yam complex, sago, Musa bananas on the coast and Eumusa and Australimusa bananas in the Highlands, and pandanus. Taro is now seen as indigenous to Papua New Guinea, although new strains may have arrived from south-east Asia, and northern Australia may also have been included in the natural distribution of wild taro (Matthews 1990; Yen 1995: 835). Some crops indigenous to Papua New Guinea and which might have been domesticated there, such as sago, sugar and *Altilis artocarpus* (the progenitor of the breadfruit) either were never found in Australia or were not found at the time of white settlement. However, four of the six most important domesticated trees in Papua New Guinea were found in northern Australia, including *Canarium baileyanum*, a source of food from the Kimberleys to Cape York, and *Terminalia* species also found in Cape York (Yen 1995: 838–41). Some tree crops, notably the bunya nut, which are found in both Papua New Guinea and Australia are only used as a source of food in the latter area. The major sources of food in Australia which were unused as far as we know in Papua New Guinea, although they occurred there, were the grasses. The least understood and most intriguing history is that of the yams, widely used in both places and which may have been both part of the pre-human flora of the larger continent and have seen later introductions and movements by people through both areas (Yen 1995: 841).

There are thus important contrasts between our emerging understanding of the complex situation of plant foods in Australia and Papua New Guinea and the movements of farming into areas occupied by hunter-gatherers in

Europe. In the European case all the major cereal crops, sheep/goat and probably cattle were domesticated in the Middle East and introduced into Europe, so that their use required the modification of the environment to suit their needs. In Papua New Guinea many of the major plant foods were indigenous and locally domesticated. Those that were introduced prehistoric-ally could be treated in similar ways to the indigenous crops, by and large, and thus they fitted within and extended existing systems. The only animal of real importance introduced into Papua New Guinea was the pig, although the dog and the chicken were of some minor importance. In Australia the only introduced animal was the dog, only rarely a source of food although important for hunting. The received wisdom has been that no plant foods were introduced prior to white settlement, but Yen's recent data may challenge that assumption. Yen (1995: 843) sees the north coast and islands of Papua New Guinea as centres of domestication of trees like *Canarium*, sago and *Artocarpus*, some of which may have been introduced into northern Australia as well as other areas of Papua New Guinea and the Pacific. Similarly, some of the Australian yams may have originated in Papua New Guinea, although in both cases more genetic work is needed to sort out the exact relations between the distributions of plants today. Furthermore, wild taro probably had a natural distribution which covered Papua New Guinea and northern Australia. Domesticated forms of taro became central to farming strategies in Papua New Guinea, in contrast to the minor use of the wild form in Australia.

We have a complex pattern here of acceptance and rejection in which some plants were moved to, and adopted in, Australia, but many others were not. Similarly the pig was never adopted by Aboriginal communities, nor were 'Neolithic' items of material culture such as pottery and polished stone axes. However, a simple dichotomy between the two areas is difficult to sustain when we consider that many of the elements of the Neolithic package have an uneven distribution within Papua New Guinea. Pottery, the quintessential element of Neolithic material culture since Childe, is absent from the Highland valleys, which have the most intensive farming systems in the western Pacific. No area of Papua New Guinea combines all the root and tree crops together and all areas specialize in some species to the exclusion of others. Forty per cent of New Guinea as a whole is classified as low intensity of subsistence production by Brookfield with Hart (1971), but many of these sustain complex exchanges of material culture and foods.

If we take polar opposites, such as the populations of the New Guinea Highlands and Australian desert groups, it is easier to maintain the stereotype of difference; but, if we consider Australia and New Guinea as a whole, complex forms of land management are practised with considerable variability and with different links to other areas of life. One potential area of commonality we would like to stress is the possibility of a long continuity in people's attachment to land throughout Sahul.

THE DREAMING IN PAPUA NEW GUINEA

Aboriginal groups conceive of Dreamtime heroes and their tracks of creation which can be followed from one cultural group to the next, the result being a common track which co-ordinates the origin traditions of diverse groups over hundreds of kilometres. Wagner (1996) has pointed out that in some parts of Papua New Guinea similar phenomena occur, especially along the south coasts of Western and Gulf Provinces, coastal Irian Jaya, Torres Strait Islands and south Simbu Province. He cites particularly an origin hero known under a variety of names, such as Sido, Souw, Soida, etc., whose story is found from the Purari River in the west to Kumbe River in the east. Sido is connected to the creation of features of the landscape, issues of human mortality, fertility and reproduction and the origins of food production (Wagner 1996: 286–7). Sido and his cognates may be linked in to other sets of myths in other areas of the interior of Papua New Guinea and Irian Jaya. There are also similarities at a general and a specific level with Aboriginal origin myths, such as the links between birds and snakes (Wagner 1996: 292).

As is mentioned below, similar sets of ancestral tracks are found amongst the Tari and their neighbours in the southern Highlands. Wassman is pursuing a similar line of argument for the Yupno and has spelt out the importance of mnemonics and stories connected with ancestral paths and village movements. These few examples indicate that there may be a larger body of historical similarities between Papua New Guinea and Australia, and these certainly need pursuing further.

However, links to land are just one element of life. As we outlined above, the matrix of connections to be obtained through considering myth, history, land and material culture greatly simplifies reality, but already provides a very complex set of connections with which the investigator must deal. In the rest of the chapter we attempt to show how this mix of factors may have produced different cultural forms in various parts of Australia and New Guinea, in both the present and prehistory, and that these broader comparisons provide a more satisfying place to start than the simple dichotomy between farming and hunter-gathering.

THREE COMPARISONS: WEST NEW BRITAIN, THE SOUTHERN HIGHLANDS, AND NORTH-CENTRAL ARNHEM LAND

From the early 1960s onwards Jane Goodale and Ann Chowning have worked with rainforest groups, primarily the Sengseng and the Kaulong, in the interior of the province of West New Britain (Chowning 1978; Goodale 1995). The Sengseng and Kaulong live in low population densities and are very mobile, resisting many attempts by the colonial administration to make them settle in villages. The interior Kaulong derive up to 60 per cent of their food from hunting and gathering (Goodale 1995: 69). They also garden taro, plus a variety of local and introduced crops, and keep pigs which are left to forage in the forest, as well as being fed. Among the Kaulong, Sengseng and other neighbouring groups garden sites are not specifically owned by individuals or groups. Gardens were located near to hamlets and Goodale recorded no instances of conflict over garden land (1995: 74). More attachment was shown to taro, and either descent groups or individuals owned, used and traded particular varieties. Taro and pigs, as well as shells and other valuables, are involved in complex forms of ceremonies and exchange partnerships. These exchanges are vital to people's sense of themselves and the community's regard for them. Goodale paints a poignant picture of people who love the cool and calm of the forest, but are forced into hamlets and garden plots in order to engage in production and exchange so as to make themselves fully human and to raise their reputations.

Comparison with the broader ethnography of West New Britain shows similar forms of life found throughout the Province and beyond, prior to colonial influence (Chinnery 1928; Chowning 1978; Harding 1967). Archaeology has demonstrated that this form of life has an antiquity of at least a millennium and maybe more (Gosden and Webb 1994). The mobile nature of life and lack of fixed attachment to individual plots of land has created a rather ephemeral set of archaeological evidence and one which is clearly different from the preceding period, prior to 1500 BP.

From the Tari Basin of the Southern Highlands of New Guinea comes a very different picture. Here the work of Ballard (1994), which might be characterized as historical ethnography, has revealed a picture in which people have a very definite attachment to land. This attachment is anchored in genealogies which are remarkable in their time-depth, going back some twenty-four generations and telling a consistent story which can be traced over large areas of the Tari Basin. Over a maximum period of 500 years the genealogies outline rights to the ditches which are used to drain the swamps of the Tari Basin, plus the ability of individuals to participate in ritual and trade. Individual ditches are named after known individuals, often the people who dug them, so that a map of the ditches also contains a map of a historical social landscape. These ditches were used for growing taro, which only in the last two centuries has been supplemented by sweet potato, and this forms the basis for pig herds, which are central to exchange systems in Tari. Ritual and trade are linked by a concern with directions and lines of power which are ritually charged. These lines of power, known as *dindi pongone*, are seen to be the tracks of ancestral spirits who created the present-day features of the landscape and obviously have parallels with dreaming tracks. Certain rituals have to be carried out at cosmologically important spots on the landscape, using material culture obtained from particular ritually charged directions, or substances like pig fat which have the correct properties to hold back the forces that lead the world to decline physically or cosmologically.

In addition to the oral history and limited amount of archaeology done in Tari, which indicate some antiquity for the ditched systems, we know from the work of Golson at Kuk in the Wahgi Valley that these systems may well go back to before the split between Australia and Papua New Guinea, as the first evidence at Kuk swamp dates to 9,000 years ago (Golson 1989). The nature of the drainage at Kuk has changed continuously over this period and indicates much change in the social formations creating it (Bayliss-Smith and Golson, Chapter 11, this volume). However, there is also an indication of a fixed attachment to land over a long period of time, which has been integral to many other aspects of life, such as the ritual and trading systems.

Moving now across the Arafura Sea to north-central Arnhem Land, where Altman's work has documented the economic and social life of the Gungwingu (Kunwinjku) people of the Mann river area. The Gungwingu aim is to accumulate ritual knowledge rather than material wealth, even though they engaged in the local and long-distance exchange of stone spear points, axes and ochres in pre-colonial times (Altman 1987: 222). Ceremonies are of different degrees of openness: exchange ceremonies can be attended by anyone, mortuary rituals are partly closed and ritual cults are entirely closed. Approximately 15 per cent of people's time is spent in large ceremonial activities, and during these periods both the unity of the group and its political hierarchy are most obvious, with most status accruing to those with most ritual knowledge and who can direct various elements of the ceremony. Ceremonies are seen to be vital to the maintenance and powers of increase of the land, and the group and Gungwingu people make no differentiation between the ceremonial system and the economic system of hunting and gathering (Altman 1987: 217).

Taçon's work on rock art in the Mann river area shows that the distribution of different motifs correlates with linguistic boundaries between eastern and western Gungwingu speakers, and that these distributions have an antiquity of some thousands of years, with some of the motifs still being used on modern bark paintings (Taçon 1994). Looking at Arnhem Land rock art more broadly, Taçon and Brockwell (1995) indicate that rock art has an antiquity of at least 13,000 years and that a number of different styles can be identified since that date with the origins of recent art going back 4,000 to 6,000 years. They also make the point that the overall history of the art is an additive one with new elements being incorporated, a process which continued over the last few hundred years with Macassan and European symbols appearing in the art (Taçon and Brockwell 1995: 693). As the art and the ritual system are closely linked in the present there is the possibility of understanding the antiquity of that system and its changes through the art, which can then complement a rather thin artefactual record.

DISCUSSION

The first point to make about these brief examples is that the New Guinean and the Australian cases do not group together in any straightforward manner. To be sure, West New Britain rainforest groups and the Huli in Tari are joined by the use of pigs and taro, but other elements of their life are very different. The Sengseng and Kaulong have a generalized attachment to land which is rather like the estates and parishes of the Gungwingu and which contrasts markedly with the Huli obsession with land ownership. On the other hand, the ritual tracks of the Huli are extremely similar to the Dreaming tracks of the Gungwingu, as are the complex of ceremonies surrounding them. The Sengseng cultivate gardens, but gain 60 per cent of their nutritional requirements from wild animals and plants. This gives them a subsistence base not far different from the Aboriginal groups who encouraged the growth of roots and/or lived in close proximity to fruit and nut-bearing trees.

Our argument is not to say that New Guinean and Australian groups were the same, although there may have been more similarities than have been perceived until now, or that Aboriginal groups were on the same trajectory as New Guinean ones but a few millennia behind (to pastiche the intensification argument). Rather we would use the notion of culture as a relational field in which the important aspect is not individual similarities and differences as such, but the overall structure of life which provides context for attachments to land and material culture and the use of ritual and exchange. Where individual elements of life are important is as possible indicators of ancient forms of inheritance reworked in different ways in tune with local circumstances. The obvious example of a possible form of ancient inheritance is the existence of Dreaming tracks in New Guinea, as well as Australia, which, as the Huli case shows, may coexist in tension with an emphasis on exchange of pigs and other valuables as a route to personal prestige quite antithetical to an Aboriginal disdain for material wealth.

The matrix of possibilities, deriving from Rumsey's distinction between myth and history we discussed in theoretical terms above, immediately becomes more complex and interesting as soon as actual cases are considered. The Huli balance an attachment to land and to material things, with a rich remembered history being created through a mixture of the two and on the basis of persistent myths. The Sengseng appear to have the most fluid of forms of life, with a light attachment to land and changing configurations of exchange, with this changeable history deriving from a less constricting and formalized set of mythological structures. The dynamic histories of Arnhem Land are anchored in a long continuity of myth which changes slowly over a period of millennia as indicated by the rock art.

Balancing myth and history, continuity and change allows us to probe anew the nature of changes, and here recent changes may provide insightful into those of the past. There has been considerable debate within New

Guinean prehistory concerning the timing and impact of the introduction of the pig and the sweet potato and their subsequent spread throughout the region. Conversely, pottery, which is a vital element of many coastal exchange systems, has never been used in the central Highlands. Aboriginal groups have generally been seen as resistant to introductions, not having incorporated the pig or sweet potato into their rosters of potential foods. On the other hand, as Taçon and Brockwell (1995: 693) have shown, the history of rock art has been one of continuous incorporation of new elements. Furthermore, Rose (1995) has shown that introduced animals which have become feral and thus important sources of food have become incorporated into systems of knowledge: 'Wild pussy from here, some rabbit from here too. Pussy cat got Dreaming, some wild pussy cat got Law' (quoted in Rose 1995: 122). In such cases Aboriginal people will often oppose eradication programmes. As Chase (1989) shows, such recent acceptances are partly a result of the devastation and complexity caused by colonial usurpation, but historical change is also mediated through pre-existing systems of knowledge.

If we suspend prior belief in the essential difference of Australia and New Guinea then together they form a broad canvas of comparison through which to investigate questions of continuity and change. Forms of subsistence become elements of life to be developed and deployed within the overall structure of practice, rather than the crucial basis for all other forms of action. It is obvious in our exploration of this broad canvas that we are still travelling towards, rather than having arrived at, any definite conclusions. But the following questions seem worth posing. Is it accidental that a stress on Dreaming tracks is most pronounced to the north and south of the Arafura Sea, the area which saw most environmental change due to rising sea levels between 15,000 and 8000 BP, and are these tracks some means of maintaining continuity in an otherwise fast-changing world? How far has the changing position of New Britain within an Oceanic world caused it to modify its older inheritances?

The results of such comparisons and questions will only derive from detailed analysis. However, we hope to have shown the benefit of giving up the old well-known forms of history, deriving from a division between Australia and New Guinea in exchange for tales of the unexpected.

ACKNOWLEDGEMENT

We are very grateful to Peter White for critical comments on this chapter.

REFERENCES

Altman, J. 1987. *Hunter-gatherers Today: an Aboriginal economy in north Australia.* Canberra: Institute of Aboriginal Studies.

Appadurai, A. 1981. Gastro-politics in Hindu south Asia, *American Ethnologist* 8, 494–511.

Attwood, B. 1989. *The Making of the Aborigines.* Sydney: Allen and Unwin.

Ballard, C. 1994. The centre cannot hold. *Archaeology in Oceania* 29, 130–48.

Beaton, J. 1983. Evidence for coastal occupation time-lag at Princess Charlotte Bay (north Queensland) and implications for coastal colonisation and population growth theories in Aboriginal Australia. *Archaeology in Oceania* 20, 73–80.

Binford, L.R. 1968. Post-Pleistocene adaptations. In *New Perspectives in Archeology*, S.R. Binford and L.R. Binford (eds), 313–41. Chicago: Aldine.

Brookfield, H.C. with D. Hart. 1971. *Melanesia: a geographical interpretation of an island world.* London: Methuen.

Chase, A. 1989. Perceptions of the past among north Queensland Aboriginal people: the intrusions of Europeans and subsequent social change. In *Who needs the past? Indigenous values and archaeology*, R. Layton (ed.), 169–79. London: Unwin Hyman.

Chinnery, E.W.P. 1928. *Certain Natives of South New Britain and Dampier Straits.* Territory of New Guinea Anthropological Report, no. 3. Melbourne: Government Printer.

Chowning, A. 1978. Changes in west New Britain trading systems in the twentieth century. *Mankind* 11, 296–307.

Codrington, R.H. 1891. *The Melanesians.* Oxford: Clarendon Press.

Davidson, I. 1989. Is intensification a condition of the fisher-hunter-gatherer way of life? *Archaeology in Oceania* 24, 75–8.

Frankel, D. 1984. Who owns the past? *Australian Society* 3, 14–15.

Golson, J. 1989. The origins and development of New Guinea agriculture. In *Foraging and Farming: the origin of plant domestication*, D. Harris and G. Hillman (eds), 678–87. London: Unwin Hyman.

Goodale, J.C. 1995. *To Sing with Pigs is Human.* Seattle: University of Washington Press.

Gosden, C. 1994. *Social Being and Time,* Oxford: Basil Blackwell.

Gosden, C. and J. Webb. 1994. Creating a Papua New Guinean landscape: results of archaeological and geomorphological work in the Arawe islands, West New Britain. *Journal of Field Archaeology* 21, 29–51.

Haddon, A.C. 1924. *The Races of Man and Their Distribution.* Halifax, Yorkshire: Milner and Co.

Harding, T.G. 1967. *Voyagers of the Vitiaz Strait,* Seattle: University of Washington Press.

Harris, D.R. 1977. Substance strategies across the Torres Strait. In *Sunda and Sahul: prehistoric studies in Southeast Asia, Melanesia and Australia,* J. Allen, J. Golson and R. Jones (eds), 421–63. London: Academic Press.

Harris, D.R. 1995. Early agriculture in New Guinea and the Torres Strait divide. *Antiquity* 69, 848–54.

Hodder, I. 1990. *The Domestication of Europe.* Oxford: Basil Blackwell.

Horton, D.R. 1982. The burning question: Aborigines, fire and Australian ecosystems. *Mankind* 13, 237–251.

Ingold, T. 1980. *Hunters, Pastoralists and Ranchers.* Cambridge: Cambridge University Press.

Ingold, T. 1986. *The Appropriation of Nature.* Manchester: Manchester University Press.

Ingold, T. 1994. Introduction to culture. In *Companion Encyclopedia of Anthropology*, T. Ingold (ed.), 329–49. London: Routledge.

Jones, R. 1975. The Neolithic, Palaeolithic and the hunting gardeners: man and land in the Antipodes. In *Quaternary Studies. Selected papers from IX Inqua congress, Christchurch N.Z. 1973*, R.P. Suggate and M.M. Cresswell (eds), 21–34. Christchurch: Royal Society NZ.

Jones, R. 1992. Philosphical time travellers. *Antiquity* 66, 744–57.

Livingstone, D. 1992. *The Geographical Tradition. Episodes in the History of a Contested Enterprise*. Oxford: Basil Blackwell.

Lourandos, H. 1980. Change or stability? Hydraulics, hunter-gatherers and population in temperate Australia. *World Archaeology* 11, 245–64.

Lourandos, H. 1983. Intensification: a late pleistocene – Holocene archaeological sequence from southwestern Victoria. *Archaeology in Oceania* 18, 81–94.

Lourandos, H. 1997. *A Continent of Hunter Gatherers*. Cambridge: Cambridge University Press.

Lourandos, H. and A. Ross, 1994. The great 'Intensification Debate': its history and place in Australian archaeology. *Australian Archaeology* 39, 54–62.

Lubbock, J. 1870. *The Origin of Civilisation and the Primitive Condition of Man*. Chicago: University of Chicago Press.

Matthews, P.J. 1990. The origins, dispersal and domestication of taro. Unpublished Ph.D. thesis, Australian National University.

Morgan, L.H. [1877] 1907. *Ancient Society, or researches in the lines of human progress from savagery through barbarism to civilization*. New York: Henry Holt and Co.

Mulvaney, D.J. 1990. The Australian Aborigines 1606–1929: opinion and fieldwork. In *Through White Eyes*, S. Janson and S. Macintyre (eds), 1–44. Sydney: Allen and Unwin.

Murray, T. 1992. Tasmania and the constitution of 'the dawn of humanity'. *Antiquity* 66, 730–43.

Peschel, O. 1876. *The Races of Man and Their Geographical Distribution*. London: Henry King and Co.

Prichard, J.C. 1855. *The Natural History of Man; comprising inquiries into the modifying influence of physical and moral agencies on the different tribes of the human family*. London: H. Balliere.

Ratzel, F. 1896. *The History of Mankind*. London: Macmillan and Co.

Rose, D.B. 1995. *Land Management Issues: attitudes and perceptions amongst Aboriginal people in central Australia*. Alice Springs: Central Land Council.

Rumsey, A. 1994. The Dreaming, human agency and inscriptive practice. *Oceania* 65, 116–30.

Sollas, W.J. 1915. *Ancient Hunters and Their Modern Representatives*. London: Macmillan and Co.

Taçon, P.S.C. 1994. Socializing landscapes: the long-term implications of signs, symbols and marks on the land. *Archaeology in Oceania* 29, 117–29.

Taçon, P.S.C. and S. Brockwell. 1995. Arnhem Land prehistory in landscape, stone and paint. *Antiquity* 69, 676–95.

Thomas, J. 1996. The cultural context of the first use domesticates in continental Central and Northwest Europe. In *The Origins and Spread of Agriculture and Pastoralism in Eurasia*, D.R. Harris (ed.), 310–22. London: UCL Press.

Turner, T. 1988. Ethnohistory: myth and history in native South American representations of contact in western society. In *Rethinking History and Myth*, J.D. Hill (ed.), 235–81. Urbana and Chicago: University of Illinois Press.

Tylor, E.B. 1891. *Primitive Culture: Researches into the development of mythology, philosophy, religion, language, art, and custom*. London: John Murray.

Wagner, R. 1996. Mysteries of origin: early traders and heroes in the Trans-Fly. In *Plumes from Paradise*, P. Swadling, 285–98. Boroko and Coorparoo: Papua New Guinea National Museum, in association with R. Brown.

White, J.P. 1971. New Guinea and Australian prehistory: the 'Neolithic Problem'. In

Aboriginal Man and Environment in Australia, D.J. Mulvaney and J. Golson (eds), 182–95. Canberra: Australian National University Press.

Williams, N.M. 1986. *The Yolngu and their Land: a system of land tenure and the fight for its recognition*. Canberra: Australian Institute of Aboriginal Studies.

Yen, D. 1995. The development of Sahul agriculture with Australia as a bystander. *Antiquity* 69, 831–47.

Zvelcbil, M. 1986. *Hunters in Transition: Mesolithic societies of temperate Eurasia and the transition to farming*. Cambridge: Cambridge University Press.

Zvelebil, M. 1996. The agricultural frontier and the transition to farming in the circum-Baltic region. In *The Origins and Spread of Agriculture and Pastoralism in Eurasia*, D. R. Harris (ed.), 323–45. London: UCL Press.

13 From the swamp to the terrace: intensification of horticultural practices in New Caledonia, from first settlement to European contact

CHRISTOPHE SAND

INTRODUCTION

Prehistoric evidence from the island group of New Caledonia demonstrates the development of one of the most intensive prehistoric subsistence regimes known from Melanesia. Recent evidence also throws light on the regional diversity throughout New Caledonia and the complexity of reasons lying behind the acceptance or rejection of new crops and practices. Although land use was intensive, two of the major features of subsistence and consumption elsewhere in the western Pacific, the pig and kava, do not appear to have been present in prehistoric New Caledonia. Finally the prehistoric evidence can help throw new light on the impact of European contact and cause us to think again about the usefulness of recent ethnographies for interpreting prehistoric periods.

This chapter presents the first diachronic view of the evolution of the plant-based subsistence systems from the southernmost archipelago of Melanesia – New Caledonia – and focuses on results obtained in the last five years by our local Department of Archaeology. We are now able to look at the transformation of cultivation techniques, in relation to the first introduction of plants, and to landscape and sociopolitical changes, population and political pressure. This exercise might allow us to present a more accurate and archaeologically sound view of the prehistory of plants than was attempted from ethnobotanical data some decades ago (Barrau 1965).

General background
The New Caledonian archipelago is located at the southern end of the Melanesian chain (between 20° and 22° south) (Figure 13.1). It comprises the Grande Terre, about 400 km long and 50 km wide, the Loyalty Islands made of raised coral (Mare, Lifou, Ouvéa) and smaller islands (Île des Pins, Bélep). The main characteristic of the Grande Terre is its complex geological formation, with one-third of the island covered by peridotites, composed of rich

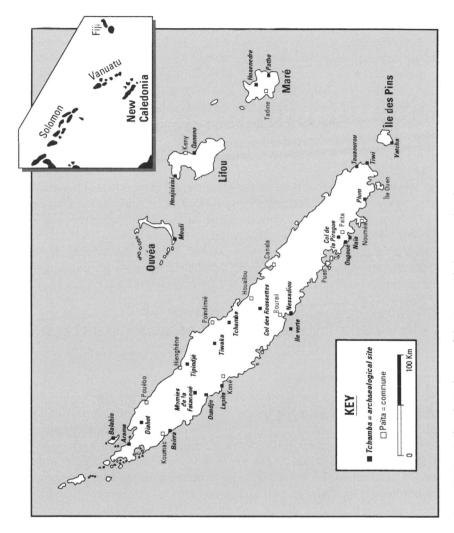

Figure 13.1 Archaeological map of the New Caledonian archipelago.

mineral elements (nickel, iron, chrome, etc.) which produce infertile soils. The mountainous ridge running down the centre of the island, separating it in two, has led to the formation of small valleys in the eastern windward coast and large plains on the dry leeward coast. The early separation of the New Caledonia plate from the Gondwanan landmass allowed the development of a very rich endemic fauna and flora.

Although the Grande Terre was one of the first islands of Melanesia to be subject to archaeological research after World War II (Gifford and Shutler 1956), most of the work carried out until the early 1990s has focused on ceramic chronology (Galipaud 1988; Sand 1995a). This recently led Kirch and Lepofsky in their survey of the irrigation systems of the Pacific, to write that 'certainly the most technically complex pondfield irrigation within Melanesia is that of New Caledonia . . . the antiquity of the New Caledonian terracing technology . . . remains wholly enigmatic' (Kirch and Lepofsky 1993: 191).

The completion of a first general survey program by the local Department of Archaeology has, in the last few years, allowed us to study the landscape as a whole, showing agricultural structures, monumental architecture and old villages, organised in an unexpected variety of combinations (Sand 1996d, 1997). Some of these sites have been excavated and dated, allowing the first study of the evolution of settlement patterns and the development of complex horticultural constructions.

THE PREHISTORIC CHRONOLOGY OF HORTICULTURAL PRACTICES

The first millennium of settlement

The northern islands of Melanesia were colonized more than 30,000 years ago (Allen *et al.* 1988), with the use of wild taro crops indicated as early as 28,000 BP (Loy *et al.* 1992). For New Caledonia in particular and for southern Melanesia in general, the dates of human colonization seem to be much later, starting at about 3000 BP (Sand 1995b, 1996c). This human dispersal is related to the movement of Austronesian populations into far Oceania (Green 1979) and is best demonstrated by the presence of Lapita pottery.

In New Caledonia, the first millennium of human occupation, the Koné period (Galipaud 1992), is principally characterized by the development of beach sites and the presence of three major types of ceramics: Lapita (dentate stamped pottery), Podtanean (paddled impressed wares) and Puen (incised vessels) (Sand 1996e; Sand and Ouetcho 1993d). Linguistic and botanical reconstructions indicate that the colonizing populations introduced horticultural products. Most of the major Koné period sites on the Grand Terre, and also in the Loyalty Islands, are located at the front of swamps (Sand 1995b): this is the case for example for the WKO013 site of Lapita in Koné, the WBR001 site of Nessadiou in Bourail, the KVO003 site of Vatcha in Île des Pins and the LMA020 site of Patho on Maré. This probably allowed wet cultivation of tubers, as has been emphasized on the NKM001 site of Boirra in Koumac (Frimigacci 1980, pers. comm. 1989); here, the excavations and subsequent analyses (Sand 1990) have shown the presence of large pits filled with compost and surrounded by beach rock slabs (Galipaud 1988). The exact age of these pits is still unclear, but they clearly seem to be associated with horticultural practices.

The first form of cultivation may have been a simple shifting technique with long fallow and most communities cultivating in their immediate vicinity at the back of the beaches. However, very soon people started to use a wider area around the habitation sites, burning the natural landscape. In the swamp of St Louis on the south-west coast of the Grande Terre, this landscape transformation, probably due to shifting cultivation, started around 3000 BP with the replacement in the pollen diagrams of trees by grass, and also the beginning of massive filling-in of the swamps due to erosion caused by humans (Stevenson and Dodson 1995).

Barrau's major ethnobotanical collection work in the 1950s in Melanesia (1958), and especially in New Caledonia (1956), led him to identify the presence on the Grande Terre of archaic species (1981). In the north, Barrau noticed the ancient introduction of breadfruit (*Artocarpus altilis* Fosb.), sugar-cane (*Saccharum* sp.) and of the banana tree *fe'i* (*Musa troglodytarum* L.). People still collect nuts (three species of *Aleurites moluccana* Willd.), wild fruits (Ebenacae, Liliacae), make flour with ovules of *Cycas rumphii* Miq. and cakes with the fruit of mangrove trees (*Bruguiera eriopetala* W. and Arn.). Primitive species of yams are characterized as *Dioscorea bulbifera* (cultivated in simple fallow) and *Dioscorea glabra* (a semi-gathered species). In the centre of the Grand Terre people still cultivate a primitive yam species (*Dioscorea nummularia*) and eat the bark of edible hibiscus species (*Hibiscus tiliaceus* L.). The use of some taro (*Colocasia esculenta* (L.) Schott) for medical purposes seems to indicate a long history of cultivation in this region. In the very distinctive cultural *cèmuhi* region (north-central Grande Terre), are still found two plants which are probably very old: the yam *Dioscorea glabra* Roxb. and the taro *Amorphophallus campanulatus* (Rox.) Bl. Barrau links these plants to early groups of the Grand Terre. On linguistic grounds, Haudricourt (1971) believes that the yam *Dioscorea alata* L. was one of the first tubers brought to New Caledonia by the Austronesian settlers.

Soon after initial settlement on the coast, some groups began to leave the shores and move inland. It is probable that the initial reason was hunting. In the oldest dated sites there is the presence of bones of endemic species like the megapode *Sylviornis neocaledoniae* which were rapidly hunted to extinction (Balouet 1986). The discovery of hammerstones with two pitched faces (Figure 13.2), forming tools which have been interpreted in

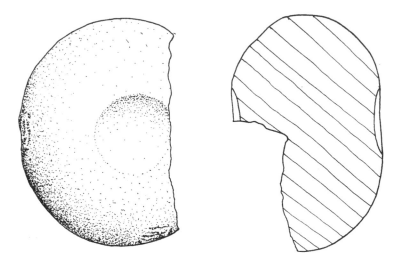

Figure 13.2 Hammerstone with the two pitched faces, from site WKO013B of Lapita, occupied around 1000 BC.

other archaeological sites of the Pacific as nut-cracking stones (Birks and Birks 1972; Kirch 1988: figure 127; Spennemann 1989: 146–50), is a new indication of the possible early presence of nuts in the diet. Nut species were still used at the arrival of the first European sailors, as the kanaks consume some varieties of nuts such as *Aleurites moluccana* and *Calophyllum inophyllum* L. (Bourret 1978, 1981; Cherrier 1990), contrary to what has sometimes been stated (Yen 1990: 268; Gosden 1992: 63).

The first millennium BC also saw the beginning of the settlement of the interior of the valleys. Regular occupation of a rock shelter in the middle Koumac valley, at approximately 5 km from the coast, seems to start at about 700 BC (Sémah *et al*. 1995). In the upper Tiwaka valley, about 15 km from the east coast, charcoal layers interpreted as the first indications of burning – and covered by more than 150 cm of alluvium – have been dated to the second half of the first millennium BC (Sand and Ouetcho 1993a), indicating the first human impact on the landscape in the mountains.

In summary, we now have clear indications of the use of the landscape, probably mostly for horticultural purposes, from the beginning of the ceramic chronology 3,000 years ago. Human predation led to the disappearance of elements of the local fauna like the megapode, a land crocodile (*Mekosuchus inexpectatus*), a horned turtle (*Meilania mackayi*) and a lizard (*Varanus* sp.) (Balouet 1984, 1986). The archaeological data show that the first settlers of New Caledonia had a diverse diet, based not only on marine products but also with a reliance on the natural flora and fauna, complemented probably by the cultivation of root crops.

The first millennium AD: a period of major changes

The first millennium AD probably witnessed the major settlement of the interior of the Grande Terre. This led, in some areas, to a massive transformation of the landscape, with the filling-in of valley bottoms and the creation of swamps through soils eroding from the hills deforested through burning. In Moindou on the west coast, for example, a layer dated by pottery to around the beginning of the first millennium AD is today covered by more than 6 m of alluvium (Avias 1950). In the Néra valley of Bourail (west coast), handled vessels of the Plum tradition, dated to the first millennium AD, were discovered under 4 m of alluvium at the end of the last century (Glaumont 1889). In the Ouamenie valley, a habitation site formerly near the sea and dated to 450–640 cal. AD (Beta-92761), with handled pottery, is today covered by more than 150 cm of alluvium (Sand 1996a: 7–11). These landscape transformations doubtless had consequences for settlement patterns, and also caused changes in cultivation techniques. The hills which suffered soil-loss became less fertile, needing longer fallow periods, and the valley bottoms collected huge amounts of fertile soils.

The first millennium AD was probably also a period of rapid population growth (Sand 1995b). This may have led to a partial failure of the techniques of long fallow needed for shifting cultivation, in areas where population density became too high. In the coral islands people began to enclose their fields. On the Grande Terre, one method to limit the fallow period was to construct terraces on the hills to trap the fertile soil and stop its erosion. In some narrow valleys, people began to divide up the landscape with dry terracing. This can be observed in different parts of the Grande Terre, where a large amount of dry terracing has been recognized, with the construction of retaining walls sometimes more than 2 m high (Sand 1995b). No specific archaeological study has until now been conducted on these particular sites. On the island of Maré (Loyalties) the construction of monumental structures started around AD 250, with walls 500 m long, 10 m wide and more than 4 m high, constructed of huge coral blocks, some over 2 m long (Sand 1996f; Sand and Ouetcho 1993b).

Generally the emphasis on the Grande Terre was on wet cultivation terraces, primarily for taro (*Colocasia esculenta*) (Figure 13.3). People of the Grande Terre, unlike in other island groups, constructed terraces on relatively steep slopes, up to 70 per cent in angle. The principle was the same as the rice terraces of South-east Asia, which meant the presence of long water channels to supply the terraces, and a complex network of channels to allow the water to flow from one terrace to the others (Barrau 1956).

This kind of horticultural construction required more time and effort, but it allowed people to shorten the fallow period in an important way. In the taro pond fields of Col de la Pirogue, on the south-west coast of the Grande Terre, excavations in 1993 uncovered for the first time in New Caledonia, on this kind of site, a layer of a probable wet cultivation terrace, dated to 1210 ± 70 BP (Beta-61956, CAMS-6499), calibrated to AD 690 (810) 975 (Sand 1994:

Figure 13.3   Example of present-day taro terraces at various stages of use (Atéou tribe).

60). This is the first direct date for terrace cultivation in the Archipelago, most probably for taro crops. This date matches well the idea of the appearance of complex cultivation sites at a period when demographic problems and the possibility of some kind of overpopulation appears in the prehistoric evidence. Demographic pressure was certainly not the only reason for the appearance of terraced structures in New Caledonia (Yen 1973; Kirch 1994), but I still believe that it was one of the major causes of its massive development.

Intensification of the horticultural landscape during the second millennium AD
During the next millennium, before the arrival of European sailors, people progressively constructed terraced cultivation sites in most of the suitable areas of the Grande Terre. In the Païta-Mont Dore region, on the south-west coast, such sites covered most of the hills of the peridotite chain between 50 m and 400 m. Mapping of the Païta commune has shown that the terraces cover more than 1,150 hectares (Sand 1994: 74). People even constructed terraces in unfavourable areas, probably bringing soil from other parts to create soils for cultivation. The lowest layer of one of these sites – WPT059 – has been dated to 300 ± 120 BP (Beta-59963), calibrated to AD 1450 (1640) 1954, with the most recent layer cultivated up to the beginning of the nineteenth century (Sand 1994:63). This clearly indicates the ongoing construction of terraced sites up to European arrival. These sites, of which more than 150 are known at present, represent hundreds of thousands of terraces (Figure 13.4).

Figure 13.4 Partial view of abandoned terraced taro-pond fields at Col des Roussettes (Bourail).

An example of the major importance of artificially created areas of cultivation comes from the mountainous centre of the Grande Terre, where flat valleys are absent. The sites ETO046 in Bounou and ETO045 in Kaden are located at the limit of the cultivable soils, at the foot of the Kunten mountain, formed by peridotite rocks and acid red soils (Sand and Ouetcho 1993a: 40–5). The great majority of the cultivation structures, be they long mounds for dry farming or terraces for wet taro cultivation, have been constructed in the fertile parts of the plateaux (Figure 13.5). In order to reserve the greatest part of the soils for cultivation, people have constructed their habitation mounds in the rocky parts of the plateau and have even used the peridotite red slopes of the Kunten mountain, although this must have been a very unfavourable area to live on.

This intensification of landscape use, shown from hill occupations, is also visible in a multitude of valley bottoms, where people have constructed in the lowest and most humid part of the base of the valley dry cultivation structures, sometimes more than 2 m high, 10 m wide and more than 100 m long.

On the east coast, some valley bottoms seem to have been completely sculpted by people, with the presence of high dry cultivation structures, mainly for yam (*Dioscorea* spp.) and wet raised taro fields, only interrupted occasionally by the house platforms of prehistoric settlements. To illustrate the importance of these structures, we may take the example of a small part of the lower Tiwaka valley, an area about 1 km long and 250 m wide (Sand

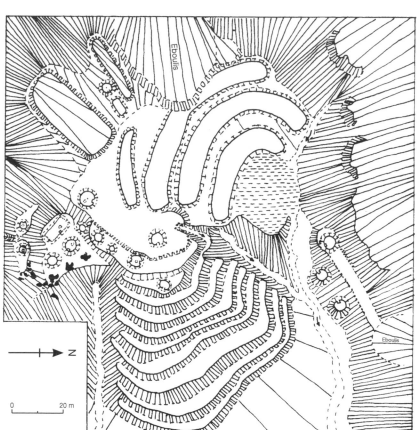

Figure 13.5 Map of the site ETO045 in Kaden, with the long raised yam fields, the taro terraces and the round habitation mounds in the surrounding rocky areas.

and Ouetcho 1993a): the density of the horticultural structures is so great (Figure 13.6) that the area of artificially constructed cultivation beds is a total of about 10 m wide, 1 m high and 17 km long (Sand 1995b).

Similar intensification of the use of the landscape can also be found in more unfavourable areas like the uplifted coral platforms in the Loyalty Islands and on the east coast, where people created gardens separated by multiple walled enclosures (Sand and Ouetcho 1994; Sand 1995b). On the partial atoll of Ouvéa, in the northern Loyalty Islands, people excavated into the sand dunes to reach the water lens to cultivate wet taro and dry-loving plants in composted soil: the biggest of these sites is 250 m wide, 4 km long and 3 m deep (Sand and Ouetcho 1993c). Finally, on the narrow south-east coast, people constructed huge dams, some more than 100 m long and 4 m high, to redirect small rivers so as to drain swamps for cultivation (Sand and Ouetcho 1992).

Figure 13.6 Aerial photograph of part of the Tiwaka plain, showing the multiple horticultural structures and some round habitation mounds in between.

DISCUSSION

This is a rapid synopsis of the presently known evolution of horticultural practices in New Caledonia over 3,000 years of prehistory and the way people adapted their cultural strategies to meet the problems of environmental change and altering human needs. On the Grande Terre these developments have created a landscape without precedent in Melanesia (Barrau 1958). Looking at the prehistoric period, two aspects of human behaviour can be investigated in the case of New Caledonia: one is of adaptation to environmental change and social influences; the other is considerable isolation from outside influences resulting in a local historical trajectory and regionally specific cultural choices.

ADAPTATION AND INFLUENCES

The evolution of cultural action related to horticultural practices following first settlement goes hand in hand with the evolution of settlement patterns, population growth and change in material culture (especially pottery) (Sand 1995b, 1996c). This led to a transformation of the landscape due to the destruction of the forests, initially to create a long fallow swidden system, and then to the modelling of the landscape and the building up of permanent horticultural structures. Seeing natural factors as the sole cause of change is limiting, although the clear definition of cultural reasons underlying these changes is always difficult. As Yen says 'the rate of change may be largely dependent on the socio-political environment, having its fundamental basis in population numbers and their change' (Yen 1973: 81). The development of the horticultural structures of the Grande Terre, which could allow for the creation of surplus as well as the presence of monumental structures in some areas of the Loyalty islands (Sand and Ouetcho 1993b; Sand 1996f), indicates that the evolution of the political structures over time was important (Sand *et al.* 1999). A major task is to define the sorts of political entities and forms of hierarchy that existed in later prehistory.

This question is linked to the problems of indigenous development and outside influence. Some archaeological and ethnographic data show that during the prehistoric period outside influences and new human arrivals led to novel adaptations (Sand 1995b). But it is difficult to link these changes directly to innovations in horticultural practices. For example, we do not know whether the particular type of steep wet terrace cultivation on the Grande Terre was of local or foreign origin. We can say it was different to those developed in most of the other great island groups of the Pacific which have a wetter climate, and that it probably needed a greater intensity of labour. This is the case for all the complex cultivation techniques of Remote Oceania. Some people favour an early introduction of the concept during the first Austronesian expansion from South-east Asia to the south-west Pacific 3,500–3,000 years ago (Spriggs 1982); others, on linguistic grounds, favour a 're-invention' in tropical Oceania (Kirch and Lepofsky 1993). In the region of Houaïlou on the east coast of the Grande Terre, myths say that it was ancestors, the Panyamanya, who taught the local inhabitants how to construct terraces. The existence of terrace cultivation in other areas of Melanesia, as far east as Fiji, points to a regional rather than a local innovation during the last 1,500 years, although it is on the Grande Terre of New Caledonia that this technique was the most intensively used. A regional influence may also account for the existence of big cultivation pits on Ouvéa Island, very similar to those found on the atolls of Micronesia and East Polynesia (Chazine 1985).

Spriggs has recently (1995) argued for the introduction of some nut trees, such as *Canarium*, in the south-west Pacific during the first Austronesian expansion. This might have been possible for New Caledonia, but here the colder climate would not have been suitable for some of the species – as in other areas of Melanesia (Gosden 1992: 63) – leading to a diversity in food management.

The cultivation of plants has symbolic as well as environmental influences: some groups are linked to species of tubers or other cultivated plants (Di Piazza 1995). In the case of New Caledonia, we can present the case of Xetriwaan, a group said to come mainly from the island of Aneytium in southern Vanuatu, and which was able, between the seventeenth and eighteenth centuries, to gain power in most of the Loyalty Islands, in the Île des Pins, and in some regions of the Grande Terre. Although, according to oral tradition, the political influence of this group in the last centuries before European arrival was important, archaeologically no sign of change in the cultural material can be found (Sand 1995b). The only introduction related to the Xetriwaan groups is the arrival of a new species of banana tree, named Kiamu after the old name of the island of Aneytium (Guiart 1963: 325). This tree still enables the related groups of Xetriwaan today to know that they are of the same origin.

Finally, European colonization also brought many new crops. To make a complete study of these in relation to the kanak society is not the subject of this chapter, but we can simply cite important trees like the mango tree, which can be seen in some traditional kanak habitation sites of the nine-teenth century (Sand 1997), or root crops like manioc (*Manihot esculenta* Crantz), which are of major importance in present-day gardens.

ISOLATION AND NON-INTRODUCTION

The reasons for the acceptance of newly introduced crops are complex. The existence of shrines near fields, where the masters of the gardens made prayers to the ancestors, and of magic stones connected to the most important plants and put in cultivated areas to speed growth, show that the acceptance of a new plant was only possible if it could be fitted within sets of complex religious beliefs.

Some outside species were definitely introduced during the prehistoric period in New Caledonia. However, in some cases plants were not accepted at all, or only found a minor place in the rosters of economically useful or symbolically potent species. If it is difficult archaeologically to identify failed introductions of plants, more recent introductions of tubers from surrounding areas, like the sweet potato (*Ipomoea batatas*) – said to have been introduced in the few centuries before European arrival by sailors from Tonga to the Île des Pins (Guiart 1963: 210) – can be studied more easily. The introduction of sweet potato was unimportant in New Caledonia and, contrary to what happened in the New Guinea Highlands (Yen 1973), sweet potato gained no central economic, symbolic and cultural role in the kanak gardens before European colonization.

There is also an absence in New Caledonia of two of the most important items of the Pacific: the pig and kava. Remains of pigs (*Sus scrofa*) are known in various Lapita sites throughout the south-west Pacific (Nagaoka 1988). This indicates that the Austronesians introduced this animal during their first expansion 3,500–3,000 years ago, out to Western Polynesia. In New Caledonia, no pig bones have been definitely identified in well-stratified prehistoric layers (however, see pp. 264–5). The absence of pigs seems to continue until first contact with Captain James Cook in 1774 on the north-east coast of the Grande Terre (Beaglehole 1961). The kanaks knew the existence of the pig, which was of major importance in the society of neighbouring Vanuatu and of the islands of Western Polynesia, but they clearly had chosen not to adopt this animal. The reasons may be multiple: for cultural reasons, such that pigs were not accepted in society; or for horticultural reasons, because people had to protect their gardens from the depredations of pigs in this infertile archipelago. In this regard, it is possible that future excavations of Lapita sites in New Caledonia will show the introduction of this animal during the first millennium BC and its later disappearance to be a cultural choice. Cases of disappearance of introduced animals, like the pig, the chicken and the dog, are known elsewhere in the Pacific (see Yen 1990 for a review).

The absence of the use of kava in New Caledonia is a second clear difference to the surrounding island groups. Kava (*Piper methysticum* Forst. f.), has a probable origin in northern Vanuatu as early as the first millennium BC and has a rich corpus of myths and histories connected to it (Lebot 1989). It was probably spread as far as Fiji and Western Polynesia soon after its discovery, and has retained there a central role in ceremonial practices, both as a cultural item and a drink. It appears that although it has ancient origins in the north of the Vanuatu archipelago, kava was probably much more recently given a cultural importance in southern Vanuatu (Bonnemaison 1985). Clearly, this importance was never transferred to kanak culture and society. The arrival during the last centuries before European contact of groups from Western Polynesia, like Uvea and Tonga (where kava was of central importance in the culture), did not change this situation. The newcomers had to adapt to local cultural norms and failed in the introduction of this part of their cultural heritage. Clearly, there were strong cultural markers in some Austronesian societies, and to imagine these island groups as permanently adopting new cultural products does not take into account the great variability of social action.

The variety of social action

These two examples show the complexity of factors influencing the cultural acceptance or rejection of crops or practice. Having said that, for New Caledonia as a whole the historical trajectory is clear, showing a process of agricultural intensification and the absence or unimportance of some cultural and economic items which had gained a central status in other archipelagos of the region.

But if we now look at a more local level, the archaeological data seem to be much more diverse. For example, a preliminary survey of part of the north-east coast of the Grande Terre, in Tiouandé (Sand 1996b), has shown the presence of a wall approximately 4 km long, starting from one side of a river mouth (Ouépouaie), climbing to the watershed of the hills and going down again to the next river-mouth (Tipindjé). It clearly separates a sea front region from more inland areas. The wall, mostly 1.5 m high, cannot have been used as a military defence: part of the time, it is simply the border of the hill which has been marked out with a stone wall, indicating that this was an attempt to prevent movement in from the sea and not, as is held by some local histories, to prevent cattle from the interior of the Tipindjé valley moving to the sea. Morphologically, this structure is very like the pig walls found in some Polynesian islands (Frimigacci 1990: 187; Kirch 1994: 184). The first European sailors noted in the area of Hienghène, of which Tiouandé is part, the presence of important seashore groups speaking Polynesian languages (Guiart 1966: 112), so that the discovery of this wall may indicate the introduction of the pig by some Polynesian communities before its introduction by Captain Cook in Balade. If future archaeological excavations confirm this hypothesis, as some preliminary analysis seems to indicate for the excavation of site WKO026 of Oundjo (Green and Mitchell 1983: 58), then it may be that the pig was already present in some areas of the Grande Terre before European contact.

This hypothesis is strengthened by one of the earliest texts written on the south-east coast of the Grande Terre, by the first members of the London Missionary Society in the early 1840s. Listing local resources, the Rarotongan teacher Ta'unga names chickens, pigs and the giant taro (Kapé – *Alocasia macrorrhiza*), 'in great abondance' (Crocombe and Crocombe 1962: 35). It is impossible to say for the moment if pigs were a post-contact introduction or whether in this region they were part of an older cultural stock, but the situation appears to be different in the south of the archipelago from what is known in the north. The mention of the giant taro is also important, as this tuber is not cultivated nowadays and has no place in the tales about the pre-European society. Other cultivated plants may have lost their importance during the last century, as the sugar-cane, which seems to have had a central symbolic position in relation to the yam in some areas.

These two examples, chosen from many possible ones, show that the cultural situations in Melanesian societies have to be studied at a very small scale to be realistic. In this respect, they follow the same path and the same variability as appears in the diversification of language (Dutton 1995). The explanation of cultural and political choices is complex, and to attempt to see them in a narrow framework of adaptation, borrowing and isolation seems not to be as effective as first thought when attempting to explain such diverse local histories.

CONCLUSION: RECONSTRUCTING PREHISTORIC COMPLEXITY

The few radiocarbon dates we have, and the texts of the first Europeans in New Caledonia, clearly indicate that most of the horticultural structures of the archipelago, irrespective of the reason and date of construction, were used up until the nineteenth century. Looking at the general prehistoric situation in New Caledonia, it seems that the common view of around 50,000 kanaks living in New Caledonia at European contact (Roux 1990), with a semi-egalitarian political system (Guiart 1963, 1983), is not supported by archaeological data. This would represent less than seven people per square km on good soil (Sand 1995b), which does not tally with the type or number of sites we have. Using the many complex horticultural sites and habitation sites as a starting point, I have raised the possibility of an important population collapse in New Caledonia between James Cook's discovery of the island in 1774 and the middle of the nineteenth century, when France took over the archipelago. This led to the collapse of the prehistoric society and its organization long before the first ethnographic studies (Sand 1995b).

Such a scenario would mean that the so-called traditional kanak social structure, characterized mainly by small groups of people always in movement around the landscape, as has been reconstructed by ethnographers (Guiart 1963, 1983; Bensa 1981), is not a prehistoric situation but is mainly linked to the first contacts with European sailors. As Gosden says for Polynesia, 'European contact brought about drastic changes in Polynesian society. Recent surveys are consequently of a state of society greatly changed from pre-contact days, and attempts to view prehistoric communities in a recent light might be suspect' (1987: 446). The prehistoric society of the mid-eighteenth century in New Caledonia might have been much more characterized by what Barrau has named 'horticultural sedentism' (1956: 56) than by the semi-nomadic societies observed 150 years later by the first ethnographers.

Nowadays, the great majority of these archaeological structures, indicative of 3,000 years of transformation and intensification of landscape use, are abandoned. However, their continued presence shows evidence of forms of life unlike those of the contemporary world and provides us the means of studying a past which still contains many surprises.

REFERENCES

Allen, J., C. Gosden, R. Jones, and J.P.White. 1988. Pleistocene dates for the human occupation of New Ireland, Northern Melanesia. *Nature* 331, 707–09.

Avias, J. 1950. Poteries canaques et poteries préhistoriques en Nouvelle-Calédonie. Contribution à l'archéologie et à la préhistoire océanienne. *Journal de la Société des Océanistes* 6, 111–39.

Balouet, J.C. 1984. Paléonthologie des vertébrés terrestres de Nouvelle-Calédonie et paléogéographie du pacifique sud-ouest. Unpublished Thèse de 3e cycle, Université Curie (Paris VI).

Balouet, J.C. 1986. Premiers colons de Nouvelle-Calédonie. *L'Univers du vivant* 7, 35–47.

Barrau, J. 1956. *L'agriculture vivrière autochtone de la Nouvelle-Calédonie*. Nouméa: Comission du Pacifique Sud.

Barrau, J. 1958. *Subsistence Agriculture in Melanesia*. Honolulu: B.P. Bishop Museum Bulletin 219.

Barrau, J. 1965. Histoire et préhistoire horticoles de l'Océanie tropicale. *Journal de la Société des Océanistes* 21, 55–78.

Barrau, J. 1981. *Ethnobotanique (Planche 17)*. *Atlas ORSTOM de la Nouvelle-Calédonie*. Paris: ORSTOM.

Beaglehole, J.C. 1961. *The Journal of Captain James Cook on his Voyages of Discovery. The voyage of the* Resolution *and adventure 1772–1775*. Cambridge: Cambridge University Press.

Bensa, A. 1981. *Clans autochtones: situation pré-coloniale (Planche 18, III)*. *Atlas de la Nouvelle-Calédonie et Dépendances*. Paris: Editions ORSTOM.

Birks, L. and H. Birks. 1972. Stone artifacts from Tonga and Fiji. *Asian Perspectives* XV, 93–6.

Bonnemaison, J. 1985. *L'arbre et la pirogue*. Paris: Editions ORSTOM.

Bourret, D. 1978. *Les 'racines' canaques*. Collection EVEIL no. 9. Nouméa: D.E.C.

Bourret, D. 1981. *Ethnobotanique (Planche 17)*. *Atlas de la Nouvelle-Calédonie et Dépendances*. Paris: Editions ORSTOM.

Chazine, J.M. 1985. Du présent au passé: questions d'ethnoarchéologie. Les fosses de culture des Tuamotu. *Techniques et culture* 6, 85–98.

Cherrier, J.F. 1990. *Utilisation de la flore indigene par les Mélanésiens à l'époque pré-européenne en Nouvelle-Calédonie*. Centre Technique Forestier Tropical (Report).

Crocombe, R.C. and M. Crocombe. 1962. *The Works of Ta'unga*. Canberra: Pacific History Series.

Di Piazza, A. 1995. Les paysagistes océaniens: De la socialisation de la nature. In *Milieux, sociétés et archéologues*, A. Marliac (ed.), 24–33. Paris: ORSTOM–KARTHALA.

Dutton, T. 1995. Language contact and change in Melanesia. In *The Austronesians: historical and comparative perspectives*, P. Bellwood, J. Fox and D. Tryon (eds), 192–213. Canberra: ANU.

Frimigacci, D. 1980. Localisation éco-géographique et utilisation de l'espace de quelques sites Lapita de Nouvelle-Calédonie: essai d'interprétation. *Journal de la Société des Océanistes* 66–67, 5–11.

Frimigacci, D. 1990. *Aux temps de la terre noire: ethno-archeologie des îles Futuna et Alofi*. Leuven, Belgium: Editions Peters. SELAF 321.

Galipaud, J.C. 1988. La poterie préhistorique néo-calédonienne et ses implications dans l'étude du processus de peuplement du pacifique occidental. Unpublished Ph.D. thesis, Université Paris I.

Galipaud, J.C. 1992. Un ou plusieurs peuples potiers en Nouvelle-Calédonie. *Journal de la Société des Océanistes* 95, 185–200.

Gifford, E.W. and D. Shutler Jr. 1956. *Archaeological Excavations in New Caledonia*. Anthropological Records 18. Berkeley and Los Angeles: University of California Press.

Glaumont, G. 1889. Fouilles à Bourail. *Revue d'Ethnographie* 8, 214–15.

Gosden, C. 1987. Comment. In History, phylogeny, and evolution in Polynesia, P.V. Kirch and R.C. Green. *Current Anthropology* 28, 446–7.

Gosden, C. 1992. Production systems and the colonisation of the Western Pacific. *World Archaeology* 24, 55–69.

Green, R.C. 1979. Lapita. In *The Prehistory of Polynesia*, J. Jennings (ed.), 27–60. Cambridge, Mass.: Harvard University Press.

Green, R. C. and J.S. Mitchell. 1983. New Caledonian culture history: a review of the archaeological sequence. *New Zealand Journal of Archaeology* 5, 19–67.

Guiart, J. 1963. *La Chefferie en Mélanésie du Sud*. Paris: Institut d'Ethnologie, Musée de l'Homme.

Guiart, J. 1966. *Mythologie du masque en Nouvelle-Calédonie*. Paris: Publication de la Société des Océanistes 18.

Guiart, J. 1983. *La terre est le sang des morts*. Paris: Editions Anthropos.

Guiart, J. 1992. *Structure de la chefferie en mélanésie du sud*. Paris: Institut d'Ethnologie.

Haudricourt, A.G. 1971. New Caledonia and the Loyalty islands. *Current Trends in Linguistics* 8, 359–96.

Kirch, P.V. 1988. *Niuatoputapu. The prehistory of a Polynesian chiefdom.* Seattle: T. Burke Memorial Washington State Museum Monograph 5.

Kirch, P.V. 1994. *The Wet and the Dry. Irrigation and agricultural intensification in Polynesia.* Chicago and London: The University of Chicago Press.

Kirch, P.V. and D. Lepofsky. 1993. Polynesian irrigation: archaeological and linguistic evidence for origins and development. *Asian Perspectives* 32, 183–204.

Lebot, V. 1989. L'histoire du Kava commence par sa découverte. *Journal de la Société des Océanistes* 88–89, 89–114.

Loy, T.H., M. Spriggs and S. Wickler. 1992. Direct evidence for human use of plants 28,000 years ago: starch residues on stone artifacts from the northern Solomon Islands. *Antiquity* 66, 898–912.

Nagaoka, L. 1988. Lapita subsistence: the evidence of non-fish archaeofaunal remains. In *Archaeology of the Lapita Cultural Complex: a critical review*, P.V. Kirch and T.L. Hunt (eds), 117–34. Seattle: T. Burke Memorial Washington State Museum Research Report 5.

Roux, J.C. 1990. Traditional Melanesian agriculture in New Caledonia and pre-contact population distribution. In *Pacific Production Systems*, D. Yen and J.M.J. Mummery (eds), 161–73. Canberra: ANU, Occasional Papers in Prehistory 18.

Sand, C. 1990. Prospection électrique sur le site archéologique de Boirra (Koumac): les premiers résultats. Unpublished report, ORSTOM Nouméa.

Sand, C. 1994. *Entre mer et montagne. Inventaire archéologique de la Commune de Païta (Province Sud).* Nouméa: Les Cahiers de l'Archéologie en Nouvelle-Calédonie 4.

Sand, C. 1995a. *Archaeology in New Caledonia. Archaeological research up to the early 1990s and future orientations.* Nouméa: Publication ADCK-CTRDP.

Sand, C. 1995b. *'Le temps d'avant' – La préhistoire de la Nouvelle-Calédonie.* Paris: Editions l'Harmattan.

Sand, C. 1996a. *Inventaire des sites archéologiques de la Commune de Boulouparis (Province Sud): premiers résultats.* Nouméa: Département Archéologie du Service des Musées et du Patrimoine de Nouvelle-Calédonie.

Sand, C. 1996b. *Nouveau corpus de sites archéologiques de Nouvelle-Calédonie.* Nouméa: Département Archéologie du Service des Musées et du Patrimoine de Nouvelle-Calédonie.

Sand, C. 1996c. Recent developments in the study of New Caledonia's prehistory. *Archaeology in Oceania* 31, 45–71.

Sand, C. 1996d. Archaeological structures, socio-political complexity and population density: new insight into the prehistory of the New Caledonian archipelago. In *Oceanic Culture History: essays in honour of Roger Green*, J. Davidson, J. Irwin, B.F. Leach, A. Pawley and D. Brown (eds), 287–95. Auckland: New Zealand Journal of Archaeology Special Publication.

Sand, C. 1996e. *Le début du peuplement austronésien de la Nouvelle-Calédonie. Données archéologiques récentes.* Nouméa: Les Cahiers de l'Archéologie en Nouvelle-Calédonie 6.

Sand, C. 1996f. Structural remains as markers of complex societies in southern Melanesia during prehistory: the case of the monumental forts of Maré Island, New Caledonia. *In Indo-Pacific Prehistory: the Chiang Mai papers*, I.C. Glover and P. Bellwood (eds), 37–44. Canberra: Bulletin of the Indo-Pacific Prehistory Association 15.

Sand, C. 1997. Variété de l'habitat ancien en Nouvelle-Calédonie: étude de cas sur des vestiges archéologiques du Centre-Nord de la Grande Terre. *Journal de la Société des Océanistes* (Paris) 104, 39–66.

Sand, C., J. Bolé and A. Ouetcho. 1999. L'apport de l'archéologie à la reconstitution des caractéristiques des sociétés pré-européennes de Nouvelle-Calédonie et des mécanismes de leur transformation historique. *Etudes des sociétés kanak: systèmes sociaux en devenir*. Paris: Publication ESK, 139–56.

Sand, C. and A. Ouetcho. 1992. *Bwede ko-tchon tchuvan-vare kein (des rivières déviées par les ancêtres). Premier inventaire archéologique de la commune de Yaté, Province Sud de la Nouvelle-Calédonie*. Nouméa: Les Cahiers de l'Archéologie en Nouvelle-Calédonie 1.

Sand, C. and A. Ouetcho. 1993a. *Etude d'impact de la transversale Koné-Tiwaka sur le patrimoine archéologique*. Nouméa: Les Cahiers de l'Archéologie en Nouvelle-Calédonie 2.

Sand, C. and A. Ouetcho. 1993b. *Etudes archéologiques sur les îles Loyauté*. Nouméa: Les Cahiers de l'Archéologie en Nouvelle-Calédonie 3.

Sand, C. and A. Ouetcho. 1993c. *Inventaire archéologique d'Ouvéa. (1) Mouly, Fayawa et Lékine*. Nouméa: Département Archéologie du Service des Musées et du Patrimoine de Nouvelle-Calédonie.

Sand, C. and A. Ouetcho. 1993d. Three thousand years of settlement in the south of New Caledonia: some recent results from the region of Païta. *New Zealand Journal of Archaeology* 15, 107–30.

Sand, C. and A. Ouetcho. 1994. Le site ancien STY7 de Pwékina. Etude archéologique d'une plaine de bord de mer du sud-est de la Grande-Terre (Nouvelle-Calédonie). *Bulletin de la Société des Etudes Mélanésiennes* 29, 16–35.

Sémah, F., A.M. Sémah and H. Forstier. 1995. Nouvelles données sur le peuplement ancien de la Nouvelle-Calédonie: la vallée de Koumac (Grande-Terre). *Compte-rendu de l'Académie des Sciences de Paris* 320, 539–45.

Spennemann, D. 1989. 'ata 'a Tonga mo 'ata 'o Tonga: early and later prehistory of the Tongan Islands. Unpublished Ph.D. thesis, Australian National University, Canberra.

Spriggs, M. 1982. Taro cropping systems in the Southeast Asian–Pacific region: archaeological evidence. *Archaeology in Oceania* 17, 7–15.

Spriggs, M. 1995. The Lapita culture and Austronesian prehistory in Oceania. In *The Austronesians: historical and comparative perspectives*, P. Bellwood, J. Fox and D. Tryon (eds), 112–33. Canberra: ANU.

Stevenson, J. and J. Dodson. 1995. Palaeoenvironmental evidence for human settlement of New Caledonia. *Archaeology in Oceania* 30, 36–41.

Yen, D.E. 1973. The origins of Oceanic agriculture. *Archaeology and Physical Anthropology in Oceania* 8, 68–85.

Yen, D.E. 1990. Environment, agriculture and colonisation of the Pacific. In *Pacific Production Systems*, D. Yen and J.M.J. Mummery (eds), 258–77. Canberra: ANU, Occasional Papers in Prehistory 18.

14 Warfare and intensive agriculture in Fiji

ROBERT KUHLKEN

Agricultural intensification has been a major theme for cultural–ecological studies within a number of disciplines. Demographic pressure on resources is the starting point for many hypotheses attempting to explain higher inputs of labour to given areas of land, often leading to irrigation systems or other forms of intensive agricultural land use. The relationship between population and the environment as expressed through agricultural change is central to a body of theory articulated most fluently by Boserup, Geertz, and Brookfield. Boserup (1965) saw agricultural intensification as triggered by population increase exerting a strain on existing food production capacity. Using a case study from Java, Geertz (1966) illustrated how only certain agrosystems are capable of absorbing higher inputs of labour and technological skill, given the constraint of a land base that remains constant. And based on research on Pacific Islands, Brookfield (1972) revealed evidence for different purposes of production, with social or ritual needs and trade requirements assuming a substantial share of yields; he concluded that 'the relation of population density to agricultural intensity in the Pacific is by no means clear' (Brookfield 1972: 36). Pacific agricultural landscapes appear to be a particularly rewarding area for exploring causal links between cultural or ecological systems and regional evolution of social and political structures. I shall argue, however, that Fiji offers the basis for quite a different interpretation.

Intensive agriculture in Fiji was only one tactic within a broad subsistence strategy that also included swidden cultivation and the exploitation of marine resources. Although agricultural intensification and expansion of intensively cultivated areas may have been caused by population increase, a more likely explanation is the impetus created by social conflict and warfare. This chapter presents several examples from historical landscapes in Fiji that serve to illustrate this idea. In the areas discussed, chronic warfare instigated a need to locate high-yielding gardens adjacent to isolated and defensible settlements. The provision of staple food crops for gatherings of warriors also stimulated agricultural intensification.

WARFARE AND SUBSISTENCE

There have been wide-ranging studies of organized aggression and conflict, especially in the context of so-called 'primitive' rather than 'modern' warfare (Davie 1929; Wedgewood 1930; Turney-High [1949]1991). A few historical works have even examined connections between warfare and agriculture (Hanson 1983; Keegan 1994). Other research has concentrated on the relationship between warfare and sociopolitical development (Webster 1975; Johnson and Earle 1987). Causality, in most cases, was seen as flowing from sedentary agriculture and population increase towards warfare, as in this passage by Hassan (1983: 204): 'Although hunters and gatherers may engage in feuds and violent confrontations, the emergence of systematic warfare, fortifications, and weapons of destruction follows the path of agriculture and the concentration of wealth.' Some scholars posit a three-way relationship linking population, warfare, and agricultural intensification. Golson (1972: 27) viewed population pressure on resources as the ultimate cause for agricultural intensification, but operating by way of the demographic stresses that induce warfare: 'instances of prehistoric fortifications, of settlement in less desirable areas, and of agriculture in marginal conditions . . . suggest the build-up of population'. Addressing these same issues, Carneiro (1970) set forth an ecologically based theory of political evolution, which holds that 'territorial circumscription' of limited arable land creates hostile competition that ultimately results in the formation of the state. Using case studies from the valleys of coastal Peru, Carneiro claimed that population increase in areas of 'circumscribed agricultural land' prompted significant cultural–ecological changes: 'tilling of land already under cultivation was intensified, and, new previously unusable land was brought under cultivation by means of terracing and irrigation' (1970: 735). Continued population pressure led to warfare over land, and, ultimately, to political integration. In a more recent paper, Carneiro (1990: 190) specifically elucidates the Fijian situation with regards to 'the centrality of war in political evolution'.

Inspired by the seminal *War in Ecological Perspective* (Vayda 1976), the tone of recent anthropological assessments of conflict has been cultural materialist, with warfare being an adaptive strategy or a requisite feedback loop in an otherwise unbalanced system (Ferguson 1984). But the idea that social aggression could determine the look and character of the landscape has largely been ignored. Turner and Harrison (1983: 255) stated and rejected the possibility when explaining Mayan raised fields in Belize: 'early use of wetlands at Albion Island may reflect local circumstances of land restriction, either by coercion or by choice . . . there is no evidence to support the coercion theme, such as confinement of people to the island by a hostile force'. Social hostility was, however, very much evident in the Fiji Islands. And coercion may well be the leading cause for intensive agriculture there. Perhaps not coincidentally, a clear example of warfare stimulating higher inputs of labour to agrosystems was documented on another Pacific archipelago. In the Hawaiian Islands, Kirch and Sahlins (1992) found that agricultural intensity in the Anahulu valley increased from 1804 to 1812, during Kamehameha's second occupation of O'ahu. The monarch was then preparing for an invasion of Kaua'i that never took place, but the food requirements for his mustered army provided an additional impetus to boost wet taro production beyond local subsistence requirements.

FIJIAN LAND AND LIFE

Fijian culture began when Austronesian people identified with Lapita pottery established the founding population in these islands some 3,500 years ago. Archaeological evidence for avifaunal extinctions and exploitation of marine species from both pelagic and reef environments points to hunting and gathering technologies, although horticulture was also a component of the subsistence base from the beginning (Hunt 1981). Following the character-istic agricultural ecology that developed throughout the Pacific, root crops were generally the most important cultigens tended by Fijians. Yams (*Dioscorea* spp.), taro (*Colocasia esculenta*), and giant swamp taro (*Cyrtosperma chamissonis*) were the most common tubers cultivated (Seemann 1973; Quain 1948). These staples responded well to higher labour inputs, with greater yields and food security provided through the practices of mounding, raised fields, and irrigated terraces.

In general, land was held communally by kinship groups. Brewster (1922: 290), who lived among the Fijians for over thirty years and was a keen observer of their customs, stated that 'except in a few isolated instances there is no individual proprietorship in land in Fiji, which is held by the unit of the family and the tribe'. Colonial administrators seeking to protect indigenous land rights during the latter part of the nineteenth century based their regulations on a standardized version of social relations which offered a consistent basis for determining territorial claims. As reflected in this model, society was organized in a nested hierarchy of kinship groups, starting with the extended household, a number of which formed a larger group known as *mataqali*, translated as 'clan' by early ethnographers. Several *mataqali* typically banded together in a tribal arrangement known as *yavusa*, and this formed the social unit of the village. It is through the traditions of their *yavusa* that Fijians are able to trace their connections with the land. But these connections were often reconstituted with each movement of the village, or as a result of divisions among the *mataqali*. As Derrick (1957: 9) related, '*yavusa* were subjected to the disruptive influences of war, internal strife, and migration'. Territorial claims applied only to those lands currently occupied by each *yavusa*, rather than to a specific ancestral domain. Using archival records from the 1890s, France (1969) revealed that because of this mobility,

> the various social units were unable to produce a body of tradition

identifying themselves with particular localities . . . their evidence told of ceaseless tribal skirmishing and a constant ebb and flow of population allowing for no permanent relationship between Fijians and the land across whose face they moved as the fortunes of war dictated.

(France 1969: 138)

Indeed, Chapelle (1976: 60) argued that Fijians were not so much tied to specific parcels of land as they were fiercely attached to land in general.

Perhaps partly resulting from the fragmenting nature of these relations, a wider polity evolved that was inclusive, and was termed *vanua*, a complex word that can also mean either 'the land' or the symbiotic relationship of people to the land. In sociopolitical parlance, *vanua* can be translated as 'chiefdom', with a territory comprising several villages within a district. Further indigenous political integration resulted in the formation of confederated high chiefdoms, or *matanitu*. Derrick (1957) explained the process:

> Many of the original *yavusa* were broken, scattered, merged wholly or in part with others; aggregations of their people formed, under stress of circumstances, new groups or confederations, called *vanua*, each under a paramount chief strong enough to seize and hold the position, which thereafter became hereditary. As the political structure developed, certain of the *vanua* were united, by conquest or accretion, into kingdoms (*matanitu*).

(Derrick 1957: 9)

Thus, political evolution had approached the formation of the state, particularly in eastern Fiji, where Polynesian influence was strongest. Hierarchical levels of authority had developed from kinship structures, and hereditary chiefs became powerful leaders of groups of villages, smaller islands, and eventually, entire regions. By the time Europeans arrived in the islands during the early 1800s, the diverse alliances and local coalitions had combined allegiances into seven powerful and often competing *matanitu*, with the three most powerful being Verata, Rewa, and Bau.

THE ROLE OF WARFARE

Warfare was a common and widespread occurrence in Fiji. Social relationships among tribal clans (*mataqali*) and larger groups (*yavusa* and *vanua*) during the several centuries leading up to the historic period were marked by mutual hostility. This may not have always been the case, of course. Some sources refer to a more peaceful past, with warfare only becoming prevalent within the last few hundred years. Conducting research among the Lauans of eastern Fiji, Thompson (1938: 183) found that 'their traditions contain no reference to warfare and there was apparently little rivalry between groups or individuals'. Some sources blame Tongan arrivals as instigators of conflict (while others blame the Fijians for taking warfare to Tonga!). Frost (1979: 74) reported evidence from Taveuni that indicated a period of building hilltop fortifications between AD 1200 and 1400. Rechtman (1992), conducting archaeological research on Wakaya, noted a 'pattern of increasing warfare and cannibalism'. Whatever may have been its causes and development, warfare in Fiji, by the time of European contact, had become an institution, and Waterhouse (1978: 315) was compelled to remark that 'Fijians, as a people, are addicted to war.'

Political elaboration induced corresponding changes in the nature of warfare in Fiji. Early observers noted there were two types of war – the 'ambuscades and desultory skirmishing in the bush' which went on all the time (Allardyce 1904: 71), and the larger-scale conflict which missionary John Hunt termed 'war of the chiefs' (Tippett 1973: 76–7). Fighting between neighbouring tribes, while common, did not actually cause many deaths. This type of war was more of a social performance than a politically motivated act (Tippett 1954). Ambush was the favoured tactic, and the ritual need to indulge in cannibalism may have provided an impetus for sending out raiding parties. Frequently it was enough to bring home a body or two for a symbolic feast. The chiefly confrontations, on the other hand, were associated with the rise of the greater polities, as the various *matanitu* competed with one another for power and influence. Both the frequency and ferocity of such wars seem to have escalated with European contact and the introduction of muskets, although Sahlins (1993: 22) has recently argued that the effect of these typically untrustworthy firearms was not as profound as earlier writers had assumed.

What concerns us here is the effect warfare may have had upon the process of agricultural intensification. Carneiro (1990: 207) noted that in Fiji the prowess of the warrior was self-validating, and resulted in the rise of chiefs rather than chiefdoms: 'success in war at the chiefdom level often did more to increase the power and status of the paramount chief than it did to enlarge his domain'. This would seem to indicate that competition over land and agricultural resources may not have played a major role after all. Viewing this tripartite relationship from another perspective, Thomas (1986) suggested that warfare arose not as a direct result of population pressure on resources, but as a consequence of the political evolutionary process itself:

> The endemic warfare arose not from the Fijian mind, but from the particular character of the system of social reproduction. It is notable that there appears to be a consistent basal date of around 1200 A.D. for Fijian fortifications. It may be that this was about the time the *matanitu* initially developed.
>
> (Thomas 1986: 63)

Regarding these fortifications, Frost (1979: 71) noted 'the densest distributions [of forts] fall where two important food resources, *dalo* (taro) and *via kana* (a tarolike plant) are intensively cultivated today'. Thus, the location of fortified sites exhibits an intriguing coincidence with areas of intensive root crop cultivation. Defensive settlements were often surrounded by taro gardens – drained fields and raised beds around ring-ditch forts on flat terrain, and irrigated terraces adjacent to ridgetop forts (Palmer 1969; Clunie 1977). This implies that agricultural intensification was triggered by warfare rather than population pressure. The necessity for keeping subsistence production in close proximity to secure habitation sites could be directly responsible for intensive agricultural landforms such as terracing and raised fields, and an end to hostilities could very well explain their abandonment.

Hostile relations influenced subsistence activities in several ways. Both the siting and situation of agricultural landscapes responded to the repercussions of warfare. As Lewis (1951) reported:

> In Fiji some of the villages are regular fortresses, elaborately fortified with earthworks ... the gardens and fields of the inhabitants are usually nearby, but may be at some distance; and the paths, both to the village and the gardens, may be concealed and difficult to find.
>
> (Lewis 1951: 48–9)

Food resources were recognized as a legitimate target by Fijian warriors. Uprooting plantations was often a prelude to laying siege to a village, and attacking agricultural lands was a typical and expected mode of operation in the heat of battle. Missionary Joseph Waterhouse was an eyewitness to a clash between Bau and Verata:

> Like a lawless troop of robbers and murderers, they destroyed many plantations, burned two settlements, killed two hundred and sixty of the inhabitants, and made prisoners of many women and children ... during several days the victors were devouring the slain, like infuriated wolves and hyænas.
>
> (Waterhouse [1866] 1978: 371)

On another occasion, after Bauan troops had lent assistance in the Vuna versus Somosomo war on Taveuni, they returned home via the south shore of Vanua Levu, 'where they amused themselves by destroying plantations' (Waterhouse [1866]1978: 138).

Chronic conflict could result in villages or even entire *vanua* (districts) being abandoned. MacDonald (1857: 237), journeying up the eastern Viti Levu rivers in 1856, noted that the Waimanu passes through 'a very populous district' but that the Rewa, 'from Navuso to Naitasiri, is very scantily populated'. He recorded the absence of coconut trees, and remarked that 'this is attributable to the continued warfare of former times: when a town was besieged the resources of the people, including breadfruit and coconut trees, were cut off by the enemy' (MacDonald 1857: 237). A bleak homecoming awaited released prisoners from a formerly prosperous area following disturbances in the upper Ba River, where 'villages had been destroyed, the plantations ravaged, and cultivated land allowed to return to scrub' (Derrick 1957: 228). For regions embroiled in internecine struggles, the cycle of ruin and repair could only end with an offer of submission by the defeated district. Burns (1963) described a characteristic scenario illustrative of such tactics:

> The villages of the conquered people would be burnt and their crops destroyed, but many of the vanquished would escape and return after the departure of the victors to build their villages again . . . it might, however, be necessary for them to pay tribute to their conquerors, in foodstuffs or in women, to escape further molestation, and this would continue until some change in the balance of power made it safe for them to evade this obligation.
>
> (Burns 1963: 29)

Defensive postures had their own price, and avoidance of the dangers of warfare could have tragic ramifications. Derrick (1957: 89) related the situation facing the inhabitants of Bua, where 'for years they had been prevented by war from giving due attention to planting, and mothers were said to have destroyed their children because there was not enough food to nourish them'.

Settlement patterns responded to strategic imperatives. This was expressed most clearly in the following statement by Douglas Oliver:

> We shall probably never discover what set of historical, environmental, and other conditions led to the initial establishment of Fiji's nucleated settlement pattern, but one factor that undoubtedly helped to maintain and perhaps even intensify it was the people's propensity for warfare. In line with this propensity was the widespread practice to space a community's dwellings close together and in defensible locations such as hilltops and peninsulas.
>
> (Oliver 1989: 339)

Many villages chose to locate in inaccessible and often lofty locations. The word 'eyrie' comes to mind. Lawry (1850: 209) described one such scene in Ra Province: 'The sloping high land hereabouts is very rocky, and in some places, very abrupt . . . such were the places selected to build upon; it matters not how high, or craggy, or precipitous it may be, there is their town on the crag of the rock.' The mountainous landscapes of most Fijian islands are punctuated with these old village sites (*na koro makawa*). Ward (1964: 485) noted the 'prevalence of warfare frequently made isolation from neighbors a desirable characteristic.' Surrounding their villages Fijians often constructed defensive earthworks. Much of this artificial terrain foreshadows modern counterparts: trenches, war pits resembling fox holes, and booby traps.

These defensive postures affected agricultural activities, a fact that was recognized by the early British consular officials:

> Jealousy that made every village distrustful of its neighbours compelled the inhabitants to fortify themselves on the most inaccessible heights, and prevented them from cultivating any land beyond the few feet around each man's dwelling, if more were required, the cultivator afraid to descend into the plain discovered some spot in the recesses of the mountains where he might plant his yams secure from molestation.
>
> (COC 1864)

The consequences of trying to grow subsistence crops in a landscape charged with potential conflict may be responsible for many of the intensive agricultural landforms found in Fiji. Bellicose conditions throughout the archipelago resulted in the necessity of building fortified settlements, not only in mountainous terrain but also in low-lying areas such as the Rewa and Navua deltas. The following examples represent diverse environments from the main island of Viti Levu (Figure 14.1).

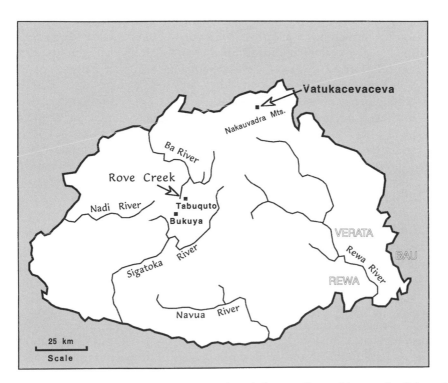

Figure 14.1 Viti Levu, largest island in Fiji. Selected places as discussed in text. Confederated chiefdoms (*matanitu*) indicated by outline type

The Rewa delta

The Rewa river is Fiji's largest; its tributaries drain the entire eastern half of Viti Levu. Parts of its delta consist of rich soils created by successive flooding and the deposition of transported material from the uplands. Other areas, closer to the sea, constitute a swampy lowland requiring drainage for both settlement and agriculture. This area was the home of a powerful *matanitu* that successfully challenged Verata for supremacy and subsequently engaged Bau in its longest competitive struggle. Sahlins (1991: 51) remarked that 'Rewa was a kingdom of established status and of agricultural rather than maritime orientation.' The Rewa delta may have witnessed the most concentrated population densities in pre-contact Fiji (Parry 1977). Still discernible in the landscape are vestiges of village fortifications and associated gardens where giant swamp taro was intercropped with taro in raised fields. Parry (1977: 69) stated that the Rewa delta 'presented one of the most difficult agricultural environments of the South Pacific because of the high water table and the frequency of flooding'. Nevertheless, early Fijians prospered here, and peppered the region with a dense pattern of moated settlements known as ring-ditches. Palmer (1969: 182) defined a ring-ditch as 'a circular ditch and bank line of defence enclosing a habitation area,' and referred to MacDonald's (1857) tally of ninety-five such defended villages extant in the Rewa delta during the middle of the nineteenth century. In addition to providing a measure of security, these water-filled trenches furnished ideal growing conditions for the edible aroids that were the basis of subsistence. Beyond these domestic perimeters, complex patterns of raised fields known as *vuci* completed the subsistence landscape. Based on painstaking aerial photographic analysis, Parry (1977, 1979) estimated the area of these gardens at 5,200 ha, which 'represents 21 percent of the total area of the delta and a massive investment of time and labour' (1979: 49). Warfare in the delta took the form of the typical raiding and ambush pattern found throughout the islands, but in 1843 culminated, perhaps inevitably, in a great 'war of the chiefs' between Rewa and Bau, a conflict that was 'centuries old before it began' (Sahlins 1987: 305). A valuable target of Bau's tributary demands, the peculiar form of intensive agriculture in the Rewa delta was both utilitarian and strategic. The maze of ditches and raised garden beds around the fortified villages served to impede and confuse Bau's marauding armies but were also a response by the people of Rewa to the need for safeguarding and intensifying food production.

Rove Creek valley

The headwaters of the Ba river rise in the convoluted terrain of the island's central highlands. Inhabiting this remote region were the *kai Colo* ('mountain tribes') who responded with armed resistance to European settlement and the Christianization of their culture. They specialized in the construction of hillside terraces to irrigate taro (Parry 1987; Hashimoto 1990). The main course of the upper Ba, along with several tributaries, exhibits a number of abandoned terrace systems (Kuhlken 1994a). I focus here on two systems in the upper Rove Creek drainage, using a published historical document, ethnographic oral accounts, and my own field observations.

Bukuya is the main village of the district of Magodro, in Ba Province. Its name can be translated as 'knot', referring to the twisted landscape where three major rivers find their source: the Ba, the Sigatoka and the Nadi. The *koro makawa* ('old village') sits atop a ridge overlooking the present village. Overgrown *yavu* (stone foundations) and eroded embankments now mark the site of the old fortified settlement. Beatrice Grimshaw, a peripatetic Irish novelist who toured the backcountry of Fiji around the turn of the century, visited the village of Bukuya, and described the irrigated taro gardens there:

> Just on my left rose, tier after tier, a strange erection of terraces, decorated with handsome, large-leaved water plants standing in an inch or so of clear water. From terrace to terrace, a tiny stream slipped downward, losing itself at last in the river below . . . this really beautiful piece of landscape gardening was a ndalo bed, where the ndalo, one of Fiji's most important roots, was grown in the slowly running water that suited it best.
>
> (Grimshaw 1907: 48–9)

These gardens were constructed adjacent to the old fortified village site in order to provide a secure source of food during times of hostility. Although the terraces were still being used in the early 1900s (Parry 1987: 83), I visited the site in October 1991 and found them abandoned. Bukuya farmers now rely on dryland plantings, and there was no intention of reviving the irrigation works.

Farther downstream, in the hills behind the village of Tabuquto, is another, larger terrace system, likewise now neglected. Tabuquto is the oldest village in Magodro, predating even Bukuya, and is situated on Rove Creek where spring-fed perennial branches enter the main stream channel. The use of irrigated taro gardens by the people of Tabuquto probably stretches back into prehistory, but informants there told me of the expansion of this particular set of terraces for a very specific purpose. At some point in the not too distant past, the people of Magodro were involved in a war with the people from Naloto, a neighbouring area to the north-west. War began when the people of Naloto tried to depose a chief who was married to a woman from Magodro. The people of Tabuquto created these terraces to serve as a larder for the Magodro warriors and their assembled allies. This is one very specific example of the effects of warfare on the process of agricultural intensification in Fiji.

Nakauvadra

The largest complex of agricultural terraces ever constructed in Fiji is situated on the northern flanks of the Nakauvadra Mountains, in Ra

Province, near the northernmost point of Viti Levu. Geographer Roger Frazer estimated this group of terraces once covered an area of 325 hectares (Frazer 1961: 164). No longer utilized, this extensive set of gardens and canals is still discernible as an artificially shaped and contoured landscape now covered by reeds and tall grasses. The larger, contoured hillside terraces remain a prominent feature on open mid-elevation slopes, from 150–250 m above sea level. Smaller terraced streamside garden areas were constructed along creekbeds and at higher elevations, adjacent to several old village sites where secondary forest has now reclaimed the land (Kuhlken 1994b). Recent excavations conducted at one of these upper terraces resulted in a radiocarbon determination corresponding to the probable date for construction. A sample of wood charcoal from a depth of 60 cm in the garden fill material yielded a date of 160 ± 70 years BP (Beta-64461; Kuhlken and Crosby, in press.). Although the wide margin of error precludes chronological precision, based on corroborating oral histories of the *yavusas* involved, it would appear that these terraces were built around the time of, or not long before, European contact (Kuhlken 1994a). Conspicuously apparent in the proto-historical geography of Nakauvadra was the avoidance of the fertile valley floor, both for habitation and cultivation.

Oral historical and archival evidence regarding this area points to a formerly larger population engaged in subsistence gardening prior to European contact. Frazer (1973: 82) located a number of fortified villages situated on the upper slopes, and I was able to find several more during the course of fieldwork. Most of these populations shifted to the valley floor during the early colonial period and consolidated within the village of Vatukacevaceva, although some *mataqali* migrated to the coast. Warfare was undoubtedly a determinant in the original siting of these old settlements and, by association, of the terraced gardens. There are several aspects of both the site and situation of the Nakauvadra terraces and associated habitation areas which bear testament to the need for wariness. First, the relative location of the terrace systems tells of implementing the preliminary line of defence: that of concealment. The position of these gardens several kilometres up a small river valley, virtually hidden from coastal view by an intervening ridge, suggests a strategic imperative. Given the volatile nature of inter-tribal relations in this area, it was essential to maintain productive garden areas next to defensible settlement sites. The villages themselves were likewise situated in rocky areas on steep slopes. Large natural boulders were used to define the boundaries of habitation areas, and rock walls were constructed along site perimeters. The elevation of every *koro makawa* exceeded 300 m. Some of the smaller hamlets were located even higher up the slopes, indicating more of a refuge function. Remnants of surrounding defensive earthworks provide still another clue to the milieu within which these people went about their lives in precarious balance with their neighbours. Several sets of ramparts and berms were discovered during reconnaissance surveys of this area. Tippett had earlier reported on these features: 'When I climbe the narrow way to the top of Nakauvadra in Ra, I crossed several war pits' (1968: 58).

At Nakauvadra, in the absence of a major chiefdom or *matanitu*, the forces of conflict operating were largely inter-tribal and provincial. Frazer (1961: 22) identified two types of warfare that occurred in Ra during the prehistoric period: 'continued outward pressure of the Colo tribes of the mountainous interior on the dwellers in the lowlands [and] internal feuds among the 21 *vanua*, with continuously changing factions'. Wilkinson (1908: 10) also spoke of the 'jealousies between the Colo and the coast tribes'. These hostile relations prevailed well into the nineteenth century. Forbes (1875) painted a stark and vivid portrait of the people of coastal Ra during the late 1860s:

> The inhabitants are hemmed in on one side by the ocean, on the other by the mountains and the warlike tribes they contain. Compared with Fijians from other parts of the group these lowlanders are a degraded and miserable set of men. With them the struggle for existence degenerates into a mere struggle for food. I have often seen them stalking along the seashore like gaunt spectres, searching with wolfish eyes for something to eat. But besides food these people stand in need to defend themselves against their cannibal neighbors who occupy mountain fastnesses in a chain of lofty mountains.
>
> (Forbes 1875: 79)

On 20 September 1850, the Reverend Walter Lawry sailed along the coast of northern Ra and uttered this lament: 'We passed along the coast of Ragi Ragi, and in sight of the Kauvadra mountains; but the Gospel makes little way among so many "little wars"' (Lawry 1851: 209). Violent skirmishing was simply a way of life for the Nakauvadra settlements. Allegiance to a greater polity was not required for participation in this particular free-for-all. But evolution of more complex chiefdoms then created a series of extra-territorial conflicts when these eastern coastal powers mounted expeditions seeking tribute or demanding submission to their authority. While earlier musketry may have been ineffectual elsewhere in Fiji, the frequent inter-tribal conflict that characterized the pre-contact cultural landscapes of Ra Province escalated and intensified with the introduction of firearms provided by European cotton planters. Later, on the eve of colonial rule, even further manifestations of warfare may be found just across the ridge to the west, where Kaplan and Rosenthal (1993) recently reported archaeological findings pointing to evidence for agricultural intensification and profound changes to the settlement landscape caused by hostile relations with the Cakobau government.

Informants in the village of Vatukacevaceva stressed that because of the potential for enemy attack or ambush, nobody lived in the valley prior to Christianity, even though it afforded much better soils. Ward (1964: 487) stressed that taro 'required soil of relatively high fertility', and Williams (1858), noted typical cultivation practices:

> Irrigated taro beds are generally oblong, and prepared with much labour . . . the most approved soil is a stiff, rich clay, which is worked into the consistency of mortar, and watered carefully, and often with skill. Valleys are preferred for these beds; but sometimes they *have to be cut on the mountain slopes* . . . [italics added].
>
> (Williams 1858: 61)

Soils underlying the terraces at Nakauvadra are slope soils or lithosols composed of shallow, rocky clays derived from parent materials of basalt and andesite. Although of relatively high nutrient content, there is a potential for 'severe sheet erosion' of these soils (Twyford and Wright 1965: 321). Thus, they are not as advantageous for agricultural use as the soils found on the valley floor. But because of warfare, taro gardens were placed adjacent to the series of hillside fortified villages located along the Nakauvadra escarpment. The rich alluvial soils of the valley bottom now support the cash cropping of sugar-cane and the diversified gardens of Indo-Fijian smallholders.

ADDITIONAL EVIDENCE

One way to further test the hypothesis connecting warfare with intensive agriculture in Fiji is to review the evidence for agricultural *disintensification* following colonial takeover by Great Britain. Of course, there are many reasons that can be assigned to the decline of intensive agriculture, and to the subsequent abandonment of intensive agricultural landforms in Fiji. Ward (1982: 14) has argued that 'the diminishing supply of available labour was a major factor in the decline of these specialized systems'. Indeed, the imposition of plantation agriculture and the later introduction of additional cash-cropping systems displaced labour from traditional subsistence activities. Other factors involve the adoption of introduced root crops such as American taro (*Xanthosoma* spp.) and cassava (*Manihot esculenta*), which are tolerant of less humid environments, poorer soils and reduced labour inputs. But cessation of hostilities, along with depopulation associated with exotic diseases, likewise exerted a negative influence on the continuation of intensive agricultural practices. Regarding the villages that depended on the raised fields of the Rewa delta, Parry (1979: 47) wrote that these 'ring-ditch settlements are now largely abandoned as a result of the peaceful conditions following Cession of the islands to Britain and the dramatic decline in population due to the epidemic diseases of the late nineteenth century'. For intensive agriculture on upland slopes, Netting (1993: 30) remarked in general, 'Once the pressure that keeps dense populations in the hills is relaxed . . . the extra labour of terrace building and maintenance may become superfluous, and an orderly artificial landscape may dissolve into silt and flooding.' Frazer (1961) linked the end of warfare with new cultigens when explaining terrace abandonment at Nakauvadra:

> the principal factor allowing the abandonment of these terraces and hillside plantations would appear to be the availability of better lands – both wet and dry – due to the peaceful conditions, and the introduction of food crops which did not require irrigation or wet situations.
>
> (Frazer 1961: 166)

And peaceful conditions at Rove Creek likewise have allowed swidden systems to supplant the wet taro formerly cultivated in terraces there.

The end of warfare was, of course, a gradual process, and Fijians in most areas did not feel secure enough to vacate relatively inaccessible and defensible village sites (with their adjoining garden areas) until after the 1874 Cession. Even before colonial rule, village relocation was common, as Ward (1964) has specified, but it was only *Pax Brittanica* that allowed many settlements finally to shift to more convenient and accessible sites:

> Prior to 1874, villages often moved because of war, internal disputes, sickness, population changes, and perhaps soil depletion . . . the establishment of peace during the 19th century led to the abandonment of many hilltop villages and the building of new settlements beside the rivers or on the coasts.
>
> (Ward 1964: 492)

This describes the situation pertaining not only to the Nakauvadra settlements that relocated and coalesced as the contemporary village of Vatukacevaceva, but also to numerous sites in the upper Ba and Sigatoka watersheds where abandoned terracing is notably apparent.

DISCUSSION

This chapter has presented evidence that challenges prevailing assumptions regarding political development, warfare, population pressure on resources, and the process of agricultural intensification. Complex relationships emerge between such highly variable components of the cultural–ecological equation, and it is often difficult to determine causality. Moreover, to successfully disentangle these factors, it becomes necessary to learn the unique historical geographies of many different places. Only when armed with this ground truth can we pick our way across the uncertain territory of hypothetical contexts.

The theoretical constructs of Carneiro accounted for agricultural intensification as a direct result of population pressure in circumscribed territory, creating a situation that eventually leads to warfare and political integration. Thus, in Fiji, the terraced landscapes within circumscribed valleys politically may represent an intermediate, perhaps penultimate level on an evolutionary journey towards statehood. We know that such an endpoint had almost, though not quite fully, developed in the islands during the early historic period. In Fiji, however, warfare was a constant, as even Carneiro (1990) acknowledged. Fear of enemies permeated all aspects of pre-Cession life and livelihood. This fear was transmitted to the landscape through the construction of fortified villages and ridge forts which served as temporary places of refuge during those times when danger of attack was imminent. Agricultural intensification resulted from the hostile social environment that was ubiquitous prior to European contact and control. The traditional and normal state of war *forced* Fijian settlement patterns towards a condition of isolation and territorial circumscription, thereby inverting Carneiro's ideal-ized mechanism of socio-spatial evolution. Intensive agriculture in Fiji developed as a defensive strategy.

Warfare in Fijian society was truly an indigenous phenomenon. Even without the graphic accounts of cannibalism, early reports by missionaries and others were replete with the atrocities of inter-tribal fighting and present a clear picture of prevailing antagonistic conditions. Although modified and in some cases exacerbated by pre-colonial European contact, conflict among *matanitu* had become a well-established form of interaction at least as far back as AD 1400. Archaeological evidence of fortifications on several islands matches oral histories that record the wanderings of various *yavusa* across contested terrain. Agrarian systems adapted to an adverse environment, and prime agricultural lands were avoided in the interest of security. It took an epidemic of religious conversion and political submission to a reluctant Great Britain to bring about change.

Once colonial rule was formally instituted, most Fijians relinquished their fortified villages and migrated onto the rich alluvial bottomlands in the valleys or along the coast. This village relocation played no small part in the abandonment of intensive agricultural landforms. As Farrell (1972: 59) has written, 'cessation of local warfare . . . has been of major consequence in modifying the Pacific *genre de vie*, the look of the land, and relations with it'. These examples from Fiji bear witness to the role of war as an independent variable that had profound influence upon social structure, settlement patterns, and subsistence activities. Intensive agricultural landscapes most likely reflected cohesive social organization and control within core areas of the major chiefdoms (e.g., the expanse of *vuci* on the Rewa delta), or represented specific expressions of social and political ecology (e.g., the terraces constructed as a larder for the upper Rove Creek tribes during the Naloto war, or the monumental Nakauvadra irrigated terrace systems). Such findings suggest the possibility of conflict as a causal agent in other regions where intensive agricultural landforms have been documented.

ACKNOWLEDGEMENTS

I wish to thank Terence Young for helpful comments on an earlier draft of this chapter, and Andrew Crosby for providing additional references and insights. Fieldwork in Fiji during 1992 was generously supported by a Fulbright fellowship.

REFERENCES

Allardyce, W. 1904. The Fijians in peace and war. *Man* 4, 69–73.

Boserup, E. 1965. *The Conditions of Agricultural Growth: the economics of agrarian change under population pressure.* London: Allen and Unwin.

Brewster, A. 1922. *The Hill Tribes of Fiji.* Philadelphia: J.B. Lippincott Co. (1967 reprint. New York: Johnson Reprint Corporation.)

Brookfield, H. 1972. Intensification and disintensification in Pacific agriculture: a theoretical approach. *Pacific Viewpoint* 13, 30–48.

Burns, A. 1963. *Fiji.* London: Her Majesty's Stationery Office.

Carneiro, R. 1970. A theory of the origin of the state. *Science* 169, 733–8.

Carneiro, R. 1990. Chiefdom-level warfare as exemplified in Fiji and the Cauca valley. In *The Anthropology of War,* J. Haas (ed.), 190–235. Cambridge: Cambridge University Press.

Chapelle, T. 1976. Land and race in Fiji: the administration of Sir Everard im Thurn, 1904–1910. Unpublished Ph.D. thesis, University of the South Pacific.

Clunie, F. 1977. *Fijian Weapons and Warfare.* Suva: Fiji Museum, Bulletin No. 2.

COC (Consular Outwards Correspondence). National Archives of Fiji, Suva.

Davie, M. 1929. *The Evolution of War: a study of its role in early societies.* New Haven: Yale University Press.

Derrick, R. 1957. *A History of Fiji.* 3rd edition. Suva: Government Printing Office.

Farrell, B. 1972. The alien and the land of Oceania. In *Man in the Pacific Islands,* R. Ward (ed.), 34–73. Oxford: Clarendon Press.

Ferguson, R. (ed.). 1984. *Warfare, Culture, and Environment.* Orlando: Academic Press.

Forbes, L. 1875. *Two Years in Fiji.* London: Longmans, Green and Co.

France, P. 1969. *The Charter of the Land: custom and colonization in Fiji.* New York: Oxford University Press.

Frazer, R. 1961. Land use and population in Ra Province, Fiji. Unpublished Ph.D. thesis, Australian National University.

Frazer, R. 1973. The Fijian village and the independent farmer. In *The Pacific in Transition: geographical perspectives on adaptation and change,* H. Brookfield (ed.), 75–95. London: Edward Arnold.

Frost, E. 1979. Fiji. In *The Prehistory of Polynesia,* J. Jennings (ed.), 69–81. Cambridge, Mass.: Harvard University Press.

Geertz, C. 1966. *Agricultural Involution: the process of ecological change in Indonesia.* Berkeley: University of California Press.

Golson, J. 1972. The Pacific Islands and their prehistoric inhabitants. In *Man in the Pacific Islands,* R. Ward (ed.), 5–33. Oxford: Clarendon Press.

Grimshaw, B. 1907. *Fiji and its Possibilities.* New York: Doubleday, Page and Co.

Hanson, V. 1983. *Warfare and Agriculture in Classical Greece.* New York: Alfred A. Knopf.

Hashimoto, S. 1990. Irrigated cultivation of taro in the Sigatoka Valley, Fiji. *Essays of Faculty of Letters of Kansai University* 39, 1–19.

Hassan, F. 1983. Earth resources and population: an archaeological perspective. In *How Humans Adapt: a biocultural odyssey*, D. Ortner (ed.), 191–216. Washington, DC: Smithsonian Institution Press.

Hunt, T. 1981. New evidence for early horticulture in Fiji. *Journal of the Polynesian Society* 90, 259–66.

Johnson, A. and T. Earle. 1987. *The Evolution of Human Societies: from foraging group to agrarian state*. Stanford: Stanford University Press.

Kaplan, M. and M. Rosenthal. 1993. Battlements, temples and the landscape of *Tuka*: the archaeological record of a cultural transformation in 19th-century Fiji. *Journal of the Polynesian Society* 102, 121–45.

Keegan, J. 1994. *A History of Warfare*. New York: Alfred A. Knopf.

Kirch, P. and M. Sahlins. 1992. *Anahulu: the anthropology of history in the kingdom of Hawaii*. Chicago: University of Chicago Press, 2 volumes.

Kuhlken, R. 1994a, Agricultural terracing in the Fiji Islands. Unpublished Ph.D. thesis, Louisiana State University.

Kuhlken, R. 1994b. *Tua tua ni Nakauvadra*: a traditional Fijian taro agrosystem. In *Science of Pacific Island Peoples, Vol. 2: Land Use and Agriculture*, J. Morrison, P. Geraghty and L. Crowl (eds), 51–62. Suva: Institute of Pacific Studies.

Kuhlken, R. and A. Crosby. In press. Agricultural terracing at Nakauvadra, Viti Levu: a late prehistoric irrigated agrosystem in Fiji. *Asian Perspectives*.

Lawry, W. 1850. *Friendly and Feejee Islands: a missionary visit to various stations in the South Seas in the year 1847*. London: Charles Gilpin.

Lawry, W. 1851. *A Second Missionary Visit to the Friendly and Feejee Islands in the Year 1850*. London: John Mason.

Lewis, A. 1951. *The Melanesians*. Chicago: Natural History Museum.

MacDonald, J. 1857. Proceedings of the expedition for the exploration of the Rewa river in Na Viti Levu, Fiji Islands. *Journal of the Royal Geographical Society* 27, 232–68.

Netting, R. McC. 1993. *Smallholders, Householders: farm families and the ecology of intensive, sustainable agriculture*. Stanford: Stanford University Press.

Oliver, D. 1989. *Oceania: the native cultures of Australia and the Pacific Islands, Vol. 1*. Honolulu: University of Hawaii Press.

Palmer, B. 1969. Ring-ditch fortifications on windward Viti Levu. *Archaeology and Physical Anthropology in Oceania* 4, 181–97.

Parry, J. 1977. *Ring-ditch Fortifications of the Rewa Delta, Fiji: air photo interpretation and analysis*. Suva: Fiji Museum, Bulletin No. 3.

Parry, J. 1979. Pre-European ring-ditch fortifications, taro gardens, in the Rewa delta, Viti Levu, Fiji. *Revue Photo-interpretation* 79, 47–50.

Parry, J. 1987. *The Sigatoka Valley: pathway into prehistory*. Suva: Fiji Museum, Bulletin No. 9.

Quain, B. 1948. *Fijian Village*. Chicago: University of Chicago Press.

Rechtman, R. 1992. The evolution of sociopolitical complexity in the Fiji Islands. Unpublished Ph.D. dissertation, University of California – Los Angeles.

Sahlins, M. 1987. War in the Fiji Islands: the force of custom and the custom of force. In *International Ethics in the Nuclear Age*, R. Myers (ed.), 299–328. Lanham, Md.: University Press.

Sahlins, M. 1991. The return of the event, again; with reflections on the beginnings of the great Fijian war of 1843 to 1855 between the kingdoms of Bau and Rewa. In *Clio in Oceania: toward a historical anthropology*, A. Biersack (ed.), 37–99. Washington, DC: Smithsonian Institution Press.

Sahlins, M. 1993. Goodbye to *tristes tropes*: ethnography in the context of modern world history. *Journal of Modern History* 65, 1–25.

Seemann, B. 1973. *Viti: an account of a government mission to the Vitian or Fijian Islands 1860–61*. Folkestone: Dawsons of Pall Mall.

Thomas, N. 1986. *Planets Around the Sun: dynamics and contradictions of the Fijian matanitu*. Sydney: Oceania Monograph No. 31.

Thompson, L. 1938. The culture history of the Lau Islands. *American Anthropologist* 40, 181–99.

Tippett, A. 1954. The nature and social function of Fijian war. *Transactions of the Fiji Society* 5 (4), 137–55.

Tippett, A. 1968. *Fijian Material Culture*. Honolulu: Bishop Museum, Bulletin No. 232.

Tippett, A. 1973. *Aspects of Pacific Ethnohistory*. Pasadena: William Carey Library.

Turner, B.L., II. and P. Harrison. 1983. *Pulltrouser Swamp: ancient Maya habitat, agriculture, and settlement in northern Belize*. Austin: University of Texas Press.

Turney-High, H. [1949]1991. *Primitive War*. Columbia: University of South Carolina Press.

Twyford, I. and Wright, A. 1965. *The Soil Resources of the Fiji Islands*. Suva: Government Printer.

Vayda, A. 1976. *War in Ecological Perspective: persistence, change, and adaptive processes in three Oceanian societies*. New York: Plenum Press.

Ward, R. 1964. Cash cropping and the Fijian village. *Geographical Journal* 130, 484–506.

Ward, R. 1982. Dilemmas in South Pacific agriculture. *South Pacific Journal of Natural Science*, vol. 3: Proceedings of CASAS Seminar.

Waterhouse, J. [1866] 1978. *The King and People of Fiji*. New York: AMS Press.

Webster, D. 1975. Warfare and the evolution of the state. *American Antiquity* 40, 464–70.

Wedgewood, C. 1930. Some aspects of warfare in Melanesia. *Oceania* 1, 5–33.

Wilkes, C. 1845. *Narrative of the United States Exploring Expedition, Vol. 3*. Philadelphia: Lea and Blanchard. (1985 Reprint. Suva: Fiji Museum.)

Wilkinson, D. 1908. Origin of the Fijian race. *Transactions of the Fiji Society* 1908: 7–17.

Williams, T. 1858. *Fiji and the Fijians. Volume I: The islands and their inhabitants*. (1982 reprint. Suva: Fiji Museum.)

15 Whose land is it anyway? An historical examination of land tenure and agriculture in northern Jordan

CAROL PALMER

The way land is held profoundly affects agricultural practice. For farmers in northern Jordan, land tenure is a central factor affecting contemporary crop and animal management. Older farmers often contrast practices associated with the former pattern of communal agricultural landholding, under the system of *mushā'*, with contemporary practices associated with the system of individual title. In the last 150 years, northern Jordan has been a part of Ottoman Greater Syria, British-mandated Transjordan and now, the Hashemite Kingdom of Jordan. Each regime has implemented land reforms, with the most far reaching brought in by the Ottomans and the British. Each reform has implications for agricultural practice.

This chapter seeks to emphasize that agriculture cannot be understood simply through the examination of crop rosters, weed assemblages, or animal bone counts. The social and economic background into which farming fits, within the social organization of decision-making, work, and marketing, is also key. In this, land tenure is central, being the point at which many of these factors meet. This chapter provides a historical example of changes in land tenure and explores its implications for the farming regime as a whole and tries to show how many of these factors may have operated in earlier archaeological periods.

INTRODUCTION

The area under study is situated in the north-west corner of modern Jordan (Figure 15.1). It stretches from the Yarmouk river in the north to 'Ajlun in the south and from the upper slopes of the Jordan Valley in the west across to Ramtha. The study area broadly consists of hills and plains. The plains lie to the north and east, and the hills combine areas to the north where there is a rapid descent westward towards the Jordan Valley, and, to the south-west, where the land dramatically rises up to the massif around 'Ajlun before plunging down again to the Jordan Valley. In the hills, cultivation is situate

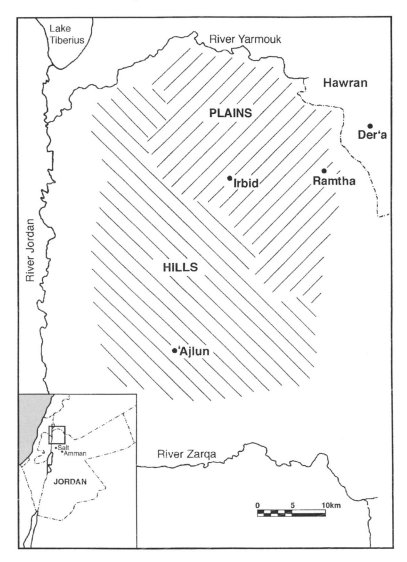

Figure 15.1 Northern Jordan. Hills and plains of the study area and major place-names mentioned in the text.

in patches on the summits, slopes and wadi floors of the area between forest, scrub and scree. The virtually uninterrupted nature of the plains, on the other hand, allows for almost continuous cultivation. The study area produces the highest dry-farmed grain yields in contemporary Jordan.

Environmental setting

North-western Jordan has an essentially Mediterranean climate and vegetation. Hot dry summers alternate with a rainy season in the winter months (Tomaselli 1977). The majority of the area is semi-arid (al-Eisawi 1985: 49), although 'Ajlun is slightly wetter and cooler and, with an average of 550 mm of precipitation each year (15-year average: 1976–90), enjoys the second highest level of precipitation in Jordan (al-Eisawi 1985: 47). On the plains, the main town of Irbid receives comparatively good precipitation, but only 15 km to the east, average annual precipitation drops dramatically to 221 mm (1976–87) – a figure just within the limits for cereal cultivation. The average annual precipitation figures camouflage a high degree of variability in precipitation from year to year (Qasem and Mitchell 1986).

As with the climate, the vegetation of the study area has a principally Mediterranean character. In the hills, there are large stretches of evergreen oak (*Quercus calliprinos*) forest and open parkland, although much of it is heavily degraded (Zohary 1973: 501). There is also remnant deciduous oak forest (*Q. ithaburensis* s.l.) situated at lower altitudes (al-Eisawi 1985). Wild olive is a minor constituent of the deciduous oak forest (Neef 1990). At and below this level most of the land is either cultivated or heavily grazed. The area contains some good soils (for example, the vertisols) which are particularly extensive on the plains, have a high potential for agriculture and a high water-holding capacity (FitzPatrick 1983: 174).

Historical background

The study area lies within the south-eastern section of Ottoman Syria and almost exactly corresponds to the former district of 'Ajlun. Ottoman rule began after the defeat of the Mamluks in 1516 and ended in 1918 following the defeat of the Ottomans in the First World War. There are tax records for the early Ottoman period documenting significant agricultural productivity in the district of 'Ajlun, and it appears to have been the most economically important area east of the River Jordan (Hütteroth and Abdulfattah 1977: 85). After the end of the sixteenth century, however, Ottoman authority and influence declined and for 250 years, a period spanning through to the mid-nineteenth century, the region lay largely outside the Ottoman order (Rogan 1991: 8).

In 1851, during the Ottoman Tanzimat (period of reform), 'Ajlun was the first south-eastern district to be reincorporated into the administrative apparatus of the Ottoman province of Syria (Fischbach 1990: 26; Rogan 1991: 11; 1994: 35). Reassertion of Ottoman authority worked in favour of the settled population and the extent of the cultivated zone expanded (Lewis 1987).

Land reform was an important component of late nineteenth-century Ottoman rule. As part of it, the Ottomans set about systematically registering all land, although 'Ajlun was the only district to be systematically registered in what was to become Transjordan (Rogan 1991: 307). Agricultural lands were given priority during registration – a fact which has given rise to the suggestion that 'the village was perceived primarily in terms of its agricultural productivity' (Mundy 1992: 221). The Ottoman land reforms encapsulated many aspects of the local prevailing system of communal land tenure an allowed its key aspects to remain in place. Examination of late Ottoman land registers gives clues to local village society and economy (Mundy 1996).

Following the First World War and the defeat of the Ottoman army in 1918, the Allied powers divided the Middle East into 'spheres of influence' according to the Sykes–Picot agreement of 1916. In 1921, Adbullah, second son of Sharif Hussein of Mecca, became Emir of the recently British-mandated territory of Transjordan (Lewis 1987: 200). The British authorities and Emir Abdullah then proceeded to create an administration and state apparatus separate from Syria and Palestine, for what was to become in 1946 the independent Hashemite Kingdom of Jordan.

The mandate authorities saw agriculture as the most important part of Transjordan's economy and hoped that it would make the new territory self-supporting. Like the Ottomans before them, they identified land reform as critically important. They viewed individual land ownership as the key to changing what they considered inefficient and unproductive methods of farming. The shift from communal to private ownership, and its implications for agriculture, is the focus of this chapter.

Agricultural fertility

Northern Jordan is agriculturally fertile. During the Ottoman period, the Hawran, of which the district of 'Ajlun was a part, was late Ottoman Syria's 'granary' (Issawi 1988: 214). The plains zone of the study area is an extension of the Syrian Hawran plains which run south of Damascus and have their regional centre at Der'a. 'Ajlun appears to have been the most productive wheat district in 1901 (see Table 15.1). Cuinet reports that relative wheat returns for the Hawran districts were 10 to 1 in 'Ajlun (but cf. Table 15.1), 15 to 1 in Jebel Druze and 20 to 1 on the Hawran plain around Der'a (Cuinet 1896: 345). The accuracy of the very high returns has been questioned recently (cf. Tabak 1991: 143), but the main point remains – yields were comparatively good. 'Ajlun also exported its surplus grain (unfortunately, the quantities are unknown) to Damascus and at the very end of the Ottoman period, after the opening of the Haifa branch line of the Hijaz railway in 1907, to the Palestine coast and, presumably, Europe (Rogan 1991: 254). The value of the study area as a grain producer was an important factor in explaining why the Ottomans were eager to re-establish authority.

Table 15.1 Grain production figures for the Hawran districts, 1901

District	Population	Area under cultivation (acres)	Wheat (bushels)	Barley (bushels)
Hawran	53,540	297,175	1,063,741	447,708
Jebel Druze	33,090	245,140	791,700	416,967
'Ajlun	30,000	225,000	1,680,000	420,000

Source: From Issawi 1988: 313

Following the establishment of Transjordan, grain continued to be exported, in increasing quantities, to Palestine (Konikoff 1943: 47). During the 1930s, the area around 'Ajlun was also the centre of unirrigated vegetable growing (chiefly okra, tomatoes and cucumbers). It possessed, along with the area around the town of Salt, the best vineyards in the country (Konikoff 1943: 48). Today, although agricultural production in the study area is the highest for the dryland sector in Jordan, average yields have not dramatically risen above the levels attained during the Ottoman period, despite the adoption of some modern farming techniques.

Social Organization and Land Tenure

Modes of existence and ties of kinship

The study area has for most of the last 400 years existed on the socially fluctuating margin between sedentary and nomadic modes of existence. Over those years, a complex relationship has existed between the largely sedentary farming population, the *fallahīn* (from *fallaha*, to cultivate), or fellaheen, and the *badw*, the bedouin. The two groups, however, should not be viewed as entirely distinct – there existed a continuum in modes of existence between farming and pastoralism. For the longest period, during the years of waning Ottoman authority, the fellaheen were submissive to the area's powerful nomadic groups who extracted a heavy 'tax' (the *khuwwa*) from allied village communities in return for protection (Rogan 1991: 14). The reassertion of Ottoman authority promoted the expansion of the agricultural mode of existence and worked to the detriment of the region's powerful nomadic groups. The Ottoman land reforms of the nineteenth century also helped to change the pattern of land use in favour of the agriculturalists and served to increase agricultural production (Amadouny 1993: 76).

Kinship affiliations have always been strong in the study area. The main social unit in the villages is the *'ā'ila*. Classically, this is a patrilineal descent group whose blood relations can be traced back five generations (Taminian 1990: 19). The *'ā'ila* was crucial in the former system of land ownership. The *'ā'ila* link together to form the *'ashīra*, a word normally translated as 'tribe'. Rather than representing purely bloodlines, kinship was, and still is, a network from which people could draw support and resolve conflicts. The kinship ties of nomadic groups appear to be better defined than those of principally agricultural groups, and the histories traced, particularly for the latter, are not always consistent (cf. Antoun 1972: 46). Kinship ties have grown less strong this century, partially as a result in the change in landholding.

This century, both the fellaheen and the bedouin have moved away from their traditional lifestyles to work in the army, in offices, universities, and abroad. Only a minority of people whose families once farmed or moved flocks still do so. Where practised, farming generally only supplements house-hold income (cf. Mundy and Smith 1990), but of those who do cultivate, particularly people growing crops in the hills, many still use traditional farming equipment and techniques.

Land tenure and land reform

One of the main features of former agricultural organization in the study area was that agricultural land was held communally under the system of *mushā'*. Firestone (1981: 813) refers to *mushā'* as 'the most important system of land tenure in the nineteenth century Levant'. Both the Ottomans and the British implemented land reforms which affected communal farming, but it was the British who finally privatized the ownership of agricultural lands in Palestine and Transjordan. The following account of *mushā'* largely refers to nineteenth-century accounts and contemporary recollections of some of the study area's oldest inhabitants.

One of the key components of *mushā'* was that plots of land were reallocated, on an 'egalitarian' basis, between *'ā'ila* (who then allocated plots to households) at regular intervals – apparently on an annual, biennial or up to five-yearly basis. It is called egalitarian because all included in the division shared in all classes of land, from rocky ground to flat, fertile plains (Fischbach 1990: 27). At the end of the last century, Bergheim observed the way village lands were divided for cases known to him in Palestine:

> supposing there are 20 *faddan* [in this instance, shares] of land . . . this land is first divided into four divisions (northern, southern, western and eastern) . . . Each of these divisions is then again divided into 20 equal portions and this time by measurement; a line or rope is sometimes used, and not infrequently a long reed or ox goad, which measures generally about nine feet.
>
> (Bergheim 1894: 193)

The overriding principle was that land of varying qualities was divided equally between farmers without bias (Weuleresse 1946: 99). Under this system of allotment, one man may end up cultivating many different strips of land (also see Neil 1890: 161). Furthermore, 'due to the scrupulous application of the principle of equality' (Patai 1949: 439), parcels of land tended to be long and narrow so that in one village plots were recorded as being 2,300 yards long but only 5 yards wide (Waschitz 1947: 47, quoted in Patai 1949: 439 and Latron 1936: 193).

Individual cultivators did not have the exclusive right to choose what to cultivate on each strip of land. Rather, the decision of what to grow where was taken by agreement. Neil states 'a man may not sow any crop which he pleases on his strip or strips, but is compelled to grow the same produce as the rest of his fellow-farmers are growing in the field or district where his allotments lie' (Neil 1890: 160). Thus, for example, an area would be given over to wheat and barley, and others to legume crops and summer vegetables. There would also be an area left without crops (i.e., fallow) for grazing.

Villagers paid heavy taxes to the Ottoman tax collectors. After ten years of observation on the Sharon plain in Palestine, Bergheim estimated that the tithe rarely, if ever, averaged under one-third of the whole crop (Bergheim 1894: 198). Firestone (1981: 826, referring to Wilson 1906: 291–2) argues that, while positions varied, the village as a whole was responsible for the payment of the tithe and that individual responsibility for paying taxes was one of the main changes resulting from the Ottoman Land Code of 1858. In 'Ajlun, farmers paid a fixed sum according to the value of their share (Fischbach 1994: 84; and from local oral accounts), but other areas seemed to have paid a percentage of the value of their crops. The nineteenth- and early twentieth-century estimates of grain production suggest that it was a profitable area from which to collect taxes.

The Land Code of 1858 aimed to regularize and modernize landholding within the Ottoman Empire and increase tax revenues. The reforms are considered an attempt by the state to privatize land rights, break down the system of communal landholding and undermine the power and influence of tax-farmers and fief holders (cf. Firestone 1981: 826). Such dramatic social aims, however, were beyond the scope of the basically conservative Land Code (Gerber 1987: 71; Rogan 1991: 303). Instead, it is viewed simply as a regularizing reform, embodying many already existing developments (Mundy 1992: 218; 1994: 59) and agrarian laws (Gerber 1987: 71). There was also, as mentioned above, the important fact that the Code would provide more tax receipts. The aim of the Ottoman authorities to raise more tax revenues has been forcibly argued by Sluggett and Farouk-Sluggett (1984). In terms of dissolving communal ownership, new interpretations of the Land Code suggest that the new legislation 'neither contradicted co-ownership nor required its dissolution' (Firestone 1990: 106).

The Ottomans registered shares in arable lands rather than ownership of particular units (Mundy 1994, 1996). The British, in contrast, opted for the complete privatization of arable land (Amadouny 1993: 78; Fischbach 1994: 93). Early assessments of the farming conditions in Transjordan pinpointed *mushā'* as a system which retarded agricultural development and kept the agricultural population poor – largely because it retarded investment (Patai 1949: 440–1).

Land settlement involved the partitioning of *mushā'* lands into individually held plots with permanent boundaries and conferred title primarily on local people. It was the most significant and ambitious policy of the Mandate. For the villagers in 'Ajlun, 92 per cent of land was registered to local inhabitants (Fischbach 1990: 26). At the date of settlement (1933–40), there were over 34,000 landowners in the whole of Transjordan, averaging 57 dunums each. By 1949, with increasing population and the local custom of divided inheritance, the number of landowners had increased to 42,000, each owning an average of 49 dunums (Fischbach 1990: 27).

Land settlement brought a profound change in the relationship between farmers and their land. Each held a consolidated plot, or plots, with fixed boundaries and the ability to cultivate what they desired as, for example, an individual or nuclear family. Effectively, settlement broke up social control of land and cultivation (Fischbach 1994: 95). Agricultural decision-making was transferred from broader alliances (tribal or village based) to smaller, more independent units. Land settlement, however, was apparently popular amongst cultivators – assuring ownership and solving inter-village conflicts – but it ultimately allowed outside merchants and moneylenders to take over land and allowed for more inequality in wealth. It also deepened the state's involvement with the cultivators and was important in helping to establish the authority of the state (Gerber 1987; Fischbach 1994).

Farmers today have an entirely different relationship with their land to that of a hundred years ago – instead of holding a share in communal agricultural lands, farmers now own their plots of land outright. The change in land tenure has helped to shift the operative emphasis of the prevailing social structure from kin-networks to households (cf. Mundy and Smith 1990).

CHANGES IN AGRICULTURE

The farming regime

The traditional suite of Old World crops is cultivated in northern Jordan; primarily: wheat, barley, lentil, bitter-vetch and chick-pea. The agricultural year traditionally commences in November when the first rains are expected and the winter cereals are sown. Barley and wheat are, even today, generally both broadcast sown. Bitter-vetch and lentil are planted after cereals, usually from December through to February (especially in the higher altitudes). Chick-pea, a so-called summer crop, is sown last and is planted in early spring.

Fallow is a critical component of the traditional farming regime in the study area. It is a technique generally used in the Mediterranean region to help improve soil moisture and restore fertility (Semple 1932: 386; Grigg 1974: 125). The greatest value of fallow, specifically what may be termed 'cultivated fallow', occurs when a wet year is followed by a dry year (Harris 1989: 151) and does not always greatly benefit yields in successive wet or dry years. Thus fallow appears to operate best as a 'buffering' mechanism (cf. Halstead and O'Shea 1989) against the severe annual variations in precipitation experienced in the Mediterranean region. Summer crops, which have a short growing season and are less exhaustive for the land, can be grown during the latter part of a fallow year (cf. Forbes 1976).

Farmers in the study area practice crop rotation and generally use two principal rotation regimes. The first is a two-year regime and involves planting a winter crop (usually a cereal) every alternate year and using fallow with summer crops in the off year. As summer crops are frequently planted in

the fallow year, this type of rotation is frequently referred to as a winter/
summer (*shatawī/ṣayfī*) rotation regime. The summer year is considered as
krāb – that is, fallow. The second pattern is a three-course rotation regime,
locally known as *muthalatha* (derived from 'triple'), and generally runs cereal–
legume–fallow. Broadly speaking, the people in the hills practise two-course
rotations; whereas, three-year regimes predominate on the plains. These
regimes appear to have a long history in the area; at least they are fixed in the
minds of the older fellaheen.

Under the system of *mushā'*, farmers acquiesced to a communally agreed,
more-or-less fixed, crop rotation regime and during any one year large
expanses of village lands were sown with each type of crop. Now farmers
more regularly cultivate legumes in the fallow, or summer, year of the typical
two-year regime. Both in the hills and on the plains, because fallow is no
longer communal grazing territory, farmers can obtain a crop from the land
every year – an intensification of land use. Summer crops are now almost
always grown in the fallow (Figure 15.2). On the plains, some farmers are
omitting legume crops, which are notoriously labour intensive, from their
traditional regime in response to local short-falls in labour availability.

Crops are no longer cultivated in large continuous areas around the village.
Instead, the landscape has a 'patchwork' appearance where cereals, legumes
and summer crops are grown on smaller plots. Settlement has also been able

Figure 15.2   Cultivation of summer crops (okra, sesame) on fallow land.

to spill out of the villages onto former agricultural land. None of these changes would have been possible without the change in the way land is held.

With land settlement and registration, there has been a reduction in the amount of grazing available for village flocks because the fallow is no longer communal grazing territory. In addition, as part of land registration, the forests, which had been an important source of grazing, were expropriated by the authorities (Fischbach 1994: 96). The shortage of grazing has contributed to farmers changing their rotation regime to grow more fodder crops. In increasing numbers, however, the fellaheen are selling their animals due to insufficient grazing.

Not all land in northern Jordan is farmed by its owner or individually owned. After land settlement, some farmers simply sold their land. Others used their land as security for a loan – often forced to do so for survival – and lost it to moneylenders when the original loan could not be paid back (Fischbach 1990). Today, farmers who rent agricultural land in northern Jordan are also less likely to invest in it. Thus, for example, they are less likely to practise regular fallowing and do not usually weed or manure their crops. They are generally less concerned with the long-term fertility of the land. Changes in crop rotation regime often go hand in hand with changes in the crops that are cultivated. These are discussed further below.

The crops cultivated

After privatization of landholding has come increasing commercialization. Farmers are growing a larger proportion of crops for sale. These crops are not always sold entirely for profit, especially by small-scale farmers. Rather, growing them for oneself means that they do not have to be purchased from elsewhere and any unwanted surplus can be sold. There has been a huge increase in the cultivation of summer crops – crops which are planted in the spring and harvested in the summer of the fallow year – such as melons, tomatoes, okra, sesame, and sorghum. In 1930, Pinner (1930: 52) noted that fallow with summer crops was not very common in the Hawran, but this is not the case today. The cultivation of summer and tree crops was encouraged by British Mandate officials to promote the private sector (Amadouny 1993; and see pp. 291–2 under 'Agricultural fertility').

Summer crops have the additional advantage that because they are grown after winter rains, farmers are better able to assess how much moisture is stored in the soil and, therefore, exactly what crop the land is able to support. Consequently, there is a reduced risk of failure. It is less easy to predict the success of winter-sown crops. The increased use of summer crops is linked to their good monetary value, a decreased reliance on subsistence crops in the area and, of course, the release of the land from communal management which meant that the fallow land was required for grazing.

Farmers also cultivate tree crops because of their good monetary value, but this is not the only reason. Farmers who own land are keen to invest in it 'for their grandchildren' and one of the most popular ways is to plant trees, particularly olives. In northern Jordan, large tracts of former prime arable land, as well as less favourable plots, are now covered with olives (Figure 15.3). Olive cultivation has a long history within the study area dating from the Bronze Age and possibly earlier (Neef 1990), but there has been a huge increase in their cultivation in recent years both in the hills and on the plains. There are many factors influencing the proliferation of olives, but the release of arable land from communal ownership and regular reallotment allowed for this important change.

Farmers favour olive cultivation, in part, because they consider olive trees easier to cultivate than cereals. The busiest time is during harvest in October when whole families go into the fields to help with the work (Figure 15.3). This usually takes place after work or school in the evening. Members of the family who work abroad may also come home at this time to help. Farmers may even hire labourers at this time. Although olives require tending at other times of the year – weeds have to be removed by ploughing and the trees have to be pruned – they are considered an easier crop to grow. Oil extraction is now usually carried out by small mechanized oil plants in each village.

For most of the study area, olive trees were private property in the

Figure 15.3 Family harvesting olives near Irbid, October 1991. Relatively young olive trees planted on former arable land.

Ottoman land registers, even if they were planted on communally owned land, and the numbers of trees held by a villager were exactly recorded (Mundy 1994, 1996). Owners were taxed for the number of trees they owned, but trees could be sold and exchanged 'in a manner unknown for houses or land' (Mundy 1994: 75). Trees, therefore, were a form of personal wealth. The British, however, did not tax farmers in this way and it would appear that, after land settlement, villagers took advantage of the more favourable taxation system and planted more trees. The fact that trees have a history of representing personal wealth may also be another reason why farmers today invest in them. Even if, by the rules of divided inheritance, plots of land become divided into ever-smaller parcels, people will be leaving a certain number of trees to their descendants, each one of which brings individual wealth. In addition, trees carry weighty symbolism, representing both ownership and longevity, which is very important to farmers.

The above factors appear to override some of the disadvantages of olive cultivation: the unpredictability of yields and their tendency only to produce good yields biennially, plus the long time it takes for them to become established (Foxhall 1990). The investment in olives, on both good and less favourable land, has been facilitated by the privatization of landholding and encouraged by the wealth they represent, the monetary value of the oil, their perceived ease of management, plus the fact that olive planting has, particularly in recent years, been the subject of government-sponsored schemes to support what has become a cash crop.

The adoption of technology, which may in turn affect what crops are grown, is also dependent upon the prevailing system of land tenure and social organization. Under the communal system of land tenure, although local farmers possessed the knowledge to terrace land and irrigate (this was done in local orchards; people also collected water for human and animal consumption in cisterns), they were prevented by the tenural system from implementing these changes on arable land. Since privatization, more land has been terraced for olives. Terracing schemes are often undertaken in co-operation with government and international organizations as individual households are not normally able to raise the capital for large-scale improvements.

Agricultural labour

Privatization of landholding has contributed to local shortages of labour for agricultural tasks. Villages and 'ā'ila no longer organize farming activities together; old farmers are less able to draw on extended family members for assistance. Older farmers in the study area often complain about this, appalled by the fact that people no longer work together as they formerly did.

There is also the very human factor that working communally relieves much of the burden and encourages people to work harder. Harvesting together, for example, helps to maintain morale for a hard job which has to be done quickly. In a small survey of farmers in the study area conducted by the author, farmers who held their land with other family members were more likely to exercise good crop management practices, such as weeding, because there was the collective responsibility to manage the land well (Palmer 1994). Older farmers often said that this was one of the main advantages of the previous system. Another advantage was that it gave individuals a certain amount of mobility. For example, both Firestone (1981, 1990) and Tabak (1991: 150) comment that holding shares in land allowed a considerable degree of movement for labour. Shares would be farmed by other members of the family, who would receive most of the produce, until the official shareholder returned. This kept agricultural land productive and helped maintain the prevailing kin-based social structure. Today, where land is individually held, land may remain uncultivated if the owner is absent for any length of time.

ARCHAEOLOGICAL IMPLICATIONS

The practice of communal farming in the Levant provides an important example of collective farming and demonstrates that private ownership should not be assumed for the past. Extensively farmed units of land can be managed without the presence of an estate manager, overlord, or ruling elite (cf. Halstead 1992). Mushā' seems to have been a strategy which coped with the constraints of the environment, promoted internal social solidarity by curbing the differential accumulation of wealth, and enabled communities to bear the dangers of bedouin raids or Ottoman tax burdens. Although criticized for inefficiency, there are advantages to communal farming and collective property rights, and decision-making can be quite consistent with private wealth maximization and also mean increased productivity (Fleming 1985: 138–43). Principally, there are economies of scale which are highly advantageous; for example, a guard can be hired by the group to police and maintain crops and boundaries for relatively little individual cost, and a communal shepherd is a low-cost method of herding (Dahlman 1980).

In northern Jordan, villages farming under the communal system were nucleated and the arable land, due to its regular redistribution, did not have permanent field boundaries. An archaeological landscape where villages are nucleated, but with little evidence of field boundaries may suggest a system of communal land management in the past. Organization of building and storage facilities within an ancient nucleated settlement may also provide evidence for communal farming, based on households, but this requires further investigation. Attempts to link weed seeds found with ancient crops with ancient crop management practices, particularly crop rotation regimes, may provide additional clues (Jones 1992; Palmer 1994; Jones et al. 1995). In this way, it may be possible to distinguish between continuous cropping, associated with private land ownership in this study, and fallow, a practice more strongly connected to communal farming practices.

Examination of recent rural history and archaeology provides increasing examples of how land tenure affects cropping regimes and settlement patterns. For the Ottoman period in Greece, Davis (1991) suggests that the system of land tenure on Keos in the Cycladic islands prevented the employment of intensive agricultural practices such as the cereal–legume rotation regimes suggested by Halstead (1987). Because land ownership was held dually – with one 'owner', usually a member of the island elite, who retained grazing rights and another who cultivated it – integration between animal husbandry and agricultural production was prevented (Davis 1991: 195–6).

Politically motivated agendas entailing land redistribution are not only a recent phenomenon. Davis (1991) cites Greek examples from the Middle Byzantine period and the fifth century BC. In the latter example, the installation of colonists at Karystos, at the southern end of the island of Euboia, resulted in the establishment of isolated farmhouses, spaced at regular intervals in the landscape (Keller and Wallace 1987, in Davis 1991: 202). It is also important to note that land reforms are not always centrally directed (e.g., Whitelaw 1991) and, indeed, *mushā'* is a good example of a non-centrally imposed system of land management. The complex system of Ottoman land ownership (Issawi 1988) probably has a deeper history in the Eastern Mediterranean region. Its implications remain to be explored. It is also interesting to speculate upon the role of land tenure during the periods of intensification and abatement (cf. sedentarization and nomadization) interpreted by LaBianca (1990) over the past 3,500 years at Hesban, near Madaba on the central Transjordanian plateau.

The ownership and management of land is an important factor affecting the adoption of crops. As well as this example, there are other historical cases from the Levant: although *dhura* (sorghum) was known in Syria from the seventh century AD, its cultivation dramatically increased during the seventeenth century due to its association with *çiftliks* (managed estates) and the market-oriented transformation of agrarian structures that followed their rise (Tabak 1991: 143–6). Incidentally, many summer crops (including types from the New World) became a regular part of crop rotation regimes in the western, particularly coastal, Levant at this time. This reflects the summer crops' good marketable value. The proliferation of summer crops in northern Jordan in recent years also parallels the privatization and commercialization of agriculture in this area. Marketable, or exchangeable crops, are important for paying taxes whether they take the form of grain, oil or a collected resource. Grain was important to villagers in the study as a source of money to pay the Ottoman tax collectors.

Olive cultivation is important for the whole Mediterranean basin. Investment in olives is a practice known from Antiquity. Wealthy Athenians are known to have increased both the capital value of their land and its productivity by planting olives (Foxhall 1990: 66–8). The adoption of olives by farmers in northern Jordan is linked to the release of land from communal tenure, the value of the crop itself, its symbolism in terms of ownership, and the easier tax regime of the later period. The suitability of olives for seasonal work was noted by Mattingly (1988: 51–2) who suggests that seasonal workers (from pastoral groups), rather than slaves, were a vital factor in North African olive-oil production.

CONCLUSIONS

The transfer of land from communal to private ownership has profoundly changed the pattern of agricultural management in northern Jordan. Organization of agriculture is now largely based on the household, rather than the extended kin-based group. Released from the communal regime, farmers are able to adopt new patterns of rotation and farm the land more intensively if they desire. Farmers today are more likely to plant summer crops and legumes on fallowed land. As an investment, many farmers are planting olives on land that was formerly only for arable cultivation. Although ownership has given households direct control over the means of production, by helping to break down kin-networks, it has also helped to reduce the amount of labour available for agriculture and this has implications for the crops grown and the animals held.

The role of land tenure in agriculture has been underestimated by archaeologists. The complex Ottoman tax system deserves further attention, both for itself and also because it probably reflects and derives from earlier forms. The shift from communal to individual title illustrates the fundamental importance of land tenure to farming. Levantine communal tenure is important, not only as a system of land and crop management but also because it represents an embodiment of local social order. The rural transformation described here for northern Jordan is just one example of agrarian change in the region. Such transformations have been viewed as the key to understanding contemporary political structures in the Middle East (Gerber 1987). The same is equally true for the past.

ACKNOWLEDGEMENTS

I am grateful to Mike Charles and Chris Gosden for suggesting that I contribute to this volume. The majority of this research I undertook as part of a Ph.D. thesis funded by the Science and Engineering Research Council. Fieldwork was also funded by the British Institute at Amman for Archaeology and History (BIAAH), the Wainwright Fund, the Robert Kiln Fund and the Palestine Exploration Fund. Thanks are extended to the staff at BIAAH, especially Alison McQuitty, for their assistance during all stages of fieldwork. I am grateful to Chris Gosden, Paul Halstead, Chris Knüsel and Robert Schick for incisive editorial comments on earlier versions. Any outstanding errors remain my own responsibility. Paul Maclean improved and computerized Figure 15.1. The Meteorological Department of the Hashemite Kingdom of Jordan kindly provided meteorological information. Finally, my greatest debt is to the people of northern Jordan who extended such generous hospitality to me and who answered my many questions with great patience and humour.

REFERENCES

Amadouny, V.M. 1993. The British role in the development of an infrastructure in Transjordan during the Mandate Period, 1921–1946. Unpublished Ph.D. thesis, University of Southampton.

Antoun, R.T. 1972. *Arab Village: a social structural study of a Trans-Jordanian peasant community*. Bloomington: Indiana University Press.

Bergheim, S. 1894. Land tenure in Palestine. *Palestine Exploration Fund, Quarterly Statement* 20, 191–9.

Cuinet, V. 1896. *Syrie, Liban et Palestine: géographie administrative, statistique et raisonnée*. Paris: Ernest Leroux.

Dahlman, C.J. 1980. *The Open Field System and Beyond: a property rights analysis of an economic institution*. Cambridge: Cambridge University Press.

Davis, J. 1991. Contributions to a Mediterranean rural archaeology: historical case studies from the Ottoman Cyclades. *Journal of Mediterranean Archaeology* 4, 131–216.

al-Eisawi, D.M. 1985. Vegetation in Jordan. In *Studies in the History and Archaeology of Jordan II*, A. Hadidi (ed.), 45–57. Amman: Department of Antiquities, Hashemite Kingdom of Jordan.

Firestone, Y. 1981. Land equalisation and factor scarcities: holding size and the burden of impositions in imperial central Russia and the Late Ottoman Levant. *Journal of Economic History* 41, 813–33.

Firestone, Y. 1990. The land equalising *musha'* village: a reassessment. In *Ottoman Palestine 1800–1914*, G.G. Gilbar (ed.), 91–129. Leiden, F.J. Brill.

Fischbach, M.R. 1990. Observations and land ownership in liwa' 'Ajlun during the Mandate. *Al-Nadwan* 2, 26–30.

Fischbach, M.R. 1994. British land policy in Transjordan. In *Village, Steppe and State: the social origins of modern Jordan*, E.L. Rogan and T. Tell (eds), 80–107. London: British Academic Press.

FitzPatrick, E.A. 1983. *Soils. Their formation, classification and distribution*. London: Longman.

Fleming, A. 1985. Land tenure, productivity and field systems. In *Beyond Domestication in Prehistoric Europe*, G. Barker and C. Gamble (eds), 125–45. London: Academic Press.

Forbes, F.A. 1976. 'The thrice-ploughed field': cultivation techniques in ancient and modern Greece. *Expedition* 19, 5–11.

Foxhall, L. 1990. Olive cultivation within Greek and Roman agriculture: the ancient economy revisited. Unpublished Ph.D. thesis, University of Liverpool.

Gerber, H. 1987. *The Social Origins of the Modern Middle East*. Boulder, Colo.: Lynne Rienner Publishers.

Grigg, E.C. 1974. *The Agricultural Systems of the World: an evolutionary approach*. Cambridge: Cambridge University Press.

Halstead, P. 1987. Traditional and ancient rural economy in Mediterranean Europe: plus ça change? *Journal of Hellenic Studies* 107, 77–87.

Halstead, P. 1992. Agriculture in the Bronze Age Aegean. In *Agriculture in Ancient Greece. Towards a model of palatial economy*, B. Wells (ed.), 105–17. Stockholm: Paul Åströms Förlag.

Halstead, P. and O'Shea, J. 1989. *Bad Year Economics: cultural responses to risk and uncertainty*. Cambridge: Cambridge University Press.

Harris, H.C. 1989. Productivity of crop rotations. In *Farm Resource Management Program: Annual Report 1989*, 137–166. Aleppo, Syria: ICARDA.

Hütteroth, W.-D. and K. Abdulfattah. 1977. *Historical Geography of Palestine, Transjordan and Southern Syria in the Late Sixteenth Century*. Erlangen: Erlanger Geographische Arbeiten.

Issawi, C. 1988. *The Fertile Crescent, 1800–1914*. Oxford: Oxford University Press.

Jones, G. 1992. Weed phytosociology and crop husbandry: identifying a contrast between ancient and modern practice. *Review of Palaeobotany and Palynology* 73, 133–43.

Jones, G., M. Charles, S. Colledge and P. Halstead. 1995. Towards the archaeobotanical recognition of winter-cereal irrigation: an investigation of modern weed ecology in northern Spain. In *Res Archaeobotanica: Ninth Symposium of the International Work Group for Palaeoethnobotany*, H. Kroll and R. Pasternak (eds), 49–68. Kiel.

Konikoff, A. 1943. *Trans-Jordan: an economic survey*. Jerusalem: Jewish Agency for Palestine.

LaBianca, Ø.S. 1990. *Sedentarization and Nomadization: food system cycles at Hesban and vicinity in Transjordan*. Hesban 1. Berrien Springs, Mich: Institute of Archaeology and Andrews University Press.

Latron, A. 1936. *La Vie Rurale en Syrie et au Liban*. Beirut: Mémoires de L'Institut Français de Damas.

Lewis, N.N. 1987. *Nomads and Settlers in Syria and Jordan, 1800–1980*. Cambridge: Cambridge University Press.

Mattingly, D.J. 1988. Oil for export? A comparison of Libyan, Spanish and Tunisian olive oil production in the Roman empire. *Journal of Roman Archaeology* 1, 33–56.

Mundy, M. 1992. Shareholders and the state: representing the village in the late nineteenth century registers of the southern Hawran. In *The Syrian Land in the Eighteenth and Nineteenth Century*, T. Philipp (ed.), 217–38. Stuttgart: Franz Steiner Verlag, Berliner Islamstudien, Bd. 5.

Mundy, M. 1994. Village land and individual title: *Musha'* and Ottoman land registration in the 'Ajlun district. In *Village, Steppe and State: the social origins of modern Jordan*, E.L. Rogan and T. Tell (eds), 58–79. London: British Academic Press.

Mundy, M. 1996. *Qada' 'Ajlun* in the late nineteenth century: interpreting a region from the Ottoman land registers. *Levant* 28, 77–95.

Mundy, M. and R.S. Smith. 1990. *Part-Time Farming: agricultural development in the Zarqa River Basin, Jordan*. Irbid, Jordan: Institute of Archaeology and Anthropology, Yarmouk University.

Neef, R. 1990. Introduction, development and environmental implications of olive culture: the evidence from Jordan. In *Man's Role in the Shaping of the Eastern Mediterranean Landscape*, S. Bottema, G. Entjes-Nieborg and W. van Ziest (eds), 295–306. Rotterdam: Balkema.

Neil, J. 1890. Land tenure in ancient times as preserved by the present village communities in Palestine. *Journal of the Transactions of the Victoria Institute* 24, 155–203.

Palmer, C. 1994. Reconstructing and interpreting ancient crop management practices: ethnobotanical investigations into traditional dryland farming in northern Jordan. Unpublished Ph.D. thesis, University of Sheffield.

Patai, R. 1949. *Musha'* tenure and co-operation in Palestine. *American Anthropologist* 51, 436–45.

Pinner, L. 1930. Wheat culture in Palestine. *Bulletin of The Palestine Economic Society* 5 (2).

Qasem, S. and M. Mitchell. 1986. The problems of rainfed agriculture. In *Agricultural Policy in Jordan*, A. Burrell (ed.), 30–40. London: Ithaca Press.

Rogan, E.L. 1991. Incorporating the periphery: the Ottoman extension of direct rule over Southeastern Syria (Transjordan) 1867–1914. Unpublished Ph.D. thesis, Harvard University.

Rogan, E.L. 1994. Bringing the state back: the limits of Ottoman rule in Jordan, 1840–1910. In *Village, Steppe and State: the social origins of modern Jordan*, E.L. Rogan and T. Tell (eds), 32–57. London: British Academic Press.

Semple, E.C. 1932. *The Geography of the Mediterranean Region and its Relation to Ancient History*. London: Constable and Co. Ltd.

Sluggett, P. and M. Farouk-Sluggett. 1984. The application of the 1858 Land Code in Greater Syria: some preliminary observations. In *Land Tenure and Social Transformation in the Middle East*, T. Khalidi (ed.), 409–21. Beirut: American University of Beirut.

Tabak, F. 1991. Agrarian fluctuations and modes of labour control in the western arc of the Fertile Crescent, c. 1700–1850. In *Landholding and Commercial Agriculture in the Middle East*, C. Keyder and F. Tabak (eds), 135–54. Albany: State University of New York Press.

Taminian, L. 1990. 'Ain. In *Part-Time Farming: agricultural development in the Zarqa River Basin, Jordan*. M. Mundy and R.S. Smith (eds), 13–59. Irbid, Jordan: Institute of Archaeology and Anthropology, Yarmouk University.

Tomaselli, R. 1977. Degradation of the Mediterranean maquis. In *Mediterranean Forests and Maquis: ecology, conservation and management*, MAB Technical Notes 2, 33–72. Paris: UNESCO.

Weuleresse, J. 1946. *Paysans de Syrie et du Proche-Orient*. Paris: Gallimard.

Whitelaw, T. M. 1991. The ethnoarchaeology of recent rural settlement and land use in northwest Keos. In *Landscape Archaeology as Long-Term History: northern Keos in the Cycladic Islands from earliest settlement until modern times*, J.F. Cherry, J.L. Davis and E. Mantzourani (eds), 403–54. Los Angeles: Institute of Archaeology, University of California, Monumenta Archaeologica 16.

Wilson, C.T. 1906. *Peasant Life in the Holy Land*. London: Murray.

Zohary, M. 1973. *Geobotanical Foundations of the Middle East*. Stuttgart: Gustav Fischer Verlag. 2 volumes.

16 Getting a life: stability and change in social and subsistence systems on the North-West Frontier, Pakistan, in later prehistory

KEN THOMAS

Marginal environments, especially arid or semi-arid zones, have long attracted scholars interested in the dynamics of human subsistence systems. Ecological factors – or constraints – have usually been the main focus of such studies, with social and cultural aspects being incorporated into broadly 'environmentalist' adaptive models.

A small topographical basin in a climatically marginal zone in north-west Pakistan (Figure 16.1) is the focus of this study. The Bannu basin is of interest not only because of its 'marginality' for agriculture but also, being surrounded by hills and mountains, it straddles important routes of migration and trade (Figure 16.2) between the Greater Indus (therefore India) and Afghanistan (therefore central Asia), routes which have been used in the historic and prehistoric past (Thomas and Knox 1994; Verma 1978). It is an area which, while offering environmental constraints to agro-pastoral production, was open to outside social influences. The area was selected for study as a potential 'model' situation for examining the dynamics of subsistence and social systems.

RECENT SETTLEMENT AND SUBSISTENCE IN BANNU

There is a marked difference between the western and eastern parts of the Bannu area in terms of recent settlement and subsistence patterns, as noted by Thomas (1986a). These differences relate to climate, the east having significantly less 'effective' rainfall for agricultural purposes because of higher temperatures and therefore greater rates of evapotranspiration. The area has a mean annual rainfall of some 320 mm. Summer temperatures up to 40°C cause huge losses of water from soils and streams and although winter rainfall levels are generally lower than those of the summer monsoon, lower winter temperatures (up to 25°C) compensate for this imbalance.

Agrarian systems vary from intensive double- and multiple-cropping in the irrigated areas to single-cropping in the rain-fed (dry farming) areas. In the

Figure 16.1 Location of the Bannu area (in black) in Pakistan

dry farming areas, such as those to the west of Bannu, the main crops grown are wheat, barley and chick-peas, as well as recent additions such as maize. Productivity of fields in these areas is not readily predictable from year-to-year because of variations in both the quantity and spatial distribution of winter and early spring rains. More fields are sown than produce a viable harvest and, in consequence, land use and landholding patterns of individual farmers tend, where possible, to be spatially diversified so as to spread the risk, although population growth in recent decades makes spatial diversification of land holding very difficult to achieve. Agriculture based on the 'traditional' western Asian package of wheat, barley, lentils, and chick-peas still predominates in the rain-fed areas and is a markedly seasonal activity, with winter planting and late spring harvesting. It is not possible to grow any of these crops in the summer to autumn period (unlike the more recently introduced millets, maize, cotton, etc.).

In consequence of both the risky nature of rain-fed farming, and its highly seasonal labour pattern, pastoralism and pastoral production tend to be relatively more important in these areas than they are in the irrigated areas. Agrarian production in these rain-fed areas has, up to quite recent times, been dominated by the environmentally tolerant cereal barley, compared with wheat. Wheat bread is a higher-ranked food than barley bread, but some of

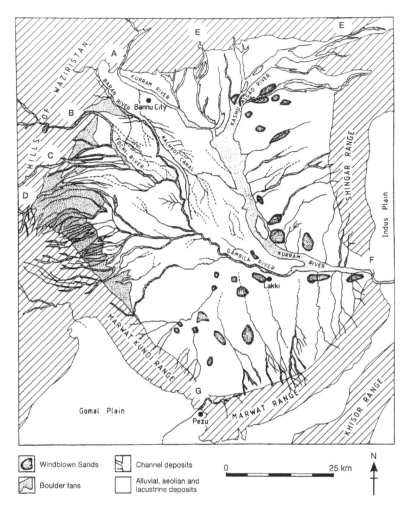

Figure 16.2   Geomorphological map of the Bannu basin. The various passes leading into and through the region are indicated on this map, as follows: A: Kurram; B: Tochi; C: Khaisor; D: Shaktu; E: passes to the Kohat plateau; F: Darrah Tang; G: Pezu Kotal.

the older workers at some of our excavations at sites in the rain-fed areas recall that barley bread (*retta*) was a staple in their childhood.

PATTERNS OF HUMAN EXPLOITATION OF THE BANNU FRONTIER ZONE

The area in the west of Bannu is of particular interest because all the later prehistoric sites are located there. This area is also immediately adjacent to the 'frontier zone', a marked physiographic barrier of hills and mountains which is cut by river valleys which, along with the high passes, afford routes of movement for people and their flocks. The main categories of exploitation of this frontier zone, based on ethnographic and ethnohistorical studies (e.g. Raverty [1878]1976; Robinson [1934]1978) and personal observations, are:

1   Pastoral nomads from Afghanistan who, until very recent times, made annual migrations between Afghanistan and the Indian subcontinent. Their movement out of Afghanistan takes place in the autumn to avoid the extreme cold and snows of winter. These nomads move with their families and flocks of animals, seeking pasture wherever it can be found or purchased. Robinson ([1934]1978: 2–3) identified various occupations among these nomads: nomadic pastoralists who are driven by climate to seek pastures on the other side of the frontier zone; merchants who trade between Afghanistan and India and whose migrations are due as much to economic causes as to climatic pressures; and other categories such as landless nomads who seek work in India (the first and last of these categories also engage in small amounts of trade).

     These people migrate back to Afghanistan in the spring to avoid the summer heat of the plains of the Indian subcontinent, when the pasture lands become scorched (and when there would be competition with settled inhabitants for restricted pasture). Their annual migrations have been severely curtailed in recent years because of the situation in Afghanistan.

2   Waziri semi-nomadic pastoral tribes living in the valleys within the frontier zone who also sow and harvest crops, according to opportunity, on the alluvial soils of the valleys. These people regularly visit the plains for employment, trade and, until recent times (and even occasionally today), plunder.

3   Under present tribal conditions it is rarely possible for settled inhabitants on the Bannu side to enter the frontier zone in order to engage in transhumant pastoralism. This pattern of exploitation, whereby a segment of a settled community takes flocks into the hills for access to pastures during some of the hot dry summer months, should not, however, be ruled out for earlier periods (see below).

PAST ENVIRONMENTS IN THE BANNU BASIN

It is evident that there have been marked and numerous changes in the behaviour of rivers and streams in the basin and many depositional sequences exist showing a complex record of incision, aggradation and changes in the direction of flow of stream channels. It is not essential to invoke climate change to account for the numerous phases of hydrological and depositional change in the Bannu basin. Such changes can entirely be the consequence of the inherently unstable and unpredictably torrential hydrological regime of this area, possibly enhanced by other factors such as episodic tectonic events (the area is still undergoing uplift as a consequence of the northwards movement of the Indian plate against the central Asiatic plate) and/or the impact of human modification of the landscape. Thomas (1986a: 21–4) discussed other aspects of past environments, including climates, in Bannu and concluded that there is no clear evidence to suggest that climate has changed markedly over the last 4–5 millennia. In truth, there is no clear evidence either way and the question of possible climatic shifts needs further investigation because the region is in a 'climatic tension zone' between Mediterranean-type winter depression systems to the west and monsoon-type summer rain systems to the south and east. A slight geographic shift in the transition zone between these weather systems could have had dramatic consequences for past subsistence systems in Bannu and the frontier zone.

Despite the uncertainties about past climatic regimes, environments have changed dramatically in terms of hydrology, soils and vegetation. There is little reason to doubt that the vegetation patterns visible in and around the basin today are a reflection of millennia of exploitation by people. Plants, especially woody species, were probably more diverse and abundant in the prehistoric past than they are today; the hills surrounding the basin were certainly more densely forested, even in historical times.

LATER PREHISTORIC SITES IN THE BANNU FRONTIER ZONE

The known archaeological sites of all periods in Bannu have been reviewed by Khan (1986); subsequent discoveries of prehistoric sites, and of excavations at some of them, have been discussed by Khan et al. (1987, 1988, 1989, 1991a). To date, all the known later prehistoric sites in the Bannu basin are located in the north-west (Figure 16.3). The various cultural phases represented by these sites, and their chronologies, are given in Table 16.1. Although sites of Kot Dijian (sometimes termed Early Harappan) affinities are known in the Bannu area, there are no sites known of the mature (urban) Harappan phase.

Some of the sites listed in Table 16.1 are small village sites which may have been occupied all year round (see discussion below). A few, notably Barrai Khuarra I, possibly Girdai, and a number of small 'sites' to the west of Lak Largai (see Figure 16.3), are only surface scatters of relatively small numbers of potsherds and a few other types of artefacts and probably represent short-term occupations.

In this chapter I intend to compare sites of the Sheri Khan Tarakai culture phase with those of the later Rehman Dheri and Kot Diji culture phases (see Table 16.1).

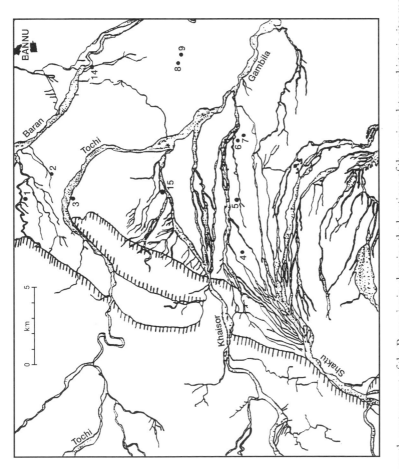

Figure 16.3 Map of the north-western part of the Bannu basin, showing the locations of the various later prehistoric sites mentioned in this chapter (see Table 16.1 for details of chronology). The hatched line marks the eastern limit of the Hills of Waziristan.

Key: Site no. 2: Islam Chowki; 3: Tarakai Qila; 4: Tarakai Ghurdai; 5: Sheri Khan Tarakai; 6: Barrai Khuarra 1; 7: Lak Largai; 8: Lewan; 9: Seer Dherai; 14: Ter Kala Dherai; 15: Girdai. (Sites 1 and 10–13 are early prehistoric sites not discussed in this chapter.)

Table 16.1 Later prehistoric sites in the Bannu basin

Cultural phase	Type site	Bannu sites	Date ranges*
Early Harappan	Kot Diji (Sind)	Islam Chowki	2500–2040 BC
		Tarakai Qila	None available
		Tarakai Ghundai	,, ,,
		Lewan	,, ,,
		Seer Dherai	,, ,,
Pre-Harappan (Chalcolithic)	Rehman Dheri (Phase I)	Islam Chowki	2870 BC
		Lak Largai	2885–2625 BC
		Lewan	None available
		Ter Kala Dherai	3110–2660 BC
Early Chalcolithic/ Late Neolithic	Sheri Khan Tarakai	Sheri Khan Tarakai	4240–2915 BC
		Barrai Khurra I	None available
		Ter Kala Dherai	,, ,,
		Girdai	,, ,,

Note: *These calibrated date ranges are summaries of data derived from radiocarbon determinations of charred organic samples from various statigraphic units on each site. The radiocarbon determinations have been calibrated to calendar dates using the curve of Pearson *et al.* (1986). Details of the radiocarbon determinations on which the above summaries are based are given in Khan *et al.* (1991a), except for the new dates for Sheri Khan Tarakai (quoted here), which will be published in *Radiocarbon* in due course (Ambers *et al.* forthcoming). The dates for Ter Kala Dherai have been published by Hedges *et al.* (1997: 258).

THE SHERI KHAN TARAKAI CULTURE PHASE

The site of Sheri Khan Tarakai has been the major focus of fieldwork since it was discovered in 1985 (Khan *et al.* 1986, 1990, 1991a, 1991b, 1992). It shows quite clearly the range of complex networks of social and, possibly, economic interactions which existed across a huge area of central and northern South Asia in the fourth millennium BC. Although the inhabitants of Sheri Khan Tarakai appear to have been settled there for most, if not all, of each year, there is evidence for contact with other sites in the local region as well as inter-regional contacts with populations in northern Baluchistan (to the south) and through to southern Turkmenistan to the north-west (Khan *et al.* 1992).

Other sites of this phase (Table 16.1 and Figure 16.3) include Barrai Khuarra I, which consists of a superficial scatter of artefacts on a river terrace; Girdai, a small shallowly stratified site located on the boulder conglomerate fan system; and Ter Kala Dheri, a site which has been virtually destroyed by recent land use but which yielded an interesting array of Sheri Khan Tarakai types of pottery and terracotta figurines alongside evidence of a transition between these and Rehman Dheri types of pottery and figurines (Thomas *et al.* 1997). Another site of this cultural phase, the first one reported outside the Bannu area, has recently been discovered by the Department of Archaeology,

University of Peshawar, to the south of the Bannu basin in Dera Ismail Khan District.

THE REHMAN DHERI AND KOT DIJI CULTURE PHASES

The type site of Rehman Dheri is located to the north of the modern city of Dera Ismail Khan, to the south of the Bannu basin. Rehman Dheri is a very large site which has been claimed to be 'urban' or, at least, 'proto-urban' (Durrani 1982, 1988). Sites in Bannu with material culture of Rehman Dheri type are at Islam Chowki, Lak Largai, Lewan, and Ter Kala Dheri. All these are well-stratified sites (although the latter has, as noted above, been virtually destroyed in recent years) which appear to be permanently settled villages. In contrast to most sites of Sheri Khan Tarakai type, they are not located on conglomerate fans but on the plains near to rivers, or in the interfluves between rivers. A few superficial scatters of pottery on the river terrace near Lak Largai (also near to the scatter at Barrai Khuarra I, see above) attest to the existence of transitory encampments. The Rehman Dheri cultural phenomenon has the same rather limited geographic extent as the antecedent Sheri Khan Tarakai one, which is in marked contrast to the Kot Diji phase which follows it.

The type site of Kot Diji is far to the south in Sind Province, and sites with this type of cultural assemblage are known from each Pakistan province: Sind, Baluchistan, Punjab and the Bannu and Dera Ismail Khan regions of the North-West Frontier. The Kot Dijian cultural horizon, sometimes described as the 'early Harappan', covers a huge geographic area and attests to a considerable degree of cultural homogeneity and, supposedly, social (and political?) integration during this period. In Bannu, sites with Kot Diji types of material culture (defined mainly by pottery and terracotta figurines) include Islam Chowki, Lewan, Tarakai Qila, Tarakai Ghundai and Seer Dherai. The latter site is small and, as the name Seer (= red), suggests, it is covered in pottery. The site has huge numbers of over-fired sherds and a considerable quantity of pottery slag, but limited numbers of other categories of artefacts, mainly struck stone but little ground stone and few terracottas, which are always so abundant on settlement sites. It is thought to be a specialist pottery-producing site, although this has yet to be confirmed by excavation.

SUBSISTENCE SYSTEMS OF THE SHERI KHAN TARAKAI, REHMAN DHERI AND KOT DIJI CULTURE PHASES IN BANNU

Large assemblages of charred plant remains are available from Sheri Khan Tarakai and Tarakai Qila, with smaller numbers of samples from Lak Largai,

Islam Chowki, and Tarakai Qila. In addition, animal bone assemblages are available from Sheri Khan Tarakai, Tarakai Qila and Lewan, with small collections from Lak Largai and Islam Chowki. These are undergoing detailed analysis, but some general results are apparent. The subsistence systems of the later cultural phases have been discussed in some detail by Thomas (1983a, 1983b, 1986b, 1989) and Khan et al. (1991c) and will only be summarized here.

The charred plant assemblages from Sheri Khan Tarakai are dominated by grains of barley (both hulled and naked varieties), with much smaller numbers of grains of wheat. Evidence from remains of chaff suggests that both these cereals were being processed at the site, and were probably grown near to the site. In addition, there are a few seeds of wild plants. The plant assemblages from both the Rehman Dheri and Kot Diji phases are also dominated by grains of barley. Wheat is present, but in much smaller quantities. Again, there is evidence of crop processing, suggesting that these cereals were being grown and harvested by the inhabitants of the various sites. At Tarakai Qila charred seeds of lentil were also found, but not in large numbers. In short, in all assemblages from all the cultural periods considered here, barley dominates, both in terms of near ubiquity of representation in the range of samples and in abundance of grains within samples.

The assemblages of animal bones show a little more variety between the culture phases, at least between the earliest and the two later ones. At Sheri Khan Tarakai there is a wide variety of larger mammals, including both wild and domesticated species. The domesticates at Sheri Khan Tarakai are cattle, sheep and goat (the relative proportions of these are still being analysed). There are also significant numbers of wild ass (onager), gazelle and (probably) mountain goat. The assemblages of animal bones from the later culture phases (Rehman Dheri and Kot Diji) contain few wild species (a few bones of onager, wild pig and a possible wild cat from Tarakai Qila, and part of a rhinoceros from Lak Largai), while water buffalo becomes a component of the domesticated species alongside cattle, sheep and goat. The assemblages from Tarakai Qila and Lewan have been best studied, so far, and indicate that cattle dominated, followed by sheep and goats. Actually, at Tarakai Qila cattle and sheep/goat were in equal abundance, with some 30 per cent of the sheep/ goats being young animals which were probably slaughtered for their meat. The cattle and water buffalo from these two sites are nearly all adults, suggesting their probable use for secondary produce (milk or traction). One proximal phalanx of a water buffalo from Lewan had a pathological condition which has been linked to traction (Thomas 1986b: 134).

The general pattern emerging from studies of these subsistence systems is:

1   Throughout the period under consideration, agriculture appears to have been wholly based on the 'borrowed' western Asiatic package of wheat and barley, with lentils present in some charred plant assemblages at one of the later sites.

2   This package is associated with distinct seasonality of the agrarian year, with autumn/winter sowing and late spring harvesting.

3   The dominance of barley among the assemblages of charred plant remains is indicative of the environmental hazards associated with rain-fed farming in this area in the past.

4   In the earliest phase, domesticated animals are cattle, sheep and goats. Water buffalo is added to this list in the later phase.

5   There is evidence that cattle and water buffalo in the later phase were used primarily for secondary products such as milk and work (including traction). Probably there was a greater 'integration' in the farming system in the later phases, with animals being used to promote agrarian production (traction, dung for manure, transport of harvest, possibly threshing) as well as for their own primary and secondary products.

6   Hunted wild animals, especially onager, gazelle and mountain goat, are more important in animal bone assemblages from the earliest phase than in the later phases.

IMPLICATIONS FOR PAST SOCIAL, SETTLEMENT AND SUBSISTENCE SYSTEMS

Emerging from this comparative study is a model of changing settlement and subsistence from the early to the later phases. Specifically, this entails a shift from at least seasonally pastoral nomadism or transhumance in the earlier phase to more sedentary existence later. It should be noted, however, that these changes represent shifts in focus or emphasis: both earlier and later phases involved combinations of (probable) all-year-round sedentism at some sites linked to seasonal pastoral transhumance.

What is the evidence and how is it interpreted? As usual with archaeological data, nothing is unequivocal. For the Sheri Khan Tarakai culture phase, the interpretation of seasonal pastoral transhumance involves a number of circumstantial pieces of evidence. Some of these point to contacts with other ecological zones away from the main habitation sites, such as bones of wild animals indicating hunting in the dry semi-arid low plains (onager and gazelle) as well as in the hills and uplands (mountain goat, which is also the only animal represented in pottery motifs in this period); wood charcoals indicate acquisition of wood resources not only from local vegetation zones but also from the low hill, the higher hill and the lower mountain zones (Cartwright and Thomas, in prep.). Woody taxa identified so far include *Tamarix, Calligonum, Salvadora* and *Zizyphus* (representative of the 'ry thorn habitats around the site today), *Acacia, Olea, Celtis,* and *Pistacia* (taxa ɔm the low and higher hill zones), and *Quercus* (from the temperate dry oak est, up to altitudes of 2,500 m). Wood from most of the local taxa must come to the site as fuel or for building materials, but that from taxa which occur well into the frontier zone could have been brought in (or acquired by exchange) as artefacts.

Other sources of evidence for contact outside the immediate area of the site point to inter-regional connections which need not, of course, arise from any pastoralist movements from the settled sites. At the site of Sheri Khan Tarakai, alongside the huge number of locally made types of hand-made (coil technique) pottery, were found a few fine red-slipped sherds of wheel-thrown pots which were clearly 'alien' and which were subsequently found to be identical to forms from sites in northern Baluchistan (Periano Ghundai and Rana Ghundai). A small number of 'alien' forms in the large and diverse array of terracotta figurines are equivalent to types from Periano Ghundai, whilst the terracotta 'cones' have equivalences in sites in southern Turkmenistan. Fragments of chank shell show links ultimately leading to the Arabian Sea, whilst lapis lazuli is ultimately from north-eastern Afghanistan. Some or even all of these materials (including the wood) could have been brought in by trade or exchange involving 'other peoples', of whom we otherwise know nothing.

Sites of this early period tend to be variable in terms of structure and, probably, function. The type site has evidence of relatively substantial structures of mud-brick with boulder footings in its latest phase, but before that structures were much less substantial, being of pressed mud with walls and roofs of wattle and daub. Other sites consist only of surface scatters of characteristic artefacts and have been interpreted as temporary encampments. One such, Barrai Khuarra I, is located on a river terrace along which there are other such sites of later periods, and which has been used by recent pastoral nomads in their movements into and out of the Bannu basin.

The subsistence remains for this phase also attest to the difficulties of farming in the area, with charred grain assemblages being overwhelmingly dominated by the more environmentally tolerant barley compared to wheat. This assemblage also indicates a strongly seasonal aspect, involving winter to spring cultivation and harvesting. The rest of the year, including the long, hot unproductive summer could have been given over to pastoral production, which probably had a strong transhumant element to it.

Against these arguments should be placed the existence of unbaked clay structures at Sheri Khan Tarakai which have been interpreted (by analogy with remarkably similar structures in the nearby modern village) as grain storage silos. This attests to human presence at the site in the post-harvest period, so at the very least not all the population would have been involved in hot-weather transhumant pastoralism. Despite the seemingly transient nature of the early occupation structures at the site, most had multiple micro-layers of mud plaster on their floors, attesting to multiple use (although this need not preclude re-use after a pastoralist period of absence from the site). The huge quantities of artefacts found in the site, especially pottery (clearly made on site, judging by the abundance of 'kiln wasters') and quern stor and grinding stones, attests to an intensity of effort and production not ea compatible with the site being wholly abandoned seasonally for pastoralist purposes.

So, what are the options for interpreting the earlier phase? The first is to have people living at their sites all-year-round, engaging in trade or exchange with more mobile groups bringing in from outside all sorts of 'alien' materials, including wood. The second is to have the site occupied all-year-round by part of the population and for another segment to be involved in hot-weather pastoral nomadism in the hills and mountains. Some foreign materials (mountain goat, wood) could have been brought to the site from this activity, whilst more distant materials could have been acquired by exchange either during such pastoralist episodes, or by other nomadic groups coming into the Bannu area. I prefer this second more complex model, based as it is on a diversity of human behaviours performed, in substantial part, by actors of whom we have some (albeit limited) archaeological knowledge.

What of the later phases considered above? Again, the evidence is not clear, but there are reasons for thinking that settled farming was more important relative to transhumant seasonal pastoralism. Sites show evidence for more substantial structures, with walls of mud-brick built on foundations of two or more courses of river-rolled boulders. Floors have multiple micro-layers of mud plaster, attesting to frequent re-use. Pottery assemblages are homogeneous, with forms having been made locally rather than showing evidence of longer-distance connections. However, the pottery also shows evidence of craft specialization, in the form of potters' marks, and there is evidence that one site, Seer Dherai, could have been a specialist pottery production site during the Kot Diji phase (see p. 313). Decorative motifs with 'ecological connotations' on the pottery, such as depictions of cattle, water buffalo, leaves of the lowland pipal tree, and fish from the rivers of the plains, contrast with the wild mountain goats of the preceding phase. The assemblages of charred seeds are, again, dominated by barley, attesting to the environmental hazards associated with dry farming in this area, but include lentils as well as wheat. Possibly lentils were used as part of an inter-cropping system, which would also have had beneficial effects on soil fertility and hence crop production. The domestic animals include a new species, the water buffalo, which is quite unsuited to pastoral nomadism in hills or mountains and which must have been tended near to rivers or swamps because the animal has to keep its skin moist, or plastered in mud, to prevent damage by cracking. There is also evidence that cattle and water buffalo animals were used for traction and possibly secondary food products derived from milk processing, which would have increased local production. Finally, steatite seals have been found in some sites, attesting to the probable control of access to stored products. All these factors point to the likelihood that populations were largely sedentary, with craft specialization at least for pottery production, and showing social ratification or inequalities, through evidence of control of storage systems. Closer integration of pastoral and agrarian modes of production, and developments in the farming system to increase productivity (even if barley continued to be the most successful crop), could have eased seasonal food constraints and lessened the need for hot-weather pastoral transhumance to the hills.

Against these arguments should be placed the fact that some sites of these later phases are only surface scatters of artefacts suggesting temporary encampments of mobile groups. Some of these are scattered along the river terrace below the major site of Lak Largai, along a route used into recent times by transhumant pastoralists. Chank shell and lapis lazuli are found in these sites, attesting to connections leading ultimately to the Arabian sea or north-eastern Afghanistan (although greater cultural homogeneity on a wide geographic scale is evidenced by the Kot Diji culture phase, attesting to long-distance connections and suggesting probable social and political integration or 'control'). Lastly, wood charcoals from some sites suggest the exploitation of phytological zones in the hills and low mountains.

For the later phases therefore there appears to be greater emphasis on, or commitment to, a more integrated farming system which might have increased productivity and, through controlled storage of surpluses, lessened the seasonal hazards associated with a long hot season. This greater cohesion wrought in the subsistence system seems to have been associated with more substantial settlements, craft specialization, greater controls over stored products, and a greater degree of regional and (in the latest phase) trans-regional social and political integration. Despite this, production was still uncertain, as evidenced by the continued dominance of barley, and pastoralism was still an important part of the subsistence system. It is very likely that seasonal pastoral transhumance continued to be practised in these later phases, involving movements of part of the human population (perhaps by now specialist flock herders?) into the hills and mountain pastures during the summer period. These movements would have increased social contacts, leading to exchange of goods, and to a range of 'alien' materials being brought into the permanent settlements.

CONCLUSION

Conditions for existence in this frontier zone are difficult and complex. The area straddles two conflicting climatic zones, which are both attentuated here, making it marginal for successful agriculture. Settled life was always a risky business and diversification of landscape exploitation for agrarian and pastoral purposes has been one important way to spread risks. Agrarian production was highly seasonal, essentially a winter/late spring activity, with unpredictable outcomes. Only the tolerant cereal barley seems to have been predictably successful, as attested by its dominance in the charred assemblages of plant remains from the various sites discussed. Summer seasonal pastoral transhumance to the hills and upland pastures is thought to have been a important strategy throughout the period considered, but especially in t' earlier phase. Social and cultural changes in the later phases appear to have brought about a change in focus away from the hills and mountains and towards the plains, associated with a more integrated mixed farming system which might have been significantly more productive, or at least have more stable levels of production. Despite this, seasonal pastoral transhumance is still conceived as having been an important feature in this phase, leading to external contact and exchange with other social and cultural groups.

The Bannu region also straddles a number of important routes for trade, exchange, and the movement of people between Afghanistan and central Asia and the plains of the Greater Indus. So, in both environmental and social terms, there was great potential for instability. This is reflected somewhat in the evolutionary shift of the subsistence system, although the essential components remain relatively constant throughout. Significant technological innovation (e.g., irrigation) or introduction of new cultigens (such as millets, which might have added a summer–autumn dimension to the cropping system) did not happen and so agricultural production remained risky. In contrast, social and cultural systems were subject to significant change, suggesting that while people were open to new ideas affecting their ideology and material culture, there were few incentives or opportunities to change significantly the broad pattern of their subsistence strategies. There were, of course, changes in how the various elements of the subsistence system were managed, which reflect strategic decisions made by the various social groups concerned.

NOTE

Ideally, the answers to problems relating to pastoral transhumance during the various cultural phases considered here could be gained by field surveys in the hills and valleys of the 'frontier zone', and by looking for sites on the Afghan side. In practice, both these alternatives are impossible; the latter for obvious reasons and the former because of severe constraints on access to the Tribal Areas of North and South Waziristan. We are therefore forced to work, for the foreseeable future, with data from only the Bannu side of the frontier zone.

ACKNOWLEDGEMENTS

I am grateful to my colleagues in the Bannu Archaeological Project: Professor Farid Khan and Robert Knox. Mr Feroze Khan of Bannu City has given help in many ways. Caroline Cartwright, of the Department of Scientific Research at the British Museum, undertook the analysis of the wood charcoals. Marcello Mannino was a source of critical support. The main financial sponsors of the Bannu Archaeological Project are the Trustees of the British Museum and the Society for South Asian Studies (British Academy).

REFERENCES

Ambers, J. et al. Forthcoming. Radiocarbon dates from the British Museum Research Laboratory. *Radiocarbon.*

Durrani, F.A. 1982. Rehman Dheri and the birth of civilization in Pakistan. *Bulletin of the Institute of Archaeology, London* 18, 191–207.

Durrani, F.A. 1988. Excavations in the Gomal Valley. Rehman Dheri Excavations Rep. 1, *Ancient Pakistan* 6, 1–232.

Hedges, R.E.M., P. Pettitt, C. Bronk Ramsey and G.J. Van Klinken. 1997. Radiocarbon dates from the Oxford AMS system: *Archaeometry* datelist 23. *Archaeometry* 39, 247–62.

Khan, F. 1986. Archaeological sites in the Bannu basin. In *Lewan and the Bannu Basin,* F.R. Allchin, B. Allchin, F.A. Durrani and F. Khan (eds), 183–95.Oxford: BAR.

Khan, F., J.R. Knox and K.D. Thomas. 1986. Sheri Khan Tarakai: a new site in the North-West Frontier Province of Pakistan, *Journal of Central Asia* 9, 13–34.

Khan, F., J.R. Knox and K.D. Thomas. 1987. The Bannu Archaeological Project: a study of prehistoric settlement in Bannu District, Pakistan, *South Asian Studies* 3, 83–90.

Khan, F., J.R. Knox and K.D. Thomas. 1988. Prehistoric and protohistoric settlements in Bannu District. *Pakistan Archaeology* 23, 99–148.

Khan, F., J.R. Knox and K.D. Thomas. 1989. New perspectives on early settlement in Bannu District, Pakistan. In *South Asian Archaeology 1985,* K. Frifelt and P. Sorenson (eds), 281–91. London: Curzon Press.

Khan, F., J.R. Knox and K.D. Thomas. 1990. The Bannu Archaeological Project: investigations at Sheri Khan Tarakai 1987–9. *South Asian Studies* 6, 241–7.

Khan, F., J.R. Knox and K.D. Thomas. 1991a. *Explorations and Excavations in Bannu District, North-West Frontier Province, Pakistan, 1985–1988.* London: The British Museum.

Khan, F., J.R. Knox and K.D. Thomas. 1991b. Sheri Khan Tarakai: a neolithic village in Bannu District, NWFP. In *South Asian Archaeology 1987,* M. Taddei and P. Calieri (eds), 111–27. Rome: Istituto Italiano per il Medio ed Estremo Oriente.

Khan, F., J.R. Knox and K.D. Thomas. 1991c. Towards a model for protohistoric subsistence systems in Bannu District, Pakistan. In *South Asian Archaeology 1987,* M. Taddei and P. Calieri (eds), 129–41. Rome: Istituto Italiano per il Medio ed Estremo Oriente.

Khan, F., J.R. Knox and K.D. Thomas 1992. Tradition, identity and individuality: exploring the cultural relationships of Sheri Khan Tarakai, *Pakistan Archaeology* 26, 156–74.

Pearson, G.W., J.R. Pilcher, M.G.L. Baillie, D.M. Corbett and F. Qua. 1986. High precision C measurement of Irish oaks to show the natural C variations from AD 1840–5210 BC. *Radiocarbon* 28, 911–34.

Raverty, H.G. [1878]1976. *Notes on Afghanistan and Baluchistan.* Lahore: Sang-e-Meel Publications.

Robinson, J.A. [1934]1978. *Notes on Nomad Tribes of Eastern Afghanistan.* Quetta: Nissa Traders.

Thomas, K.D. 1983a. Tarakai Qila: site, economy and environment. In *Site, Environment and Economy,* B. Proudfoot (ed.), 127–44. Oxford: BAR.

Thomas, K.D. 1983b. Agricultural and subsistence systems of the third millennium BC in north-west Pakistan: a speculative outline. In *Integrating the Subsistence Economy,* M. Jones (ed.), 279–314. Oxford: BAR.

Thomas, K.D. 1986a. Environment and subsistence in the Bannu basin. In *Lewan an the Bannu Basin,* F.R. Allchin, B. Allchin, F.A. Durrani and F. Khan (eds), 13–3 Oxford: BAR.

Thomas, K.D. 1986b. Palaeobiological investigations. In *Lewan and the Bannu Basin*, F.R. Allchin, B. Allchin, F.A. Durrani and F. Khan (eds), 121–36. Oxford: BAR.

Thomas, K.D. 1989. Hierarchical approaches to the evolution of complex agricultural systems. In *The Beginnings of Agriculture*, A. Milles, D. Williams and N. Gardner (eds), 55–73. Oxford: BAR.

Thomas, K.D. and J.R. Knox. 1994. Routes of passage: later prehistoric settlement and exploitation of a frontier region in northwestern Pakistan, *Bulletin of the Institute of Archaeology, London* 31, 89–104.

Thomas, K.D., J.R. Knox and F. Khan. 1997. Technology transfer and culture change: an example from northwest Pakistan. In *South Asian Archaeology 1995*, Volume 1, R. Allchin and B. Allchin (eds), 237–51. New Delhi: Oxford and IBH.

Verma, H.C. 1978. *Medieval Routes to India: Baghdad to Delhi. A study of trade and military routes*. Calcutta: Naya Prokash.

17 Interaction of maritime and agricultural adaptations in the Japan Sea basin

Yuri E. Vostretsov

The cultural evolution of prehistoric populations in coastal zones of different regions of the world shows a similarity of features of economic and social development. The Japan Sea basin is one of the unique areas of the world's oceans where a complicated interaction of ancient cultures connected with maritime and agricultural adaptation occurred.

Such factors as the location of the Japan Sea between 30° and 40°N, the presence of warm and cold currents, the monsoonal nature of the climate and a complicated continental relief led to a combination of both tropical and subarctic features of climate and the high productivity of maritime and terrestrial ecosystems. Climatic contrasts between the northern and southern parts of the basin explain the modern division of adjoining territories into a millet-dominated northern zone and rice-dominated southern area, a division originating in ancient times. Part of the purpose of this chapter is to explain how this division came about.

The region is unevenly studied. However, the existing data allow us to determine the stages and trajectories of the interaction of maritime and agricultural adaptations in the Japan Sea basin and to find some features of similarity and difference in the various areas of the region. In the Early and Middle Holocene different variants of two types of adaptation dominate in the Japan Sea basin. The first of these is connected with the exploitation of plants and hunting in terrestrial-riverine ecosystems. The second is connected with non-specialized fishing, hunting and gathering in the coastal zones. The first adaptation is represented by sites in western Japan and western Korea. The second by sites in the south of the Korean peninsula, eastern Japan, and the north-west sector of the Japan Sea basin.

The warming, and sharp rise in sea level of between 2–4 m higher than the present, from the Early to Middle Holocene has submerged various cases of Early Holocene maritime adaptation (Korotkii 1985: 297). The exceptions are the shell midden at Natsushima (Aikens and Higuchi 1982: 114–20) and the first level of the Tonsondong site (Sample 1974: 117). However, maritime adaptations have deep roots in the region. By the Middle Holocene people had accumulated a rich experience of the exploitation of different maritime ecosystems in the whole of the Japan Sea basin. This is evidenced by cultural remains at sites in eastern Korea (So 1986) and sites connected with the Boisman cultural tradition: Ragin; Posyet-1; Hansi-1, 2; Zaisanovka-1, 3, 4; Boisman-1, 2, 3; and Sibiryakov-1, in the Primorsky Territory of Russia. In Japan there are the sites of the Early Jomon (Ikawa-Smith 1986: 208). The sites of this period manifest a rather non-specialized use of marine resources.

By 5000 BP, at the end of the Atlantic phase, there was considerable cooling of the climate which led to the disappearance of certain types of animals (e.g., deer and water buffalo) and a change in the plant communities in the coastal zone. A marine regression and considerable change in landscape and seascape took place which led to the disappearance of lagoons and deep bays and to the creation of alluvial valleys at river estuaries (Korotkii 1994: 39). The changes in environment undermined the usual resource base and made the population look for new adaptive situations. It was this period of cultural changes in the region which led to the disappearance of some cultural traditions and the appearance of others. In Korea and the southern Dunbay the comb-marked impressed ceramic tradition changed to the comb-marked incised ceramic tradition. From that time began the first stage in the adoption of agriculture in the region. The first evidence of cultivation is found in western Korea, where it entered from the neighbouring Dunbay area (northern China) where agriculture had been practised much earlier (Choe 1990: 4, 10).

Some evidence of cultivation of millet (*Setaria italica*) in north-west Korea is apparently found in an earlier period as well (So 1986: 79). However, the change of climate made the population of western Korea increase the proportion of cultivated plants in the diet (Choe 1990: 4). Although at first this contribution was not large and did not lead to notable changes in the life of the people as a whole, we can see a tendency towards the permanent enlarging of its role during the Middle and Late Chulmun. The diverse and rich plant resources of the continental zone prevented the rapid adoption of cultivation in western Korea.

In the north-west sector of the Japan Sea and eastern Korea, the intensification of maritime adaptation strategies is connected with the cooling and regression of the sea. Intensification of exploitation of maritime resources took place by means of specialized fishing in forest-estuary and forest-bay ecosystems. In the north-west sector of the Japan Sea (the estuary of the Tumen river), the transformation of the Boisman cultural tradition (impressed pottery) into the Zaisanovsky tradition (incised pottery) took place. The latter tradition in the coastal zone is connected with the appearance of specialized fishing, an increase in the size and density of population and in larger dwellings as compared to the previous period.

At the same time we can see a growth in the number of sites of the Zaisanovsky cultural tradition in continental zones on the middle reaches of rivers. Apparently the movement of population inland from the coastal zone can be connected with the appearance of cultivation as one of the components of subsistence systems. However, so far there are no palaeobotanic data to support this supposition. A similar situation at the same time is seen in western Japan where swidden agriculture of millet in the Late Jomon is considered possible by some scientists (Rowley-Conwy 1984). In eastern Japan, complex fishing-hunting-gathering economies continued to predominate (Aikens and Higuchi 1982: 182–6).

By the end of the first stage of the adoption of agriculture, the Final Jomon, the Bronze and Early Iron Age in Korea and Dunbay, cultivation probably followed a number of stages of intensification and we can see much evidence of cultivation in the region (So 1986). Apparently swidden agriculture began to be used.

In the southwest of the Korean peninsula and northern Kyushu between 3000–2600 BP, there appeared evidence of rice cultivation (Aikens and Higuchi 1982; Nelson 1982, Chapter 8 in this volume). In the coastal zones of this region the technologies oriented towards the exploitation of maritime resources in diverse ecosystems reached their culmination (Final Jomon in Japan and Yankovskay culture in the north-west part of the Japan Sea) (Akazawa 1986; Andreeva et al. 1986).

Thus the first stage in the adoption of agriculture is characterized by the appearance and enlargement of the role of cultivated plants in favourable zones, along with the parallel development of diverse hunting-gathering-fishing adaptations which continued to dominate in most of the Japan Sea basin. The second stage of the adoption of cultivation in the Japan Sea basin began around 2400–2300 BP and is connected with the spreading of rice cultivators (the Yayoi culture) in the south and millet, barley and wheat cultivators in the north (the Krounovsky culture). From that time a new stage in the social and economic history of the region begins, leading to the domination of agriculture in the economy. This process, which finally led to the formation of early states in the region, had many similar features in the south and north despite the absence of any cultural contacts between them.

The expansion of both cultures, with no direct contacts between them, began approximately simultaneously, which leads us to suppose that there was a similar motivation for this change. The start of the expansion could have been initiated by changes in ecological and social circumstances. What changes in environment took place at that time? On the basis of palaeogeographic data from the Primorsky Territory of Russia we can suggest the following reconstruction of events.

Between 2500–2200 BP a considerable cooling of the climate took place. This was accompanied by a strengthening of its continental conditions, with colder winters and drier, warmer summers. Precipitation was less than at present. In the first part of summer droughts became more pronounced, especially in continental areas. The cooling was accompanied by a sharp fall in sea level from 1.5 m above the present sea level to between 0.8 and 1.5 m below it. Initially it led to the formation of over-deepened river beds, and the drying up and disappearance of most lagoons. At the period of lowest sea level, between 2100–1900 BP, the first overflood terraces were formed in the lower and middle reaches of rivers, while in the estuaries marshes dried up and alluvial plains with meadow soils were formed (Korotkii 1994: 36–7, 40).

These changes in environment are similar to those which took place in Japan, and probably explain the following:

1   Why the degradation of Jomon marine economies was greater in western Japan than in eastern Japan.
2   Why the expansion of rice cultivators began in the third century BC, rather than between the tenth and sixth centuries BC when they first appeared in northern Kyushu.
3   Why the expansion of the Yayoi population occurred first through the coastal area (in estuary zones) and only later up the valleys of the rivers.

Akazawa (1982: 157–60) describes two stages of the expansion of rice cultivators (Figure 17.1), which can be connected with the environmental changes described above. In the first stage, rice cultivation came from the continent in the Final Jomon to the north of Kyushu Island. But rice cultivation became widespread from around the third century BC in the Early Yayoi and continued up to 100 BC. At that period the Yayoi population (according to the Chinese chronicles these were the people referred to as 'Wa' (Aikens and Higuchi 1982: 247)) lived in simple rural communities and inhabited areas along the wide coastal plain of Kyushu Island and southern Honshu in the places where the decline of weak Jomon marine economies took place, and where there appeared new types of landscape suitable for rice cultivation. In the second stage (100 BC–AD 300) Middle and Late Yayoi sites spread into the interior valleys in western and eastern Japan. The density and social complexity of the population increased.

Although the Yayoi spread and its social results have been widely discussed by scholars (Akazawa 1982, 1986; Rowley-Conwy 1984; Rouse 1986: 67–105), the simultaneous events in the north-west region of the Japan Sea basin are a new subject for discussion. Let us therefore consider them in detail. Krounovsky culture sites date from *c.* 500 BC to at least AD 200–300, the upper limit being not fixed yet. This is due to the absence of direct references in chronicles and insufficient radiocarbon dates.

In China this culture is named Tuanjie (Kuang 1982; Lin 1985: 8). Chinese scholars connect the Krounovsky–Tuanjie culture with the Woju tribes, which later were brought into the Koguryo state and also the later Pokhai, based on the coincidence of area and time and some features of the economy and social life (Lin 1985: 19). They were simple rural communities without notable social stratification. They probably had individual land ownership and an advanced system of agriculture, using beds[1] for cultivating millet, barley and wheat (Yanushevich *et al.* 1990: 5–7; Vostretsov 1987a, 1987b).

The nucleus of the Krounovsky culture is the continental area of Dunbay

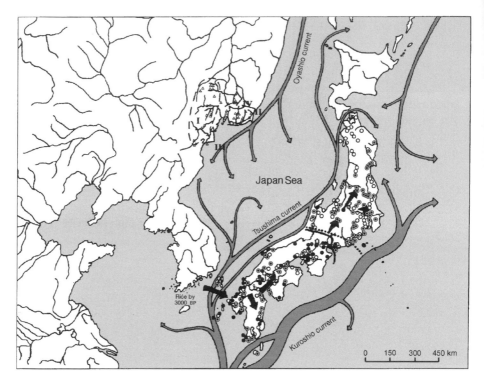

- ➡ – First rice expansion
- → – Second rice expansion
- —— – Approximate limits of the first rice expansion
- · · · · – Approximate limits of Tottaimon-type pottery
- ● – Early Yayoi sites (300–100 BC)

- ◉ – Middle Yayoi sites (100 BC– AD 100)
- ○ – Late Yayoi sites (AD 100–300)
- △ – sites
- ⟨Ⅰ⟩ – nuclear area
- ⟹Ⅱ – direction of expansion

Figure 17.1 Map illustrating: (i) expansion of rice cultivators in Japan (redrawn from Akazawa 1982, fig 4.6); (ii) expansion of Krounovsky–Tuanjie culture c.500 BC–300 AD

near the border with Russia, from the Tumen River to Lake Khanka. Sites were located along the middle reaches of rivers (Figure 17.2). We now know of more than forty sites, and eight sites of the Krounovsky culture have been excavated by the author, using fine-scale recovery techniques such as flotation. Based on the results of archaeological research in the Primorsky Territory of Russia, two chronological stages of the Krounovsky culture are now distinguished. Within these stages we can also distinguish three groups of sites, on the basis of their economy or ecological situation. These sites are located in different ecological zones with different resource bases, which affected their subsistence systems, material culture, settlement patterns and

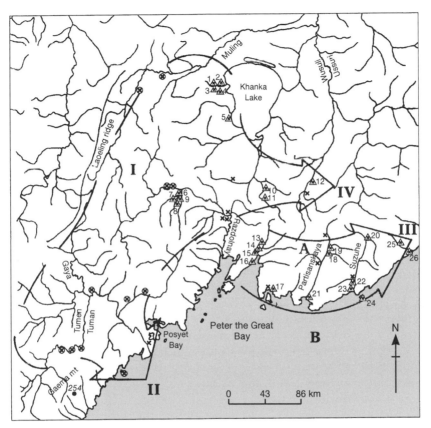

⟨I⟩   – nuclear area

⊃⇢ II   – direction of expansion

×   – sites of the Krounovsky culture in the Primorsky Territory of Russia

⚠   – sites of the Krounovsky culture in the Primorsky Territory of Russia
       with catchment area studied

⊗   – sites of the Tuanjie culture (Lin 1985: 15)

Figure 17.2   Map illustrating the expansion of the Krounovsky–Tuanjie culture

socio-demographic characteristics (see Figures 17.3, 17.4) (Vostretsov 1987a, 1987b).

In the first stage, Krounovsky sites were located in the nuclear area, the continental zone (Figure 17.1: 1). In the second stage (300–100 BC) there began a migration in three directions: south, east and south-east into the coastal zone of the Primorsky Territory of Russia (Figure 17.2: II, III, IV). Archaeological evidence, such as the stratigraphic features of the sites, the phases of occupation of the sites, and the evolution of ceramic styles, allows the conclusion that the migration was in waves, of a pulsating character

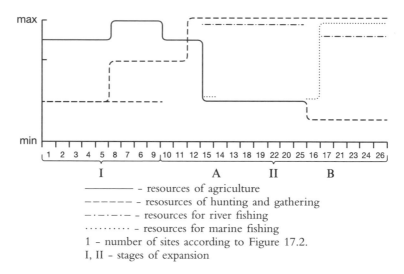

1 - number of sites according to Figure 17.2.

I, II - stages of expansion

Figure 17.3 Changes of resources within the catchment area of sites (radius 5 km) of Krounovsky culture during migration

(Vostretsov 1987b; Zhushchikhovskaya 1994: 92–5). The following factors influenced the beginning of the migration.

The cooling climate, the fall in sea level to between 0.8 and 1.5 m lower than the present and radical changes in coastal landscapes, led to the decline of the Yankovsky population, the economy of which was oriented to the exploitation of maritime resources from different maritime ecosystems. While earlier sites of the Yankovsky culture spread from the north Hamgyong to the north-east, including Peter the Great Bay, later they survived only along the most productive area of the coast from the Tumen river estuary to the Razdolnaya river estuary.

On the other hand the areas located near the coast, and some areas of the coast itself, became more attractive for cultivators: the marshes were drained, wide coastal plains were formed, and in the coastal areas the risk of drought decreased (a problem for agriculture in Dunbay) as compared to inland regions where the climate became colder and dryer. Thus the interaction of forced emigration and positive attractions led to the movement of part of the population of the Krounovsky culture to the coastal zone.

Besides natural factors, there apparently existed internal reasons for the beginning of migration such as population pressure on resources. The Krounovsky sites in the nuclear area were located in clusters close to each other and were rather large (up to 12,000 square metres). Populations at individual sites varied from 120 (Semipiatnova-1) to 500 (Krounovska-1) (Figure 17.2: 1, 8). According to ethnological data such population levels could be close to the upper limit for sites using cultivation in beds. Deterioration of cultivation conditions, along with the relatively high density of population, could be the reason for the beginning of the migration of part of the population to already depopulated coastal areas beginning around 300–200 BC.

Migration from the nuclear area went in three directions. The first was towards the estuary of the Tumen river (Figure 17.2). We know little of it. The second was to the south-east and east (Figure 17.2). Let us consider its socioeconomic consequences: Figure 17.3 shows how the proportion of potential resources in site catchments changed during the migration. In nuclear areas (Figures 17.2: I, 17.3: I) agricultural resources predominated. With migration to the east the balance of resources changed in favour of gathering, hunting and fishing. This stage can be characterized as a period of stress for groups on the move. This made the migrants take different adaptive decisions, which we can see in the changes of subsistence systems and the settlement pattern.

Part of the population (Figure 17.2: II-A) settled in subcontinental areas on the middle reaches of rivers. They created small sites (up to 2,000 square metres), located some distance apart, the population of which continued to practise agriculture, but in a changed form. In contrast to nuclear areas where cultivation of barley and wheat predominated, millet cereals began to dominate which gave more stable yields in the subcontinental zone. At the same time the role of diverse wild plants such as walnut (*Junglans manshurica*), hazelnut (*Corylus avelana*), Brassicaceae sp., *Chenopodium album*, Setaria sp., Amarantus sp., Rumex sp., Polygonaceae sp. increased in importance and river fishing played a larger role (Vostretsov 1987a: 127, 132).

The other part of the population inhabited estuary areas in coastal zones (Figure 17.2: II-B). Here we can also see small sites (up to 3,000 square metres) located some distance apart. Their inhabitants continued to practise agriculture. However, we cannot yet estimate the role of agriculture against the background of the increase of the river fishing and the appearance of marine fishing. The other direction of expansion was to the east into areas close in landscape structure and resources to the nuclear area. Here the subsistence system and settlement pattern changed only a little as compared with the nuclear area (Figure 17.2: IV) (Vostretsov 1987a).

Thus we can see that the changes in subsistence systems correspond to the peculiarities of the environment, while agriculture remained the basic strategy of adaptation. We can make an attempt to estimate the socio-demographic consequences of migration of part of the Krounovsky population to the east. In nuclear areas (Figure 17.4: I) the population inhabited large sites located in clusters. The sites were characterized by sizeable dwellings (from 48 to 115 square metres) for one nuclear family or extended family, with low density of people per dwelling (7–9 square metres per person). In the migration to the south-east (Figure 17.4: II-A, B) the settlement pattern changed. The Krounovsky population inhabited small, separate sites of 50–70 people each. The sites were characterized by small dwellings (from 10 to 26 square metres) for one nuclear family, with high density of people per dwelling (2–4 square metres per person). In addition,

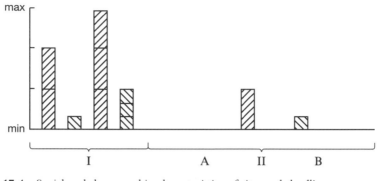

Figure 17.4   Social and demographic characteristics of sites and dwellings
◪ – size of sites
◩ – nuclear family

the diversity of material culture reduced. We find less decoration on tools, pottery became more primitive, and there were fewer iron items.

The greatest adaptive success was achieved by the Krounovsky population in nuclear areas where, probably, it continued up to the formation of the Pokhai state (AD 698). Nevertheless, at that time agriculture began to dominate in the economy of the region and this later led to the formation of early states. There was a definite similarity in the expansion of cultivators in the south and north of the Japan Sea basin. This similarity involves time, causes, stages, and the fact that rapid expansion of cultivation is connected with the appearance of new cultural groupings. However, the second stage of agricultural expansion was more difficult in the north of the region because of natural limitations, and did not lead to a rapid rise in social complexity of the sort we can see from Middle to Late Yayoi.

Thus, the processes of adopting agriculture in different parts of the Japan Sea basin had much in common, resulting from the ecological situation, and they occurred slowly in constant competition with highly developed marine economies.

ACKNOWLEDGEMENT

I would like to thank Peter Rowley-Conwy for his help during the writing of this chapter.

NOTE

1 Climatic conditions of relevance to agriculture in Korea and Dunbay are determined by the monsoonal nature of the climate, with cold winters, a late

spring, and an arid first half of summer. The second half of summer (mid-August) is characterized by typhoons, bringing up to 80 per cent of the annual precipitation. As a result, cultivators have a short growing season, this necessitating a specific agricultural system: cultivation in beds.

At the end of the nineteenth century bed cultivation was as follows:

(i) Beds were formed by a mound of soil 0.2–0.3 m high, up to 0.7 m wide and with ditches between the rows of mounds up to 0.7 m wide. The size of beds and intervening ditches varied from 0.25–1.00 m.

(ii) Sowing was carried out in one or two lines (depending on the kind of plants).

(iii) Every year the beds were moved, with the spaces between rows elevated to form the new beds. Thus the bed system was like a 1.5–2 field system.

(iv) Crops were rotated, usually using five kinds of plants.

(v) Organic fertilizers, such as dung and compost, were used.

(vi) Plants with short period of growth were preferred.

(vii) Weeding was carried out 3–4 times per summer.

(viii) This agricultural system required hand labour using simple tools.

Points (i), (ii), (vi) and (vii) aimed to maximize the short growing season, while points (iii), (iv) and (v) aimed to maintain the fertility of the soil.

The agricultural system in beds was distinguished by high crop yields of up to 1.5–2 times (according to some data 3–4 times) more than in the contemporaneous eastern European system of agriculture used by Russian peasants. When using agricultural beds for subsistence one nuclear family needed from 0.5–1 hectare of land. This system led to a high density of population and the formation of a clustered settlement pattern.

REFERENCES

Aikens, M. C. and T. Higuchi. 1982. *The Prehistory of Japan*. New York: Academic Press.

Akazawa, T. 1982. Cultural change in prehistoric Japan: receptivity to rice agriculture in the Japanese archipelago. In *Advances in World Archaeology* Vol. 1, F. Wendorf and A.E. Close (eds), 151–211. New York: Academic Press.

Akazawa, T. 1986. Regional variation in procurement systems of Jomon hunter-gatherers. In *Prehistoric Hunter-gatherers in Japan: new research methods*. Bulletin No. 27, T. Akazawa and C.M. Aikens (eds), 73–89. Tokyo: University of Tokyo.

Andreeva, J.V., I.S. Zhushchikhovskaya and N.A. Kononenko. 1986. *The Yankovsky Culture*. Moscow: Nauka.

Choe, C.-P. 1990. Origins of agriculture in Korea. *Korean Journal* 30, 4–14.

Ikawa-Smith, F. 1986. Late pleistocene and early holocene technologies. In *Windows on the Japanese Past: studies in archaeology and prehistory*, R.L. Pearson (ed.), 199–216. Ann Arbor: Michigan University Press, Center for Japanese Studies.

Korotkii, A.M. 1985. Quaternary sea-level fluctuation on the northwestern shelf of the Japan Sea. *Journal of Coastal Research* 1, 293–8.

Korotkii, A.M. 1994. Fluctuations of Japan Sea level and landscapes of coastal zone (stages of development and trends). *Bulletin of the Far Eastern Branch of the Russian Academy of Sciences* 1, 25–42. (In Russian.)

Kuang, Y. 1982. Zhanguo zhi liang han-di bei woju wenhua (The culture of Northern Woju between the Zhanguo and Han dynasties). *Heilongjiang wenwu congkan* 1, 25–31. (In Chinese.)

Lin, Y. 1985. Lun tuanjie wenua (About the Tuanjie culture). *Beifang wenwu* 1, 8–20. (In Chinese.)

Nelson, S.M. 1982. Recent progress in Korean Archaeology. In *Advances in World Archaeology* Vol. 1, F. Wendorf and A.E. Close (eds), 99–149. New York: Academic Press.

Rouse, I. 1986. *Migrations in Prehistory. Inferring population movement from cultural remains*. New Haven: Yale University Press.

Rowley-Conwy, P. 1984. Postglacial foraging and early farming economies in Japan and Korea: a west European perspective. *World Archaeology* 16, 28–42.

Sample, L.L. 1974. Tongsandong: a contribution to Korean neolithic culture history. *Arctic Anthropology* 11, 1–125.

So, K.T. 1986. *The Neolithic of Korea*. Pyongyang: Social Science Institute. (In Korean.)

Vostretsov, Y.E. 1987a. The dwellings and the sites of the Iron Age of the Russian Far East: The Krounovsky culture. Unpublished Ph.D. thesis, St. Petersburg, Institute of the History of Culture Material. (In Russian.)

Vostretsov, Y.E. 1987b. *The Dwellings and the Sites of the Iron Age: The Krounovsky culture*. St. Petersburg: Nauka. (In Russian.)

Yanushevich, Z.V., Y.E. Vostretsov and S.V. Makarova. 1990. *Palaeoethnobotanical finds at Primorie (Russia)*. Vladivostok: Nauka. (In Russian.)

Zhushchikhovskaya, I.S. 1994. Pottery-making of the prehistoric cultures of South of Russian Far East as palaeoeconomic phenomena. In *The Problems of Historical Interpretation of Archaeological Data*, Z.V. Andreeva, N.A. Kononenko and I.S. Zhushchikhovskaya (eds), 8–31. Moscow: Nauka.

18 Invisible pastoralists: an inquiry into the origins of nomadic pastoralism in the West African Sahel

KEVIN MACDONALD

Madame Dieterlen . . . gave me coffee in her caravan on the edge of the Dogon cliff. I asked her what traces the Bororo Peul – cattle herders of the Sahel – would leave for an archaeologist once they had moved off a campsite.

She thought for a moment, and answered, 'They scatter the ashes of their fires. No. Your archaeologist would not find those. But the women do weave little chaplets from grass stems and hang them from the branches of their shade tree.'

Bruce Chatwin, *The Songlines*

nomad – a member of a tribe roaming from place to place in search of pasture

The Concise Oxford Dictionary

INTRODUCTION: INVISIBILITY AND ARCHAEOLOGY

The origins of nomadic pastoralism in West Africa, *sensu stricto*, is a topic which has remained relatively unexplored archaeologically. That cattle keepers existed in the Sahara from at least 5000 BC, and in the Sahel from at least 2000 BC, is well attested by osteological remains and rock art depictions (cf. Blench and MacDonald in press). This lengthy pastoral heritage has already inspired detailed considerations of nomadic origins in north-eastern and eastern Africa (Sadr 1991; Marshall 1990a). However, in the western Sahel there are few archaeologically significant data points for the seasonal mobility, economic interactions, and degree of livestock dependence for ancient cattle keepers. In this preliminary enquiry, I will focus on two Malian material case studies: one from the second millennium BC, another from the first millennium AD. Primary questions to be addressed will include how relatively 'invisible' ancient nomadic populations may be perceived, and how diverse economic adaptations may be archaeologically recognized and classified.

Much has been written about the virtual invisibility, in an archaeological sense, of temporary nomadic encampments (cf. Bradley 1992; Cribb 1991). Although not as dire in their portent as Chatwin's anecdotal conversation with Germaine Dieterlen, they sound a strong note of caution that nomadic encampments, after the passage of millennia, will not be readily visible to the archaeologist. Indeed, Bradley's ethnoarchaeological investigations predicted that nomadic camps and activities would be:

> virtually invisible archaeologically in the seasons of maximum mobility, and marginally visible in those of minimum mobility. The location of the latter would correspond to areas habitable by sedentarists, and the remains of nomadic groups would thus be liable to masking by those of the sedentary groups with whom they interacted.
>
> (Bradley 1992: 214)

Add to this the fact that the existing nomadic peoples of Sahelian West Africa (the Peul, the Tuareg, and the Maure) do not, except where settled, possess their own unique ceramic industries, and our difficulties increase still further (Gallay et al. 1996; Nicolaisen and Nicolaisen 1997; Huysecom, pers. comm.).[1] Modern West African pastoralists have few distinct, durable 'ethnic markers' save Tuareg and Maure metalwork. In the pre-metallurgical past, if nomadic pastoralists did not make their own pottery, then we could only hope for specific, but as yet poorly defined, lithic industries. Unfortunately, these might not be very visible archaeologically. Thus, any archaeological inquiry into nomadic pastoralism must first cope with the perception of that particular economy in the archaeological landscape.

The 'invisibility' of peoples and economies in a landscape has, as a notion, received little attention in archaeology. The old chestnut 'absence of evidence is not evidence of absence' is about as far as discussion of the topic usually proceeds. But, as Ebbert (1992) has interestingly pointed out, archaeological sites per se are only loci of intense human depositional activity, with the greater landscape being also – in its totality – an archaeological site, albeit with lesser depositional density. Thus the term 'archaeological site' is misleading, particularly when dealing with mobile peoples, or the remains of their behaviour which is depositionally meagre. This thought is still not comforting to surveyors wading through grassland overgrowth and wondering whether or not to record an eroded potsherd or an undiagnostic lithic which has crossed their path as a 'locality.' In a region where ceramics have existed for nearly ten millennia and the landscape is still trodden daily by substantial herds and their herders, the utility of dating non-diagnostic, loose, unconcentrated finds, can easily be brought into question. True, there are the Saharan steinplätze of Gabriel (1987) – ephemeral stone groupings, ash lenses and bone scatters in the Central Sahara mostly dated to between 8000 and 4000 bp and are associated with mobile pastoral groups – but their preservation is an artefact of the quasi-abandonment of this vast region –

leaving its archaeological sites in a state of splendid, preserved isolation. In the Sahel, the archaeologist is not so 'lucky' and hydraulic, faunal, floral, and human activity continue apace, blurring the archaeological landscape.

Thus, in making a preliminary inquiry into the origins of Sahelian nomadism in West Africa, I am obliged to concentrate on evidence from loci of more concentrated activity, being: seasonal aggregations of pastoralists, burial grounds/monuments, or, more usually, places of their interaction with sedentarists. Eventually, it is hoped, purposefully gathered survey data will allow a consideration of the more mobile phases of ancient pastoral existence in the western Sahel.

WEST AFRICAN PASTORAL ECONOMIES: THEIR CLASSIFICATION AND ANTIQUITY

The classification of the historic and living pastoral economies of the world has not been a very consensual process, and there have been several different schemes in use over recent decades (e.g., Goldschmidt 1979; Barth 1973; Cribb 1982; Khazanov 1984). These sources have all been usefully reviewed by Sadr (1991) and a further classificatory scheme proposed. Here, I will synthesize the schemes of Barth (1973), Cribb (1982) and Sadr (1991), eliminating aspects which assume the pre-existence of state structures and central markets before nomadism, and introducing some further changes to increase their clarity and potential archaeological utility. These four economic classes include the extremes of live stock-keeping in terms of relative mobility and ethnic interaction:

1   *Mixed or household economies* – where both cultivation and stock-keeping are undertaken at the household level. This category would include agricultural societies with limited household stock-keeping and assumes full sedentism, with only limited movement of stock around the settlement or the stall-rearing of animals.

    Archaeological assumptions based on ethnographic analogies: deep accumulations of settlement debris and/or large settlements with evidence for both pastoral and agricultural production at a household/village level; site location should always be in fertile zones.

2   *Segmented or agropastoral economies* – where herding and cultivation or gathering is practised by two discrete social segments of one self-sufficient ethnic group (via either caste, age, or gender division). Here it is assumed that herd sizes exceed that which can be carried by one locality. Thus, one segment of society undertakes a seasonal round with the cattle, spending only part of the year with the more localized cultivating or gathering segment.

    Archaeological assumptions based on ethnographic analogies: a (probable) single tradition of material culture with a distribution in varied ecological zones, having both ephemeral campsites (shallow and/or small) and seasonal aggregations (large settlements).

3 *Symbiotic economies of nomad and sedentarist* – where two or more distinct ethnic/linguistic groups form a single economic unit, with at least one being specialized, nomadic herders and the other(s) specialized, sedentarist cultivators. Such a situation can exist as either a biased (patron and client) symbiosis or as a true (unbiased) symbiosis.

Archaeological assumptions based on ethnographic analogies: as segmented economies, but with material culture differences between the two groups being more likely. Thus one might expect two technologically or stylistically different lithic and/or pottery assemblages in one contemporary 'sedentary' deposit.

4 *Full or independent pastoral nomads* – where a fully mobile pastoral group sustains itself principally from the produce of its herd and only occasionally from hunting and gathering activities (no cultivation). Trade with other groups does not form an essential part of the subsistence economy, but it does sometimes occur.

Archaeological assumptions based on ethnographic analogies: little durable material culture made by the group itself, no large sedentary camps or debris accumulations, primarily visible through trade in stock to sedentarists.

Categories 1 and 4 are particularly important. The first subsumes the multiple categories of Cribb (1982) and Sadr (1991) for specialized agricultural (with rare stock-keeping) and predominantly agricultural (with limited stock-keeping) which are merely clinal, and almost indistinguishable archaeologically. The fourth category is a variation on previous categorizations, as it purposefully leaves room for a type of non-state-dependent, almost purely pastoral economy which does not exist in West Africa today but might have existed during prehistory. Indeed, for the fourth category the only possible African analogue is the Masaai of Kenya (cf. Jacobs 1975), but even their independence may be debatable, and one must admit that such a 'pure' pastoral economic system might never have existed in Africa.

It is becoming gradually apparent that some form of pastoral production long preceded cereal agriculture in most of Africa. Whilst this might come as a shock to generations of archaeologists schooled on the truism that agriculture precedes pastoralism, Africanists have been facing up to the consequences of an entirely new set of data (Blench and MacDonald in press). Not only does it now seem probable, on the basis of DNA and mounting archaeological evidence, that cattle domestication was an indigenous African innovation at *c.* 8000 + bp (Wendorf and Schild 1994; Bradley *et al.* 1996), but extensive palaeobotanical searches of the western Sahel show no definite agricultural evidence (or even evidence for field clearance) before 3500 bp (Ballouche and Neumann 1995), with livestock being present in arid West Africa from *c.* 6500 bp (Gautier 1987; MacDonald and MacDonald in press).

Admittedly, some form of cultivation of crops without domestication may have been practised in North-east Africa from $c.$ 6000 bp (Haaland 1995). But one must then pose the question, what was the economic organization of Saharan and Sahelian pastoralists during the millennia before fully developed cereal agriculture?

MIXED, SEGMENTED, SYMBIOTIC OR INDEPENDENT?: DHAR TICHITT AND THE MIDDLE NIGER (2000–800 BC)

In recent years, research into Middle Niger pre-iron-using societies has concentrated on two desiccated basins to the north-west and south-east of the modern Inland Delta: the Méma and the Gourma (Figure 18.1). In both of these regions there is evidence for cattle-keeping, and for cultural diversity during the second millennium BC[2] (MacDonald 1996a, 1996b). Here we will focus on the more northerly Méma region, which supplies a puzzling case study of the development of early pastoral economies in West Africa.

The principal archaeological facies relevant to this inquiry is the Ndondi Tossokel facies, an aspect, or regional variant, of the larger Tichitt tradition (MacDonald 1996a). The original centre of the Tichitt tradition was along the Dhar Tichitt and Dhar Walata escarpments in south-western Mauritania. There, quasi-or proto-urban settlements, ranging up to $c.$ 95 ha in area and built of dry stone, flourished from $c.$ 1350–800 BC (Munson 1971, 1976, 1980, 1989; Holl 1986, 1993). Economically, people of the Tichitt tradition herded cattle and small livestock and grew domestic millet. However, the limited nature of field investigations in the area has not allowed the clear definition of the economic organization of Tichitt. In other words, on the basis of sites in Mauritania we have little to tell whether farming and herding were undertaken contemporaneously by different segments of a single society, or even whether the Tichitt polity was composed of more than one ethnic group. On the other hand, fieldwork across the border in Mali seems to give a hint about this economic organization.

The fact that Tichitt tradition settlements existed beside the ancient Inland Niger Delta, in an area known as the Méma, is relatively recent news (cf. MacDonald 1994, 1996a; MacDonald and Van Neer 1994). Although Tichitt tradition ceramics have been recorded near the present delta (the site of Tondodie, near Diafarabé), in western Mali (near Kayes), and in Méma region (around Nampala), it is only in the Méma that intensive and systematic investigation has been conducted.

There would appear to have been at least two contemporary facies in the Méma dating to the second millennium BC: that of Ndondi Tossokel (derivative of the Tichitt tradition), and that of Kobadi (part of a tradition by that same name). Sites from this period documented by survey and excavation in the Méma are of three principal types: (1) small, shallow accumulations of debris at the edge of, or just within, the palaeo-floodplain

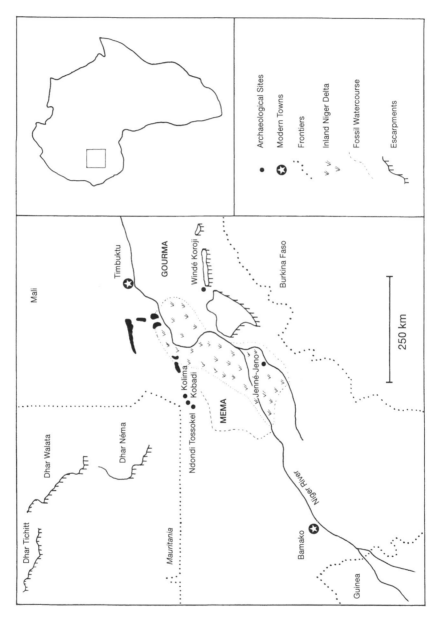

Figure 18.1 Map of south–eastern Mauritania and the Middle Niger region of Mali, showing localities referred to in the text.

with only Tichitt (Ndondi Tossokel) ceramics and thinly scattered livestock and fish remains; (2) fairly large (1–8 ha) fish-bone and shell middens within the floodplain having only Kobadi tradition ceramics; and (3) larger and more deeply stratified aggregated sites possessing mixed ceramic assemblages of Tichitt (Ndondi Tossokel) and Kobadi wares, with masses of fish-bone (e.g. c. 20,000 identifiable fragments from excavations) and small quantities of cattle and ovicaprine bone (only 17 identifiable elements from the excavations) (Table 18.1). All sites feature polished tools/ornaments and chipped stone tools fashioned from Mauritanian phthanite and chert, most of it already imported in a finished form.

The Kobadi tradition would appear to have been of an entirely fisher-hunter-gatherer economic orientation, and has been documented in the Malian Sahara and throughout most of the Middle Niger and Niger bend area (e.g. Raimbault and Dutour 1989; Togola and Raimbault 1991; MacDonald and Van Neer 1994; MacDonald 1996b; Raimbault 1996). Kobadi ceramics differ greatly from those of Tichitt, having entirely different rim forms (simple rather than everted), decorative tools (comb and spatula rather than cord-wrapped stick), and fabric (sand and sponge temper rather than chaff) (Walicka Zeh and MacDonald in prep.) (Figure 18.2).

At the aggregate sites, excavation has shown that Kobadi ceramics preceded those of Tichitt. At Kolima-Sud, a date of 3365 ± 70 bp (1740–1530 BC), is associated with the earliest (layer V, Kobadi) occupation layer of the site. The appearance of Tichitt tradition ceramics, cattle and ovicaprine bones, and cattle figurines begins in layer III, with a date at the layer II/III transition falling at 3084 ± 73 bp (1420–1230 BC). Kobadi tradition ceramics then appear to continue alongside the Tichitt ceramics until abandonment (MacDonald 1996a).

One interesting facet of the 'Méma expression' of the Tichitt tradition (the Ndondi Tossokel facies), is that unlike the principal Tichitt sites where all ceramics without exception are chaff tempered, those of the Méma are not – being grog tempered instead (MacDonald 1996a, 1996b). This may be economically significant, since the majority of grain impressions on post-1300 BC Tichitt pottery are of domestic millet (Munson 1976, Amblard and Pernès 1989). This important difference may be explained in a variety of ways. It may be that this temper choice is an element of 'technical

Table 18.1 Size (in hectares) and location of Kobadi, Ndondi Tossokel and aggregate sites (with material culture elements of both traditions)

Facies/location	>1 ha	1–3 ha	4–8 ha	8–12 ha
Kobadi (within floodplain)	—	1	1	—
Aggregate sites (within floodplain)	—	1	2	1
Ndondi Tossokel (within floodplain)	1	1	—	—
Ndondi Tossokel (edge of floodplain)	9	2	1	—

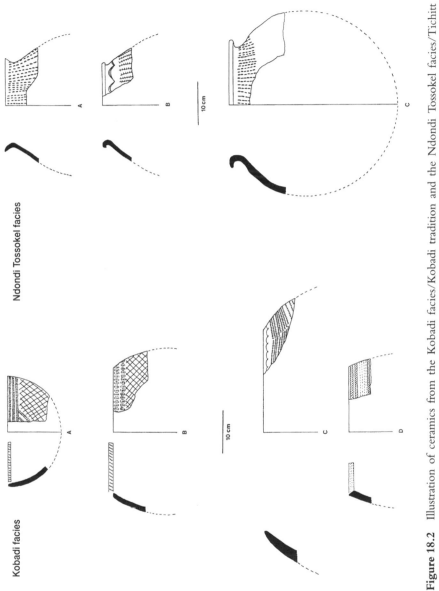

Figure 18.2 Illustration of ceramics from the Kobadi facies/Kobadi tradition and the Ndondi Tossokel facies/Tichitt tradition: provenance of the Kobadi ceramics: A&B = 1251-1, C = Bérétouma 1121-2, D = Tiabel Goudiodié; provenance of the Ndondi Tossokel ceramics: A = Kolima-Sud, B = 1251-2, C = Ndondi Tossokel 1119-1.

Kobadi facies

Ndondi Tossokel facies

style' differing between two castes or ethnicities of the broader Tichitt tradition. Alternatively, it could have something to do with the season of firing of the Ndondi Tossokel facies pottery (e.g., it could have been fired outside the autumnal harvest season). Or, it may be that the segment of the Tichitt society living in, or seasonally visiting, the Méma did not themselves practise cultivation, perhaps because at that time the Méma was perpetually swampy and thus unsuitable for millet agriculture.

It is tempting to opt for the third option for a variety of reasons. First, there are no exclusively Ndondi Tossokel settlements exceeding 6 ha in size. This is in sharp contrast to the large 30–95 ha settlements known from the Mauritanian Tichitt–Walata region. The Ndondi Tossokel settlements' small size and low artefact density would seem to indicate more ephemeral occupations.

Second, there is the question of stone raw materials. The Méma, being a floodplain composed of reworked dunes, lacks any significant raw materials in its proximity, save sandstone from the low ridge of Boulel. Thus its 'Late Stone Age' occupation features little evidence of stone-working and fairly impoverished lithic industries (most formal tools of the Kobadi tradition are in bone or imported stone) (Raimbault and Dutour 1989; MacDonald 1994). The use of Mauritanian raw materials (Phthanite – a type of siltstone, and chert) at both Kobadi and Ndondi Tossokel sites indicates an active exchange network in stone materials necessitating frequent contact with the relatively 'raw material rich' zones of the Mauritanian escarpments.

Finally, ecological conditions in the Méma during the second millennium BC would not have been favourable for cattle all year around. Faunal samples from the sites of Kobadi and Kolima-Sud indicate that at least from 2000 BC the region was as swampy as the modern Inland Niger Delta if not more so (Raimbault et al. 1987; MacDonald and Van Neer 1994). Indeed, faunal samples from Kolima-Sud indicate only aquatic animals until post-c. 1500 BC, with numerous fish remains indicative of shallow- and deep-water fishing, as well as hippo, waterbuck and sitatunga (an aquatic antelope now only existing in the forest regions of West and Central Africa; cf. Kingdon 1997). After 1500 BC there is an increase in shallow water taxa, and also a wider range of antelope taxa. It is possible that a hydrological change at that time, from almost continual lacustrine innundation to a more seasonal innundation, allowed the entrance of herds into the Méma for the first time. As Tichitt–Walata, due to the recent Holocene arid trend, was suffering from shrinking bodies of permanent water and grazing land, a seasonal run for herds to the edge of the Inland Niger Delta would have become desirable if not essential (Person et al. 1996). During the wet season, any cattle in the region would have been exposed to a greater risk from waterborne diseases and hoof-rot. So, just as today in the Inland Delta, prehistoric pastoralists could have visited seasonally at the time of low-waters, grazing on the rich floodplain grasses and trading with its sedentary inhabitants (cf. Gallais 1967, 1984). Although most settlement would keep to the edge of the floodplain, allowing access to floodplain resources while minimalizing disease risk, some groups may have lived side by side with fisherfolk in their principal villages on the floodplain, as evidenced by material culture distributions, and current settlement (Gallais 1967; McIntosh 1993).

What then was the pastoral economic system of the Ndondi Tossokel facies? With the limited data at hand, the most elegant argument possible for relative mobility would be a seasonal presence of pastoral 'Tichitt–Walata populations' along the ancient Inland Niger Delta. They could have been a segment of the population set off by sex or age group (e.g. young adult men), or they could have been a discrete 'pastoral' caste or ethnicity within Tichitt–Walata society. The contemporary inter-mixing of Kobadi and Tichitt artefacts at many sites argues for interaction and exchange between the two entities, and perhaps some eventual form of symbiosis. At Kolima-Sud, cattle remains are found in the same middens as massive numbers of fish remains, possibly attesting to animals traded to the Kobadi 'fisherfolk' in exchange for fish and wild(?) grain. Future research on the ephemeral edge of floodplain scatters of the Ndondi Tossokel facies, could give valuable evidence concerning the timing of developments in the Méma, since it is possible that seasonal migrations were made to the edge of the floodplain before any real interaction between the Kobadi and Tichitt traditions developed. Thus, the material culture 'alliance' to the sendentary Tichitt polity, and evident exchange with the Kobadi fisherfolk, would seem to indicate either a segmented agro-pastoral system or a symbiotic pastoral one, with the former possibly trending towards the latter over time.

NOMADS AND URBAN CENTRES: THE CASE OF JENNÉ-JENO (AD 450–1450)

Jenné-Jeno is perhaps the best known and most completely published urban site yet excavated in West Africa. Three major research seasons have been undertaken there (1977, 1981, 1996/7) by Roderick and Susan McIntosh (McIntosh and McIntosh 1993; McIntosh 1995). The 33 ha mud-brick settlement mound of Jenné-Jeno has over five metres of deposits, stretching in date from c. 200 BC to AD 1450. The site was at its full size of 33 ha, with several substantial outlying settlements, at or before AD 450 (McIntosh 1995). During the late 1980s I had the opportunity to analyse the fauna of this site (excluding the fish remains, analysed by Wim Van Neer), and have since published the results (MacDonald 1995). The most substantive, and relevant, faunal samples come from occupation Phases III (AD 450–850) and IV (AD 850–1450). Metric data on cattle from these periods allow interesting insights into cattle populations and some of the ancient economic interactions of the city.

Although measurable elements from West African sites are usually scarce, there is some marked metrical divergence visible in such cattle remains as have been published. From these there would appear to be at least three broad cattle size classes present in West Africa between 2000 BC and AD 1400. A large size class is known from the site of Windé Koroji Ouest (2200–950 BC), Gao Sany (AD 900–1200) and Siouré Phase IV–V (AD 950–1400) and is comparable in height to the large cattle of Ngamuriak, Kenya (Marshall 1990b). These may pertain to the now largely interbred native African longhorn breeds. The middle group, documented by the famous 'Adrar Bous cow' (Carter and Clark 1976), the Kolima-Sud cattle (MacDonald 1994) and the Middle Senegal Valley assemblages (Siouré, Cubalel and Tulel Fobo, c. AD 0–950) are comparable in size to modern Ndama breeds (MacDonald and MacDonald n.d.; Van Neer and Bocoum 1991). The smaller type, as documented at Kintampo, is close to that of the West African dwarf shorthorn (Carter and Flight 1972)[3].

Although the faunal sample from the early phases of Jenné Jeno's occupation are too small to be of use, it would appear on the basis of size distributions that at least two distinctive cattle populations were being consumed at the site during its floruit (Phase III, AD 450–850) (Figure 18.3).[4] During this phase both 'middle-sized' and 'small' breeds are present, and it should be noted that this is also the case for sheep and goats for which both 'dwarf' and 'savanna' varieties are present (MacDonald 1995). However, during Phase IV (AD 850–1400) there is only evidence of a single 'small' breed cattle population. Since faunal samples came from five different exposures spread widely over the site, this is unlikely to be an artefact of sampling.

This metric distribution may be a fascinating clue – almost a calling-card – for intensive interaction with nomadic pastoral populations during this period, which would otherwise be invisible. As noted above, today transhumant Fulani/Peule pastoralists make a seasonal incursion into the Inland Niger Delta, during the time of the low waters, trading their cattle into urban centres and grazing on the grass of the delta (Gallais 1967, 1984). The presence of the Fulani/Peule in the delta, and this system, dates back at least to the fifteenth century AD, although other groups may have practised a similar system earlier (Belcher 1997).

There is no material culture evidence to indicate any ethnic diversity at Jenné-Jeno during its occupation (McIntosh 1995), although social factors may have conspired to mask the material expression of different perceived identities. As noted previously, modern pastoral nomads in West Africa do not usually make their own ceramics, leaving that to their sedentary trading partners or 'slaves/serfs' (e.g., the Bella and the Rimaibé for the Tuareg and Fulani respectively). So other than their animals, and now long-decayed leather and basketry work, there would be little distinctive trace of them in the ancient urban milieu. Interestingly, Annette Schmidt (pers. comm.) has recorded numerous pottery and bone scatters with no architectural traces on dune-tops around the margins of larger settlements in the Inland Niger Delta.

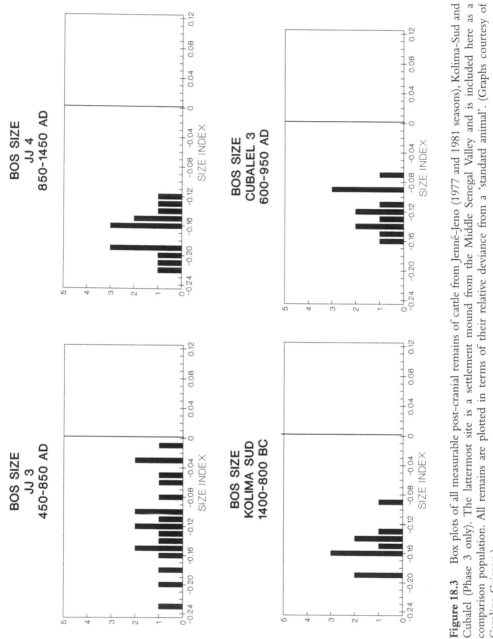

Figure 18.3 Box plots of all measurable post-cranial remains of cattle from Jenné-Jeno (1977 and 1981 seasons), Kolima-Sud and Cubalel (Phase 3 only). The lattermost site is a settlement mound from the Middle Senegal Valley and is included here as a comparison population. All remains are plotted in terms of their relative deviance from a 'standard animal'. (Graphs courtesy of Caroline Grigson.)

Likewise, during the 1989/90 Méma survey Téréba Togola and myself observed many small 'iron age' pottery scatters at some remove from mud-brick towns (Togola 1993; MacDonald 1994). These small scatters may have been the remains of small farming hamlets, or they could have been pastoral camps utilizing pottery obtained from neighbouring settlements; excavation is needed to test these hypotheses.

We know very little about the first millennium AD pastoralists from West Africa. Travellers' tales and later histories refer to large cattle herds either in the lands or the cities of the 'Empire of Ghana' (c. AD 300–1170), but there is little specific mention of the people who were keeping them (Lewicki 1974). Before the advent of the Fulani/Peule in the Middle Niger, scholars have generally assumed the existence of a specialized pastoral component in the region's economy (Levtzion, pers. comm.), and certainly there is evidence for mobile pastoral populations in the Sahara and Sahel before 1000 BC (see below). However, the period of c. 800 BC–AD 1400 is rather obscure. Pastoral Maure and Berber populations existed in the Sahara during this period, but there is little clear evidence for their presence in proximity to the Inland Delta. Still, since ecological factors limit the keeping of anything other than waterborne-disease-resistant dwarf cattle in the delta all year round, the presence of larger breeds argues for incoming cattle from the Sahel. Thus, one does not know whether this was a mobile segment of Middle Niger's population, or a discrete ethnic group in symbiosis with deltaic populations, although modern and historic analogy would support the latter.

CONCLUSIONS

In this chapter I have primarily concentrated on two case studies from the past 4,000 years in Mali, but it should be remembered that cattle-keeping populations have been active in the West African Sahara for much longer than this. In particular one can note the many tumuli of cattle-keepers dotting the deserts of Niger. In recent years many have been directly dated, and it can now be shown that they range over a vast expanse of time (c. 6000–1000 bp; Paris 1984, 1996). Settlements are, however, more difficult to locate than tumuli, and more regional survey work, coupled with test excavations, is necessary in this arid region before more detailed economic speculations can be made about these vanished peoples.

When considering both modern and archaeologicaly attested African pastoral societies, one sees persistently one of two patterns: segmented societies with a single ethnic identity, or two ethnically different societies in symbiosis. Today, and historically, the latter is more common. At least from 1500 BC onwards, our limited evidence would indicate the existence of both economic forms in the western Sahel (see also McIntosh 1993). The predominance of these two economic patterns is in part due to the particularities of West African ecology: the Sahara, the Sahel, and the inundated plains. To stay still with cattle, with the exception of dwarf animals, is virtually impossible. The seasonal round, either via splitting a single society or through the alliance of varied cultures, is an ecological imperative. Indeed, the modern Middle Niger region provides a host of examples of ethnically linked economic variants inspired by this unique ecology: Bozo and Somono fisherfolk, Fulani/Peule and Tuareg nomadic pastoralists, Soninke and Bambara cultivators, etc. (Gallais 1967, 1984). The archaeological time-depth of the resultant symbiotic, economic web is becoming an increasingly important research focus (McIntosh 1993; MacDonald 1994), but for the archaeologist the most daunting task is how to perceive those highly mobile, 'invisible' pastoralists? It is hoped that this preliminary essay will inspire debate and more focused research on this question.

ACKNOWLEDGEMENTS

The primary data used in this article derived from survey and excavations carried out in the Méma in 1989 and 1990 by Téréba Togola, Helen Haskell and myself, and from my analysis of the Jenné-Jeno faunal assemblage excavated by Roderick and Susan McIntosh in 1981. Special thanks go to David Harris and Peter Ucko for encouraging me to give the origins of West African pastoral systems further thought, and to write this chapter. Thanks also to Andrew Reid for making some useful comments on a draft of this chapter.

NOTES

1 Nicolaisen and Nicolaisen (1997, I: 336) note, 'Pastoral Tuareg of the Ahaggar acquire most of their pots from the sedentary agriculturists of their own country, but they also buy some pots of superior quality during trading expeditions to the Sudan.'
2 Throughout the text, capitalized 'BC' indicates calibrated radiocarbon dates or time ranges derived from calibrated radicarbon dates; lower case 'bc' or 'bp' indicate non-calibrated radiocarbon dates or time ranges derived from non-calibrated radiocarbon dates.
3 For information on the modern cattle breeds of West Africa, see Epstein 1971.
4 I am very grateful to Dr Caroline Grigson for her manipulation of this data, and the production of Figure 18.3, using her standard animal metric system.

REFERENCES

Amblard, S. and Pernès, J. 1989. The identification of cultivated pearl millet (*Pennisetum*) amongst plant impressions on pottery from Oued Chebbi (Dhar Oualata, Mauritania). *African Archaeological Review* 7, 117–26.
Ballouche, A. and K. Neumann. 1995. Pollen from Oursi/ Burkina Faso and charcoal

from NE Nigeria: a contribution to the Holocene vegetation history of the West African Sahel. *Vegetation History and Archaeobotany* 4, 31–9.

Barth, F. 1973. A general perspective on nomad–sedentary relations in the Middle East. In *The Desert and the Sown: nomads in a wider society,* C. Nelson (ed.), 11–22. Berkeley: University of California Press.

Belcher, S. 1997. La présence peule dans les épopées mandingue. In *Peuls et Mandingues: dialectique des constructions identitaires,* M. De Bruijn and H. Van Dijk (eds), 129–46. Paris: Karthala–ASC.

Blench, R.M. and K.C. MacDonald (eds). In press. *The Origins and Development of African Livestock.* London: UCL Press.

Bradley, D.G., D.E. MacHugh, P. Cunningham and R. T. Loftus. 1996. Mitochondrial diversity and the origins of African and European cattle. *Proceedings of the National Academy of Sciences, USA* 93, 5131–5.

Bradley, R.J. 1992. *Nomads in the Archaeological Record.* Meroitica No. 13. Berlin: Akademie Verlag.

Carter, P.L. and J.D. Clark. 1976. Adrar Bous and African cattle. In *Proceedings of the Panafrican Congress of Prehistory, Addis Ababa 1971,* A. Berhanou, J. Chevaillon and J.E.G. Sutton (eds), 487–93. Addis Ababa: Provisional Military Government of Socialist Ethiopia, Ministry of Culture.

Carter, P.L. and C. Flight. 1972. A report on the fauna from the sites of Ntereso and Kintampo rock shelter six in Ghana, with evidence for the practise of animal husbandry in the second millennium BC. *Man* 7, 277–82.

Cribb, R. 1982. The archaeological dimensions of Near Eastern nomadic pastoralism: towards a spatial model of unstable settlement systems. Unpublished Ph.D. thesis, University of Southampton.

Cribb, R. 1991. *Nomads in Archaeology.* Cambridge: Cambridge University Press.

Ebert, J.I. 1992. *Distributional Archaeology.* Albuquerque: New Mexico University Press.

Epstein, H. 1971. *The Origin of the Domestic Animals of Africa.* New York: Africana Publishing Corporation.

Gabriel, B. 1987. Palaeoecological evidence from neolithic fireplaces in the Sahara. *African Archaeological Review* 5, 93–104.

Gallais, J. 1967. *Le delta intérieur du Niger et ses bordures: étude de géographie régionale.* 2 volumes. Dakar: IFAN.

Gallais, J. 1984. *Hommes du Sahel.* Paris: Flammarion.

Gallay, A., E. Huysecom, A. Mayor and G. de Ceuninck. 1996. *Hier et Aujourd'hui: des poteries et des femmes, ceramiques traditionelles du Mali.* Document du Département d'anthropologie et d'écologie no. 22. Geneva: Département d'anthropologie et d'écologie, Université de Genève.

Gautier, A. 1987. Prehistoric men and cattle in North Africa: a dearth of data and a surfeit of models. In *Prehistory of Arid North Africa,* A. Close (ed.), 163–87. Dallas: SMU Press.

Goldschmidt, W. 1979. A general model for pastoral social systems. In *Pastoral Production and Society,* 15–28. Cambridge: Cambridge University Press.

Haaland, R. 1995. Sedentism, cultivation, and plant domestication in the Holocene Middle Nile region. *Journal of Field Archaeology* 22, 157–74.

Holl, A. 1986. *Economie et Société Néolithique du Dhar Tichitt (Mauritanie).* Editions Recherche sur les Civilisations, Mémoire no. 69. Paris: Editions Recherche sur les Civilisations.

Holl, A. 1993. Late neolithic cultural landscapes in southeastern Mauritania: an essay in spatiometrics. In *Spatial Boundaries and Social Dynamics: case studies from food-producing societies,* A. Holl and T.E. Levy (eds), 95–133. Ann Arbor: International Monographs in Prehistory.

Jacobs, A.H. 1975. African pastoralists: some general remarks. *Anthropological Quarterly* 38, 144–54.

Khazanov, A.M. 1984. *Nomads and the Outside World*. Cambridge: Cambridge University Press.

Kingdon, J. 1997. *The Kingdon Field Guide to African Mammals*. London: Academic Press.

Lewicki, T. 1974. *West African Food in the Middle Ages*. Cambridge: Cambridge University Press.

MacDonald, K.C. 1994. *Socio-economic diversity and the origins of cultural complexity along the Middle Niger* (2000 BC to AD 300). Unpublished Ph.D. thesis, University of Cambridge.

MacDonald, K.C. 1995. The faunal remains (mammals, birds, and reptiles). In *Excavations at Jenné-Jeno, Hambarketolo, and Kaniana (Inland Niger Delta, Mali), the 1981 Season*, S.K. McIntosh (ed.), 291–318. Berkeley: University of California Press.

MacDonald, K.C. 1996a. Tichitt–Walata and the Middle Niger: evidence for cultural contact in the second millenium BC. In *Aspects of African Archaeology: Papers from the 10th Congress of the Pan-African Association for Prehistory and Related Studies*, G. Pwiti and R. Soper (eds), 429–40. Harare: University of Zimbabwe Publications.

MacDonald, K.C. 1996b. The Windé Koroji complex: evidence for the peopling of the eastern Inland Niger Delta (2100–500 BC). *Préhistoire Anthropologie Méditerranéennes* 5, 147–65.

MacDonald, K.C. and R.M. MacDonald. In press. The origins and development of domesticated animals in arid West Africa. In *The Origins and Development of African Livestock*, R.M. Blench and K.C. MacDonald (eds). London: UCL Press.

MacDonald, K.C. and R.H. MacDonald. n.d. Report on the mammalian, avian and reptilian remains from the 1990 season at the sites of Cubalel and Siouré (Sénégal). Unpublished manuscript on file, Department of Anthropology, Rice University, Houston.

MacDonald, K.C. and W. Van Neer. 1994. Specialised fishing peoples in the Later Holocene of the Méma region (Mali). In *Fish Exploitation in the Past*, W. Van Neer (ed.), 243–51. Annales du Musée Royal de l'Afrique Centrale, Sciences Zoologiques, No. 274. Tervuren: Musée Royal de l'Afrique Centrale.

McIntosh, R.J. 1993. The pulse theory: genesis and accommodation of specialization in the Middle Niger. *Journal of African History* 34, 181–220.

McIntosh, S.K. (ed.). 1995. *Excavations at Jenné-Jeno, Hambarketolo, and Kaniana (Inland Niger Delta, Mali), the 1981 Season*. Berkeley: University of California Press.

McIntosh, S.K. and R.J. McIntosh. 1993. Cities without citadels: understanding urban origins along the Middle Niger. In *The Archaeology of Africa: food, metals and towns*, T. Shaw, P. Sinclair, B. Andah and A. Okpoko (eds), 622–41. London: Routledge.

Marshall, F. 1990a. Origins of specialized pastoral production in East Africa. *American Anthropologist* 92, 873–94.

Marshall, F. 1990b. Cattle herds and caprine flocks. In *Early Pastoralists of South-western Kenya*, P. Robertshaw (ed.), 205–60. Memoir 11, The British Institute in Eastern Africa. Nairobi: British Institute in Eastern Africa.

Munson, P.J. 1971. The Tichitt tradition: a late prehistoric occupation of the southwestern Sahara. Unpublished Ph.D. thesis, University of Illinois at Urbana-Champaign.

Munson, P.J. 1976. Archaeological data on the origins of cultivation in the south-western Sahara and their implications for West Africa. Origins of African plant domestication. In *Origins of African Plant Domestication*, J. De Wet and A. Stemmler (eds), 187–209. The Hague: Muton.

Munson, P.J. 1980. Archaeology and the prehistoric origins of the Ghana empire. *Journal of African History* 21, 457–66.

Munson, P.J. 1989. About economie et Société Néolithique du Dhar Tichitt (Augustin Holl). *Sahara* 2, 107–9.

Nicolaisen, J. and I. Nicolaisen. 1997. *The Pastoral Tuareg*. 2 volumes. London: Thames and Hudson.

Paris, F. 1984. *La Région d'In Gall – Tegidda N Tesemt (Niger): Programme Archéologique d'urgence 1977–1981. III. Les Sépultures du Néolithique Final à l'Islam*. Etudes Nigériennes No. 50. Niamey: Institut de Recherches en Sciences Humaines.

Person, A., S. Amblard-Pison, N. Saoudi, J.-F. Saliège and M. Gérard. 1996. Les Dhars de la Mauritanie sud-orientale: environnements refuges sahariens au Néolithique. *Préhistoire Anthropologie Méditerranéennes* 5, 119–34.

Raimbault, M. 1996. L'impact de la dégradation climatique Holocène sur les Néolithiques du Sahara malien et les données du faciès sahélien de Kobadi. *Préhistoire Anthropologie Méditerranéennes* 5, 135–46.

Raimbault, M. and Dutour, O. 1989. Les Nouvelles Données du Site Néolithique de Kobadi dans le Sahel malien: la mission 1989. *Travaux du LAPMO* 1989, 175–83.

Raimbault, M., C. Guérin and M. Faure. 1987. Les Vertébrés du gisement Néolithique du Kobadi. *Archaeozoologia* 1, 219–38.

Sadr, K. 1991. *The Development of Nomadism in Ancient Northeast Africa*. Philadelphia: University of Pennsylvania Press.

Togola, T. 1993. Archaeological investigations of iron age sites in the Méma region. Unpublished Ph.D. thesis, Department of Anthropology, Rice University.

Togola, T. and M. Raimbault. 1991. Les Missions d'inventaire dans le Méma, Kareri et Farimaké (1984 et 1985). In *Recherches Archéologiques au Mali*, M. Raimbault and K. Sanogo (eds), 81–90. Paris: Karthala.

Van Neer, W. and H. Bocoum. 1991. Etude archéozoologique de Tulel-Fobo, site protohistorique (IVe–Xe siècle) de la moyenne vallée du Fleuve Sénégal (République du Sénégal). *Archaeozoologia* 4, 93–114.

Walicka Zeh, R. and K.C. MacDonald. In prep. Sponge Spicule Temper and the Second Millennium BC pottery assemblages of the Middle Niger (Mali).

Wendorf, F. and R. Schild. 1994. Are the early holocene cattle in the eastern Sahara domestic or wild? *Evolutionary Anthropology* 3, 118–28.

19   Evidence for agricultural change in the Balikh basin, northern Syria

WILLEM VAN ZEIST

INTRODUCTION

The discussion presented in this chapter is based upon plant remains retrieved from settlement sites in the upper Balikh valley of northern Syria: Tell Hammam et-Turkman, Tell Sabi Abyad I and nearby Tell Sabi Abyad II (Figures 19.1 and 19.2). These sites provide good archaeobotanical evidence of possible agricultural change in this important area. Together the sites have yielded a long archaeological record of plants, from the Later Pre-Pottery Neolithic to the Late Bronze Age, although the record is not continuous. In addition, environmental conditions are the same for Sabi Abyad and

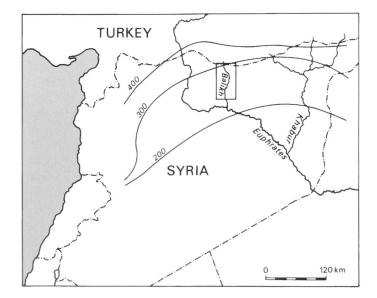

Figure 19.1 Location map. The framed area is shown in Figure 19.2. The isohyets for northern Syria are drawn after Alex (1984).

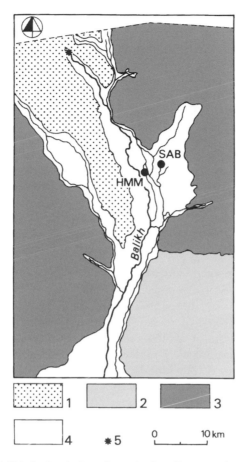

Figure 19.2   The Balikh basin: 1. Interfluve; 2. Gypsiferous soils; 3. Calcareous soils; 4. Alluvial valley sediments; 5. Spring of Ain al-Arous. (HMM = Hammam et-Turkman; SAB = Sabi Abyad.) After Boerma (1988).

Hammam et-Turkman, less than 5 km apart. The periods represented in the archaeobotanical record are listed in Table 19.1.

The sites

Tell Sabi Abyad I and Tell Sabi Abyad II are part of a cluster of four prehistoric mounds. The largest of these mounds, Tell Sabi Abyad I, measures 240 by 170 m at its base and is up to 10 m high. Since 1986, excavations at the site have been directed by Dr P.M.M.G. Akkermans, formerly under the auspices of the University of Amsterdam but since 1991 on behalf of the National Museum of Antiquities, Leiden. Sabi Abyad I was a major prehistoric settlement in the sixth millennium bc (see Table 19.1 note). Pre-Halaf neolithic levels of occupation have been exposed on a limited scale ~ly. The late sixth millennium occupation (Transitional period, Early Halaf:

Table 19.1   Archaeological periods represented at Sabi Abyad and Hammam et-Turkman.

Period	Site	Dating
Pre-Pottery Neolithic B	Sabi Abyad II	6500–6000 bc
Pre-Halaf Neolithic	Sabi Abyad I	5800/5700—5200 bc
Transitional period	Sabi Abyad I	5200–5100 bc
Early Halaf	Sabi Abyad I	5100–5000 bc
Ubaid	Hammam	4500–3700 bc
Late Chalcolithic	Hammam	3700–3000 bc
Early Bronze IV	Hammam	2400/2500–2000 bc
Middle Bronze	Hammam	2000–1550 bc/BC
Late Bronze	Hammam/Sabi Abyad I	1550–1250 BC
Parthian/Roman/Byzantine	Hammam	200 BC–AD 700

Note: The excavators of Sabi Abyad and Hammam use conventional (uncalibrated) radiocarbon dates and, for the later periods, traditional historical dates which may be in conflict with calibrated radiocarbon dates (for the Hammam C14 dates, see Mook and van Loon 1988). The present author decided to follow the excavators' forms, but instead of the notation 'BC' prefers to give the dates in years bc (as is usual for uncalibrated C14 dates). Only for the Late Bronze Age does a dating in years BC (in calendar years) seem justified. Occasionally, uncalibrated radiocarbon dates are given in years BP (Before Present = 1950).

see Table 19.1) consisted of rectangular, multi-roomed houses and circular structures, so-called tholoi, which probably served for storage. Remains of Middle Assyrian (Late Bronze II) occupation, dating from the second half of the thirteenth century BC, included a huge, monumental building, referred to as the Fortress, and domestic structures. It is likely that Late Bronze Sabi Abyad was an Assyrian border garrison town (Akkermans and Rossmeisl 1990; Akkermans 1993; Akkermans et al. 1993; Akkermans and Verhoeven 1995).

Tell Sabi Abyad II measures 125 by 75 m and rises about 4.5 m above the surrounding fields. Fieldwork at Sabi Abyad II started as a sideline of the excavations at Sabi Abyad I. The stratigraphic sequence of the tell was investigated in a 'stepped trench' consisting of three N–S oriented trenches (9 by 2 m). Traces of rectangular architecture and ovens were uncovered. On the basis of the artefacts the site is dated to the final stages of the Pre-Pottery Neolithic B period, second half of the seventh millennium bc (Verhoeven 1994). The archaeological dating is confirmed by the radiocarbon date obtained for the lowermost occupation level of the site: 8530 ± 60 BP (GrN-21319).

Tell Hammam et-Turkman is a large mound, *c.* 500 m in diameter and up to 45 m high. Excavations at Hammam were carried out from 1981–8 by a team of the University of Amsterdam under the direction of Professor M.N. van Loon and Dr D.J.W. Meijer. Since 1992 excavations at Hammam have been continued by Dr Meijer, now on behalf of the University of Leiden. The earliest levels of occupation date from the Ubaid period. Other archaeological periods represented at Hammam are Late Chalcolithic, Early Bronze IV, Middle Bronze and Late Bronze I (for dates, see Table 19.1). I addition to domestic architecture, remains of large buildings came to lig such as a temple dated to about 3200 bc (final stages of the Late Chalcolithic period), a Middle Bronze administrative building and a Late Bronze palace. These prestigious buildings illustrate the importance of Hammam. For millennia, from Late Chalcolithic to Late Bronze I times, Tell Hammam et-Turkman must have been the political and administrative centre of the upper Balikh basin, with some interruptions when the site was temporarily abandoned. After about 1350 BC Hammam seems to have been largely deserted. Remains of Parthian/Roman/Byzantine occupation are found on top of the mound (Meijer 1986, 1988; van Loon and Meijer 1987, 1988; van Loon 1988).

Environmental conditions

The information on the environmental conditions presented in this section has been taken mainly from Akkermans (1993: chapter 2) and Boerma (1988).

The Balikh, a tributary of the Euphrates (Figure 19.1), is a small perennial river, on average 6 m wide. It is a strongly meandering stream which has its main spring at Ain al-Arous, at the Syro-Turkish border (Figure 19.2). This spring is fed by subterranean streams. In the wet season several wadis carry water to the Balikh, but for the greater part of the year they are dry. The average flow of the Balikh is only about 6 m^3/sec., increasing to a maximum of about 12 m^3/sec. after the winter rains (Wirth 1971). At present, a large part of the river is dry in summer, due to the large-scale extraction of water in the upper Balikh region for the irrigation of cotton fields.

The Balikh basin is 1–12 km wide, with an average width of 5 km. As is clear from Figure 19.2, Sabi Abyad and Hammam are situated in an area where the valley has its greatest width. The valley is made up of alluvial, highly calcareous, clayey deposits covered with loam. A distinction can be made between the lowest Balikh terrace of (early-)Holocene age and the narrow, actual floodplain of relatively recent date. The many ancient settlement sites in the Balikh region are virtually all situated on the Holocene terrace. The upland (plateau) soils in the Hammam/Sabi Abyad area have developed on limestone and marls. As a result these soils are highly calcareous. Soils in the interfluve of Balikh and Qaramokh are also highly calcareous, with a loamy-clayey texture. Gypsiferous plateau soils are found further south (see Figure 19.2).

No weather records are available for the Hammam/Sabi Abyad area. Estimated mean annual precipitation is about 250 mm (see Figure 1). The rainy season lasts from October to April. Precipitation shows great annual fluctuations. Thus, at Raqqa, *c.* 60 km further south, annual precipitation varied from 95 to 366 mm (mean 213.8 mm) during sixteen years of observation (Alex 1985). Summers are hot and dry, with mean July temperatures of about 30°C, while winters are relatively mild, with mean January temperatures of about 7°C. The climate of the area is defined as arid, evaporation greatly exceeding precipitation.

The natural vegetation of the plateau is steppe. At present, the steppe is dominated by *Artemisia* and other dwarf shrubs, but originally it must have been grass steppe. Due to over-grazing the grass steppe gave way to dwarf-shrub steppe. Charcoal analysis suggests that the narrow, annually inundated floodplain was originally covered by riverine forest with *Populus* (poplar), *Ulmus* (elm) and *Fraxinus* (ash).

Conditions for plant cultivation

The calcareous soils in the Hammam/Sabi Abyad area are in principle well suited for plant cultivation; this is in contrast to the gypsiferous plateau soils to the south which lack nutrients. The limiting factor for rain-fed agriculture in the Balikh region is precipitation. A mean annual rainfall of 250 mm, as is estimated for the Hammam/Sabi Abyad area, is assumed to be the minimum for dry farming. Thus, further south, with decreasing amounts of rainfall, only irrigation agriculture is possible, whereas in the upper Balikh region dry farming is practised. Here, rain-fed fields are left fallow every other year to increase the moisture content of the soil. However, a mean annual precipitation of 250 to 300 mm is rather marginal for dry farming. Because of the considerable annual fluctuations in rainfall, crop failures occur commonly under these climatic conditions. In this connection it may be mentioned that in upland Iraq, 200 mm of rain is considered to be the minimum required for the growth of cereals and that the 200 mm *reliable* rainfall isohyet has been found to coincide roughly with the 300 mm *average* rainfall isohyet (Oates and Oates 1976).

One wonders to what extent in ancient times, in the period covered by the Hammam/Sabi Abyad plant record, climatic conditions may have been more favourable for plant growing. Information on past climatic conditions can be inferred from palynological data. A long pollen record has been obtained from sediment in the Ghab valley of north-western Syria, *c.* 275 km from the Hammam/Sabi Abyad area. The pollen evidence from the Ghab suggests that in the early Holocene, between 10,000 and 8000 BP, precipitation in northern Syria may have been higher than nowadays. Thus, at the time of the occupation of aceramic Neolithic Sabi Abyad II, the climate may have been somewhat more humid than at present, implying more favourable conditions for dry farming. The palynological examination of sediment cores from the Balikh and Khabur valleys and the Bouara salt marsh led Gremmen and Bottema (1991) to the conclusion that the climate of the Syrian Jazira, and consequently of the Hammam/Sabi Abyad area, has not changed significantly in the last 6,000 years.

Points for attention

Below some questions are listed which have a bearing on the topic of agricultural change. A major question will be to what extent the archaeobotanical data contribute to the elucidation of these points:

- Is there archaeobotanical evidence for changes in crop plant assemblages and/or shifts in crop plant proportions, and to what extent can possible changes be related to political, economic and/or demographic (population) factors?

- As has been mentioned above, a mean annual precipitation of *c.* 250 mm is rather marginal for rain-fed agriculture. In the valley, irrigation could be practised without undue efforts. In fact, there is textual evidence for the utilization of Balikh water for agricultural purposes in the Middle Bronze Age (Dossin 1974). Does the archaeobotanical record provide evidence for irrigation agriculture in the past?
- The relatively moist stream valley must have been most suitable for plant cultivation. Are there indications of expansion of the arable acreage to the plateau outside the valley? On the plateau, irrigation was not possible in ancient times.
- Does the position of Tell Hammam et-Turkman as a regional centre find expression in the archaeological plant record?

MATERIAL AND METHODS

The samples

During fieldwork at Hammam and the two Sabi Abyad sites, samples for botanical examination were secured routinely, partly by the botanist assigned to the excavation, partly by other members of the excavation team. Two main types of samples are distinguished here: samples of more or less pure grain deposits and samples from habitation contexts. In the latter deposits seeds are usually not visible with the naked eye. Samples of occupational fill were not randomly taken, but, as a rule, ashy features were selected for sampling. The soil samples were floated in the field (manual water separation) to recover charred vegetable remains.

Grain deposits may provide a fair picture of the quality of the crop, but those uncovered at Hammam and Sabi Abyad are not very informative on the cornfield weed flora. They appeared to be the charred remains of fairly thoroughly cleaned supplies. The samples of occupational fill, on the other hand, are usually much richer in weed seeds and other remains, such as chaff, but the botanical contents of these deposits are mostly of diverse origins, which seriously handicaps the interpretation in terms of vegetations of the past. Moreover, only a few seed types could be identified to the species level.

The botanical examination of Hammam and Sabi Abyad has not yet been completed, and the present discussion is based upon the state of the investigation in spring 1995. A preliminary report on the examination of samples of the 1982 and 1984 campaigns at Hammam has been published (van Zeist *et al.* 1988), so too has the report on Neolithic Sabi Abyad I (van Zeist and Waterbolk-van Rooijen 1996).

In this chapter the term 'seeds' has been used somewhat loosely and may also denote anatomically defined fruits.

The presentation of the results

To permit a comparison between the botanical records of the various archaeological periods represented at Hammam and Sabi Abyad, samples of a given period are taken together and the total seed frequencies are expressed as percentages. In this exercise only samples of occupational soil were utilized. With one exception (Late Bronze Sabi Abyad I, see below), samples of more or less pure grain supplies were left out. With respect to the calculation of the percentages the following should be mentioned.

First, for each taxon the numbers of seeds in the samples of a given group (archaeological period) were added up. Then, the total numbers of seeds, crop plants and wild plant taxa in turn in the group concerned were determined. The percentages were calculated, on the understanding that the crop plant proportions are based upon the sum of crop plant seeds and the wild plant proportions upon the sum of wild plant seeds.

The proportions of crop plant species and of a selected number of wild plant taxa are presented in Table 19.2. Some of the samples were left out of the calculation of the percentages of either crop plants or wild plant taxa because of an anomalously large number of one or two seed types in the sample concerned. This explains the differences in the 'Number of samples included' between crop plants and wild plants in some of the periods. For Late Bronze Sabi Abyad I (right-hand column in Table 19.2) no proportions could be determined for lack of reasonably good samples of occupational soil. In this case the relative frequency indications are based upon charred grain samples.

The Late Chalcolithic is not represented in Table 19.2 because only three samples are available for this period. The evidence obtained from Parthian/Roman/Byzantine levels of occupation at Hammam (see Table 19.1) will not be discussed in this chapter.

A first glance at Table 19.2 shows that some seed types display considerable fluctuations in mean values between periods. With the aim of making changes in relative frequencies and possible correlations between two or more taxa more clearly visible, several graphs (Figs 19.4–8) have been prepared.

SOME COMMENTS ON CROP PLANT REMAINS

By far the majority of the crop plant remains at Hammam and Sabi Abyad is made up of barley and wheat.

In addition to the grains of barley and wheat, appreciable quantities of chaff (spikelet forks, glume bases, rachis internodes) were retrieved. Most of the cereal-type culm (stem) remains are probably of cereals, although it cannot be excluded that some are of reed. The non-grain cereal remains are not shown in Table 19.2.

Barley

Almost all barley recovered from the Balikh sites under consideration is of the hulled type. A few grains have been attributed to naked barley, *Hordeum vulgare* var. *nudum*. This barley species was probably not grown here as a crop in its own right but may have occurred as an admixture to hulled barley.

The shape of fairly well preserved hulled barley grains points to the two-rowed form, *Hordeum distichum*: straight, symmetrical kernels. The identification of two-rowed barley is confirmed by the rachis internode remains. Several internodes could confidently be identified as *Hordeum distichum*. A characteristic feature of these internodes are the basal, stalk-like parts of the sterile, lateral spikelets.

With one exception, among the better preserved grains no distinctly lop-sided specimens, characteristic of six-rowed barley, were observed. Equally no rachis internode remains which are clearly of six-rowed barley could be demonstrated. Only at Late Bronze Sabi Abyad I is there evidence of six-rowed barley, *Hordeum vulgare*. Here, in addition to two-rowed barley, the six-rowed form was cultivated.

Hulled wheat

The hulled or glume wheats *Triticum dicoccum* (emmer wheat) and *T. monococcum* (einkorn wheat) are represented as well as free-threshing (naked) wheat. As a rule, the grains of emmer wheat can easily be distinguished from those of einkorn. However, there are exceptions. The difference in shape between the grains of the two glume wheats is due to the fact that in emmer wheat usually two kernels are formed in a spikelet and in einkorn wheat only one. The presence of two-seeded einkorn wheat can be a complicating factor.

A large cereal grain deposit, uncovered at Sabi Abyad I in the remains of a building attributed to the Transitional period, consisted largely of two-seeded einkorn wheat (van Zeist and Waterbolk-van Rooijen 1996: table 7). Since in two-seeded einkorn wheat two grains develop in a spikelet, the ventral side is straight in side view, just as in emmer wheat. The grains of the Sabi Abyad two-seeded einkorn wheat are distinguishable from those of emmer wheat by their size (they are notably smaller, on average), their greater slenderness and their fairly narrow apical (upper) and basal (lower) ends (Figure 19.3).

Naked wheat

The grains of free-threshing wheat can, as a rule, be differentiated with certainty from those of emmer wheat. Only in the case of serious deformations may the distinction be problematic. The identification of the grains is supported by rachis internode remains of free-threshing wheat. Two naked wheat species come into consideration; namely, tetraploid hard wheat (*Triticum durum*) and hexaploid bread wheat (*T. aestivum*). For practical reasons tetraploid *T. turgidum* is left out of consideration here, but where *T. durum* is mentioned, it should, in fact, read *T. durum/turgidum*. The charred grains do

Table 19.2 Proportions of crop plants and wild plant taxa in various archaeological periods (for explanation, see text)

Period / Site	PPNB SAB II	PreHal SAB I	TrPer SAB I	EHalaf SAB I	Ubaid HMM	EBr IV HMM	MBr HMM	LBr I HMM	LBr II SAB I
Triticum monococcum	1.1	2.0	3.6	5.4	0.9	0.3	—	0.4	—
Triticum dicoccum	24.7	27.2	39.6	78.8	23.4	4.0	0.7	1.6	x
Triticum durum/aestivum	7.9	0.7	1.2	—	16.2	9.4	17.7	12.2	xxx
Triticum spec.	—	—	—	—	—	—	0.7	—	—
Hordeum distichum	12.4	66.2	47.2	8.5	39.6	84.2	76.3	83.6	—
Hordeum distichum/vulgare	—	—	—	—	—	—	—	—	xxx
Hordeum vulgare var. *nudum*	—	—	—	—	0.4	—	0.3	—	—
Lens culinaris	9.0	0.7	0.4	2.3	9.4	0.5	1.3	1.0	—
Pisum sativum	—	—	0.4	0.2	0.4	0.6	0.1	—	—
Lathyrus sativus	—	2.0	—	—	0.9	0.8	0.4	0.8	—
Vicia ervilia	—	—	—	0.2	0.9	0.3	2.4	0.4	—
Linum usitatissimum	44.9	1.3	7.2	4.7	8.1	—	—	—	—
Sesamum indicum	—	—	—	—	—	—	—	—	x
Sum of crop plant seeds	89	151	250	485	235	651	705	499	
Number of samples included	10	6	15	9	7	12	22	11	

Aegilops	3.9	0.9	1.2	0.9	1.2	4.3	5.9	7.4	x
Bromus	0.4	—	2.2	1.7	2.8	3.2	1.6	1.2	—
Cynodon	—	—	—	3.1	0.1	—	7.2	0.6	x
Eremopyrum	0.3	0.5	0.5	0.5	—	11.7	9.9	18.7	x
Hordeum wild	0.9	1.2	4.8	5.4	—	0.3	0.6	1.8	x
Lolium	31.0	8.7	26.6	32.3	17.2	1.0	0.9	0.8	x
Phalaris	0.6	0.7	3.6	7.3	16.3	3.3	4.9	11.1	—
Trachynia distachya	—	—	—	—	—	0.5	0.9	0.2	—
Other Gramineae	2.2	1.2	8.9	3.1	5.7	9.1	6.0	14.2	x
Astragalus	6.4	23.4	14.6	1.9	4.5	5.0	1.8	1.0	x
Coronilla	—	—	—	—	—	0.4	1.8	1.2	—
Medicago	—	—	—	0.7	0.6	0.1	1.1	0.3	—
Melilotus	16.7	0.5	2.2	—	2.3	0.2	0.6	0.8	—
Prosopis	—	0.9	3.4	0.2	1.4	0.9	1.2	1.0	—
Trigonella astroites type	0.4	2.3	0.7	0.2	—	11.9	6.5	2.3	x
Vicia spec.	0.3	2.1	4.3	3.3	0.8	0.3	0.1	0.1	—
Other Leguminasae	15.4	17.1	8.9	13.2	16.7	8.4	13.6	4.5	x
Σ Caryophyllaceae	0.4	0.9	0.2	3.5	0.7	1.9	1.1	1.5	—
Centaurea	—	—	1.2	—	0.6	2.5	1.2	1.5	x
Σ Cruciferae	0.1	0.2	0.2	0.2	—	1.8	2.5	2.9	x
Carex	3.0	5.4	1.7	0.5	8.8	0.9	0.7	—	—
Scirpus maritimus	2.4	1.9	0.2	0.5	2.0	4.7	4.6	2.2	x
Polygonum	—	0.2	—	0.2	0.3	0.5	1.9	0.7	—
Rumex	0.8	2.6	4.8	12.5	0.8	1.3	3.8	0.6	x
Galium	0.3	1.6	1.0	3.8	1.6	6.8	11.7	9.4	x
Σ Umbelliferae	—	—	1.2	0.5	—	1.2	0.5	0.5	x
Sum of seeds of wild plants	787	427	417	424	861	2,185	2,443	1,208	
Number of samples included	10	6	20	14	7	12	19	11	

Note: Full names of periods are given in Table 19.1. SAB = Sabi Abyad; HMM = Hammam et-Turkman. x = present; xxx = much.

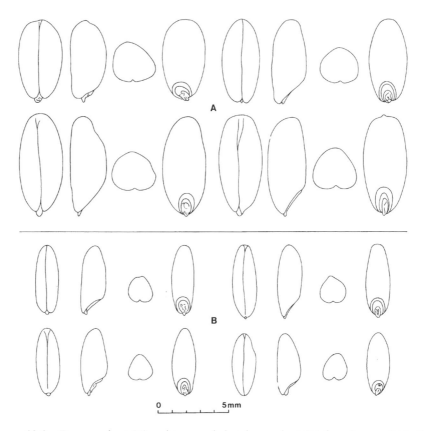

Figure 19.3   Emmer wheat (A) and two-seeded einkorn wheat (B) from late neolithic Sabi Abyad.

not allow a distinction between the two naked wheats. The rachis internodes, on the other hand, should in principle allow us to determine the ploidy level. Jacomet (1987: 47) lists the criteria thought to differentiate between the two free-threshing wheats. Many of the reasonably well preserved rachis internodes at Hammam (the majority of the rachis remains are strongly fragmented) are morphologically more or less intermediate between *T. durum* and *T. aestivum*, following Jacomet's criteria. Some of the rachis internodes are typical of *durum* wheat and a few others could confidently be attributed to *T. aestivum*. As the rachis internode remains suggest that in addition to *durum* wheat, *aestivum* wheat is represented, the free-threshing wheat at Hammam (and Sabi Abyad) is indicated here as *Triticum durum/aestivum*.

Hard wheat and bread wheat have different ecological requirements. *Durum* wheats are well adapted to the Mediterranean-type climate with mild, rainy winters and warm, dry summers. *Aestivum* wheats, on the other hand, are more adapted to extreme continental conditions and to sub-humid temperate climates (Zohary 1971). Consequently, on ecological grounds *T.*

durum would be the most likely candidate for the Balikh area. However, in this respect some caution should be observed: Jansen (1986: table 6) reports that in present-day north-eastern Syria, bread wheat is cultivated in addition to hard wheat.

Flax (linseed)

The crop plant record of Sabi Abyad II is characterized by a conspicuously high proportion of flax (linseed). The samples included in the calculation of the percentages are from successive levels in one of the three 9 × 2 m trenches (see p. 352 on the sites). One of the few botanical samples taken from the other two trenches yielded a very large number of linseeds: the charred remains of a linseed supply. It can clearly be assumed that at aceramic Sabi Abyad flax was cultivated and that the linseeds had not been gathered from the wild. This assumption is supported by the size of the Sabi Abyad seeds, which points to domesticated flax, *Linum usitatissimum* (unpublished data).

CROP PLANT PROPORTIONS

Cereals

The proportions of the cereal species in the various periods are shown in Figure 19.4. With respect to this graph, it should be mentioned that the

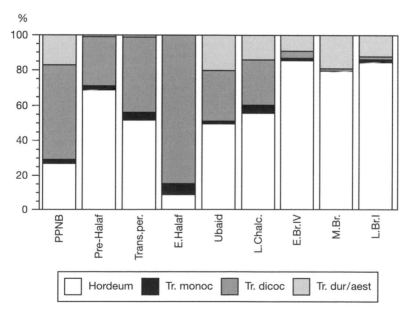

Figure 19.4 Cereal grain proportions: PPNB = Pre-Pottery Neolithic B; Pre-Halaf = Pre-Halaf Neolithic; Trans.per. = Transitional period; E.Halaf = Early Halaf; L.Chalc. = Late Chalcolithic; E.Br.IV = Early Bronze IV; M.Br. = Middle Bronze; L.Br.I = Late Bronze I.

percentages shown here are based upon the total numbers of cereal grains (and not of all crop plant seeds) in each of the groups concerned. Naked barley, which was only rarely found, is included in the *Hordeum* proportions. Although based upon three samples only, the Late Chalcolithic cereal proportions are shown in Figure 19.4; they fit with general trends.

Pre-Pottery Neolithic Sabi Abyad II stands somewhat isolated due to a considerable time gap (*c.* 1,500 radiocarbon years) from the next period represented in Figure 19.4 (Pre-Halaf). The main difference with Late Neolithic Sabi Abyad I (Pre-Halaf, Transitional period, Early Halaf) is the comparatively high value for free-threshing wheat (*Triticum durum/aestivum*) at Sabi Abyad II, whereas at Sabi Abyad I this wheat is hardly represented.

With respect to the almost total disappearance of free-threshing wheat, the examination of two samples from Early Pottery Neolithic Damishliyya (early sixth millennium bc), a small settlement close to Tell Hammam et-Turkman, is of particular interest. These samples provide firm evidence for naked wheat at Damishliyya (van Zeist *et al.* 1988: table 154), indicating that until at least 5700 bc this wheat was grown in the area. One wonders whether in the course of the 6th millennium bc, climatic conditions became less favourable for the cultivation of free-threshing wheat. As has been discussed above, the early Holocene climate of northern Syria may have been somewhat more humid than afterwards. In the sixth millennium bc, a distinct change occurred in the crop plant assemblage of the farmers in the Hammam/Sabi Abyad area.

The archaeobotanical record suggests that during the Late Neolithic, hulled wheat became the most important cereal at Sabi Abyad. In Early Halaf the proportion of barley had decreased to less than 10 per cent. This does not necessarily imply that the wheat acreage had increased at the expense of barley, but it could be that fresh land had been taken into cultivation. It is most likely that only the river valley, with comparatively favourable moisture conditions, was suitable for wheat growing.

As usual, at Late Neolithic Sabi Abyad, emmer wheat was quantitatively far more important than einkorn wheat. The einkorn wheat at Sabi Abyad deserves some special attention because of the presence of the two-seeded form (Figure 19.3). As has already been discussed, a cereal grain supply of predominantly two-seeded einkorn was found in a Transitional period context. The two-seeded einkorn wheat at Sabi Abyad is remarkable, for there is no other evidence of the cultivation of this wheat as a crop in its own right in the Near East. At least for the time being, the Sabi Abyad two-seeded einkorn wheat is an isolated case. Wild two-seeded einkorn wheat (*Triticum boeoticum* ssp. *thaoudar*) occurs in massive stands on basaltic soil in south-eastern Anatolia (Harlan and Zohary 1966). Could the species have been taken into cultivation there, after which the new cultivar was introduced in adjacent northern Syria? There is no evidence of two-seeded einkorn in Halaf and younger levels, suggesting that in the Hammam/Sabi Abyad area its cultivation must have been of relatively short duration. Apparently, this new crop did not come up to expectations and was therefore abandoned.

At Ubaid Hammam et-Turkman free-threshing wheat again formed part of the crop plant assemblage. In view of the suggestion made above that the almost total absence of free-threshing wheat from Late Neolithic Sabi Abyad was due to a change to a somewhat drier climate, one wonders how conditions for the cultivation of naked wheat could again have become more favourable. Without indications of a more humid climate, the only reasonable assumption is that some kind of irrigation was carried out. In the valley, this could have been done rather easily by damming the river and diverting the water over the fields. The problem of finding botanical evidence for irrigation in ancient times will be discussed below.

From Ubaid times, naked wheat was cultivated. At first, emmer wheat was at least as important as *durum/aestivum* wheat, but since the Bronze Age emmer wheat played a minor role only. That the latter continued to be grown as a crop in its own right is demonstrated by a few finds of emmer wheat supplies.

The Bronze Age (Early Bronze IV, Middle Bronze, Late Bronze I) crop plant record from Hammam is characterized by a strong predominance of barley. How can this apparent preference be explained, or was it a necessity dictated by the environmental conditions? One could speculate that the need for corn had increased considerably. In this connection it should be borne in mind that Hammam had developed into a large regional centre with a substantial population. In the river valley there was no room for extending the cereal acreage, so there was no alternative to taking the plateau into cultivation. Here, without the possibility of irrigating the fields, only barley could have been grown. Barley makes less high demands upon climate and soil than wheat; it is more drought-resistant. The extra barley may have been necessary, not only to meet the food requirements of a growing population but also for feeding the numerous pack-animals following the caravan route along the Balikh.

Arable farming at Bronze Age Hammam may have been distinguishable from that of the preceding periods by the large-scale exploitation of the plateau.

At Middle Assyrian (Late Bronze II) Sabi Abyad I, concentrations of cereal grains were uncovered in the fortress and a domestic building. It seems that barley and wheat were equally important (van Zeist 1994: table 4). The size of the grains suggests that the corn had been grown in irrigated fields. Irrigation agriculture within the valley, without use of the plateau, could have been due to a smaller population or to a demand for the best quality grain available by the Assyrian occupants of the site and that these corn finds are not representative for the whole of the area.

Pulses

Pulse crop proportions are plotted in Figure 19.5. Lentil is the most regularly occurring species, and a few relatively large total pulse crop percentages are occasioned by lentil. As is clear from Table 19.2 and Figure 19.5, there are no indications of significant changes in pulse crop cultivation. The role of pulses

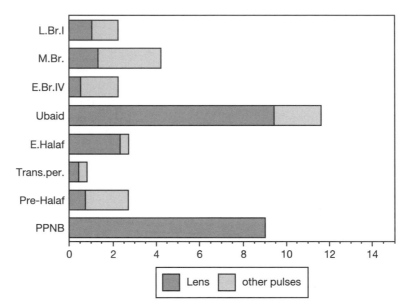

Figure 19.5   Pulse seed proportions. For full names of periods, see caption of Figure 19.4.

in the agrarian economy is difficult to evaluate. Were they grown on small (garden) plots only or in fields of larger dimensions?

Oil crops

The exceptionally high percentage of flax at Pre-Pottery Neolithic Sabi Abyad II (Table 19.2, Figure 19.6a) is puzzling, and the role of this crop in the economy of the site is not clear. Only a minor part of the site (27 × 2 m) has been excavated and this may have been the area where linseed was processed or stored. Was Sabi Abyad II perhaps some kind of specialized flax-growing site? In this connection it may be mentioned that according to Akkermans (1993: 163), the clustering of small sites into larger agglomerations was a characteristic feature of the earliest Neolithic in the area. Thus, Sabi Abyad II formed part of a cluster of three aceramic Neolithic sites.

At least up to Ubaid times, flax continued to be cultivated in the area, but it is virtually absent from the bronze age record. The disappearance of flax from the regular crop plant assemblage constituted a distinct change in the agrarian economy. Had linen perhaps been replaced by wool? As a matter of fact, from the seeds one cannot tell whether flax was grown primarily for its fibres or for its oleaginous seeds. Flax must have been cultivated on relatively moist soil in the valley. Could it be that this prime soil was needed for the production of high-quality corn?

Table 19.2 lists sesame (*Sesamum indicum*) for Late Bronze Sabi Abyad. The evidence consists of six damaged seeds only, but nevertheless it indicates that this oil crop of Indian origin was cultivated in the area. Textual evidence of sesame in Mesopotamia dates back to the middle of the third millennium (Bedigian 1985), but the earliest actual seed finds are of a much later date. The introduction of sesame may have entailed a change in the agrarian system in that, in contrast to barley, wheat and flax, this species is a typical summer crop. In the first millennium BC other summer crops, such as broomcorn millet (*Panicum miliaceum*) and foxtail millet (*Setaria italica*), would follow (Nessbit and Summers 1988).

FIELD WEEDS

Charred remains of unprocessed crop supplies should provide reliable and detailed information on the ancient weed flora. Unfortunately, this ideal situation is only rarely encountered. As has aleady been mentioned, the Hammam/Sabi Abyad charred grain samples are the remains of fairly thoroughly cleaned supplies which yielded only small numbers of weed seeds. For information on the Hammam/Sabi Abyad arable weed flora we depend particularly on samples from occupational layers. With regard to vegetation of the past, one is faced with the usual problems when interpreting the evidence obtained from this type of sample. A great number of charred seeds cannot be identified to the species level, and no ecological conclusions can be drawn from seed types which may include species from different habitats. Another handicap is the fact that in the occupational soil, plant remains of diverse origins are usually found together. Seeds of arable weeds may have been carried in together with the (cereal) crop processed on the site. In threshing and subsequent cleaning, chaff, weed seeds and other contaminants were separated from the crop and either stored for animal fodder or dumped as refuse. Substantial numbers of seeds may have been brought to the site in animal dung that was used as fuel (Bottema 1984; Miller and Smart 1984). It is likely that sheep grazed in the steppe outside the cultivated area, but also on the fields after the harvest and in any other place where there was plant growth. This implies that species of different habitats were represented in sheep dung (and that of other domestic animals). In one and the same sample seeds of arable weeds, ruderal species and steppe plants may be found in addition to crop plant remains.

In reconstructing the ancient segetal flora from archaeological plant remains, much profit is gained from information on the flora of traditionally cultivated fields of the recent past. No reconstruction of the ancient arable weed flora of the Hammam/Sabi Abyad area will be presented here. Instead, in focusing on agricultural change, special attention will be paid to a few selected taxa.

Figure 19.6a shows a fair correlation between *Linum* (flax) and *Lolium* (rye-grass). The obvious conclusion that rye-grass must have been a common weed of flax fields is supported by the large number of *Lolium* seeds in the linseed supply recovered from PPNB Sabi Abyad II. Here 460 *Lolium* seeds

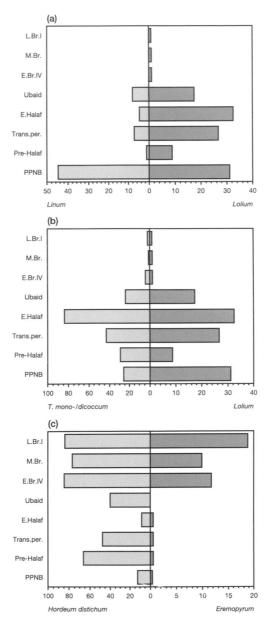

Figure 19.6 Comparisons between proportions of cultivated and wild plants (arable weeds). For full names of periods, see caption of Figure 19.4.

were counted against 1,200 linseeds, whereas other (potential) field weeds occurred in low numbers only. The *Lolium* seeds are of the *Lolium perenne/rigidum* type and not of *Lolium remotum*, which much later would become a characteristic weed of flax fields.

Lolium may have been the most common flax-field weed, but it was probably not confined to this crop plant. A comparison of hulled wheat (*Triticum monococcum* and *dicoccum*) and rye-grass proportions (Figure 19.6b) suggests a correlation at least as good as that between flax and rye-grass. It is tempting to assume that in general, *Lolium* was a common weed of comparatively moist fields in the river valley. It was on these soils that flax and wheat must preferably have been grown.

The high barley proportions at Bronze Age Hammam may have been the consequence of the large-scale utilization of the plateau for the production of corn. Barley was probably the only cereal that could profitably be grown under wholly rain-fed conditions. To what extent is the expansion of barley cultivation to the plateau soils reflected in the field weed proportions? Most striking in this respect is the behaviour of the grass *Eremopyrum* (*bonaepartis*). This taxon is scarcely represented in earlier periods, but shows high values in the Bronze Age (Figure 19.6c). It looks as though *Eremopyrum* did very well in the rain-dependent barley fields on the plateau. *Galium* values are highest in the bronze age periods, suggesting that this taxon was also common in the barley fields on the plateau (Figure 19.7a). *Galium* includes a great number of species, and the species that grew on the plateau may have been different from those in the river valley. The variation in size of the *Galium* seeds recovered indicates the presence of several species.

Trigonella astroites type shows a fair correlation with barley (Figure 19.7b). This leguminous seed type displays very high proportions at Early Bronze Tell Raqa'i, located on the Khabur of north-eastern Syria (van Zeist, manuscript). Near Raqa'i, almost all cereal cultivation must have taken place on the plateau because of the locally narrow valley of the Khabur. A mean annual precipitation of *c.* 250 mm at Raqa'i is the same as that in the Hammam/Sabi Abyad area. The Raqa'i evidence suggests that the *Trigonella astroites* type seeds were very well adapted to dry arable fields. This may explain the relatively high proportions of this seed type at Bronze Age Hammam. Comparatively high values for *Hordeum distichum* and *Trigonella astroites* type at Pre-Halaf Sabi Abyad (Figure 19.7b) could point to a temporary expansion of arable farming to the plateau.

A correlation of *Triticum durum/aestivum* with one or more weed types is more problematic. Free-threshing wheat could have been grown in the river valley only, and, in later periods, probably only in irrigated fields. It has been suggested above that *Lolium* was a common weed in arable fields with a reasonably good moisture content during the growing season, implying that in fields of free-threshing wheat *Lolium* occurred commonly. Indeed, in Pre-Pottery Neolithic and Ubaid levels, both *Lolium* and free-threshing wheat show relatively high values, but in the Bronze Age a positive correlation appears to be absent (Figure 19.7c). Figure 19.7c gives occasion to the following speculations: relative to *Lolium*, *Phalaris* shows a gradual increase; in Ubaid levels, *Phalaris* had reached about the same mean value as *Lolium*, and in the Bronze Age it must have been more common than rye-grass. Could it

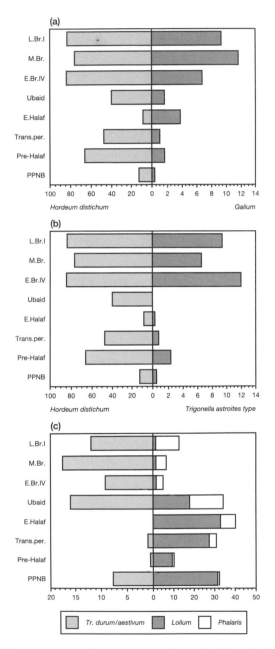

Figure 19.7 Further comparisons between proportions of cultivated and wild plants (arable weeds). For full names of periods, see caption of Figure 19.4.

be that in the river valley, *Lolium* was largely replaced by *Phalaris* as a segetal weed and that this was one of the effects of irrigation? One may object that in the bronze age levels, *Phalaris* proportions are rather small, which is not in conformity with the comparatively high free-threshing wheat frequencies. These relatively low *Phalaris* values could, at least in part, have been occasioned by the large numbers of weed seeds originating from the rain-fed plateau fields.

Admittedly, the above is very speculative, but it leads us to the question of to what extent irrigation agriculture finds expression in the archaeobotanical record. Zohary (1973: 643–4) lists a number of species which occur in periodically irrigated fields, but of these taxa only *Cynodon* (*dactylon*) was recorded more than occasionally, be it rather irregularly (Table 19.2). Scarcely represented at Hammam are *Amaranthus* spec., *Setaria viridis/verticillata* and *Echinochloa* spec. (not listed in Table 19.2). If one takes the line that *Cynodon* is indicative of irrigation, it would imply that already in Early Halaf times, 5100–5000 bc, irrigation was practised in the Balikh valley, which is very early but not unimaginable. There is convincing evidence for irrigation at Samarran Choga Mami in eastern Iraq, dated to *c*. 5000 bc (Oates and Oates 1976). On the other hand, the (near-)absence of *Cynodon* from Ubaid and Early Bronze Hammam, both with fairly high naked wheat proportions, makes one doubt whether this grass is a real indicator of irrigation farming. Dependable archaeobotanical evidence for irrigation in the ancient Near East is still a problematic issue.

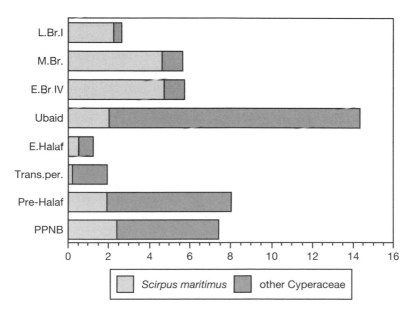

Figure 19.8 Cyperaceous seed proportions. For full names of periods, see caption of Figure 19.4.

Marsh plants, such as *Scirpus maritimus* (sea clubrush) and other Cyperaceae, are often regarded as indicators of irrigation. Along irrigation ditches marsh plants could expand up to the edges of the arable fields. The Hammam/Sabi Abyad Cyperaceous values fluctuate rather wildly (Figure 19.8), but there appears to be no clear correlation with crop plant proportions. The fairly good representation of Cyperaceae at Hammam and Sabi Abyad may be seen as evidence of the exploitation of the herbaceous ground flora of the Balikh valley. Sedge (*Carex*) and sea clubrush could have been used as litter for bedding, and sea clubrush also for matting. In addition, it is likely that domestic animals grazed in the valley, which may have resulted in the incorporation of Cyperaceous seeds in the occupational deposits.

CONCLUSIONS

The following summarizing remarks can be made:

1 Various shifts in crop-plant assemblages are evident from the archaeo-botanical record. Conspicuous changes include the almost total disappearance of flax after the Ubaid period and the reappearance of free-threshing wheat in Ubaid levels. Cultivation of two-seeded einkorn wheat at Late Neolithic Sabi Abyad was apparently of short duration only. In the Bronze Age, the economic importance of emmer wheat had greatly declined, whereas barley had become the most widely grown corn.

2 The marked expansion of barley cultivation at Bronze Age Hammam is thought to have been to feed growing numbers of people as well as animals. A considerable increase in cereal production could be achieved only by extending the arable acreage onto the plateau. Here, without the possibility of irrigation, only barley could profitably have been grown. *Eremopyrum* (*bonaepartis*) probably was a common weed in the rain-fed barley fields, and so may have been the species that produced the *Trigonella astroites* type seed.

3 It is suggested that the cultivation of free-threshing wheat in Ubaid times and later required additional watering of the fields. Irrigation may have effected the replacement of *Lolium* by *Phalaris* as a segetal weed. Of the species reported as weeds in the present-day, periodically irrigated fields, only *Cynodon* (*dactylon*) is more than occasionally represented. However, it is questionable whether this species is a dependable indicator of irrigation in ancient times. The excellent quality of the corn at Middle Assyrian Sabi Abyad points to cultivation in irrigated fields.

4 The position of Tell Hammam et-Turkmam as a cultural and administrative centre hardly finds expression in the plant remains recovered. Admittedly, the botanical contents of the samples included in

Table 19.2 largely reflect common domestic activities such as crop processing, food preparation and heating (dung fuel). However, samples of food supplies are no more indicative of anything extraordinary. The only exception is the find of a cache of fruit-stones of *Prunus mahaleb* (St. Lucie cherry), which must have been brought in from quite some distance (van Zeist and Waterbolk-van Rooijen 1992). No olive stones were found, although olives could easily have been imported from the Mediterranean region. Equally, evidence of fig (*Ficus carica*) is conspicuously absent from Bronze Age Hammam.

ACKNOWLEDGEMENTS

The author wishes to acknowledge the co-operation of the following: Dr P.M.M.G. Akkermans and Dr D.J.W. Meijer provided information on the sites and the samples. Rita M. Palfenier-Vegter, Mien Waterbolk-van Rooijen and G.J. de Roller assisted in the archaeobotanical examination. The drawings were prepared by G. Delger and J.H. Zwier. Sheila M. van Gelder-Ottway improved the English text.

REFERENCES

Akkermans, P.M.M.G. 1993. *Villages in the Steppe: Later neolithic settlement and subsistence in the Balikh valley, northern Syria*. Michigan: Ann Arbor, International Monographs in Prehistory. Archaeological Series 5.

Akkermans, P.M.M.G. and I. Rossmeisl. 1990. Excavations at Tell Sabi Abyad, Northern Syria: a regional centre on the Assyrian frontier. *Akkadica* 66, 13–60.

Akkermans, P.M.M.G. and M. Verhoeven. 1995. An image of complexity: the burnt village at late neolithic Sabi Abyad, Syria. *American Journal of Archaeology* 99, 5–32.

Akkermans, P.M.M.G., J. Limpens and R.H. Spoor. 1993. On the frontier of Assyria: excavations at Tell Sabi Abyad, 1991. *Akkadica* 84/85, 1–52.

Alex, M. 1984. *Vorderer Orient. Mittlere Jahresniederschläge und Variabilität 1: 8 000 000. Tübinger Atlas des Vorderen Orients, Karte A IV 4*. Wiesbaden: Ludwig Reichert Verlag.

Alex, M. 1985. *Klimadaten ausgewählter Stationen des Vorderen Orients. Beihefte zum Tübinger Atlas des Vorderen Orients, Reihe A (Naturwissenschaften) 14*. Wiesbaden: Ludwig Reichert Verlag.

Bedigian, D. 1985. Is še-giš-ì sesame or flax? *Bulletin of Sumerian Agriculture* 2, 159–78.

Boerma, J.A.K. 1988. Soils and environment of Tell Hammam et-Turkman. In *Hammam et-Turkman I. Report on the University of Amsterdam's 1981–1984 Excavations in Syria*, M.N. van Loon (ed.), 1–11. Istanbul: Nederlands Historisch-Archaeologisch Instituut.

Bottema, S. 1984. The composition of modern charred seed assemblages. In *Plants and Ancient Man*, W. van Zeist and W.A. Casparie (eds), 207–12. Rotterdam/Boston: Balkema.

Dossin, G. 1974. Le site de Tuttul-sur-Balih. *Revue d'Assyriologie et d'Archéologie Orientale* 68, 25–34.

Gremmen, W.H.E. and S. Bottema. 1991. Palynological investigations in the Syrian

Gazira. In *Die rezente Umwelt von Tall Seh Hamad und Daten zur Umweltrekonstruktion der assyrischen Stadt Dur-Katlimmu*, H. Kühne (ed.), 105–16. Berlin: Dietrich Reimer Verlag.

Harlan, J.R. and D. Zohary. 1966. Distribution of wild wheats and barley. *Science* 153, 1074–80.

Jacomet, S. 1987. *Prähistorische Getreidefunde.* Basel: Botanisches Institut der Universität.

Jansen, A.-E. 1986. *Art und Bedeutung der Segetalflora im Weizenanbau Nordost-Syriens unter besonderer Berücksichtigung des traditionellen Anbausystems.* Aichtal: Josef Markgraf.

Meijer, D.J.W. 1986. Tell Hammam in Noord-Syrië. Een vluchtig overzicht van de architectuur uit vier campagnes. *Phoenix* 32, 31–47.

Meijer, D.J.W. 1988. Tell Hammam: architecture and stratigraphy. In *Hammam et-Turkman I. Report on the University of Amsterdam's 1981–1984 Excavations in Syria*, M.N. van Loon (ed.), 9–127. Istanbul: Nederlands Historisch-Archaeologisch Instituut.

Miller, N.F. and T.L. Smart. 1984. Intentional burning of dung as fuel: a mechanism for the incorporation of charred seeds into the archaeological record. *Journal of Ethnobiology* 2, 15–28.

Mook, W.G. and M.N. van Loon. 1988. Radiocarbon dates. In *Hammam et-Turkman I. Report on the University of Amsterdam's 1981–1984 Excavations in Syria*, M.N. van Loon (ed.), 703–4. Istanbul: Nederlands Historisch-Archaeologisch Instituut.

Nessbit, M. and G.D. Summers. 1988. Some recent discoveries of millet (*Panicum miliaceum* L. and *Setaria italica* (L.) P.Beauv.) at excavations in Turkey and Iran. *Anatolian Studies* 38, 85–97.

Oates, D. and J. Oates. 1976. Early irrigation agriculture in Mesopotamia. In *Problems in Economic and Social Archaeology*, G. de Sieveking, I.H. Longworth and K.E. Wilsom (eds), 109–35. London: Duckworth.

van Loon, M.N. (ed.) 1988. *Hammam et-Turkman I. Report on the University of Amsterdam's 1981–1984 Excavations in Syria.* 2 volumes. Istanbul: Nederlands Historisch-Archaeologisch Instituut.

van Loon, M.N. and D.J.W. Meijer. 1987. Hammam et-Turkman on the Balikh: First results of the University of Amsterdam's 1986 excavation. *Akkadica* 52, 1–9.

van Loon, M.N. and D.J.W. Meijer. 1988. Conclusions. In *Hammam et-Turkman I. Report on the University of Amsterdam's 1981–1984 Excavations in Syria*, M.N. van Loon (ed.), 697–701. Istanbul: Nederlands Historisch-Archaeologisch Instituut.

van Zeist, W. 1994. Some notes on second millennium BC plant cultivation in the Syrian Jazira. In *Cinquante-deux réflexions sur le Proche-Orient ancien offertes en hommage à Léon De Meijer*, H. Gasche and M. Tanret (eds), 541–53. Leuven: Peeters.

van Zeist, W. The plant husbandry of Tell al-Raqa'i. In press, in H.H. Curvers and G.M. Schwartz (eds), Tell al-Raqa'i, volume 1).

van Zeist, W. and W. Waterbolk-van Rooijen. 1992. Two interesting floral finds from third millennium B.C. Tell Hammam et-Turkman, northern Syria. *Vegetation History and Archaeobotany* 1, 157–61.

van Zeist, W. and W. Waterbolk-van Rooijen. 1996, The cultivated and wild plants. In *Tell Sabi Abyad: the later neolithic settlement*, P.M.M.G. Akkermans (ed.), 521–50. Istanbul: Nederlands Historisch-Archaeologisch Instituut.

van Zeist, W., W. Waterbolk-van Rooijen and S. Bottema. 1988. Some notes on the plant husbandry of Tell Hammam et-Turkman. In *Hammam et-Turkman I. Report on the University of Amsterdam's 1981–1984 Excavations in Syria*, M.N. van Loon (ed.), 705–15. Istanbul: Nederlands Historisch-Archaeologisch Instituut.

Verhoeven, M. 1994. Excavations at Tell Sabi Abyad II, a later Pre-Pottery Neolithic B village in the Balikh valley, northern Syria. *Orient Express* 1994, 9–12.

Wirth, E. 1971. *Syrien, eine geographische Landeskunde.* Wissenschaftliche Länderkunden, Band 4/5. Darmstadt: Wissenschaftliche Buchgesellschaft.

Zohary, D. 1971. Origin of south-west asiatic cereals: wheats, barley, oats and rye. In *Plant Life of South-West Asia*, P.H. Davis (ed.), 235–63. Edinburgh: Botanical Society of Edinburgh.

Zohary, M. 1973. *Geobotanical Foundations of the Middle East.* 2 volumes. Stuttgart/ Amsterdam: Gustav Fischer/Swets and Zeitlinger.

Part IV

PLANTS AND PEOPLE

20 Tracking the banana: its significance in early agriculture

EDMOND DE LANGHE AND PIERRE DE MARET

[W]e need to focus research more on the evolutionary history of individual crops . . .

David R. Harris (1996)

INTRODUCTION

Considerable progress has been made during recent decades into the investigation of early stages of agriculture in the tropics. However, the ubiquitous banana crop[1] is rarely dealt with by the disciplines involved and it is hardly mentioned in the fast expanding literature, thus giving the impression that bananas provide little evidence of importance.

It is certainly difficult to find material traces of a herbaceous plant which generally produces neither seeds nor pollen. But the same holds for taro and yam which do regularly figure in the literature.

This contribution shows how attempts at combining botanical and genetical features with the input of linguistic, anthropological, and archaeological data may open new prospects for understanding how, where and when the crop evolved from its wild relatives. It also shows that this crop may have played, in various parts of the tropics, a much greater role in the evolution of subsistence systems than previously thought.

We shall argue that more research on the past of banana as a crop could be helpful for a better grasp of the early history of tropical agriculture. Because of the complexity of its domestication process, a rather elaborate explanation of the botanical and genetical background of the crop is necessary.

DOMESTICATION OF THE FE'I BANANA

The genus *Musa* is classified in four sections, of which two are basic to the crop: *Australimusa* (2n = 20 chromosomes) and *Eumusa* (2n = 22 chromosomes in the wild form).

The Fe'i banana cultivars,[2] which are grown in the Pacific only, belong to the section *Australimusa*. The relatively few species of this section are rather majestic plants, with pseudostems from 7 up to 12 m high. They can be found on alluvial soils, but also in mountains up to 2,000 m where, however, seed-setting becomes rare. Knowledge of variation in the Section is satisfactory, due to an extensive study of the wild bananas in Papua New Guinea (Argent 1976). An analogous study in the Indonesian part of New Guinea, Irian Jaya, is still required for a complete picture. On Figure 20.1, the names of the species are roughly placed in the zone of their occurrence.[3]

Domestication in *Australimusa* was a relatively linear process involving the progressive acquisition of parthenocarpy and seed sterility, followed by somatic mutations. Seed formation is still frequent in several cultivars, which explains why Fe'i plants can occur in semi–wild state.

The species *Musa maclayi*, of which the varieties show a more or less erect inflorescence, is considered as the most likely wild relative of the Fe'i bananas (Simmonds 1956, [1959]1966). The cultivation zone of 'Fe'i' is actually confined to a tiny series, stretching from some islands around western New Guinea, where they are rare, to the Marquesas in the Pacific, where diversity is large. They probably never became important north of the equator, in Hawaii or in Kusaie, the extreme east of the Carolines (Simmonds [1959] 1966, 1962).

Of interest is the fact that Fe'i bananas appear in a semi–cultivated condition only in mainland New Guinea and that they may not have been known there in the past (Simmonds 1956). Hence, the beginning of domestication could have taken place in the Solomon Islands, where *Musa maclayi* ssp. *maclayi* var. *erecta* with blunt apex fruits is endemic, rather than in New Guinea.

Study of the *Musa* phytoliths from the archaeological deposits at the Kuk site in mainland New Guinea led to the conclusion that they probably do not belong to the *Australimusa* section (Wilson 1985). It will become clear from the following paragraphs that the endemic *M. acuminata* subspecies *banksii* is the more likely source.

EDIBLE BANANA DIPLOID GENERATION: THE MAJOR STEP IN BANANA DOMESTICATION[4]

In the section *Eumusa*, the hundreds of banana cultivars form a very heterogeneous group and their phenotypes are the reflection of a ramified pattern of domestication more or less coupled with genome combinations, polyploidization and somatic mutations.

Domestication must have started in *Musa acuminata*, one of the two *Eumusa* species which played a basic role in the genesis of banana and plantain (Simmonds 1962). The species in its wild state covers a huge area,

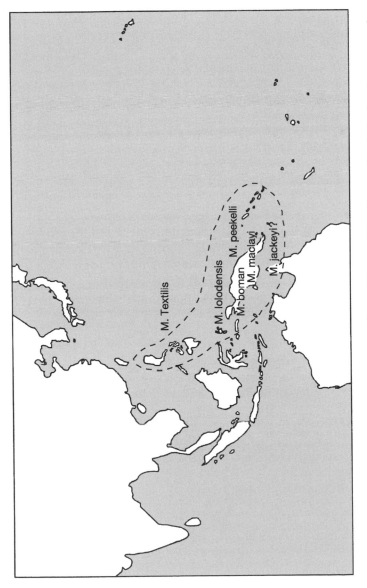

Figure 20.1 The wild species of the Section *Australimusa*. *Musa maclayi*, with several varieties showing more or less erect bunches, is the probable parent species for the 'Fe'i' bananas in the Pacific.

M. Textilis

M. lolodensis

M. peekelli

M. boman

M. maclayi

M. jackeyi?

from New Guinea in the east to Myanmar in the west, with a consequent variation in phenotype which has been classified into a number of subspecies.

The original phase in the domestication process may well have needed several thousands of years for the progressive increase in parthenocarpy and of seed sterility leading to the generation of comestible *acuminata* diploids, for which the conventional term 'edible AA' has been adopted. The large number of edible AAs found in New Guinea and surrounding areas, which is the area of the subspecies *banksii*, is in sharp contrast with the few other edible relatives of *M. acuminata* found in the *acuminata* area.

The *banksii* area itself is rather large, and includes New Guinea, some neighbouring islands, part of eastern Island South-east Asia and the Philippines (Figure 20.2).[5] Somatic mutation certainly played a great subsequent role for the phenotypic diversity in the edible *banksii* AA.

HYBRIDS AND POLYPLOIDS

The next step in banana domestication was a combination of polyploidization and intra/inter-specific hybridization. Many edible diploids, when profusely pollinated, can produce viable seeds, and many offspring appear to be seed-sterile triploids. Thus, when cultivated in the neighbourhood of wild relatives, the edible AA produced seeds containing new *acuminata* combinations, including inter-subspecific AA hybrids, and the basic AAA triploids. Intensive vegetative propagation provoked somatic mutations, thus creating the cultivars.

Hybridization with the other basic *Eumusa* species, *Musa balbisiana*, again followed by somatic mutation, produced some AB cultivars and numerous AAB and ABB triploids.[6] Because banana triploids are generally more robust than edible AA, they must have supplanted the latter in many regions of origin.

M. balbisiana covers an area more to the north, including drier regions as far as south China. Some AAB and most ABB are rather drought-resistant. Variation within the species is small, in sharp contrast with the variation in *M. acuminata*.

This second step in the domestication of bananas would not have required a long period. As soon as edible AA were grown in the proximity of wild relatives, production of viable seeds and seedlings of ensuing triploids and hybrids must have been (and still can be) a fast process, whereby farmers detected, selected and subsequently cloned the most vigorous or attractive plants.

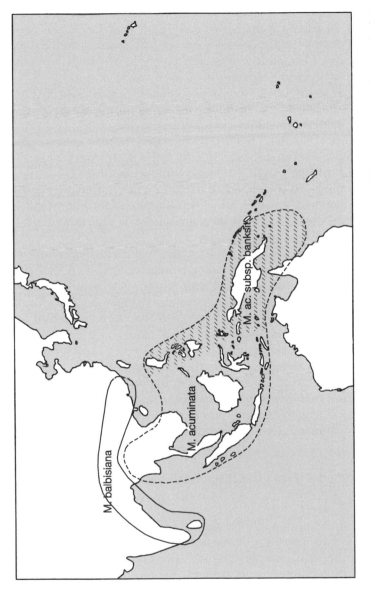

Figure 20.2 Distribution of the *Eumusa* species basic to the banana and plantain. The *M. acuminata* subspecies *banksii* played a fundamental role in the initial domestication.

THE HUMAN STAMP ON EXTREME CULTIVAR DIVERSITY: PLANTAINS AND 'MAIA MAOLI'

Since seed- and pollen-deficient banana plants cannot propagate by natural means, their diffusion is due to human intervention, and they are consequently an excellent marker of early food production and agriculture. The initial creation of intra- and inter-specific hybrids and cultivars was somehow followed by anthropogenic movement both within and beyond the wild *Musa* area in various directions.

Of course, some cultivars are nowadays almost omnipresent in the tropics, and a search for their initial 'pathway', from that area of origin to the places of current cultivation, looks impossible. Two groups, however, each containing about one hundred cultivars with a similar general phenotype in each, appear to have a particular significance for early agriculture. The first group is that of the AAB plantains with great diversity in rainforests: Africa and probably also in South India. The other group, that of the AAB 'Maia-maoli/popoulu' bananas, which is called hereafter 'the MMP-group',[7] is grown in Polynesia. MMP is virtually absent in the traditional Plantain growing zone and vice versa.

The reasonable explanation for the exceptional intra-group diversity is that basic hybrids and cultivars underwent a long series of additional somatic mutations in regions of intensive cultivation, thus producing numerous 'secondary' cultivars which were carefully maintained by cloning (i.e., vegetative propagation). Such a process calls for early cultivation and both groups indeed seem to have been part of local cultures for a very long time, as testified by traditions and legends.

But the most intriguing aspect of the impressive diversity of plantains and of MMPs in humid Africa and in Polynesia respectively, is its manifestation in areas so far away from the original *Musa* diversity centre, and its relative rarity in all other places with the exception of the plantains of South India. Yet both groups are genetically very proximal, as the following item will illustrate.

THE DIFFICULT DISTINCTION BETWEEN PLANTAIN AND MMP

The two groups cannot easily be distinguished, even when growing on the same field. It is no surprise, then, that MMP cultivars growing in Colombia, such as 'Pompo', are confounded with plantains (Cardenosa 1954).[8] The vegetative parts are quite similar, with the yellowish tinge of the green leaves somewhat more pronounced in plantains. Typical fruits of MMP are plump with a completely blunt apex in the 'Popoulu' subgroup.[9] Typical plantain fruits are generally slender with pronounced ribs and a salient apex. But the characteristic is not reliable since some plantain cultivars grow fruits with blunt apexes as well and some 'Maia' cultivars have a rather tapering apex.[10]

Even the colour of the compound tepal, which is yellow-orange in typical plantains, and white in MMP, is subject to confusing ecological variation.

Consequently, one is left with a rough, general picture of the inter-group difference, but also a regional description. Plantains with complete inflorescence (the so-called French plantains)[11], always have persistent bracts hiding the pendulous male axis, while the MMP bracts are dehiscent, leaving the male axis naked. On average, the plantain fruits are slender and angular, while those of MMP are plump and rounded.

The difficulty of finding a number of simple and reliable discriminant morphologic characters is clearly a reflection of an amply shared genetical background. This has now been confirmed by molecular techniques.

IN SEARCH OF THE CRADLE OF PLANTAINS AND MMP

Peninsular India lies in the wild *Musa* area, and, since no other important plantain diversity had been reported in other parts of the area, it was previously presumed that plantains originated in India. The fact that 'French plantains' were missing to the east of India was an indirect, but strong, indication in support of the hypothesis (Simmonds [1959]1966). But at least one 'French plantain' has since been detected in the Philippines, near Baguio (Luzon), and probably more are to be found where the Aeta people are still practising itinerant agriculture (Allen 1965; De Langhe and Valmayor 1979).

For the 'MMP' group, and on the base of a phenotypically similar cultivar grown in the Philippines, Simmonds suggested that the basic cultivars of the group originated there, and that diversification occurred on the way to, and within, Polynesia, the actors being the currently called Austronesian-speaking people (Simmonds 1962).

The hard facts needed for clarifying these problems are now coming from research in molecular genetics of the genus *Musa*. DNA polymorphism of plantain and MMP clones was studied via restriction fragment length polymorphism (RFLP) and it was found that their two A-genomes are very close to that of the subspecies *banksii*, while no relation with any other *acuminata* genome could be found (Carreel 1994). Consequently, the *M. acuminata* subspecies *banksii* is the most plausible source of the AA genomes in both these AAB groups.

Since variation in *Musa balbisiana* is by no means as pronounced as in *Musa acuminata*, the resulting AABs indeed must have about the same genetical constitution. It is, then, no surprise that the groups can hardly be distinguished on morphological grounds.

As *Musa balbisiana* exists in eastern New Guinea, as a consequence there should be plenty of plantains and MMPs in that country. However, neither of the two groups form part of the traditional agriculture in New Guinea, so that the role of *M. balbisiana* in this region is unclear.

MUSA BALBISIANA AND THE AUSTRONESIAN-SPEAKING POPULATIONS

Simmonds discovered that *M. balbisiana* was not native in Thailand, peninsular Malaysia and Indonesia, although it was found 'in the wild state' in many remote places (Simmonds 1956).

The plant is semi-cultivated for many purposes in these countries, as well as in Vietnam and the Philippines (Nguyen Dang Khoi and Valmayor 1995; Brewbaker and Umali 1956; Brewbaker *et al.* 1956). Leaves are used as wrapping material; the pseudostems are a source of fibres, as well as food for pigs; the male bud is consumed as a vegetable, and the fruits are said to possess medicinal value. Such plants remain fully fertile and have the capacity to colonize the environment. Hence the concept of *M. balbisiana* as being naturalized in these countries, and not native.[12]

It was accepted, with some hesitation, that the plant is native in the Philippines, in eastern New Guinea and in New Britain: 'it seems to be truly native – certainly it is widespread and locally abundant in "natural" habitats' (Simmonds 1956: 473). But the lack of morphological variation in this species, which covers such a vast area, is intriguing when compared with the wide spectrum in *Musa acuminata*.

However, the 'native' status of the species in New Guinea was revisited more recently and anthropogenic introduction was favoured (Argent 1976). A strong argument for introduction by people is the fact that the rare AAB and ABB hybrids in New Guinea may be considered for the most part as 'alien' (Simmonds [1959]1966). If the numerous edible AAs of that country have been growing for a long time in the proximity of truly wild *M. balbisiana*, many original hybrids would have been generated.

In the Philippines, the AABs are again in a small minority when compared with the numerous edible AAs and the AAAs, and they too appear to have been mostly introductions (Valmayor *et al.* 1981). The same holds for the ABBs, with the notable exception of the 'Saba' group for which the BBB constitution has been defended (see also note 12). Semi-cultivation in many places points to massive, if not exclusive, human influence on the *M. balbisiana* germplasm.

It is thus very likely that *Musa balbisiana* is endemic to a restricted zone of mainland South-east Asia (Figure 20.2), and that people were responsible for its considerable expansion since ancient times over the rest of Mainland South-east Asia, Island South-east Asia, and parts of Melanesia and of Polynesia (Figure 20.3). This would help explain the lack of variation in the species mentioned above.

The presence of 'wild' *M. balbisiana* in the Mapulehu valley at Hawaii allows us to construct a scenario of human intervention. It is inconceivable that the plant could be part of the original flora, and it must have been brought there by the Hawaiian ancestors. Checking the places where the species has been recorded outside Mainland South-east Asia, one finds an area

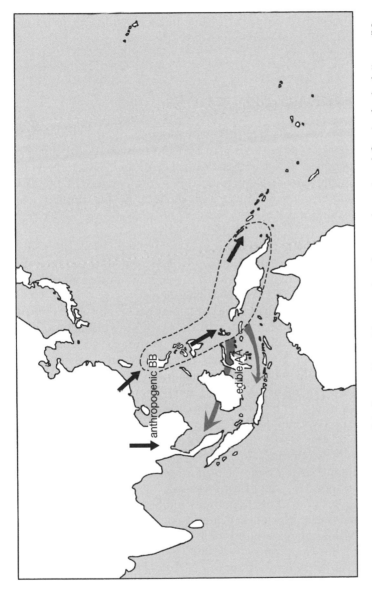

Figure 20.3 Starting from well before 3500 BP, *Musa acuminata* became domesticated first in the *banksii* area (New Guinea and probably the Philippines) and later progressively in Island and Mainland South-east Asia. Human populations were also responsible for the considerable expansion of a semi-wild *Musa balbisiana* area.

that roughly coincides with the presumed route taken by the predecessors of the Polynesians: the Philippines, Bismarck archipelago and eventually Hawaii. Other Austronesian-speaking people would have moved *M. balbisiana* south of the Philippines and then to the West.[13]

Consequently, the expansion of the Austronesian-speaking population seems to have been the instrument of the anthropogenic expansion of *Musa balbisiana*, with major consequences for the subsequent generation of important cultivar groups.

MULTIDISCIPLINARY DEDUCTIONS

The anthropogenic *M. balbisiana* (BBant) hypothesis sheds a new light on the problem of the origin of the AAB plantains and the MMPs explained earlier. The rarity or complete absence of traditional AAB and ABB in New Guinea is explained by the fact that Austronesians – the carriers of the BBant – probably were never in close contact with the local people, and did not move inland into a well-populated area where the mass of the edible AAs are found.[14]

The southward moving BBant through the Philippines and the Moluccas would have met with the edible '*banksii*'- AAs, and thus produce the first AAB hybrids, the plantains and the Maia maoli/Popoulus, or at least the basic cultivars of these groups (Figures 20.3 and 20.4).

The fact that each group had a very different geographical destiny calls for their generation at two distinct zones. In contrast to the plantains, of which at least a few cultivars are still grown all over Indonesia, no cultivars of the MMP group have ever been reported there, or for that matter anywhere further west in the Old World. The plantains, on the other hand, are by no means part of the Polynesian banana group. Therefore, while both groups would have originated within, or close to, the non-New Guinea part of the *Musa acuminata* subspecies *banksii* zone, the specific cradle of the MMP group may have been more to the north-east of the plantains.

We suggest New Britain and neighbouring islands, with perhaps the southern Philippines as the zone of origin for the MMP group – this group remaining confined to the Proto-Oceanic speaking people since its generation (Figure 20.4). This hypothesis implies the possibility that only a part of the central-east Malayo-Polynesian-speaking people moved down in the Sulawesi-Malukku area around 4500 BP, while another part already may have moved to the east from (southern?) Philippines, in contrast with the supposed later move eastward of the east Malayo-Polynesian groups, the latter presumably centred on the islands in Cenderawasih Bay off West New Guinea (Spriggs 1989). The alternative, that plantains were not yet in existence, can hardly be defended since many plantain cultivars show more progressed floral degeneration characteristics than the MMPs do, a signal of their more remote past. One realizes how the recording of even a single

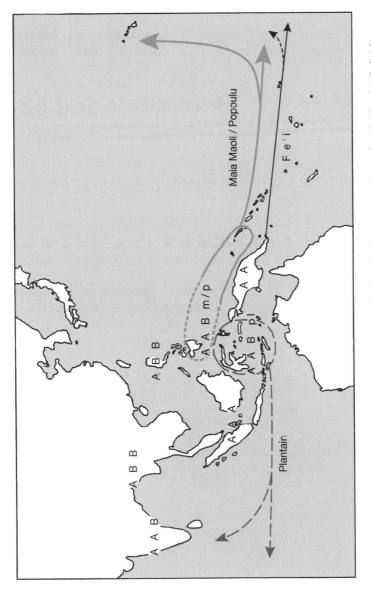

Figure 20.4 By 3500 BP, the first AAB Plantain (AABpl) and Maia-maomi/Popoulu (AABm/p) hybrids were generated in restricted zones, from where they were carried to remote regions by Austronesian-speaking populations. Meanwhile, a large number of other triploids and hybrids came into existence along the routes of expansion of the edible *acuminata* varieties.

cultivar of the MMP group in this critical zone could be of considerable significance for confirmation versus reconsideration of the hypothesis.

In connection with the theories of the Austronesian expansion, the period of origin of the plantains and of the Maia maoli/Popoulus can thus be estimated between 4500 and 3500 BP.

Meanwhile, the expansion to the west of the edible AAs would have allowed for new edible AA combinations and even for the first AAAs, such as the Cavendish for example (Figure 20.4). The actors here were agriculturists of Austroasiatic origin of whom linguistic traces have been found in Sumatra, western Borneo and possibly Sumbawa (Bellwood 1996).

The many plantain cultivars in South India should consequently be seen as composing a secondary centre of diversity. This poses an interesting question: could Austronesian people have brought the basic cultivars there? By what alternative mechanism did these plantains reach India?

Only at a later stage did the edible AA reach mainland South-east Asia where the AABs (India principally) and ABBs were produced. Meanwhile, a great number of new AAA came into being in Indonesia (Figure 20.4).

THE PLANTAIN IN AFRICA

It was thought until recently that the banana did not arrive in East Africa prior to the first centuries of our era, and that its diffusion through Equatorial Africa would have been completed by around AD 500 (Vansinna 1990: 64). Ideally adapted to evergreen rainforests, the banana must have had a major impact on the way of life in this area and would have soon become the staple crop for agriculture.

However, it has since been suggested that plantains reached Africa by 3000 BP (De Langhe et al. 1994–5). It was also argued that Madagascar could not have been the 'port of entry' of traditional bananas and plantains into Africa. Plantains would have reached the continent along the east coast, in a first wave, well before the other bananas.

This hypothesis, derived from botanical and linguistic evidence, has now unexpectedly received strong confirmation during archaeological research carried out in West-Central Africa. In the vicinity of Yaoundé, in rainforest Cameroon, some Musaceae phytoliths were observed on several occasions at the bottom of large refuse pits firmly dated 840–350 BC (Mbida 1996; Mbida et al. 1997). Exhaustive comparative observations by optical and scanning electron microscopy of phytoliths from the genus *Musa* and *Ensete* allow us to rule out the possibility that the phytoliths belong to the latter genus.

Such first evidence of the antiquity of plantains in Africa has far-reaching implications. It could well explain the very significant increase in village densities in the forest at that time and be directly connected with yet another major population movement, this time in Africa: the Bantu expansion. Indeed, the latter is believed to have taken place during that period. Here again the banana may have been a major factor in a larger pattern of subsistence.

The supposed arrival of plantains in Africa at such early dates thus calls for special attention. The localization of the plantain homeland in eastern Island South-east Asia leads to the presumption that the basic cultivars of this group could not have been carried by Austronesian-speaking people before 4000 BP. But while trans-oceanic movements of people are readily imagined over the last 2,000 years, the idea of navigators crossing the entire Indian Ocean some 1,000–1,500 years earlier is a daring one indeed.

Yet these people should have been well acquainted with long-distance seafaring since an impressive lexicon dealing with the outrigger canoe complex already existed in Proto-Malayo-Polynesian (Blust 1995). Expeditions in search of suitable land should then not be totally excluded. Besides, the possible first visit to South India by 'Austronesians' could have meant an intermediary phase in a voyage to Africa, allowing for the pioneers to learn more about trade winds and currents in the Indian Ocean.

THE SEEDY PEMBA *ACUMINATA*: A WRONG TRACK

A modest population of (semi-)wild *Musa* plants with all the basic characteristics of *M. acuminata* has been recorded in Pemba island, off the East African coast and north of Zanzibar, and thus very distant from the main area of diversity for the species. On the basis of its crossing behaviour, the population shows an affinity with *acuminata* forms within Indonesia (Simmonds 1962). It could thus be a remainder of the *Musa* package brought over by the Austronesian people, which certainly must have contained edible AA and perhaps semi-domesticated AA varieties besides the plantain.

No such 'wild' population has ever been found in continental Africa, in contrast with a number of edible AA still cultivated by farmers such as the Chagga in Tanzania (Baker and Simmonds 1951; Shepherd 1957; Philippson 1984). Consequently, the Pemba *acuminata* has not played a role in the presence of African banana and plantain cultivars.

WHAT WAS THE HOSTING SYSTEM FOR PLANTAIN IN AFRICA?

It has been suggested that *Ensete* populations, which once covered a much larger area in Africa, may have been semi-cultivated close to the east coast and that the similar morphology of the plantains would have made such integration easy (De Langhe *et al.* 1994–5). Cultivation of *Ensete ventricosum* is practised in Ethiopia, sometimes in close proximity to the wild populations. Both cultivated and wild populations are conserved in a ritual sanctuary among the Omotic Ari people, who are bringing into cultivated populations new genotypes sprouting from natural crosses between the two (Shigeta 1990).

There appears to exist some sort of relation in the Bantu languages of eastern and southern Africa between *Ensete* and *Musa* through a number of reflexes that would point to *gomb(w)a* as a proto-word. The term frequently designates the vegetative parts of the plants, rather than the fruit, but the relation should be considered with caution because the Swahili word 'mgomba' for 'banana tree' is found in several languages as a loan-word as well (Philippson and Bahuchet 1994–5).

Much of what is known of East African prehistory relies on the archaeological study of grains and animal bones and of the related artefacts. Such study is of course carried out in areas which have never been hospitable to root and tuber crops and bananas.

At any rate, the impressive number of plantain cultivars grown in the whole rainforest zone, as well as the presence there of numerous cultivars with almost completely degenerated inflorescence, do form a massive indication of the very ancient adoption of the plant in the middle of the continent (De Langhe 1961, 1964a, 1964b).

If plantains arrived in Africa with early Austronesian speakers, some other crops such as taro, yam, and sugar-cane would probably have been part of the subsistence package. But no evidence for early introduction of these crops exists.

THE BANANA AS A TOOL FOR UNCOVERING THE OBSCURE PAST OF VEGECULTURE

Traces of deliberate vegeculture by hunter-gatherers or mobile horticulturalists are very hard to find. The plants in question are herbaceous; inflorescences were and still are consumed in an immature stage (*Colocasia* and *Musa* in Asia and the Pacific), and many domesticated forms became seed-sterile and even lack pollen. Circumstantial evidence is equally very weak. Stone tools were not necessarily required for the clearing of plots in primary forests (Orme 1981). Evidence of fences in the form of post-holes, for protection against pigs, or deer and the like, are characteristic of only a part of the tropical zone, and are not a regular practice in the African rainforest for instance. Remains of villages become conspicuous only when the latter had a long duration – that is, when itinerant agriculture could be sustained in one place for a long time, or when agriculture became sedentary. The same holds for indications of forest burning.

Even more challenging is the attempt to reconstruct the initial domestication stages of a crop. Archaeologists with a vast experience in research into early agriculture estimate that, at least for the New Guinea– Melanesia area, late pleistocene/early holocene populations were transplanting particular taxa 'in ways that foreshadowed the later development of "house-garden" horticulture' (Harris 1995). With the example of the anthropogenic *Musa balbisiana* in mind, one realizes that both semi-wild and vegetative propagation may have co-existed for a considerable time.

However, the recent progress in archaeobotany proves that, while the potential of pollen diagrams may be limited, identification of phytoliths and the analysis of charcoal and of coprolites can be very rewarding indeed (Hather 1994). Remains of palms, of *Canarium* and of other trees in a vague cultural context, can put the archaeologist on a promising track. Identification of carbonized tissues of roots and tubers such as taro and sweet potato in the Pacific has recently been of great help in unravelling the prehistory of these crops there (Hather and Kirch 1991; Hather 1992).

Most promising for the reconstruction of the early past of a crop could be the combination of these techniques with sufficient knowledge about the botanical and genetical framework in which a wild plant can evolve into a cultivated crop. Questions such as which wild species are likely to have played the initial role, which palaeoenvironments were favourable, and which species could have interacted for the generation of the crop, and how, can only be answered with the help of such knowledge. Unfortunately, this knowledge is meagre in the case of yam and taro. For the latter crop, its wild relatives are not even known. One can only continue to hope that interest will emerge for a systematic botanical and genetical investigation of these crops.

The banana has the advantage of partly being a commercial crop, and genetic improvement has been undertaken since the beginning of this century. The result is a detailed knowledge of its botanical and genetical background which is now rapidly extending to the entire *Musa* germplasm, with the great help of molecular techniques.

The present chapter offers an example of how this vast and still increasing knowledge could stimulate research on the crop's early history. The interdisciplinary 'dialogue' of all the scientists involved, with the implied control and correction of formulated hypotheses, seems to be the only method of finding satisfactory answers to many unanswered questions. In many cases early vegeculture relied on at least three crops: banana, yam and taro. Consequently, the progress in interdisciplinary research on bananas could be of great help for deducing what may have happened with the other two crops in the remote past.

For Africa, such evidence might cause a reformulation of the whole complex formed by both the 'hunter–gatherer systems' and the 'itinerant agriculture systems'. That could lead to the search in appropriate palaeo-environments for possible transition phases to agriculture, thereby exploiting the possibilities of archaeobotany and a multidisciplinary approach.

CONCLUSIONS

In this updated reconstruction of the possible evolution of bananas, particular attention was paid to AAB plantains and AAB bananas in Polynesia, because they appear to form part of traditional culture for many millennia.

The following review of the suggested salient features in the domestication and further evolution of the banana should be considered. It proposes a number of facts which are open to critical, but focused, research with the aim of moving the hypothesis to the level of a more solid explanatory framework, after the necessary corrections and reconsiderations.

1 Domestication of the Fe'i bananas started in the Solomon Islands and evolved further to the east, with Proto-Polynesian people as the agents.

2 Domestication of all other bananas started well before 4500 BP in New Guinea, eastern Indonesia and perhaps the Philippines.

3 This domestication first produced the comestible *acuminata* diploids (edible AA), the area of which expanded westwards through the rest of Indonesia and then mainland South-east Asia, whereby new (inter-subspecific) edible AA and *acuminata* triploids (AAA) came into existence. Ancestors of Austro-Asiatic-speaking people were the actors behind the process.

4 From about 4500 BP, Proto-Austronesian-speaking people, during their colonization of the Philippines, eastern Indonesia and the long series of islands (and northern New Guinea?) to the east, were responsible for the related considerable expansion of the anthropogenic *Musa balbisiana* (BBant), which remained in a semi-wild seed-bearing stage.[15]

5 Natural crossing between this BBant and edible AA produced the first AAB plantain hybrids in eastern Indonesia, and the basic stock of the Polynesian Maia maoli/Popoulu, probably in the Bismarck archipelago. Many new AAA as well as other AAB and ABB hybrids were subsequently produced everywhere the edible AA came into contact with other subspecies of *M. acuminata*, with BBant and eventually with the original BB, when diffusion of the AA reached the drier areas of mainland Asia.

6 Starting about 3500 BP, pioneers among the ancestral Central Malayo-Polynesian-speaking populations undertook expeditions across the Indian Ocean (perhaps avoiding the rest of Indonesia, already colonized by the western branch?), reaching the south of peninsular India, and East Africa. They brought plantains, water yam and taro with them.[16]

7 During the same period, the central-east branch of the Malayo-Polynesians, after establishing the Lapita culture in the Bismarck archipelago, undertook expeditions to the east and found unoccupied islands which they colonized, thereby diversifying the 'Maia' germplasm through somatic mutations. They may be the same people who met

with the first Fe'i bananas in the Solomons, and who diversified the latter in southern Polynesia (Marquesas) before the more attractive Maia maoli/Popoulu dominated during their later colonizations.[17]

8 During all this time and down to the period of first contacts with Europeans, agriculture in New Guinea (except perhaps the northern fringes where Austronesians settled), remained isolated. The only bananas were the edible AA of which some cultivars acquired an extreme expression of the cumulated parthenocarpy, leading to the production of fruits that are as large as those of normal triploids. This may be the reason that the latter had no success, in marked contrast with the sweet potato.

In the areas where plantain and MMP cultivars are supposed to have been introduced by Austronesian-speaking people, the search for *Musa* phytoliths in relevant horizons would be very useful since their presence could in most cases unequivocally point to early agriculture.[18] Of the other crops which could have been part of the 'Austronesian package', neither the water-yams nor taro produce phytoliths, and their domesticated forms rarely bear seeds.[19]

This contribution hopefully shows the pertinence of the botanical and genetical background of a crop in the search into its early history and the beginnings of vegeculture; an interdisciplinary approach is of the essence.

NOTES

1 For reasons of convenience, in this text the term 'banana' covers the totality of edible fruit-bearing plants of the genus *Musa,* with the exclusion of the 'Fe'i banana(s)'. The terms 'banana crop' and 'crop' apply for both categories.

2 'Cultivars' is in the present context the term for the different clones reflecting a phenotypical variation which is maintained by people through vegetative propagation. The term 'varieties' is confined to the natural variation at the lowest rank, occurring in the wild state within a species. When this variation is artificially maintained through vegetative propagation (for example in botanical gardens), the neutral term 'clones' is preferred.

3 One additional species, *Musa bukensis* Argent,was found in Bougainville island of the Solomons only (Argent 1976).

4 For a comprehensive theory which is now firmly established, see Simmonds (1962). The explanation in the present text is focused on the origin of plantains and of other relevant cultivar groups, with some consequent adaptation of the theory.

5 The wild AA in the Philippines is sometimes qualified as *Musa acuminata* subsp. *errans,* but that status is questioned by others (Shepherd 1988). On the basis of molecular marker analysis of a few representative clones, it was found that both have a rather similar nuclear profile but that the cytoplasmic genomes could be different. On the other hand, the edible AAs of both the Philippines and New Guinea form one vast phenotypical complex, quite distinct from the other edible AAs (Carreel 1994). Within a third, *M. acuminata microcarpa*, the clone 'Borneo' may be genetically very close to subsp. *banksii*, but its exact taxonomic position in *Musa acuminata* needs further study. In the present contribution, the

'Borneo' clone is ignored, and the subsp. *errans* is included as part of the subsp. *banksii*.

6 The distribution of the two species as on Figure 20.1 does not show areas of mutual overlap. This would restrict the zone of hybridization to a part of mainland South-east Asia only. Explanations *sub* item '*Musa balbisiana* and the Austronesian-speaking people' will clarify the potential problem. A few tetraploid hybrids do exist but their occurrence does not interfere with the present exposé.

7 The group frequently named the Pacific plantains. Confusion around the term 'plantain' subsists in the literature, despite the description and classification by Simmonds, unanimously accepted by the taxonomists, of the only AAB subgroup that deserves the name (Simmonds [1959]1966). At least two other groups are known for their diversity, but to a much lesser extent: the ABB 'Saba' in and around the Philippines and the ABB 'Bluggoe's' in India.

8 These could well be vestiges of a once-made 'visit' of Polynesians to the South American coast, although a recent origin via exchange between collections cannot be excluded (Simmonds [1959]1966).

9 Distinctions between 'Maia maoli' and 'Popoulu' conform to the classification established by Simmonds ([1959]1966), who stressed that much taxonomical work is needed for comprehensive and reliable classification. Hence the 'Maia maoli/Popoulu' connotation in the present text.

10 The latter are grouped by the Hawaiian farmers under the name 'Maia iholena'. 'Maia' means 'banana'.

11 Numerous plantain cultivars do indeed lack the male part of the inflorescence, and are called 'Horn plantain' because of the very long and curved fruits resembling the horns of cows, buffaloes, etc. Such bunch morphology has never been reported in MMP, even if at least one MMP cultivar also lacks male flowers (but keeps normal finger size and form). The morpho-taxonomy of the latter group still needs more systematic study, and exhaustive comparative study of both groups on the same field would of course be ideal.

12 Since the 1950s a debate developed on whether some of these semi-cultivated *M. balbisiana* clones became parthenocarpic and semi-sterile or not. Several scientists, having worked in the Philippines, are of the opinion that parthenocarpic BBBs (e.g., some 'Saba' clones) do exist. If this process occurs, its progress should be much slower than with *M. acuminata*.

13 The sequence of Austronesian language development is according to the currently accepted theory (Blust 1995).

14 The relative lack of a firm Austronesian colonization of the lowlands of New Guinea is in fact as yet unexplained (Bellwood 1996).

15 Identifying *balbisiana* seeds in lower horizons during excavations in countries such as Thailand, Vietnam, the Philippines, New Guinea (the neighbouring islands such as New Britain) and even in Polynesia, would not only confirm the hypothesis but would also shed some light on the cultural pattern of human populations connected to the reconstructed Proto-Austro-Asiatic and Proto-Austronesian lexicons or their ramifications. These seeds have a unique and thus very characteristic morphology (Simmonds 1962).

16 If they returned to base they may have reported that the lands discovered were occupied, and actual colonization would thus have been discouraged – with the absence of consistent archaeological vestiges as a result, but with the plantains, the water yam, taro (and perhaps sugar-cane?) as witness of their visit.

17 It should be noticed that the present-day distribution of the Austronesian languages (South-Halmahera, West New Guinea, Central Malayo-Polynesian, West Malayo-Polynesian and Oceanic) closely parallel the major area of this reconstructed history of banana domestication.

18 This would certainly be the case in continental Africa, and probably in the Kerala zone of India as well. For the Pacific zone the need for morphological distinction between *Australimusa* and *Eumusa* phytoliths is imperative, but at least one attempt looks encouraging (Wilson 1985).

19 Taro starch residues have been found on stone tools from the Solomon Islands dating to 28,000 BP (Loy *et al.* 1992). Beyond the considerable expertise involved in such research, there is the question of whether the use of stone artefacts always indicates areas where vegeculture occurred.

REFERENCES

Allen, P.H. 1965. Annotated index of Philippine *Musaceae*. *Philippine Agriculture* 49, 320–411.

Argent, G.C.G. 1976. The wild bananas of Papua New Guinea. *Notes from the Botanic Garden Edinburgh* 35, 77–114.

Baker, R.E.D. and N.W. Simmonds. 1951. Bananas in East Africa. Pt. I The botanical and agricultural status of the crop. *Emp. J. exp. Agric.* 19, 283–90.

Bellwood, P. 1996. The origins and spread of agriculture in the Indo-Pacific region: gradualism and diffusion or revolution and colonization? In *The Origins and Spread of Agriculture and Pastoralism in Eurasia*, D.R. Harris (ed.), 465–98, London: UCL Press.

Blust, R. 1995. The prehistory of the Austronesian-speaking peoples: a view from language. *Journal of World Prehistory* 9, 453–510.

Brewbaker, J.L. and D.L. Umali. 1956. Classification of Philippine *Musae*. I. The genera *Musa* L. and *Ensete* Horan. *The Philippine Agriculturist* 40, 231–41.

Brewbaker, J.L., D.D. Gorrez and D.L. Umali. 1956. Classification of Philippine *Musae*. II. Canton and Minay, putative hybrid forms of *Musa textilis* and *Musa balbisiana*. *The Philippine Agriculturist* 40, 242–57.

Cardenosa, R. 1954. *El genero Musa en Colombia*. Palmira: Minist. Agric. Ganad.

Carreel, F. 1994. Etude de la diversité génétique des bananiers genre Musa à l'aide des marqueurs RFLP. Thèse, Institut National Agronomique, Paris-Grignon.

De Langhe, E. 1961. La taxonomie du bananier plantain en Afrique équatoriale. *J. Agric. Trop. Bot. Appl.* 8, 417–49.

De Langhe, E. 1964a. The origin of variation in the plantain banana. *Mededelingen van de Landbouwhogeschool en de Opzoekingsstations van de Staat te Gent.* 29, 45–80.

De Langhe, E. 1964b. Influence de la parthénocarpie sur la dégénérescence florale chez le bananier. *Fruits* 19, 239–57, 311–22.

De Langhe, E. and R.V. Valmayor. 1979. French plantains in Southeast Asia. *IBPGR Newsletter for South-east Asia*, 3–4.

De Langhe, E., R. Swennen and D. Vuylsteke. 1994–5. Plantain in the early Bantu world. *Azania* 29–30, 147–60.

Harris, D.R. 1995. Early agriculture in New Guinea and the Torres Strait divide. *Antiquity* 69, 848–54.

Harris, D.R. 1996. Introduction: themes and concepts in the study of early agriculture. In *The Origins and Spread of Agriculture and Pastoralism in Eurasia*, D.R. Harris (ed.) 1–9. London: UCL Press.

Hather, J.G. 1992. The archaeobotany of subsistence in the Pacific. *World Archaeology* 24, 70–81.

Hather, J.G. (ed.). 1994. *Tropical Archaeobotany*. London: Routledge.

Hather, J.C. and P.V. Kirch. 1991. Prehistoric sweet potato *Ipomea batatas* from Mangaia Island, Central Polynesia. *Antiquity* 65, 887–93.

396 E. DE LANGHE AND P. DE MARET

Loy, T.H., M. Spriggs and S. Wickler. 1992. Direct evidence for human use of plants 28,000 years ago: starch residues on stone artifacts from the northern Solomon Islands. *Antiquity* 66, 898–912.
Mbida, C. 1996. L'émergence de communautés villageoises en Cameroun meridional. Etude archéologique des sites de Nkang et de Ndindan. Unpublished Ph.D. thesis. Faculté de Philosophie et de Lettres, Université Libre de Bruxelles (ULB).
Mbida, C., H. Doutrelepont, L. Vrydaghs, Rony Swennen, Rudy Swennen, H. Beeckman, E. De Langhe and P. de Maret. 1997. First archaeological evidence of banana cultivation in central Africa during the third millennium before present. Submitted for publication.
Nguyen Dang Khoi and R.V. Valmayor. 1995. Collection, characterization, evaluation and conservation of the indigenous *Musa* germplasm of Viet Nam – a progress report. *InfoMusa*, INIBAP 4, 3–4.
Orme, B. 1981. *Anthropology for Archaeologists: an introduction*. London: Duckworth.
Philippson, G. 1984. *Gens des Bananeraies*. Paris: Editions Recherche sur les Civilisations.
Philippson, G. and S. Bahuchet. 1994. Cultivated crops and Bantu migrations in central and Eastern Africa: a linguistic approach. *Azania* 29–30, 103–20.
Shepherd, K. 1957. Banana cultivars in East Africa. *Tropical Agriculture* 34, 277–86.
Shepherd, K. 1988. Observations on *Musa* taxonomy. In *Identification of Genetic Diversity in the Genus Musa*, R.L. Jarrelt (ed.), Rome: IBPGR Publications. INIBAP, 158–65.
Shigeta, M. 1990. Folk *in-situ* conservation of Ensete *Ensete ventricosum* Welw. E.E. Cheesman: towards the interpretation of indigenous agricultural science of the Ari, southwestern Ethiopia. *African Study Monographs* 10, 93–107.
Simmonds, N.W. 1956. Botanical results of the banana expedition, 1954–5. *Kew Bulletin* 1956, 463–90.
Simmonds, N.W. [1959]1966. *Bananas*. London: Longmans.
Simmonds, N.W. 1962. *The Evolution of the Bananas*. London: Longmans.
Spriggs, M. 1989. The dating of the Island Southeast Asian Neolithic: an attempt at chronometric hygiene and linguistic correlation. *Antiquity* 63, 587–613.
Valmayor, R.V., F.N. Rivera and F.M. Lomuljo. 1981. *Philippine Banana Cultivar Names and Synonyms*. Los Bânos: NPGRL, Institute of Plant Breeding, University of the Philippines.
Vansinna, J. 1990. *Paths in the Rainforests*. Madison: University of Wisconsin Press.
Wilson, S.M. 1985. Phytolith analysis at Kuk, an early agricultural site in Papua New Guinea. *Archaeology in Oceania* 20, 90–7.

21 *The puzzle of the late emergence of domesticated sorghum in the Nile valley*

RANDI HAALAND

This chapter concerns the pathways underlying the evolution of domesticated sorghum, and its distribution in time and space. In our present state of knowledge the following statements appear reasonable starting points for the discussion:

1 The first domesticated sorghum known archaeologically is evidence for a long preceding process (pathway) of evolution.
2 This process was shaped by selection pressures operating on wild sorghum.
3 A fundamental factor in these pressures was human activity primarily in the form of intensified use of wild sorghum.
4 One precondition for such pressures to be effective is that they continuously operate on a plant population.
5 Such continuous pressures are likely to be brought about by increased sedentism.
6 Another factor which is necessary in order for selection pressures to be effective is that the plant population on which they operate is isolated as a gene-pool in order to avoid back crossing to the wild forms.
7 Such isolation of the gene-pool is most likely achieved if wild sorghum is cultivated outside its natural habitat.

GATHERING IN THE MIDDLE NILE VALLEY

The starting point for my discussion of possible trajectories in the transition from wild to domesticated forms of sorghum is empirical material from sites excavated between Atbara and Khartoum.

The earliest sites showing evidence for gathering of wild sorghum are from three mesolithic sites (Abu Darbein, El Damer and Aneibis) located in the Atbara region (Figure 21.1). Material from these sites has been presented in some detail elsewhere (Haaland 1995; Haaland and Magid 1995), and I shall

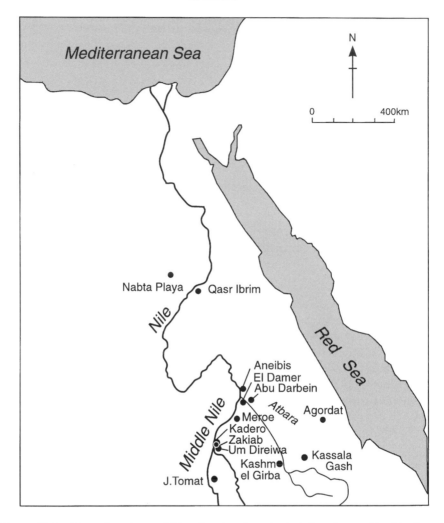

Figure 21.1 Map of north-east Africa, showing the principal sites discussed in this chapter.

therefore only mention some crucial facts. The earliest date from these sites is 8600 BP, but most dates cluster around 8000 BP. These were large sites ranging from 6,000 to 10,000 square m. The inhabitants of these sites exploited a broad spectrum of resources through hunting and gathering, but with a heavy emphasis on aquatic resources. The osteological material shows that at least thirty different species were exploited, as well as large quantities of molluscs. Peters (1995), who has analysed the faunal remains, argues that the species composition indicates that the inhabitants were using nets and exploiting deep-water fish. They would thus have had a boat technology, and small disc-shaped pottery artefacts which could have been used as net sinkers have been recovered. The many harpoons found also attest to the importance of aquatic resources. Hunting activities are shown by the presence of both large and small mammals (large mammals such as giraffe, elephant and various types of small gazelles).

Remains of the cereals *Sorghum verticilliflorum*, *Setaria* and *Pannicum* have been recovered as imprints on pottery (Magid 1995). These cereals are all from wild plants – there is no indication of any morphological changes. The presence of fragments of grinders indicates that these may have been used for processing these wild growing cereals, since cereals have to be processed before being eaten (Magid 1995). The grinders recovered are not numerous when compared to material recovered from the later sites, the highest number of fragments (around 200) coming from the site of El Damer. The evidence indicates the exploitation of plants, probably gathered and not cultivated. Huge quantities of pottery were found. Pottery was probably used both for cooking and storage. Both the large quantities and size of the pottery have implied constraints on mobility (Figure 21.2 shows the type of pottery manufactured). The very high artefact densities and thick cultural deposits suggest long-term permanent occupancy. Several pieces of wattle and daub suggest the presence of more permanent huts or houses. Another set of data which supports this interpretation is the presence of graves (seven graves were excavated at the site of El Damer). The problem of the

Figure 21.2 Potsherds from the Atbara sites (Aneibis), decorated with typical dotted wavy-line decoration.

permanency of the sites has been discussed by Close (1995), who doubts that the population had become sedentary. It is, however, difficult to interpret these data otherwise than that they reflect a trend towards a more sedentary way of life.

In an earlier article (Haaland 1995) I argue that a sedentary way of life based on a broad spectrum of resources, but with an emphasis on intensive exploitation of aquatic resources, was a precondition for the adoption of cultivation because sedentarization would have created conditions which would have been conducive to stimulate population growth (see also Rafferty 1985; Haaland 1987, 1995). With a growing population, the scarcity of plants would have increased and thus stimulated people to intensify use of plant resources. I consider sedentism followed by population increase as an important factor in the origin of agriculture (Smith and Young 1972, 1983; Miller 1992; Haaland 1995).

On the basis of my interpretation of this material I shall argue that an important pathway leading from wild to domesticated sorghum consists in the transition from the gathering of this wild plant to activities which can be characterized as cultivation as early as 6,000 years ago. However, before proceeding with this discussion it is necessary to clarify a few points.

CULTIVATION AND DOMESTICATION: A BASIC DISTINCTION

In trying to understand and identify domestication through archaeological evidence, we are confronted with great difficulties. The first requirement is a clarification of our concept of domestication. Some forms of plants are clearly recognized as domesticated, and the question of the origin of domestication can be solved by tracing such plants back to their wild forms. Domestication is, from this perspective, defined according to criteria of plant morphology and these criteria are used to indicate domestication.

However, domestication is a process, and the forms we identify as domesticated are the outcome of long-lasting human activities in the natural environment. If we want to increase our understanding of domestication we have to grasp the nature of these activities and their relation to domesticated forms.

A critical problem here is to distinguish between those results of intentional human activities, e.g. gathering wild cereals, and the unintended consequences of these activities. Because the results of domestication were far-reaching, and since purposeful creation of new domesticated forms through techniques of modern plant breeding has a long historical record, it is almost unavoidable that we think of the emergence of domesticated plants as intended results. It is unlikely that people had a clear concept of the end result of domestication and worked towards that. In my opinion, it is much more likely that domesticated forms were the unintended consequences of human activities. If this is the case, it is important to understand the results people intended which produced such revolutionary, though unintended, results. The main aim, I assume, was the maintenance of the vegetal component in their diet. With increasing pressure on plant resources, the amount of labour required to satisfy the requirements of the vegetal component increased.

It is possible that this would lead to activities such as planting, weeding, winnowing, threshing, and storing, focusing attention on specific plants. The processing of cereals by grinding, which was one of the most labour-demanding tasks, started at a much earlier stage within a gathering type of economy. These new activities must have changed selection pressures in the natural environment, in a direction which favoured the reproduction of plants which were felt to be superior, having, for example, a higher yield. The unintended outcome of altered selective pressures would have been the emergence of domesticated plants, species which were dependent on human activities for their reproduction. The social implications of cultivation must have been far-reaching, most importantly with reference to the evolution of systems of property. When labour is invested in a process of production where the results are harvested 4–6 months later, one generally finds some kind of institutionalized rights in the standing crop. Ownership of plots of land usually arises at a later stage in the evolution of cultivation systems based on higher labour intensity and permanent cropping. The typical pattern in African shifting agriculture today can best be described as communal rights in land, and individual rights in the crops cultivated (Goody 1968; Maquet 1970; Boserup 1981). It is reasonable to expect that early property systems were similar.

The most important step in the emergence of agriculture is thus cultivation and not domestication. It is expected that by the time we recover the domesticated plants, people were highly dependent on cultivated wild cereals. It is important to distinguish between cultivation as a socioeconomic process relating to people's activities, and domestication as a biological process relating to morphological changes in the plants with cultivation originating prior to domestication (Haaland 1981, 1987, 1995; Bar-Yosef et al. 1991; Miller 1992). This has been forcefully advocated by Harris who has long argued (1984, 1989, 1996) that it is important to look at the agricultural system of plant utilization, which includes cultivation as well as domestication.

I will base my argument on archaeological material from the middle Nile valley during the Holocene period from the ninth to the second millennium BP.

CULTIVATION OF WILD SORGHUM IN THE MIDDLE NILE VALLEY

In the middle Nile region we can observe an increase over time in the number of sites found (Caneva 1988: 334). We can also observe an increase in the size of the settlements. At the beginning of the sixth millennium BP, we can see sites, such as Kadero 1 (Figure 21.1), as large as 30,000 square metres (Krzyzaniak 1978).

Based on the material from the middle Nile region I shall argue that the intensified use of resources led to cultivation of morphologically wild sorghum during the sixth millennium BP. The material relevant to the hypothesis about cultivation of pre-domesticated sorghum during the sixth millennium BP will be based mainly on three sites located in the Khartoum area: Kadero 1, Um Direiwa and Zakiab. The first site was excavated by Kryzaniak (1978, 1991) and the others by Tigani and myself (Haaland 1981, 1987; Tigani 1988). The same broad spectrum of resources was exploited on these sites as was observed on the older sites.

However, people had adopted animal husbandry such as sheep/goat and cattle (Haaland 1981, 1987; Krzyzaniak 1978, 1991; Tigani 1988). The plants recovered from these three sites indicate that several species of grasses were utilized to a significant extent (Stemler 1990). However, the only cereal which we have reason to believe was cultivated is sorghum, twenty imprints of which have been identified (Figure 21.3). The plants recovered are found as imprints on pottery, except for the remains of Celtis and Zizyphus (remains of tree fruits) which were recovered as pips in the settlement debris. The absence of carbonized plant remains may be explained by the nature of the sediments in the sites that are not conducive to the preservation of organic material. Charcoal is almost non-existent. All radiocarbon dates are based upon shell. The froth flotation technique was used but did not yield reliable results – most of the plant remains recovered seem to be recent, and from species existing in the area today. The same negative results were experienced by Clark (1984, 1989) and Krzyzaniak (pers. comm.).

ETHNOBOTANICAL COMPARISON

I will first very briefly discuss the grass seeds recovered which are still harvested today by different people in sub-Saharan Africa and which were never domesticated: Panicum sp. Digitaria type, Eragrostis, Cenchrus cf. biflorus, Paspalum and Setaria. Harvesting of these wild grasses is still known among several groups in the Sahara and savannah zone at the present time (Harlan 1989a). Harlan's survey of grass seeds which are still used also contains grasses found on our sites. Today most of these seeds are famine or scarcity food, or they are harvested casually and opportunistically. However, several of the species he discusses can provide large quantities of food and do actually serve as staples for some tribes. Different harvesting methods were used, several of which are of interest to us; for example, beating into a container, rubbing with the hands into a basket, using a swinging basket or calabash, sweeping or raking off the ground. These harvesting techniques would not constitute a selection pressure that could result in evolution of domesticated cereals

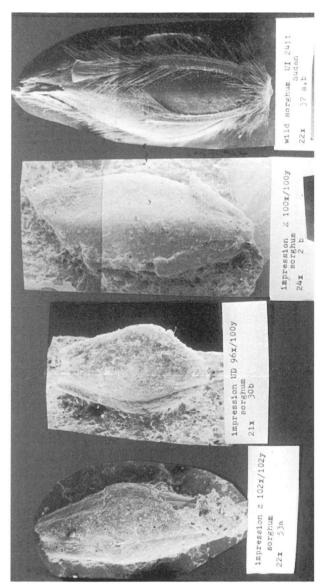

Figure 21.3 Imprints of cereals (*sorghum verticilliflorum*) in potsherds. The three imprints on the left are from the neolithic sites Zakiab and Um Direiwa, the imprint on the right is from recent wild sorghum. (Scanning microscope photo by Ann B.L. Stemler.)

because such harvesting methods are not sufficiently different from natural seeding (Stemler 1990). It is only when people uses sickles or knives to harvest the cereal that they are treating the harvested grain in a way which is different from the natural dispersal mechanisms (Stemler 1990).

On the three sites, tools that could have been used as sickles are almost absent. The only tools recovered which could have been used as sickles are the lunates. However, lunates lack sickle gloss, are small, and few in number. The size of these lunates is on average c. 10–15 mm, a few reaching 20 mm. Even when several are hafted together, they do not seem to be functional as harvesting tools for cutting the thick stalks of the sorghum. Furthermore, over time, as cereal grasses seem to have increased in importance, this type of tool decreases.

ARCHAEOLOGICAL INDICATIONS OF PRE-DOMESTICATED CULTIVATION

The argument that the people inhabiting these three sites were cultivating wild cereals such as sorghum is based on the enormous quantities of broken grinders recovered on these sites.

On one of the sites (Um Direiwa) 30,000 fragments of worn grinders were recovered (Figure 21.4), from 148 square metres excavated. Elsewhere I have discussed in detail the type and quantity of the material excavated (Haaland 1987, 1995). The broken grinders have signs of quite heavy use (Figure 21.5). Ethnographic fieldwork I carried out in West Sudan in 1978 shows that grindstones would last on average about three years. This was partly due to the grindstones being worn down by the grinding activity itself, but the main factor was that the grinders had to be regularly re-pecked to roughen the surface. I will argue that the large number of worn-out grinders is strong evidence for heavy reliance on cereals. When compared with the earlier mesolithic sites (El Damer), where we recovered around two hundred pieces at most, this shows an increased reliance on grain food. I will further hypothesize that the inhabitants of these three sites were cultivating wild sorghum. It is not a change in tool-kit which indicates cultivation, it is the change in frequency of certain tools. In Haaland (1981) I argued that the use of specialized cutting tools, such as sickles, was a necessary condition for the emergence of domesticated varieties. In central Sudan the making of tools for cutting could occur with the transition to an iron technology during the Meroitic period by the end of the third millennium BP.

PERSPECTIVE FROM PLANT GENETICS

However, as has been forcefully argued by Magid (1989), in order for technological changes to be operative as an efficient selective pressure the

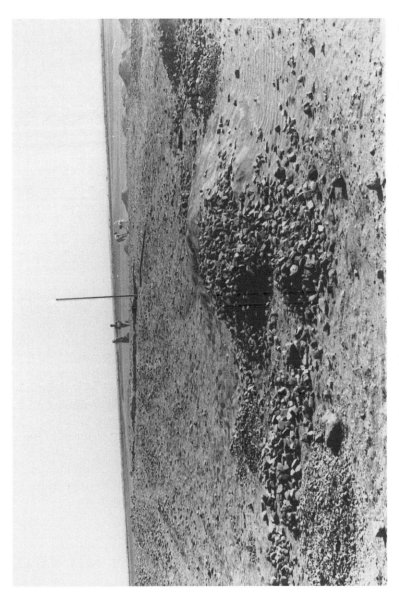

Figure 21.4 Um Direiwa site with some of the excavated grindstone fragments in the foreground. The site can be seen as a low settlement mound elevated above the alluvial flood plain. The Nile is visible in the background. (Photo: Randi Haaland.)

Figure 21.5 Um Direiwa, fragments of worn-out sandstone grinders. (Photo: Randi Haaland.)

isolation of the gene-pool was also essential. He claims this isolation was brought about by the emergence of groups who relied more heavily on animal husbandry and who had brought wild grains with them for cultivation in areas outside the natural habitat of wild sorghum. A similar argument has been presented for the Middle East by Flannery (1965).

If the gene-pool had not been isolated, cross-pollination would have prevented the morphological changes characteristic of domesticated varieties becoming prevalent in a plant population. Wild sorghum outcross frequently (18–30 per cent) compared with domestic ones (5–10 per cent), and thus diverge by a process of disruptive selection (Doggett 1976: 113; 1988: 6). The high level of outcrossing of the genetically wild form will prevent genetic changes among cultivated sorghum. The late emergence of conditions conducive to such isolation in central Sudan may thus be a factor explaining the late appearance of domestic sorghum in the Nile valley.

DOMESTICATED SORGHUM IN THE MIDDLE NILE VALLEY

The available data indicate a late occurrence of domestic sorghum (*Sorghum bicolor*). The earliest dates recorded are from two sites in Sudan, from Jebel Tomat, dated to AD 245 ± 69 (Clark and Stemler 1975; Magid 1989), and from Meroe dated to 20 ± 127 BC (Stemler and Falk 1981). From Qasr Ibrim, in the southern part of Egypt, which has a long settlement history dating from 3000 BC to the medieval period, the plant remains recovered are quite extensive. These have been identified by Rowley-Conwy who concludes that domesticated sorghum was present by AD 100. It is rather interesting to note that during the Napatan period 800–600 cal. BC, no *Sorghum bicolor* was found. It appears only to have gained a widespread distribution around the beginning of the Christian period (Rowley-Conwy 1991).

It should be mentioned that claims have been made for earlier domesticated sorghum in eastern Sudan, including the Gash Delta. Constantini has identified impressions of domestic sorghum on potsherds estimated to date from the second millennium BC collected during a survey (Constantini *et al.* 1983). Only preliminary publications of these findings have appeared and it is thus difficult to judge their importance. Harlan, in his survey of the earliest evidence for domesticated sorghum, does not refer to this find (Harlan 1989b, 1992).

To sum up, our material from the middle Nile valley shows that sorghum has been exploited for a long period by people in the Nile valley – first as a gathered wild cereal at the site of Abu Darbein 8600 BP, then as cultivated wild cereal at the sites of Kadero, Um Dureiwa and Zakiab around 6000 BP, and finally at Jebel el Tomat around AD 250.

THE GLOBAL SCENE

If we had confined our study to the African savannah we might reasonably have seen this as an example of local evolution. This notion becomes very problematic when we place the material in a more global context and look at this question from the savannah, Eygpt, southern Arabia and the Indus (Figure 21.6).

Looking at Eygpt first, excavation at the site of Nabta Playa in the western desert of Egypt has brought to light large quantities of carbonized sorghum grains which have been dated to 8000 BP. These finds are interesting as they are found so far north, outside the Sudanese savannah, which at present is the natural habitat area of wild sorghum and the area where domestication is thought to have initially occurred (Harlan 1989b). Harlan and Stemler (1976) have suggested that the past distribution of sorghum may have been different. Changes in climate could have shifted vegetation zones north. Based on these finds it looks as if we now must widen the geographical area for the distribution and exploitation of sorghum.

An interesting aspect of these finds from Nabta Playa is that they are morphologically wild 'but the lipid fraction of the sorghum grains shows a closer relationship to domesticated than to wild varieties' (Wendorf *et al.* 1992: 721). Could the inhabitants at Nabta Playa have been cultivating sorghum at this early stage? Can the slight morphological changes that we observed on sorghum, both at Nabta Playa 8,000 years ago and from Um Direiwa 2,000 years later, be due to problems of isolating the gene-pools of

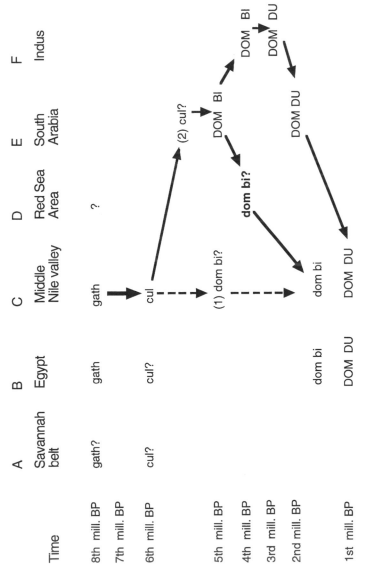
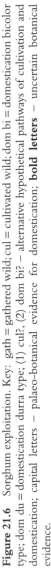

Figure 21.6 Sorghum exploitation. Key: gath = gathered wild; cul = cultivated wild; dom bi = domestication bicolor type; dom du = domestication durra type; (1) cul?, (2) dom bi? – alternative hypothetical pathways of cultivation and domestication; capital letters – palaeo-botanical evidence for domestication; **bold letters** – uncertain botanical evidence.

cultivated sorghum and back-crossing between cultivated and wild-growing sorghum? I leave these questions open for the moment.

DOMESTICATED SORGHUM IN SOUTH ARABIA AND INDIA

The more challenging problem arises when we move to southern Arabia and India (Figure 21.6). The archaeological evidence that we have available at present indicates that domestic sorghum is earlier in both southern Arabia and the Indus valley than it is in Africa (Figure 21.7).

Several imprints of sorghum in potsherds have been found at sites in Yemen, and the reliable dates are 3800 ± 80 BP. The dates we have from (Oman) are much earlier – from 5000 BP. The site of Hili 8 is important here. The material recovered from this site includes charred seeds from several domesticated species: bread wheat, emmer, two- and six-row barley, hulled barley, and, most importantly in this context, *Sorghum bicolor* (Potts 1993: 182). If this date is correct it is the earliest ever recorded. However, doubts about the identification have been raised (Gordon Hillman and Mark Nesbit, pers. comm.). These doubts are similar to those raised on the domesticated sorghum found as imprints on mud-brick dated to 2900 BC. It thus seems that the earliest reliable identification and dates of domestic sorghum in southern Arabia are around 4000 BP. The presence of domesticated sorghum in Yemen seems to be quite clear (George Willcox, pers. comm.). Early dates of *Sorghum bicolor* have been obtained from Harappan sites in the Indus valley, and beyond; these are dated to 2000 cal. BC (Possehl 1986, 1996; Kajale 1991).

Meadow (1996) discussed how African cereals were introduced to India as important summer-growing crops within a complex agricultural regime. He does not limit his discussion to sorghum but mentions finger millet and pearl millet as well. He suggests that the introduction from Africa of the three cereal types spanned a millennium. Finger millet seems to have been introduced first, followed by sorghum and then pearl millet. The oldest finds date back to the last part of the third millennium cal. BC. Sorghum is dated to the beginning of the second millennium cal. BC (Meadow 1996).

The present evidence indicates that *Sorghum bicolor* was earlier in both South Arabia and the Indus Valley than in Africa, where it does not appear in the record before the birth of Christ.

A PARADOX TO BE EXPLAINED

Since wild sorghum is not found in Asia, the domesticated varieties we find on the early sites here must somehow be derived from the African wild varieties. This leaves us with two main hypotheses.

The first is that wild sorghum was domesticated much earlier in Africa than

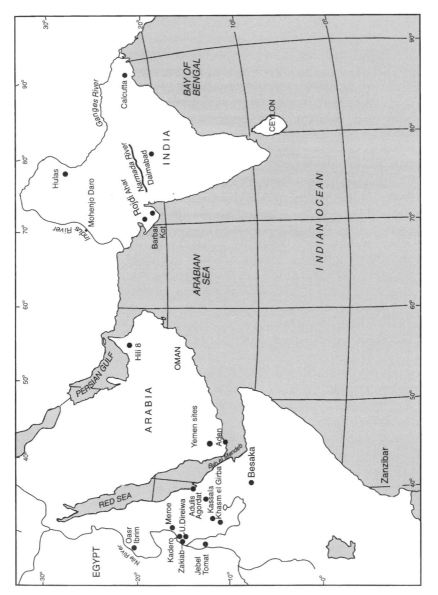

Figure 21.7 Map of East Africa, the Arabian peninsula and the Indian subcontinent showing the principal sites mentioned in this chapter.

our evidence shows. Harlan (1992) reviews the earliest finds of domesticated *Sorghum bicolor* and argues that, since it appears in India during the first millennium BC, it must be earlier than 3000 BP in Africa. (However, since we now have finds from South Arabia as old as 5000 BP Harlan would have to argue that an original domestication in Africa must go back to at least this date.) He furthermore suggests the area within the Chad–Sudan savannah (see Figure 21.6), as the place for the development of domesticated *Sorghum bicolor* (Harlan 1992: 63). Harlan does not refer to the possible finds of domesticated sorghum from eastern Sudan, the Gash delta. This might be due to fact that the publications have appeared as short preliminary reports only, and it is somewhat difficult to judge the validity of these finds.

This hypothesis suggests that *Sorghum bicolor* evolved in an area close to the natural habitat of wild sorghum in Africa, and that it spread from there to Arabia and Asia through processes of diffusion or migration. Even if earlier dates of domesticated sorghum are available from the Sudan savannah, the absence of such finds in the areas lying between the western savannah and Arabia would still pose a puzzle.

The second is that the practice of cultivating wild sorghum spread from people practising a broad spectrum type of economy (with aquatic resources being important) along inland African waterways to populations with a similar broad-based economy along the coast of the Red Sea and the Horn of Africa and from there further east to southern Arabia. The diffusion to India was later and probably involved long-distance trading between more complex societies.

One thus has to consider the possibility that domestication took place outside the natural growing habitat of this cereal – such as southern Arabia, with the Indus valley less likely. Since the dates from Oman are the earliest and the distance from the Horn of Africa to southern Arabia is quite short, southern Arabia may have been the place of domestication. It is interesting to observe that the oldest trace of teff (the cereal which grows wild only in Ethiopia) is found not in Ethiopia but in South Yemen, at Hajar bin Humeid (van Beek 1969; Phillipson 1993). This clearly shows the very close connections between the Horn of Africa and southern Arabia.

The problem with this second hypothesis is that we have no evidence for the presence of wild cultivated sorghum in South Arabia and India which could have served as the gene-pools from which the *Sorghum bicolor* evolved. There is, however, some supporting evidence. Rowley-Conwy has pointed out that the botanical evidence that we have from the Nile valley is quite substantial (Rowley-Conwy, pers. comm.) and that it is evident that domesticated sorghum is not present here during the Napatan period (800–600 cal. BC) while it is well documented from about the birth of Christ. Recent DNA results on *Sorghum bicolor* and durra from Qasr Ibrim suggest that these are closely related. This could be taken as a support of my hypothesis that both *Sorghum bicolor* and durra was domesticated outside Africa; on the other hand it could also indicate that both races were domesticated in Africa (Rowley-Conwy *et al.* in press).

The crucial evidence which could settle the issue – earlier dates of domesticated sorghum in Africa, or finds of wild cultivated sorghum in South Arabia and India – is lacking and we have to leave the question of the origin of domesticated sorghum, as well as the pathways of its later dispersal, unresolved. However, both hypotheses presuppose early contacts between the continents.

PATHWAYS OF DIFFUSION

There is evidence of contact between the Nile and the coast. This is shown by the presence of marine shells at such sites as Kadero, dated to the sixth millennium BP (Krzyzaniak 1991). The marine shells recovered at Kadero are found mainly in rich furnished graves. These shells could have reached the Nile valley as gift exchange through indirect contact, or through direct contact between people with a similar adaptation. The three sites discussed from the middle Nile region had an adaptation based on food production, cultivation of sorghum, animal husbandry (sheep/goat, cattle) and a continuing heavy reliance on aquatic exploitation. This was an adaptation which could be sustained from the Nile valley to the coast of the Red Sea. It can be incorporated in what Sutton calls the aquatic civilization of Africa (Sutton 1977), where populations adapted to a broad spectrum and an aquatic-oriented economy can be found spread along now extinct rivers and lakes from west Sahara to the Nile and East Africa. These types of sites are dated to the Early to Mid-Holocene period. Up until recently evidence of boats was lacking. However, Breunig (1996) reports a dugout canoe at the site of Dufuna, Nigeria, dated to the middle of the eighth millennium BP (7260 ± 55 and 7670 ± 110 BP). This clearly suggests what type of vessels could have been used for water transport, and quite probably indicates the use of this type of vessel by people throughout Africa.

Archaeological material has been surveyed and excavated in the area of Khasm el Ghirba and Erkowit (in the Red Sea Hills) which shows cultural similarities with finds from the Nile valley stretching from the seventh to the third millennium BP (Fattovich et al. 1984; Marks et al. 1985; Marks 1987). Similarities in cultural remains, such as pottery, clearly indicate a long history of contact between the Nile and the coast. During the fifth millennium BP one can observe a development in the Khasm el Girba area of large village-like sites, the sizes of which range from 45,000 to 120,000 square metres. Only a few domestic animals are found, with a heavy emphasis on aquatic resources and exploitation of savannah animals. Large quantities of ground tools were recovered, although only slight evidence of plant remains. Sorghum is found, although whether wild or domesticated is still uncertain. However, the size of the sites and the nature of the deposits, in addition to the large quantities of ground tools, is strong evidence for the cultivation of cereals such as sorghum. The archaeological remains (from this so-called Kassala phase) seems to stretch as far north as Erkowit in the Red Sea Hills and east to the Baraka valley of Agordat in Eritrea. Phillipson (1993) in his survey of material from Ethiopia–Eritrea for the Neolithic period, has pointed out that the archaeological material is exceedingly scant. He also refers to the site of Agordat in Eritrea as showing cultural affinities with sites from the Nile valley, where a surface collection was done by Arkell (1954). Coastal sites do not seem to have been found from this period. However, it is interesting to note that a site dated to the late Pleistocene (19,000 BP) on Lake Besaka in central Ethiopia shows evidence for contact between the inland of Ethiopia and the coast. Brandt, who excavated the site, recovered two cowry shells which may represent the earliest dated occurrence in East Africa of inland contact with the sea (Brandt 1986). The later early Holocene sites from the Lake Besaka area show a significant increase in the density of archaeological deposits, and the faunal material attests to the adaptation of abundant aquatic resources such as fish, hippos and crocodiles. This is the same adaptation as that witnessed along the Nile and elsewhere in Africa – along Saharan inland lakes and East African lakes (Sutton 1977; Haaland 1992). The paucity of archaeological remains from the coastal regions of the Horn of Africa is probably due to lack of archaeological research, as one would expect to find sites of a similar type. Furthermore, obsidian artefacts, found on the Red Sea island of Dahlak Kebir off the coast of Eritrea, must have been brought to the island by boat. Brandt (1986) tentatively dates these finds to the Early Holocene, and this could also suggest contact and flow of commodities other than obsidian at an early period.

Along the coast of southern Arabia several sites have been recorded and excavated which show that the inhabitants had a broad spectrum type of economy, some with a heavy emphasis on aquatic resources (Potts 1993). In an aquatic adaptation it is likely that the water between the Horn of Africa and the Arabian peninsula has been a medium of contact not division. For later periods contact among people on both sides of the Red Sea is manifested both culturally and linguistically from the fourth millennium BP (Fattovich 1990; Munroe-Hay 1993). In the discussion of the rise of complex societies in East Africa, such as the pre-Axumite kingdom, the contact between the two regions is manifested in written sources, in linguistic terms and archaeological material, besides the notion that complex societies were involved in long-distance trading. However, when discussing cultural development during earlier periods there is a tendency to look at the Horn of Africa as belonging to the African continent and the Arabian peninsula as belonging to Asia. Thus our modern geographical classification tends to bias our interpretation of culture history. One tends to see food-gatherers and early food-producers as isolated, in contrast to complex societies with their items of long-distance trade.

The distance across the sea from the Horn of Africa to the Arabian peninsula is less than 20 km, so that the diffusion of both cultural features and people in an aquatic-oriented economy would pose no problem.

Archaeological material, such as pottery and beads, shows contact eastwards between Oman and Iran–Mesopotamia during the third millennium cal. BC (Potts 1993). That there was a further contact between Iran–Mesopotamia and the Indus valley during the third millennium BC is documented in finds such as seals (Crawford 1973). Crawford refers to finds at Ur of Indian and Bahreini seals (Crawford 1973). Edens (1992) has convincingly argued that the Gulf trade connected Mesopotamia with societies in the Arabian Gulf and the Indus Valley for several millennia. This Gulf trade included a wide variety of both luxury and consumption goods. The most important commodity mentioned by Edens is cereal, chiefly barley, part of what Crawford (1973) terms the invisible and bulky goods. Edens discusses how trade items change over time from luxury items to necessities. Cereals, like barley, are mentioned as an example of such a change. It is within this context that one can see how sorghum could easily have been spread as one commodity among others.

Objects from Africa found in the Near East or India are very rare. It is thus very interesting to note that a pendant of copal has been identified from Mesopotamia dated to *c*. 2500–2400 cal. BC. Copal of this sort has been identified as originating from the East African coast: from Zanzibar, Madagascar or Mozambique. As pointed out by Meyer *et al.* (1991), this type of object does not in itself suggest direct contact between East Africa and Mesopotamia but rather trade from north to south Arabia and thence up the Persian Gulf to Mesopotamia. The early dispersal of sorghum within this so-called 'trickle trade' is thus quite likely. The copal pendant was excavated several decades ago and was originally identified as amber; however, new techniques have made it possible to reidentify the object (Meyer *et al.* 1991). I expect that future research will give us more data in support of this type of early contact.

No matter which way the early dispersal of sorghum was carried out, it seems certain that the later emergence of a new sorghum type – durra – took place in India (Harlan 1992) and from there was diffused back to Africa, probably during Islamic times (Harlan 1989b, 1992).

CONCLUSION

This chapter has focused on the long process of domestication of sorghum in Africa. I have argued that cultivation emerged long before cereals were domesticated in Africa and that these activities constituted the selection pressure which was a necessary condition for the biological evolution of domesticated cereals.

I have also argued that the tendency to focus on small areas, and to see temporal changes as a result of local 'evolution', has prevented us from grasping the large-scale processes within which local developments are embedded. For researchers working in Africa, there has hardly been any attempt to place their local sites in wider, more global contexts. The few attempts made to consider local sites in relation to developments taking place in other continents are usually confined to events which have taken place after the rise of complex societies – that is, in periods when we have overwhelming evidence to demonstrate that long-distance trade and politics connected localities scattered on different continents in ramifying systems of interdependence.

The material presented here shows that local sequences even at early dates do not make sense if they are not seen as brought about by processes operating within such intercontinental contexts. The presence of the early domesticated sorghum varieties in South Arabia supports my argument for the earlier phase of cultivation of wild sorghum: without such a phase the occurrence of domesticated varieties outside the natural habitat of sorghum is incomprehensible.

I have ended up with two possible pathways of regional dispersal – both of them plausible on the basis of available evidence and current theoretical positions in ecology and social science. Although my feeling is that domestication of sorghum first occurred in Africa, the present data seem to lend more support to the Asian origin. In the end, as more material is available, neither of the hypotheses may be true, but they will have served the purpose of directing attention to the collection of material which may serve as evidence to refute them and for the formulation of more adequate hypotheses.

ACKNOWLEDGEMENTS

This chapter was written when I was on sabbatical leave at Clare Hall College, University of Cambridge. I want to thank the staff at Clare Hall for their support during my stay. A shorter version of this chapter was given as a lecture at the Department of Archaeology, University of Cambridge, May 1996. I am grateful to Gregory Possehl who very generously shared his ideas with me during his visit to Cambridge in July 1996. Many thanks to Peter Rowley-Conwy for taking time to read the manuscript and for making important comments on it. I would like to thank Rachel Hutton MacDonald, Kevin MacDonald and Rosemarie Luff for fruitful discussions during my stay in Cambridge. Last, but not least, my thanks to Gunnar Haaland for helpful comments. The research in Sudan was funded by the Norwegian Development Agency (NORAD).

REFERENCES

Arkell, A.J. 1954. Four occupation sites at Agordat. *Kush* 2, 33–62.
Bar-Yosef, O., A. Gopher, B. Tchernov and M.K. Kislev. 1991. Netiv Hagdud: an early neolithic village site in the Jordan valley. *Journal of Field Archaeology* 18, 405–25.

Boserup, E. 1981. *Population and Technological Change.* Chicago: The University of Chicago Press.

Brandt, S. 1986. The Upper Pleistocene and Early Holocene prehistory of the Horn of Africa. *African Archaeological Review* 4, 41–82.

Breunig, P. 1996. The 8000 year old dugout canoe from Dufuna (NE Nigeria). In *Aspects of African Archaeology*, G. Pwiti and R. Soper (eds), 461–9. Zimbabwe: Zimbabwe University Press.

Caneva, I. 1988. Prehistoric settlements along the Nile between Geili and Kabbashi. In *El Geili: the history of a middle Nile environment 7000 B.C.–A.D. 1500*, I. Caneva (ed.), 321–44. Oxford: Cambridge Monographs in African Archaeology 29.

Clark, J.D. 1984. Prehistoric cultural continuity and change in the Central Sudan in the early Holocene period. In *From Hunters to Farmers*, J.D. Clark and S. Brandt (eds), 113–26. Berkeley: University of California Press.

Clark, J.D. 1989. Shabona: an early Khartoum settlement on the White Nile. In *Late Prehistory of the Nile Basin and the Sahara*, L. Krzyzaniak and M. Kobusiewicz (eds), 387–411. Poznan.

Clark, J.D. and A.B.L. Stemler. 1975. Early domesticated sorghum from central Sudan. *Nature* 25, 588–91.

Close, A.E. 1995. Few and far between: early ceramics in North Africa. In *The Emergence of Pottery*, W.K. Barnett and J.W. Hoops (eds), 23–54. Washington, DC: Smithsonian Institution Press.

Constantini, L., R. Fattovich, M. Piperno and K. Sadr. 1983. Gash Delta Archaeological Project: 1982 field season. *Nyame Akume* 23, 17–18.

Crawford, H.E.W. 1973. Mesopotamia's invisible export in the third millennium. *World Archaeology* 5, 232–42.

Doggett, H. 1976. Sorghum. In *Evolution of Crop Plants*, N.W. Simmons (ed.), 112–17. London: Longman.

Doggett, H. 1988. *Sorghum.* 2nd edition. London: Longman.

Edens, C. 1992. Dynamics of trade in the ancient Mesopotamian 'world system'. *American Anthropologist* 94, 118–39.

Fattovich, R. 1990. Remarks on the pre-Axumite period in northern Ethiopia. *Journal of Ethiopian Studies* 23, 1–33.

Fattovich, R., A.E. Marks and A.M. Mohammed. 1984. The archaeology of the eastern Sahel, Sudan: preliminary results. *The African Archaeological Review* 2, 173–86.

Flannery, K.V. 1965. The ecology of early food production in Mesopotamia. *Science* 147, 1247–56.

Goody, J. 1968. *Tradition, Technology and State in Africa.* Oxford: Oxford University Press.

Haaland, R. 1981. Migratory herdsmen and cultivating women. The structure of Neolithic seasonal adaptation in the Khartoum Nile environment. Unpublished Ph.D. thesis, University of Bergen.

Haaland, R. 1987. *Socio-economic Differentiation in the Neolithic Sudan.* British Archaeological Reports International Series 350. Oxford: Cambridge Monographs in African Archaeology 20.

Haaland, R. 1992. Fish, pots and grain: Early and Mid-Holocene adaptations in the Central Sudan. *The African Archaeological Review* 10, 43–64.

Haaland, R. 1995. Sedentism, cultivation, and plant domestication in the Holocene middle Nile region. *Journal of Field Archaeology* 22, 157–73.

Haaland, R. and A.M. Magid. 1995. *Aqualithic Sites Along the Rivers Nile and Atbara, Sudan.* Bergen: Alma Mater.

Harlan, J.R. 1989a. Wild-grass seed harvesting in the Sahara and sub-Sahara of Africa. In *Foraging and Farming. The evolution of plant exploitation*, D.R. Harris and G.C. Hillman (eds), 79–97. London: Unwin Hyman.

Harlan, J.R. 1989b. The tropical African cereals. In *Foraging and Farming. The evolution of plant exploitation*, D.R. Harris and G.C. Hillman (eds), 336–44. London: Unwin Hyman.

Harlan, J.R. 1992. Indigenous African agriculture. In *The Origins of Agriculture, an International Perspective*, C. Wesley Cowan and P.J. Watson (eds), 59–70. Washington, DC: Smithsonian Institution Press.

Harlan, J.R. and A.B.L. Stemler. 1976. The races of sorghum in Africa. In *Origins of African Plant Domestication*, J.R. Harlan, J.M.J. de Wet and A.B.L. Stemler (eds), 465–78. The Hague: Mouton Publishers.

Harris, D.R. 1984. Ethnohistorical evidence for the exploitation of wild grasses and forbs: its scope and archaeological implications. In *Plants and Ancient Man: studies in paleoethnobotany*, W. van Zeist and W.A. Caparie (eds), 63–9. Rotterdam: Balkema.

Harris, D.R. 1989. An evolutionary continuum of people-plant interaction. In *Foraging and Farming: the evolution of plant exploitation*. D.R. Harris and G.C. Hillman (eds), 11–26. London: Unwin Hyman.

Harris, D.R. 1996. The origins and spread of agriculture and pastoralism in Eurasia: an overview. In *The Origins and Spread of Agriculture and Pastoralism in Eurasia*, D.R. Harris (ed.), 552–70. London: UCL Press.

Kajale, M.J. 1991. Current status of Indian paleoethnobotany: introduced and indigenous food plants with a discussion of the historical and evolutionary development of Indian agricultural systems in general. In *New Light on Early Farming*, J. Renfrew (ed.), 155–91. Edinburgh: Edinburgh University Press.

Krzyzaniak, L. 1978. New light on early food-production in the Central Sudan. *Journal of African History* 19, 159–72.

Krzyzaniak, L. 1991. Early farming in the middle Nile basin: recent discoveries at Kadero (central Sudan). *Antiquity* 65, 515–32.

Magid, A.M. 1989. *Plant Domestication in the Middle Nile Basin. An archaeoethnobotanical case study*. BAR. Oxford: Cambridge Monographs in African Archaeology 35.

Magid, A.M. 1995. Plant remains and their implications. In *Aqualithic Sites Along the Rivers Nile and Atbara, Sudan*, R. Haaland and A.M. Magid (eds), 147–77. Bergen: Alma Mater.

Maquet, J. 1970. Rwanda castes. In *Social Stratification in Africa*, A. Tuden and A. Plotnicov (eds), 59–92. New York: The Free Press.

Marks, A.E. 1987. Terminal pleistocene and holocene hunters and gatherers in the eastern Sudan. *The African Archaeological Review* 5, 79–92.

Marks, A.E., A.M. Ali, J. Peters and R. Robertson. 1985. The prehistory of the central Nile valley as seen from the hinterlands; excavations of Shaqadud, Sudan. *Journal of Field Archaeology* 12, 261–79.

Meadow, R.H. 1996. Agriculture and pastoralism in northwestern South Asia. In *The Origins and Spread of Agriculture and Pastoralism in Eurasia*, D.R. Harris (ed.), 390–412. London: UCL Press.

Meyer, C., J. Markley Todd and C.W. Beck. 1991. From Zanzibar to Zagros: a copal pendant from Eshnunna. *Near Eastern Studies* 50, 289–99.

Miller, N.F. 1992. The origins of plant cultivation in the Near East. In *The Origins of Agriculture. An international perspective*, C. Wesley Cowan and P.J. Watson (eds), 39–58. Washington, DC: Smithsonian Institution Press.

Munroe-Hay, S. 1993. State development and urbanism in northern Ethiopia. In *The Archaeology of Africa*, T. Shaw, P. Sinclair, B. Andah and A. Opoko (eds), 608–21. London: Routledge.

Phillipson, D.W. 1993. The antiquity of cultivation and herding in Ethiopia. In *The Archaeology of Africa*, T. Shaw, P. Sinclair, B. Andah and A. Opoko (eds), 344–57. London: Routledge.

Peters, J. 1995. Mesolithic subsistence between the 5th and the 6th Nile cataract: the archaeofaunas from Abu Darbein, El Damer, and Aneibis (Sudan). In *Aqualithic Sites Along the Rivers Nile and Atbara, Sudan*, R. Haaland and A.M Magid (eds), 178–244. Bergen: Alma Mater.

Possehl, G.L. 1986. African millets in South Asian prehistory. In *Studies in the Archaeology of India and Pakistan*, J. Jacobson (ed.), 237–56. Delhi: Oxford and IBH and the American Institute of Indian Studies.

Possehl, G.L. 1996. Prehistoric plant exchange between Africa and the Indian subcontinent. Paper presented at the Plants for Food and Medicine Cross-Cultural Plant Exchange Conference, London, July.

Potts, D.T. 1993. The late prehistoric, protohistoric, and early historic periods in eastern Arabia (ca. 5000–1200 B.C.). *Journal of World Prehistory* 7, 163–212.

Rafferty, J.E. 1985. The archaeological record on sedentariness: recognition, development, and implication. In *Advances in Archaeological Method and Theory*, M.B. Schiffer (ed.), 113–57, Orlando, Fla: Academic Press.

Rowley-Conwy, P. 1991. Sorghum from Qasr Ibrim, Egyptian Nubia, *c.* 800 BC–AD 1811; a preliminary study. In *New Light on Early Farming*, J. Renfrew (ed.), 191–212. Edinburgh: Edinburgh University Press.

Rowley-Conwy, P., O.J. Deakin and C.H. Shaw. In press. Ancient DNA from archaeological sorghum (*Sorghum bicolor*) from Qasr Ibrim Nubia: implications for domestication and evolution. Manuscript.

Smith, P.E.L. and T.C. Young Jr. 1972. The evolution of early agriculture and culture in Greater Mesopotamia: a trial model. In *Population Growth*, B. Spooner (ed.), 1–55. Cambridge, Mass: MIT Press.

Smith, P.E.L. and T.C. Young Jr. 1983. The force of numbers: population pressure in the central western Zagros 12,000– 4500 B.C. In *The Hilly Flanks and Beyond*, T.C. Young Jr., P.L. Smith and P. Mortensen (eds), 141–61. Chicago: University of Chicago, Oriental Institute.

Stemler, A.B.L. 1990. A scanning electron microscopic analysis of plant impressions in pottery from the sites of Kadero, El Zakiab, Um Direiwa and El Kadada. *Archaeologie Du Nil Moyen* 4, 87–106.

Stemler, A.B.L. and R.H. Falk. 1981. SEM of archaeological plant specimens. *Scanning Electron Microscopy* III, 191–6.

Sutton, J.E.G. 1977. The aquatic civilization of middle Africa. *Antiquity* 51, 25–33.

Tigani, A.M. 1988. *Zooarchaeology in the Middle Nile Valley: a study of four neolithic sites near Khartoum*. British International Reports 418. Oxford: Cambridge Monographs in African Archaeology 27.

van Beck, G.W. 1969. *Hajar bin Humeid; investigations at a pre-Islamic site in south Arabia*. Baltimore, Md: Johns Hopkins University Press.

Wendorf, F., A.E. Close, R. Schild, K. Wasylikowa, R.A. Housley, J.R. Harlan and K. Krolik. 1992. Saharan exploitation of plants 8,000 years BP. *Nature* 359, 721–4.

22 The impact of maize on subsistence systems in South America: an example from the Jama River valley, coastal Ecuador

DEBORAH M. PEARSALL

INTRODUCTION

Archaeologists are fascinated by maize. *Zea mays* L. has undoubtedly been the subject of more debate, more publications, and more archaeological research than any other New World crop; perhaps more than all the others put together. A recent compendium of this research (Johannessen and Hastorf 1994) illustrates the point.

Maize deserves all this interest; at the time of European contact it was the mainstay of diet of peoples from the Eastern Woodlands of the United States to the Andes of Peru and beyond. One issue of continuing interest throughout the New World is when, and under what sets of circumstances, maize came to occupy this role. As a recent overview of South American data relevant to this issue has shown (Pearsall 1994a), we are only beginning to understand this process, since we still lack good, regional archaeological sequences documenting when maize became incorporated into subsistence, and how its transition to a dietary staple occurred. It is especially important that the role of maize be considered in the context of the indigenous foraging and horticultural practices of the people who accepted it. In the case of the tropical lowlands, for example, maize was introduced into subsistence systems that were likely based primarily upon tuber and root resources and tree fruits, rather than on small-seeded annuals (Pearsall 1992a). Maize would be unlikely to supplant such indigenous plant staples until a number of key innovations occurred: maize productivity outstripped that of competing crops, maize was able to fill a previously unoccupied niche in the crop landscape or calendar, and food storage became critical for economic, political, or social reasons. In this chapter I discuss a case study from the lowlands of western Ecuador, the Jama Valley Archaeological-Palaeoethnobotanical project, to illustrate one approach to understanding this complex process of innovation in subsistence.

Before turning to the Jama study, it is necessary to discuss several issues relevant to the process of subsistence change, and how change is documented through the archaeological botanical record. First, in the case of a crop introduction, one should not assume that the 'full' impact of a new crop is felt immediately upon its appearance in the archaeological record. The importance of the crop must be documented, not assumed: ecological and cultural factors such as those discussed above may slow the process of acceptance and increased dependence; other factors may hasten it. In the case of the introduction of maize into temperate eastern North America, for example, there is a gap of a thousand years or more between an early appearance of the crop (charred remains accelerator-dated to 200 BC, Middle Woodland period, reviewed in Riley et al.. 1990, 1994) and its nearly ubiquitous occurrence in late prehistoric village sites throughout the region (Smith 1989; Johannessen 1993; Scarry 1993; Bendremer and Dewar 1994). Interestingly, the change in maize use appears to be gradual in some regions, such as southern Ontario, Canada (Katzenberg et al.. 1995), and the northern United States (Buikstra and Milner 1991), and more abrupt in others, such as parts of the southern United States (Lynott et al.. 1986). Crop introduction and innovation in subsistence are different processes, and may be widely separated in time and space.

From this distinction it follows that different methods may be necessary to document crop introduction and innovation in subsistence. The initial introduction may leave a very ephemeral mark in the archaeological record: a few charred remains (if the crop was cooked before being consumed); the appearance of a few phytoliths (opaline silica bodies) or pollen grains in refuse areas; little to no shift in the isotopic signature of human skeletal remains. If sites themselves are ephemeral (i.e., seasonal camps rather than villages), this may compound the problem of documenting the presence of a new crop. One effective way to circumvent this difficulty is to look not just at archaeological sites but at whole landscapes. Lake coring can reveal the impact of humans on vegetation on both local and regional scales (e.g., Piperno 1993, 1995); if this impact included preparing fields and growing crops, pollen, phytoliths, and even macroremains of those crop plants may be preserved in the lake core record. If the introduced crop has a major, immediate impact on subsistence, this should be clear in a regional vegetation record, even if sites are difficult to locate or have poorly preserved botanical remains. If the impact is light, studying the regional vegetation record is more likely to 'catch' the introduction than is testing at a single site in that region. Documenting the initial introduction of a crop should thus rely on multiple indicators, and include off-site data. In the case of the spread of maize from southern Mesoamerica into Central and South America, half of the early occurrences of the crop are documented in lake cores, not archaeological sites (Table 22.1; Pearsall 1995a). Without the core data, our knowledge of the spread of maize in the Neotropics would be greatly reduced. These same cores indicate when maize became important by documenting increasing abundances of maize pollen and/or phytoliths, evidence of extensive forest clearance, and appearance of weedy taxa (Pearsall 1995a).

Table 22.1 Early occurrences of corn in the New World tropics. Dates are uncalibrated C-14.

	Location	Date	Comments/Reference
Lake Cores			
Peten Lake	Guatemala	2300 BP	pollen; Vaughn *et al.* 1985
Lake Yojoa	Honduras	4770 BP	pollen; Rue 1989
Gatun Lake	Panama	4750 BP	pollen, phytoliths; Piperno 1985
La Yequada	Panama	4200 BP	pollen, phytoliths Piperno *et al.* 1990, 1991a, 1991b
Lake Wodehouse	Panama	3900 BP	phytoliths; Piperno 1994
Hacienda Lusitania	Colombia	older than 5150 BP	pollen; Monsalve 1985
Hacienda El Dorado	Colombia	6680 BP	pollen; Bray *et al.* 1987
Lake Ayauchi	Ecuador	5300 BP	pollen, phytoliths; Bush *et al.* 1989; Piperno 1990
Lake San Pablo	Ecuador	4000 BP	pollen, charred tissue; Athens 1990, 1991
Archaeological Sites			
Tehuacan	Mexico	4700 BP	dried cobs; Long *et al.* 1989
Aguadulce	Panama	4500 BP	phytoliths; Piperno 1985, 1988
Cueva de los Ladrones	Panama	6910 BP	pollen, phytoliths; Piperno 1985, 1988; Piperno *et al.* 1985
Vegas type site	Ecuador	older than 6600 BP	phytoliths; Piperno 1988; Pearsall and Piperno 1990
Real Alto	Ecuador	5200 BP	phytoliths; Pearsall 1979; Pearsall and Piperno 1990
Loma Alta	Ecuador	5000 BP	charred kernels; Pearsall 1988, 1995c

Another point illustrated by Table 22.1 is how many of these earliest finds of maize in the Neotropics are either pollen grains or phytoliths. Note that phytoliths are as important for tracing maize in the archaeological record as in lake cores. Why is the macroremain record of early maize so sparse? Each taphonomic process (i.e., amount of burning activity to produce charred remains) and set of recovery techniques (i.e., flotation technique, screen size employed) is unique, but I suggest part of the answer lies in differential preservation of charred macroremains and phytoliths. I have discussed in detail elsewhere (Pearsall 1995b) some of the factors that contribute to poor preservation of macroremains in some settings in the lowland tropics. Basically, in heavy clay soils that are wetted and dried on a regular basis (seasonally, for example), charred remains can be broken up over time, while phytoliths are unaffected. Figure 22.1 illustrates this phenomenon for macroremains from site M3D2-009 (Finca Cueva) in the Jama valley. The graph represents over 3,000 years of occupation of this village site, from terminal Valdivia (Piquigua) through Muchique 3 (E. Engwall, pers. comm., 1996). Artefact densities indicate that the site was intensely occupied during Muchique 2 and 3 (surface through 120 cm in this test pit), with a much lighter occupation for Muchique 1, Tabuchila and Piquigua (120 cm through

240 cm). Although artefact densities are high through 120 cm, note the decline in wood charcoal density beginning at 40 cm. This drop-off in charred material in a part of the sequence with dense occupational debris appears to be a taphonomic phenomenon. Phytoliths extracted from the same levels are abundant and well-preserved. In settings where macroremains are influenced by post-depositional destruction, they may not be a reliable indicator of plant abundance, or, in cases as extreme as that illustrated in Figure 22.1, even the absence of a target species such as maize may be illusory.

My point in raising these issues in the context of documenting the impact of maize on subsistence is a simple one: before charred macroremains data are used to demonstrate an apparent shift in abundances of food resources, the analyst must demonstrate that differential destruction of charred material with depth (time) has not occurred. This can be done by graphing abundance of charred material per litre of soil, by depth, as illustrated in Figure 22.1. Contexts of samples to be compared should also be similar; a change in site function or intensity of occupation may cause an increase or decrease in burning activity, and hence preservation (e.g., Pearsall 1983). Comparing data from preceramic and ceramic-using sites is especially problematic; if cooking techniques changed with the appearance of pottery, so might the ways foods enter the archaeological record. If preservation of charred botanical remains is a problem in earlier ceramic phases, as it is in the Jama valley, phytoliths provide a robust alternative source of data on early crop occurrences.

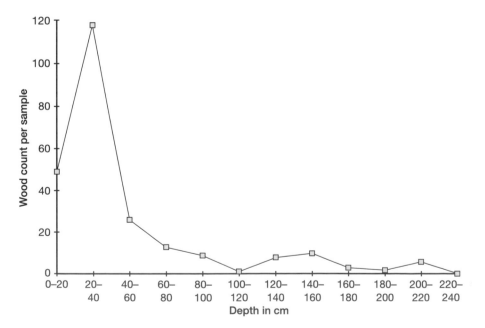

Figure 22.1   Abundance of charred wood with depth. Data from test pit 2, site M3D2-009 (Finca Cueva), Jama Valley, Ecuador.

MAIZE IN COASTAL ECUADORIAN SUBSISTENCE

It is difficult not to equate the importance of maize and the importance of agriculture when looking at palaeoethnobotanical data from coastal Ecuadorian sites, since the most important lowland root crop, manioc (*Manihot esculenta*), is nearly 'invisible' in the archaeological record. Maize is present in coastal Ecuador since the late Preceramic (Late Las Vegas phase, maize phytoliths in strata older than 4600 BC) (Piperno 1988; Pearsall and Piperno 1990). It is impossible, however, to assess the importance of the 'new' crop relative to other foods at this time period because the poor preservation of macroremains at Vegas and subsequent Valdivia (Early Formative, first ceramic phase) sites limits both precision of identification and application of quantitative measures. Bone collagen in human skeletal samples from the Vegas type site, OGSE-80, is poorly preserved, but eight samples with preserved collagen from Valdivia 1–2 strata at the Loma Alta site show no dietary impact by maize (average delta 13C, −19.0 ‰; van der Merwe *et al.* 1993). Maize kernels are rare at Loma Alta. The single Valdivia 3 sample with preserved collagen from the large Real Alto village is similar (delta 13C, −18.8 ‰). Maize phytoliths occur in many contexts at that site. The isotopic data are silent on the identity of the major plant contributors to the Vegas and Valdivia diets.

Archaeobotanical data do contribute some information on this. 'Porous' tissue that could be root remains, and phytoliths from *Canna*, a taxon producing edible tubers, at Real Alto suggest that root/tuber foods, as well as maize, were in use during the Valdivia period, along with jack beans (*Canavalia*), cotton (*Gossypium*), tree fruits, and small seed resources (Pearsall 1979; Damp *et al.* 1981; Damp and Pearsall 1994). Whether the root/tuber foods and cotton were domesticated is unknown; however, *Canna* does not occur naturally in the region, and the jack beans are likely the domesticated species, *C. plagiosperma*. Thus while we know that a variety of crops were present by the Early Formative in coastal Ecuador, we do not have good answers to two interrelated questions: was subsistence based on agriculture, and how important was maize early in coastal prehistory?

The available bone isotope data for the later Formative Machalilla and Chorrera periods document that maize had some impact on diet during Machalilla (average delta 13C, −12.3 ‰), with an increase in maize use at one Chorrera site (Loma Alta, average delta 13C, −10.1 ‰) and steady levels at another (Salango, average delta 13C, −12.5 ‰) (van der Merwe *et al.* 1993). The absence of late Valdivia samples, and the evidence of variability of isotopic signature between Chorrera sites, makes it difficult to assess whether this change in maize use was gradual or abrupt. The transition from low levels of maize use to its role as a dietary staple is still poorly documented for coastal Ecuador, complicated by poor preservation at early sites and the availability of relatively few datasets.

One of the goals of the Jama valley project was to gather data relevant to the evolution of coastal subsistence from terminal Valdivia through the contact period from one region (Zeidler and Pearsall 1994). Through a programme of valley-wide survey and site testing, such a database has been compiled. Although analyses are not completed for all sites, preliminary results are available which provide insight into agricultural evolution in this valley, and suggest a model of change in the relative importance of maize and local foods that may be applicable more widely in the lowland tropics of the New World.

The Jama valley archaeobotanical database, as it currently exists, has limitations that must be acknowledged. Because terminal Valdivia and Chorrera Formative deposits are often buried by metres of later occupation, the database for the earlier time periods is smaller both in numbers of sites and contexts tested, and in abundance of botanical remains recovered per flotation sample (Pearsall 1994b). Many Formative-age samples appear to be heavily affected by post-depositional destruction of remains, and cannot be compared quantitatively to later, better-preserved samples. The sequence immediately after the Formative in the Jama valley, the Muchique sequence (Jama-Coaque I and II), is less impacted by taphonomic factors in many cases.

Thus the Jama valley database does not provide a direct means, at this time, of testing whether the Late Formative marks an important transition in the use of maize in the coastal lowlands, as suggested by the van der Merwe *et al.*. (1993) isotope study. However, the Muchique sequence does provide some insight into the process of innovation in subsistence. If maize came to dominate subsistence during the late Formative in the Jama valley, then we should see evidence for this in the subsequent Muchique I period. In other words, maize should already be abundant at sites. If this transition occurred later in time in the Jama case, then the sequence should document changes in subsistence from Muchique 1–2 or during the Muchique 2 sequence. These issues will be discussed below. An evaluation of the overall importance of agriculture, relative to the use of wild and tended plant resources, awaits final identifications of root/tuber foods and tree fruits.

THE JAMA VALLEY PROJECT

The Jama valley Archaeological-Palaeoethnobotanical project was initiated by James A. Zeidler and myself in the mid-1980s for the purpose of conducting an interdisciplinary archaeological investigation of long-term sociopolitical change through the successive prehispanic occupations of northern Manabi province (Zeidler and Pearsall 1994). One of the major foci of the project was to investigate the process of agricultural intensification in the lowland tropics. The ultimate goal of this focus was to test models of agricultural evolution and cropping intensification by using biological data recovered from sites in the valley.

The Jama river drainage is one of the numerous river valleys flowing directly into the Pacific Ocean along the coastal strip of western Ecuador (Figure 22.2). It is situated just below the equatorial line in northern Manabi province. The Jama is the largest drainage basin of northern Manabi, and has its headwaters in the low hills of the coastal cordillera. The main channel of the river extends 75 km. The valley occupies a transitional area from dryer to wetter (coastal to inland) conditions (dry megathermic tropical to semi-humid megathermic tropical). Although the valley is largely deforested today,

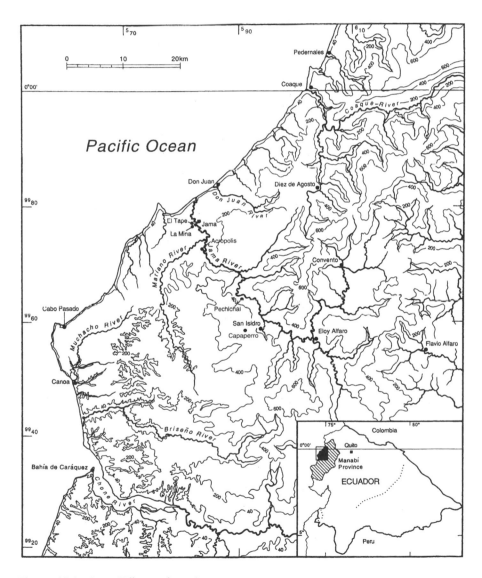

Figure 22.2 Jama Valley study region.

the natural vegetation cover is dry tropical forest along the coast and humid pre-montane tropical forest further inland (Zeidler and Kennedy 1994).

As a result of a valley-wide archaeological survey and testing programme carried out from 1989 through 1991, the cultural chronology presented in Table 22.2 (Zeidler *et al.* 1998) was established. An important feature of the chronology is the presence of three discrete tephra layers, thick deposits of wind-transported volcanic ash and pumice, throughout the valley. These tephra deposits originated from volcanic eruptions in the western Andean cordillera and were distributed onto the coastal plain by the prevailing easterly winds (Isaacson 1994). Originally blanketing the landscape, the tephras were redeposited within each coastal watershed by erosion from hill slopes into valley bottoms, where deposits up to 2 m thick were created. Ash deposition of this magnitude produces a wide range of environmental hazards, including damage to forests and crop destruction, and can lead to long-term disruption of agricultural systems, especially those that are based on cultivation of alluvial lands (Isaacson 1994).

In the case of the Jama valley, understanding the impact of tephra deposition is essential for understanding human adaptation in the valley. While the small Terminal Valdivia populations survived the first tephra fall, the valley was abandoned within a hundred years of the event, and remained unoccupied for some 550 years. Tephra II ended the Chorrera occupation of the valley, resulting in a major cultural discontinuity that is seen not only in the Jama valley, but widely in north-west Ecuador (Isaacson 1994). The valley was quickly reoccupied by Jama-Coaque I populations (Muchique 1 phase). The third tephra event, resulting in the deepest deposits, had by contrast less impact on cultural continuity in the valley than did Tephra II. A short abandonment, of perhaps a generation, occurred after Tephra III, followed by re-establishment of Jama-Coaque populations (Muchique 2 phase).

Table 22.2 Cultural chronology of the Jama River valley. Model dates (cal. BC) based on an analysis of 37 radiocarbon dates (Zeidler *et al.* 1998)

Culture	Phase	Date	Period
Campace (?)	Muchique 5	AD 1430–1640	Colonial
	Spanish conquest (AD 1532)		
Jama-Coaque II	Muchique 4	AD 1290–1430	Integration
Jama-Coaque II	Muchique 3	AD 880–1260	Integration
Jama-Coaque II	Muchique 2	AD 420–790	Integration
	Tephra III (*c.* AD 400)		
Jama-Coaque I	Muchique 1	240 BC–AD 90	Regional Developmental
	Tephra II (*c.* 750 BC)		
Chorrera	Tabuchila	1300–750 BC	Late Formative
	Hiatus		
Valdivia	Late Piquigua	1800 BC	Early Formative
	Tephra I		
	Early Piquigua	2030 BC	Early Formative

A RECONSTRUCTION OF PREHISTORIC SUBSISTENCE IN THE JAMA RIVER VALLEY

Data recovery and analysis procedures

The primary data used in this discussion are charred botanical remains recovered by water flotation of sediments from test excavations in the Jama valley. The flotation system used, an IDOT-style manual system with 0.5 mm screen (Pearsall 1989), permitted recovery of all size classes of botanical remains. Non-buoyant remains were hand-sorted in the field lab from heavy fractions, ensuring that materials of all densities were represented. Flotation samples were sorted at the University of Missouri Paleoethnobotany Lab following standard procedures (Pearsall 1989). Determining final identifications is ongoing; many small seed taxa and fruit fragments remain unidentified to species. To make a preliminary assessment of the impact of maize on subsistence, four types of remains are considered here: maize or corn, bean (*Phaseolus vulgaris*), tree fruit (palm and other wild/tended tree taxa), and root/tuber (root-like storage organ fragments, not yet identified to taxon). Since the majority of small seeds appear to be from weedy plants, they are omitted from this analysis.

It is likely that final identification of remains will result in at least three types of tubers (*Maranta*, *Canna* and *Manihot*), and as many, or more, species of tree fruits (for example, taxa in the families Palmae and Sapotaceae) being identified. This increased level of precision will allow refinement of the patterns discussed below, and may permit use of diversity measures to examine patterning in the botanical data. What is unlikely to change are patterns of bias in the data due to differences in the 'toughness' of the various classes of botanical materials. Fruit fragments, dense meats and rinds, are durable materials that are much less likely to be destroyed by wetting and drying and soil pressure than are the fragile remains of tubers. These are the remains most likely to be dramatically over- and under-represented, respectively, throughout the sequence. In broad terms, tuber-root remains are more important in subsistence than is suggested by the quantity of remains recovered, and tree fruits less so. Beans and maize fall in between, with maize kernels being more subject to destruction, and somewhat under-represented, than are dense bean cotyledons.

The botanical data discussed below pertain to seven chronological phases, and come from five sites (Table 22.3). Features (F) and Deposits (Dep. – natural stratigraphic layer) in domestic occupation debris make up the majority of the database; arbitrary levels assignable to Muchique 1 from the Don Juan site were included to augment this early period. Data from individual samples were grouped by summing raw data counts by phase.

The Muchique 1 phase is represented by materials from the Don Juan site, located at the mouth of the river of the same name (Figure 22.2). One feature from this site, Feature 7, dating to 480 BC, is examined separately, since it falls before the main Muchique 1 occupation at 355 BC. As will be

Table 22.3   Macroremain database, in chronological order

Site number (name)	Strata	Phase	C-14 date	No. litres	Wood[1]	Corn	Other food
M3B2-001 (Don Juan)	Dep. 1,2	Post-Much. 3		302.5	853	208	57
M3B3-012 (Acropolis)		Late Much. 3	AD 1150	94	395	265	44
M3B2-001 (Don Juan)	Dep. 3	Late Much. 3		151	592	162	24
M3D2-065 (Cappaperro)	F4	Early Much. 3	AD 755	51	138	162	48
M3B4-011 (Pechichal)	F5	Much. 2	AD 545	831.5	2702	3568	1922
M3B3-002 (El Tape)	F4	Early Much. 2	AD 340	184.5	8863	647	43
TEPHRA III (ca. AD 400)							
M3B2-001 (Don Juan)	Dep. 4	Much. 1		190	331	85	11
M3B2-001 (Don Juan)	F7	Early Much. 1	480 BC	18	55	9	0

Note

1   Wood, corn, and other food data are presented in counts.

discussed further, abundance of materials is lowest for the Muchique 1 phase. Two deep storage pits provide data for the Muchique 2 phase. The El Tape pit is about 200 years younger than the pit from the Pechichal site, providing an opportunity to look at change within the Muchique 2 phase. Both pits have abundant remains. The El Tape site is in the lower Jama valley; Pechichal in the upper. Three sites provide material dated to the Muchique 3 phase; the Capaperro site in the upper valley dates to early in this phase; Don Juan and the Acropolis, both in the lower valley, are later and roughly contemporary. No samples clearly attributable to Muchique 4 (AD 1250–1430) were available for this analysis, so the upper two deposits at the Don Juan site (Deposits 1 and 2), known to post-date Muchique 3, were combined to give some indication of later subsistence patterning.

A number of ways of quantifying macroremains data could be applied to the Jama valley dataset (Hastorf and Popper 1988; Pearsall 1989). To assess the degree of preservation bias, I graphed wood count per 10 litres of floated soil for each phase; abundance fluctuates, but does not decline dramatically with depth (Figure 22.3). This suggests that taphonomic phenomena have not biased the overall plant assemblage to a great extent. Wood is especially abundant in the El Tape feature samples; food remains very common in the Pechichal pit samples. Ratios of each class of food remain per 10 litres of floated soil (corn/10 litres, tree fruit/10 litres, bean/10 litres, tuber-root/10 litres) allow abundance of individual remains to be tracked over time. A direct

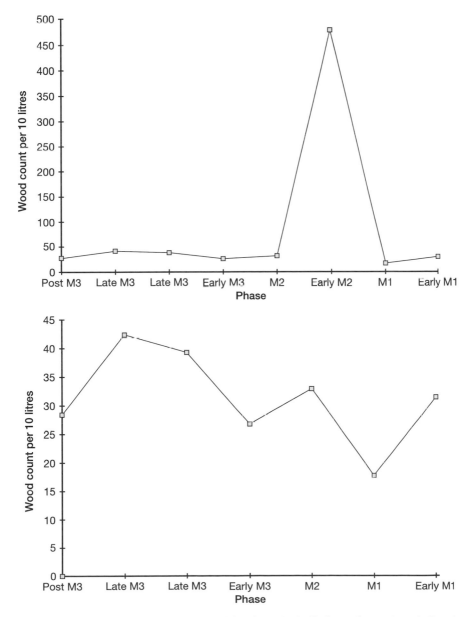

Figure 22.3 Abundance of charred wood by phase: (top) all phases; (bottom) excluding the early Muchique 2 phase in order to illustrate the pattern for the other phases more clearly.

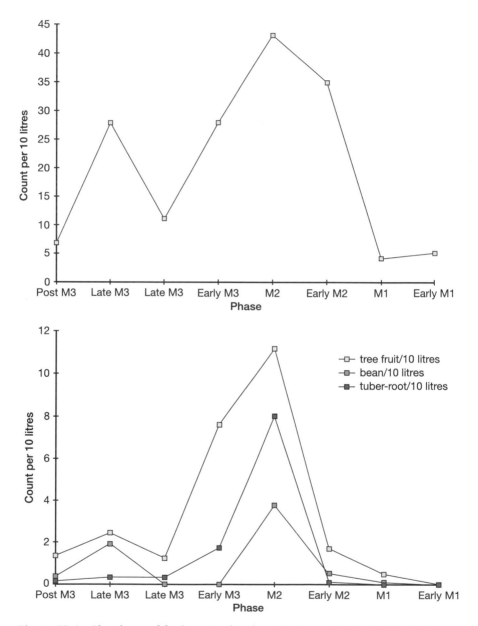

Figure 22.4 Abundance of food remains by phase: (top) corn; (bottom) other foods.

comparison of maize to all other foods (corn:other food ratio) contrasts the occurrence of the target species to all other foods as a group.[1]

Patterning in Muchique phase macroremains data

Figure 22.4 illustrates the abundance of each class of food remains by phase. All foods increase in abundance during the later Muchique 2 phase; these are the rich Pechichal pit samples. The most significant pattern, however, is that maize is present in greater abundance than other food remains in all phases. After maize, tree fruits are most abundant. The relative abundance of beans and tuber-root fragments varies by phase, with tubers being significantly more abundant than beans in the Late Muchique 3 sample from the Acropolis. Since tuber remains are extremely fragile, this is a significant finding.

Comparing maize directly to other foods (corn:other food ratio, Figure 22.5) reveals some interesting patterns. Maize is very abundant relative to other foods during the Muchique 1 and early Muchique 2 phases, increasing in abundance between them. There is then a significant drop in the relative abundance of maize; it is still the most common food remains in the later part of the Muchique 2 phase, but other foods contribute substantially to the archaeobotanical record. The corn:other food ratio goes up again, but never to the levels observed early in the sequence.

Qualitative comparisons of Muchique to Formative period data

As discussed above, the Formative macroremains database from the Jama valley project, as it currently exists, cannot be compared quantitatively to that of the Muchique sequence because of preservation and sampling problems. The best information on plants utilized for subsistence during the Formative

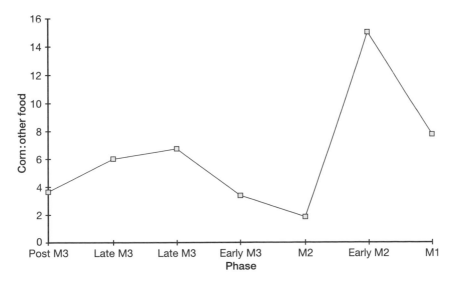

Figure 22.5 Abundance of corn relative to other foods by phase.

derives from phytoliths. It is difficult to determine the relative importance of crops from phytolith data, however, since phytolith production patterns vary widely among species (Piperno 1988; Pearsall 1989). The strength of phytolith data lies in documenting plants poorly preserved in the charred botanical record.

Phytolith data from a series of test pits in the San Isidro site (M3D2-001), the central place of the valley, document the presence of a suite of cultivated and utilized plants which remains much the same from late Valdivia through Jama-Coaque II. Maize, Marantaceae (probably *Maranta*, arrowroot tuber), and *Canna* (achira tuber) are present throughout the sequence. Palms and sedges, either cultivated or encouraged, were also consistently present, as were wild grasses, especially bamboos. Squash or gourd were identified in Formative samples (Pearsall 1992b; Pearsall and Zeidler 1994). Palm and achira phytoliths are especially abundant late in the Jama-Coaque II period; this hints at a shift in importance of these resources at San Isidro, but this requires corroboration. Chorrera phase deposits from two smaller sites, M3B4-031 and M3D2-009, essentially duplicate the plant suite documented at San Isidro.

What the phytolith data contribute for comparing Formative period and later subsistence in the Jama river valley is to (1) confirm that maize was present from the beginning of the sequence, (2) identify two of the root crops, arrowroot and achira, and document their continued presence, (3) suggest that an enhanced role for root crops and palms in the later part of the sequence be investigated, and (4) document that the variety (richness) of resources utilized stayed high throughout the sequence. The last point does not negate an increased reliance on maize during Muchique 1 and early Muchique 2, but indicates this occurred in the context of a broad-based subsistence system.

DISCUSSION

Perhaps the most striking point revealed by this preliminary look at the Jama valley archaeobotanical data is that the numbers of kinds of foods used, the richness of the resource base, remained very consistent through time. This is the major contribution of the phytolith data, which show continuity of resources present from terminal Valdivia (1700 BC) through Jama-Coaque II (AD 1532). Maintaining a broad subsistence base, a natural feature of the lowland forest environment and early subsistence systems, would be highly adaptive in a setting subjected to catastrophic events like tephra fall: the more crops/resources used, the more likely some would be to survive.

Agricultural technology would also play a role in successful human adaptation in such a setting. Even given a subsistence system characterized by richness, terminal Valdivia and Chorrera period peoples of the Jama were severely affected by tephra events. One likely contributing factor was concentration of settlements and fields on the river alluvium, which was buried deeply by redeposited tephra. Archaeological survey data show no Valdivia period settlements off the alluvium, and only a few small Chorrera and Muchique 1 sites in non-alluvium; appreciable expansion of settlement into the uplands and the beginning of upland agriculture, presumably utilizing the slash and burn technique, does not occur until Muchique 2, after the Tephra III ash fall (Pearsall and Zeidler 1994). This suggests that Muchique 2 populations took advantage of 'new' agricultural lands to weather the effects of the tephra. Population growth resulted, with a rapid increase in sites and evidence for storage, such as the pit analysed from the Pechichal site.

It is during the Muchique 2 phase that changes occur in the apparent importance of maize and other food plants. As detailed above, maize increases in abundance relative to tree fruits, beans, and root/tuber foods from Muchique 1 to early Muchique 2. The relationship of this change to the Tephra III event, which occurred between Muchique 1 and 2, is suggestive: of the available crops, was maize best adapted to the altered growing conditions in the valley; namely, very deep tephra deposits on alluvial soils that necessitated use of newly cleared fields in the uplands?

Later in the Muchique phase, maize abundance declines sharply, then rises again in subsequent phases but not to the levels seen previously. Today in the Jama valley both maize and manioc are grown in the uplands; maize first, to take advantage of soil nutrients, followed by manioc. As-yet-unanalysed agronomic data will allow more precise modelling of agricultural productivity in the valley, but perhaps a mixed cropping strategy, as suggested by the lower maize:other food ratios of late Muchique 2 and after, contributed to long-term stability of subsistence in the valley.

In what sense, then, does maize cultivation represent an innovation in subsistence in this case? First, the abundance of charred maize remains relative to other foods is highest in the early part of the Muchique sequence. If, as the van der Merwe et al. (1993) isotope study suggests, maize was important in diet beginning in the late Formative (Chorrera) in coastal Ecuador, then it is not surprising that the crop holds this position in the immediate post-Formative period (i.e., Muchique 1 in the Jama valley). While root crops such as manioc, achira, or arrowroot must be processed into flour for storage 'above ground', maize can be readily stored in the form of dried grain. The changing economic and political conditions in the valley marking the emergence of the Jama-Coaque chiefdom may have provided an impetus for maize production in the context of a broad-based subsistence system.

The Jama data also suggest, however, that maize, in combination with the opening of new agricultural lands, may have contributed to the success of the population in quickly reoccupying the valley following the catastrophic Tephra III ash fall. In this sense, an innovation in cropping was perhaps as important as the crop itself.

CONCLUSION

This chapter has presented a case study focused on the role of maize in innovation in subsistence in lowland South America. To investigate this, or any topic related to subsistence in the tropical lowlands, requires not only systematic recovery of charred macroremains but also analysis of phytoliths which are preserved under conditions where charred materials may be destroyed.[2] Because understanding the quality of preservation is critical for applying quantitative methods to macroremains data (and for knowing when not to apply such methods), these issues were discussed at length, and only one part of the Jama valley sequence, the Muchique phase, was considered from a quantitative perspective.

One of the goals of the Jama valley Archaeological-Palaeoethnobotanical project was to test when maize became important in subsistence in western Ecuador – specifically, to test whether the late Formative, the Chorrera period, marked the beginning of maize-based subsistence systems in this region. Unfortunately, the Formative period macroremains database available at this time from the Jama is not robust enough to test this model. We have documented, however, that all the elements of the subsistence system observed at contact, including maize, were in place by the Formative. Maize was the most abundant food throughout the post-Formative, Muchique phase, but was only part of a broad-based subsistence system that contributed to long-term stability. Abundance of maize relative to other foods peaked in early Muchique 2, when it may have played an important role in the rapid recolonization of the valley following a major tephra event. Innovation in coastal Ecuadorian agricultural systems will be investigated further in upcoming research in the Jama river valley.

ACKNOWLEDGEMENTS

Pearsall and Zeidler's research in the Jama river valley has been supported by grants from the National Science Foundation of the United States.

NOTES

1 The corn:other food ratio is not calculated for early Muchique 1, since only corn is present among foods.
2 This chapter has not considered pollen evidence, which in some regions can provide valuable insight into subsistence, because pollen has not been well preserved in contexts studied to date in the Jama valley (Zimmerman 1994).

REFERENCES

Athens, J.S. 1990. *Prehistoric Agricultural Expansion and Population Growth in Northern Highland Ecuador: interim report for 1989 fieldwork.* Honolulu, Hawaii: International Archaeological Research Institute, Inc.

Athens, J.S. 1991. Early agriculture in northern highland Ecuador. Paper presented at the 56th Annual Meeting of the Society for American Archaeology, New Orleans.

Bendremer, J.C.M. and R.E. Dewar. 1994. The advent of prehistoric maize in New England. In *Corn and Culture in the Prehistoric New World*, S. Johannessen and C.A. Hastorf (eds), 369–93. Boulder, Colo.: Westview Press.

Bray, W., L. Herrera, M.C. Schrimpff, P. Botero and J.G. Monsalve. 1987. The ancient agricultural landscape of Calima, Colombia. In *Pre-Hispanic Agricultural Fields in the Andean Region*, W.M. Denevan, K. Mathewson and G. Knapp (eds), 443–81. Oxford: BAR International Series 359 (ii).

Buikstra, J.E. and G.R. Milner. 1991. Isotopic and archaeological interpretations of diet in the central Mississippi valley. *Journal of Archaeological Science* 18, 319–29.

Bush, M.B., D.R. Piperno and P.A. Colinvaux. 1989. A 6000 year history of Amazonian maize cultivation. *Nature* 340, 303–5.

Damp, J.E. and D.M. Pearsall. 1994. Early cotton from coastal Ecuador. *Economic Botany* 48, 163–5.

Damp, J., D.M. Pearsall and L. Kaplan. 1981. Beans for Valdivia. *Science* 212, 811–12.

Hastorf, C., and V. Popper (eds). 1988. *Current Paleoethnobotany.* Chicago: University of Chicago Press.

Isaacson, J. 1994. Volcanic sediments in archaeological contexts from western Ecuador. In *Regional Archaeology in Northern Manabí, Ecuador, Volume 1. Environment, Cultural Chronology, and Prehistoric Subsistence in the Jama River Valley*, J. A. Zeidler and D.M. Pearsall (eds), 131–40. Pittsburgh: University of Pittsburgh Memoirs in Latin American Archaeology No. 8.

Johannessen, S. 1993 Farmers of the Late Woodland. In *Foraging and Farming in the Eastern Woodlands*, C.M. Scarry (ed.), 57–77. Gainesville: University Press of Florida.

Johannessen, S. and C.A. Hastorf (eds). 1994. *Corn and Culture in the Prehistoric New World.* Boulder, Colo.: Westview Press.

Katzenberg, M.A., H.P. Schwarcz, M. Knyf and F.J. Melbye. 1995. Stable isotope evidence for maize horticulture and paleodiet in southern Ontario, Canada. *American Antiquity* 60, 335–50.

Long, A., B.F. Benz, D.J. Donahue, A.J.T. Jull and L.J. Toolin. 1989. First direct AMS dates on early maize from Tehuacan, Mexico. *Radiocarbon* 31, 1035–40.

Lynott, M.J., T.W. Boutton, J.E. Price and D.E. Nelson. 1986. Stable carbon isotopic evidence for maize agriculture in south-east Missouri and north-east Arkansas. *American Antiquity* 51, 51–65.

Monsalve, J.G. 1985. A pollen core from the Hacienda Lusitania. In *Pro Calima* 4, 40–4.

Pearsall, D.M. 1979. *The application of ethnobotanical techniques to the problem of subsistence in the Ecuadorian Formative.* Ph.D. dissertation (Anthropology), University of Illinois. University Microfilms, Ann Arbor, Mich.

Pearsall, D.M. 1983. Evaluating the stability of subsistence strategies by use of paleoethnobotanical data. *Journal of Ethnobiology* 3, 121–37.

Pearsall, D.M. 1988. An overview of Formative period subsistence in Ecuador: palaeoethnobotanical data and perspectives. In *Diet and Subsistence: Current archaeological perspectives*. B.V. Kennedy and G.M. LeMoine (eds), 149–64. Proceedings of the Nineteenth Annual Chacmool Conference. Chacmool: The Archaeological Association of the University of Calgary, Alberta.

436 D. M. PEARSALL

Pearsall, D.M. 1989. *Paleoethnobotany. A handbook of procedures.* San Diego, Calif.: Academic Press.

Pearsall, D.M. 1992a. The origins of plant cultivation in South America. In *The Origins of Agriculture. An international perspective*, C. Wesley Cowan and P. J. Watson (eds), 173–205. Washington, DC.: Smithsonian Institution Press.

Pearsall, D.M. 1992b. Prehistoric subsistence and agricultural evolution in the Jama river valley, Manabi province, Ecuador. *Journal of the Steward Anthropological Society* 20, 181–207.

Pearsall, D.M. 1994a. Issues in the analysis and interpretation of archaeological maize in South America. In *Corn and Culture in the Prehistoric New World*, S. Johannessen and C.A. Hastorf (eds), 245–72. Boulder Colo.: Westview Press.

Pearsall, D.M. 1994b. Macrobotanical analysis. In *Regional Archaeology in Northern Manabí, Ecuador, Volume 1. Environment, Cultural Chronology, and Prehistoric Subsistence in the Jama River Valley*, J.A. Zeidler and D. M. Pearsall (eds), 149–59. Pittsburgh: University of Pittsburgh Memoirs in Latin American Archaeology No. 8.

Pearsall, D.M. 1995a. Domestication and agriculture in the New World tropics. In *Last Hunters–First Farmers: new perspectives on the prehistoric transition to agriculture*, T.D. Price and A.B. Gebauer (eds), 157–92 Santa Fe, N.Mex.: School of American Research.

Pearsall, D.M. 1995b. 'Doing' paleoethnobotany in the tropical lowlands: adaptation and innovation in methodology. In *Archaeology in the Lowland American Tropics. Current analytical methods and recent applications.* P.W. Stahl (ed.), 113–29. Cambridge: Cambridge University Press.

Pearsall, D.M. 1995c. Subsistence in the Ecuadorian Formative: overview and comparison to the central Andes. Paper presented at the Dumbarton Oaks Conference on the Ecuadorian Formative, October.

Pearsall, D.M. and D.R. Piperno. 1990. Antiquity of maize cultivation in Ecuador: summary and reevaluation of the evidence. *American Antiquity* 55, 324–37.

Pearsall, D.M. and J.A. Zeidler. 1994. Regional environment, cultural chronology, and prehistoric subsistence in northern Manabí. In *Regional Archaeology in Northern Manabí, Ecuador, Volume 1. Environment, Cultural Chronology, and Prehistoric Subsistence in the Jama River Valley*, J.A. Zeidler and D.M. Pearsall (eds), 201–16. Pittsburgh: University of Pittsburgh Memoirs in Latin American Archaeology No. 8.

Piperno, D.R. 1985. Phytolithic analysis of geological sediments from Panama. *Antiquity* LIX, 13–19.

Piperno, D.R. 1988. *Phytolith Analysis. An archaeological and geological perspective.* San Diego, Calif.: Academic Press.

Piperno, D.R. 1990. Aboriginal agriculture and land usage in the Amazon basin, Ecuador. *Journal of Archaeological Science* 17, 665–77.

Piperno, D.R. 1993. Phytolith and charcoal records from deep lake cores in the American tropics. In *Current Research in Phytolith Analysis: applications in archaeology and paleoecology*, D.M. Pearsall and D.R. Piperno (eds), 58–71. Philadelphia: MASCA, the University Museum of Archaeology and Anthropology, University of Pennsylvania.

Piperno, D.R. 1994. Phytolith and charcoal evidence for prehistoric slash-and-burn agriculture in the Darien rainforest of Panama. *The Holocene* 4, 321–5.

Piperno, D.R. 1995. Plant microfossils and their application in the New World tropics. In *Archaeology in the Lowland American Tropics. Current analytical methods and recent applications*, P. W. Stahl (ed.), 130–53. Cambridge: Cambridge University Press.

Piperno, D.R., M.B. Bush and P.A. Colinvaux. 1990. Paleoenvironments and human occupation in late-glacial Panama. *Quaternary Research* 33, 108–16.

Piperno, D.R., M.B. Bush and P.A. Colinvaux. 1991a. Paleoecological perspectives on human adaptation in central Panama. I. The Pleistocene. *Geoarchaeology* 6 (3), 201–26.

Piperno, D.R., M.B. Bush and P.A. Colinvaux. 1991b. Paleoecological perspectives on human adaptation in Central Panama. II. The Holocene. *Geoarchaeology* 6 (3), 227–50.

Piperno, D.R., K. Husam-Clary, R.G. Cooke, A.J. Ranere and D. Weiland. 1985. Preceramic maize in central Panama: phytolith and pollen evidence. *American Anthropologist* 87, 871–8.

Riley, T.J., R. Edging, and J. Rossen. 1990. Cultigens in prehistoric eastern North America. *Current Anthropology* 31, 525–41.

Riley, T.J., G.R. Walz, C.J. Bareis, A.C. Fortier and K.E. Parker. 1994. Accelerator mass spectrometry (AMS) dates confirm early *Zea mays* in the Mississippi River valley. *American Antiquity* 59, 490–8.

Rue, D.J. 1989. Archaic middle American agriculture and settlement: Recent pollen data from Honduras. *Journal of Field Archaeology* 16, 177–84.

Scarry, C.M. 1993. Variation in Mississippian crop production strategies. In *Foraging and Farming in the Eastern Woodlands*, C.M. Scarry (ed.), 78–90. Gainesville: University Press of Florida.

Smith, B.D. 1989. The origins of agriculture in eastern North America. *Science* 246, 1566–71.

van der Merwe, N.J., J.A. Lee-Thorp, J. Scott Raymond. 1993. Light, stable isotopes and the subsistence base of Formative cultures at Valdivia, Ecuador. In *Prehistoric Human Bone: archaeology at the molecular level*, J.B. Lambert and G.Grupe (eds), 63–97. Berlin: Springer-Verlag.

Vaughn, H.H., E.S. Deevy Jr. and S.E. Garrett-Jones. 1985. Pollen stratigraphy of two cores from the Petén Lake district, with an appendix on two deep-water cores. In *Prehistoric Lowland Maya Environment and Subsistence Economy*, M. Pohl (ed.), 73–89. Cambridge, Mass.: Peabody Museum of Archaeology and Ethnology, Harvard University.

Zeidler, J.A., C.E. Buck and C.D. Litton. 1998. The integration of archaeological phase information and radiocarbon results from the Jama river valley, Ecuador: a Bayesian approach. *Latin American Antiquity*, 9, 160–79.

Zeidler, J.A. and R. Kennedy. 1994. Environmental setting. In *Regional Archaeology in Northern Manabí, Ecuador, Volume 1. Environment, Cultural Chronology, and Prehistoric Subsistence in the Jama River Valley*, J.A. Zeidler and D.M. Pearsall (eds), 13–41. Pittsburgh: University of Pittsburgh Memoirs in Latin American Archaeology No. 8.

Zeidler, J. A. and D. M. Pearsall (eds). 1994. *Regional Archaeology in Northern Manabí, Ecuador, Volume 1. Environment, Cultural Chronology, and Prehistoric Subsistence in the Jama River Valley*. Pittsburgh: University of Pittsburgh Memoirs in Latin American Archaeology No. 8.

Zimmerman, L.S. 1994. Palynological analysis. In *Regional Archaeology in Northern Manabí, Ecuador, Volume 1. Environment, Cultural Chronology, and Prehistoric Subsistence in the Jama River Valley*, J.A. Zeidler and D. M. Pearsall (eds), 175–83. Pittsburgh: University of Pittsburgh Memoirs in Latin American Archaeology No. 8.

23 Starch in sediments: a new approach to the study of subsistence and land use in Papua New Guinea

MICHAEL THERIN, RICHARD FULLAGAR AND ROBIN TORRENCE

PREHISTORY OF TROPICAL AGRICULTURE

Current understanding of agricultural origins and change has been dominated by archaeological research conducted in very dry environments where ancient plants, particularly seeds, have been well preserved: e.g. Mesoamerica, Peru, and the 'fertile crescent' of South-west Asia (cf. Smith 1995; Gebauer and Price 1992; Cowan and Watson 1992). These biases in the preservation of data have provided archaeologists with a very partial view, but one which nevertheless underlies many general theories about the role of agriculture in the development of sedentary villages, hierarchical societies, etc. Not surprisingly, these theories do not fit the picture of social change that is coming to light as a result of recent discoveries in tropical regions (e.g. studies in Hather 1994b) and particularly in Papua New Guinea where agriculture was practised as early as in the traditional centres of civilization, but where it does not appear to have led society in the same directions. Since those new data are contrary to their theories, many archaeologists have ignored (e.g. Gebauer and Price 1992; Cowan and Watson 1992) or are reluctant to accept (e.g. Smith 1995) Golson's (1991a, 1991b; Golson and Gardner 1990) the discovery of agriculture in the Highlands of Papua New Guinea as early as 9,000 years ago.

Surprisingly, the prehistory of subsistence and land use in the lowland regions of Melanesia has also been influenced more by research in the northern latitude centres of agricultural origins than by the implications of Golson's important findings at Kuk swamp. Consequently, the traditional view of subsistence change in island Papua New Guinea relies on the association of agriculture and sedentism observed in other parts of the world which are located in radically different ecological settings (cf. Shoocongdej 1996 for a similar critique concerning South-east Asia). So, for example, many scholars have implied that around 3,500 years ago in lowland Melanesia there was a radical increase in the intensity of plant use as inferred from the presence of villages (i.e. sedentism). This change is usually linked to the supposed introduction of South-east Asian domesticates and Lapita–style pottery (e.g. Green 1979; Kirch 1988; cf. summaries and discussions in Yen 1982, 1991; Matthews 1990, 1995; Matthews and Terauchi 1994; Golson and Ucko 1994; Gosden and Webb 1992).

One exception to the view that agriculture is a relative latecomer to the Pacific region is Spriggs (1993) whose view was highly influenced by the finding of stone tools dated to 28,000 BP and found to have starch grains identified as *Colocasia esculenta* adhering to their edges (Loy *et al.* 1992; Loy 1994: fig. 5.7). The aim of this chapter is to introduce a new approach involving the analysis of starch grains in sediments. We argue that the frequency and composition of starch grains can be used to monitor changes in subsistence and the history of land use. Future work can then be directed toward the critique of long-held assumptions about the relationship of villages, sedentism and agriculture, such as those implicit in the traditional model for the origins of Pacific agriculture. Our arguments are developed within a case study in which the analysis of assemblages of starch grains from two archaeological sites from West New Britain Province, Papua New Guinea are used in conjunction with studies of obsidian artefacts to test competing proposals concerning the direction and rate of subsistence change.

Until recently, research on subsistence and land use in the tropical regions has been seriously hindered because, with a few notable exceptions (Hather and Kirch 1991; Hather 1992, 1994; Haberle 1995), the roots which are most likely to have formed the bulk of subsistence in these regions are invisible in the archaeological record due to poor preservation and because these plants generally lack pollen and phytoliths. In contrast, analyses of sediments and residues from the two archaeological sites of FRL at Bitokara Mission (Specht *et al.* 1988; Torrence *et al.* 1990; Torrence 1992; Fullagar 1992) and FAO on Garua Island (Barton *et al.* 1995; Barton 1994; Therin 1994; Torrence 1994a) have shown that starch grains are well-preserved at these locations (Figure 23.1). Identification to species is not yet possible but we argue that variations through time in the frequency and assemblage composition of starch grains can be used to track changes in patterns of mobility and, by implication, of strategies for subsistence in terms of land management.

We must stress, however, that the approach presented here as well as the techniques for extraction and counting of grains are in their early stages of development, and so the chapter represents an outline of broad principles rather than a definitive methodology. Limitations identified in the course of the analyses discussed here are currently being addressed through an ongoing programme of experimentation and fieldwork (Therin 1994; Lentfer 1995; Therin *et al.* 1997). Although the results for FRL and FAO must be considered as provisional, they are very provocative and justify further research into the analysis of prehistoric starch grains.

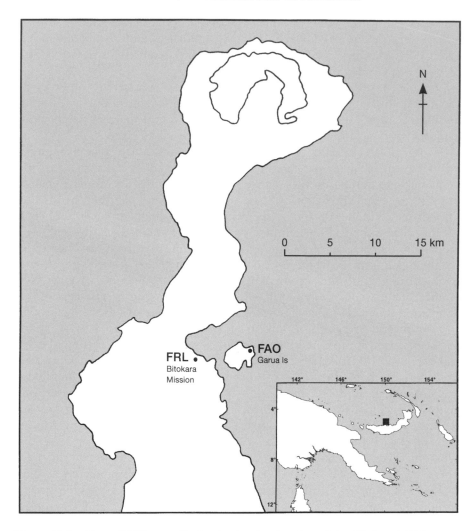

Figure 23.1   Map of Willaumez Peninsula, showing location of sites FAO and FRL.

MOBILITY AND LAND MANAGEMENT

A number of new studies have shown that many major food crops were probably domesticated locally in Melanesia and not imported from South-east Asia (e.g. Coates *et al.* 1988; Matthews 1991; Yen 1991; Matthews and Terauchi 1994; Haberle 1995). Consequently, the traditional model equating Lapita-style pottery, villages, and agricultural origins has come under attack. Current scholars have shifted the focus from looking at the origins of agriculture to trying to track the history of subsistence through focusing on patterns of forest management (e.g. Groube 1989). For instance, Torrence

(1992, 1994a, 1994b) hypothesized that in the Talasea region of West New Britain province in Papua New Guinea a slow, steady decline in mobility took place during the period from c. 6000 BP up to the present. She goes on to suggest that the increase in sedentism was caused by a gradual increase in the intensification of land management, which she defines as the extraction of increasing amounts of plant food from a decreasing amount of land (Torrence 1992: 121). Like the traditional model, Torrence implies that the emphasis on gardening increased during the time of Lapita-style pottery, but she envisages it as the result of gradual change operating over a long time frame, rather than a sudden jump due to the introduction of new crops.

A third view has been put forth by Gosden and Pavlides (1994: 169), who have proposed that radical changes in gardening practices on the south coast of New Britain did not occur during the time of Lapita-style pottery. In their view, the major period of change has taken place in the past 100 years when, due to pacification, opportunities for trade have increased markedly. In turn, large, sedentary villages have been created and gardening practices have significantly intensified, since food is the major trade item. Unlike the two previous views which imply permanent or at least long-term settlement at sites with Lapita-style pottery, they propose that these sites were visited repeatedly by small groups of people practising a fairly mobile way of life combined with a low intensity form of agriculture. So, for them Lapita sites are 'spots on the landscape to which people returned regularly and which perhaps had stands of nut bearing trees and areas of cleared land for garden plots nearby' (Gosden and Pavlides 1994: 169). These locations are also described as resulting from a continuation of 'long lasting traditions, deriving from Pleistocene forms of movement' (ibid.). Furthermore, the large amounts of erosion associated with the beginning of Lapita-style pottery is thought to indicate 'ad hoc clearance and planting' (ibid.). They suggest that this way of life based on impermanent hamlets continued until the middle of the nineteenth century.

Both the Torrence and the Gosden and Pavlides models for mobility and land use differ from the traditional model in that they conceive of subsistence during the time of Lapita pottery to be derived from previous patterns rather than imported from elsewhere. They differ from each other in the degree to which sedentism is thought to have been practised at this time, although both models are deliberately vague about how long people are supposed to have resided at the places where pottery is found. In summary, the major questions that arise from the debates over the nature of sedentism and gardening practices during the time of Lapita-style pottery are as follows: (1) is there a significant increase in the intensity of gardening practices after the beginning of Lapita-style pottery?; (2) if so, was this change sudden or part of a long-term process?; and (3) to what extent do Lapita sites represent sedentary villages? Answering these questions will have important implications for evaluating the archaeology theory concerning the relationship between sedentism and agriculture that has been derived from research in other parts of the world (e.g. Gebauer and Price 1992).

Currently available data do not allow us to answer these key questions satisfactorily due to lack of data about subsistence practices. Since it is unlikely that direct, macroscopic indicators of subsistence have been well enough preserved in the tropical setting of New Britain, new techniques are needed to shed light on the important issues discussed above concerning intensity of plant use and sedentism. In order to contribute to the ongoing debate about Pacific subsistence, our chapter presents preliminary results based on the initial stages in the development of a new methodological approach based on the analysis of starch grains extracted from archaeological sediments.

THE CASE STUDY

The Talasea region of West New Britain (Figure 23.1) is an excellent setting for a case study concerning mobility and land use practices. To begin with, open sites which span at least the past 6,000 years are commonplace here, but are rare elsewhere in New Britain. The presence of contexts both earlier and later than Lapita-style pottery from the same locations allows a test of whether the Lapita cultural material represents a sharp break within long-term processes of change. Second, a series of well-dated Holocene volcanic eruptions have blanketed the landscape with easily recognizable layers of tephra which have sealed continuous landscapes (Machida *et al.* 1996). The tephra layers provide invaluable markers for linking the stratigraphy of sites separated by many kilometres (Specht *et al.* 1991; Torrence 1994a; Torrence *et al.* 1997).

For our preliminary examination of the potential of starch grains for testing hypotheses of land use and subsistence, we have focused on two archaeological sites with comparable stratigraphy and long sequences (Figures 23.1, 23.2). Site FRL, Trench 1 (2 × 2 m), located on the mainland of New Britain at Bitokara Mission, was excavated to a depth of 3.1 m in 1988 by a team headed by Specht (Specht *et al.* 1988; Torrence *et al.* 1990). The site is situated near extensive flows of obsidian which have been extensively quarried and traded for at least the past 20,000 years (e.g. Summerhayes and Allen 1993; Summerhayes *et al.* 1993). FRL is also important for our purposes because the analysis of the obsidian assemblages recovered from the site contributed to Torrence's hypothesis about mobility changes (Torrence 1992). Fullagar (1992, 1993) has analysed the use-wear and residues on artefacts from the site, and described the distribution of starch grains on one large retouched obsidian artefact. The starch analysis of sediments from FRL were carried out by Fullagar *et al.* (1994).

Our second site, FAO, is located on Garua Island which is in the adjacent harbour within view of Bitokara (Figure 23.1). The site was excavated in

1992–3 as part of a larger project investigating changes in settlement history, resource use and exchange (Torrence 1994a). At site FAO twenty-four test pits have been excavated across the hilltop (Torrence 1997). A deep sounding to 3.5 metres within pit 1000/1000, has been the focus of subsequent detailed analysis. Michael Therin conducted the starch analyses of sediments from FAO 1000/1000 (Therin 1994; Therin *et al.* 1994), and a preliminary study of starch extracted from obsidian artefacts in this pit has also been completed (Barton *et al.* 1995).

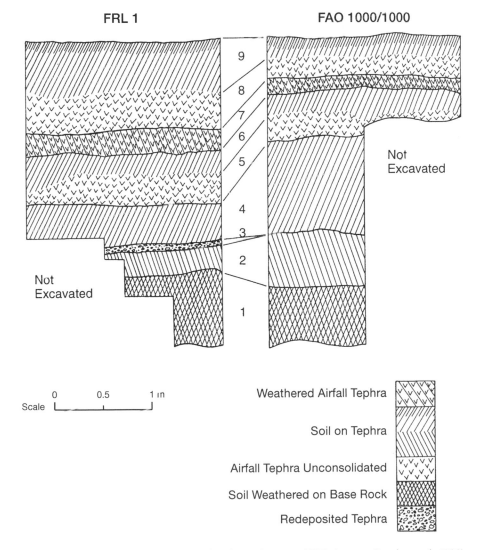

Figure 23.2 Comparison of stratigraphic layers between FRL (source: Specht *et al.* 1988) and FAO (source: Therin 1994).

As illustrated in Figure 23.2, both sites are comprised of a series of superimposed airfall tephras, two of which have well-developed soil horizons. Fortunately, it is relatively easy to recognize each of these strata in this region and therefore correlate layers between the two sites. This process has been facilitated because three of the tephras can be identified to their source volcano and relative date of eruption by using a combination of visual inspection of composition and layering (Machida *et al.* 1996) and geochemical analyses of glass shards using SEM microprobe (Torrence *et al.* 1997). The source of a fourth tephra is unknown but the geochemical signature of stratigraphically comparable layers at the two sites is identical and it resembles a tephra from the Witori group.

The stratigraphy of the two sites is composed of nine layers as shown in Figure 23.2 (cf. fuller descriptions in Specht *et al.* 1988: 8–9; Torrence *et al.* 1990: 459; Torrence *et al.* 1997).

Layer 1: Soil from weathering of bedrock; date unknown.

Layer 2: Soil developed from an unsourced airfall tephra; date unknown.

Layer 3: Airfall tephra from WK-1 eruption dated younger than *c.* 5630 ± 110 BP (Machida *et al.* 1996: 71; Specht *et al.* 1991: 282); redeposited at FRL but not present at FAO.

Layer 4: Soil developed from an unsourced tephra (possibly the WK-1 airfall tephra). Dates of 3370 ± 100 BP (SUA-2814) and 3590 ± 90 (Beta-57773) have been returned at FRL (Machida *et al.* 1996: 71; Specht *et al.* 1991: 282) and a date of 3532 ± 66 (NZA 2901) has been obtained from this layer at FAO.

Layer 5: Unconsolidated airfall tephra from the WK-2 eruption.

Layer 6: Soil formed on WK-2 airfall tephra. Dates of 2439 ± 64 BP (NZA 3738) and 2452 ± 67 BP (NZA 3729) have been obtained from the comparable soil horizon within test pits at FAO. Lapita-style pottery was recovered from this layer at FAO, but it is absent from FRL.

Layer 7: Partially developed soil derived from an airfall tephra whose source is suspected to be the Witori volcano, but whose geochemistry has not yet been correlated with a particular eruption (Torrence *et al.* 1997). The geochemistry of this layer is identical at both sites.

Layer 8: Unconsolidated airfall tephra from the Dakataua eruption dated to *c.* 1150 ± 60 BP (Machida *et al.* 1996: 71).

Layer 9: Soil formed on the Dakataua tephra.

At the FRL trench, Layer 3, the WK-1 tephra is presumed to have been washed down from the nearby hillslope; Layer 3 is not present on the hilltop at FAO, but has been located as a redeposited layer in a nearby valley. Layers 5 and 8 are unconsolidated airfall tephra and are virtually devoid of archaeological finds at both sites.

STONE TOOL ANALYSES

Previous analyses of stone tool technology (Torrence 1992) and use–wear and residues (Fullagar 1992) at FRL have supported the hypothesis of a gradual reduction in mobility over time. Torrence (1992) argued that the change from gearing up of multi-purpose tools at the obsidian sources to the expedient manufacture of unretouched flakes could be explained as the result of a shift from embedded procurement within a highly mobile subsistence pattern to special purpose trips undertaken from relatively sedentary villages. Support for this view was provided by Fullagar (1992) whose study of six sites, spread throughout West New Britain, identified a gradual shift from sites having a limited range of activities in the pre-Lapita-style pottery phases to the presence of a wider range of stone uses in the most recent levels. He interpreted the convergence in site function to mean reduced mobility of the stone users. Both these analyses depend on a series of complex inferences linking stone tools to land use. If any one of these is faulty, then the overall interpretation fails. The analysis of starch grains was therefore initiated in order to provide a more direct measure of land management practices.

Before turning to the starch results, it is useful to create a simple measure of cultural activity against which to interpret changes in the frequency and composition of starch grains. For this purpose we have chosen to use 'density' of stone artefacts, which is defined as the counts of artefacts per layer divided by the volume of soil for the relevant layer. Figure 23.3 portrays density in terms of numbers of artefacts per cubic metre of soil for each phase of FAO and FRL. The very small numbers of artefacts in layers 3, 5, and 8 are

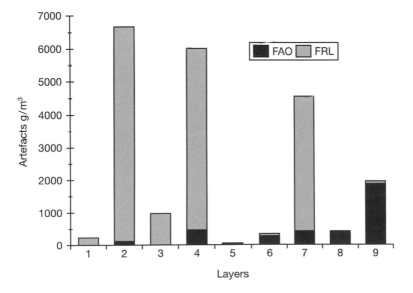

Figure 23.3   Stone artefact frequencies at FRL and FAO, by layer.

consistent with their being unconsolidated tephras. The focus of analysis should therefore be placed on layers 1, 2, 4, 6, and 7.

As seen in Figure 23.3, chronological change in artefact density at the two sites presents very different patterns. First, throughout the sequence there are markedly higher quantities of obsidian artefacts at FRL until the most recent phase. Second, the nature of changes through time varies between the two sites. The frequency of obsidian at FAO rises gradually up to layer 4 where it remains stable until layer 9 when there is another small rise. In contrast, at FRL the frequency of artefacts steadily decreases through time. In other words, having started from very different points, the sites gradually become more similar through time.

These patterns can be explained in terms of likely site function. To begin with, the much higher quantities of obsidian at FRL are consistent with its location at a major quarry. The decline in frequency of material reflects a gradual shift away from quarrying and manufacture as the primary activity on the site to one characterized by production and use in a domestic context. Layer 6 is an exception to this pattern. Possibly the site was not used during this time. It is notable that the number of artefacts in layer 6 at FAO has also diminished from the high point in layer 4. This trend is likely to reflect the abandonment of the area after the disastrous effects of the WK-2 volcanic event (Torrence et al. 1990; Machida et al. 1996: 76). The decline in relative numbers of artefacts through time at FRL supports Torrence's (1992) interpretation for a shift from production of stemmed tools for use elsewhere, a process which would generate large quantities of waste by-products, to expedient manufacture of flake tools to be used for immediate consumption by local residents.

On the contrary, in terms of obsidian artefacts FAO can be interpreted as having been a consumption site throughout its history. The overall, gradual increase through time in artefacts illustrated in Figure 23.3 is also consistent with the hypothetical shift to a more expedient strategy for maintaining tools (Torrence 1992, 1994b). The rise in artefact frequency in layer 4 is contemporary with a dramatic decline in numbers of retouched artefacts throughout the region. Using Torrence's hypothesis this shift can be explained as a change from a more to a less mobile settlement pattern. The second rise in layer 9 may signal the existence of a relatively permanent residential site in which obsidian was expediently made and used on a regular basis.

These results are more tantalizing than conclusive and derive from a very small sample. Nevertheless, the density of obsidian artefacts lends support to Torrence's (1992) and Fullagar's (1992) previous observations about changes in procurement, manufacture, and tool use in West New Britain. It is against this background, then, that we initiated attempts to develop a methodology for using starch grains to measure changes in subsistence patterns.

BACKGROUND TO STARCH ANALYSES

Starch is a semi-crystalline polymer composed of crystalline and amorphous regions. The granule is made up of two organic polymers, amylose (crystalline) and amylopectin (amorphous) (cf. Banks and Greenwood 1975). As a polymer starch granules are highly resistant to corrosion. In plants and animals starch is broken down through the use of specific enzymes which are not normally present in soils. Therefore, it is not surprising that starch grains have been preserved in a number of very ancient contexts.

Starch has been observed as part of the residues on stone artefacts for many years, but it is only since the mid-1970s that archaeologists have attempted to make use of this class of data to answer questions about prehistoric subsistence. A historical review of these early unsystematic observations can be found in Fullagar (1988) and Hall et al. (1989). With the exception of Ungent et al. (1987), who used the morphology of starch grains to argue that poorly preserved macroscopic remains of potatoes from a site in Chile represented a domesticated rather than a wild species, recent work has been dominated by Australian scholars: notably Loy (1994; Loy et al. 1992), Hall and his students (Hall et al. 1989; Robertson 1994) and Fullagar (1988; 1993). Loy's (1994; et al. 1992) work has been especially important because he has proposed a method for using size and shape of starch grains to identify the species of plant from which they were derived.

Following Loy's proposals, a series of assessments of the utility of starch grain analysis have been undertaken at the Australian Museum by a team led by Fullagar (e.g., Atchison 1994; Barton 1990, 1994; Barton and White 1993; Barton et al. 1995; Brass 1993; Fullagar 1992, 1993; Fullagar et al. 1992; Furby 1995). All these studies have attempted to identify starch grains extracted from residues on stone tools recovered from archaeological sites in Papua New Guinea and Australia. Most recently, the team has turned its attention to the study of starch grains extracted from ancient sediments (Fullagar et al. 1994; Therin 1994; Therin et al. 1994), along the lines of pollen or phytolith studies (cf. studies in Hather 1994; Haberle 1995; Powers and Gilbertson 1989) in order to provide a way to reconstruct vegetation histories at sites. Preliminary work using modern comparative material has shown that tubers, in particular, appear to produce starch grains with distinctive shapes and characters, especially when viewed in polarized light, as in the *Dioscorea nummularia* pictured in Figure 23.4, which is from modern reference material. In comparison, the grain shown in Figure 23.5, which was extracted from an archaeological sample, is not so well preserved and is therefore less distinctive, but it can nevertheless be tentatively assigned to the genus *Dioscorea* due to its size, overall elongated shape, and the character of the extinction cross. In very rare situations a cluster of starch grains has been recovered from archaeological sediments as in the case of the grains shown in Figure 23.6, which closely resemble grains of *Manioc esculenta* in our modern reference collection.

Figure 23.4 Starch grains of *Dioscorea nummularia* from modern reference material. Scale bar equals 20 microns. Photo taken with cross-polarized, transmitted light at ×500 magnification.

The overall conclusions reached in the pilot studies undertaken to date are that (1) starch grains are frequently found in abundance both in sediments and on the edges of stone tools; (2) the location and quantity of starch grains on stone tools is correlated with use-wear traces; (3) except in very rare circumstances (e.g., Figures 23.5, 23.6; cf. Barton 1990; Barton and White 1993; Therin 1994: pl. 6.4), the descriptions of starch grains from root crops presented by Loy (1994) and Loy *et al.* (1992) do not allow identification of the starch grains observed in soils or on tools from sites FRL and FAO; and (4) the raphides that are critical to the Loy *et al.* (1992) classification were almost completely absent in our samples of sediments or artefactual residues. The implications of the last two findings are either that the food crops Loy has described were not present in West New Britain or, more likely, that further work is required to greatly extend and improve the methods used to identify plants to family or genus level on the basis of the shape and size of starch grains. Consequently, the Australian Museum team has undertaken fieldwork to expand the botanical reference collection (Lentfer 1995; Torrence 1995; Therin *et al.* 1997) and is currently employing image analysis of this large dataset in order to establish a more comprehensive methodology for the identification of ancient starch grains from Australia and Papua New Guinea.

In this chapter we present some results from the early stages in our ongoing research on the interpretation of starch grains extracted from sediments. Research on stone tool residues is also in progress but presents fewer difficulties because the range of starch grains observed is much less

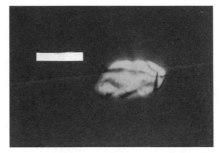

Figure 23.5 Starch grain extracted from layer at FAO most closely resembles modern reference material of *Dioscorea* sp. Scale bar equals 20 microns. Photo taken at ×500 magnification with cross-polarized, transmitted light.

restricted than in the assemblages recovered from sediments. Due to the difficulties of taxonomic identification, we have adopted a pragmatic approach similar to that used by Powers and Gilbertson (1989; cf. Powers and Padmore 1993) in the initial stages of phytolith analysis in Scotland, where a taxonomic key also had not yet been established.

In our study, frequency of starch grains per volume of sediment and the relative size of grains are used to interpret changes in local vegetation and, by implication, in site function. Combined with the previously summarized information on the densities of stone tools at FRL and FAO, these data are then used to evaluate the current models of land use in West New Britain. We now turn to a description of methods and results of two independent analyses of starch grains extracted from archaeological deposits at FRL (Fullagar *et al.* 1994) and FAO (Therin 1994).

Methods for starch extraction and interpretation

Starch grains were extracted from forty-one sediment samples from both FRL and FAO (Figure 23.2). At FRL bulk samples (approximately 1 kg dry weight each) were collected from each layer exposed in the vertical section of the excavation unit (Specht *et al.* 1988). This was a rather coarse-grained sampling method since each sample extended for at least 10 cm vertically in the trench. From these, eighteen samples were extracted and analysed. In contrast, FAO samples were removed during 1992–3 from bulk sediment samples (approximately 5 × 5 × 5 cm) collected every 5 cm down the vertical section of sample pit 1000/1000. Twenty-three samples were selected from the column for the study reported here. When more than one sediment sample has been extracted within a single layer, the starch grain frequencies have been averaged. The data discussed below are therefore equivalent to the mean frequency for each layer.

The starch extractions for FRL were undertaken as a pilot study by Fullagar with Loy and Cox (Fullagar *et al.* 1994). This technique was later modified by Therin (1994) in order to increase sample size. The two extraction procedures are summarized in Table 23.1. While the starch grain

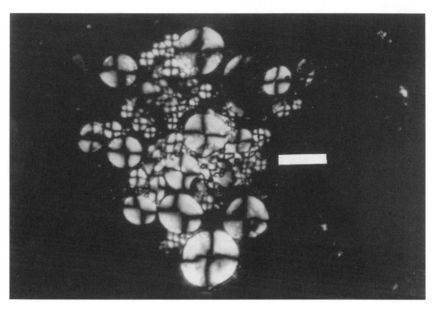

Figure 23.6   Starch grains extracted from layer at FAO resemble modern reference material of *Manioc esculenta*. Scale bar equals 20 microns. Photo taken at ×500 magnification.

frequencies for FAO and FRL are internally consistent, absolute counts are not directly comparable since Therin's (1994) procedure not only doubled the sediment sample size, but also improved the recovery rate for starch. The following analysis is therefore not based on direct comparisons of counts between sites but relies instead on relative differences between the layers at each site. Temporal trends identified at individual sites are then compared.

Frequencies were calculated in two size classes (2–5 μm and greater than 5 μm) for two reasons. In the first instance, movement of starch through sediments has been monitored by Fullagar *et al.* (1994) and in rigorous detail by Therin (1994: 68–9), under different irrigation conditions. Both studies have found that movement of starch grains down the profile occurred but at a remarkably low rate, even allowing for high rainfall conditions prevalent in West New Britain. In Therin's (1994) experiments it was found that small grains were more likely to move downward than large grains. For this reason, we have assumed that there will be a small amount of background noise comprised of small starch grains within all the sediments. Interpretation of the frequency of the small starch grains must therefore focus on large differences in magnitude.

The second reason for distinguishing these two size classes relates to uncertainties in the interpretation of small starch grains as specifically derived from plant foods, rather than general vegetation. Based on our knowledge of current reference material of over 250 species (Therin *et al.* 1997) and

Table 23.1 Summary of starch extraction techniques

I   *FRL (Fullagar* et al. *1994)*

1 Mix 1 g of dry sediment sample with 1,000 µl of aqueous CsCl (specific gravity 1.79 at 20°C).
2 Centrifuge at 400 rpm for 80 seconds.
3 Extract supernatant with starch grains
4 Use 200 µl filtered and distilled water to dilute the CsCl.
5 Centrifuge at 13,000 rpm for 60 seconds to force the starch grains to the bottom of the vial.
6 Withdraw supernatant leaving 20–50 µl in vial.
7 Repeat steps 4–7 twice to remove all CsCl.
8 Withdraw supernatant leaving 30–50 µl.
9 Vortex.
10 Remove 10 µl to microscope slide. Let dry and mount in Euparol.

II   *FAO (Therin 1994)*

1 Vortex to mix well 2 g of dry sediment with 2000 µl of aqueous CsCl (specific gravity = 1.7900 at 20°C).
2 Centrifuge for 120 sec at 400 rpm.
3 Extract supernatant and place in 1.5 ml eppendorf type vial. Using CsCl make vial up to 1.5 µl, vortex.
4 Remove two amounts of 500 µl to separate eppendorf vials.
5 Add 700 µl ultrapure water to each eppendorf.
6 Vortex briefly and then centrifuge at 13,000 rpm for 90 seconds.
7 Withdraw 1150 µl of supernatant, leaving 50 µl
8 Add another 400 µl ultrapure water and repeat step 6.
9 Withdraw 400 µl of supernatant leaving 50 µl of supernatant in vial, repeat steps 8 and 9 two more times.
10 Vortex, remove 10 µl to microscope slide. Let dry and mount in Euparol.

---

previous work by Loy *et al.* (1992), starch grains larger than about 5 µm are primarily associated with the edible portions of plants: e.g. palm pith, fruits, tubers, and seed kernels. In contrast, small starch grains (less than about 5 µm) are more likely to be found in a wide range of plant parts (including stems, leaves, roots) and to represent a much wider range of taxa, although we do note that the important root *Colocasia esculenta* is an exception which falls within the small size class of starch grains (cf. Loy *et al.* 1992).

The methodological assumptions used in the following interpretation of the starch grain frequencies from FRL and FAO are summarized below.

1 Only very large frequencies of the small size class (2–5 µm) are considered to be meaningful, since a small amount of these starch grains are potentially subject to downward movement by rain water.
2 Changes in the relative frequency of starch grains per layer, calculated as the mean number of grains per 2 g of sediment, can be used to compare temporal trends in the overall plant component represented at FAO and FRL.
3 The small size class (2–5 µm) represents general vegetation because

these grains are most likely to be derived from a wide range of plant parts.

4 The larger size class (>5 μm) represents edible starchy plants because these grains are most common in fruits and storage organs of plants (e.g., tubers).

Ongoing research on our extensive modern reference material is aimed at further testing and improving these assumptions for further work. At this preliminary stage of research, the potential of starch grain analyses of archaeological sediments can be adequately examined by accepting these simplifying assumptions.

Before undertaking the immense task of establishing a key to identify plant taxa on the basis of the morphology of starch grains, our preliminary analysis was designed to investigate the nature of variation among archaeological contexts in the frequency of starch grains of differing sizes. We argue that only when sufficient differences between archaeological contexts can be demonstrated is it worth while to undertake the very labour intensive task of establishing more precise taxonomic identifications (cf. Powers and Gilbertson 1989).

CHANGES IN FREQUENCY AND ASSEMBLAGE COMPOSITION OF STARCH GRAINS

In interpreting the data presented below, it is important to emphasize again that due to variations in the extraction methods used and initial sample sizes for the two sites, differences in absolute frequency are not meaningful. Since one is only justified in examining relative differences through time or in assemblage composition in terms of the size classes, the raw data are not presented here and we base our arguments on a series of bar graphs (Figures 23.7–9).

Beginning with the temporal pattern of starch grain frequencies at sites FAO and FRL shown in Figure 23.7, two notable features can be observed. First, the chronological trend witnessed at each site proceeds in opposite directions: in relative terms starch grain frequency decreases through time at FAO but increases at FRL. Despite this difference, the overall pattern represented at the two sites becomes more similar through time. So, for example, FAO begins with a relatively high frequency of starch grains in layer 1 and then stabilizes at a much lower level, whereas at FRL starch grains are relatively less common at the beginning of the sequence than in the most recent layer. However, from layers 4 or 5 onwards starch grain frequencies at the two sites start to track each other.

To understand how these trends relate to changes in vegetation and by implication in site usage, we turn to the distribution of small (2–5 μm) and large (>5 μm) size classes presented in Figures 23.8 and 23.9. At FRL, where fluctuations in the frequency of the total assemblage had appeared less marked than FAO in Figure 23.7, considerable variation through time can be observed when the data are divided into small and large size classes, as shown in Figure 23.8.

First, we should take notice of likely taphonomic features in the data. The

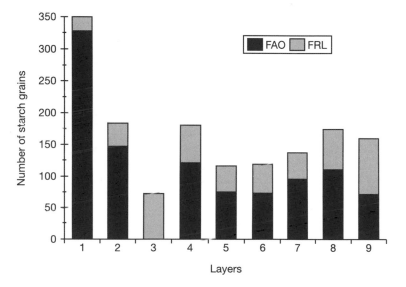

Figure 23.7   Starch grain frequencies at FRL and FAO, by layer.

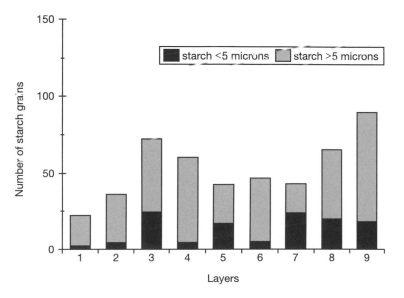

Figure 23.8   FRL starch grain frequencies for each size class (0–5 microns and >5 microns), by layer.

peaks in the frequency of small starch grains combined with a decrease in the large grains in the unconsolidated airfall tephras seem most likely to be a result of differential downward movement of grains. Along these same lines, it seems likely that the concentration of starch in layer 3 is especially likely to be a taphonomic signature since this sediment was washed down from the nearby hillside and probably incorporated a range of material during the process.

The second point to note is that even allowing for differential movement of grains, the large starch grains are always more abundant than small starch grains. This suggests that the majority of the plant products entering the archaeological record were products of plant food processing. In contrast to the densities of artefacts, which decline through time at FRL, there is an overall slight increase in large starch grains. It is also notable that the peaks in grains occur in layers 6, 7 and 8 which represent troughs in the density of artefacts. One possibility for this pattern is that there are subtle oscillations in site usage during this period, from primarily tool use (layers 6 and 8) to mainly tool production (layer 7). It is significant that Fullagar (1990) was able to refit a flake core from layer 7, but attempts at refitting of material from other layers at the site have not been so successful.

FAO presents a very different picture of changes in starch grain frequencies when broken down into the two size classes of the grains (Figure 23.9). First, it is apparent that the exceptionally high frequencies in layer 1 are largely made up of small starch grains. After layer 1, as in the sequence discussed above for FRL (Figure 23.8), large starch grains are invariably more abundant

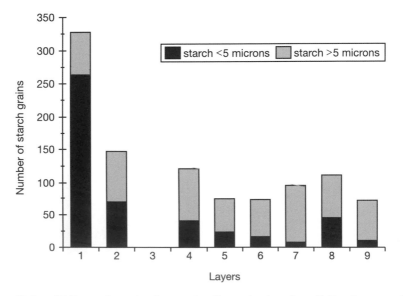

Figure 23.9   FAO starch grain frequencies for each size class (0–5 microns and >5 microns), by layer.

than small starch grains. Second, there appears to be little correlation between the high frequencies of the small class of starch grains and the tephras except for layer 8. At this stage all we can suggest is that there appears to have been less downward movement at FAO, possibly because of its location on the level top of a hill, rather than on a slight slope as at FRL. Third, at FAO the frequency of large starch grains exhibits very little variation at all, again contrasting with the pattern at FRL. Fourth, apart from a slight increase in the layer 8 tephra, the overall frequency of small starch grains gradually declines through time. Following our methodological assumptions, it is clear that the most dramatic change in localized vegetation is coincident with early use of the site, between layers 1 and 2, and then this is followed by a very gradual decrease in small grains.

At this first level of interpretation the starch grain data from FAO and FRL appear to produce conflicting results, since the former site shows very little change in the incidence of plant foods after an initial reduction in vegetation, whereas in the latter case a gradual increase in plant foods can be inferred. How can these conflicting datasets inform us about changes in land-use patterns, particularly with regard to the controversy concerning settlement and subsistence during the time of Lapita-style pottery? We argue that when the information on changes in starch grain frequencies are integrated with the data on artefact density, a number of hypotheses concerning regional changes in land use can be put forward. Furthermore, we stress that an understanding of mobility and subsistence patterns in West New Britain is only possible when the results from these various types of data are conceived of on a *regional scale*, rather than on a site by site basis (cf. Fullagar 1992).

LONG-TERM PATTERNS OF LAND USE

Within the temporal sequence represented at FRL there is steady decline in the density of obsidian artefacts (Figure 23.3) and a reduction in the proportion of retouched artefacts (Torrence 1992), compared with an increase in the range of tool uses as inferred from use-wear and residue studies (Fullagar 1992). We interpret these data to represent a gradual shift in site function from a task-specific quarry site to a domestic site where a wider, more generalized range of activities were carried out including the expedient use of obsidian. The starch record supports this inference because the frequency of large starch grains, assumed to represent the processing and consumption of plant foods, generally increases through time. During the last half of the sequence large starch grains and artefact density change in opposition to each other.

In contrast, FAO is neither a quarry nor a site for initial reduction of obsidian, and this is reflected in the much lower density of obsidian artefacts throughout its history. The relatively low rate of obsidian artefact deposition at FAO is therefore more consistent with domestic usage. We also argue that the gradual increase in artefact density can be explained as the result of a trend towards more intensive settlement which is signified by an increase in the expedient production of tools. The first appearance of obsidian artefacts at FAO in layer 2 is associated with a rapid decline in frequency of small starch grains, which can be interpreted as local clearance. In contrast, the stable, high frequency of large starch grains throughout the remainder of the sequence indicates plant food processing on site and supports the interpretation based on obsidian artefacts of domestic use of the site since initial occupation.

We therefore conclude that the technological changes witnessed at FAO and FRL are paralleled by the gross variations in starch grain assemblages from sediments, although each site has a different history of usage. FRL shifts from a special purpose quarry site to a domestic site, whereas FAO maintains its domestic function throughout the sequence. The first main point to emphasize is that the changes which we observe are gradual in nature, and the long-term trends in starch grain frequency and assemblage composition are less clear than for artefact density (Figure 23.3), technology (Torrence 1992) or function (Fullagar 1992).

Importantly, there is no sudden increase in the amount of large starch grains that would lead us to suspect a major change in plant exploitation after the WK-2 eruption and the introduction of Lapita-style pottery to this region (i.e. following layer 5). In contrast, at both sites there is a decrease in the frequency of starch grains in layer 6 from the previous occupation level of layer 4, suggesting less intense use of both sites for plant processing after the major volcanic event. In addition, the most recent period shows an increase in plant processing at FRL but a decrease at FAO. In other words, there is no clear signature showing major differences in the intensity of plant processing at any particular time as predicted in all three of the models presented at the outset of this chapter (traditional, Torrence, Gosden and Pavlides). Instead, we witness a slow, gradual intensification with a number of minor fluctuations that are difficult to interpret with the data at hand.

To understand how these two very different site histories contribute to the debate about subsistence and settlement in West New Britain, we need to incorporate the two data sites into a regional view and ask what kind of patterns would lead to a change from variability in the use of places to homogeneity across the wider landscape combined with a change from a strategy based on the gearing up of 'formal,' retouched forms to one based on the expedient manufacture of unretouched tools. We feel that the best explanation is for a gradual decline in mobility across the region, which was in turn the consequence of an increase in the intensity of forest management and, by implication, in formal gardening practices. We offer no solution to the problem of causation at this stage.

A FUTURE FOR STARCH IN SEDIMENTS?

We acknowledge that there are limitations to this preliminary study. First, differences in the sampling methods and extraction techniques used at the two sites restrict interpretations of the frequency data. Second, in many cases the number of counts per extracted sample were very low and so sampling error may have affected the nature of compositional differences among the samples. Finally, we have used only two size classes to monitor a poorly known range of variability in plant parts and taxa.

Despite these problems and the coarse nature of the data presented here, the patterns derived from the data about starch extracted from sediments are extremely important. Gross variations in starch grain frequency and assemblage composition have been demonstrated and these appear to correlate with independent data which indicate changes in site function and local land use. We have therefore fulfilled our primary aim to evaluate whether starch grain assemblages derived from ancient sediments vary significantly in different cultural settings. It appears that they do. We therefore conclude that there is great potential for analysing starch in sediments, especially in the tropics where phytoliths and pollen are not produced by major food crops. The obvious next step is to develop ways to interpret what the variation means in more specific terms.

Research on starch grains in progress at the Australian Museum includes (1) the establishment of an extensive reference collection of plants known to have been used in the local region for food, building, craft items, medicinal, religious purposes, etc. (over 250 species to date) (Lentfer 1995; Therin et al. 1997); (2) image analysis of reference material to help establish an identification key; and (3) experiments testing various methods for extracting starch from sediments. We also recognize that further work is needed to understand taphonomic processes such as the effects of bioturbation, infiltration, weathering, etc. as well as the effects on grains of different food preparation techniques such as pounding, roasting, boiling, etc.

Returning to the major issues which motivated the evaluation of starch grains as a way to study prehistoric subsistence, if the starch data tracks changes in subsistence patterns, as we have argued, then it is extremely important that there are no major breaks after the WK-2 volcanic eruption and the introduction of Lapita-style pottery to this region. Like the data on stone tool technology and function presented by Torrence (1992, 1994b) and Fullagar (1992) a decline in residential mobility, and, by implication, in the intensification of plant management (?gardening), appears to be a slow and relatively steady process, despite the impact of major volcanic events in the region. At this stage even the combination of preliminary starch grain analyses with stone tool studies are unable to resolve the debate over whether 'sites' with Lapita-style pottery represent permanent villages or not.

It is worth stressing, however, that the analysis of starch in sediments is only one of several methodological approaches which are being pursued to resolve the nature of subsistence and settlement change in West New Britain. No single technique can be expected to satisfactorily reconstruct subsistence and mobility patterns and solve the debate about the pace and nature of change in plant usage in Melanesia. Mention has already been made of our continuing research in West New Britain on stone tool technology and functional analyses based on use-wear and residue studies, but progress has already been made in developing methods for the analyses of phytoliths (Lentfer 1995; Kealhofer 1995), soil micromorphology, and erosional history (Boyd and Torrence 1996) in order to complement the findings from the ongoing starch research. The analysis of differences in inter- and intra-site patterning of artefacts using 'on site' (Torrence 1994a) and 'off-site' or distributional archaeological methods (Torrence 1997) to further illuminate mobility and settlement patterns is also being carried out.

The tropics are not an easy place to study agricultural history. Since the ecology is so different from the traditional homes of agricultural origins, it is important that archaeologists find ways to overcome the methodological obstacles of identifying plant use, particularly of tree and root crops, in a setting dominated by high rainfall and temperatures. Whatever the outcome of this ongoing multidisciplinary research, we believe that the history of plant use in Melanesia is likely to produce a very different picture to that obtained in other parts of the world, especially in terms of the much debated relationship between sedentism and gardening practices.

ACKNOWLEDGEMENTS

Richard Fullagar and Robin Torrence were supported by an ARC Fellowship and Senior Fellowship respectively. This research has been funded by the Australian Research Council, the Carlyle Greenwall Bequest, the Australia and Pacific Foundation, and the Australian Museum. We thank the West New Britain Provincial Government, Bitokara Mission, and Kimbe Bay Shipping Company for permission to work at the sites and for help with transport and accommodation. We are grateful to our affiliating institutions, the National Museum and Art Gallery and the Department of Anthropology and Social Work at the University of Papua New Guinea, and to the Institute of Papua New Guinea Studies for help with permits and fieldwork. In the field we have been greatly helped by many local residents from Bitokara Mission and Garua Plantation, as well as by a loyal band of overseas volunteers. We are also very grateful to Walindi Plantation and Resort and the West New Britain Cultural Centre (especially John Namuno and John Normu) for practical assistance and moral support. For general advice on the project or comments on the chapter we thank Bill Boyd, Steve Cox, David Gilbertson, Peter Jackson, Carol Lentfer, Peter Matthews, Tom Loy, Jim Specht and Peter White.

REFERENCES

Atchison, J.M. 1994. Analysis of food starch residues at the Jinmium archaeological site, Northern Territory. Unpublished Honours Bachelor of Environmental Science research report, University of Wollongong.

Banks, W. and C.T Greenwood, 1975. *Starch and its Components.* Edinburgh: Edinburgh University Press.

Barton, H. 1990. Raw material and tool function: a residue and use-wear analysis of artefacts from a Melanesian rock shelter. Unpublished BA (Hons) thesis, University of Sydney.

Barton, H. 1994. Report on analyses of residues from FAO 1000/1000. ms.

Barton, H., R. Torrence and R. Fullagar, 1995. A study of starch grains on used and unused obsidian flakes from Garua Island, Melanesia. Paper presented at the Annual Meeting of the Australian Archaeological Association, Gatton.

Barton, H. and J.P White, 1993. Use of stone and shell artefacts at Balof 2, New Ireland, PNG. *Asian Perspectives* 32, 169–81.

Boyd, B. and R. Torrence. 1996. Periodic erosion and human land use on Garua Island, PNG: a progress report. In *Australian Archaeology '95: Proceedings of the 1995 Australian Archaeological Association Annual Conference*, S. Ulm, I. Lilley and A. Ross (eds), Tempus 6: 265–74 St. Lucia: University of Queensland.

Brass, L. G. 1993. A residue and use-wear analysis of ethnographic and archaeological stone artefacts from the New Guinea Highlands. Unpublished BA (Hons) thesis, University of Sydney.

Coates, D.J., D.E. Yen and P.M. Gaffey. 1988. Chromosome variation in taro, *Colocasia esculenta*: implications for origin in the Pacific. *Cytologia* 53, 551–60.

Cowan, C. and P. Watson (eds). 1992. *The Origins of Agriculture.* Washington, DC: Smithsonian Institution Press.

Fullagar, R. 1988. Recent developments in Australian use-wear and residue studies. Oxford: BAR 45, 133–45.

Fullagar, R. 1990. A reconstructed obsidian core from the Talasea excavations. *Australian Archaeology* 30, 79–80.

Fullagar, R. 1992. Lithically Lapita. Functional analysis of flaked stone assemblages from West New Britain Province, Papua New Guinea. In *Poterie Lapita et Peuplement*, J.-C. Galipaud (ed.), 135–43. Noumea: ORSTOM.

Fullagar, R. 1993. Flaked stone tools and plant food production: a preliminary report on obsidian tools from Talasea, West New Britain, PNG. In *Traces et Fonction: Les Gestes Rétrouves*, P. Anderson, P. S. Beyries, M. Otte and H. Plisson (eds), 331–7. Liège: Colloque Internationale de Liège, Editions ERAUL, 50.

Fullagar, R., T. Loy and S. Cox. 1994. Starch grains in archaeological sediments: implications for vegetation history and residue studies. Paper presented at the 15th Congress of the Indo-Pacific Prehistory Association, Chiang Mai, Thailand.

Fullagar, R., B. Meehan and R. Jones. 1992. Residue analysis of ethnographic plant-working and other tools from northern Australia. In *Préhistoire de l'Agriculture: Nouvelles Approches Experimentales et Ethnographiques*, Monographie du CRA no. 6, P. Anderson-Gerfaud (ed.), 39–53. Paris: CNRS.

Furby, J.H. 1995. Megafauna under the microscope. Unpublished Ph.D. thesis, University of New South Wales.

Gebauer, A. and T. Price (eds). 1992. *Transitions to Agriculture in Prehistory.* Madison: University of Wisconsin Press.

Golson, J. 1991a. Bulmer Phase II: early agriculture in the New Guinea Highlands. In *Man and a Half: essays in Pacific anthropology and ethnobiology in honour of Ralph Bulmer*, A. Pawley (ed.), 484–91. Auckland: The Polynesian Society.

Golson, J. 1991b. The New Guinea Highlands on the eve of agriculture. *Indo-Pacific*

Prehistory 1990. Volume 2, P. Bellwood (ed.), 82–91. *Bulletin Indo-Pacific Prehistory Association* 11.

Golson, J. and D. Gardner. 1990. Agriculture and socio-political organisation in New Guinea Highlands prehistory. *Annual Review of Anthropology* 19, 395–417.

Golson, J. and P. Ucko. 1994. Foreword. In *Tropical Archaeobotony*, J. Hather (ed.), xiv–xix. London: Routledge.

Gosden, C. and C. Pavlides. 1994. Are islands insular? *Archaeology in Oceania* 29, 162–71.

Gosden, C. and J. Webb. 1992. The creation of a Papua New Guinean landscape. *Journal of Field Archaeology* 21, 29–51.

Green, R. 1979. Lapita. In *The Prehistory of Polynesia*, J. Jennings (ed.), 27–60. Cambridge, Mass. Harvard University Press.

Groube, L. 1989. The taming of the rain forests: a model for Late Pleistocene forest exploitation in New Guinea. In *Foraging and Farming: the evolution of plant exploitation*, D. Harris and G. Hillman (eds), 292–304. London: Unwin Hyman.

Haberle, S.G. 1995. Identification of cultivated *Pandanus* and *Colocasia* in pollen records and the implications for the study of early agriculture in New Guinea. *Vegetation History and Archaeobotany* 4, 195–210.

Hall, J., S. Higgins and R. Fullagar. 1989. Plant residues on stone tools. In *Plants in Australian Archaeology*, W. Beck, A. Clarke and L. Head (eds), Tempus Monograph Series, 136–60. St. Lucia: Anthropology Museum, University of Queensland.

Hather, J. 1992. The archaeobotany of subsistence in the Pacific. *World Archaeology* 24, 70–81.

Hather, J. 1994. The identification of charred root and tuber crops from archaeological sites in the Pacific. In *Tropical Archaeobotany*, J. Hather (ed.), 51–65. London: Routledge.

Hather, J. and P.V. Kirch, 1991. Prehistoric sweet potato (*Ipomoea batatas*) from Mangaia Island, central Polynesia. *Antiquity* 65, 887–93.

Kealhofer, L. 1995. A phytolith study of stone tool residues from the Willaumez peninsula, West New Britain, PNG. Report submitted to the Australian Museum.

Kirch, P.V. 1988. Long-distance exchange and island colonisation: the Lapita case. *Norwegian Archaeological Review* 21, 103–17.

Lentfer, C. 1995. Ethnobotanical research in West New Britain and the Forestry Research Institute Hermarium, Lae, PNG. Report submitted to the West New Britain Provincial Government.

Loy, T. 1994. Methods in the analysis of starch residues on prehistoric stone tools. In *Tropical Archaeobotany*, J. Hather (ed.), 86–114. London: Routledge.

Loy, T., S. Wickler and M. Spriggs, 1992. Direct evidence for human use of plants 28,000 years ago: starch residues on stone artefacts from the northern Solomon Islands. *Antiquity* 66, 898–912.

Machida, H., R. Blong, J. Specht, H. Moriwaki, R. Torrence, H. Hayakawa, B. Talai, D. Lolok and C. Pain. 1996. Holocene explosive eruptions of Witori and Dakataua caldera volcanoes in West New Britain, Papua New Guinea. *Quaternary International* 34–36, 65–78.

Matthews, P. 1990. The origins, dispersal and domestication of taro. Unpublished Ph.D. thesis, Australian National University.

Matthews, P. 1991. A tropical wild type taro: *Colocasia esculenta* var. *aquatilis*. In *Indo-Pacific Prehistory 1990. Volume 2*, P. Bellwood (ed.), 68–81. *Bulletin Indo-Pacific Prehistory Association* 11.

Matthews, P. 1995. Aroids and the Austronesians. *Tropics* 4, 105–26.

Matthews, P. and R. Terauchi. 1994. The genetics of agriculture: DNA variation in taro and yam. In *Tropical Archaeobotany*, J. Hather (ed.), 251–62. London: Routledge.

Powers, A.H. and D.D. Gilbertson. 1989. Studies of late prehistoric and modern opal phytoliths from coastal sand dunes and machair in north-west Britain. *Journal of Archaeological Science* 16, 27–45.

Powers, A.H. and J. Padmore, 1993. The use of quantitative methods and statistical analysis in the study of opal phytoliths. In *Current Research in Phytolith Analysis: applications in archaeology and paleoecology,* D.M. Pearsall and D.R. Piperno (eds), 47–56. Philadelphia: MASCA, University of Pennsylvania.

Robertson, G. 1994. An application of scanning electron microscopy and image analysis to the differentiation of starch grains in archaeological plant residues. Unpublished BA (Hons) thesis, University of Queensland.

Shoocongdej, R. 1996. Rethinking the development of sedentary villages in western Thailand. In *Indo-Pacific Prehistory: the Chiang Mai papers,* P. Bellwood (ed.), 203–15. Canberra: Indo-Pacific Prehistory Association.

Smith, B. 1995. *The Emergence of Agriculture.* New York: Freeman.

Specht, J., R. Fullagar and R. Torrence, 1991. What was the significance of Lapita pottery at Talasea? In *Indo-Pacific Prehistory 1990. Volume 2,* P. Bellwood (ed.), 281–94. *Bulletin Indo-Pacific Prehistory Association* 11.

Specht, J., R. Fullagar, R. Torrence and N. Baker. 1988. Prehistoric obsidian exchange in Melanesia: a perspective from the Talasea sources. *Australian Archaeology* 27, 3–16.

Spriggs, M. 1993. Pleistocene agriculture in the Pacific: why not? In *Sahul in Review: Pleistocene archaeology in Australia, New Guinea and Island Melanesia,* M. Smith, M. Spriggs, and B. Fankhauser (eds), 137–43. Canberra: Department of Prehistory, Research School of Pacific Studies, ANU.

Summerhayes, G.R. and J. Allen. 1993. The transport of Mopir obsidian to Late Pleistocene New Ireland. *Archaeology in Oceania* 28, 144–8.

Summerhayes, G.R., J.R. Bird, A. Katsaros, N. Shagholi, C. Gosden, R. Fullagar, J. Specht, and R. Torrence. 1993. West New Britain obsidian: production and consumption patterns. In *Archaeometry: current Australasian research,* B. Fankhauser and R. J. Bird (eds), 57–68. Canberra: Department of Prehistory, Research School of Pacific Studies, ANU.

Therin, M.J. 1994. Subsistence through starch. The examination of subsistence changes on Garua Island, West New Britain, PNG, through the extraction and identification of starch in sediments. Unpublished BA (Hons) thesis, University of Sydney.

Therin, M., R. Fullagar and H. Barton. 1994. Starch as an indicator of subsistence change. Paper presented at the 3rd World Archaeological Congress, New Delhi.

Therin, M., R. Torrence and R. Fullagar. 1997. The Australian Museum starch reference collection. *Australian Archaeology* 44, 52–3.

Torrence, R. 1992. What is Lapita about obsidian? A view from the Talasea source. In *Poterie Lapita et Peuplement,* J.C. Galipaud (ed.), 111–26. Noumea: ORSTOM.

Torrence, R. 1994a. Processes and events: differential rates of change in the Talasea region of West New Britain, Papua New Guinea. Paper presented at the 15th Congress of the Indo-Pacific Prehistory Association, Chiang Mai, Thailand.

Torrence, R. 1994b. Strategies for moving on in lithic studies. In *The Organization of Technology: North American prehistoric chipped stone technologies,* P. Carr (ed.), 123–31. Ann Arbor: University of Michigan, International Monographs in Prehistory.

Torrence, R. 1995. Archaeological and ethnobotanical fieldwork in West New Britain province, PNG. June–July 1995. Report submitted to the West New Britain Provincial Government.

Torrence, R. 1997. Distributional archaeology and buried landscapes: a new approach to tropical subsistence and settlement studies. Paper presented at the Society of American Archaeology Annual Meeting, Nashville.

Torrence, R., P. Jackson, C. Pavlides and J. Webb. 1997. Volcanic disasters and cultural continuities in the Holocene of West New Britain, Papua New Guinea. Paper presented at the Geological Society of London Conference, 'Volcanoes, Earth-quakes, and Archaeology'.

Torrence, R., J. Specht, and R. Fullagar. 1990. Pompeiis in the Pacific. *Australian Natural History* 23, 457–63.

Ungent, D., T. Dillehay and C. Ramirez. 1987. Potato remains from a late pleistocene settlement in south central Chile. *Economic Botany* 41, 17–27.

Yen, D. 1982. The history of cultivated plants. In *Melanesia: beyond diversity*, R.J. May and H. Nelson (eds), 281–95. Canberra: Research School of Pacific Studies, ANU.

Yen, D. 1991. Domestication: the lessons from New Guinea. In *Man and a Half: Essays in Pacific Anthropology and Ethnobiology in Honour of Ralph Bulmer,* A. Pawley (ed.), 558–69. Auckland: The Polynesian Society.

24 Traditional seed cropping systems in the temperate Old World: models for antiquity

ANN BUTLER

In the regions of South-west Asia and south-east Europe where there is the earliest archaeological evidence for the cultivation of grain crops in the temperate Old World, mechanized farming has largely replaced traditional technology. Here, in the 1970s and 1980s, some important pioneer documentation was undertaken of the cultivation and processing by traditional methods of cereals, and to a lesser extent pulses. Nevertheless, further data is needed for the interpretation of archaeobotanical remains, but today it is becoming increasingly difficult to find and observe any relatively unmechanized agriculture in these key regions.

The assemblage of ancient cereal and legume crops was introduced in antiquity from South-west Asia into more distantly peripheral areas of South Asia and East Africa, as well as Europe, where they continue to be utilized as plant food staples. In these regions, a wide diversity of non-mechanized, traditional agricultural systems is still practised, some of which are described here.

It is suggested that aspects of the systems found in such peripheral regions might provide a useful basis for our interpretations of ancient plant assemblages, including material recovered from archaeological sites in South-west Asia and Europe.

INTRODUCTION TO THE USE OF ETHNOGRAPHIC STUDIES OF TRADITIONAL AGRICULTURE

The interpretation of the remains of ancient food plants recovered from agrarian sites is assisted by studies of present-day traditional agriculture. The arguments for the application of modern ethnographic data to archaeo-botanical interpretation are well rehearsed (for example, Hillman 1981, 1984a; Jones 1984). In the light of the different environmental and cultural factors which are likely to have pertained in the past, the direct application of models based on recent agricultural practices is not always appropriate;

however, parallels can usefully be drawn within what appear to be similar environments.

The documentary records of farming practices which date from the earliest historical periods, as well as the later agricultural literature, seldom cover the full range of information about traditional agarian systems required by archaeobotanists. The latter may include tillage practices, plot management, the weed assemblages associated with the crop plants, the harvesting sequences prior to the processing of the crop yield and storage methods, and the farmers' rationale for their selection of the particular agronomic system employed, as well as other cultural variables. The need for archaeobotanists to compile their own ethnological data is superimposed upon a general urgency for the documentation of traditional agricultural systems, many of which are threatened with extinction – both as mechanization becomes more widespread and because of social and political unrest (Francis 1986).

THE ETHNOGRAPHIC RECORD OF AGRONOMIES COMPILED BY ARCHAEOBOTANISTS

Archaeobotanists began recording traditional seed agriculture in the Old World over twenty years ago. Studies of the crop-processing sequences for free-threshing and glume wheats in eastern Turkey and Syria (Al-Mouayad Al Azem 1991; Hillman 1972, 1973, 1981, 1984a, 1984b, 1985), similar data for a range of crops including pulses and cereals in Greece (H. Forbes, 1976; Forbes and Koster 1976; M. Forbes, 1976a, 1976b; Halstead 1987; Halstead and Jones 1989, 1995; Jones 1983, 1984, 1987) and more recent work in Spain (Peña Chocarro, 1995), typify such work. As indicated by these examples, most data have been collected from southern Europe and South-west Asia, those areas of the Old World where the earliest evidence of grain cultivation has been found.

This chapter examines a range of agronomic systems for producing grain crops in the wider temperate and subtropical regions of the Old World, with emphasis on systems of multiple cropping. Reference is made to historical and archaeological evidence where possible. The cropping patterns as defined by Andrews and Kassam (1976) and Francis (1986) are listed in Table 24.1.

CROPPING PRACTICES, REGIONALLY AND HISTORICALLY

At present, in temperate regions of the Old World the most common traditional system of agronomy employed for grain crops, both for food and animal feed, is monocropping, under which the farming resources are mainly directed towards the production of the maximum yield from a single crop on each land unit each year. This situation pertains in South-west Asia, the

Table 24.1 Summary of types of cropping system

Cropping system	Definition
Monoculture	One crop grown on the same plot for successive years
Monocropping	One crop grown on one plot in a single year
Multiple cropping	Two or more crops grown on the same plot in one year, either simultaneously or sequentially
Sequential cropping	More than one crop a year on one plot in sequence
Double/triple cropping	Two/three crops in sequence per plot per year
Intercropping	Two or more crops grown simultaneously on one plot
Mixed intercropping	Simultaneous cropping with random distribution
Row intercropping	Two or more crops per plot sown singly in separate rows
Strip intercropping	Two or more crops per plot sown singly in separate strips
Relay intercropping	Simultaneous cropping for only part of crop life-cycles
Ratoon cropping	Cultivation of crop regrowth after harvest

Source: Largely after Andrews and Kassam (1976) and Francis (1986)

peri-Mediterranean regions of southern Europe and North Africa, and northern Europe.

South-west Asia

Over the past twenty years, financial incentives to mechanize have increased the practice of monocropping, where machines can facilitate cultivation, but prior to the 1970s the multiple cropping of grain crops was relatively common in South-west Asia. Usually several varieties of a cultigen such as bread wheat, or both the wild and cultivated subspecies of a crop such as chickpea, were grown in association and sometimes mixed with other secondary crop species. Some less important component crops could be either tolerated or actively encouraged as an insurance against crop failure, as is sometimes still seen in Syria today. Since farmers typically saved seed from each harvest for the next sowing, the crop mixture was perpetuated (Plucknett and Smith 1986). Row intercropping was also practised, characteristically alternating cereals with pulses. One example from Iraq recorded in the 1930s, was a mixed crop of faba bean and barley, which could yield three products: the barley was cut for fodder several times when green and finally was allowed to mature to grain harvest, while the beans were harvested separately when the seeds were ripe (Townsend and Guest 1974). Now intercropping has become rare and the technology has changed; traditional hand implements and animal traction have largely been replaced by modern machinery.

Our knowledge of past agricultural systems is sparse. The documentary evidence for ancient cropping practices in Mesopotamia is complicated by problems in translation. The difficulties in extracting accurate and detailed information on agronomy from cuneiform tablets have been described by van Driel (1990), who has identified in the Muräsu documents a possible reference to double cropping in Iraq during the neo-Babylonian period. A number of Sumerian texts recording the cultivation of legumes have been discussed by Maekawa (1985), but no information about sowing seasons, distribution patterns or harvesting regimes appears to be included amongst descriptions of tillage practices and other data. Most of this type of documentation derives from temple archives and the private records of small landowners in large towns; these concern high value crops and tend to omit the yields produced for local consumption from small farms (van Driel 1990). More certain reference to double cropping in Iraq dates from AD 77 (Nasr 1976). Indirect evidence could be useful: for instance, since sequential cropping is associated today with the increased availability of water following the introduction of irrigation, it has been suggested that evidence of irrigation in antiquity may equate with this form of multiple cropping (Dalrymple 1971).

Europe and the northern peri-Mediterranean region

Today, in Europe as a whole, monocropping is the usual system employed for grain crops. Yet in some regions with particular needs, small-scale inter-cropping is practised, exemplified by the risk-spreading strategy in Amorgos, in Thessaly, Greece, of mixed cropping wheat with legumes (Halstead and Jones 1989), and the field-edge cultivation in Spain of legumes of erect habit, such as *Vicia faba* and some varieties of *Pisum sativum*, to reduce wind damage and prevent lodging in the mixed emmer and spelt crops; the cereals and the legumes are harvested separately for human food (Peña Chocarro 1995). Generally, however, the mixed cultivation of grain crops is rare.

Larger-scale mixed cropping is commonly confined to forage and feed crops for the yield of vegetative parts, as hay or silage, rather than for seed. The practice of planting medics and clovers with grasses for fodder is widespread; smaller grain legumes, such as *Vicia sativa,* are frequently cropped with related wild vetches for animal feed. In the recent past, *V. sativa*, pea, and faba bean were grown together for winter animal feed in Spain – the so-called Sicilian method of cultivation (Cubero 1983) – and today in some areas *Vicia ervilia, Lathyrus cicera* and *L. sativa* are cultivated in a mixture, *comuña,* for fodder (Jubete 1991). Also in northern Europe, cereal mixtures, for example rye with oats known as *maslin,* are still used. There are records of sowing wheat into clover or other cereal crops as a precaution against predation by birds (Marshall 1796, cited in Sigaut 1992), and forage legumes were sometimes included in cereal fields to smother and suppress weeds (Pretty 1990).

Roman authors have documented the establishment of mixed pasture. *Ocinum,* a mixture of vetch, fenugreek, bitter vetch and broad beans, grass pea mixed with bitter vetch, and emmer wheat mixed with vetch are some examples of fodder assemblages or *farrago* used as forage and fodder for cattle and oxen (Cato, Columella, Pliny, Varro, cited in White 1970); historical evidence indicates that legumes, both the pulses and species of the small-seeded genera, were grown singly for feed and mixed for forage (White

1970). The mixed cultivation of cereal and grain legume crops for feed in Britain was common during the medieval period (Pretty 1990) and up to the more recent past (Rider Haggard [1899]1987). Mixed cropping is believed to have been an early practice in ancient Greece. While attention has been drawn to the hazards of potential misinterpretation of some ancient crop residues due to post-depositional effects (Halstead 1989), a plant assemblage of cereals and pulses from Bronze Age Amorgos has been tentatively interpreted as the product of a mixed cropping system (Jones *et al.* 1986).

North Africa: the southern peri-Mediterranean region
Here, although farming by machine is rapidly increasing, legume cultivation in particular remains largely unmechanized, since hand-harvesting and threshing are said to provide a better yield (Zagdouni and Benatya 1990). Sequential cropping is common; for example, in Egypt the important short-season small-seeded legume fodder crop, *Trifolium alexandrinum* (berseem), is sown and harvested early in the year, to be replaced by cash crops during the main growing season (personal observation, 1992). Double cropping is documented in Egypt from about 300 BC (Nasr 1976).

To observe a wider range of currently practised cropping systems it is necessary to travel to the Indian subcontinent or sub-Saharan Africa.

South Asia
The agronomic practices in the Indian subcontinent are particularly diverse, and many of the recent investigations into the effects of multiple cropping derive from this region; but even here the need for more research has been stressed (Singh and Ahuja 1990). The usual cropping timetable follows the rainfall regime with two seasons: *kharif*, during the summer monsoon period (June–October), and *rabi* during the winter (October–March) (Kajale 1994). Legumes play an important role in Indian mixed cropping systems, where they are employed to maintain soil fertility; in the Deccan, typically several pulses, millet, and oil-seeds are sown in mixtures of at least four species, and often every fourth row is sown with a single pulse (Nicol 1935). The different crops may occupy adjacent rows or strips, or be sown alternately along rows, or even planted along sets of rows running at right angles, the two crops forming a grid pattern. In random mixed cropping, the disseminules of two or more crop species or varieties are mixed and broadcast sown together; they are commonly harvested when individually ripe, which may or may not be a synchronous operation. The latter cropping system requires minimal input of time and energy until the harvest seasons, when the labour requirement can be very high (Smith and Francis 1986).

In Nepal, the seeds of the primary crops such as grain legumes are usually broadcast in varying mixtures with mustard, linseed, barley and rice, and each crop is harvested separately as it ripens. Similar mixtures may also be broadcast into standing rice paddy (Bharati 1986), using a strategy, also common in India, known as relay cropping, when for a variable period the growing seasons of the two crops overlap, although sowing and harvesting times may not be synchronous.

The earliest evidence of grain cultivation in the subcontinent is associated with the introduction of the South-west Asian crop assemblage to Baluchistan and the Indus valley. Reports of monocropping in India from the third millenium BC have been based on the recovery of archaeobotanical remains of species which are now cultivated as winter crops (Sharma 1982). The remains of species cultivated today as summer and winter crops have been recovered together from sites dating from the second millenium BC; these have suggested the practice of double cropping during that period (Kajale 1988, 1992, 1994; Lone et al. 1993). The consistent association of the remains of both cereals and pulses, at Inamgaon in the western Maharashtra of India from 1600 BC, has prompted the suggestion that mixed cropping was practised. However, without the evidence that the crops were cultivated together in the same plot, these interpretations must remain speculative (Kajale 1988). More solid evidence of mixed cropping has been found from levels dating from the third millenium BC at Kalibangan in the Indus Valley: a grid of crossed plough lines has been excavated, which closely resembles the patterns which result from intercropping at the present time (Lal 1970).

Sub-Saharan highland Africa

In Africa as a whole, mixed systems are commonly employed as a strategy for increased yields. Ethiopia, for example, has a long history of both mixed and sequential cropping (Westphal 1974, 1975). Typically, paired combinations of cereals, cereals and legumes, or various other crops such as *Linum usitatissimum* (flax) and *Lepidium sativum* (garden cress), occupy the same plots (Okigbo and Greenland 1976; Westphal 1975). Differences in the dimensions and habits of the individual crop species are accommodated by variations in their management. Wide or tall species may overshadow a crop of smaller plants, yet be suitable companion crops as their times of maturity may differ. An example of management strategy is to broadcast sow chickpea as a maincrop and intercrop with sorghum sown in a random arrangement of clumps, a system sometimes referred to as patch intercropping; this minimizes the effects of overshading by the tall canopies of the cereal. The chickpea ripens and is harvested before the sorghum. Where associated cultigens have more similar growth habits they may be processed together; for example, in mid-altitude regions faba bean is cultivated with pea; the ripening is synchronous and the total yield of mixed grains may be treated as a single product from harvesting to its final preparation as food (Abate Tedla, pers. comm.). Alternatively, the same mixture of crop species, harvested individually by sickle, may be carefully separated in the field prior to drying, cleaning, storage and food preparation (Geletu Bejiga, pers. comm.). In the highlands, following the heavy summer rains, short-season small-seeded or grain legumes may be sown into the semi-drained land to reduce erosion and produce a harvest before the ground is sufficiently dry for the main sowing season (Abate Tedla, pers. comm.). Some interesting work in Malawi on the role of economic factors in the selection of cropping method has demonstrated that a high diversity of crops in mixed systems is dependent upon a large labour force (Shaxson and Tauer 1992).

The archaeobotanical record in East Africa is slender; excavation of early archaeological sites with plant remains is needed to reveal more about the first stages of African seed cultivation (Wetterstrom 1991).

THE POTENTIAL RELEVANCE OF MODERN TRADITIONAL AGRICULTURE TO THE ANCIENT PAST

South Asia and Africa both still have a rich diversity of agronomies, largely employing a variety of mixed cropping systems. To what extent could a study of any of these systems be applicable to the interpretation of ancient plant remains from other temperate areas? There is evidence to show that some of these systems were local developments; for instance, in some areas, double cropping is seen as a response to the monsoon rainfall (Kajale 1992). Furthermore, in certain locations, mixed cropping has been a recent introduction, or re-introduction.

Early agricultural connections between South-west Asia and both India and Ethiopia are well established, though they are undated. The route for the introduction of the South-west Asian crop assemblage to East Africa is still undefined. Various suggestions have been made, the most favoured being from the north via the Nile or across to Ethiopia from the Yemen (see Doggett 1991; Simoons 1960). An interchange of crop plants between Africa and India appears to have been taking place at least from the second millenium BC, as suggested by the remains of domesticated African millet and sorghum sometimes found with various African terracotta artefacts in sites in Saurashtra, Rajasthan and Maharashtra (Kajale 1992; Allchin and Allchin 1982; Ghosh and Lal 1963; Rao 1963; Vishnu-Mittre 1974, and others, cited by Mehra 1991), seemingly imported via Saba and Baluchistan (Mehra 1991). It seems highly likely that some cropping techniques were imported with the founder-crop assemblages, and thus some of the wide range of agronomic practices observable in India and Ethiopia today could incorporate elements developed during the early stages of cultivation in South-west Asia and Europe.

THE ADVANTAGES OF MULTIPLE CROPPING

While it is impossible to gauge accurately the past conditions which led to the development of the wide range of agronomic systems, an examination of the recognized advantages associated with particular practices in the present

Table 24.2   Advantages of mixed cropping

Advantage	Source
1 Intensification of production	de Carvalho & da Silva Leal 1991; Nasr 1976; Singh & Ahuja 1990
2 Risk management and stability (sustainability)	Chatterjee & Mandal 1992; Okigbo & Greenland 1976; Smith and Francis 1986
3 Efficient utilization of space	Wrigley 1982
4 Production of complementary food for a balanced diet	Kishk 1979; Malik 1988
5 Soil fertility, resource partitioning and the utilization of water	Davis et al. 1986; Mirchandani & Misra 1975; Wrigley 1982
6 Weed suppression	Chatterjee & Mandal 1992
7 Decreased disease and insect-damage	Chatterjee & Mandal 1992: Wrigley 1982
8 Wind protection	Peña Chocarro, pers. comm.; Radke & Hagstrom 1976; Siddoway & Barnett 1976
9 Support against lodging	Francis et al. 1976
10 Erosion control	Abate Tedla, pers comm.
11 Reduction or spread of labour	Shaxson & Tauer 1992; Wrigley 1982
12 Protection of ownership	Springborg 1990

day (see Table 24.2) can highlight some factors which could aid our understanding.

1. INTENSIFICATION OF PRODUCTION

Multiple cropping, whether simultaneous or sequential, can yield more than a single crop per unit area per year; consequently, it can be regarded as a form of intensification. Generally the total yield is greater than that of any single crop occupying the same area for a similar period (for example, de Carvalho and da Silva Leal 1991; Nasr 1976; Singh and Ahuja 1990), a factor held by many to be most important in the choice of farming strategy; even when the overall biomass resulting from multicropping may be less, the nutritional quality in terms of crude protein is commonly greater, especially when a legume species is included (Barker and Francis 1986).

2. RISK MANAGEMENT AND STABILITY (SUSTAINABILITY)

The yield in a multiple cropping system may be synchronous or require more than one harvest, and can result in a number of different products. Risk avoidance results from the increased opportunity for success, and concomitantly a lower probability of failure (Chatterjee and Mandal 1992; Okigbo and Greenland 1976). Little research has been undertaken on the relative stabilities of monocropping and multiple cropping sytems; however, it has been pointed out that no natural ecosystem remains stable over time with a low level of diversity (Smith and Francis 1986); although multiple cropping systems do not always show greater profitability in terms of total yield, they appear to have a higher likelihood of sustainability (Francis 1986).

3. EFFICIENT UTILIZATION OF SPACE

Mixed cropping maximizes the use of the available space, allowing the exploitation of different ecological niches in close proximity with minimal competition. Further, certain crops required in small quantities can be accommodated in a limited area (Wrigley 1982).

4. PRODUCTION OF COMPLEMENTARY FOOD FOR A BALANCED DIET

Single crops, such as a cereal, cannot supply all the nutrients essential for human diet. The inclusion of a secondary crop, particularly one or more pulses, can provide a nutritionally balanced food base (Kishk 1979). Thus combinations of wheat and rice cropped with grain legumes, such as lentils and faba bean throughout Pakistan, have been shown to provide near-ideal levels of dietary nitrogen (Malik 1988).

5. SOIL FERTILITY, RESOURCE PARTITIONING AND THE UTILIZATION OF WATER

Different crop species have root systems which exploit the soil resources at different depths; a crop mixture exploiting a range of depths is less likely to deplete the soil fertility (Mirchandani and Misra 1975). The nitrogen input from nodulating leguminous crops can benefit other species, particularly the cereals (Wrigley 1982). Under conditions of water depletion, drought stress is lessened when the timing of maximum water uptake differs for each crop in a mixed system (Davis et al. 1986).

6. WEED SUPPRESSION

Intercropping can result in a more complete ground cover, which deters the establishment of weeds, than may be achieved by monocropping, The effectiveness of weed suppression depends on factors such as the density and distribution of planting and the crops employed. A strategy particularly common in India is to sow a cereal main crop into a standing crop of a small-seeded perennial legume, which acts as a living mulch (Chatterjee and Mandal 1992).

7. DECREASED DISEASE AND INSECT-DAMAGE

Certain species are known to reduce the spread and hence the damage by various pathogenic agencies (Wrigley 1982). For example, the spread of airborne spores may be restricted due to a reduction in air turbulence in the crop canopy. Some crop species seem to be associated with a lowering of soil temperature, which arrests attack by certain fungal parasites. The incidence of insect pests, such as thrips and leaf miners, can be reduced in the main crop by the presence of deterrent secondary crop species (Irvine 1934), which are often legumes (Chatterjee and Mandal 1992).

8. WIND PROTECTION

A secondary crop species, when sown around the edges of plots or at right angles to prevailing winds, can act as a wind-break to protect the main crop from damage (Siddoway and Barnett 1979). Commonly, relatively tall and erect species are planted for this purpose, and may be harvested as a supplementary grain or fodder crop, exemplified, as mentioned above, in Spain by *Vicia faba* (Peña Chocarro 1995). This can be considered as a form of strip intercropping (Radke and Hagstrom 1976).

9. SUPPORT AGAINST LODGING

Non-self-supporting herbaceous taxa, such as the tendrillous or twining legumes, benefit from associations with vegetation which provides support and facilitates the provision of maximum light to the canopy. Such crops as mustard are often cultivated with grain legumes for this purpose in India.

10. EROSION CONTROL

Crops such as *Lathyrus sativus*, which have a short growing season and which tolerate waterlogged conditions, may be sown on semi-drained land following the rainy season to stabilize the soil and provide a yield prior to the sowing season of the maincrop, a sequential cropping strategy employed in the Ethiopian highlands (Abate Tedla, pers. comm.).

11. REDUCTION OR SPREAD OF LABOUR

Mixed cropping requires only one basic tillage operation per year for all the crops cultivated within that system. Although a high species diversity in mixed systems demands a high input of labour at harvesting, it has been found that labour requirements are less concentrated for mixed crops than for individual plots of the same species, and it is said that storage problems where mixed harvests are taken tend to be reduced (Wrigley 1982; Shaxson and Tauer 1992).

12. PROTECTION OF OWNERSHIP

While the ownership of a grain crop is commonly respected, forage rights are often less easy to protect. In Jordan, for example, a cereal crop is sometimes sown with a legume forage crop to provide more secure ownership rights for the grazing of the stubble and legume forage following the grain harvest (Springborg 1990).

It can be seen that a wide range of physiological, morphological, environmental and sociocultural factors can interact to govern the choice of cropping system, and presumably will have stimulated their development.

THE EARLIEST AGRONOMIES

It has been argued that in tropical regions multiple cropping systems were the earliest forms of cultivation, that roots and tubers were the first types of crop propagated, and that within these systems seed cultivation was a secondary development (Francis 1986; Sauer 1969). In temperate regions, the earliest cultivation on a garden plot scale may have included grain crops as components of multiple systems. It has been suggested that because of the difficulties inherent in the cultivation and harvesting of wild-type plants which have a high level of seed dormancy and the freely disseminating ripe grains characteristic of undomesticated species, cereals and grain legumes (pulses) were unlikely to have been amongst the first cultigens (Francis 1986). It has also been pointed out that roots and tubers are the most characteristic crop types planted in garden plot clearings in wooded areas, while grain and fruit crops cultivated in larger field systems are more typical of savannahs (Okigbo and Greenland 1976). If the latter generalization can be accepted, grain crop development may have depended on and followed the decrease in forest.

Many extant traditional agricultural systems are polycultural. As we have seen, these are now found mainly in tropical environments, but multiple cropping was more widely prevalent in the past. It has been said that specialized monocultural systems are associated with higher levels of technological complexity (Harris 1969), and therefore supposedly were developed later. However, we have no evidence that in the temperate Old World the multiple cropping of grain crops predated monocropping (Butler 1992) or that monocropping as whole was a later development. While archaeobotanists continue to be influenced largely by ethnobotanical studies from monocropping systems it is unlikely that these questions will be answered adequately.

Consequently, it is suggested that the interpretation of early archaeological crop assemblages should be based upon consideration of a number of models deriving from a wide range of cropping strategies. Primarily we need more data. As a prerequisite, detailed analyses should be made of the agronomic processes employed in, and the residues resulting from, mixed systems, similar to those collected from the monocropping systems of South-west Asia and Europe cited above. Work is needed particularly in the Indian subcontinent and North and East Africa, and this need is urgent as traditional agriculture is continually under threat from schemes of modernization in the drive for increased productivity.

Fortunately it has recently been recognized that maximum productivity does not necessarily equate with sustainability. Such mechanized techniques as deep ploughing deplete soil fertility, destroy soil structure and encourage erosion. Consequently, in some areas agronomists are now recommending the application of more conservative and even no-tillage practices (Papendick et al. 1988). These are dependent upon traditional resources and technology and, although less productive in the short term, are minimally destructive and, by definition from their long standing traditions, can be sustained in the long term. Thus there is hope that traditional multicropping systems may be retained and will enable such environmental work to be undertaken.

ACKNOWLEDGEMENTS

The personal communications of Dr Abate Tedla of the International Livestock Research Institute (ILRI), Addis Ababa, and Dr Geletu Bejiga of Alemaya University of Agriculture, Debre Zeit, Ethiopia are gratefully acknowledged. I thank Dr Sarah Mason, Institute of Archaeology, University College London, for her valuable suggestions on reading the manuscript.

REFERENCES

Al-Mouayad Al Azem, A.N. 1991. Crop storage in ancient Syria: a functional analysis using ethnographic modelling. Unpublished Ph.D. thesis, University of London.

Allchin, B. and R. Allchin. 1982. *The Rise of Civilization in India and Pakistan.* Cambridge: Cambridge University Press.

Andrews, D.J. and A.H. Kassam, 1976. The importance of multiple cropping in increasing world food supplies. In *Multiple cropping,* R.I. Papendick, P.A. Sanchez and G.B. Triplett (eds), 1–10. Madison, Wis.: American Society of Agronomy.

Barker, T.C. and C.A. Francis. 1986. Agronomy of multiple cropping systems. In *Multiple Cropping Systems,* C.A.Francis (ed.), 161–82. New York: Macmillan.

Bharati, M.P. 1986. Status of *Lathyrus sativus* among grain legumes cultivated in Nepal. In *Lathyrus and lathyrism,* A.K. Kaul and D. Combes (eds), 142–5. New York: Third World Medical Research Foundation.

Butler, E.A. 1992. Pulse agronomy: traditional systems and implications for early cultivation. In *Préhistoire de l'agriculture,* P.C. Anderson (ed.), 67–78. Paris: CNRS.

Chatterjee, B.N. and B.K. Mandal. 1992. Present trends in research on intercropping. *Indian Journal of Agricultural Sciences* 2, 507–18.

Cubero, J.I. 1983. Parasitic diseases in *Vicia faba* L. with special reference to broomrape (*Orobanche crenata* Forsk.). In *Faba Bean,* P.D. Hebblethwaite (ed.), 493–521. London: Butterworths.

Dalrymple, D.G. 1971. *Survey of Multiple Cropping in Less Developed Nations.* Washington DC.: Foreign Economic Development Service, US Department of Agriculture.

Davis, J.H.C., J.N. Woolley and R.A. Moreno. 1986. Multiple cropping with starchy roots. In *Multiple Cropping Systems,* C.A. Francis (ed.), 133–60. New York: Macmillan.

de Carvalho, H. and M. de L. da Silva Leal. 1991. Cultivares de milho e de feijão em monocultivo e em consorcio. *Pesquita Agropecuaria Brasiliera* 26, 1467–73.

Doggett, H. 1991. Sorghum history in relation to Ethiopia. In *Plant Genetic Resources of Ethiopia,* J.M.M. Engels, J.G. Hawkes and Melaku Worede (eds), 140–59. Cambridge: Cambridge University Press.

Forbes, H.A. 1976. 'We have a little of everything'. The ecological basis of some agricultural practices in Methana, Trizinia. *Annals of the New York Academy of Sciences* 268, 236–50.

Forbes, H.A. and H.A. Koster. 1976. Fire, axe and plow: human influence on local plant communities in the southern Argolid. *Annals of The New York Academy of Sciences* 268, 109–26.

Forbes, M.H.C. 1976a. Farming and foraging in prehistoric Greece: a cultural ecological perspective. *Annals of The New York Academy of Sciences* 268, 127–42.

Forbes, M.H.C. 1976b. Gathering in the Argolid: a subsistence subsystem in a Greek agricultural community. *Annals of the New York Academy of Sciences* 268, 251–64.

Francis, C.A. 1986. Introduction: distribution and importance of multiple cropping. In *Multiple Cropping Systems*, C.A. Francis (ed.), 1–19. New York: Macmillan.

Francis, C.A., C.A. Flor and S.R. Temple. 1976. Adapting varieties for intercropping systems in the tropics. In *Multiple Cropping*, R.I. Papendick, P.A. Sanchez and G.B. Triplett (eds), 235–53. Madison, Wis.: American Society of Agronomy.

Ghosh, S. S. and K. Lal. 1963. Plant remains from Rangpur. In *Excavations at Rangpur and Other Explorations in Gujurat*, S.R. Rao (ed.), *Ancient India* 18–19, 161–75.

Halstead, P. 1987. Traditional and ancient rural economy in Mediterranean Europe: plus ça change. *Journal of Hellenic Studies* 107, 77–87.

Halstead, P. and G.E.M. Jones, 1989. Agrarian ecology in the Greek islands: time stress, scale and risk. *Journal of Hellenic Studies* 109, 41–5.

Halstead, P. and G.E.M. Jones, 1995. Maslins, mixtures and monocrops: on the interpretation of archaeo-botanical crop samples of heterogeneous composition. *Journal of Archaeological Science* 22, 103–14.

Harris, D.R. 1969. Agricultural systems, ecosystems and the origins of agriculture. In *The Domestication and Exploitation of Plants and Animals*, P.J. Ucko and G.W. Dimbleby (eds), 3–15. London: Duckworth.

Hillman, G.C. 1972. Recent archaeological research in Turkey. Asvan 1971. Archaeobotanical studies. *Anatolian Studies* 22, 17–19.

Hillman, G.C. 1973. Crop husbandry and food production: modern basis for the interpretation of plant remains. *Anatolian Studies* 23, 241–4.

Hillman, G.C. 1981. Reconstructing crop husbandry practices from charred remains of crops. In *Farming Practices in British Prehistory*, R. Mercer (ed.), 123–62. Edinburgh: Edinburgh University Press.

Hillman, G.C. 1984a. Interpretation of archaeological plant remains: the application of ethnographic models from Turkey. In *Plants and Ancient Man*, W. van Zeist and W.A. Casparie (eds), 1–41. Rotterdam: Balkema.

Hillman, G.C. 1984b. Traditional husbandry and processing of archaic cereals in modern times: Part I, the glume wheats. *Bulletin on Sumerian Agriculture, Cambridge* 1, 114–52.

Hillman, G.C. 1985. Traditional husbandry and processing of archaic cereals in recent times: the operations, products, and equipment that might feature in Sumerian texts. *Bulletin on Sumerian Agriculture, Cambridge* 2, 1–31.

Irvine, F.R. 1934. *A Text-book of West African Agriculture*. London: Oxford University Press.

Jones, G.E.M. 1983. The use of ethnographic and ecological models in the interpretation of archaeological plant remains. Unpublished Ph.D. thesis, University of Cambridge.

Jones, G.E.M. 1984. Interpretation of archaeological plant remains: ethnographic models from Greece. In *Plants and Ancient Man*, W. van Zeist and W.A. Casparie (eds), 43–61. Rotterdam: Balkema.

Jones, G.E.M. 1987. Agricultural practice in Greek prehistory. *The Annual of the British School at Athens* 82, 115–23.

Jones, G.M., K. Wardle, P. Halstead and D. Wardle. 1986. Crop storage at Assiros. *Scientific American* 254, 96–103.

Jubete, F. 1991. *Los titarros: el cultivo de Lathyrus en Castilla y León*. Valladolid: Junta Castilla y León Consejería de Agricultura y Galadería.

Kajale, M.D. 1988. Plant economy. In *Excavations at Inamgaon*, Vol. I Part ii, M.K. Dhavalikar, H.D. Sankalia and Z.D. Ansari (eds), 727–821. Pune: Deccan College.

Kajale, M.D. 1992. Current status of Indian palaeoethnobotany: introduced and indigenous food plants with a discussion of the historical and evolutionary development of Indian agriculture and agricultural systems in general. In *New Light on Early Farming*, J. Renfrew (ed.), 154–89. Edinburgh: University of Edinburgh Press.

Kajale, M.D. 1994. Archaeobotanical investigations on a multicultural site at Adam, Maharashtra, with special reference to the development of tropical agriculture in parts of India. In *Tropical Archaeobotany*, J.G. Hather (ed.), 34–50. London: Routledge.

Kishk, F. 1979. The role of the IDRC in food legume improvement research. In *Food Legume Improvement and Development*, G.C. Hawtin and G.J. Chancellor (eds), 192–3. Ottawa: ICARDA and IDRC.

Lal, B.B. 1970. Perhaps the earliest ploughed field so far excavated anywhere in the world. *Puratattva*. 4, 1–3.

Lone, F.A., M. Khan and G.M. Buth. 1993. *Palaeoethnobotany*. Rotterdam: Balkema.

Maekawa, K. 1985. Cultivation of legumes and mun-gazi plants in Ur III Girsu. *Bulletin on Sumerian Agriculture, Cambridge* 2: 97–118.

Malik, B.A. 1988. Problems and prospects of winter cereals and food legumes in the high-elevation areas of Pakistan. In *Winter Cereals and Food Legumes in Mountainous Areas,* J.P. Srivastava, M.C. Saxena, S. Varma and M. Tanir (eds), 211–19. Aleppo: ICARDA.

Marshall, G. 1796. *The Rural Economy of Yorkshire*. London: G. Nicol.

Mehra, K.L. 1991. Prehistoric Ethiopia and India: contacts through sorghum and millet genetic resources. In *Plant Genetic Resources of Ethiopia*, J.M.M. Engels, J.G. Hawkes and Melaku Worede (eds), 60–168. Cambridge: Cambridge University Press.

Mirchandani, T.J. and D.K. Misra. 1975. Associated growth of cereals and legumes. *Indian Journal of Agronomy* 1, 237–43.

Nasr, H.N. 1976. Multiple cropping in some countries of the Middle East. In *Multiple Cropping,* R.I. Papendick, P.A. Sanchez and G.B. Triplett (eds), 117–27. Madison, Wis.: American Society of Agronomy.

Nicol, H. 1935. Mixed cropping in primitive agriculture. *Empire Journal of Experimental Agriculture* 3, 189–95.

Okigbo, B.N. and D.J. Greenland. 1976. Intercropping systems in tropical Africa. In *Multiple Cropping*, R.I. Papendick, P.A. Sanchez and G.B. Triplett (eds), 63–101. Madison, Wis.: American Society of Agronomy.

Papendick, R.I., S.L. Chowdhury and C. Johansen. 1988. Managing systems for increasing productivity in dryland agriculture. In *World Crops: cool season food legumes,* R.J. Summerfield (ed.), 237–55. Dordrecht: Kluwer.

Peña Chocarro, L. 1995. Prehistoric agriculture in southern Spain: the application of ethnographic models. Unpublished Ph.D. thesis, University of London.

Plucknett, D.L. and N.J.H. Smith. 1986. Historical perspectives on multiple cropping. In *Multiple Cropping Systems*, C.A. Francis (ed.), 20–39. New York: Macmillan.

Pretty, J.N. 1990. Sustainable agriculture in the Middle Ages: the English manor. *Agricultural History Review* 38, 1–19.

Radke, J.K. and R.T. Hagstrom. 1976. Strip intercropping for wind protection. In *Multiple Cropping*, R.I. Papendick, P.A. Sanchez and G.B. Triplett (eds), 201–22. Madison, Wis.: American Society of Agronomy.

Rao, S.R. (ed.). 1963. *Excavations at Rangpur and Other Explorations in Gujurat, Ancient India*, 18–19, 5–207. New Delhi.

Rider Haggard, H. [1899]1987. *A Farmer's Year.* London: the Cresset Library.

Sauer, C.O. 1969. *Agricultural Origins and Dispersals: the domestication of animals and foodstuffs.* 2nd edition. Cambridge, Mass.: MIT Press.

Sharma, A.K. 1982. Excavations at Gufkral 1979–1980. *Puratattva* 11, 19–25.

Shaxson, L. and L.W. Tauer. 1992. Intercropping and diversity: an economic analysis of cropping patterns on smallholder farms in Malawi. *Experimental Agriculture* 28, 211–28.

Siddoway, F.H. and A.P. Barnett. 1976. Water and wind erosion control aspects of multiple cropping. In *Multiple Cropping*, R.I. Papendick, P.A. Sanchez and G.B. Triplett (eds), 317–36. Madison, Wis.: American Society of Agronomy.

Sigaut, F. 1992. Rendements, semis et fertilité: signification analytique des rendements. In *Préhistoire de l'agriculture. Nouvelles approches expérimentales et ethnographiques,* P. Anderson (ed.), 395–403. Paris: CNRS.

Simoons, F.J. 1960. *North-west Ethiopia.* Madison, Wis.: University of Wisconsin Press.

Singh, S.P. and Ahuja, K.N. 1990. Intercropping of grain sorghum with fodder legumes under dryland conditions in North-Western India. *Indian Journal of Agronomy* 35, 287–96.

Smith, M.E. and C.A. Francis. 1986. Breeding for multiple cropping systems. In *Multiple Cropping Systems,* C.A. Francis (ed.), 219–49. New York: Macmillan.

Springborg, R. 1990. Human constraints in extending the use of forage legumes in Mediterranean areas. In *The Role of Legumes in the Farming Systems of the Mediterranean Areas,* A.E. Osman, M.H. Ibrahim and M.A. Jones (eds), 283–94. Dordrecht: Kluwer.

Townsend, C.C. and E. Guest, 1974. *Flora of Iraq.* Volume 3. Baghdad: Ministry of Agriculture.

van Driel, G. 1990. Neo-Babylonian agriculture III: cultivation. *Bulletin on Sumerian Agriculture, Cambridge* 5, 219–66.

Vishnu-Mittre. 1974. The beginnings of agriculture, palaeobotanical evidence in India. In *Evolutionary Studies in World Crops: diversity and change in the Indian sub-continent,* J.B. Hutchinson (ed.), 3–30. Cambridge: Cambridge University Press.

Westphal, E. 1974. *Pulses in Ethiopia, their Taxonomy and Agricultural Significance.* Wageningen: Centre for Agricultural Publishing and Documentation, PUDOC.

Westphal, E. 1975. *Agricultural Systems in Ethiopia.* Wageningen: Centre for Agricultural Publishing and Documentation, PUDOC.

Wetterstrom, W. 1991. Fleshing out early agriculture. In *Origins and Development of Agriculture in East Africa: the ethnosystems approach to the study of food production in Kenya,* R.E. Leakey and L.J. Slikkerveer (eds), 219–33. Iowa: Iowa State University Research Foundation.

White, K.D. 1970. *Roman Farming.* London: Thames and Hudson.

Wrigley, G. 1982. *Tropical Agriculture: the development of production.* New York: Longman.

Zagdouni, L. and D. Benatya, 1990. Mechanisation and agricultural employment in arid and semiarid zones of Morocco: the case of Upper Chaouia. In *Labor, Employment and Agricultural Development in West Asia and North Africa,* D. Tully (ed.), 103–40. Dordrecht: Kluwer.

25　Agrarian change and the beginnings of cultivation in the Near East: evidence from wild progenitors, experimental cultivation and archaeobotanical data

GEORGE WILLCOX

INTRODUCTION

This chapter examines the change in the subsistence system in the Near East from a gathering economy to one of production (the beginnings of cereal and pulse cultivation), in the light of observations made during the experimental cultivation of primitive cereals at Jalès (France), together with field observations of wild cereals in their natural habitat at a number of stations in Syria. These observations are compared to recent archaeobotanical data.

Since the publications by Kislev on the difficulties of distinguishing wild and domestic emmer wheats (1989: 148, and 1992), Hillman and Davies's (1990) publication on rates of domestication and Baruch and Bottema's (1991) work on climatic change, which Moore and Hillman (1992) suggest might be a contributing factor in the emergence of cereal cultivation, a number of new sites have been published and others are in the process of being analysed. Sites with well-preserved plant remains from the crucial period between 10,500 and 9000 BP are rare and frequently this period is represented only at the base of tells where extensive sampling has not been possible (Cayönü, Aswad and Cafer Höyük). Sites (see Figure 25.1) such as Cafer Höyük (de Moulins 1997) and Cayönü (van Zeist and de Roller 1994) have recently been published, and others such as Jerf al Ahmar, Dja'de (Willcox 1996), Nevali Cori (Pasternak 1995), Qermez Dere, M'lefaat, Hallan Cemi, and Nemrik (Nesbitt 1995) are now being analysed. In addition new evidence is coming to light on the distributions of wild cereals in Syria.

Experimental results from the cultivation of wild einkorn indicate that selective pressures in favour of domestic traits, such as the solid rachis, can be variable depending on harvesting techniques, and may be low (Hillman and Davies 1990; Willcox 1995). This is in contrast to the more conventional view that domestic traits were promptly selected for (Zohary 1992, 1996) once the progenitor was brought into cultivation. Low selective pressures could explain recent archaeobotanical finds which indicate that domestic and

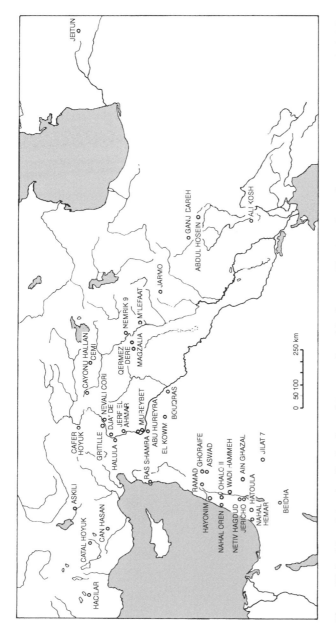

Figure 25.1 Map giving the distribution of sites mentioned in the text. The site of Franchti cave in Greece is not included for reasons of scale.

wild cereals occurred as mixtures on several early neolithic sites over a period of at least a millennium. Archaeobotanical finds and field studies confirm that late epipalaeolithic and early neolithic distributions of wild cereals were more extensive (Hillman 1996) and environmental differences (soil types and humidity) between sites are reflected in the cereal assemblages at, and perhaps just after, the gathering stage (barley on poor dry soils for example). But once cultivation began, favourable soils would be chosen as would preferred crops. For example, emmer becomes more widespread at the expense of einkorn.

It is argued here that subsistence change in the Near East was a gradual process, proceeding over millennia rather than centuries, and that the adoption of cultivation required little innovation because, on the one hand, the 'tool kit' already existed and, on the other, the natural life cycle of the plants concerned had been exploited for some considerable time. After a period of small-scale cultivation an organized production economy was established, crops would have evolved more rapidly and village size could increase and societies develop in new ways.

PRESENT-DAY WILD CEREALS

The evolutionary paths which led to present-day wild and domestic cereals are not fully understood. For example we do not know when sterility barriers developed between *T. urartu* and *T. boeoticum*. Both species are present in the Levant today but we cannot tell how these compare genetically to the wild einkorn identified at sites such as Mureybet (van Zeist and Bakker-Heeres 1984a) and Abu Hureyra (Hillman *et al.* 1989). Even the BB genome donor is disputed (Konarev and Konarev 1993). Cytogenetic studies of modern populations are still providing new evidence for the early evolution of domesticates. A major limiting factor in the study of early crop evolution is the fact that we cannot know the cytogenetic relationships of ancient populations, particularly given the possibility of rapid evolution under domestication which may have led to a large number of extinctions of ancient domestic varieties. In addition genetic exchange between different wild populations will have occurred over the last 10,000 years.

The distribution of wild cereals is well known in Turkey and Iraq (Davies 1985; Bor 1968), but has been somewhat neglected for Syria where primary stands of all four wild wheats are more widespread than has been previously suspected (Valkoun 1992, and pers. comm., author's field studies in 1995). These populations, which are being studied by members of ICARDA (International Centre for Agricultural Research in Dry Areas, Aleppo), show high diversity and it is probable that genetic exchange between these closely related taxa occurs, despite the fact that they are predominantly inbreeders. *Triticum urartu* (AA donor for the tetraploid wheats) and *T. boeoticum* appear to be relatively common in areas with 300 mm of rain per annum but can occur occasionally in areas with as little as 250 mm. A number of recent discoveries have been made by J. Valkoun (1992) of ICARDA, and his results will be published in detail at a later date.

In northern Syria the present author collected *T. urartu* and *T. boeoticum* in the north-western part of the Jeseri at several stations near Ain al Arab. Mouterde (1966: 143) reports that he found wild einkorn on the Jebel Aziz (*Triticum thaoudar* Reut.). West of Aleppo several populations, which include *T. urartu*, *T. dicoccoides*, *T. boeoticum* and *T. araraticum* have been found. A population of *T. urartu* was located north of Homs by J. Valkoun (pers. comms.). In the south, on the Jebel Druze, which is a basaltic massif rising to 1,800 metres, one can find vast stands of *T. urartu*, *T. dicoccoides* and *T. boeoticum* in their primary habitat. Finally, Valkoun (pers. comms.) reports that he has found a population of *T. urartu* as far south as Beida in southern Jordan. All these populations appear to be restricted to deep, rich, decalcified soils, such as *terra rossa* formed on limestone, or soils derived from basalt. But in higher rainfall areas they may occur on poorer soils. Wild wheats in Syria occur in open habitats, beyond the eastern margins of the Mediterranean vegetation zone, where they colonize open habitats with a continental climate. The four wild wheats found in Syria appear to occur in similar ecological zones; at certain locations they may occur as mixed populations, or in other cases will form pure stands. In either case they frequently grow with *Aegilops* spp. such as *A. speltoides*, *A. searsi*, *A. crassa* and *A. tauschii*, and form what might be described as a rich prairie habitat. In Syria wild einkorn penetrates the steppe habitat, whereas further north in Turkey it occupies the open deciduous oak parkland, described by Zohary (Zohary and Hopf 1988: 32) as the typical habitat for wild einkorn. This latter habitat does not exist in Syria today, but it is possible that this association was more widespread in the past and recent studies have indicated that deciduous oak charcoal is present on sites in Syria – not just from the Neolithic but also from the Bronze Age and later periods (Willcox 1991a, 1995, 1996). In southern Syria deciduous oak forests have been progressively replaced by evergreen oak forests (Willcox forthcoming) since the Bronze Age.

How far does the present-day distribution and ecology relate to the early Neolithic period? It is clear that today the wild wheats are restricted to favourable soil types. In addition, wild wheat populations appear to be very susceptible to grazing and occur only in areas where grazing is restricted. Thus what is seen today is likely to be a much-reduced distribution; with less human pressure and perhaps a more favourable climate, wild wheats may have covered a much wider zone during the Epipalaeolithic and Neolithic periods. This is indeed confirmed by the archaeobotanical finds from what is today arid steppe in that part of northern Syria which flanks the Euphrates (see also Hillman 1996 for a reinterpretation of post-glacial forest-steppe colonization).

The fact that these closely related species of wild wheat are found together has led to high genetic variability, although this may not be identifiable archaeobotanically. However, regional differences between populations of wild cereals, where different species (barley, einkorn, emmer and rye) are dominant, should show up archaeobotanically at the collecting stage during the Epipalaeolithic; but once cultivation and domestication began one might expect specialization and selection at the species level and ultimately the development of a weed flora. This would result in more uniform assemblages on a regional scale.

EXPERIMENTAL CULTIVATION RESULTS AND SELECTIVE TENDENCIES

In 1985, following discussions between G. Hillman, P. Anderson, J. Cauvin and the present author, it was decided to set up experiments using primitive wheats, and in particular wild einkorn, in order to test their behaviour under cultivation. An important aspect was the recording of spikelet loss under different harvesting techniques in order to estimate selection pressures and the rapidity of the domestication process. Hillman and Davies in their article (1990) discuss a wide range of possibilities for pre-domestic agriculture using a mathematical model. It emerges that spikelet loss during harvesting is one of the crucial elements which influence selective pressures and affect rates of domestication. Thus in 1989 a large-scale experiment was set up to test this aspect of the model. The reader is referred to the original article by Hillman and Davies which discusses in detail the different variables concerned, a wide range of scenarios and the mathematical model used to calculate the experimental results given here.

The principal population of *Triticum boeoticum* was collected in 1986 in eastern Anatolia near Karaçadag between Diyarbakir and Siverek at an altitude of approximately 800 metres above sea level, in a region where there is an annual rainfall of approximately 600 mm. This wild population prospers under the climatic and edaphic conditions at Jalès, which is situated at the extreme southern limit of the Ardèche in southern France. The difference in altitude (Jalès 130 metres above sea level) appears to be compensated for by the difference in latitude (5.5°) between the two locations.

The wild population that was collected in its natural habitat showed a high diversity in, for example, gliadin analyses, and in morphological features such as glume colouring and hairiness. This original population contained low frequencies of wild emmer and *Aegilops speltoides*; the latter remained in the population for several years while the former died out after two generations.

In addition a number of other populations of both wild and domestic cereals were cultivated. The populations which were obtained from plant breeders were single-line, true-breeding populations, and are therefore less representative of early farming practices.

Before discussing the principal experiment, set up in 1989 to examine selection rates, it is necessary to present the techniques used and some relevant results obtained during the first years (between 1986 and 1989). Additional results can be found elsewhere (Willcox 1991b, 1992).

Sowing

In their natural habitat wild cereals sow themselves immediately after ripening. Thus the time of sowing is dependent on the altitude and latitude of any particular ecotype in question. Timing of natural dispersion will therefore vary from May to August, depending on the relative ripening times in different geographical areas. The advantage of early sowing for the farmer is that there is less chance of loss from vermin during storage (our samples were attacked by weevils), and the young plants get a better start and give good tillering.

Vernalization is the major factor controlling whether barley and wheat are spring or autumn sown. All wheats and barleys can be planted in the winter, but only those which lack the need for vernalization may be planted in the spring. Wild cereals exhibit varying degrees of vernalization requirement (Mathon 1985). In 1987/8 we planted *T. boeoticum aegilopoides* in both winter and spring. The spring-sown crop exhibited poor tillering. The emmer crop when spring-planted gives a highly diminished yield. We conclude that in a Mediterranean climate primitive cereals would have been predominantly winter-sown. Thus it would appear that by following the natural life-cycle the best results are obtained, though of course this could result in diminishing selective pressure.

Seed was broadcast by hand at high density in its hulled condition, that is to say the equivalent of about 140 kilos per hectare once the weight of the chaff is removed. We do not know how the earliest farmers sowed, although we do know that by the beginning of the third millennium in Mesopotamia, cereals were sown in carefully spaced rows using a seed-drill (Postgate 1984: 102).

Dormancy/inhibition of germination

Germination tests were carried out by the local agricultural college at Aubenas on samples of our seed grain under laboratory conditions. Observations on 100 grains were made at seven and fourteen days; the grains were kept humid at a temperature of 18°C. Table 25.1 gives the results of germination tests from 7–21 October 1987.

The results from the germination tests indicate that:

1 in the case of wild einkorn, a crop harvested before maturity, still green, gives viable seed for planting the following autumn;
2 the glumes in the twinned-grained einkorns tend to inhibit the germination of the 'second grain' over a fourteen-day period and there was no twinned germination in sample number 122;
3 wild emmer and wild barley gave poor results, perhaps because of strong germination inhibitors;

Table 25.1 Results of germination tests carried out over a fourteen-day period. Tests were made at varying degrees of ripeness to test the viability of harvests carried out before maturity. It is clear that naked caryops gave good germination rates, while in the hulled state the glumes inhibited germination and in all but one sample only one grain germinated.

Species	Ref. no.	Naked grain %	Hulled %	Double %	Comments
T. monococcum	12	92	80	0	
T. dicoccoides	18	56	17.5	0	Only 40 spikelets
T. b. thaoudar	122	82	80	0	Green
,, ,,	62	42	0	0	Half green (mouldy)
,, ,,	92	90	0	0	Ripe
,, ,,	77	94	94	0	Green
,, ,,	98	96	18	0	Half green
,, ,,	92	84	46	0	Ripe
,, ,,	38	92	98	16	Green
,, ,,	100	95	10	0	Half green
,, ,,	100	100	20	0	Ripe
T. urartu	59	82	94	6	Ripe
T. compactum	13	90	—	—	Free threshing
H. spontaneum	33	97.5	58	—	Ripe
,, ,,	52	54	—	—	Green

4   sample number 77 appears to lack the dormancy factor when harvested ripe. This sample, which appears to be a single-line (true-breeding) population, also tends to have a more solid rachis.

Dormancy was shown to exist in the laboratory experiments but these tests were only carried out over a fourteen-day period. Thus it was necessary to test whether dormant grains could germinate in the field and provide a harvest the following year. In 1989/90 we harvested a plot of wild einkorn before the grains were formed to eliminate self-seeding. The following two years saw no new germination. Thus the dormancy period under the conditions at Jalès was less than a year. However, under drier conditions germination may be inhibited for longer periods.

Uneven ripening and the brittle rachis
Wild cereals exhibit uneven ripening between different plants. In the case of wild einkorn grown at Jalès at least a month may elapse between the earliest and the latest maturation in the same field. Uneven ripening also occurs between spikelets on the same ear, which mature progressively, with the uppermost spikelets ripening first. Primitive domestic cereals such as spelt, emmer and einkorn retained this trait which indicates that it was not selected against during the early stages of domestication.

If the fallen grain survives to be harvested with part of the crop kept back for sowing the fragile rachis continues to be selected for in the population. The germination tests given above show that a premature harvest before ripening produces viable grain, but because of uneven ripening a small proportion of ripe grain will in fact fall (see Table 25.2). If this self-sown seed is harvested then selective pressures in favour of uniform ripening and against uneven ripening would have been minimal.

Self-seeding and its effect on domestication

The domestication experiment was set up in 1989 and continued until 1993. Eight plots, A to H, each measuring 5 × 5 metres, were planted in August with 1.2 kilos of third-generation hulled wild einkorn. The quantity sown may seem high but it must be remembered that the chaff fraction represents well over half of the total weight. The first harvest took place during the last two weeks of June. Two variables were tested: method of reaping (shaking, sickle, hand picking and uprooting) and the degree of maturity, which was measured by the level of humidity. The results are given in Table 25.2. The main aim of these experiments was to test grain loss through self-seeding under differing conditions and to estimate its effect on the domestication process.

It was found that the combined traits of uneven ripening and brittle rachis resulted in a certain amount of grain falling during harvest regardless of the technique (see Table 25.2). This occurred particularly during the harvest of the last plots which were riper than those harvested earlier. In theory, loss through fallen spikelets during the harvest results in an increase in selective pressure in favour of solid-rachised domestic plants. Loss was measured by collecting fallen spikelets from a randomly chosen square metre for each twenty-five metre square. As can be seen, loss is highly variable depending on the conditions of harvesting.

The plots were left fallow and the following year, 1990, a second harvest was obtained and the effects of spontaneous sowing were measured. Harvests were continued through to 1993 by which time competition, essentially from perennial grasses, seriously reduced the yield. As can be seen in Table 25.2, the first year of grow-back in 1991 represents a reasonable harvest. On the one hand, if early farmers opened up new fields, they could hardly ignore the spontaneously sown fallow fields; on the other, if they worked and replanted the same fields the effects of even short-term dormancy would mean that a reasonable proportion of viable spikelets would in fact survive. Given the results obtained it would appear reasonable to assume that harvests could have contained 25 per cent of self-seeded plants. This 25 per cent could come from continuously cultivated fields, or from fallow fields.

This estimate does not include any spikelets which may have been harvested from natural stands, which is probable during the transition period, because the annual rainfall may not have been reliable. Under the present-day climate the rainfall for the Near East is irregular, particularly in the Euphrates valley, and years with low rainfall are frequent (Traboulsi 1981; Kerbe 1987). This may well have been the case 10,000 years ago. Thus, in poor years, whether due to such climatic abnormalities, disease or social upheaval, gathering from the wild could have supplemented the cultivated harvests. If

Table 25.2 Results obtained from experimental cultivation of wild einkorn as part of a CNRS project. The experiments were devised to test rates of spikelet loss under different harvesting conditions. Initially rates were put forward in predominantly model form by Hillman and Davies (1990), but see also Willcox (1991a, 1992). Spikelet loss was measured using two variables, maturity measured by the humidity and harvesting technique (column two). Selection coefficients (using Hillman and Davies's calculation) based on losses during the first year's harvest indicate that domestication would proceed. But if we take into account the quantity harvested in 1991 from spontaneously sown plants, this would seriously reduce selection coefficients.

Plot	Methods	m^2	Date	1989	Hum. (%)	1990	l/m^2	l (%)	s/c	1991	S (%)	1992	SI (%)	1993
A	Shaking	12.5	26.6	0.65	10.36	0.169	0.242	94.5	0.114	2.05		1.76		0.34★
B	Sickle	25	19.6	1.2		5.5	0.027	10.93		2.3	37.27	1.55	75.6	
C	Hand	25	21.6	1.2	31.16	1.55	0.088	58.6			148.38	1.49	64.7	
D	Sickle	12.5	12.6	0.65	50.86	3.3	0.015	5.36	0.106	2.06	31.21†	1.01	49	
d	Sickle	12.5	29.5	0.65	57.40‡									
E	Sickle	25	12.6	1.2	52.68‡	7.5	0.018	5.6	0.105	1.56	20.8			
F	Hand	25	13.6	1.2	53.00‡	5.5	0.057	20.57	0.134	2.25	40.9			
G	Uprooting	12.5	14.6	0.65	49.81	2.55	0.020	8.92	0.110	1.04	18.57†			
g	Uprooting	12.5	19.6	0.65		3.35	0.022	7.58	0.112					
H	Sickle	12.5	13.5	0.65	47.50	2.25	0.018	9.09	0.111	1.97	51.16†			
h	Sickle	12.5	21.6	0.65		1.6	0.031	19.47	0.130					
Poc	Sickle	15	11.6			3	0.011	5.21						
Lf	Sickle	91	21.6		33.59	14.8	0.093	36.8						

Key: 1989 = weight sown 1989
Hum. % = percentage of humidity at time harvest
1990 = weight harvested 1990
l/m^2 = loss per square metre
m^2 = area planted in square metres
l (%) = percentage lost (i.e. fallen after harvest)
s/c = selection coefficient after Hillman's model <0.1 no domestication
1991 = weight harvested in 1991
S (%) = percentage of 1991 zero planting harvest compared to the 1990 harvest
1992 = weight of 1992 harvest with no planting
SI (%) = percentage of 1992 zero planting harvest compared to the 1991 harvest
1993 = average of all plots compared for 1993 harvest weight in kilos of hulled grain

Notes: ★ combined result; † two half plots combined; ‡ estimation

the gathered cereal became mixed with the seed grain it would have slowed down the rate of domestication. Keeping morphologically identical populations apart would have been difficult. Thus there are at least three factors which would slow selection rates and the process of domestication: (1) supplementary gathering, (2) spontaneous sowing under cultivation and (3) introgression (Zohary 1969).

We observed the presence of accidentally self-seeded cereals occurring in and around threshing areas at Jalès. This phenomenon must also have occurred during the gathering stage millennia before domestication, when cereals or legumes were displaced for processing, storage or consumption; such unintentional cultivation could have led to the extension of natural stands during the gathering stage.

Problems of identifying morphological domestication

Observations of a wide range of material reveal certain problems when identifying archaeobotanical remains. While it is well known that distortion by carbonization can lead to overlap between einkorn and emmer (this we have confirmed by experimentation), it is less well known that the proportion of single-grained spikelets in twinned-grained einkorn and emmer is extremely variable. This can lead to confusion. In one modern sample of *T. boeoticum thaoudar*, single-grained spikelets considerably outnumbered double-grained ones (Table 25.3). The reduction in number of grains appears to be related to stress caused, for example, by high sowing density or drought. These observations indicate that domestication criteria based on grain morphology alone could be misleading, particularly if based on a limited number of grains.

The abscission layer which is formed well before maturity causes the spikelets to dehisce on drying, even when harvested green. The early harvest does not affect the mechanism which causes the rachis to break up. However, as pointed out by Hillman (1981) and Kislev (1992) and confirmed among our populations, about 10 per cent of wild barley rachis fragments show solid domestic-type fused basal internodes. Thus, 10 per cent or less of domestic

Table 25.3 The ratio of single- to double-grained spikelets in three wheat species. The variability appears to correlate with varying environmental conditions.

		Double : single
T.b. thaoudar	1987	2.6 : 1
	1988	3.6 : 1
	1991 d	1 : 5.3
	g	1.7 : 1
	c	1.9 : 1
T. urartu	1988	1 : 1
	1987	4.5 : 1
T.b. aegilopoides	1988	0 : 1
T. dicoccum	1993	1.2 : 1

types is not necessarily indicative of domestication. If harvesting occurred late, with many of the upper spikelets already fallen, the percentage could be higher.

The distinction between domestic and wild wheats is based on the dissarticulation scar. The break occurs in the same place, and in modern material one is rough and the other smooth. However, in ancient carbonized remains the surface is very often too poorly preserved to allow this distinction. The semi-solid rachis in barley has not been recognized archaeologically; however, although not generally known, varieties do exist. The author has collected specimens of semi-solid rachis, two-rowed 'black' barley near Bosra in southern Syria. The dissarticulation scar is similar to that of the wild barleys.

Yield

The relevance of crop yield in cultivation (i.e., harvest weight compared to planted area) is likely to have been of limited interest to early farmers, who would have been more concerned with the return from a given amount of grain seed regardless of the planted area (yield ratio). Constant return, despite natural environmental fluctuations, would also have been favoured. Results obtained at Jalès are given by Willcox (1992: 176). Wild einkorn gave variable results in 1986; for example, a plot of 130 square metres gave a yield equivalent to 500 kg per hectare including chaff, but the ratio of harvest to seed corn was 8.6:1. In 1989 1.2 kg was sown for 25 square metres which in the best plot gave 7.5 kg, which is the equivalent of 3,000 kg per hectare but only 6.25:1 for the harvest/seed ratio. According to our cultivation results and results obtained in the field, wild einkorn can give between 0.5 and 1.5 tons of threshed grain per hectare. To take the totally hypothetical example of 200 grams of grain per day, per person (72 kilos per annum) one hectare would supply enough grain for 7–21 people. Unfortunately it is not possible to estimate the population of early neolithic village sites. But one might speculate that a small farming community of fifty people would need between 2.5 and 7 hectares for their cereals.

Conclusions based on experimental data

Traits such as dormancy and uneven ripening are not as disadvantageous as expected when cultivating wild cereals (Zohary 1996). Losses due to spikelets falling before and during the harvest are unavoidable, but these lead to germination and greatly reduce the chances of a mutant solid rachised type being kept back for sowing and increase its chances of ending up on the dinner table, thus diluting selective pressures in favour of a solid ear. In addition, early farmers may have encouraged a system where minimal seed corn gave a maximum return, which would also lead to a higher proportion of lost mutants on the dinner table. In this respect our estimates for the proportion of grain held back for sowing may be too high.

During the initial stages of cultivation, one might expect field size to be relatively small with a high risk of contact with wild populations at the periphery leading to introgression. In order for selection rates to be high enough to favour a solid rachis population, wild and cultivated populations would have to be separated. In reality this would prove difficult, given the spontaneous germination of fallen spikelets and the probability that gathering from wild populations would be needed in poor years to supplement harvests from cultivated fields which had failed.

The results thus indicate that selective pressures in favour of domestication vary according to the proportions of self-seeded (including wild seed grain) and harvested seed grain from deliberately sown plots. It is clear that once the level of wild seed dropped below 15 or 10 per cent, domestication would advance relatively quickly (Hillman and Davies 1990). For this to occur communities would have to be almost totally reliant on sown crops and have a well-organized farming system; if not, selective tendencies would be too low and cultivation might continue indefinitely without domestication taking place.

ARCHAEOBOTANICAL RESULTS COMPARED TO OBSERVATIONS BASED ON PRESENT-DAY POPULATIONS

A summary of archaeobotanical results is given in Table 25.4. The earliest evidence for cereal exploitation dates from 19,000 BP at Oholo II near the sea of Galilee where wild barley and emmer were recovered (Kislev *et al.* 1992). For the later Epipalaeolithic period (12,000–10,000 BP), there is more information. Small village sites such as Mureybet and Abu Hureyra on the Euphrates in Syria, Hayonim in Israel, Wadi Hammeh in Jordan, Franchthi cave in Greece and Qermez Dere, Nemrik 9 and M'lefaat in northern Iraq indicate that wild cereals were exploited together with a number of edible fruits and pulses. Indirect evidence from glossed tools indicates that plants with high silica contents were harvested at the Epipalaeolithic sites of Nahal Oren, Hatula, and Kebara in Israel, and Beidha in Jordan where plant remains were not recovered (Anderson 1994: 292, and pers. comm.). It is clear that morphologically wild progenitors of Old World cereals and legumes were exploited for several millennia before the appearance of their domestic counterparts. The geographical extent is impressive, stretching from northern Iraq to the southern Levant, and perhaps Western Anatolia, since we have the site of Franchthi in Greece. As was expected from observations of modern distributions, strong regional differences can be seen between Epipalaeolithic sites. Einkorn is dominant at Mureybet and Abu Hureyra (which also has wild oats, rare elsewhere); barley and some emmer are present at Ohalo II. Rye is also present at a number of these sites (Hillman *et al.* 1993).

The pre-pottery neolithic A (PPNA: 10,000–9600 BP) sites are less frequent but the architecture of small round houses is more substantial. No unequivocal morphological evidence for domestication at sites such as

Table 25.4 The major cereals, pulses and tree species from sites in the eastern Mediterranean (adapted from Nesbit and Samuel 1996). There is considerable chronological overlap between sites, particularly for the later periods. Note that lentils are very frequent; however, domestication appears over a wide area during the last half of the tenth millennium BP. Lentils are common on most sites. Oak is also well represented.

Site	Phase	Date BP non cal.	einkorn (w)	emmer (w)	barley (w)	einkorn (d)	emmer (d)	naked wheat (d)	barley 2r (d)	barley 6r (d)	aegilops (w)	lentil (?)	pea (?)	bitter vetch (?)	oak (w)	almond (w)	pistacia (w)	flax (?)	Reference
Ohalo II		19,000	O		O							O	O		A		O		Kislev et al. 1992
Franchthi		12,400–9000			O							O	O	O		O	O		Hansen 1991
Hayonim		12,300–11,900			O							O	O	O			O		Hopf and Bar Yosef 1987
Wadi Hammeh 27		12,200–11,900			O							O			W		O		Colledge 1994; Willcox 1991a
Abu Hureyra		11,000–10,000	O		O							O	O	O	W	W	O		Hillman et al. 1989
Hallan Cemi		10,600–9900	O									O	O	O		W	O		Rosenberg et al. 1995
Mureybet I	I–III	10,200–9500	O		O							O	O	O	W		O		van Zeist and Bakker-Heeres 1984a
Qermez Dere		10,100–9700										O	O	O			O		Nesbitt 1995
Netiv Hagdud		10,000–9400		O								O	O				O		Bar-Yosef et al. 1991
Jerf el Ahmar		9800–9700	O		O							O	O		W	O	O		Willcox 1996
M'lefaat		9800–9600	?									O	O	O			O		Nesbitt 1995
Tell Aswad	Ia	9700–9600			O				?		O	O	O	O	W		O		van Zeist and Bakker-Heeres 1984b
Dj'ade		9600–9000	O		?							O		O	W		O		Willcox 1996
Cayönü rh		9500–9200	?	?	?						O	O	O				O		van Zeist and de Roller 1994
Jericho	PPNA	9500–9000	O		O	O	O				O	O	O	O			O		Hopf 1983
Mureybet	IV	9400–8500	O	O		O	O					O	O	O	W	O	O		van Zeist and Bakker-Heeres 1984a
Cafer Höyük	XIII–X	9400–9000	O			O	O		?			O	O	O	W	O	O		de Moulins 1997; Willcox 1991c
Tell Aswad	Ib	9300–8800	O		O	O	O					O	O	O			O		van Zeist and Bakker-Heeres 1984b
Cayönü	gp bp c	9200–8500	O			O	O		?		O	O	O	O	W	O	O	O	van Zeist and de Roller 1994
Nevali Cori		9200										O	O	O			O	O	Pasternak 1995
Ain Ghazal		9000–8500			O	O	O	O				O	O	O	W	O	O	O	Rollefson et al. 1985
Jericho	PPNB	9000–8500			O	O	O	O				O	O	O		O	O	O	Hopf 1983
Cafer Höyük	IX–VI	9000–8400	O		O		O					O			W	W	O		de Moulins 1997
Nahal Hemar		9000–8200					O	O	O			O			A	O	O		Kislev 1988

Site		Date		References
Bheida		8900–8700		Helbaek 1966
Ganj Dareh	BM	8900–8200		van Zeist *et al.* 1986
Ali Kosh		8800–8000		Helbaek 1969
Jilat 7		8800–8400		Colledge 1994
Asikli		8800–8400		van Zeist 1995
Abu Hureyra PPNB		8800–8000		de Moulins 1997
Tell Aswad	II	8700–8400		van Zeist and Bakker-Heeres 1984b
Ghoraife	I	8700–8100		van Zeist and Bakker-Heeres 1984b
Abdul Hosein		8700–7500		Hubbard 1990; Willcox 1990
Halula		8700		Willcox 1996
Magzalia		8600–7800		Willcox in preparation
Gritille		8500–7700		Voigt 1984
Can Hassan III		8500–7600		French *et al.* 1972
Jarmo		8500		Braidwood and Braidwood 1983

Key: w = wild, d = domestic, ? = wild and/or domestic, O = present, ? = identification based on small number of poorly preserved finds, W = identification based on wood, A = acorn.

Mureybet, Jerf al Ahmar and Netiv Hagdud is forthcoming. For the very earliest levels at Aswad IA and Jericho, remains are numerically too meagre to be certain of domestication, but what is clear for this period is that the plant/crop assemblages vary remarkably between sites. Emmer is dominant at Aswad (van Zeist and Bakker-Heeres 1984b), einkorn at Mureybet, barley at Jerf el Ahmar in northern Syria (Table 25.5). This suggests that the inhabitants of these sites were still gathering local cereals, but this does not exclude small-scale cultivation as described by Harris (1996: 553) using locally available wild cereals as seed stock. Lentils are common on most sites even in the most arid zones.

During the next chronological period (Early PPNB 9600–9000 BP) architecture is distinctly rectangular. Emmer domestication has been reported for sites such as Cafer Hüyök and Cayonü in eastern Anatolia and for Aswad near Damascus (however, some researchers prefer to rely on the solid rachis in barley and the naked wheats as sure evidence for domestication, especially when samples size is small). At Aswad, between 9730 and 8560 BP (PPNA and early PPNB), 26 per cent of the barley rachis fragments are solid domestic types, but it is not clear if they occur in the earliest levels. At Dja'de (Willcox 1996) preliminary studies indicate that the cereals are not yet domesticated, but indirect evidence of weed associations strongly suggests the presence of cultivation and similar assemblages are seen at Awad, Cayonü and Cafer Hüyök.

The Middle PPNB (9200–8600 BP) sites are more extensive, more frequent and cover a wider geographical area comprising central Anatolia (Asikli Höyük) and Cyprus (Shillourokambos). Crop evolution and morphological domestication are clearly shown by the appearance of a solid rachis in barley and naked wheat – for example, at Aswad West phase II (van Zeist and Bakker-Heeres 1984b) and at Halula (Willcox 1995, 1996). For the first time there is evidence for the introduction of crops plants into new areas. Domestic emmer was introduced to the middle Euphrates at Abu Hureyra and Halula. But wild types remain at significant frequencies, which is evidenced at Cayönü, Cafer Höyük (wild wheats), Aswad, Ganj Dareh (wild barley), Halula (wild wheats and barley) and also in the Azraq basin (Colledge 1994). These mixed finds could be interpreted in three ways: (1) as evidence of the exploitation of wild stands, (2) as unwanted weeds, and (3) as an

Table 25.5 Comparison of percentages of cereals at four PPNA sites. The differences indicate that the inhabitants were still using local cereals rather than introduced crops, which start to appear in the Middle PPNB.

	Jerf el Ahmar (%)	Mureybet (%)	Aswad 1a (%)	Netiv Hagdud (%)
Einkorn	15.80	96	0	0
Emmer	0	0	89.50	Present
Barley	84.20	4	10.50	Dominant

integral part of the crop consisting of a mixture of wild and domestic cereals. The relatively high proportion of wild types and the lack of pure finds of domesticates suggest that the wild plants may have been considered as a useful part of the crop, as opposed to unwanted weeds. This suggests cultivation of wild and domestic types together but does not exclude gathering from wild stands in a kind of mixed economy. Even during later periods (Late PPNB: 8600–8000 BP), for example at Ramad between 8210 and 7880 BP, domestic barley rachis fragments are only at 52 per cent. A similar situation was noted at Magzalia (Willcox unpublished report). However at other contemporary sites such as Bouqras (van Zeist and van Waterbolk 1985) and Ras Shamra (phase Vc) wild types are rare or absent. These sites also contain naked wheat. During the Late PPNB, einkorn becomes a minor component and could be interpreted as a weed for most of the Near East. However, it reappears as a major component later at Jeitun in Central Asia (Harris *et al.* 1992) and at many sites in Europe.

Experimental results indicate that particular agricultural conditions are necessary in order for domestication to occur. As Hillman and Davies (1990: 213) point out, both seed corn from the wild, or that originating from fallen spikelets during the harvest, must be kept apart, and in reality this is not easy. This could explain why significant mixtures occur over a period of at least a millennium and would appear to indicate that selective pressures stayed relatively low. If this interpretation is correct, then it follows that cultivation without domestication would have occurred for some considerable time prior to the appearance of the solid rachis. If this is indeed the case, then archaeobotanists need to look for indirect indicators. Hillman examined the possibility of identifying a weed assemblage from Epipalaeolithic Abu Hureyra (Hillman *et al.* 1989: 253). His results were negative. Preliminary results from a later site, Dja'de, on the Euphrates (Willcox 1996), look more promising. Van Zeist examined the problem for later sites and the possibility of identifying weeds of irrigated fields (van Zeist 1993); he also points out that a number of taxa present at Cayönü are potential field weeds.

EVIDENCE FOR *IN SITU* EVOLUTION UNDER CULTIVATION

At sites with long sequences such as Aswad and Cayönü it is possible to trace evolutionary trends. At Cayönü wild-type emmer grains are progressively replaced by domestic types (van Zeist and de Roller 1994), whereas at Aswad and near-by Ghoraifé, as already mentioned, wild-type barley rachis internodes are replaced progressively by solid-type domestic rachis fragments (van Zeist and Bakker-Heeres 1984b). The period of time necessary to recognize these changes appears to be about a millennium; that is to say, between the early tenth and early ninth millennia. Other sites such as Mureybet show no evolutionary trends; however taxa which are interpreted as weed assemblages at other sites are present. For example at Cayönü similar taxa are considered by van Zeist to be potential field weeds; these taxa also occur at other PPNA sites, suggesting predomestic agriculture.

CONCLUSIONS

Archaeobotanical evidence indicates that wild cereals were exploited in the Near East for several millennia before the appearance of domestic types. Specialized gathering and especially storage of cereals and pulses would have provided a secure subsistence base, making possible a sedentary existence. In the northern Levant it is not clear whether early tenth millennium cereals were domesticated. During the second half of the tenth millennium there is evidence of emmer domestication. However, a millennium after the appearance of domestication wild types still persisted at frequencies which suggest they were part of the crop rather than unwanted weeds. Experimental cultivation indicates that cereal cultivation need not necessarily lead to rapid domestication. Selective pressures were found to be low because wild types continued to propagate under cultivation through spontaneous sowing. Further dilution could occur from occasional gathering from the wild and through crosses with wild populations. However, a number of scholars insist that domestication was a rapid process suggesting that after the appearance of a given mutation the establishment of mutant lines could take place in a few years (McCorriston and Hole 1991, Zohary 1992, 1996). They therefore see the appearance of domestication as simultaneous with the beginnings of cultivation.

The area occupied by these sites is vast, which suggests the possibility that domestication could have occurred independently in different localities. Indeed genetic evidence points to at least two different origins for barley, and according to Zohary emmer and the pulses were taken into cultivation perhaps 'once or at most only very few times' (Zohary 1996: 155). However, still other varieties may have been taken into cultivation but subsequently died out or do not show up because of genetic modifications which have occurred over the last 10,000 years.

The point at which people started to cultivate remains elusive, but small-scale or intermittent cultivation of pulses and perhaps cereals may have occurred over a long period (PPNA and earlier) without leading to domestication, as suggested by Kislev (1992). Not until large-scale cereal cultivation in the Middle PPNB do we see the appearance of domestic barley and naked wheat and the spread of emmer. As for the identification of predomestic cultivation the best evidence would appear to come from weed assemblages.

How much can we say about cultural change in subsistence systems from the observations we have made? It would appear that the transition was gradual, as there is no evidence for an abrupt change. During the period of transition there was little need for innovation in material culture. The tools for processing of gathered and cultivated cereals remain essentially the same. Storage, and storage structures, could be the same for both economic systems. During the late Epipalaeolithic one might consider the possibility that natural wild stands were to some extent managed to avoid over-exploitation. Then occasional sowing was adopted. As we have seen, inadvertent or accidental sowing around crop processing areas during the collecting stage is inevitable and could hardly have been totally ignored. Sowing would be enhanced if the soil was worked, and it is possible that suitable tools already existed for other activities such as collecting earth for building or digging up roots and tubers.

The change from a subsistence system to a production economy in the Near East has also been correlated with climatic change, notably the return of a cooler, dryer period (Younger Dryas) between 11,000 and 10,000 BP which, it is suggested, could have been a contributing factor to the subsequent development of agriculture (Moore and Hillman 1992). Movement of populations into drier areas might have the same effect. Given the steep gradient in isohytes between the Mediterranean vegetation zone and the interior steppe zone, even a small climatic change in the marginal areas would have a profound effect.

The evolution towards and the adaptation to a production economy with resulting domestication required certain pre-conditions. In other words it required a combination of complex circumstances leading to an evolutionary path which resulted in an economy dependent on cereal cultivation. On the one hand the plants had to have the right biological attributes (see Zohary 1996), and on the other humans had to have prerequisite behavioural attributes. They would have to be sedentary gatherers of wild progenitors with a minimum village size and a storage system. As pointed out by Cauvin, humans would have to be culturally ready (Cauvin 1994). Once all these conditions were fulfilled a full-scale farming economy (symbiosis) becomes inevitable. This would provide a subsistence system where production was guaranteed to supply demand (and/or surplus) in an expanding economy, ultimately leading to an irreversible process. We are not in a position to say whether cultural change played a more important role than climatic change. To assume that a single factor such as climatic change could have led to the adoption of plant husbandry is too simplistic.

The archaeobotanical remains, as we have seen, indicate that the change to a production economy was slow. The biological process of domestication appears to require that sowing be systematically carried out and that spontaneously sown seed be kept to a minimum. This would require that the soil be worked rigorously and fields systems be carefully managed. Cultivation of pulses and cereals during the early stages, even during the eleventh and tenth millennia, could have been an occasional option, but not necessarily systematically adopted. If occasional domesticates arose they may not have survived in the long term. But ultimately social organization developed to a point where farming became more and more organized, leading to high selective pressures for domestic types. Archaeological evidence during the Middle PPNB indicates the simultaneous emergence of rectilinear architecture, considerable increase in village size, the consistent appearance of domesticated cereals and the domestication of sheep and goat. Could these changes be correlated with a more developed and organized sociocultural system which became increasingly reliant on a highly managed agricultural system? This could have coincided with the adoption of rectangular field systems. Ultimately the process led to irreversible domestication combined with a steep rise in population. It appears that these changes were gradual and occurred more or less simultaneously over a wide area; that is to say the Euphrates valley, eastern Anatolia, the southern Levant and the Zagros foothills. Differences in material culture over the area as a whole are slight and contact across the region between geographically widely separated populations has been shown to occur from finds of marine shells and obsidian, which were traded across vast distances. If the area as a whole went through the pre-domestic cultivation stage then it is highly probable that domestication of the so-called founder crops occurred independently in different areas. However, at some sites, for example at Mureybet, only wild cereals were exploited during the Middle PPNB, while at the majority of sites, for this period, domestic cereals were predominant.

ACKNOWLEDGEMENTS

I would like to thank first and foremost G. Hillman for giving us the original ideas and plan for the experiments at Jalès, and P. Anderson who helped organize the project with me and was of invaluable help in both the theoretical and administrative fields. I would like to express my appreciation and warm thanks to all members of the Antiquities Department of the Syrian Arab Republic from the Damascus, Palmyra and Aleppo museums who during my numerous visits to Syria gave me a warm-hearted welcome, full backing and kind guidance. I would also like to thank J. Valkoun of ICARDA for showing me a large number of wild wheat populations in Syria, and J. Cauvin for his archaeological advice. Finally I am most grateful to W. van Zeist for his numerous publications and his pioneering work on Near Eastern archaeobotany without which much of this chapter would not have been possible.

REFERENCES

Anderson, P. 1994. Insights into plant harvesting and other activities at Hatoula, as revealed by microscopic functional analysis of selected chipped stone tools. In *Le gisement de Hatoula en Judée occidentale, Israël*, M. Lechevallier and A. Ronen (eds), 277–93. Memoires et travaux du centre de recherche Français de Jerusalem No. 8. Paris: Association Paléorient.
Baruch, U. and S. Bottema. 1991. Palynological evidence for climatic changes in the

Levant ca. 17,000–9,000 B.P. In *The Natufian Culture in the Levant*, O. Bar-Yosef, and F. Valla (eds), 11–20. International Monographs in Prehistory, Ann Arbor: University of Michigan Press.

Bar-Yosef, O., A. Gopher, E. Tchernov and M. Kislev. 1991. Nativ Hagdud: an early neolithic village site in the Jordan valley. *Journal of Field Archaeology* 18, 405–26.

Bor, N.L. 1968. Gramineae. In *Flora of Iraq*. Volume 9, C.C. Townsend, E. Guest and A. Al-Rawi (eds), 1–588. Glasgow: University of Glasgow Press, MacLehose.

Braidwood, L. and R. Braidwood. 1983 *Prehistoric Archaeology Along the Hilly Flanks*. Chicago: University of Chicago Oriental Institute Publications Volume 103.

Cauvin, J. 1994. *Naissance des divinités: Naissance de l'agriculture*. Paris: CNRS Editions.

Colledge, S. 1994. *Plant exploitation on Epipalaeolothic and early Neolithic sites in the Levant*. Unpublished Ph.D. thesis, Department of Archaeology and Prehistory, University of Sheffield.

Davies, P. H. 1985. *Flora of Turkey and the Aegean Islands*. Volume 9. Edinburgh: Edinburgh University Press.

de Moulins, D. 1997. *Agriculture Changes at Euphrates and Steppe Sites in the Mid-8th to the 6th Millennium B.C.* Oxford: BAR.

French, D., G.C. Hillman, S. Payne and J.R. Payne. 1972. Excavations at Can Hassan III 1969–1970. In *Papers in Economic Prehistory*, E.S. Higgs (ed.), 181–90. Cambridge: Cambridge University Press.

Hansen, J. 1991. *Excavations at Franchthi cave, Greece. Fascicule 7: The Palaeoethnobotany*. Bloomington: Indiana University Press.

Harris, D. R. 1996. The origins and spread of agriculture and pastoralism in Eurasia: an overview. In *The Origins and Spread of Agriculture and Pastoralism in Eurasia*, D. Harris (ed.), 552–74. London: UCL Press.

Harris, D. R., V.M. Masson, Y. E. Berezkin, M.P. Charles, C. Gosden, G.C. Hillman, A.K. Kasparov, G.F. Korobkova, K. Kurbansakhatov, A.J. Legge and S. Limbrey. 1992. Investigating early agriculture in Central Asia: new research at Jeitun, Turkmenistan. *Antiquity* 67, 324–8.

Helbaek, H. 1966. Pre-pottery neolithic farming at Bheida: a preliminary report. *Palestine Exploration Quarterly* 98, 61–6.

Helbaek, H. 1969. Plant collecting, dry farming, and irrigation in prehistoric Deh Luran. In *Prehistoric and Human Ecology of the Deh Luran Plain. An early village sequence from Khuzistan, Iran*. F. Hole, K. Flannery and J. Neely (eds), 383–426. Memoirs of the Museum of Anthropology 1. Ann Arbor: University of Michigan Press.

Hillman, G.C. 1981. Reconstructing crop husbandry practices from charred remains of crops. In *Farming Practices in British Prehistory*, R. Mercer (ed.), 123–62. Edinburgh: Edinburgh University Press.

Hillman, G. 1996. Late Pleistocene changes in wild plant-foods available to hunter-gatherers of the northern Fertile Crescent: possible preludes to cereal cultivation. In *The Origins and Spread of Agriculture and Pastoralism in Eurasia*, D. Harris (ed.), 159–203. London: UCL Press.

Hillman, G.C., S.M. Colledge and D.R. Harris. 1989. Plant food economy during the Epi-palaeolithic period at Tell Abu Hureyra, Syria: dietary diversity, seasonality and modes of exploitation. In *Foraging and Farming: the evolution of plant exploitation*, D.R. Harris and G.C. Hillman (eds), 240–68. London: Unwin Hyman.

Hillman, G. and S. Davies. 1990. Measured domestication rates in wild wheats and barley under primitive cultivation, and their archaeological implications. *Journal of World Prehistory* 4, 157–219.

Hillman, G., S. Wales, F. McLaren, J. Evans and A. Butler. 1993. Identifying problematic remains of ancient plant foods: a comparison of the role of chemical, histological and morphological criteria. *World Archaeology* 25, 94–121.

Hopf, M. 1983. Jericho plant remains. In *Jericho Volume V: The pottery phases of the tell and other finds* (Appendix B), K. Kenyon and T. Holland (eds), 576–621. London: British School of Archaeology in Jerusalem.

Hopf, M. and O. Bar-Yosef. 1987. Plant remains from Hayonim cave, western Galilee. *Paléorient* 13 (1), 117–120.

Hubbard, R.N.L.B. 1990. Carbonised seeds from Tepe Abdul Hosein: results of preliminary analyses. In *Tepe Abdul Hosein*, J. Pullar (ed.), 217–22. Oxford: BAR International Series 562.

Kerbe, J. 1987. *Climat, hydrologie et aménagements hydro-agricoles de Syrie*. Bordeaux: Presses Universitaires de Bordeaux.

Kislev, M. 1988. Nahal Hemar cave desiccated plant remains: an interim report. *Atiqot* 18, 76–81.

Kislev, M. 1989. Pre-domesticated cereals in the Pre-Pottery Neolithic A period. In *People and Cultural Change*, I. Hershkovitz (ed.), 147–51. Oxford: BAR International Series 508 (i).

Kislev, M. 1992. Agriculture in the Near East in the VIIth millennium B.C. In *Préhistoire de l'agriculture*, P. Anderson (ed.), 87–94. Monographie du CRA no. 6. Paris: Editions CNRS.

Kislev, M.E., D. Nadel and I. Carmi. 1992. Epipalaeolithic (19,000 bp) cereal and fruit diet at Ohalo II, Sea of Galilee, Israel. *Review of Palaeobotany and Palynology* 73, 161–6.

Konarev, A.V. and V.G. Konarev. 1993. The use of genome-specific antigens and prolamin electrophoresis in the evaluation of wheat and its wild relatives. In *Biodiversity and Wheat Improvement*, A. B. Damania (ed.), 259–72. Chichester: Wiley and Sons.

McCorriston, J. and F. Hole. 1991. The ecology of seasonal stress and the origins of agriculture in the Near East. *American Anthropologist* 93, 46–69.

Mathon, C.-C. 1985. La recherche du patrimone sur quelques blés traditionnels du sud-est de la France. *Supplément au Bulletin mensuel de la Société Linnéenne de Lyon* 4, 7–34.

Moore, A.M.T. and G.C. Hillman. 1992. The Pleistocene to Holocene transition and human economy in southwest Asia : the impact of the Younger Dryas. *American Antiquity* 57, 482–94.

Mouterde, P. 1966. *Nouvelle flore du Liban et la Syrie*. Volume I Beyrouth: Presse Catholique.

Nesbitt, M. 1995. Clues to agricultural origins in the northern Fertile Crescent. *Diversity: a news journal for the international genetic resources community* 11, 142–3.

Nesbitt, M. and D. Samuel. 1996. From a staple crop to extinction. The archaeology and history of the hulled wheats. In *Hulled Wheats. Proceedings of the First International Workshop on Hulled Wheats*, P. Sadulosi, K. Hammer and J. Heller (eds), 41–100. Rome: IPGRI.

Pasternak, R. 1995. Die botanischen Funfe aus Nevali Cori, Türkei (Akeramisches Neolithikum) – Ein Vorbericht. In *Res archaeobotanicae: International Workgroup for Palaeoethnobotany. Proceedings of the Ninth Symposium Kiel 1992*, H. Kroll and R. Pasternak (eds). Kiel: Herangegeben.

Postgate, N. J. 1984. The problems of yields in the cuneiform record. *Bulletin on Sumerian Agriculture* 1, 97–102.

Rollefson, G., A. Simmons, M. Donaldson, W. Gillespie, Z. Kafafi, I. Kohler-Rollefson, E. McAdam, S. Ralston and K. Tubb. 1985. Excavations at the pre-pottery Neolithic B. village of 'Ain Ghazal (Jordan), 1983. *Mittelugen der Deutschen Orient-Gesellschaft zu Berlin* 117, 69–116.

Rosenberg, M., M. Nesbitt, R.W. Redding and T.F. Strasser. 1995. Hallen Cemi Tepesi: some preliminary observations concerning early Neolithic subsistence in eastern Anatolia. *Anatolia* 21, 1–12.

Traboulsi, M. 1981. *Le climat de la Syrie: exemple de dégradation vers l'aride du climat méditerranéen.* Thèse du Troisième Cycle, Université de Lyon 2.

Valkoun, J. 1992. Exploration mission for wild cereals in Syria. *Genetic Resources Unit Annual Report for 1991*, 16–18. Aleppo: International Center for Agricultural Research in Dry Areas.

van Zeist, W. 1993. Archaeobotanical evidence of the bronze age field weed flora of northern Syria. *Festschrift Zoller, Dissertationes Botanicae* 196, 499–511.

van Zeist, W. and J.A. Bakker-Heeres. 1984a. Archaeobotanical studies in the Levant 3. Late Palaeolithic Mureybet. *Palaeohistoria* 26, 171–99.

van Zeist, W. and J.A. Bakker-Heeres. 1984b. Archaeobotanical studies in the Levant 1. Neolithic sites in the Damascus basin: Aswad, Ghoraife, Ramad. *Palaeohistoria* 24, 165–256.

van Zeist, W. and G. de Roller. 1994. The plant husbandry of aceramic Cayönü, SE Turkey. *Palaeohistoria* 33/34, 65–96.

van Zeist, W. and G. de Roller. 1995. Plant remains from Asikli Höyük, a pre-pottery neolithic site in central Anatolia. *Vegetation History and Archaeobotany* 4, 179–85.

van Zeist, W., P. Smith, R. Palfenier, M. Suwijin and W. Casparie. 1986. An archaeobotanical study of Ganj Dareh Tepe, Iran. *Palaeohistoria* 26, 201–24.

van Zeist, W. and R. van Waterbolk. 1985. The palaeobotany of Tell Bouqras. *Paléorient* 11, 131–47.

Voigt, M. 1984. Village on the Euphrates. Excavations at neolithic Gritille in Turkey. *Expedition* 27, 10–24.

Willcox, G. 1990. Charcoal remains from Tepe Abdul Hosein. In *Tepe Abdul Hosein: a neolithic site in western Iran. Excavations 1978*, J. Pullar (ed.), 223–7. Oxford: BAR.

Willcox, G. 1991a. Exploitation des espèces ligneuses au Proche-Orient. *Paléorient* 17, 117–26.

Willcox, G. 1991b. La culture inventée, la domestication inconsciente: le début de l'agriculture au Proche Orient. In *Rites et Rythmes agraires*, M.-C. Cauvin (ed.), 9–31. Lyon: Travaux de la Maison de L'Orient 20.

Willcox, G., 1991c. Cafer Höyük (Turquie): Les Charbons de bois néolithiques. *Cahiers de l'Euphrate* 5–6, 139–50. Paris: Editions Recherche sur les Civilisations.

Willcox, G. 1992. Archaeobotanical significance of growing Near Eastern progenitors of domestic plants at Jalès (France). In *Préhistoire de l'agriculture: Nouvelles approches expérimentales et ethnographiques*, P. Anderson (ed.), 159–78. Monographie du CRA No. 6. Paris: Editions du CNRS.

Willcox, G. 1995. Wild and domestic cereal cultivation: new evidence from early neolithic sites in the northern Levant and south-eastern Anatolia. *ARX World Journal of Prehistoric and Ancient Studies* 1, 9–16.

Willcox, G. 1996. Evidence for plant exploitation and vegetation history from three early neolithic pre-pottery sites on the Euphrates (Syria). *Vegetation History and Archaeobotany* 5, 143–52.

Willcox, G. Forthcoming. Charcoal analysis and vegetation history in southern Syria. *Quaternary Studies Reviews.*

Zohary, D. 1969. The progenitors of wheat and barley in relation to domestication and agricultural dispersals in the Old World. In *The Domestication of Plants and Animals*, G.W. Dimbleby and P. Ucko (eds), 35–46. London: Duckworth.

Zohary, D. 1992. Domestication of the neolithic crop plant assemblage. In *Préhistoire de l'agriculture: Nouvelles approches expérimentales et ethnographiques*, P. Anderson (ed.), 159–78. Monographie du CRA No. 6. Paris: Editions du CNRS.

Zohary, D. 1996. The mode of domestication of the founder crops of Southwest Asian agriculture. In *The Origins and Spread of Agriculture and Pastoralism in Eurasia*, D.R. Harris (ed.), 159–203. London: UCL Press.

Zohary, D. and M. Hopf. 1988. *Domestication of Plants in the Old World*. Oxford: Duckworth.

Index

Aborigines: agriculture, their
non-adoption of 235; ancestral tracks,
presence of in the landscape 244;
Dreamtime, characteristics of 244;
Dreamtime, its role in the
non-adoption of agriculture 235; early
ethnographic constructions of 237;
environment, its perceived role in
determining Aboriginal culture 238;
myth, presence of in the landscape
235–6, 244; property concepts of 238,
239; ritual attachment to land, its role
in the non-adoption of agriculture
235; ritual, its relationship to landscape
235; social memory, its place in the
landscape 235–6; see also Gungwingu
Abu Darbein: wild sorghum, gathering of
at 397; see also Middle Nile Valley
Abu Hureyra: cereal exploitation, early
evidence of at 489; domesticated
emmer, introduction of at 492;
einkorn, dominance of at 489; weed
assemblage of, analysis of 493
achira: connotations of 49; distribution of
49; origins of 43; Peru, its introduction
into 47
Acropolis: post-Muchique 3 phase of 428,
431; see also Jama valley
Africa: Bantu, role of in the dispersal of
plantains 388–9; cattle, indigenous
domestication of 336; dispersal of
domesticated plants to India from 139,
142, 144–5; finger millet, introduction
to India from 409, 469; pastoralism, its

predating of cereal production 336;
plantains, diversity of 382; plantains,
introduction of to 388–90, 392; see also
Méma, Middle Nile valley, West Africa
agrarianism: see agriculture
agriculture: Aborigines, their
non-adoption of agriculture 235;
agricultural intensification and the
environment, relationship between
270; crop dispersals, process of 28–31;
crop innovation, process of 420; crop
introductions, process of 129, 130–1,
420; demographic pressure, its role in
agricultural intensification 270;
dichotomy between hunter-gatherers
and farmers, discussion of 99, 117–18,
237–9; India, origins of agriculture in
139, 142 5; interaction between
agricultural regimes, discussion of
28–9; introduction of, process of 36;
kinship, its relationship to the origins
of 39–40; land tenure systems, their
effects on agricultural regimes 288,
293, 295–300, 301, 302; milk
production, incentive for 23–4; origins
of, models of 23, 28, 37; pastoralism,
relationship between 15, 16; secondary
farming, development of in south-west
Asia 23–8; sedentism, its association
with 15; social conflict, its role in
agricultural intensification 270, 271–2;
social consequences of the adoption of
21, 147, 160, 401; spread of 23, 24, 25,
28, 166–7; technology, its role in crop